LABOUR RELA'
STATUTES AND MATERIALS

AUSTRALIA AND NEW ZEALAND
The Law Book Co. Ltd.
Sydney : Melbourne : Perth

CANADA AND U.S.A.
The Carswell Company Ltd.
Agincourt, Ontario

INDIA
N. M. Tripathi Private Ltd.
Bombay
and
Eastern Law House Private Ltd.
Calcutta and Delhi
M.P.P. House
Bangalore

ISRAEL
Steimatzky's Agency Ltd.
Jerusalem : Tel Aviv : Haifa

MALAYSIA : SINGAPORE : BRUNEI
Malayan Law Journal (Pte.) Ltd.
Singapore

PAKISTAN
Pakistan Law House
Karachi

SWEET & MAXWELL'S
LABOUR RELATIONS STATUTES AND MATERIALS

SECOND EDITION

Edited by

Sweet & Maxwell's Legal Editorial Staff

Advisory Editors

B. A. HEPPLE, M.A., LL.B.
of Gray's Inn, Barrister; Professor of
English Law, University of London at
University College London; a Chairman of
Industrial Tribunals (England and Wales)

PAUL O'HIGGINS, M.A., Ph.D.
of the King's Inns and Lincoln's Inn, Barrister;
Reader, Christ's College; University Lecturer
in Law, Cambridge

LORD WEDDERBURN OF CHARLTON, M.A., LL.B., F.B.A.
of Middle Temple, Barrister;
Cassel Professor of Commercial Law,
University of London at the London School of Economics

LONDON
SWEET & MAXWELL
1983

First Edition 1979
Second Edition 1983

Published in 1983 by
Sweet & Maxwell Ltd. of
11 New Fetter Lane, London.
Computerset by
Promenade Graphics Ltd.,
Cheltenham
and printed in Scotland.

British Library Cataloguing in Publication Data
Sweet & Maxwell's labour relations statutes and materials.—2nd ed.
  1. Labor laws and legislation—Great Britain
  I. Hepple, B.A.   II. O'Higgins, Paul
  III. Wedderburn of Charlton, Kenneth William
  Wedderburn, *Baron*   IV. Sweet & Maxwell.
  Legal Editorial Staff
  344.104'1'02632   KD3040.A3

ISBN 0–421–32010–9

*All rights reserved.
No part of this publication may be
reproduced or transmitted, in any form
or by any means, electronic, mechanical,
photocopying, recording or otherwise, or
stored in any retrieval system of any
nature, without the written permission
of the copyright holder and the publisher,
application for which shall be made to
the publisher.*

©
Sweet & Maxwell Limited
1983

PREFACE

Once again, in compiling this edition of *Labour Relations Statutes and Materials*, the two overriding considerations have been the question of timing and the crucially important selection of materials.

The speed and volume of change in the field of labour relations make the decision as to the optimum time for publication almost impossible. This edition has proved no exception. Whilst the collection was in production proposals for further legislation covering trade union elections, ballots before strikes and the political activities of trade unions were issued in a press notice from the Department of Employment on July 12, 1983. In addition, it is understood that the government propose to repeal the Truck Acts and associated legislation and replace them by new legislation designed to protect workers from arbitrary deductions from wages. We believe, however, that we are right to press on and produce an updated version of the materials or face the prospect of holding back indefinitely whilst further legislative developments are in train.

With regard to the selection of materials, we have been concerned to include the most important and relevant sections of all labour related statutes. Nevertheless, this edition benefits from a timely reappraisal of the materials and their strict relevance to the subject. Accordingly several of the statutes relating to specific employments have been left out this time and from the Social Security legislation only the sections most indispensable to a study of labour law have been included in the collection. The Truck Acts remain in, pending their repeal and notable additions to the statutes section include the text of the Employment Act 1982 and relevant sections of the Companies Act 1981 and the Social Security and Housing Benefits Act 1982.

As in the previous edition and supplement the statutes and materials are presented chronologically to assist with speedy reference. The format has been improved by the division of the contents into five separate sections, namely Statutes, Statutory Instruments, European Materials, Repealed Legislation and Appendices containing Codes of Practice and other non-statutory material, all fully indexed. Of these the most fundamental innovation to the manual is the new section of repealed provisions of labour law statutes. It is every lawyer's experience that an understanding of some aspects of labour law is almost impossible without a knowledge of what preceded the existing statutes. Undoubtedly this new section will be of great assistance to students and practitioners alike.

We have been able to include at a late stage in production the amendments made to the Equal Pay Act 1970 and related legislation by the Equal Pay (Amendment) Regulations 1983 as well as the Code of Practice on Race Relations in employment, issued by the Commission for Racial Equality and effective from April 1, 1984. Regrettably there has been no sign of the new rules of industrial tribunal procedure and we are therefore unable to include them.

Finally, we are most grateful to our three eminent Advisory Editors, Professor B. A. Hepple, Dr. Paul O'Higgins and Professor Lord

Wedderburn of Charlton for their careful guidance and patient deliberations over the difficult selection of material to be included or excluded. Their combined expertise drawn from academic, administrative and legislative experience of the subject has been of invaluable assistance. A comprehensive index has been prepared by Robert Spicer and a detailed table of contents setting out exactly which sections of the Acts are included is to be found at the front of the book.

September 1, 1983   SWEET & MAXWELL

CONTENTS

	Page
Preface	v
PART I STATUTES	*Para*
Truck Act 1831 ss. 1–6, 8–9, 13, 14, 20, 23–25, 27	1–001
Apportionment Act 1870 ss. 1–7	1–017
Conspiracy and Protection of Property Act 1875 ss. 1, 5–8, 10, 11, 13, 15–21	1–025
Truck Amendment Act 1887 ss. 1–15, 18	1–041
Truck Act 1896 ss. 1–6, 8–10, 12	1–058
Bankruptcy (Scotland) Act 1913 s. 118	1–069
Trade Union Act 1913 ss. 1–8, Sched.	1–070
Bankruptcy Act 1914 ss. 33–34	1–082
Industrial Courts Act 1919 ss. 4, 5, 7–10, 13, 14	1–084
Sex Disqualification (Removal) Act 1919 s. 1	1–093
Emergency Powers Act 1920 ss. 1–3	1–094
Bankruptcy (Amendment) Act 1926 s. 2	1–098
Truck Act 1940 ss. 1, 3	1–099
Companies Act 1947 ss. 91, 115(1)	1–102
Companies Act 1948 ss. 154, 319, 358, 359	1–105
Payment of Wages Act 1960 ss. 1–7, 9	1–110
Trade Union (Amalgamations, etc.) Act 1964 ss. 1–11, Scheds. 1, 2	1–119

Contents

Companies Act 1967
ss. 8, 26   1–133

Equal Pay Act 1970
ss. 1–7, 9–11   1–135

Health and Safety at Work etc. Act 1974
ss. 2–4, 6–9, 18–25, 46, 48, 79   1–146

Trade Union and Labour Relations Act 1974
ss. 1–4, 7–13, 15–31, Scheds. 1–5   1–165

Rehabilitation of Offenders Act 1974
s. 4   1–200

Social Security Pensions Act 1975
s. 31   1–202

Sex Discrimination Act 1975
ss. 1–21, 37–43, 47–77, 80–87, Scheds. 2–4   1–203

Employment Protection Act 1975
ss. 1–10, 17–21, 40, 97, 99–108, 110–111, 114–119, 121–129, Scheds. 1, 9–10, 12–18   1–275

Race Relations Act 1976
ss. 1–16, 28–38, 40–56, 58–66, 68–69, 71–80, Scheds. 1–2   1–347

Patents Act 1977
ss. 39–43   1–414

Criminal Law Act 1977
ss. 1–5   1–420

State Immunity Act 1978
s. 4   1–426

Employment Protection (Consolidation) Act 1978
ss. 1–2, 4–6, 8–76A, 77–96, 98–142, 144–146, 148–160, Scheds. 1–17   1–427

Wages Councils Act 1979
ss. 1–32, Scheds. 1–7   1–616

Companies Act 1980
ss. 46–47, 54, 61, 63, 74, 87   1–656

Employment Act 1980
ss. 1–5, 14, 16–17, 19–21, Scheds. 1–2   1–664

Companies Act 1981
ss. 6(1)(2), 16(1), 42, Sched. 1, paras. 52 and 56   1–678

Employment Act 1982
ss. 2, 12–18, 20–22, Sched. 1   1–682

Social Security and Housing Benefits Act 1982
ss. 1–10, 20, 26, Scheds. 1, 2(2)   1–695

PART II STATUTORY INSTRUMENTS

No.

1965/1101	Industrial Tribunals (England and Wales) Regulations	2–001
1974/1925	Industrial Tribunals (Improvement and Prohibition Notices Appeals) Regulations	2–010
1975/1023	Rehabilitation of Offenders Act 1974 (Exceptions) Order	2–015
1975/1993	Sex Discrimination (Formal Investigations) Regulations	2–021
1975/2048	Sex Discrimination (Questions and Replies) Order	2–024
1976/660	Labour Relations (Continuity of Employment) Regulations	2–027
1976/663	Industrial Tribunals Awards (Enforcement in case of Death) Regulations	2–028
1977/500	Safety Representatives and Safety Committees Regulations	2–029
1977/841	Race Relations (Formal Investigations) Regulations	2–033
1977/842	Race Relations (Questions and Replies) Order	2–036
1977/1094	Industrial Tribunals (Non-Discrimination Notices Appeals) Regulations	2–039
1978/216	Patents Rules	2–041
1980/884	Industrial Tribunals (Rules of Procedure) Regulations	2–042
1980/1252	Funds for Trade Union Ballots Regulations	2–047
1980/2035	Employment Appeal Tribunal Rules	2–052
1981/1794	Transfer of Undertakings (Protection of Employment) Regulations	2–063
1982/894	Statutory Sick Pay (General) Regulations	2–076
1982/953	Funds for Trade Union Ballots Order	2–098

PART III EUROPEAN MATERIALS

Text of EEC Treaty, Arts. 117–122	3–001
Council Directive 75/117	3–007
Council Directive 75/129	3–018
Council Directive 76/207	3–024
Council Directive 77/187	3–036
European Convention on Human Rights and Fundamental Freedoms 1953, Arts. 9–11, 14	3–041

x   *Contents*

    European Social Charter 1965, Arts. 6, 8   3–042

PART IV   REPEALED LEGISLATION

    Trade Union Act 1871
      ss. 2–4   4–001

    Conspiracy and Protection of Property Act 1875
      ss. 3, 4   4–005

    Trade Disputes Act 1906
      ss. 2–5   4–008

    Trade Union and Labour Relations Act 1974
      ss. 13(2) (3), 14, 15, 29(1)   4–013

PART V   APPENDICES

1. EAT Practice Direction – Appeal Procedure   5–001
2. Codes of Practice:
    Industrial Relations Act 1971   5–006

    Disciplinary Practice and Procedures in
       Employment   5–009

    Disclosure of Information to Trade Unions
       for Collective Bargaining Purposes   5–018

    Time off for Trade Union Duties and Activities   5–025

    Health and Safety Commission's Code of
       Practice on Safety Representatives   5–032

    Picketing   5–045

    Closed Shop Agreements and Arrangements   5–058

    Race Relations   5–078/1
3. TUC Disputes Principles and Procedures   5–079

Index   681

PART I
STATUTES

Truck Act 1831

1–001

(1 & 2 WILL. 4, C.37)

An Act to prohibit the payment, in certain trades, of wages in goods, or otherwise than in the current coin of the realm.

[15th October, 1831]

AMENDMENT
The words omitted immediately following "artificer" and "labour" throughout the Act were repealed by the Statute Law Revision Act 1891 (54 & 55 Vict, c. 67).

Contracts for the hiring of artificers must be made in the current coin of the realm

1–002

1. In all contracts hereafter to be made for the hiring of any artificer . . . or for the performance by any artificer of any labour . . . the wages of such artificer shall be made payable in the current coin of this realm only, and not otherwise; and that if in any such contract the whole or any part of such wages shall be made payable in any manner other than in the current coin aforesaid, such contract shall be and is hereby declared illegal, null, and void.

No stipulations shall be inserted as to the manner in which the wages shall be expended

1–003

2. If in any contract hereafter to be made between any artificer . . . and his employer, any provision shall be made directly or indirectly respecting the place where, or the manner in which, or the person or persons with whom, the whole or any part of the wages due or to become due to any such artificer shall be laid out or expended, such contract shall be and is hereby declared illegal, null, and void.

All wages shall be paid to the artificer in coin

1–004

3. The entire amount of the wages earned by or payable to any artificer . . . in respect of any labour by him done . . . shall be actually paid to such artificer in the current coin of this realm, and not otherwise; and every payment made to any such artificer by his employer, of or in respect of any such wages, by the delivering to him of goods, or otherwise than in the current coin aforesaid, except as herein-after mentioned, shall be and is hereby declared illegal, null, and void.

Artificers may recover wages, if not paid in the current coin

1–005

4. Every artificer . . . shall be entitled to recover from his employer . . . in the manner by law provided for the recovery of servants' wages, or by any other lawful ways and means, the whole or so much of the wages earned by such artificer . . . as shall not have been actually paid to him by such his employer in the current coin of this realm.

In an action brought for wages no set-off shall be allowed for goods supplied by the employer, or by any shop in which the employer is interested

1–006   5. In any action, suit, or other proceeding to be hereafter brought or commenced by any artificer against his employer, for the recovery of any sum of money due to any such artificer as the wages of his labour . . . the defendant shall not be allowed to make any set-off, nor to claim any reduction of the plaintiff's demand, by reason or in respect of any goods, wares, or merchandise had or received by the plaintiff as or on account of his wages or in reward for his labour, or by reason or in respect of any goods, wares, or merchandise sold, delivered, or supplied to such artificer at any shop or warehouse kept by or belonging to such employer, or in the profits of which such employer shall have any share or interest.

No employer shall have any action against his artificer for goods supplied to him on account of wages

1–007   6. No employer of any artificer . . . shall have or be entitled to maintain any suit or action in any court of law or equity against any such artificer, for or in respect of any goods, wares, or merchandise sold, delivered, or supplied to any such artificer by any such employer, whilst in his employment, as or on account of his wages or reward for his labour, or for or in respect of any goods, wares, or merchandise sold, delivered, or supplied to such artificer at any shop or warehouse kept by or belonging to such employer, or in the profits of which such employer shall have any share or interest.

. . . . . .

Not to invalidate the payment of wages in bank notes, if artificer consents

1–008   8. Provided always, . . . that nothing herein contained shall be construed to prevent or to render invalid any contract for the payment, or any actual payment, to any such artificer as aforesaid, of the whole or any part of his wages, either in the notes . . . of the Bank of England, or in the notes of any person or persons carrying on the business of a banker, and duly licensed to issue such notes in pursuance of the laws relating to his Majesty's revenue of stamps, or in drafts or orders for the payment of money to the bearer on demand, drawn upon any person or persons carrying on the business of a banker, being duly licensed as aforesaid, within fifteen miles of the place where such drafts or orders shall be so paid, if such artificer shall be freely consenting to receive such drafts or orders as aforesaid, but all payments so made with such consent as aforesaid, in any such notes, drafts, or orders as aforesaid, shall for the purposes of this Act be as valid and effectual as if such payments had been made in the current coin of the realm.

Penalties on employers entering into contracts hereby declared illegal

1–009   9. Any employer of any artificer . . . who shall, by himself or by the agency of any other person or persons, directly or indirectly enter into any contract or make any payment hereby declared illegal, shall [be liable on summary conviction to a fine not exceeding £200].

AMENDMENT
   The words in square brackets were substituted by the Criminal Law Act 1977 (c. 45), ss.15 and 30 and Sched. 1.

A partner not to be liable in person for the offence of his copartner, but the partnership property to be so liable

13. No person shall be liable to be convicted of any offence against this Act committed by his or her copartner in trade, and without his or her knowledge, privity, or consent; but it shall be lawful, when any penalty, or any sum for wages, or any other sum, is ordered to be paid, under the authority of this Act, and the person or persons ordered to pay the same shall neglect or refuse to do so, to levy the same by distress and sale of any goods belonging to any copartnership concern or business in the carrying on of which such charges may have become due or such offence may have been committed; and in all proceedings under this Act to recover any sum due for wages it shall be lawful in all cases of copartnership for the justices, at the hearing of any complaint for the nonpayment thereof, to make an order upon any one or more copartners for the payment of the sum appearing to be due; and in such case the service of a copy of any summons or other process, or of any order, upon one or more of such copartners, shall be deemed to be a sufficient service upon all.

1–010

How summonses are to be served

14. In all cases it shall be deemed and taken to be sufficient service of any summons to be issued against any offender or offenders by any justice or justices of the peace, under the authority of this Act, if a duplicate or true copy of the same be left at or upon the place used or occupied by such offender or offenders for carrying on his, her, or their trade or business, or at the place of residence of any such offender or offenders, being at or upon any such place as aforesaid, the same being directed to such offender or offenders by his, her, or their right or assumed name or names.

1–011

Saving as to domestics

20. Nothing herein contained shall extend to any domestic servant or servant in husbandry.

1–012

Particular exceptions to the generality of the law

23. Nothing herein contained shall extend or be construed to extend to prevent any employer of any artificer, or agent of any such employer, from supplying or contracting to supply to any such artificer any medicine or medical attendance, or any fuel, or any materials, tools, or implements to be by such artificer employed in his trade or occupation, if such artificers be employed in mining, or any hay, corn, or other provender to be consumed by any horse or other beast of burden employed by any such artificer in his trade and occupation; nor from demising to any artificer, . . . the whole or any part of any tenement at any rent to be thereon reserved; nor from supplying or contracting to supply to any such artificer any victuals dressed or prepared under the roof of any such employer, and there consumed by such artificer; nor from making or contracting to make any stop-

1–013

page or deduction from the wages of any such artificer, for or in respect of any such rent; or for or in respect of any such medicine or medical attendance; or for or in respect of such fuel, materials, tools, implements, hay, corn, or provender, or of any such victuals dressed and prepared under the roof of any such employer; or for or in respect of any money advanced to such artificer for any such purpose as aforesaid: provided always, that such stoppage or deduction shall not exceed the real and true value of such fuel, materials, tools, implements, hay, corn, and provender, and shall not be in any case made from the wages of such artificer, unless the agreement or contract for such stoppage or deduction shall be in writing, and signed by such artificer.

Employers may advance money to artificers for certain purposes

1–014
24. Nothing herein contained shall extend or be construed to extend to prevent any such employer from advancing to any such artificer any money to be by him contributed to any friendly society or bank for savings duly established according to law, nor from advancing to any such artificer any money for his relief in sickness, or for the education of any child or children of such artificer, nor from deducting or contracting to deduct any sum or sums of money from the wages of such artificers for the education of any such child or children of such artificer, . . .

Definition of terms

1–015
25. In the meaning and for the purposes of this Act, . . . all masters, bailiffs, foremen, managers, clerks, and other persons engaged in the hiring, employment, or superintendence of the labour of any such artificers, shall be and be deemed to be "employers"; and within the meaning and for the purposes of this Act, any money or other thing had or contracted to be paid, delivered, or given as a recompense, reward, or remuneration for any labour done or to be done, whether within a certain time or to a certain amount, or for a time or an amount uncertain, shall be deemed and taken to be the "wages" of such labour; and that within the meaning and for the purposes aforesaid, any agreement, understanding, device, contrivance, collusion, or arrangement whatsoever on the subject of wages, whether written or oral, whether direct or indirect, to which the employer and artificer are parties or are assenting, or by which they are mutually bound to each other, or whereby either of them shall have endeavoured to impose an obligation on the other of them, shall be and be deemed a "contract."

. . . . . .

To extend over Great Britain

1–016
27. The provisions of this Act shall extend over the whole of . . . Great Britain.

Apportionment Act 1870

(33 & 34 VICT. c.35)

An Act for the better Apportionment of Rents and other periodical Payments.

[1st August 1870]

Short title

1. This Act may be cited for all purposes as "The Apportionment Act 1870."

Rents, &c. to be apportionable in respect of time

2. All rents, annuities, dividends, and other periodical payments in the nature of income (whether reserved or made payable under an instrument in writing or otherwise) shall, like interest on money lent, be considered as accruing from day to day, and shall be apportionable in respect of time accordingly.

Apportioned part of rent, &c. to be payable when the next entire portion shall have become due

3. The apportioned part of any such rent, annuity, dividend, or other payment shall be payable or recoverable in the case of a continuing rent, annuity, or other such payment when the entire portion of which such apportioned part shall form part shall become due and payable, and not before, and in the case of a rent, annuity, or other such payment determined by re-entry, death, or otherwise when the next entire portion of the same would have been payable if the same had not so determined, and not before.

Persons shall have the same remedies for recovering apportioned parts as for entire portions with proviso as to rents reserved in certain cases

4. All persons and their respective heirs, executors, administrators, and assigns, and also the executors, administrators, and assigns respectively of persons whose interests determine with their own deaths, shall have such or the same remedies at law and in equity for recovering such apportioned parts as aforesaid when payable (allowing proportionate parts of all just allowances) as they respectively would have had for recovering such entire portions as aforesaid if entitled thereto respectively; provided that persons liable to pay rents reserved out of or charged on lands or other hereditaments of any tenure, and the same lands or other hereditaments shall not be resorted to for any such apportioned part forming part of an entire or continuing rent as aforesaid specifically, but the entire or continuing rent, including such apportioned part, shall be recovered and received by the heir or other person who, if the rent had not been apportionable under this Act, or otherwise, would have been entitled to such entire or continuing rent, and such apportioned part shall be recoverable from such heir or other person by the executors or other parties entitled under this Act to the same by action at law or suit in equity.

Interpretation

5. In the construction of this Act—

The word "rents" includes rent service, rentcharge, and rent seck, and also tithes and all periodical payments or renderings in lieu of or in the nature of rent or tithe.

The word "annuities" includes salaries and pensions.

The word "dividends" includes (besides dividends strictly so called) all payments made by the name of dividend, bonus, or otherwise out of the revenue of trading or other public companies, divisible between all or any of the members of such respective companies, whether such payments shall be usually made or declared at any fixed times or otherwise; and all such divisible revenue shall, for the purposes of this Act, be deemed to have accrued by equal daily increment during and within the period for or in respect of which the payment of the same revenue shall be declared or expressed to be made, but the said word "dividend" does not include payments in the nature of a return or reimbursement of capital.

Act not to apply to policies of assurance

1–023   6. Nothing in this Act contained shall render apportionable any annual sums made payable in policies of assurance of any description.

Act not to apply where stipulation made to the contrary

1–024   7. The provisions of this Act shall not extend to any case in which it is or shall be expressly stipulated that no apportionment shall take place.

1–025   # Conspiracy and Protection of Property Act 1875

(38 & 39 Vict. c.86)

An Act for amending the Law relating to Conspiracy, and to the Protection of Property, and for other purposes.

[13th August 1875]

Short title

1–026   1. This Act may be cited as "The Conspiracy, and Protection of Property Act 1875."

. . . . .

Breach of contract involving injury to persons or property

1–027   5. Where any person wilfully and maliciously breaks a contract of service or of hiring, knowing or having reasonable cause to believe that the probable consequences of his so doing, either alone or in combination with others, will be to endanger human life, or cause serious bodily injury, or to expose valuable property whether real or personal to destruction or serious injury, he shall on conviction thereof by a court of summary jurisdiction, [. . .], be liable either to pay a penalty not exceeding twenty pounds, or to be imprisoned for a term not exceeding three months, with or without hard labour.

AMENDMENT
The words omitted in this section were repealed by the Criminal Law Act 1977 (c. 45), s.65 and Sched. 13.

Miscellaneous

Penalty for neglect by master to provide food, clothing, &c., for servant or apprentice

6. Where a master, being legally liable to provide for his servant or apprentice necessary food, clothing, medical aid, or lodging, wilfully and without lawful excuse refuses or neglects to provide the same, whereby the health of the servant or apprentice is or is likely to be seriously or permanently injured, he shall on summary conviction be liable either to pay a penalty not exceeding twenty pounds, or to be imprisoned for a term not exceeding six months, with or without hard labour.

1–028

Penalty for intimidation or annoyance by violence or otherwise

7. Every person who, with a view to compel any other person to abstain from doing or to do any act which such other person has a legal right to do or abstain from doing, wrongfully and without legal authority,—

1. Uses violence to or intimidates such other person or his wife or children, or injures his property; or,
2. Persistently follows such other person about from place to place; or
3. Hides any tools, clothes, or other property owned or used by such other person, or deprives him of or hinders him in the use thereof; or
4. Watches or besets the house or other place where such other person resides, or works, or carries on business, or happens to be, or the approach to such house or place; or,
5. Follows such other person with two or more other persons in a disorderly manner in or through any street or road,

shall, on conviction thereof by a court of summary jurisdiction, [. . .], be liable either to pay a penalty not exceeding twenty pounds, or to be imprisoned for a term not exceeding three months, with or without hard labour.

1–029

AMENDMENT
The words omitted in this section were repealed by the Criminal Law Act 1977 (c. 45), s.65 and Sched. 13.

Reduction of penalties

8. Where in any Act relating to employers or workmen a pecuniary penalty is imposed in respect of any offence under such Act, and no power is given to reduce such penalty, the justices or court having jurisdiction in respect of such offence may, if they think it just so to do, impose by way of penalty in respect of such offence any sum not less than one-fourth of the penalty imposed by such Act.

1–030

. . . .

Proceedings before a court of summary jurisdiction

10. Every offence under this Act which is made punishable on conviction by a court of summary jurisdiction or on summary conviction, and every penalty under this Act recoverable on summary conviction, may be prose-

1–031

Regulations as to evidence

1–032 **11.** Provided, that upon the hearing and determining of any indictment or information under sections [. . .], five, and six of this Act, the respective parties to the contract of service, their husbands or wives, shall be deemed and considered as competent witnesses.

AMENDMENT
  The words omitted from this section were repealed by the Industrial Relations Act 1971 (c. 72), s.133 and Sched. 9.

. . . . . .

Definitions

General definitions

1–033 **13.** In this Act,—
  The expression "court of summary jurisdiction" means—
  (1) As respects the city of London, the Lord Mayor or any alderman of the said city sitting at the Mansion House or Guildhall justice room; and
  (2) As respects any police court division in the Metropolitan police district, any Metropolitan police magistrate sitting at the police court for that division; and
  (3) As respects any city, town, liberty, borough, place, or district for which a stipendiary magistrate is for the time being acting, such stipendiary magistrate sitting at a police court or other place appointed in that behalf; and
  (4) Elsewhere, any justice or justices of the peace to whom jurisdiction is given by the Summary Jurisdiction Act: Provided that, as respects any case within the cognisance of such justice or justices as last aforesaid, an information, under this Act shall be heard and determined by two or more justices of the peace in petty sessions sitting at some place appointed for holding sessions.
  Nothing in this section contained shall restrict the jurisdiction of the Lord Mayor or any alderman of the city of London, or of any metropolitan police or stipendiary magistrate, in respect of any act or jurisdiction which may now be done or exercised by him out of court.

. . . . . .

Definition of "maliciously"

1–034 **15.** The word "maliciously" used in reference to any offence under this Act shall be construed in the same manner as it is required by the fifty-eighth section of the Malicious Damage Act 1861 to be construed in reference to any offence committed under such last-mentioned Act.

Saving Clause

Saving as to sea service

16. Section 5 of this Act does not apply to seamen.

1–035

AMENDMENT

This section was substituted prospectively by the Merchant Shipping Act 1970 (c. 36), s.100(1) and Sched. 3, para. 1.

Repeal

Enforcement of order for wages

17. Any order for wages or further sum of compensation in addition to wages made in pursuance of section sixteen of the Summary Jurisdiction (Ireland) Act 1851 may be enforced in like manner as if it were an order made by a court of summary jurisdiction in pursuance of the Employers and Workmen Act 1875, and not otherwise.

1–036

Application of Act to Scotland

Application to Scotland

18. This Act shall extend to Scotland, with the modifications following; that is to say,
(1) [*Repealed by the Industrial Relations Act 1971 (c. 72), s.133 and Sched. 9.*]
(2) [*Repealed by the Statute Law Revision Act 1894 (c. 54).*]
(3) The expression "the court of summary jurisdiction" means the sheriff of the county or any one of his substitutes.

1–037

Recovery of penalties, &c., in Scotland

19. In Scotland the following provisions shall have effect in regard to the prosecution of offences, recovery of penalties, and making of orders under this Act:
(1) [*Repealed by the Criminal Law Act 1977 (c. 45), s.65 and Sched. 13*]:
(2) [*Repealed by the Criminal Law Act 1977 (c. 45), s.65 and Sched. 13*]:
(3) Every person found liable on conviction to pay any penalty under this Act shall be liable, in default of payment within a time to be fixed in the conviction, to be imprisoned for a term, to be also fixed therein, not exceeding two months, or until such penalty shall be sooner paid; and the conviction and warrant may be in the form of No. 3 of Schedule K. of the Summary Procedure Act 1864:
(4) In Scotland all penalties imposed in pursuance of this Act shall be paid to the clerk of the court imposing them, and shall by him be accounted for and paid to the Queen's and Lord Treasurer's Remembrancer, and be carried to the Consolidated Fund.

1–038

Appeal in Scotland

20. In Scotland it shall be competent to any person to appeal against any order or conviction under this Act to the High Court of Justiciary in the manner prescribed by and under the rules, limitations, conditions, and restrictions contained in the Heritable Jurisdictions (Scotland) Act 1746, in

1–039

12 Conspiracy and Protection of Property Act 1875

regard to appeals to circuit courts in matters criminal, as the same may be altered or amended by any Acts of Parliament for the time being in force.

Application of Act to Ireland

1–040 21. This Act shall extend to Ireland, with the modifications following; that is to say,

. . . . .

The expression "municipal authority" shall be construed to mean the town council of any borough for the time being subject to the Municipal Corporations (Ireland) 1840, and any commissioners invested by any general or local Act of Parliament, with power of improving, cleansing, lighting, or paving any town or township.

1–041 # Truck Amendment Act 1887

(50 & 51 VICT. c.46)

An Act to amend and extend the law relating to truck.

[16th September, 1887]

Short title

1–042 1. This Act may be cited as the Truck Amendment Act 1887.

AMENDMENT
By virtue of this section which has been repealed by the Statute Law Revision Act 1908, references in this Act to "the principal Act" were references to the Truck Act 1831, *ante*.

Application of principal Act to workman as defined by 38 & 39 Vict. c. 90

1–043 2. The provisions of the principal Act shall extend to, apply to, and include any workman [. . .], and the expression "artificer" in the principal Act shall be construed to include every workman [. . .], and all provisions and enactments in the principal Act inconsistent herewith are hereby repealed.
[In this section "workman" does not include a seaman or a domestic or menial servant but means any other person who, being a labourer, servant in husbandry, journeyman, artificer, handicraftsman, miner, or otherwise engaged in manual labour, whether under the age of eighteen years or above that age, has entered into or works under a contract with an employer, whether the contract be made before or after the passing of this Act, be express or implied, oral or in writing, and be a contract of service or a contract personally to execute any work or labour.]

AMENDMENT
The words omitted in the first paragraph of this section were repealed by the Statute Law (Repeals) Act 1973, Sched. 2. The second paragraph was added by the Statute Law (Repeals) Act 1973, Sched. 2.

Advance of wages

1–044 3. Whenever by agreement, custom, or otherwise a workman is entitled to receive in anticipation of the regular period of the payment of his wages an advance as part or on account thereof, it shall not be lawful for the employer to withhold such advance or make any deduction in respect of such advance on account of poundage, discount, or interest, or any similar charge.

Saving for servant in husbandry

4. Nothing in the principal Act or this Act shall render illegal a contract with a servant in husbandry for giving him food, drink, not being intoxicating, a cottage, or other allowances or privileges in addition to money wages as a remuneration for his services.

1–045

Order for goods as a deduction from wages illegal

5. In any action brought by a workman for the recovery of his wages, the employer shall not be entitled to any set off or counterclaim in respect of any goods supplied to the workman by any person under any order or direction of the employer, or any agent of the employer, and the employer of a workman or any agent of the employer, or any person supplying goods to the workman under any order or direction of such employer or agent, shall not be entitled to sue the workman for or in respect of any goods supplied by such employer or agent, or under such order or direction, as the case may be.

1–046

Provided that nothing in this section shall apply to anything excepted by section twenty-three of the principal Act.

No contracts with workman as to spending wages at any particular shop, etc.

6. No employer shall, directly or indirectly, by himself or his agent, impose as a condition, express or implied, in or for the employment of any workman any terms as to the place at which, or the manner in which, or the person with whom, any wages or portion of wages paid to the workman are or is to be expended, and no employer shall by himself or his agent dismiss any workman from his employment for or on account of the place at which, or the manner in which, or the person with whom, any wages or portion of wages paid by the employer to such workman are to be expended or fail or is expended.

1–047

Deduction for education

7. Where any deduction is made by an employer from a workman's wages for education, such workman on sending his child to any state-inspected school selected by the workman shall be entitled to have the school fees of his child at that school paid by the employer at the same rate and to the same extent as the other workmen from whose wages the like deduction is made by such employer.

1–048

In this section "state-inspected school" means any elementary school inspected under the direction of the Education Department in England or Scotland or of the Board of National Education in Ireland.

Deduction for sharpening tools, etc.

8. No deduction shall be made from a workman's wages for sharpening

1–049

or repairing tools, except by agreement not forming part of the condition of hiring.

Audit of deductions

1–050   9. Where deductions are made from the wages of any workman for the education of children or in respect of medicine, medical attendance, or tools, once at least in every year the employer shall, by himself or his agent, make out a correct account of the receipts and expenditure in respect of such deductions, and submit the same to be audited by two auditors appointed by the said workmen, and shall produce to the auditors all such books, vouchers, and documents, and afford them all such other facilities as are required for such audit.

Artificer to be paid in cash and not by way of barter for articles made by him

1–051   10. Where articles are made by a person at his own home, or otherwise, without the employment of any person under him except a member of his own family, the principal Act and this Act shall apply as if he were a workman, and the shopkeeper, dealer, trader, or other person buying the articles in the way of trade were his employer, and the provisions of this Act with respect to the payment of wages shall apply as if the price of an article were wages earned during the seven days next preceding the date at which any article is received from the workman by the employer.

This section shall apply only to articles under the value of five pounds knitted or otherwise manufactured of wool, worsted, yarn, stuff, jersey, linen, fustian, cloth, serge, cotton, leather, fur, hemp, flax, mohair, or silk, or of any combination thereof, or made or prepared of bone, thread, silk, or cotton lace, or of lace made of any mixed materials. Where it is made to appear to Her Majesty the Queen in Council that, in the interests of persons making articles to which this section applies in any county or place in the United Kingdom, it is expedient so to do, it shall be lawful for Her Majesty, by Order in Council, to suspend the operation of this section in such county or place, and the same shall accordingly be suspended, either wholly or in part, and either with or without any limitations or exceptions, according as is provided by the Order.

Offences

1–052   11. If any employer or his agent contravenes or fails to comply with any of the foregoing provisions of this Act, such employer or agent, as the case may be, shall be guilty of an offence against the principal Act, and shall be liable to the penalties imposed by section nine of that Act as if the offence were such an offence as in that section mentioned.

Fine on person committing offence for which employer is liable, and power of employer to exempt himself from penalty on conviction of actual offender

1–053   12.—(1) Where an offence for which an employer is, by virtue of the principal Act or this act, liable to a penalty has in fact been committed by some agent of the employer or other person, such agent or other person shall be liable to the same penalty as if he were the employer.

(2) Where an employer is charged with an offence against the principal Act or this Act he shall be entitled, upon information duly laid by him, to have any other person whom he charges as the actual offender brought before the court at the time appointed for hearing the charge, and if, after the commission of the offence has been proved the employer proves to the satisfaction of the court that he had used due diligence to enforce the execution of the said Acts, and that the said other person had committed the offence in question without his knowledge, consent, or connivance, the said other person shall be summarily convicted of such offence, and the employer shall be exempt from any penalty.

When it is made to appear to the satisfaction of [an officer appointed by the Secretary of State to enforce the provisions of the principal Act or this Act,] or in Scotland a procurator fiscal, at the time of discovering the offence, that the employer had used due diligence to enforce the execution of the said Acts, and also by what person such offence has been committed, and also that it had been committed without the knowledge, consent, or connivance of the employer, then [the officer] or procurator fiscal shall proceed against the person whom he believes to be the actual offender in the first instance without first proceeding against the employer.

AMENDMENT
The words in square brackets were substituted by the Truck Acts 1831 to 1896 (Enforcement) Regulations 1974 (S.I. 1974 No. 1887).

Recovery of penalties
13.—(1) [*Repealed by the Criminal Law Act 1977 (c. 45), s.65 and Sched. 13.*]
(2) [*Repealed by the Truck Acts 1831 to 1896 (Enforcement) Regulations 1974.*]
(3) [*Repealed by the Criminal Law Act 1977 (c. 45), s.65 and Sched. 13.*]
(4) In Scotland—
    (*a*) The procurators fiscal of the sheriff court shall, as part of their official duty, investigate and prosecute offences against the principal Act or this Act. [. . .]
    (*b*) All offences against the said Acts shall be prosecuted in the sheriff court.

1–054

AMENDMENT
The words omitted from subs. (4)(*a*) were repealed by the Truck Acts 1831 to 1896 (Enforcement) Regulations 1974 (S.I. 1974 No. 1887).

Definitions
14. In this Act, unless the context otherwise requires . . . expressions have the same meaning as in the principal Act.

1–055

Disqualification of justice
15. . . . .
A person engaged in the same trade or occupation as an employer charged with an offence against the principal Act or this Act shall not act as a justice of the peace in hearing and determining such charge.

1–056

AMENDMENT
The words omitted were repealed by the Statute Law (Revision) Act 1908 (8 Edw. 7, c. 49), Sched. L.

Application of Acts to Ireland

1-057   18. The principal Act, so far as it is not hereby repealed, and this Act shall extend to Ireland, subject to the following provisions—
  (1) [*Repealed by the Statute Law Revision Act* 1963 (*c.* 30).]
  (2) Penalties recovered under the principal Act or this Act shall be applied in the manner directed by the Fines (Ireland) Act 1851, and the Acts amending the same.

1-058

Truck Act 1896

(59 & 60 VICT. c.44)

An Act to amend the Truck Acts.

[14th August, 1896]

Deductions or payments in respect of fines

1-059   1.—(1) An employer shall not make any contract with any workman for any deduction from the sum contracted to be paid by the employer to the workman, or for any payment to the employer by the workman, for or in respect of any fine, unless—
  (*a*) the terms of the contract are contained in a notice kept constantly affixed at such place or places open to the workmen and in such a position that it may be easily seen, read, and copied by any person whom it affects; or the contract is in writing, signed by the workman; and
  (*b*) the contract specifies the acts or omissions in respect of which the fine may be imposed, and the amount of the fine or the particulars from which that amount may be ascertained; and
  (*c*) the fine imposed under the contract is in respect of some act or omission which causes or is likely to cause damage or loss to the employer, or interruption or hindrance to his business; and
  (*d*) the amount of the fine is fair and reasonable having regard to all the circumstances of the case.

(2) An employer shall not make any such deduction or receive any such payment, unless—
  (*a*) the deduction or payment is made in pursuance of, or in accordance with, such a contract as aforesaid and
  (*b*) particulars in writing showing the acts or omissions in respect of which the fine is imposed and the amount thereof are supplied to the workman on each occasion when a deduction or payment is made.

(3) This section shall apply to the case of a shop assistant in like manner as it applies to the case of a workman.

Deductions or payments in respect of damaged goods

1-060   2.—(1) An employer shall not make any contract with any workman for

any deduction from the sum contracted to be paid by the employer to the workman, or for any payment to the employer by the workman for or in respect of bad or negligent work or injury to the materials or other property of the employer, unless—
- (*a*) the terms of the contract are contained in a notice kept constantly affixed at such place or places open to the workmen and in such a position that it may be easily seen, read, and copied by any person whom it affects; or the contract is in writing, signed by the workman; and
- (*b*) the deduction or payment to be made under the contract does not exceed the actual or estimated damage or loss occasioned to the employer by the act or omission of the workman, or of some person over whom he has control, or for whom he has by the contract agreed to be responsible; and
- (*c*) the amount of the deduction or payment is fair and reasonable, having regard to all the circumstances of the case.

(2) An employer shall not make any such deduction or receive any such payment unless—
- (*a*) the deduction or payment is made in pursuance of, or in accordance with, such a contract as aforesaid; and
- (*b*) particulars in writing showing the acts or omissions in respect of which the deduction or payment is made and the amount thereof are supplied to the workman on each occasion when a deduction or payment is made.

Deductions or payment in respect of materials

3.—(1) An employer shall not make any contract with any workman for any deduction from the sum contracted to be paid by the employer to the workman, or for any payment to the employer by the workman for, or in respect of, the use or supply of materials, tools or machines, standing room, light, heat, or for or in respect of any other thing to be done or provided by the employer in relation to the work or labour of the workman unless—
- (*a*) the terms of the contract are contained in a notice kept constantly affixed at such place or places open to workmen, and in such a position that it may be easily seen, read, and copied by any person whom it affects; or the contract is in writing signed by the workman; and
- (*b*) the sum to be paid or deducted under the contract in respect of materials, tools or machines, standing room, light, heat, or any other thing, does not exceed, in the case of materials, or tools supplied to the workman, the actual or estimated cost thereof to the employer, or in the case of the use of machinery, light, heat, or any other thing in this section mentioned, a fair and reasonable rent or charge, having regard to all the circumstances of the case.

(2) An employer shall not make any such deduction or receive any such payment unless—
- (*a*) the deduction or payment is made in pursuance of, and in accordance with, such a contract as aforesaid; and
- (*b*) particulars in writing showing the things in respect of which the deduction or payment is made and the amount thereof are supplied

1–061

to the workman on each occasion when a deduction or payment is made.

Penalty

1–062   **4.** If any employer enters into any contract contrary to this Act, or makes any deduction or receives any payment contrary to this Act, he shall be guilty of an offence against the Truck Act 1831 and shall be liable to the penalties imposed by section nine of that Act as if the offence were an offence in that section mentioned.

Recovery of payments or deductions

1–063   **5.** Any workman or shop assistant may recover any sum deducted by or paid to his employer contrary to this Act, provided that proceedings for such recovery are commenced within six months from the date of the deduction or payment sought to be recovered, and that where he has consented to or acquiesced in any such deduction or payment, he shall only recover the excess which has been deducted or paid over the amount, if any, which the court may find to have been fair and reasonable, having regard to all the circumstances of the case.

Production of contract

1–064   **6.**—(1) Every employer who has made any contract purporting or intending to operate as a contract under this Act shall, on demand in writing by one of Her Majesty's inspectors of factories or of mines, produce the contract or a true copy thereof at any convenient time and place to be named by the inspector, and the inspector shall be at liberty to take a copy of the same or of any part thereof, and the employer of any workman or shop assistant who is party to any such contract shall at the time of making the contract give the workman or shop assistant a copy of the contract or of the notice containing its terms.

(2) A workman or shop assistant who is party to any such contract shall be entitled, on request, to obtain from his employer free of charge a copy of the contract or of the notice containing its terms.

(3) Every employer who has made any contract purporting or intending to operate as a contract under section one of this Act shall keep a register of deductions or payments, and shall enter therein every deduction or payment for or in respect of any fine purporting to be made under any such contract, specifying the amount and nature of the act or omission in respect of which the fine was imposed, and this register shall be at all times open to inspection by one of Her Majesty's Inspectors of Factories or of Mines.

(4) If any person fails to comply with this section he shall be liable on summary conviction to a fine not exceeding forty shillings.

. . . . . .

Saving as to contracts and payments illegal under existing Acts

1–065   **8.** Nothing in this Act shall make lawful any contract or payment which is illegal under the Truck Acts 1831 and 1887, or under the Hosiery Manufacture (Wages) Act 1874, or affect the provisions of the Coal Mines Regulation Act 1887, or any amending Act, with respect to persons employed in mines and paid according to weight, or make lawful any deduction from payments made to those persons.

. . . . . .

Power to exempt from provisions of Act

9.—(1) The Secretary of State, if satisfied that the provisions of this Act are unnecessary for the protection of the workmen employed in any trade or business, or in any branch or department of any trade or business, either generally or within any specified area, may by order under his hand grant an exemption from those provisions in respect of the persons engaged in that trade, business, branch or department, either generally or within that area.

(2) The Secretary of State may at any time amend or revoke any such order.

(3) Every order made under this section shall be laid as soon as may be before both Houses of Parliament, and if either House within the next forty days after the order has been so laid before that House resolves that the order ought to be annulled, the order shall, after the date of that resolution, be of no effect, without prejudice to the validity of anything done in the meantime under the order or to the making of a new order.

1–066

Duties of inspectors

10.—[(1) The Secretary of State, with the approval of the Minister for the Civil Service as to numbers and salaries, may appoint such officers as he thinks necessary for the purpose of enforcing the provisions of this Act and of the Truck Acts 1831 and 1887 and the persons so appointed shall for that purpose have the powers conferred on them by subsection (3) of this section.

(2) Every appointment under the preceding subsection shall be made by an instrument in writing and an officer appointed thereunder shall, if so required when exercising or seeking to exercise any power conferred on him by subsection (3) of this section, produce his instrument of appointment or a duly authenticated copy thereof.

(3) An officer appointed under subsection (1) of this section may, for the purpose there mentioned, exercise any of the following powers:—

- (a) at any reasonable time to enter any premises where any person is or has been employed whom he has reason to believe is a workman to whom the said Acts apply or applied and, at any reasonable time, to enter any premises from which work in connection with the business carried on at those premises is given out to outworkers to whom he has reason to believe the said Acts apply;
- (b) to require the production of, inspect, and take copies of or of any entry in any wage sheets or other records of wages kept by an employer, and records of payments made to outworkers by persons giving out work;
- (c) to require any person giving out work and any outworker to give any information which it is in his power to give with respect to the names and addresses of the persons to whom the work is given out or from whom the work is received, as the case may be, and with respect to the payments to be made for the work;

1–067

(d) to inspect and copy the whole or any material part of any list of outworkers kept by an employer or person giving out work to outworkers;

(e) to require any person whom he has reasonable cause to believe to be able to give any information relevant to his investigation under the said Acts to answer (in the absence of persons other than a person nominated by him to be present and any persons whom the officer may allow to be present) such questions as the officer thinks fit to ask and to sign a declaration of the truth of his answers, so however that no one shall be required under this provision to answer any question tending to criminate himself or, in the case of a person who is married, his or her wife or husband.

(4) In England and Wales, an officer appointed under subsection (1) of this section, if authorised in that behalf by the Secretary of State may, although not of counsel or a solicitor, prosecute before a magistrates' court proceedings for an offence under any of the said Acts.

(5) If any person in purported compliance with a requirement imposed under this section—

(a) produces or furnishes or causes or knowingly allows to be produced or furnished any wages sheet, record, list or other document which he knows to be false in a material particular; or

(b) makes any statement which he knows to be false in a material particular or recklessly makes a statement which is so false,

he shall be guilty of an offence and liable on summary conviction to a fine not exceeding £100 or to imprisonment for a term not exceeding three months or to both such fine and such imprisonment.

(6) If any person intentionally obstructs an officer appointed under subsection (1) of this section in the exercise or performance of his powers or duties or fails to comply with any requirement imposed by such an officer in the exercise of his powers, he shall be guilty of an offence and liable on summary conviction to a fine not exceeding £20.]

AMENDMENTS
The words in square brackets were substituted by the Truck Acts 1831 to 1896 (Enforcement) Regulations 1974 (S.I. 1974 No. 1887), reg. 2(6).

. . . . . .

Short title and construction

1-068 **12.** This Act may be cited as the Truck Act 1896; and the Truck Acts 1831 and 1887 and this Act shall be construed together as one Act and may be cited collectively as the Truck Acts 1831 to 1896.

1-069

Bankruptcy (Scotland) Act 1913

(3 & 4 GEO. 5, c.20)

. . . . . .

Preferential payments

118.—(1) In the division of a bankrupt's estate under the provisions of this Act the following shall be paid in priority to all other debts:—

. . . . . .

(b) All wages or salary of any clerk or servant in respect of service rendered to the bankrupt during four months before the said date not exceeding [eight hundred] pounds to any one clerk or servant;

(c) All wages of any workman or labourer not exceeding [eight hundred] pounds to any one workman or labourer, whether payable for time or for piece work, in respect of services rendered to the bankrupt during [four] months before the said date. Provided that, where any labourer in husbandry has entered into a contract for the payment to him of a portion of his wages in a lump sum, the priority under this section shall extend to the whole of such sum or a part thereof as the court may decide to be due under the contract proportionate to the time of service up to the said date;

. . . . . .

[(f) All the debts specified in section 153(2) of the Social Security Act 1975; Schedule 3 to the Social Security Pensions Act 1975, and any corresponding provisions in force in Northern Ireland.]

(2) The foregoing debts shall rank equally among themselves and shall be paid in full, unless the assets are insufficient to meet them, in which case they shall abate in equal proportions.

. . . . . .

(4) The date hereinbefore referred to in this section is the date of the award of sequestration, and, in the case of the sequestration of the estates of a deceased debtor, the date of his death, and, where sequestration has not been awarded, the date of the concourse of diligence for distribution of the estate of a party being notour bankrupt.

AMENDMENT
The words in square brackets in paras. (b) and (c) were substituted by the Companies Act 1947, s.115, and the Insolvency Act 1976, s.1. Para. (f) was substituted by the Social Security Pensions Act 1975 (c. 60), Sched. 4.

Trade Union Act 1913

(2 & 3 GEO. 5, c.30)

An Act to amend the Law with respect to the objects and powers of Trade Unions.

[7th March 1913]

NOTE
In this Act, the words in square brackets have been substituted by the Trade Unions and Labour Relations Act 1974 (c. 52), Scheds. 3 and 5.

Amendment of law as to objects and powers of trade unions

1-071   **1.**—(1): [*Repealed by the Industrial Relations Act* 1971 (*c.* 72), *Sched.* 9.]
(2) For the purposes of this Act, the expression "statutory objects" means [. . .] the regulation of the relations between workmen and masters, or between workmen and workmen, or between masters and masters, or the imposing of restrictive conditions on the conduct of any trade or business, and also the provision of benefits to members.

AMENDMENT
   The words omitted from this section were repealed by the Industrial Relations Act 1971 (c. 72), Sched. 9.

Definition of [organisation to which this Act applies]

1-072   **2.**—[(1) In this Act, except so far as the context otherwise requires, "trade union" means an organisation (whether permanent or temporary) which either—
   (*a*) consists wholly or mainly of workers of one or more descriptions and is an organisation whose principal purposes include the regulation of relations between workers of that description or those descriptions and employers or employers' associations; or
   (*b*) consists wholly or mainly of—
      (i) constituent or affiliated organisations which fulfil the conditions specified in paragraph (*a*) above (or themselves consist wholly or mainly of constituent or affiliated organisations which fulfil those conditions), or
      (ii) representatives of such constituent or affiliated organisations;
   and in either case is an organisation whose principal purposes include the regulation of relations between workers and employers or between workers and employers' associations, or include the regulation of relations between its constituent or affiliated organisations.
(1A) In this Act, except so far as the context otherwise requires, "employers' association" means an organisation (whether permanent or temporary) which is unincorporated and either—
   (*a*) consists wholly or mainly of employers or individual proprietors of one or more descriptions and is an organisation whose principal purposes include the regulation of relations between employers of that description or those descriptions and workers or trade unions; or
   (*b*) consists wholly or mainly of—
      (i) constituent or affiliated organisations which fulfil the conditions specified in paragraph (*a*) above (or themselves consist wholly or mainly of constituent or affiliated organisations which fulfil those conditions), or
      (ii) representatives of such constituent or affiliated organisations;
   and in either case is an organisation whose principal purposes include the regulation of relations between employers and workers or between employers and trade unions, or include the regulation of relations between its constituent or affiliated organisations.]
(2) [*Repealed by the Industrial Relations Act* 1971 (*c.* 72), *Sched.* 9.]

AMENDMENT
The words in square brackets in subss. (1) and (1A) were added by the Trade Union and Labour Relations Act 1974 (c. 52), Sched. 3, para. 2(2) and Sched. 5.

Restriction on application of funds for certain political purposes

3.—(1) The funds of [a trade union] shall not be applied, either directly or in conjunction with any other [trade union], association, or body, or otherwise indirectly, in the furtherance of the political objects to which this section applies (without prejudice to the furtherance of any other political objects), unless the furtherance of those objects has been approved as an object of the [union] by a resolution for the time being in force passed on a ballot of the members of the [union] taken in accordance with this Act for the purpose by a majority of the members voting; and where such a resolution is in force, unless rules, to be approved, [. . .] by the [Certification Officer] are in force providing—

(*a*) That any payments in the furtherance of those objects are to be made out of a separate fund (in this Act referred to as the political fund of the [union] and for the exemption in accordance with this Act of any member of the [union] from any obligation to contribute to such a fund if he gives notice in accordance with this Act that he objects to contribute; and

(*b*) That a member who is exempt from the obligation to contribute to the political fund of the [union] shall not be excluded from any benefits of the [union], or placed in any respect either directly or indirectly under any disability or at any disadvantage as compared with other members of the [union] (except in relation to the control or management of the political fund) by reason of his being so exempt, and that contribution to the political fund of the [union] shall not be made a condition for admission to the [union].

(2) If any member of [a trade union] alleges that he is aggrieved by a breach of any rule made in pursuance of this section, he may complain to the [Certification Officer], and the [Certification Officer], after giving the complainant and any representative of the [union] an opportunity of being heard, may, if he considers that such a breach has been committed, make such order for remedying the breach as he thinks just under the circumstances; and [any such order of the [Certification Officer] [. . .] on being recorded in the county court, may be enforced as if it had been an order of the county court. In the application of this provision to Scotland the sheriff court shall be substituted for the county court, [. . .].

(3) The political objects to which this section applies are the expenditure of money—

(*a*) on the payment of any expenses incurred either directly or indirectly by a candidate or prospective candidate for election to Parliament or to any public office, before, during, or after the election in connexion with his candidature or election; or

(*b*) on the holding of any meeting or the distribution of any literature or documents in support of any such candidate or prospective candidate; or

(*c*) on the maintenance of any person who is a member of Parliament or who holds a public office; or

(*d*) in connexion with the registration of electors or the selection of a candidate for Parliament or any public office; or

(e) on the holding of political meetings of any kind, or on the distribution of political literature or political documents of any kind, unless the main purpose of the meetings or of the distribution of the literature or documents is the furtherance of statutory objects within the meaning of this Act.

The expression "public office" in this section means the office of member of any county, county borough, district, or parish council, or board of guardians, or of any public body who have power to raise money, either directly or indirectly, by means of a rate.

(4) A resolution under this section approving political objects as an object of the [union] shall take effect as if it were a rule of the [union] and may be rescinded in the same manner and subject to the same provisions as such a rule.

(5) The provisions of this Act as to the application of the funds of [a union] for political purposes shall apply to [a union] which is in whole or in part an association or combination of other unions as if the individual members of the component unions were the members of that [union] and not the unions; but nothing in this Act shall prevent any such component [union] from collecting from any of their members who are not exempt on behalf of the association or combination any contributions to the political fund of the association or combination.

AMENDMENT
The words omitted from this section were repealed by the Trade Union and Labour Relations Act 1974 (c. 52), Sched. 3, para. 2(4) and Sched. 5, and words inserted by *ibid.* Sched. 3, para. 2(3).
The words "Certification Officer" in this section replace the title "Register of Friendly Societies" by virtue of the Employment Protection Act 1975 (c. 71), s.7(2)(*a*).

Approval of rules

1–074   **4.**—(1) A ballot for the purposes of this Act shall be taken in accordance with rules of the [union] to be approved for the purpose, [. . .] by the [Certification Officer], but the [Certification Officer] shall not approve any such rules unless he is satisfied that every member has an equal right, and, if reasonably possible, a fair opportunity of voting, and that the secrecy of ballot is properly secured.

(2) If the [Certification Officer] is satisfied, and certifies, that rules for the purpose of a ballot under this Act or rules made for other purposes of this Act which require approval by the [Certification Officer], have been approved by a majority of members of [a trade union] [. . .], voting for the purpose, or by a majority of delegates of such [a trade union] voting at a meeting called for the purpose those rules shall have effect as rules of the [union], notwithstanding that the provisions of the rules of the [union] as to the alteration of rules or the making of new rules have not been complied with.

AMENDMENT
The words omitted from this section were repealed by the Trade Union and Labour Relations Act 1974. The words in square brackets were substituted by the Trade Union and Labour Relations Act 1974; the title "Certification Officer" replaces "Registrar of Friendly Societies" by virtue of the Employment Protection Act 1975 (c. 71), s.7(2)(*a*).

Notice of objection to contribute towards political object

1–075   **5.**—(1) A member of [a trade union] may at any time give notice, in the form set out in the Schedule to this Act or in a form to the like effect, that he objects to contribute to the political fund of the [union], and, on the adoption of a resolution of the [union] approving the furtherance of political objects as an object of the [union], notice shall be given to the members of the [union] acquainting them that each member has a right to be exempt from contributing to the political fund of the [union], and that a form of exemption notice can be obtained by or on behalf of a member either by application at or by post from the head office or any branch office of the [union] or the office of the [Certification Officer].

Any such notice to members of the [union] shall be given in accordance with rules of the [union] approved for the purpose by the [Certification Officer], having regard in each case to the existing practice and to the character of the [union].

(2) On giving notice in accordance with this Act of his objection to contribute, a member of the [union] shall be exempt, so long as his notice is not withdrawn, from contributing to the political fund of the [union] as from the first day of January next after the notice is given, or in the case of a notice given within one month after the notice given to members under this section on the adoption of a resolution approving the furtherance of political objects, as from the date on which the member's notice is given.

AMENDMENT

The words in square brackets in this section were substituted by the Trade Union and Labour Relations Act 1974 (c. 52), Sched. 3; the title "Certification Officer" replaces "Registrar of Friendly Societies" by virtue of the Employment Protection Act 1975 (c. 71), s.7(2)(*a*).

[Appeals

5A. An appeal shall lie, in accordance with [section 136(2) of the Employment Protection (Consolidation) Act 1978], to the Employment Appeal Tribunal on any question of law arising in any proceedings before or arising from any decision of the Certification Officer under section 3, 4 or 5 of this Act.]

1–076

AMENDMENT

This section was added by the Employment Protection Act 1975 (c. 71), s.125(1), Sched. 16, and amended by the Employment Protection (Consolidation) Act 1978 (c. 44), Sched. 16.

Mode of giving effect to exemption from contributions to political fund

6. Effect may be given to the exemption of members to contribute to the political fund of [a trade union] either by a separate levy of contributions to that fund from the members of the [union] who are not exempt, and in that case the rules shall provide that no moneys of the [union] other than the amount raised by such separate levy shall be carried to that fund, or by relieving any members who are exempt from the payment of the whole or any part of any periodical contributions required from the members of the [union] towards the expenses of the [union], and in that case the rules shall provide that the relief shall be given as far as possible to all members who are exempt on the occasion of the same periodical payment and for enabling each member of the [union] to know as respects any such periodical contribution, what portion, if any, of the sum payable by him is a contribution to the political fund of the [union].

1–077

AMENDMENT
The words in square brackets in this section were substituted by the Trade Union and Labour Relations Act 1974 (c. 52), Sched. 3.

[Application of sections 3 to 6 to employers' associations

1–078   **6A.** Sections 3 to 6 of, and the Schedule to, this Act shall apply, with the necessary modifications, in relation to unincorporated employers' associations as they apply in relation to trade unions.]

AMENDMENT
This section was added by the Trade Union and Labour Relations Act 1974 (c. 52), Sched. 3, para. 2.

[Definition of Certification Officer

1–079   **7.** In this Act references to the "Certification Officer" are references to the officer appointed under section 7 of the Employment Protection Act 1975.]

AMENDMENT
This section was substituted by the Employment Protection Act 1975 (c. 71), s.125(1), Sched. 16, para. 2(4).

Short title and construction

1–080   **8.** This Act may be cited as the Trade Union Act 1913 and shall be construed as one with the Trade Union Acts 1871 and 1876; and this Act and the Trade Union Acts 1871 to 1906 may be cited together as the Trade Union Acts 1871 to 1913.

1–081

SCHEDULE
FORM OF EXEMPTION NOTICE

Name of Organisation

POLITICAL FUND (EXEMPTION NOTICE)
I hereby give notice that I object to contribute to the Political Fund of the
Union, and am in consequence exempt, in manner provided by the Trade Union Act 1913, from contributing to that fund.

                A.B.
                        Address
    day of   19   .

1–082

Bankruptcy Act 1914

(4 & 5 GEO. 5, C.59)

An act to consolidate the law relating to Bankruptcy.

[10th August 1914]

. . . . . .

Priority of debts

33.—(1) In the distribution of the property of a bankrupt there shall be paid in priority to all other debts—

. . . . . .

(b) All wages or salary of any clerk or servant in respect of services rendered to the bankrupt during four months before the date of the receiving order, not exceeding [eight hundred] pounds;

(c) All wages of any labourer or workman not exceeding [eight hundred] pounds, whether payable for time or for piece work, in respect of services rendered to the bankrupt during [four] months before the date of the receiving order: Provided that, where any labourer in husbandry has entered into a contract for the payment of a portion of his wages in a lump sum at the end of the year of hiring, the priority under this section shall extend to the whole of such sum, or a part thereof, as the court may decide to be due under the contract, proportionate to the time of service up to the date of the receiving order;

. . . . . .

[(f) All the debts specified in section 153(2) of the Social Security Act 1975; Schedule 3 to the Social Security Pensions Act 1975 and any corresponding provisions in force in Northern Ireland.]

(2) The foregoing debts shall rank equally between themselves and shall be paid in full, unless the property of the bankrupt is insufficient to meet them, in which case they shall abate in equal proportions between themselves.

AMENDMENT

The words in square brackets in paras. (b) and (c) were substituted by the Companies Act 1947 (c. 47), s.115, and the Insolvency Act 1976 (c. 60), s.1. Para. (f) was substituted by the Social Security Pensions Act 1975 (c. 60), Sched. 4.

Preferential claim in case of apprenticeship

34.—(1) Where at the time of the presentation of the bankruptcy petition any person is apprenticed or is an articled clerk to the bankrupt, the adjudication of bankruptcy shall, if either the bankrupt or apprentice or clerk gives notice in writing to the trustee to that effect, be a complete discharge of the indenture of apprenticeship or articles of agreement; and, if any money has been paid by or on behalf of the apprentice or clerk to the bankrupt as a fee, the trustee may, on the application of the apprentice or clerk, or of some person on his behalf, pay such sum as the trustee, subject to an appeal to the court, thinks reasonable, out of the bankrupt's property, to or for the use of the apprentice or clerk, regard being had to the amount paid by him or on his behalf, and to the time during which he served with the bankrupt under the indenture or articles before the commencement of the bankruptcy, and to the other circumstances of the case.

(2) Where it appears expedient to a trustee, he may, on the application of any apprentice or articled clerk to the bankrupt, or any person acting under the preceding provisions of this section, transfer the indenture of apprenticeship or articles of agreement to some other person.

Industrial Courts Act 1919

(9 & 10 Geo 5, c.69)

An Act to provide for the establishment of an Industrial Court and Courts of Inquiry in connection with Trade Disputes, and to make other provision for the settlement of such disputes.

[20th November 1919.]

NOTE

In this Act, the words in square brackets were substituted by the Industrial Relations Act 1971 (c. 72), Sched. 8, continued by the Trade Union and Labour Relations Act 1974 (c. 52), Sched. 3, para. 3.

For the words "Minister" read "Secretary of State" throughout this Act as amended by the Secretary of State for Trade and Industry Order 1970 (S.I. 1970 No. 1537).

. . . . . .

PART II

COURTS OF INQUIRY

Inquiry into trade disputes

4.—(1) Where any trade dispute exists or is apprehended, the Minister may, [. . .], inquire into the causes and circumstances of the dispute, and, if he thinks fit, refer any matters appearing to him to be connected with or relevant to the dispute to a court of inquiry appointed by him for the purpose of such reference, and the court shall, either in public or in private, at their discretion, inquire into the matters referred to them and report thereon to the Minister.

(2) A court of inquiry for the purposes of this Part of this Act (in this Act referred to as "a court of inquiry") shall consist of a chairman and such other persons as the Minister thinks fit to appoint, or may, if the Minister thinks fit, consist of one person appointed by the Minister.

(3) A court of inquiry may act notwithstanding any vacancy in their number.

(4) The Minister may make rules regulating the procedure of any court of inquiry, including rules as to summoning of witnesses, quorum, and the appointment of committees and enabling the court to call for such documents as the court may determine to be relevant to the subject-matter of the inquiry.

(5) A court of inquiry may, if and to such extent as may be authorised by rules made under this section, by order require any person who appears to the court to have any knowledge of the subject-matter of the inquiry to furnish, in writing or otherwise, such particulars in relation thereto as the court may require, and, where necessary, to attend before the court and give evidence on oath, and the court may administer or authorise any person to administer an oath for that purpose.

AMENDMENT

The words omitted in subs. (1) were repealed by the Employment Protection Act 1975 (c. 71), s.125(1), Sched. 16.

Reports

5.—(1) A court of inquiry may, if it thinks fit, make interim reports.   1–086

(2) Any report of a court of inquiry, and any minority report, shall be laid as soon as may be before both Houses of Parliament.

(3) The Minister may, whether before or after any such report has been laid before Parliament, publish or cause to be published from time to time, in such manner as he thinks fit, any information obtained or conclusions arrived at by the court as the result or in the course of their inquiry:

Provided that there shall not be included in any report or publication made or authorised by the court or the Minister any information obtained by the court in the course of their inquiry as to any trade union or as to any individual business (whether carried on by a person, firm, or company) which is not available otherwise than through evidence given at the inquiry, except with the consent of the secretary of the trade union or of the person, firm, or company in question, nor shall any individual member of the court or any person concerned in the inquiry, without such consent, disclose any such information.

. . . . . .

PART IV

GENERAL

Remuneration and expenses

7. Any expenses incurred by the Minister in carrying this Act into operation, including the expenses [. . .] of any court of inquiry, shall be paid out of moneys provided by Parliament.   1–087

AMENDMENT
The words omitted in this section were repealed by the Employment Protection Act 1975 (c. 71), s.125(1), Sched. 16.

[Interpretation

8. In this Act the expression "trade dispute" and "worker" have the same meaning as in the Trade Union and Labour Relations Act 1974.]   1–088

AMENDMENT
This section was substituted by the Employment Protection Act 1975 (c. 71), s.125(1), Sched. 16.

Rules as to appearance by counsel or solicitor

9. Provision shall be made by rules under this Act with respect to the cases in which persons may appear by counsel or solicitor on proceedings under this Act [. . .] before a court of inquiry, and except as provided by those rules no person shall be entitled to appear on any such proceedings by counsel or solicitor.   1–089

AMENDMENT
The words omitted in this section were repealed by the Employment Protection Act 1975 (c. 71), s.125(1), Sched. 16.

Employment under the Crown

1-090 [**10.**—(1) Subject to lthe following provisions of this section, the provisions of this Act shall have effect in relation to Crown employment and to workers who are Crown employees as they have effect in relation to other employment and to other workers.

(2) In this section "Crown employment" means, subject to subsection (3) of this section, employment under or for the purposes of a government department or any officer or body exercising on behalf of the Crown functions conferred by any enactment.

(3) This section does not apply to service as a member of the naval, military or air forces of the Crown or of any women's service administered by the Defence Council, but does not apply to employment by any association established for the purposes of the Auxiliary Forces Act 1953.

(4) A Minister of the Crown may exempt from the provisions of this section employment of a specified description or the employment of a particular person by certificate stating that such exemption is required for the purpose of safeguarding national security; and any document purporting to be such a certificate shall, unless the contrary is proved, be deemed to be such a certificate.]

AMENDMENT
This section was substituted by the Employment Protection Act 1975 (c. 71), s.125(1), Sched. 16.

. . . . . .

Report to Parliament

1-091 13. The Minister shall from time to time present to Parliament a report of his proceedings under this Act.

Short title

1-092 14. This Act may be cited as the Industrial Courts Act 1919.

Sex Disqualification (Removal) Act 1919

1-093

(9 & 10 GEO 5, c.71)

An Act to amend the Law with respect to disqualifications on account of sex.

[23rd December 1919]

Removal of disqualification on grounds of sex
1. A person shall not be disqualified by sex or marriage from . . . entering or assuming or carrying on any civil profession or vocation, . . .

Emergency Powers Act 1920

1-094

(1920 c.55)

An Act to make exceptional provision for the Protection of the Community in cases of Emergency.

[29th October 1920.]

Issue of proclamations of emergency

1.—(1) If at any time it appears to His Majesty that [there have occurred, or are about to occur, events of such a nature] as to be calculated, by interfering with the supply and distribution of food, water, fuel, or light, or with the means of locomotion, to deprive the community, or any substantial portion of the community, of the essentials of life, His Majesty may, by proclamation (hereinafter referred to as a proclamation of emergency), declare that a state of emergency exists.

1–095

No such proclamation shall be in force for more than one month, without prejudice to the issue of another proclamation at or before the end of that period.

(2) Where a proclamation of emergency has been made the occasion thereof shall forthwith be communicated to Parliament, and, if Parliament is then separated by such adjournment or prorogation as will not expire within five days, a proclamation shall be issued for the meeting of Parliament within five days, and Parliament shall accordingly meet and sit upon the day appointed by that proclamation, and shall continue to sit and act in like manner as if it had stood adjourned or prorogued to the same day.

AMENDMENT
The words in square brackets were substituted by the Emergency Powers Act 1964 (c. 38), s.1.

Emergency regulations

2.—(1) Where a proclamation of emergency has been made, and so long as the proclamation is in force, it shall be lawful for His Majesty in Council, by Order, to make regulations for securing the essentials of life to the community, and those regulations may confer or impose on a Secretary of State or other Government department, or any other persons in His Majesty's service or acting on His Majesty's behalf, such powers and duties as His Majesty may deem necessary for the preservation of the peace, for securing and regulating the supply and distribution of food, water, fuel, light, and other necessities, for maintaining the means of transit or locomotion, and for any other purposes essential to the public safety and the life of the community, and may make such provisions incidental to the powers aforesaid as may appear to His Majesty to be required for making the exercise of those powers effective:

1–096

Provided that nothing in this Act shall be construed to authorise the making of any regulations imposing any form of compulsory military service or industrial conscription:

Provided also that no such regulation shall make it an offence for any person or persons to take part in a strike, or peacefully to persuade any other person or persons to take part in a strike.

(2) Any regulations so made shall be laid before Parliament as soon as may be after they are made, and shall not continue in force after the expiration of seven days from the time when they are so laid unless a resolution is passed by both Houses providing for the continuance thereof.

(3) The regulations may provide for the trial, by courts of summary jurisdiction, of persons guilty of offences against the regulations; so, however, that the maximum penalty which may be inflicted for any offence against

any such regulations shall be imprisonment with or without hard labour for a term of three months, or a fine of one hundred pounds, or both such imprisonment and fine, together with the forfeiture of any goods or money in respect of which the offence has been committed: Provided that no such regulations shall alter any existing procedure in criminal cases, or confer any right to punish by fine or imprisonment without trial.

(4) The regulations so made shall have effect as if enacted in this Act, but may be added to, altered, or revoked by resolution of both Houses of Parliament or by regulations made in like manner and subject to the like provisions as the original regulations [. . .]

(5) The expiry or revocation of any regulations so made shall not be deemed to have affected the previous operation thereof, or the validity of any action taken thereunder, or any penalty or punishment incurred in respect of any contravention or failure to comply therewith, or any proceeding or remedy in respect of any such punishment or penalty.

AMENDMENT
The words omitted in this section were repealed by the Statute Law Revision Act 1963 (c. 30), Sched.

Short title and application

3.—(1) This Act may be cited as the Emergency Powers Act 1920.
(2) This Act shall not apply to Ireland.

Bankruptcy (Amendment) Act 1926

(16 & 17 GEO. 5, c.7)

An Act to amend the Bankruptcy Act 1914.

[16th June 1926.]

. . . . . .

Explanation of the Bankruptcy Act 1914, s.33
2. For the removal of doubts it is hereby declared that the priority given by section thirty-three of the principal Act to the wages or salary of any clerk or servant in respect of services rendered to a bankrupt during four months before the date of the receiving order, not exceeding fifty pounds, applies to any such wages or salary as aforesaid whether or not earned wholly or in part by way of commission.

Truck Act 1940

(3 & 4 GEO. 6, c.38)

An Act to restrain legal proceedings under the Truck Acts 1831 to 1896 in respect of certain transactions heretofore effected which might lawfully have been effected in another form, and to remove doubts as to whether persons employed under contracts rendered illegal by those Acts are or were to be regarded for purposes other than those of the said Acts as employed under contracts of service.

[10th July, 1940]

Restraint on proceedings under 1 & 2 Will. 4, c. 37, and removal of doubts as to effect of illegality of contracts

1.—(1) [*This subsection was repealed by the Statute Law (Repeals) Act 1973, Sched. 1.*]

(2) For the removal of doubt it is hereby declared that in determining for any purpose other than the purposes of the Truck Acts 1831 to 1896 whether a person is or was before the commencement of this Act employed under a contract of service, the person shall not be deemed not to be or not to have been so employed by reason only of the contract being or having been illegal, null, or void under the said Acts.

(3) [*This subsection was repealed by the Statute Law (Repeals) Act 1973, Sched. 1.*]

1–100

. . . . . .

Short title, citation and extent

3.—(1) This Act may be cited as the Truck Act 1940, and this Act and the Truck Acts 1831 to 1896 may be cited together as the Truck Acts 1831 to 1940.

(2) [. . .] this act shall not extend to Northern Ireland.

1–101

AMENDMENT
The words omitted in subs. (2) were repealed by the Statute Law (Repeals) Act 1973 (c. 39), Sched. 1.

Companies Act 1947

1–102

(10 & 11 GEO. 6, C.47)

An Act to amend the law relating to companies and unit trusts and to dealing in securities, and in connection therewith to amend the law of bankruptcy and the law relating to the registration of business names.

[6th August 1947]

. . . . . .

PART V

WINDING UP

. . . . . .

Amendments as to preferential payments

1–103   91.—(1) The maximum amount to which, under subsection (1) of section two hundred and sixty-four of the principal Act, priority is to be given—
   (a) to a debt for the wages or salary of a clerk or servant; or
   (b) to a debt for the wages of a workmen or labourer; or
   (c) to any sum ordered under the Reinstatement in Civil Employment Act 1944, to be paid by way of compensation;
shall be two hundred pounds (instead of being fifty pounds in the cases referred to in paragraphs (a) and (c) of this subsection or twenty-five pounds in the case referred to in paragraph (b) thereof).

(2) The period within which services must have been rendered by a workman or labourer for his wages in respect thereof to have priority under the said subsection (1) shall be the same as in the case of a clerk or servant, that is to say, four months (instead of two months).

(3) [*Repealed by the Companies Act* 1948 (*c.* 38), *s.*459 *and Sched.* 17, *Part* I.]

(4) For the purposes of the said section two hundred and sixty-four any remuneration in respect of a period of holiday or of absence from work through sickness or other good cause shall be deemed to be wages in respect of services rendered to the company during that period.

(5) The debts which are to be paid in priority under the said section two hundred and sixty-four shall include all accrued holiday remuneration becoming payable to a clerk, servant, workman or labourer (or in the case of his death to any other person in his right) on the termination of his employment with the company before or by the effect of the winding up order or resolution;

(6) For the purposes of this section—
   (a) the expression "accrued holiday remuneration" includes in relation to any person, all sums which, by virtue either of his contract of employment or of any enactment (including any order made or direction given under any Act), are payable on account of the remuneration which would in the ordinary course have become payable to him in respect of a period of holiday had his employment with the company continued until he became entitled to be allowed the holiday; and
   (b) references to remuneration in respect of a period of holiday include any sums which, if they had been paid, would have been treated for the purposes of the National Insurance Act 1946, or any enactment repealed by that Act as remuneration in respect of that period.

(7)(8) [*Repealed by the Companies Act* 1948 (*c.* 38), *s.*459 *and Sched.* 17, *Part* I.]

Part VIII

Amendments etc. of Acts other than principal Act

Bankruptcy

1–104   115.—(1) Subsection (1) of section thirty-three of the Bankruptcy Act 1914, and subsection (1) of section one hundred and eighteen of the Bankruptcy (Scotland) Act 1913, shall have effect subject to the like amendments as are by [section ninety-one of this Act] made in relation to the winding up of a company but with the substitution for references to the company and to the winding up order or resolution of references to the bankrupt and to the receiving order or, in the case of a person dying insolvent, to the deceased and to his death.

Companies Act 1948

1–105

(11 & 12 GEO. 6, C.38)

Meaning of "holding company" and "subsidiary"

154.—(1) For the purposes of this Act, a company shall, subject to the provisions of subsection (3) of this section, be deemed to be a subsidiary of another if, but only if,—

1–106

   (*a*) that other either—
      (i) is a member of it and controls the composition of its board of directors; or
      (ii) holds more than half in nominal value of its equity share capital; or
   (*b*) the first-mentioned company is a subsidiary of any company which is that other's subsidiary.

(2) For the purposes of the foregoing subsection, the composition of a company's board of directors shall be deemd to be controlled by another company if, but only if, that other company by the exercise of some power exercisable by it without the consent or concurrence of any other person can appoint or remove the holders of all or a majority of the directorships; but for the purposes of this provision that other company shall be deemed to have power to appoint to a directorship with respect to which any of the following conditions is satisfied, that is to say—

   (*a*) that a person cannot be appointed thereto without the exercise in his favour by that other company of such a power as aforesaid; or
   (*b*) that a person's appointment thereto follows necessarily from his appointment as director of that other company; or
   (*c*) that the directorship is held by that other company itself or by a subsidiary of it.

(3) In determining whether one company is a subsidiary of another—

   (*a*) any shares held or power exercisable by that other in a fiduciary capacity shall be treated as not held or exercisable by it;
   (*b*) subject to the two following paragraphs, any shares held or power exercisable—
      (i) by any person as a nominee for that other (except where that other is concerned only in a fiduciary capacity); or
      (ii) by, or by a nominee for, a subsidiary of that other not being a subsidiary which is concerned only in a fiduciary capacity;
   shall be treated as held or exercisable by that other;
   (*c*) any shares held or power exercisable by any person by virtue of the provisions of any debentures of the first-mentioned com-

pany or of a trust deed for securing any issue of such debentures shall be disregarded;

(*d*) any shares held or power exercisable by, or by a nominee for, that other or its subsidiary (not being held or exercisable as mentioned in the last foregoing paragraph) shall be treated as not held or exercisable by that other if the ordinary business of that other or its subsidiary, as the case may be, includes the lending of money and the shares are held or power is exercisable as aforesaid by way of security only for the purposes of a transaction entered into in the ordinary course of that business.

(4) For the purposes of this Act, a company shall be deemed to be another's holding company if, but only if, that other is its subsidiary.

(5) In this section the expression "company" includes any body corporate, and the expression "equity share capital" means, in relation to a company, its issued share capital excluding any part thereof which, neither as respects dividends nor as respects capital, carries any right to participate beyond a specified amount in a distribution.

. . . . .

Preferential payments

1–107 319.—(1) In a winding up there shall be paid in priority to all other debts—

. . . . .

(*b*) all wages or salary (whether or not earned wholly or in part by way of commission) of any clerk or servant in respect of services rendered to the company during four months next before the relevant date and all wages (whether payable for time or for piece work) of any workman or labourer in respect of services so rendered;

(*c*) any sum ordered under the Reinstatement in Civil Employment Act 1944, to be paid by way of compensation where the default by reason of which the order for compensation was made occurred before the relevant date, whether or not the order was made before that date;

(*d*) all accrued holiday remuneration becoming payable to any clerk, servant, workman or labourer (or in the case of his death to any other person in his right) on the termination of his employment before or by the effect of the winding-up order or resolution;

. . . . .

(*f*) unless the company is being wound up voluntarily merely for the purposes of reconstruction or of amalgamation with another company, or unless the company has, at the commencement of the winding up, under such a contract with insurers as is mentioned in section seven of the Workmen's Compensation Act 1925, rights capable of being transferred to and vested in the workman, all amounts due in respect of any compensation or liability for compensation under the said Act, being amounts which have accrued before the relevant date in satisfaction of a right which arises or has arisen in respect of employment before the fifth day of July, nineteen hundred and forty-eight (that is to say, the day appointed for the purposes of the National Insurance (Industrial Injuries) Act 1946);

(g) the amount of any debt which, by virtue of subsection (5) of section three of the Workmen's Compensation (Coal Mines) Act 1934 is due from the company to an insurer in respect of a liability in respect of the satisfaction of a right falling within the last foregoing paragraph.

(2) Notwithstanding anything in paragraphs (b) and (c) of the foregoing subsection, the sum to which priority is to be given under those paragraphs respectively shall not, in the case of any one claimant, exceed [eight hundred] pounds:

Provided that where a claimant under the said paragraph (b) is a labourer in husbandry who has entered into a contract for the payment of a portion of his wages in a lump sum at the end of the year of hiring, he shall have priority in respect of the whole of such sum, or a part thereof, as the court may decide to be due under the contract, proportionate to the time of service up to the relevant date.

(3) Where any compensation under the Workmen's Compensation Act 1925 is a weekly payment, the amount due in respect thereof shall, for the purposes of paragraph (f) of subsection (1) of this section, be taken to be the amount of the lump sum for which the weekly payment could, if redeemable, be redeemed if the employer made an application for that purpose under the said Act.

(4) Where any payment has been made—
    (a) to any clerk, servant, workman or labourer in the employment of a company, on account of wages or salary; or
    (b) to any such clerk, servant, workman or labourer or, in the case of his death, to any other person in his right, on account of accrued holiday remuneration;

out of money advanced by some person for that purpose, the person by whom the money was advanced shall in a winding up have a right of priority in respect of the money so advanced and paid up to the amount by which the sum in respect of which the clerk, servant, workman or labourer, or other person in his right, would have been entitled to priority in the winding up has been diminished by reason of the payment having been made.

(5) The foregoing debts shall—
    (a) rank equally among themselves and be paid in full, unless the assets are insufficient to meet them, in which case they shall abate in equal proportions; and
    (b) in the case of a company registered in England [or Scotland], so far as the assets of the company available for payment of general creditors are insufficient to meet them, have priority over the claims of holders of debentures under any floating charge created by the company, and be paid accordingly out of any property comprised in or subject to that charge.

(6) Subject to the retention of such sums as may be necessary for the costs and expenses of the winding up, the foregoing debts shall be discharged forthwith so far as the assets are sufficient to meet them, and in the case of the debts to which priority is given by paragraph (e) of subsection (1) of this section formal proof thereof shall not be required except in so far as is otherwise provided by general rules.

(7) In the event of a landlord or other person distraining or having distrained on any goods or effects of the company within three months next

before the date of a winding up order, the debts to which priority is given by this section shall be a first charge on the goods or effects so distrained on, or the proceeds of the sale thereof:

Provided that, in respect of any money paid under any such charge, the landlord or other person shall have the same rights of priority as the person to whom the payment is made.

(8) For the purposes of this section—

(*a*) any remuneration in respect of a period of holiday or of absence from work through sickness or other good cause shall be deemed to be wages in respect of services rendered to the company during that period;

(*b*) the expression "accrued holiday remuneration" includes, in relation to any person, all sums which, by virtue either of his contract of employment or of any enactment (including any order made or direction given under any Act), are payable on account of the remuneration which would, in the ordinary course, have become payable to him in respect of a period of holiday had his employment with the company continued until he became entitled to be allowed the holiday;

(*c*) references to remuneration in respect of a period of holiday include any sums which, if they had been paid, would have been treated for the purposes of the [Social Security Act 1975 or the Social Security (Northern Ireland) Act 1975] [as earnings paid in that period and];

(*d*) the expression "the relevant date" means—

(i) in the case of a company ordered to be wound up compulsorily, the date of the appointment (or first appointment) of a provisional liquidator, or, if no such appointment was made, the date of the winding-up order, unless in either case the company had commenced to be wound up voluntarily before that date; and

(ii) in any case where the foregoing sub-paragraph does not apply, means the date of the passing of the resolution for the winding up of the company.

(9) This section shall not apply in the case of a winding up where the relevant date as defined in subsection (7) of section two hundred and sixty-four of the Companies Act 1929 as originally enacted, occurred before the commencement of this Act, and in such a case the provisions relating to preferential payments which would have applied if this Act had not passed shall be deemed to remain in full force.

AMENDMENTS

In subs. (8)(*c*) the words in square brackets were substituted by the Social Security Act 1973 (c. 38), s.100(2), Sched. 27, and the Social Security (Consequential Provisions) Act 1975 (c. 18), s.1(3), Sched. 2. The limit of £200 for preferential status under s.1(*b*)(*c*) is increased to £800 by the Insolvency Act 1976 (c. 60), s.1, Sched. 1, and subs. (2) is amended accordingly.

. . . . . .

Preferential payments in stannaries cases

358.—(1) In the application to companies within the stannaries of the provisions of this Act with respect to preferential payments, the following modifications shall be made:—

(*a*) in the case of a clerk or servant of such a company, the priority with respect to wages and salary given by this Act shall not extend to the principal agent, manager, purser or secretary;

(*b*) all wages in relation to the mine of a miner, artisan, or labourer employed in or about the mine, including all earnings by a miner arising from any description of piece or other work, or as a tributer or otherwise, but not exceeding an amount equal to four months wages, shall be included amongst the payments which are, under this Act, to be made in priority to other debts;

(*c*) the following debts, that is to say:—

(i) wages of any miner, artisan or labourer and accrued holiday remuneration becoming payable to or in right of any miner, artisan or labourer as mentioned in paragraph (*d*) of subsection (1) of section three hundred and nineteen of this Act, being wages or remuneration unpaid at the commencement of the winding up;

(ii) all such amounts due in respect of contributions payable in respect of a miner under the enactments mentioned in paragraph (*e*) of the said subsection (1) as are given priority by that paragraph; and

(iii) all such amounts due in respect of any compensation or liability for compensation under the Workmen's Compensation Act, 1925, payable to a miner or the dependants of a miner as are given priority by paragraph (*f*) of the said subsection (1);

shall be paid by the liquidator forthwith in priority to all costs, except (in the case of a winding up by the court) such costs of and incidental to the making of the winding up order as in the opinion of the court have been properly incurred, and to all claims by mortgages, execution creditors, or any other persons, except the claims of clerks and servants in respect of their wages or salary or accrued holiday remuneration due to them;

(*d*) subject as aforesaid, the court may, by order, charge the whole or any part of the assets of the company, in priority to all claims and to all existing mortgages or charges thereon, with the payment of a sum sufficient to discharge the debts to be paid in priority under the last foregoing paragraph, together with interest thereon at a rate not exceeding five per cent. per annum, and this charge may be made in favour of any person who is willing to advance the requisite amount or any part thereof, and as soon as the said sum has been so advanced, the said debts shall be paid without delay so far as the amount advanced extends, and in such order of payment as the court directs;

(*e*) the provision giving a right of priority to a person who has advanced money for the making of payments on account of wages, salary or accrued holiday remuneration shall have effect subject to the modifications contained in this section.

(2) References in the foregoing subsection to wages shall be construed as including references to such remuneration in respect of a period of holiday or absence from work as is deemed for the purposes of section three hundred and nineteen of this Act to be wages, and for the purposes of that subsection the expression "accrued holiday remuneration" has the same meaning as it has for the purposes of that section.

(3) The foregoing provisions of this section shall not apply in the case of such a winding up as is mentioned in subsection (9) of the said section three

hundred and nineteen, and in such a case the provisions which, by virtue of that subsection, are deemed to remain in force shall have effect in their application to companies within the stannaries subject to the modifications subject to which they would have had effect if this Act had not passed.

Provisions as to mine club funds

1-109   359.—(1) On the winding up of a company within the stannaries, contributions of the miners, artisans or labourers for the purpose of a mine club, or accident, or sick, or benefit fund shall not be deemed to be, or be applied as part of the assets of the company in liquidation of the debts of the company or otherwise, but shall be accounted for by the purser or any other person in possession of the fund to the liquidator, and shall be recoverable by him, and be applied in accordance with the rules of the club.

(2) Where the winding up is a voluntary winding up, any person claiming to be entitled to any such contributions or fund shall have the same right as the liquidator of applying to the court for directions, or to determine any question arising in the matter.

1-110

Payment of Wages Act 1960

(8 & 9 ELIZ. 2, c.37)

An Act to remove certain restrictions imposed by the Truck Acts 1831 to 1940 and other enactments, with respect to the payment of wages; and for purposes connected therewith.

[2nd June, 1960]

NOTE
References in the Act to the Minister of Labour should now be read as references to the Secretary of State for Employment, by virtue of the Secretary of State for Trade and Industry Order 1970 (S.I. 1970 No. 1537).

Request for payment of wages otherwise than in cash

1-111   1.—(1) If an employed person requests his employer to pay his wages in a way specified in the request, being one of the ways authorised by this Act, and the employer agrees to that request, nothing in the enactments mentioned in the next following subsection shall operate—

(*a*) so as to render that request, or the employer's agreement thereto, unlawful, or

(*b*) so as to render unlawful or invalid any payment of wages to which the request applies if, at a time while the request and agreement remain in force, the payment is made in the way specified in the request and the requirements of the next following section are fulfilled in relation thereto.

(2) The said enactments (hereafter in this Act referred to as "the specified enactments") are—

(*a*) sections one and three of the Truck Act 1831 (which render unlawful and invalid any contract to pay, or payment of, wages to an artificer otherwise than in the current coin of the realm);

(*b*) section one of the Hosiery Manufacture (Wages) Act 1874 (which requires all contracts for wages to which that Act applies to make the wages payable in the current coin of the realm), and section three of that Act (which imposes penalties) except in so far as it relates to deductions from wages; and

(c) section twelve of the Stannaries Act 1887 (which relates to the payment of wages to miners to whom that Act applies).

(3) The following ways of payment are authorised by this Act, that is to say,—
- (a) payment into an account at a bank, being an account standing in the name of the person to whom the payment is due, or an account standing in the name of that person jointly with one or more other persons;
- (b) payment by postal order;
- (c) payment by money order;
- (d) payment by cheque:

[. . .]

(4) Any request made by an employed person as mentioned in subsection (1) of this section shall be made by notice in writing given to his employer.

(5) An employer may signify his agreement to such a request either by notice in writing given to the employed person or by paying the wages in the way specified in the request.

(6) Any such request—
- (a) shall cease to have effect if, before the end of the period of fourteen days beginning with the day on which the notice containing the request is given, the employer gives to the employed person notice in writing that he refuses the request, and
- (b) in any other case, shall cease to have effect at the end of that period unless before the end thereof the employer has signified his agreement to the request as mentioned in the last preceding subsection.

(7) A request under subsection (1) of this section may be made in respect of part of the wages of an employed person; and, in relation to any such request, any reference in this Act to a payment of wages shall be construed as a reference to a payment of such part of the wages as may be specified in the request.

AMENDMENT

The words omitted in this subsection were repealed by the Statute Law (Repeals) Act 1977 (c. 18), Sched. 1, Pt. XIX.

Requirements applicable to payments authorised by s.1

2.—(1) A request that any wages may be paid into an account at a bank shall specify the bank and the branch thereof at which the account is kept and the person or persons in whose name or names the account stands; and a payment of wages in accordance with such a request does not fulfil the requirements of this section unless it is made into the account so specified.

(2) A payment of wages by cheque does not fulfil the requirements of this section unless the cheque is made payable to, or to the order of, the person to whom the wages are due.

(3) A payment of wages in any of the ways authorised by this Act does not fulfil the requirements of this section if, in calculating the payment, any deduction from the gross amount of the wages is made by reason that the payment is made in that way.

(4)–(8) [*Repealed by the Employment Protection Act* 1975, *Sched.* 18.]

Cancellation of request or of employer's agreement

1-113   3.—(1) Subject to the provisions of this section—
  (*a*) an employed person who has made such a request as is mentioned in section one of this Act may at any time cancel that request by notice in writing given to his employer;
  (*b*) an employer who has agreed to such a request may at any time cancel his agreement thereto by notice in writing given to the person who made the request.

(2) A notice under this section shall take effect at (but not before) the end of the period of four weeks beginning with the day on which the notice is given.

(3) Without prejudice to the exercise of any power conferred by subsection (1) of this section, where such a request and an employer's agreement thereto are for the time being in force, the employer and the employed person may at any time, by agreement in writing, cancel that request and agreement as from such date as may be specified in the agreement made under this subsection.

Payment of wages otherwise than in cash in cases of absence

1-114   4.—(1) The provisions of this section shall have effect where, at the time when an employed person's wages fall to be paid, he is absent from the proper or usual place for the payment thereof, or for the payment of so much thereof as is not covered by a request and agreement under section one of this Act, and no notice excluding him from the operation of this section is in force at that time.

(2) If no part of those wages is covered by a request and agreement under section one of this Act, and either—
  (*a*) the employed person has duties in connection with his employment which require him to be absent as mentioned in the preceding subsection, and the employer has reasonable grounds for believing that he is absent in order to carry out those duties, or
  (*b*) the employer has reasonable grounds for believing that the employed person's absence is on account of his being ill or having sustained a personal injury
nothing in the specified enactments shall operate so as to render unlawful or invalid any payment of those wages, if they are paid by postal order or money order [. . .].

(3) If part of the wages in question is covered by a request and agreement under section one of this Act, and the conditions mentioned in paragraph (*a*) or paragraph (*b*) of the last preceding subsection are fulfilled, nothing in the specified enactments shall operate so as to render unlawful or invalid any payment of any part of those wages not covered by such a request and agreement, if it is paid by postal order or money order [. . .].

(4) If an employed person, by notice in writing given to his employer, declares that he does not wish to have any of his wages paid to him by postal order or money order, that notice—

(a) shall remain in force until cancelled by the employed person by a further notice in writing given to his employer, and
(b) while it remains in force, shall have effect for the purposes of subsection (1) of this section as a notice excluding him from the operation of this section.

(5) For the purposes of this section wages, or part of wages, shall be taken to be covered by a request and agreement under section one of this Act if a request and agreement, as mentioned in that section, are for the time being in force with respect to those wages or that part thereof, as the case may be.

AMENDMENT
The words omitted were repealed by the Employment Protection Act 1975 (c. 71), Sched. 18.

Provisions as to notices and statements

5.—(1) Anything which, in accordance with any of the preceding provisions of this Act, may be done by an employed person by notice in writing given to his employer may be done by such a notice given either by the employed person himself or by a person authorised by him to act on his behalf; and anything which, in accordance with subsection (3) of section three of this Act, may be done by agreement in writing may be done by such an agreement made by the employer either with the employed person himself or with a person so authorised.   1–115

(2) Any such notice as is mentioned in the preceding subsection, whether given by or on behalf of an employed person,—
(a) may be given by being delivered to the employer, or sent by post addressed to him at the place of business where that person is employed, or
(b) if arrangements in that behalf have been made by the employer, may be given by being delivered to a person designated by the employer in pursuance of the arrangements, or left for such a person at a place so designated, or sent by post to such a person at an address so designated.

(3) Any notice or statement which by any provision of this Act is authorised or required to be given by an employer to an employed person may be given by being delivered to the employed person, or left for him at his usual or last-known place of residence, or sent by post addressed to him at that place.

(4) Any notice or statement which, in accordance with any provision of this section, is left for a person at a place or address referred to in that provision shall, unless the contrary is proved, be presumed to have been received by him on the day on which it was left there.

(5) Nothing in subsection (1) or subsection (2) of this section shall be construed as affecting the capacity of an employer to act by a servant or agent for the purposes of any provision of this Act, including either of those subsections.

Supplementary provisions

6.—(1) Where, in the case of any wages to which the Truck Act 1831 applies, a payment of the wages or part thereof is made in circumstances falling within subsection (1) of section one of this Act, or falling within sub-   1–116 section (2) or subsection (3) of section four of this Act, section four of that Act (which confers a right of recovery in respect of wages not actually paid in current coin of the realm) shall not confer any right of recovery in respect of so much of those wages as has been paid in those circumstances, or as represents a lawful deduction taken into account in calculating that payment.

(2) For the purposes of section nine of the Truck Act 1831 (whereby it is an offence to enter into any contract or make any payment thereby declared illegal),—

(a) no such request and agreement as are mentioned in subsection (1) of section one of this Act, and

(b) no payment falling within paragraph (b) of the said subsection (1), or falling within subsection (2) or subsection (3) of section four of this Act,

shall be treated as a contract or payment declared illegal by that Act.

(3) For the purposes of section five of the Hosiery Manufacture (Wages) Act 1874 (which precludes any action or set-off for any contract thereby declared illegal), no such request and agreement as are mentioned in subsection (1) of section one of this Act shall be treated as a contract declared illegal by that Act.

(4) For the purposes of subsection (1) of section fourteen of the Wages Councils Act 1959 (which relates to the computation of remuneration) any amount paid or to be paid to a person in any of the ways mentioned in subsection (3) of section one of this Act (whether that person is an employed person within the meaning of this Act or not) shall be treated as an amount obtained or to be obtained by him in cash, and the provisions of Part II of that Act as to payment of remuneration shall be construed accordingly:

Provided that nothing in this subsection shall affect the rights of any person except in so far as they are rights conferred by that Part of that Act.

(5) The following provisions shall have effect with respect to payment by post, that is to say,—

(a) a request under section one of this Act for payment by cheque shall not, unless it expressly so provides, be taken to imply a request that cheques in payment of the wages shall be sent by post;

(b) a request under that section for payment by money order or postal order shall, unless it otherwise expressly provides, be taken to imply a request that money orders or postal orders in payment of the wages shall be sent by post;

(c) in determining, for the purpose of that section, whether a payment is made in the way specified in a request, it is immaterial whether the payment is or is not sent by post;

(d) in the case of any payment sent by post, any requirement of this Act that a statement relating thereto shall be given at or before the time when the payment is made shall (if not complied with apart from this paragraph) be treated as complied with if a statement containing the requisite particulars is sent by post together with the payment.

(6) Subject to the preceding provisions of this section, nothing in this Act—

(a) shall render unlawful or invalid any agreement or payment which apart from this Act is lawful and valid, or

(b) shall render lawful or valid any agreement or payment which, apart from this Act, is unlawful or invalid otherwise than by virtue of any of the specified enactments;

and, in relation to any payment made in any of the ways authorised by this Act, nothing in this Act shall be construed as rendering lawful a deduction which would not be a lawful deduction if the payment had been made to the employed person in cash.

(7) Nothing in this Act shall operate so as to enable an employed person to be required, by the terms or conditions of his employment or otherwise, to make such a request as is mentioned in section one of this Act, or to refrain from cancelling such a request.

Interpretation

7.—(1) In this Act, except in so far as the context otherwise requires, the following expressions have the meanings hereby assigned to them respectively, that is to say:—

"account" includes both a current account and a deposit account (whether described by that name or as a deposit or in any other way);

"the appointed day" means such day as the Minister of Labour may appoint by order made by statutory instrument;

"bank" includes a savings bank;

"branch", in relation to a bank, includes the head office of the bank;

"employed person" (subject to the next following subsection) means any person who is an artificer within the meaning of the Truck Acts 1831 to 1940, or of the Hosiery Manufacture (Wages) Act 1874, or a company within the meaning of the Stannaries Act 1887;

"money order" means a money order issued by the Postmaster General or the Post Office;

"postal order" means a postal order so issued;

"the specified enactments" has the meaning assigned to it by subsection (2) of section one of this Act;

"wages" (subject to the next following subsection) means any amount which constitutes wages within the meaning of the Truck Acts 1831 to 1940, or of the Hosiery Manufacture (Wages) Act 1874, or which constitutes wages within the meaning of the Stannaries Act 1887, including subsist as defined in section eleven of that Act.

(2) Section ten of the Truck Amendment Act 1887 (which applies the provisions of the Truck Act 1831, and of that Act to certain outworkers not directly employed) shall have effect for the purposes of this Act as it has effect for the purposes of those Acts, and references in this Act to employed persons, to employers and to wages shall be construed accordingly.

(3) [*Repealed by the Employment Protection Act 1975, Sched. 18.*]

(4) References in this Act to a deduction do not include a part of an employed person's wages which is paid in any of the ways authorised by this Act.

(5) References in this Act to any enactment shall, except where the context otherwise requires, be construed as references to that enactment as amended or extended by or under any other enactment.

(6) In this section "savings bank" means any of the following, that is to say,—

1–117

(a) any trustee savings bank within the meaning of the Trustee Savings Banks Act 1954;
(b) any bank to which the Savings Bank (Scotland) Act 1819 applies;
(c) any organisation established (whether as a separate body or otherwise) under a local or private Act, in pursuance of a provision in that Act expressly describing it as a savings bank;
(d) any organisation formed in the United Kingdom (whether before or after the passing of this Act) which does not fall within any of the preceding paragraphs, but, being an organisation in the nature of a bank, accepts deposits of money for the benefit of the persons making the deposits, and, in the case of all deposits so accepted,—
  (i) accumulates the produce of the deposits (so far as not withdrawn) at compound interest, and
  (ii) returns the deposits and produce to the depositors after deducting any necessary expenses of management but without deriving any benefit from the deposits or produce.

. . . . .

Short title, commencement and extent

1–118   9.—(1) This Act may be cited as the Payment of Wages Act 1960.

(2) Section four of this Act, and in their application for the purposes of that section (but not otherwise) sections two, five, six and seven of, and the Schedule to, this Act, shall come into operation at the end of the period of one month beginning with the day on which this Act is passed.

(3) Subject to the last preceding subsection, this Act, except the last preceding section, shall come into operation at the end of the period of six months beginning with the day on which it is passed.

(4) This Act, [. . .], shall not extend to Northern Ireland.

AMENDMENT
The words omitted in this section were repealed by the Northern Ireland Constitution Act 1973 (c. 36), Sched. 6.

1–119   # Trade Union (Amalgamations, etc.) Act 1964

(1964 c.24)

An Act to amend the law relating to the amalgamation of trade unions, the transfer of engagements from one trade union to another, and the alteration of the name of a trade union.

[25th March, 1964]

AMENDMENTS
In this Act (unless otherwise indicated) the words in square brackets were substituted by the Trade Union and Labour Relations Act 1974 (c. 52), Sched. 3, and the Employment Protection Act 1975 (c. 71), s.125 and Sched. 16.

References in this Act to functions performed by the Chief Registrar of Friendly Societies or any assistant registrar are, by the Employment Protection Act 1975 (c. 71), s.7(2), to be performed by the "Certification Officer" created by that Act. Parts I and III of Sched. 1 to that Act set out the constitution of that body and remuneration of its members.

Conditions necessary for amalgamations and transfers of engagement of [trade unions]

1.—(1) Subject to this section—
  (a) two or more [trade unions] to which this Act applies may amalgamate and become one [trade union], with or without a division or dissolution of the funds of any one or more of those [unions], but shall not do so unless, in the case of each of the amalgamating [unions], a resolution which approves an instrument of amalgamation approved by the [Certification Officer] has been passed on a vote taken in a manner which satisfies the conditions specified in subsection (2) of this section;
  (b) [a trade union] may transfer its engagements to any other [trade union] which undertakes to fulfil those engagements, but shall not do so unless, in the case of the transferor [union], a resolution which approves an instrument of transfer approved by the [Certification Officer] has been passed on a vote taken in a manner which satisfies the said conditions.

[(1A) Subject to any express provision of this Act with respect to employers' associations, this Act shall apply, with the necessary modifications, in relation to unincorporated employers' associations as it applies in relation to trade unions.]

(2) The conditions referred to in the foregoing subsection are the following, that is—
  (a) every member of [the union] must be entitled to vote on the resolution;
  (b) every member of [the union] must be allowed to vote without interference or constraint and must, so far as is reasonably possible, be given a fair opportunity of voting;
  (c) the method of voting must involve the marking of a voting paper by the person voting;
  (d) all reasonable steps must have been taken by [the union] to secure that, not less than seven days before voting on the resolution begins, every member of [the union] is supplied with a notice in writing approved for the purpose by the [Certification Officer.]

(3) The notice referred to in subsection (2)(d) of this section—
  (a) shall either set out in full the instrument of amalgamation or transfer to which the resolution relates, or give an account of it sufficient to enable those receiving the notice to form a reasonable judgment of the main effects of the proposed amalgamation or transfer; and
  (b) if it does not set out the instrument in full, shall state where copies of the instrument may be inspected by those receiving the notice;

and both the instrument and the notice shall comply with the requirements of any regulations for the time being in force under this Act.

(4) Before a resolution to approve an instrument of amalgamation or transfer is voted on by the members of [a trade union]—
  (a) that instrument, and

1–120

(b) the notice proposed to be supplied to members of [the union] in accordance with subsection (2)(d) of this section,

shall be submitted to the [Certification Officer] and the [Certification Officer] shall approve them respectively on being satisfied that they comply with the requirements of subsection (3) of this section.

(5) An instrument of amalgamation or transfer shall not take effect before it has been registered by the [Certification Officer] under this Act, and shall not be so registered before the expiration of a period of six weeks beginning with the date on which an application for its registration is sent to the [Certification Officer].

(6) No such amalgamation or transfer as is mentioned in subsection (1) of this section shall prejudice any right of any creditor of [any trade union] party thereto.

Manner of voting on, and majority required for, resolution

1–121   2.—(1) Section 1 of this Act shall apply in relation to every amalgamation or transfer of engagements notwithstanding anything in the rules of any of the [trade unions] concerned or in the following provisions of this section.

(2) For the purposes of the passing of a resolution to approve an instrument of amalgamation or transfer, the committee of management or other governing body of [a trade union] shall, unless the rules of that [union] expressly provide that this subsection shall not apply in relation to that [union], have power, notwithstanding anything in the rules of the [union], to arrange for a vote of the members of that [union] to be taken in any manner which that body think fit.

(3) Where, in the case of [a trade union], a vote is taken (whether under arrangements made under subsection (2) of this section or under provisions in the rules of the [union]) on a resolution to approve an instrument of amalgamation or transfer, a simple majority of the votes recorded shall be sufficient to pass the resolution, notwithstanding anything in the rules of the [union] and, in particular, notwithstanding anything in those rules which, but for the subsection, would require the resolution—

(a) to be passed by a majority greater than a simple majority, or
(b) to be voted on by not less than a specified proportion of the members of the [union]:

Provided that the foregoing provisions of this subsection shall not apply in the case of [a union] whose rules expressly provide that this subsection shall not apply in relation to that [union].

Power to alter rules of transferee organisation for purposes of transfer of engagements

1–122   3. Where [a trade union] proposes to transfer its engagements to another [trade union], and an alteration of the rules of the transferee [union] is necessary to give effect to provisions in the instrument of transfer, the committee of management or other governing body of the transferee [union] shall, unless the rules of that [union] expressly provide that this section shall not apply in relation to that [union], have power, notwithstanding anything in the rules of that [union], by memorandum in writing to alter the rules of that [union] so far as is necessary to give effect to those provisions; but an alteration of the transferee [union's] rules under this section shall not take effect unless or until the instrument of transfer takes effect.

Complaints to [Certification Officer] as regards passing of resolution

4.—(1) A member of [a trade union] which passes or purports to pass a resolution approving an instrument of amalgamation or transfer may complain to the [Certification Officer] on one or more of the following grounds, that is—

(a) that the manner in which the vote on the resolution was taken did not satisfy the conditions specified in section 1(2) of this Act; or

(b) where that vote was taken under arrangements made under section 2(2) of this Act, that the manner in which it was taken was not in accordance with the arrangements; or

(c) where that vote was taken under provisions in the rules of the [union], that the manner in which it was taken was not in accordance with those rules; or

(d) that the votes recorded did not have the effect of passing the resolution.

(2) A complaint under this section may be made at any time before, but shall not be made after, the expiration of a period of six weeks beginning with the date on which an application for registration of the instrument of amalgamation or transfer is sent to the [Certification Officer]; and where a complaint is made under this section, the [Certification Officer] shall not register the instrument under this Act before the complaint is finally determined.

(3) Where a complaint is made under this section the [Certification Officer] may either dismiss it or, if after giving the complainant and [the trade union] an opportunity of being heard he finds the complaint to be justified, may either—

(a) so declare, but make no order under this subsection thereon, or

(b) make an order specifying the steps which must be taken before he will entertain any application to register the instrument of amalgamation or transfer, as the case may be.

(4) It shall be the duty of the [Certification Officer] to furnish a statement, either written or oral, of the reasons for any decision which he gives on a complaint under this section.

(5) The [Certification Officer] may from time to time by order vary any order made under subsection (3) of this section, and after making an order under that subsection in relation to an instrument of amalgamation or transfer shall not entertain any application to register that instrument unless he is satisfied that the steps specified in the order (or, where the order has been varied, in the order as varied) have been taken.

(6) Schedule 1 to this Act shall apply in relation to complaints under this section.

(7) Subject to subsection (8) of this section, the validity of a resolution approving an instrument of amalgamation or transfer shall not be questioned in any legal proceedings whatsoever (except proceedings before the [Certification Officer] under this section or any proceedings arising out of such proceedings) on any ground on which a complaint could be, or could have been, made to the [Certification Officer] under this section.

[(8) An appeal shall lie, in accordance with [section 136(2) of the Employment Protection (Consolidation) Act 1978,] at the instance of the complainant or the trade union to the Employment Appeal Tribunal on any question of law arising in any proceedings before, or arising from any decision of, the Certification Officer under this section.]

1–123

(9) It is hereby declared that the Arbitration Act 1950 does not apply to proceedings on a complaint under this section.

(10) For the purposes of this section a .complaint which is withdrawn shall be deemed to be finally determined at the time when it is withdrawn.

(11) [*Repealed by the Industrial Relations Act* 1971 (*c.* 72), *s.*169(*a*) *and Sched.* 9.]

AMENDMENT

Subs. (8) was substituted by the Employment Protection Act 1975 (c. 71), s.125(1), Sched. 16, and amended by the Employment Protection (Consolidation) Act 1978, s.159(2), Sched. 16.

Disposal of property on amalgamation or transfer

1–124   **5.**—(1) Subject to this section, where an instrument of amalgamation or transfer takes effect, the property held—
  (*a*) for the benefit of any of the amalgamating [trade unions] or for the benefit of a branch of any of those [unions], by the trustees of the [union] or branch, or
  (*b*) for the benefit of the transferor [trade union] or for the benefit of a branch of the transferor [union], by the trustees of the [union] or branch,
shall without any conveyance, assignment or assignation vest, on the instrument taking effect, or on the appointment of the appropriate trustees, whichever is the later, in the appropriate trustees.

(2) The foregoing subsection shall not apply—
  (*a*) to property excepted from the operation of this section by the instrument of amalgamation or transfer, or
  (*b*) to stocks and securities in the public funds of the United Kingdom or Northern Ireland.

(3) In this section "the appropriate trustees" means—
  (*a*) in the case of any property to be held for the benefit of a branch of the amalgamated [trade union] or for the benefit of a branch of the transferee [union], the trustees of that branch, unless the rules of the amalgamated or transferee [union] provide that the property to be so held shall be held by the trustees of the [union], and
  (*b*) in any other case, the trustees of the amalgamated or transferee [union].

(4) For the removal of doubt it is hereby declared that if, in the case of an amalgamation of two or more [trade unions] each qualified under section 3 of the Trade Union Act 1913 to operate such a fund as is mentioned in subsection (1)(*a*) of that section, the rules of the amalgamated [union] in force immediately after the amalgamation include such rules as are required by that section, that [union] is to be treated for the purposes of that section as having immediately after the amalgamation passed such a resolution as is mentioned in subsection (1) of that section, with power to rescind it under subsection (4) thereof.

Change of name of organisation

1–125   **6.**—(1) Subject to this section, [a trade union] may change its name by any method of doing so expressly provided for by its rules or, if its rules do not expressly provide for a method of doing so, by adopting in accordance with its rules an alteration of the provision in them which gives [the union] its name.

[(2) If the name of a trade union or employers' association is for the time being entered in the list of trade unions or employers' associations under section 8 of the Trade Union and Labour Relations Act 1974, a change of its name shall not take effect until approved by the [Certification Officer] under this Act; and the [Certification Officer] shall not approve a change of name if it appears to him that the proposed new name is the same as one entered in either list as the name of another trade union or employers' association or is a name so nearly resembling such a name as to be likely to deceive the public.]

(3) Where [a trade union] changes its name, the change of name shall not affect any right or obligation of [the union] or of any of its members, and any pending legal proceedings may be continued by or against the trustees of [the union] or any other officer of [the union] who can sue or be sued on its behalf, notwithstanding its change of name.

Regulations

7.—(1) The Minister of Labour may make regulations as respects— 1–126
   (a) applications to the [Certification Officer] under this Act;
   (b) the registration under this Act of any document or matter;
   (c) the inspection of documents kept by the [Certification Officer] [. . .] under this Act;
   (d) the charging of fees in respect of such matters, and of such amounts, as may with the approval of the Treasury be prescribed by the regulations,

and generally for carrying this Act into effect.

(2) Regulations under this section may in particular—
   (a) require any application for the registration of an instrument of amalgamation or transfer or a change of name to be accompanied by such statutory declarations or other documents as may be specified in the regulations;
   (b) make provision as to the form or content of any document required by this Act or by the regulations to be sent or submitted to the [Certification Officer] and the manner in which any such document is to be signed or authenticated;
   (c) authorise the [Certification Officer] to require notice to be given or published in such manner as he may direct of the fact that an application for registration of an instrument of amalgamation or transfer has been or is to be made to him.

(3) Regulations under this section may make different provision for different circumstances and, in particular, different provision with respect to cases where a Northern Ireland union is, and cases where a Northern Ireland union is not, party to an amalgamation or transfer of engagements.

(4) Any regulations under this section shall be made by statutory instrument subject to annulment in pursuance of a resolution of either House of Parliament.

Power of Registrar to delegate functions

8. Anything which is required or authorised to be done by or to the 1–127

Registrar under this Act or under any regulations made thereunder may be done by or to any assistant registrar whom he may appoint for the purpose.

Interpretation

1–128   9.—[(1) In this Act, unless the context otherwise requires—
"amalgamating unions" and "amalgamated union", in relation to a proposed amalgamation, mean respectively the trade unions proposing to amalgamate and the trade union which is to result from the proposed amalgamation;
["Certification Officer" means the officer appointed under section 7 of the Employment Protection Act 1975;]
[. . .]
"employers' association" has the same meaning as in the Trade Union and Labour Relations Act 1974;
"Northern Ireland union" has the meaning assigned to it by section 10 of this Act;
[. . .]
"transferor trade union" and "transferee trade union", in relation to a proposed transfer of engagements, mean respectively the trade union proposing to transfer its engagements and the trade union proposing to accept them.]
(2) References in this Act to any other enactment are references to that enactment as amended or applied by or under any other enactment.

Provisions as to Northern Ireland

1–129   10.—(1) This Act, [. . .], shall not extend to Northern Ireland.
(2) This Act shall have effect in relation to amalgamations and transfers of engagements to which both [a trade union] and a Northern Ireland union are parties subject to the modifications specified in Schedule 2 to this Act.
(3) In so far as any provision of this Act is capable of applying, as part of the law of England and Wales or of Scotland, to persons or property in Northern Ireland, subsection (1) of this section shall not affect the operation of that provision, as part of that law, in relation to persons or property in Northern Ireland.
(4) [*Repealed by the Northern Ireland Constitution Act* 1973 (*c.* 36).]
(5) In this Act "Northern Ireland union" means a trade union within the meaning of the enactments relating to trade unions in Northern Ireland, being either—
   (*a*) a union which is, or for the purpose of any of those enactments is deemed to be, registered in Northern Ireland, or
   (*b*) an unregistered union whose principal office is situated in Northern Ireland.
(6) In this section "the enactments relating to trade unions in Northern Ireland means all or any of the following enactments, that is to say, the Trade Union Acts 1871 to 1971 as for the time being in force in Northern Ireland, and any enactments of the Parliament of Northern Ireland (whether passed before or after the passing of this Act) whereby those Acts or any provisions thereof were or are amended or superseded.

AMENDMENT
   The words omitted from this section were repealed by the Northern Ireland Constitution Act 1973 (c. 36).

Short title, citation, repeals, saving and commencement

11.—(1) This Act may be cited as the Trade Union (Amalgamations, etc.) Act 1964 and may be cited together with the Trade Union Acts 1871 to 1913 as the Trade Union Acts 1871 to 1964.

(2) (3) [*Repealed by the Statute Law (Repeals) Act* 1969 (*c.* 52).]

(4) This Act shall come into force on such date as the Minister of Labour may by order made by statutory instrument appoint, and different dates may be appointed under this subsection for different provisions of this Act or for different purposes.

SCHEDULES

Section 4   SCHEDULE 1

PROVISIONS SUPPLEMENTAL TO S.4

1. On a complaint made under section 4 of this Act the Registrar may—
    (*a*) require the attendance of the complainant or of any officer of [the trade union], and may, on the application of the complainant or any such officer, require the attendance of any person as a witness;
    (*b*) require the production of any documents relating to the matters complained of;
    (*c*) administer oaths and take affirmations, and require the complainant, any officer of [the trade union] or any person attending as a witness to be examined on oath or affirmation;
    (*d*) grant to the complainant or to any officer of [the trade union] such discovery as to documents and otherwise, or such inspection of documents, as might be granted by the county court;
    (*e*) order the whole or any part of the expenses of hearing the complaint, as certified by the Registrar, to be paid either out of the funds of [the trade union] or by the complainant; and
    (*f*) order [the trade union] to pay the complainant out of the funds of [the union], or the complainant to pay to [the union], either a specified sum in respect of the costs incurred by the complainant or [the union], as the case may be, or the taxed amount of those costs.

2. A person who, on the application of any person, is required to attend before the Registrar as a witness in proceedings on a complaint under section 4 of this Act shall be entitled to be paid by the person on whose application he is so required—
    (*a*) such sum in respect of loss of time and travelling expenses as he would be entitled to on being served with a summons to attend as a witness in the county court, and
    (*b*) if he duly attends, a sum equal to the further allowances, if any, to which he would be entitled if attending as a witness in proceedings in the county court.

3. If any person without reasonable excuse fails or refuses to comply with any requisition of the Registrar under sub-paragraphs (*a*) to (*c*) of paragraph 1 of this Schedule or any order of the Registrar made in pursuance of sub-paragraph (*d*) of that paragraph, he shall be liable on summary conviction to a fine not exceeding fifty pounds or to imprisonment for a term not exceeding three months, or to both:

Provided that a person shall not be convicted of an offence under this paragraph by reason of failure or refusal on his part to comply with a requisition to attend as a witness before the Registrar unless any sum to which he is entitled under paragraph 2(*a*) of this Schedule has been paid or tendered.

4. Any costs required by an order under paragraph 1(*f*) of this Schedule to be taxed may be taxed in the county court according to such of the scales prescribed by county court rules for proceedings in the county court as may be directed by the order or, if the order gives no direction, by the county court.

5. Any sum payable by virtue of an order under paragraph 1(*e*) or (*f*) of this Schedule shall, if the county court so orders, be recoverable by execution issued from the county court or otherwise as if payable under an order of that court.

6. In relation to proceedings in Scotland this Schedule shall have effect subject to the following modifications—

(a) in paragraph 1(d), for the references to discovery as to documents and to the county court there shall be substituted respectively references to recovery of documents and to the sheriff court;
(b) for paragraph 1(f) there shall be substituted the following—
"(f) order that the expenses of the proceedings incurred by the complainant or by [the trade union] shall be paid by [the union] out of its funds or by the complainant as the case may be, and may tax or settle the amount of any expenses to be paid under any such order or direct in what manner they are to be taxed";
(c) in paragraph 2, for sub-paragraphs (a) and (b) there shall be substituted the following—
"(a) such sum as he would be entitled to on being cited as a witness in civil proceedings in the sheriff court, and
(b) if he duly attends, a sum equal to the fees and further allowances to which he would be entitled if attending as a witness in civil proceedings in the sheriff court."; and
(d) paragraphs 4 and 5 shall not apply.

1–132 Section 10 SCHEDULE 2

MODIFICATIONS OF ACT AS APPLYING TO AMALGAMATIONS AND TRANSFERS OF ENGAGEMENTS INVOLVING NORTHERN IRELAND UNIONS

1. Subject to this Schedule, any reference to [a trade union] (except in section 6) shall include a reference to a Northern Ireland union.

2.—(1) The requirements of section 1 of this Act as to the approval of the instrument of amalgamation or transfer by a resolution of [the trade union or unions concerned] shall not apply to any Northern Ireland union, but the Registrar shall not under section 1(5) of this Act register the instrument unless he is satisfied that the instrument will be effective under the law of Northern Ireland.

(2) In accordance with the foregoing sub-paragraph, nothing in section 2 or section 4 of this Act shall apply in relation to the passing of a resolution by a Northern Ireland union.

3. Nothing in section 3 of this Act shall apply in relation to the alteration of the rules of a Northern Ireland union.

4. Where an instrument of amalgamation or transfer is submitted to the Registrar for his approval under section 1(4) of this Act, the Registrar shall not give his approval unless the instrument states which of the bodies concerned is a Northern Ireland union, and, in the case of an instrument of amalgamation, shall not give his approval unless the instrument also states whether the resultant body [is, or is not to be] a Northern Ireland union.

1–133

Companies Act 1967

(1967 c.81)

An Act to amend the law relating to companies, insurance, partnerships and moneylenders.

[27th July 1967]

. . . . .

Particulars in accounts of salaries of employees receiving more than [£20,000] a year

8.—(1) In any accounts of a company [prepared under section 1 of the Companies Act 1976], or in a statement annexed thereto, there shall be shown by reference to each pair of adjacent points on a scale whereon the lowest point is [£20,000] and the succeeding ones are successive integral multiples of [£5,000] beginning with that in the case of which the multiplier is five, the number (if any) of persons in the company's employment whose several emoluments exceeded the lower point but did not exceed the higher, other than,—
(a) directors of the company; and

(b) persons, other than directors of the company, being persons who,—
  (i) if employed by the company throughout the financial year to which the accounts relate, worked wholly or mainly during that year outside the United Kingdom; or
  (ii) if employed by the company for part only of that year, worked wholly or mainly during that part outside the United Kingdom.

(2) For the purposes of this section, a person's emoluments shall include any paid to or receivable by him from the company, the company's subsidiaries and any other person in respect of his services as a person in the employment of the company or a subsidiary thereof or as a director of a subsidiary thereof (except sums to be accounted for to the company or any of its subsidiaries) and "emoluments", in relation to a person, includes fees and percentages, any sums paid by way of expenses allowance in so far as those sums are charged to United Kingdom income tax, and the estimated money value of any other benefits received by him otherwise than in cash.

(3) The amounts to be brought into account for the purpose of complying with subsection (1) above as respects a financial year shall be the sums receivable in respect of that year, whenever paid, or in the case of sums not receivable in respect of a period, the sums paid during that year, so, however, that where—
  (a) any sums are not brought into account for the relevant financial year on the ground that the person receiving them is liable to account therefor as mentioned in the last foregoing subsection, but the liability is wholly or partly released or is not enforced within a period of two years; or
  (b) any sums paid to a person by way of expenses allowance are charged to United Kingdom income tax after the end of the relevant financial year;
those sums shall, to the extent to which the liability is released or not enforced or they are charged as aforesaid, as the case may be, be brought into account for the purpose of complying with subsection (1) above on the first occasion on which it is practicable to do so.

(4) If, in the case of any accounts, the requirements of this section are not complied with, it shall be the duty of the auditors of the company by whom the accounts are examined to include in their report thereon, so far as they are reasonably able to do so, a statement giving the required particulars.

(5) References in subsection (2) above to a company's subsidiary—
  (a) in relation to a person who is or was, while employed by the company a director, by virtue of the company's nomination, direct or indirect, of any other body corporate, shall, subject to the following paragraph, include that body corporate, whether or not it is or was in fact the company's subsidiary; and
  (b) shall be taken as referring to a subsidiary at the time the services were rendered.

AMENDMENT
The words in square brackets in subs. (1) were substituted by the Companies Act 1980 (c. 22), Sched. 3, para. 41 and the figures in square brackets were substituted by the Companies (Accounts) Regulations 1979 (S.I. 1979 No. 1618).
Also, see below Companies Act 1981 (c. 62), s.6(1)(d).

. . . . . .

Directors' service contracts, or memorandum thereof, to be open to inspection by company's members

1–134   **26.**—(1) Subject to the provisions of this section, every company shall keep at an appropriate place—

(*a*) in the case of each director whose contract of service with the company is in writing, a copy of that contract;

(*b*) in the case of each director whose contract of service with the company is not in writing, a written memorandum setting out the terms of that contract;

[(*c*) in the case of each director who is employed under a contract of service with a subsidiary of the company, a copy of that contract or, if it is not in writing, a written memorandum setting out the terms of that contract;]

and all copies and memorandums kept by a company in pursuance of this subsection shall be kept at the same place.

(2) The following shall, as regards a company, be appropriate places for the purposes of the foregoing subsection, namely,—

(*a*) its registered office;

(*b*) the place where its register of members is kept (if other than its registered office);

(*c*) its principal place of business, provided that that is situate in England, in a case in which the company is registered in England, and in Scotland, in a case in which the company is registered in Scotland.

(3) Every company shall send notice [in the prescribed form] to the registrar of companies of the place where copies and memorandums required by subsection (1) above to be kept by it and of any change in that place, save in a case in which they have at al times been kept at its registered office.

[(3A) Subsection (1) above shall not apply in relation to a director's contract of service with the company or with a subsidiary of the company if that contract required him to work wholly or mainly outside the United Kingdom, but the company shall keep a memorandum—

(*a*) in the case of a contract of service with the company, setting out the name of the director and the provisions of the contract relating to its duration;

(*b*) in the case of a contract of service with a subsidiary of the company, setting out the name of the director, the name and place of incorporation of the subsidiary and the provisions of the contract relating to its duration,

at the same place as copies and the memorandums are kept by the company in pursuance of subsection (1) above.]

(4) Every copy and memorandum required to be kept by subsection (1) above shall, during business hours (subject to such reasonable restrictions as the company may in general meeting impose, so that not less than two hours in each day be allowed for inspection), be open to the inspection of any member of the company without charge.

(5) If default is made in complying with subsection (1) above, or if an inspection required under the last foregoing subsection is refused, the company and every officer of the company who is in default shall be liable to a fine not exceeding £500 and further to a default fine; and, if defaultis made for fourteen days in complying with subsection (3) above, the com-

pany and every officer of the company who is in default shall be liable to a default fine.

(6) In the case of a refusal of an inspection required under subsection (4) above of a copy or memorandum, the court may by order compel an immediate inspection thereof.

(7) Subsection (1) of this section shall apply to a variation of a director's contract of service with a company as it applies to the contract.

(8) This section shall not require there to be kept—
    (*a*) [*Repealed by the Companies Act* 1980, *Sched.* 4];
    (*b*) a copy of, or memorandum setting out the terms of, a contract or a copy of, or memorandum setting out the terms of a variation of, a contract at a time at which the unexpired portion of the term for which the contract is to be in force is less than twelve months or at a time at which the contract can, within the next ensuing twelve months, be terminated by the company without payment of compensation.

AMENDMENTS
  Subs. (1), para. (*c*), and subs. (3A) were inserted by the Companies Act 1980. In subs. (3), the words in square brackets were added by the Companies Act 1976, Sched. I.
  Also, see below Companies Act 1980, ss.47, 54 and 61.

Equal Pay Act 1970

1–135

(1970 c.41)

An Act to prevent discrimination, as regards terms and conditions of employment, between men and women.

[29th May 1970]

Requirement of equal treatment for men and women in same employment

1.—[(1) If the terms of a contract under which a woman is employed at an establishment in Great Britain do not include (directly or by reference to a collective agreement or otherwise) an equality clause they shall be deemed to include one.

1–136

(2) An equality clause is a provision which relates to terms (whether concerned with pay or not) of a contract under which a woman is employed (the "woman's contract"), and has the effect that—
    (*a*) where the woman is employed on like work with a man in the same employment—
        (i) if (apart from the equality clause) any term of the woman's contract is or becomes less favourable to the woman than a term of a similar kind in the contract under which that man is employed, that term of the woman's contract shall be treated as so modified as not to be less favourable, and
        (ii) if (apart from the equality clause) at any time the woman's contract does not include a term corresponding to a term benefiting that man included in the contract under which he is employed, the woman's contract shall be treated as including such a term;

(b) where the woman is employed on work rated as equivalent with that of a man in the same employment—

(i) if (apart from the equality clause) any term of the woman's contract determined by the rating of the work is or becomes less favourable to the woman than a term of a similar kind in the contract under which that man is employed, that term of the woman's contract shall be treated as so modified as not to be less favourable, and

(ii) if (apart from the equality clause) at any time the woman's contract does not include a term corresponding to a term benefiting that man included in the contract under which he is employed and determined by the rating of the work, the woman's contract shall be treated as including such a term.

[(c) where a woman is employed on work which, not being work in relation to which paragraph (a) or (b) above applies, is, in terms of the demands made on her (for instance under such headings as effort, skill and decision), of equal value to that of a man in the same employment—

(i) if (apart from the equality clause) any term of the woman's contract is or becomes less favourable to the woman than a term of a similar kind in the contract under which that man is employed, that term of the woman's contract shall be treated as so modified as not to be less favourable, and

(ii) if (apart from the equality clause) at any time the woman's contract does not include a term corresponding to a term benefiting that man included in the contract under which he is employed, the woman's contract shall be treated as including such a term.]

[(3) An equality clause shall not operate in relation to a variation between the woman's contract and the man's contract if the employer proves that the variation is genuinely due to a material factor which is not the difference of sex and that factor—

(a) in the case of an equality clause falling within subsection 2(a) or (b) above, must be a material difference between the woman's case and the man's; and

(b) in the case of an equality clause falling within subsection 2(c) above, may be such a material difference.]

(4) A woman is to be regarded as employed on like work with men if, but only if, her work and theirs is of the same or a broadly similar nature, and the differences (if any) between the things she does and the things they do are not of practical importance in relation to terms and conditions of employment; and accordingly in comparing her work with theirs regard shall be had to the frequency or otherwise with which any such differences occur in practice as well as to the nature and extent of the differences.

(5) A woman is to be regarded as employed on work rated as equivalent with that of any men if, but only if, her job and their job have been given an equal value, in terms of demand made on a worker under various headings (for instance effort, skill, decision), on a study undertaken with a view to evaluating in those terms the jobs to be done by all or any of the employees in an undertaking or group of undertakings, or would have been given an equal value but for the evaluation being made on a system setting different values for men and women on the same demand under any heading.

(6) Subject to the following subsections, for purposes of this section—
  (a) "employed" means employed under a contract of service or of apprenticeship or a contract personally to execute any work or labour, and related expressions shall be construed accordingly;
  (b) [Repealed by the Sex Discrimination Act 1975 (c. 65);]
  (c) two employers are to be treated as associated if one is a company of which the other (directly or indirectly) has control or if both are companies of which a third person (directly or indirectly) has control.

[and men shall be treated as in the same employment with a woman if they are men employed by her employer or any associated employer at the same establishment or at establishments in Great Britain which include that one at which common terms and conditions of employment are observed either generally or for employees of the relevant classes.]

(7) [Repealed by the Sex Discrimination Act 1975 (c. 65).]

[(8) This section shall apply to—
  (a) service for purposes of a Minister of the Crown or government department, other than service of a person holding a statutory office, or
  (b) service on behalf of the Crown for purposes of a person holding a statutory office or purposes of a statutory body,

as it applies to employment by a private person, and shall so apply as if references to a contract of employment included references to the terms of service.

(9) Subsection (8) does not apply in relation to service in—
  (a) the naval, military or air forces of the Crown, or
  (b) any women's service administered by the Defence Council.

(10) In this section "statutory body" means a body set up by or in pursuance of an enactment, and "statutory office" means an office so set up; and service "for purposes of" a Minister of the Crown or government department does not include service in any office in Schedule 2 (Ministerial offices) to the House of Commons Disqualification Act 1975 as for the time being in force.]

[(11) For the purposes of this Act it is immaterial whether the law which (apart from this subsection) is the proper law of a contract is the law of any part of the United Kingdom or not.

(12) In this Act "Great Britain" includes such of the territorial waters of the United Kingdom as are adjacent to Great Britain.

(13) Provisions of this section and [sections 2 and 2A] below framed with reference to women and their treatment relative to men are to be read as applying equally in a converse case to men and their treatment relative to women.]

AMENDMENT

Throughout this Act except where otherwise indicated, the words in square brackets were inserted by the Sex Discrimination Act 1975 (c. 65).

Para.(c) to subsection (2) was inserted by the Equal Pay (Amendment) Regulations 1983 and subsection (3) was substituted by *ibid*. The words in square brackets in subsection (13) were substituted by the Equal Pay (Amendment) Regulations 1983.

Disputes as to, and enforcement of, requirement of equal treatment

2.—[(1) Any claim in respect of the contravention of a term modified or included by virtue of an equality clause, including a claim for arrears of remuneration or damages in respect of the contravention, may be presented by way of a complaint to an industrial tribunal.]

[(1A) Where a dispute arises in relation to the effect of an equality clause the employer may apply to an industrial tribunal for an order declaring the rights of the employer and the employee in relation to the matter in question.]

(2) Where it appears to the Secretary of State that there may be a question whether the employer of any women is or has been [contravening a term modified or included by virtue of their equality clauses] but that it is not reasonable to expect them to take steps to have the question determined, the question may be referred by him [as respects all or any of them] to an industrial tribunal and shall be dealt with as if the reference were of a claim by the women [or woman] against the employer.

(3) Where it appears to the court in which any proceedings are pending that a claim or counter-claim in respect of the operation of an [equality clause] could more conveniently be disposed of separately by an industrial tribunal, the court may direct that the claim or counter-claim shall be struck out; and (without prejudice to the foregoing) where in proceedings before any court a question arises as to the operation of an [equality clause,] the court may on the application of any party to the proceedings or otherwise refer that question, or direct it to be referred by a party to the proceedings, to an industrial tribunal for determination by the tribunal, and may stay or sist the proceedings in the meantime.

(4) No claim in respect of the operation of an [equality clause] relating to a woman's employment shall be referred to an industrial tribunal otherwise than by virtue of subsection (3) above, if she has not been employed in the employment within six months preceding the date of the reference.

(5) A woman shall not be entitled, in proceedings brought in respect of a failure to comply with an [equality clause] (including proceedings before an industrial tribunal), to be awarded any payment by way of arrears of remuneration or damages in respect of a time earlier than two years before the date on which the proceedings were instituted.

(6) [*Repealed by the Sex Discrimination Act* 1975 (*c*. 65).]

(7) [*Repealed by the Employment Protection (Consolidation) Act* 1978 (*c*. 44).]

[Procedure before industrial tribunal

2A.—(1) Where on a complaint or reference made to an industrial tribunal under section 2 above, a dispute arises as to whether any work is of equal value as mentioned in section 1(2)(*c*) above the tribunal shall not determine that question unless—

(*a*) it is satisfied that there are no reasonable grounds for determining that the work is of equal value as so mentioned; or

(*b*) it has required a member of the panel of independent experts to prepare a report with respect to that question and has received that report.

(2) Without prejudice to the generality of paragraph (*a*) of subsection (1) above, there shall be taken, for the purposes of that paragraph, to be no reasonable grounds for determining that the work of a woman is of equal value as mentioned in section 1(2)(*c*) above if—

(*a*) that work and the work of the man in question have been given dif-

ferent values on a study such as is mentioned in section 1(5) above; and
   (b) there are no reasonable grounds for determining that the evaluation contained in the study was (within the meaning of subsection (3) below) made on a system which discriminates on grounds of sex.

(3) An evaluation contained in a study such as is mentioned in section 1(5) above is made on a system which discriminates on grounds of sex where a difference, or coincidence, between values set by that system on different demands under the same or different headings is not justifiable irrespective of the sex of the person on whom those demands are made.

(4) In paragraph (b) of subsection (1) above the reference to a member of the panel of independent experts is a reference to a person who is for the time being designated by the Advisory, Conciliation and Arbitration Service for the purposes of that paragraph as such a member, being neither a member of the Council of that Service nor one of its officers or servants.]

AMENDMENT
This section was inserted by the Equal Pay (Amendment) Regulations 1983.

Collective agreements and pay structures
3.—(1) Where a collective agreement made before or after the commencement of this Act contains any provision applying specifically to men only or to women only, the agreement may be referred, by any party to it or by the Secretary of State, to [the Central Arbitration Committee] constituted under [section 10 of the Employment Protection Act 1975] to declare what amendments need to be made in the agreement, in accordance with subsection (4) below, so as to remove that discrimination between men and women.

(2) Where on a reference under subsection (1) above [the Central Arbitration Committee] have declared the amendments needing to be made in a collective agreement in accordance with that subsection, then—
   (a) in so far as the terms and conditions of a person's employment are dependent on that agreement, they shall be ascertained by reference to the agreement as so amended, and any contract regulating those terms and conditions shall have effect accordingly; and
   (b) [if an award or determination is, or has been, made under any enactment requiring an employer to observe the collective agreement, that award or determination shall have effect by reference to the agreement as so amended.]

(3) On a reference under subsection (1) above [the Central Arbitration Committee] may direct that all or any of the amendments needing to be made in the collective agreement shall be treated as not becoming effective until a date after their decision, or as having been effective from a date before their decision but not before the reference to them, and may specify different dates for different purposes; and subsection (2) above and any different dates for different purposes; and subsection (2) above and any such contract, award or determination as is there mentioned shall have or be deemed to have had effect accordingly.

(4) Subject to section 6 below, the amendments to be made in a collective agreement under this section shall be such as are needed—
   (a) to extend to both men and women any provision applying specifically to men only or to women only; and
   (b) to eliminate any resulting duplication in the provisions of the agree-

ment in such a way as not to make the terms and conditions agreed for men, or those agreed for women, less favourable in any respect than they would have been without the amendments;
but the amendments shall not extend the operation of the collective agreement to men or to women not previously falling within it, and where accordingly a provision applying specifically to men only or to women only continues to be required for a category of men or of women (there being no provision in the agreement for women or, as the case may be, for men of that category), then the provisions shall be limited to men or women of that category but there shall be made to it such amendments, if any, as are needed to secure that the terms and conditions of the men or women of that category are not in any respect less favourable than those of all persons of the other sex to whom the agreement applies.

(5) For purposes of this section "collective agreement" means any agreement as to terms and conditions of employment, being an agreement between—

(a) parties who are or represent employers or organisations of employers or associations of such organisations; and

(b) parties who are or represent organisations of employees or associations of such organisations;

but includes also any award modifying or supplementing such an agreement.

(6) Subsections (1) to (4) above (except subsection (2)(b) and subsection (3) in so far as it relates to subsection (2)(b)) shall have effect in relation to an employer's pay structure as they have effect in relation to a collective agreement, with the adaptation that a reference to [the Central Arbitration Committee] may be made by the employer or by the Secretary of State; and for this purpose "pay structure" means any arrangements adopted by an employer (with or without associated employer) which fix common terms and conditions of employment for his employees or any class of his employees, and of which the provisions are generally known or open to be known by the employees concerned.

(7) In this section the expression "employment" and related expressions, and the reference to an associated employer, shall be construed in the same way as in section 1 above, and section 1(8) shall have effect in relation to this section as well as in relation to that section.

Wages regulation orders

1–139 4.—(1) Where [an order under] [section 14 of the Wages Councils Act 1979] made before or after the commencement of this Act contains any provision applying specifically to men only or to women only, the order may be referred by the Secretary of State to [the Central Arbitration Committee] to declare what amendments need to be made in the order, in accordance with the like rules as apply under section 3(4) above to the amendment under that section of a collective agreement, so as to remove that discrimination between men and women; and when the [Committee] have declared the amendments needing to be so made, [it shall be the duty of the wages council or statutory joint industrial council, by a further order coming into operation not later than five months after the date of the Committee's decision, either to make those amendments in the order referred to by the Committee or otherwise to replace or amend that order so as to remove the discrimination.]

[(1A) Where a wages council or statutory joint industrial council certifies that the effect of an order under] [section 14 of the Wages Councils Act 1979] [is only to make such amendments of a previous order as have under this section been declared by the Central Arbitration Committee to be needed, or to make such amendments as aforesaid with minor modifications or modifications of limited application, or is only to revoke and reproduce with such amendments a previous order, then the wages council or statutory joint industrial council may instead of complying with] [subsections (4) and (5) of the said section 14] [give notice of the proposed order in such manner as appears to the council expedient in the circumstances, and may make the order at any time after the expiration of seven days from the giving of the notice.]

(2) [An order under] [section 14 of the Wages Councils Act 1979] [shall be referred to the Central Arbitration Committee under this section if the Secretary of State is requested so to refer it either—
   (a) by an employers' association for the time being entitled to nominate for membership of the wages council or statutory joint industrial council in question persons representing employers (or, if provision is made for any of the persons representing employers to be elected instead of nominated, then by a member or members representing employers); or
   (b) by a trade union for the time being entitled to nominate for membership of the wages council or statutory joint industrial council in question persons representing workers (or, if provision is made for any of the persons representing workers to be elected instead of nominated, then by a member or members representing workers);
or if in any case it appears to the Secretary of State that the order may be amendable under this section.]

(3) Where by virtue of [section 15(1) or (2) of the Wages Councils Act 1979] a contrast between a worker and an employer is to have effect with modifications specified in [section 15(1) or (2)], then (without prejudice to the general savings in [section 14(12)] of that Act for rights conferred by or under other Acts) the contract as so modified shall have effect subject to any further term implied by virtue of section 1 above.

(4) [*Repealed by the Employment Protection Act* 1975 (*c.*71).]

AMENDMENTS
In this section the words in square brackets are substituted by the Employment Protection Act 1975 (c. 71), Sched. 16, and the Wages Councils Acts 1979 (c. 12), s.31(2), Sched. 6.

Agricultural wages orders

5.—(1) Where an agricultural wages order made before or after the commencement of this Act contains any provision applying specifically to men only or to women only, the order may be referred by the Secretary of State to [the Central Arbitration Committee] to declare what amendments need to be made in the order, in accordance with the like rules as apply under section 3(4) above to the amendment under that section of a collective agreement, so as to remove that discrimination between men and women; and when [the Central Arbitration Committee] have declared the amendments needing to be so made, it shall be the duty of the Agricultural Wages Board, by a further agricultural wages order coming into operation not later than five months after the date of the Court's decision, either to make those amendments in the order referred to [the Central Arbitration Com-

1–140

mittee] or otherwise to replace or amend that order so as to remove the discrimination.

(2) Where the Agricultural Wages Board certify that the effect of an agricultural wages order is only to make such amendments of a previous order as have under this section been declared by [the Central Arbitration Committee] to be needed, or to make such amendments as aforesaid with minor modifications or modifications of limited application, or is only to revoke and reproduce with such amendments a previous order, then the [Agricultural Wages Board] may instead of complying with paragraphs 1 and 2 of Schedule 4, or in the case of Scotland paragraphs 1 and 2 of Schedule 3, to the Agricultural Wages Act give notice of the proposed order in such manner as appears to the [Agricultural Wages Board] expedient in the circumstances, and may make the order at any time after the expiration of seven days from the giving of the notice.

(3) An agricultural wages order shall be referred to [the Central Arbitration Committee] under this section if the Secretary of State is requested so to refer it either—

(*a*) by a body for the time being entitled to nominate for membership of the Agricultural Wages Board persons representing employers (or, if provision is made for any of the persons representing employers to be elected instead of nominated, then by a member or members representing employers); or

(*b*) by a body for the time being entitled to nominate for membership of the [Agricultural Wages Board] persons representing workers (or, if provision is made for any of the persons representing workers to be elected instead of nominated, then by a member or members representing workers);

or if in any case it appears to the Secretary of State that the order may be amendable under this section.

(4) In this section "the Agricultural Wages Board" means the Agricultural Wages Board for England and Wales or the Scottish Agricultural Wages Board, "the Agricultural Wages Act" means the Agricultural Wages Act 1948 or the Agricultural Wages (Scotland) Act 1949 and "agricultural wages order" means an order of the Agricultural Wages Board under the Agricultural Wages Act.

Exclusion from ss.1 to 5 of pensions etc.

6.—[(1) Neither an equality clause nor the provisions of section 3(4) above shall operate in relation to terms—

(*a*) affected by compliance with the law regulating the employment of women, or

(*b*) affording special treatment to women in connection with pregnancy or child birth.

(1A) An equality clause and those provisions shall not operate in relation to terms related to death or retirement, or to any provision made in connection with death or retirement.]

(2) Any reference in this section to retirement includes retirement, whether voluntary or not, on grounds of age, length of service or incapacity.

AMENDMENT
The words in square brackets are substituted by the Sex Discrimination Act 1975 (c. 65), Sched. I, Pt. I, para. 3.

Service pay
7.—(1) The Secretary of State or Defence Council shall not make, or recommend to Her Majesty the making of, any instrument relating to the terms and conditions of service of members of the naval, military or air forces of the Crown or of any women's service administered by the Defence Council, if the instrument has the effect of making a distinction, as regards pay, allowances or leave, between men and women who are members of those forces or of any such service, not being a distinction fairly attributable to differences between the obligations undertaken by men and those undertaken by women as such members as aforesaid.

(2) The Secretary of State or Defence Council may refer to [the Central Arbitration Committee] for their advice any question whether a provision made or proposed to be made by any such instrument as is referred to in subsection (1) above ought to be regarded for purposes of this section as making a distinction not permitted by that subsection.

1-142

AMENDMENT
The words in square brackets are substituted by the Employment Protection Act 1975 (c. 71) Sched. 16, Pt. IV, paras. 13(2) and 13(3).

. . . . . .

Commencement
9.—(1) [. . .] the foregoing provisions of this Act shall come into force on the 29th December 1975 and references in this Act to its commencement shall be construed as referring to the coming into force of those provisions on that date.

(2) [*Repealed by the Sex Discrimination Act* 1975 (*c.* 65).]

1-143

Preliminary references to Central Arbitration Committee
10.—(1) A collective agreement, pay structure or order which after the commencement of this Act could under section 3, 4 or 5 of this Act be referred to [the Central Arbitration Committee] to declare what amendments need to be made as mentioned in that section may at any time not earlier than one year before that commencement be referred to the [Committee] under this section for their advice as to the amendments to be so made.

(2) A reference under this section may be made by any person authorised by section 3, 4 or 5, as the case may be, to make a corresponding reference under that section, but the Secretary of State shall not under this section refer an order to [the Central Arbitration Committee] unless requested so to do as mentioned in section 4(2) or 5(3), as the case may be, nor be required to refer an order if so requested.

(3) A collective agreement, pay structure or order referred to [the Central Arbitration Committee] under this section may after the commencement of this Act be again referred to the [Committee] under section 3, 4 or 5; but at that commencement any reference under this section (if still pending) shall lapse.

(4) [*Repealed by the Sex Discrimination Act* 1975.]

1-144

AMENDMENT
The words in square brackets were susbstituted by the Employment Protection Act 1975 (c. 71), Sched. 16, Pt. IV, paras. 13(2) and 13(3).

Short title, interpretation and extent

1–145　11.—(1) This Act may be cited as the Equal Pay Act 1970.

(2) In this Act the expressions "man" and "woman" shall be read as applying to persons of whatever age.

(3) This Act shall not extend to Northern Ireland.

1–146

Health and Safety at Work etc. Act 1974

(1974 c.37)

. . . . .

General Duties

General duties of employers to their employees

1–147　2.　　. . .

(3) Except in such cases as may be prescribed, it shall be the duty of every employer to prepare and as often as may be appropriate revise a written statement of his general policy with respect to the health and the safety at work of his employees and the organisation and arrangements for the time being in force for carrying out that policy and to bring the statement and any revision of it to the notice of all of his employees.

(4) Regulations made by the Secretary of State may provide for the appointment in prescribed cases by recognised trade unions (within the meaning of the regulations) of safety representatives from amongst the employees, and those representatives shall represent the employees in consultations with the employers under subsection (6) below and shall have such other functions as may be prescribed.

(5) [. . .]

(6) It shall be the duty of every employer to consult any such representatives with a view to the making and maintenance of arrangements which will enable him and his employees to co-operative effectively in promoting and developing measures to ensure the health and safety at work of the employees, and in checking the effectiveness of such measures.

(7) In such cases as may be prescribed it shall be the duty of every employer, if requested to do so by the safety representatives mentioned in [subsection (4)] [. . .] above, to establish, in accordance with regulations made by the Secretary of State, a safety committee having the function of keeping under review the measures taken to ensure the health and safety at work of his employees and such other functions as may be prescribed.

AMENDMENT

Subs. (5) was repealed by the Employment Protection Act 1975, ss.116 and 125 (3), Sched. 15, para. 2 and Sched. 18. The words in square brackets in subs. (7) were substituted, and the words omitted were repealed, by the Employment Protection Act 1975, ss.116 and 125(3), Sched. 15, para. 2 and Sched. 18.

General duties of employers and self-employed to persons other than their employees

3.—(1) It shall be the duty of every employer to conduct his undertaking in such a way as to ensure, so far as is reasonably practicable, that persons not in his employment who may be affected thereby are not thereby exposed to risks to their health or safety.

1–148

(2) It shall be the duty of every self-employed person to conduct his undertaking in such a way as to ensure, so far as is reasonably practicable, that he and other persons (not being his employees) who may be affected thereby are not thereby exposed to risks to their health or safety.

(3) In such cases as may be prescribed, it shall be the duty of every employer and every self-employed person, in the prescribed circumstances and in the prescribed manner, to give to persons (not being his employees) who may be affected by the way in which he conducts his undertaking the prescribed information about such aspects of the way in which he conducts his undertaking as might affect their health or safety.

General duties of persons concerned with premises to persons other than their employees

4.—(1) This section has effect for imposing on persons duties in relation to those who—

1–149

(*a*) are not their employees; but

(*b*) use non-domestic premises made available to them as a place of work or as a place where they may use plant or substances provided for their use there,

and applies to premises so made available and other non-domestic premises used in connection with them.

(2) It shall be the duty of each person who has, to any extent, control of premises to which this section applies or of the means of access thereto or egress therefrom or of any plant or substance in such premises to take such measures as is reasonable for a person in his position to take to ensure, so far as is reasonably practicable, that the premises, all means of access thereto or egress therefrom available for use by persons using the premises, and any plant or substance in the premises or, as the case may be, provide for use there, is or are safe and without risks to health.

(3) Where a person has, by virtue of any contract or tenancy, an obligation of any extent in relation to—

(*a*) the maintenance or repair of any premises to which this section applies or any means of access thereto or egress therefrom; or

(*b*) the safety of or the absence of risks to health arising from plant or substances in any such premises;

that person shall be treated, for the purposes of subsection (2) above, as being a person who has control of the matters to which his obligation extends.

(4) Any reference in this section to a person having control of any premises or matter is a reference to a person having control of the premises or matter in connection with the carrying on by him of a trade, business or other, undertaking (whether for profit or not).

General duties of manufacturers, etc., as regards articles and substances for use at work

6.—(1) It shall be the duty of any person who designs, manufactures, imports or supplies any article for use at work—

(a) to ensure, so far as is reasonably practicable, that the article is so designed and construed as to be safe and without risks to health when properly used;

(b) to carry out or arrange for the carrying out of such testing and examination as may be necessary for the performance of the duty imposed on him by the preceding paragraph;

(c) to take such steps as are necessary to secure that there will be available in connection with the use of the article at work adequate information about the use for which it is designed and has been tested, and about any conditions necessary to ensure that, when put to that use, it will be safe and without risks to health.

(2) It shall be the duty of any person who undertakes the design or manufacture of any article for use at work to carry out or arrange for the carrying out of any necessary research with a view to the discovery and, so far as is reasonably practicable, the elimination or minimisation of any risks to health or safety to which the design or article may give rise.

(3) It shall be the duty of any person who erects or installs any article for use at work in any premises where that article is to be used by persons at work to ensure, so far as is reasonably practicable, that nothing about the way in which it is erected or installed makes it unsafe or a risk to health when properly used.

(4) It shall be the duty of any person who manufactures, imports or supplies any substance for use at work—

(a) to ensure, so far as is reasonably practicable, that the substance is safe and without risk to health when properly used;

(b) to carry out or arrange for the carrying out of such testing and examination as may be necessary for the performance of the duty imposed on him by the preceding paragraph;

(c) to take such steps as are necessary to secure that there will be available in connection with the use of the substance at work adequate information about the results of any relevant tests which have been carried out on or in connection with the substance and about any conditions necessary to ensure that it will be safe and without risks to health when properly used.

(5) It shall be the duty of any person who undertakes the manufacture of any substance for use at work to carry out or arrange for the carrying out of any necessary research with a view to the discovery and, so far as is reasonably practicable, the elimination or minimisation of any risks to health or safety to which the substance may give rise.

(6) Nothing in the preceding provisions of this section shall be taken to require a person to repeat any testing, examination or research which has been carried out otherwise than by him or at his instance, in so far as it is reasonable for him to rely on the results thereof for the purposes of those provisions.

(7) Any duty imposed on any person by any of the preceding provisions of this section shall extend only to things done in the course of a trade,

business or other undertaking carried on by him (whether for proft or not) and to matters within his control.

(8) Where a person designs, manufactures, imports or supplies an article for or to another on the basis of a written undertaking by that other to take specified steps sufficient to ensure, so far as reasonably practicable, that the article will be safe and without risks to health when properly used, the undertaking shall have the effect of relieving the first mentioned person from the duty imposed by subsection (1)(*a*) above to such extent as is reasonable having regard to the terms of the undertaking.

(9) Where a person ("the ostensible supplier") supplies any article for use at work or substance for use at work to another ("the customer") under a hire-purchase agreement, conditional sale agreement or credit-sale agreement, and the ostensible supplier—
- (*a*) carries on the business of financing the acquisition of goods by others by means of such agreements; and
- (*b*) in the course of that business acquired his interest in the article or substance supplied to the customer as a means of financing its acquisition by the customer from a third person ("the effective supplier"),

the effective supplier and not the ostensible supplier shall be treated for the purposes of this section as supplying the article or substance to the customer, and any duty imposed by the preceding provisions of this section on suppliers shall accordingly fall on the effective supplier and not on the ostensible supplier.

(10) For the purposes of this section an article or substance is not to be regarded as properly used where it is used without regard to any relevant information or advice relating to its use which has been made available by a person by whom it was designed, manufactured, imported or supplied.

General duties of employees at work

7. It shall be the duty of every employee while at work—   **1–151**
- (*a*) to take reasonable care for the health and safety of himself and of other persons who may be affected by his acts or omissions at work; and
- (*b*) as regards any duty or requirement imposed on his employer or any other person by or under any of the relevant statutory provisions, to co-operate with him so far as is necessary to enable that duty or requirement to be performed or complied with.

Duty not to interfere with or misuse things provided pursuant to certain provisions

8. No person shall intentionally or recklessly interfere with or misuse   **1–152**
anything provided in the interests of health, safety or welfare in pursuance of any of the relevant statutory provisions.

Duty not to charge employees for things done or provided pursuant to certain specific enactments

9. No employer shall levy or permit to be levied on any employee of his   **1–153**
any charge in respect of anything done or provided in pursuance of any specific requirement of the relevant statutory provisions.

. . . . . .

Enforcement

Authorities responsible for enforcement of the relevant statutory provisions

18.—(1) It shall be the duty of the Executive to make adequate arrangements for the enforcement of the relevant statutory provisions except to the extent that some other authority or class of authorities is by any of those provisions or by regulations under subsection (2) below made responsible for their enforcement.

(2) The Secretary of State may by regulations—

(a) make local authorities responsible for the enforcement of the relevant statutory provisions to such extent as may be prescribed;

(b) make provisions for enabling responsibility for enforcing any of the relevant statutory provisions to be, to such extent as may be determined under the regulations—

(i) transferred from the Executive to local authorities or from local authorities to the Executive; or

(ii) assigned to the Executive or to local authorities for the purpose of removing any uncertainty as to what are by virtue of this subsection their respective responsibilities for the enforcement of those provisions;

and any regulations made in pursuance of paragraph (b) above shall include provision for securing that any transfer or assignment effected under the regulations is brought to the notice of persons affected by it.

(3) Any provision made by regulations under the preceding subsection shall have effect subject to any provision made by health and safety regulations [. . .] in pursuance of section 15(3)(c).

(4) It shall be the duty of every local authority—

(a) to make adequate arrangements for the enforcement within their area of the relevant statutory provisions to the extent that they are by any of those provisions or by regulations under subsection (2) above made responsible for their enforcement; and

(b) to perform the duty imposed on them by the preceding paragraph and any other functions conferred on them by any of the relevant statutory provisions in accordance with such guidance as the Commission may give them.

(5) Where any authority other than [. . .] the Executive or a local authority is by any of the relevant statutory provisions or by regulations under subsection (2) above made responsible for the enforcement of any of those provisions to any extent, it shall be the duty of that authority—

(a) to make adequate arrangements for the enforcement of those provisions to that extent; and

(b) to perform the duty imposed on the authority by the preceding paragraph and any other functions conferred on the authority by any of the relevant statutory provisions in accordance with such guidance as the Commission may give to the authority.

(6) Nothing in the provision of this Act or of any regulations made thereunder charging any person in Scotland with the enforcement of any of the

relevant statutory provisions shall be construed as authorising that person to institute proceedings for any offence.

(7) In this Part—

    (*a*) "enforcing authority" means the Executive or any other authority which is by any of the relevant statutory provisions or by regulations under subsection (2) above made responsible for the enforcement of any of those provisions to any extent; and

    (*b*) any reference to an enforcing authority's field of responsibility is a reference to the field over which that authority's responsibility for the enforcement of those provisions extends for the time being;

but where by virtue of paragraph (*a*) of section 13(1) the performance of any function of the Commission or the Executive is delegated to a government department or person, references to the Commission or the Executive (or to an enforcing authority where that authority is the Executive) in any provision of this Part which relates to that function shall, so far as may be necessary to give effect to any agreement under that paragraph, be construed as references to that department or person; and accordingly any reference to the field of responsibility of an enforcing authority shall be construed as a reference to the field over which that department or person for the time being performs such a function.

AMENDMENT

The words in square brackets in subs. (1) were repealed, by the Employment Protection Act 1975 (c. 71), ss.116 and 125(3), Sched. 15, para. 8 and Sched. 18.

Appointment of inspectors

19.—(1) Every enforcing authority may appoint as inspectors (under whatever title it may from time to time determine) such persons having suitable qualifications as it thinks necessary for carrying into effect the relevant statutory provisions within its field of responsibility, and may terminate any appointment made under this section.

(2) Every appointment of a person as an inspector under this section shall be made by an instrument in writing specifying which of the powers conferred on inspectors by the relevant statutory provisions are to be exercisable by the person appointed; and an inspector shall in right of his appointment under this section—

    (*a*) be entitled to exercise only such of those powers as are so specified; and

    (*b*) be entitled to exercise the powers so specified only within the field of responsibility of the authority which appointed him.

(3) So much of an inspector's instrument of appointment as specifies the powers which he is entitled to exercise may be varied by the enforcing authority which appointed him.

(4) An inspector shall, if so required when exercising or seeking to exercise any power conferred on him by any of the relevant statutory provisions, produce his instrument of appointment or a duly authenticated copy thereof.

Powers of inspectors

20.—(1) Subject to the provisions of section 19 and this section, an inspector may, for the purpose of carrying into effect any of the relevant statutory provisions within the field of responsibility of the enforcing authority which appointed him, exercise the powers set out in subsection (2) below.

(2) The powers of an inspector referred to in the preceding subsection are the following, namely—

(a) at any reasonable time (or, in a situation which in his opinion is or may be dangerous at any time) to enter any premises which he has reason to believe it is necessary for him to enter for the purpose mentioned in subsection (1) above;

(b) to take with him a constable if he has reasonable cause to apprehend any serious obstruction in the execution of his duty;

(c) without prejudice to the preceding paragraph, on entering any premises by virtue of paragraph (a) above to take with him—

(i) any other person duly authorised by his (the inspector's) enforcing authority; and

(ii) any equipment or materials required for any purpose for which the power of entry is being exercised;

(d) to make such examination and investigation as may in any circumstances be necessary for the purpose mentioned in subsection (1) above;

(e) as regards any premises which he has power to enter, to direct that those premises or any part of them, or anything therein, shall be left undisturbed (whether generally or in particular respects) for so long as is reasonably necessary for the purpose of any examination or investigation under paragraph (d) above;

(f) to take such measurements and photographs and make such recordings as he considers necessary for the purpose of any examination or investigation under paragraph (d) above;

(g) to take samples of any articles or substances found in any premises which he has power to enter, and of the atmosphere in or in the vicinity of any such premises;

(h) in the case of any article or substance found in any premises which he has power to enter, being an article or substance which appears to him to have caused or to be likely to cause danger to health or safety, to cause it to be dismantled or subjected to any process or test (but not so as to damage or destroy it unless this is in the circumstances necessary for the purpose mentioned in subsection (1) above);

(i) in the case of any such article or substance as is mentioned in the preceding paragraph, to take possession of it and detain it for so long as is necessary for all or any of the following purposes; namely—

(i) to examine it and do to it anything which he has power to do under that paragraph;

(ii) to ensure that it is not tampered with before his examination of it is completed;

(iii) to ensure that it is available for use as evidence in any proceedings for an offence under any of the relevant statutory provisions or any proceedings relating to a notice under section 21 or 22;

(j) to require any person whom he has reasonable cause to believe to be able to give any information relevant to any examination or investigation under paragraph (d) above to answer (in the absence of persons other than a person nominated by him to be present and any persons whom the inspector may allow to be present) such questions as the inspector thinks fit to ask and to sign a declaration of the truth of his answers;

(k) to require the production of, inspect, and take copies of or of any entry in—

(i) any books or documents which by virtue of any of the relevant statutory provisions are required to be kept; and

(ii) any other books or documents which it is necessary for him to see for the purposes of any examination or investigation under paragraph (d) above;

(l) to require any person to afford him such facilities and assistance with respect to any matters or things within that person's control or in relation to which that person has responsibilities as are necessary to enable the inspector to exercise any of the powers conferred on him by this section;

(m) any other power which is necessary for the purpose mentioned in subsection (1) above.

(3) The Secretary of State may by regulations make provision as to the procedure to be followed in connection with the taking of samples under subsection (2)(g) above (including provision as to the way in which samples that have been so taken are to be dealt with).

(4) Where an inspector proposes to exercise the power conferred by subsection (2)(h) above in the case of an article or substance found in any premises, he shall, if so requested by a person who at the time is present in and has responsibilities in relation to those premises, cause anything which is to be done by virtue of that power to be done in the presence of that person unless the inspector considers that its being done in that person's presence would be prejudicial to the safety of the State.

(5) Before exercising the power conferred by subsection (2)(h) above in the case of any article or substance, an inspector shall, consult such persons as appear to him appropriate for the purpose of ascertaining what dangers, if any, there may be in doing anything which he proposes to do under that power.

(6) Where under the power conferred by subsection (2)(i) above an inspector takes possession of any article or substance found in any premises, he shall leave there, either with a responsible person or, if that is impracticable, fixed in a conspicuous position, a notice giving particulars of that article or substance sufficient to identify it and stating that he has taken possession of it under that power; and before taking possession of any such substance under that power an inspector shall, if it is practicable for him to do so, take a sample thereof and give to a responsible person at the premises a portion of the sample marked in a manner sufficient to identify it.

(7) No answer given by a person in pursuance of a requirement imposed under subsection (2)(j) above shall be admissible in evidence against that person or the husband or wife of that person in any proceedings.

(8) Nothing in this section shall be taken to compel the production by any person of a document of which he would on grounds of legal professional privilege be entitled to withhold production on an order for discovery in an action in the High Court or, as the case may be, on an order for the production of documents in an action in the Court of Session.

Improvement notices

1-157   **21.** If an inspector is of the opinion that a person—

(*a*) is contravening one or more of the relevant statutory provisions; or

(*b*) has contravened one or more of those provisions in circumstances that make it likely that the contravention will continue or be repeated,

he may serve on him a notice (in this Part referred to as "an improvement notice") stating that he is of that opinion, specifying the provision or provisions as to which he is of that opinion, giving particulars of the reasons why he is of that opinion, and requiring that person to remedy the contravention or, as the case may be, the matters occasioning it within such period (ending not earlier than the period within which an appeal against the notice can be brought under section 24) as may be specified in the notice.

Prohibition notices

1-158   **22.**—(1) This section applies to any activities which are being or are about to be carried on by or under the control of any person, being activities to or in relation to which any of the relevant statutory provisions apply or will, if the activities are so carried on, apply.

(2) If as regards any activities to which this section applies an inspector is of the opinion that, as carried on or about to be carried on by or under the control of the person in question, the activities involve or, as the case may be, will involve a risk of serious personal injury, the inspector may serve on that person a notice (in this Part referred to as "a prohibition notice").

(3) A prohibition notice shall—

(*a*) state that the inspector is of the said opinion;

(*b*) specify the matters which in his opinion give or, as the case may be, will give rise to the said risk;

(*c*) where in his opinion any of those matters involves or, as the case may be, will involve a contravention of any of the relevant statutory provisions, state that he is of that opinion, specify the provision or provisions as to which he is of that opinion, and give particulars of the reasons why he is of that opinion; and

(*d*) direct that the activities to which the notice relates shall not be carried on by or under the control of the person on whom the notice is served unless the matters specified in the notice in pursuance of paragraph(*b*) above and any associated contraventions of provisions so specified in pursuance of paragraph (*c*) above have been remedied.

(4) A direction given in pursuance of subsection (3)(*d*) above shall take immediate effect if the inspector is of the opinion, and states it, that the risk of serious personal injury is or, as the case may be, will be imminent, and shall have effect at the end of a period specified in the notice in any other case.

Provisions supplementary to ss.21 and 22

1-159   **23.**—(1) In this section "a notice" means an improvement notice or a prohibition notice.

(2) A notice may (but need not) include directions as to the measures to

be taken to remedy any contravention or matter to which the notice relates; and any such directions—
- (a) may be framed to any extent by reference to any approved code of practice; and
- (b) may be framed so as to afford the person on whom the notice is served a choice between different ways of remedying the contravention or matter.

(3) Where any of the relevant statutory provisions applies to a building or any matter connected with a building and an inspector proposes to serve an improvement notice relating to a contravention of that provision in connection with that building or matter, the notice shall not direct any measures to be taken to remedy the contravention of that provision which are more onerous than those necessary to secure conformity with the requirements of any building regulations for the time being in force to which that building or matter would be required to conform if the relevant building were being newly erected unless the provision in question imposes specific requirements more onerous than the requirements of any such building regulations to which the building or matter would be required to conform as aforesaid.

In this subsection "the relevant building", in the case of a building, means that building, and, in the case of a matter connected with a building, means the building with which the matter is connected.

(4) Before an inspector serves in connection with any premises used or about to be used as a place of work a notice requiring or likely to lead to the taking of measures affecting the means of escape in case of fire with which the premises are or ought to be provided, he shall consult the fire authority.

In this subsection "fire authority" has the meaning assigned by section 43(1) of the Fire Precautions Act 1971.

(5) Where an improvement notice or a prohibition notice which is not to take immediate effect has been served—
- (a) the notice may be withdrawn by an inspector at any time before the end of the period specified therein in pursuance of section 21 or section 22(4) as the case may be; and
- (b) the period so specified may be extended or further extended by an inspector at any time when an appeal against the notice is not pending.

(6) In the application of this section to Scotland—
- (a) in subsection (3) for the words from "with the requirements" to "aforesaid" there shall be substituted the words—
    "(a) to any provisions of the building standards regulations to which that building or matter would be required to conform if the relevant building were being newly erected; or
    (b) where the sherrif, on an appeal to him under section 16 of the Building (Scotland) Act 1959—
        (i) against an order under section 10 of that Act requiring the execution of operations necessary to make the building or matter conform to the building standards regulations, or
        (ii) against an order under section 11 of that Act requiring the building or matter to conform to a provision of such regulations,

has varied the order, to any provisions of the building standards regulations referred to in paragraph (*a*) above as affected by the order as so varied,

unless the relevant statutory provision imposes specific requirements more onerous than the requirements of any provisions of building standards regulations as aforesaid or, as the case may be, than the requirements of the order as varied by the sheriff."

(*b*) after subsection (5) there shall be inserted the following subsection—

"(5A)In subsection (3) above 'building standards regulations' has the same meaning as in section 3 of the Building (Scotland) Act 1959."

Appeal against improvement or prohibition notice

1–160   **24.**—(1) In this section "a notice" means an improvement notice or a prohibition notice.

(2) A person on whom a notice is served may within such period from the date of its service as may be prescribed appeal to an industrial tribunal; and on such an appeal the tribunal may either cancel or affirm the notice and, if it affirms it, may do so either in its original form or with such modifications as the tribunal may in the circumstances think fit.

(3) Where an appeal under this section is brought against a notice within the period allowed under the preceding subsection, then—

(*a*) in the case of an improvement notice, the bringing of the appeal shall have the effect of suspending the operation of the notice until the appeal is finally disposed of or, if the appeal is withdrawn, until the withdrawal of the appeal;

(*b*) in the case of a prohibition notice, the bringing of the appeal shall have the like effect if, but only if, on the application of the appellant the tribunal so directs (and then only from the giving of the direction).

(4) One or more assessors may be appointed for the purposes of any proceedings brought before an industrial tribunal under this section.

Power to deal with the cause of imminent danger

1–161   **25.**—(1) Where, in the case of any article or substance found by him in any premises which he has power to enter, an inspector has reasonable cause to believe that, in the circumstances in which he finds it, the article or substance is a cause of imminent danger of serious personal injury, he may seize it and cause it to be rendered harmless (whether by desctruction or otherwise).

(2) Before there is rendered harmless under this section—

(*a*) any article that forms part of a batch of similar articles; or

(*b*) any substance,

the inspector shall, if it is practicable for him to do so, take a sample thereof and give to a responsible person at the premises where the article or substance was found by him a portion of the sample marked in a manner sufficient to identify it.

(3) As soon as may be after any article or substance has been seized and

rendered harmless under this section, the inspector shall prepare and sign a written report giving particulars of the circumstances in which the article or substance was seized and so dealt with by him, and shall—
  (*a*) give a signed copy of the report to a responsible person at the premises where the article or substance was found by him; and
  (*b*) unless that person is the owner of the aricle or substance, also serve a signed copy of the report on the owner;
and if, where paragraph (*b*) above applies, the inspector cannot after reasonable enquiry ascertain the name or address of the owner, the copy may be served on him by giving it to the person to whom a copy was given under the preceding paragraph.

(4) An order made by virtue of the preceding subsections which declares an authority to be in default may, for the purpose of remedying the default, direct the authority (hereafter in this section referred to as "the defaulting authority") to perform such of their enforcement functions as are specified in the order in such manner as may be so specified and may specify the time or times within which those functions are to be performed by the authority.

(5) If the defaulting authority fail to comply with any direction contained in such order the Secretary of State may, instead of enforcing the order by mandamus, make an order transferring to the Executive such of the enforcement functions of the defaulting authority as he thinks fit.

(6) Where any enforcement functions of the defaulting authority are transferred in pursuance of the preceding subsection, the amount of any expenses which the Executive certifies were incurred by it in performing those functions shall on demand be paid to it by the defaulting authority.

(7) Any expenses which in pursuance of the preceding subsection are required to be paid by the defaulting authority in respect of any enforcement functions transferred in pursuance of this section shall be defrayed by the authority in the like manner, and shall be debited to the like account, as if the enforcement functions had not been transferred and the expenses had been incurred by the authority in performing them.

(8) Where the defaulting authority are required to defray any such expenses the authority shall have the like powers for the purpose of raising the moneys for defraying those expenses as they would have had for the purpose of raising money required for defraying expenses incurred for the purpose of the enforcement functions in question.

(9) An order transferring any enforcement functions of the defaulting authority in pursuance of subsection (5) above may provide for the transfer to the Executive of such of the rights, liabilities and obligations of the authority as the Secretary of State considers appropriate; and where such an order is revoked the Secretary of State may, by the revoking order or a subsequent order, make such provisions as he considers appropriate with respect to any rights, liabilities and obligations held by the Executive for the purposes of the transferred enforcement functions.

(10) The Secretary of State may by order vary or revoke any order previously made by him in pursuance of this section.

(11) In this section "enforcement functions", in relation to a local authority, means the functions of the authority as an enforcing authority.

(12) In the application of this section to Scotland—
  (*a*) in subsection (2) for the words "subsections (2) to (5) of section 250 of the Local Government Act 1972" there shall be substituted the words "subsections (2) to (8) of section 210 of the

Local Government (Scotland) Act 1973", except that before 16th May 1975 for the said words there shall be substituted the words "subsections (2) to (9) of section 355 of the Local Government (Scotland) Act 1947";

(b) in subsection (5) the words "instead of enforcing the order by mandamus" shall be omitted.

. . . . .

Service of notices

46.—(1) Any notice required or authorised by any of the relevant statutory provisions to be served on or given to an inspector may be served or given by delivering it to him or by leaving it at, or sending it by post to, his office.

(2) Any such notice required or authorised to be served on or given to a person other than an inspector may be served or given by delivering it to him, or by leaving it at his proper address, or by sending it by post to him at that address.

(3) Any such notice may—
   (a) in the case of a body corporate, be served on or given to the secretary or clerk of that body;
   (b) in the case of a partnership, be served on or given to a partner or a person having the control or management of the partnership business or, in Scotland, the firm.

(4) For the purposes of this section and of section 26 of the Interpretation Act 1889 (service of documents by post) in its application to this section, the proper address of any person on or to whom any such notice is to be served or given shall be his last known address, except that—
   (a) in the case of a body corporate or their secretary or clerk, it shall be the address of the registered or principal office of that body;
   (b) in the case of a partnership or a person having the control or the management of the partnership business, it shall be the principal office of the partnership;
and for the purposes of this subsection the principal office of a company registered outside the United Kingdom or of a partnership carrying on business outside the United Kingdom shall be their principal office within the United Kingdom.

(5) If the person to be served with or given any such notice has specified an address within the United Kingdom other than his proper address within the meaning of subsection (4) above as the one at which he or someone on his behalf will accept notices of the same description as that notice, that address shall also be treated for the purposes of this section and section 26 of the Interpretation Act 1889 as his proper address.

(6) Without prejudice to any other provision of this section any such notice required or authorised to be served on or given to the owner or occupier of any premises (whether a body corporate or not) may be served or given by sending it by post to him at those premises, or by addressing it by name to the person on or to whom it is to be served or given and delivering it to some responsible person who is or appears to be resident or employed in the premises.

(7) If the name or the address of any owner or occupier of premises on

or to whom any such notice as aforesaid is to be served or given cannot after reasonable inquiry be ascertained, the notice may be served or given by addressing it to the person on or to whom it is to be served or given by the description of "owner" or "occupier" of the premises (describing them) to which the notice relates, and by delivering it to some responsible person who is or appears to be resident or employed in the premises, or, if there is no such person to whom it can be delivered, by affixing it or a copy of it to some conspicuous part of the premises.

(8) The preceding provisions of this section shall apply to the sending or giving of a document as they apply to the giving of a notice.

. . . . . .

Application to Crown

48.—(1) Subject to the provisions of this section, the provisions of this Part, except sections 21 to 25 and 33 to 42, and of regulations made under this Part shall bind the Crown.

1–163

(2) Although they do not bind the Crown, sections 33 to 42 shall apply to persons in the public service of the Crown as they apply to other persons.

(3) For the purposes of this Part and regulations made thereunder persons in the service of the Crown shall be treated as employees of the Crown whether or not they would be so treated apart from this subsection.

(4) Without prejudice to section 15(5), the Secretary of State may, to the extent that it appears to him requisite or expedient to do so in the interests of the safety of the State or the safe custody of persons lawfully detained, by order exempt the Crown either generally or in particular respects from all or any of the provisions of this Part which would, by virtue of subsections (1) above, bind the Crown.

(5) The Power to make orders under this section shall be exercisable by statutory instrument, and any such order may be varied or revoked by a subsequent order.

(6) Nothing in this section shall authorise proceedings to be brought against Her Majesty in her private capacity, and this subsection shall be construed as if section 38(3) of the Crown Proceedings Act 1947 (interpretation of references in that Act to Her Majesty in her private capacity) were contained in this Act.

. . . . . .

Amendment of Companies Acts to directors' reports

79.—(1) The Companies Act 1967 shall be amended in accordance with the followig provisions of this section.

1–164

(2) In section 16 (additional general matters to be dealt with in directors' reports) in subsection (1) there shall be added after paragraph (*f*)—

  "(*g*) in the case of companies of such classes as may be prescribed by regulations made by the Secretary of State, contain such information as may be so prescribed about the arrangements in force in that year for securing the health, safety and welfare at work of employees of the company and its subsidiaries and for protecting other persons against risks to health or safety arising out of or in connection with the activities at work of those employees."

(3) After subsection (4) of the said section 16 there shall be added—

"(5) Regulations made under paragraph (g) of subsection (1) above may—
   (a) make different provisions in relation to companies of different classes;
   (b) enable any requirements of the regulations to be dispensed with or modified in particular cases by any specified person or by any person authorised in that behalf by a specified authority;
   (c) contain such transitional provisions as the Secretary of State thinks necessary or expedient in connection with any provision made by the regulations.
(6) The power to make regulations under the said paragraph (g) shall be exercisable by statutory instrument which shall be subject to amendment in pursuance of a resolution of either House of Parliament.
(7) Any expression used in the said paragraph (g) and in Part I of the Health and Safety at Work etc. Act 1974 shall have the same meaning in that paragraph as it has in that Part of that Act and section 1(6) of that Act shall apply for interpreting that Part of that Act; and in subsection (5) above 'specified' means specified in regulations made under that paragraph."

Trade Union and Labour Relations Act 1974

1–165

(1974 c.52)

An Act to repeal the Industrial Relations Act 1971; to make provision with respect to the law relating to trade unions, employers' associations, workers and employers, including the law relating to unfair dismissal, and with respect to the jurisdiction and procedure of industrial tribunals; and for connected purposes.

[31st July 1974]

Repeal of Industrial Relations Act 1971

Repeal of Industrial Relations Act 1971 and re-enactment of certain provisions

1–166   **1.**—(1) The Industrial Relations Act 1971 is hereby repealed.
(2) Nevertheless, Schedule 1 to this Act shall have effect for re-enacting, with amendments consequential on the following sections of this Act and other amendments, the under-mentioned provisions of that Act, that is to say—
   (a) Part I of that Schedule so re-enacts sections 2 to 4 (code of practice);
   (b) [*Repealed by the Employment Protection (Consolidation) Act 1978, c. 44.*]
   (c) [*Repealed by the Employment Protection (Consolidation) Act 1978, c. 44.*]
   (d) Part IV so re-enacts sections [. . .] 155, 161 and 162 (conciliation officers, and miscellaneous and supplementary provisions).
(3) The repeal by this section of the following provisions of the 1971 Act, that is to say, sections 7(2) and (3), 11 to 18, 31, 32, 37 to 55, 76, 77, 99,

101 to 105, 111, 112, 114, 115, 129 136, 138 to 145 and 160 and Schedule 1 (jurisdiction, functions and constitution of the National Industrial Relations Court) shall take effect on the passing of this Act and on the passing of this Act that Court is hereby abolished.

Status and regulation of trade unions and employers' associations

Status of trade unions

2.—(1) A trade union which is not a special register body shall not be, or be treated as if it were, a body corporate but—
(*a*) it shall be capable of making contracts;
(*b*) all property belonging to the trade union shall be vested in trustees in trust for the union;
(*c*) [. . .] it shall be capable of suing and being sued in its own name, whether in proceedings relating to property or founded on contract or tort or any other cause of action whatsoever;
(*d*) proceedings for any offence alleged to have been committed by it or on its behalf may be brought against it in its own name; and
(*e*) any judgment, order or award made in proceedings of any description brought against the trade union on or after the commencement of this section shall be enforceable, by way of execution, diligence, punishment for contempt or otherwise, against any property held in trust for the trade union to the like extent and in the like manner as if the union were a body corporate.

(2) A trade union which is not a special register body shall not be registered as a company under the Companies Act 1948 and accordingly any registration of any such union under that Act (whenever effected) shall be void.

(3) No trade union shall be registered under the Friendly Societies Act 1896 or the Industrial and Provident Societies Act 1965 and accordingly any registration of a trade union under either of those Acts (whenever effected) shall be void.

(4) A trade union (other than a special register body) which, immediately before the commencement of this section, was a body corporate shall, on that commencement, cease to be a body corporate and the provisions of section 19 below (as well as this section and section 4 below) shall apply to the trade union on and after that commencement.

(5) The purposes of any trade union which is not a special register body and, in so far as they relate to the regulation of relations between employers and employers' associations and workers, the purposes of any trade union which is such a body, shall not, by reason only that they are in restraint of trade, be unlawful so as—
(*a*) to make any member of the trade union liable to criminal proceedings for conspiracy or otherwise, or
(*b*) to make any agreement or trust void or voidable;
nor shall any rule of a trade union which is not a special register body or, in so far as it so relates, any rule of any other trade union be unlawful or unenforceable by reason only that it is in restraint of trade.

1–167

AMENDMENT
In subs. (1)(*c*), the words omitted were repealed by the Employment Act 1982 (c. 46), Sched. 4.

Status of employers' associations

1–168   **3.**—(1) An employers' association may be either a body corporate or an unincorporated association.

(2) Where an employers' association is unincorporated—
- (a) it shall be capable of making contracts;
- (b) all property belonging to the employers' association shall be vested in trustees in trust for the association;
- (c) [. . .] it shall be capable of suing and being sued in its own name, whether in proceedings relating to property or founded on contract or tort or any other cause of action whatsoever;
- (d) proceedings for any offence alleged to have been committed by it or on its behalf may be brought against it in its own name; and
- (e) any judgment, order or award made in proceedings of any description brought against the employers' association on or after the commencement of this section shall be enforceable, by way of execution, diligence, punishment for contempt or otherwise, against any property held in trust for the employers' association to the like extent and in the like manner as if the association were a body corporate.

(3) Any employers' association which became a body corporate by virtue of section 74 of the 1971 Act shall cease to be a body corporate by virtue of that section at the expiration of the period of six months beginning with the commencement of this section and the provisions of section 19 below (as well as this section and section 4 below) shall apply to it on and after the expiration of that period, unless before the expiration of that period it has again become a body corporate.

(4) Nothing in section 434 of the Companies Act 1948 (associations of over twenty members for certain purposes must be incorporated or otherwise formed in special ways) shall be taken to prevent the formation of an employers' association which is neither registered as a company under that Act nor otherwise incorporated.

(5) The purposes of an unincorporated employers' association and, in so far as they relate to the regulation of relations between employers and workers or trade unions, the purposes of an employers' association which is a body corporate, shall not, by reason only that they are in restraint of trade, be unlawful so as—
- (a) to make any member of the association liable to criminal proceedings for conspiracy or otherwise; or
- (b) to make any agreement or trust void or voidable;

nor shall any rule of an unincorporated employers' association or, in so far as it so relates, any rule of an employers' association which is a body corporate be unlawful or unenforceable by reason only that it is in restraint of trade.

AMENDMENT

The words omitted in subs. (2)(c) were repealed by the Employment Act 1982 (c. 46), Sched. 4.

Supplementary provisions about property of trade unions and unincorporated employers' associations

1–169   **4.**—(1) Sections 39 and 40 of the Trustee Act 1925 and sections 38 and 39 of the Trustee Act (Northern Ireland) 1958 (vesting of property on retirement of trustee or appointment of new trustee) shall, in their application to trustees in whom any property is vested in trust for a trade union or an unincorporated employers' association to which this subsection applies, each have effect as if for any reference to a deed there were substituted a reference to an instrument in writing and as if in subsection (4) of section 40 of the said Act of 1925 and of section 39 of the said Act of 1958 paragraphs (*a*) and (*c*) were omitted.

(2) Subsection (1) above applies to a trade union (other than a special register body) and to an unincorporated employers' association whose name is (in either case) for the time being entered in the list of trade unions or of employers' associations under section 8 below.

(3) An instrument in writing appointing a new trustee of a trade union or unincorporated employers' association to which subsection (1) above applies is referred to in this section as an "instrument of appointment" and an instrument in writing discharging a trustee of such a union or association is referred to as an "instrument of discharge"; and for the purposes of this section (and the sections of the Acts of 1925 and 1958 applied by subsection (1) above), where a trustee of such a union or association is appointed or discharged by a resolution taken by or on behalf of the union or association, the written record of the resolution shall be treated as if it were the instrument in writing appointing or, as the case may be, discharging that trustee.

(4) Where by any enactment or instrument the transfer of securities of any description is required to be effected or recorded by means of entries in a register then, if—
   (*a*) there is produced to the person who is authorised or required to keep the register, a copy of an instrument of appointment or of an instrument of discharge which contains or has attached to it a list identifying the securities of that description held in trust for the union or association to which the instrument relates at the date of the appointment or discharge; and
   (*b*) it appears to that person that any of the securities so identified are included in the register kept by him,
he shall, notwithstanding anything in section 75 or 117 of the Companies Act 1948 or any other enactment or instrument regulating the keeping of the register, make such entries as may be necessary to give effect to the instrument of appointment or of discharge.

(5) A document which purports to be a copy of an instrument of appointment or of an instrument of discharge containing or having attached to it such a list and to be certified to be a copy of such an instrument in accordance with subsection (6) below shall be taken to be a copy of such an instrument unless the contrary is proved.

(6) The certificate referred to in subsection (5) above shall be given by the president and general secretary (or persons occupying positions equivalent to those of president and general secretary) of the union or association to which the instrument relates and, in the case of an instrument to which the list of securities is attached, shall appear both on the instrument and on the list.

(7) Nothing done for the purposes of or in pursuance of subsection (4) above shall be taken to affect any person with notice of any trust or to impose on any person a duty to inquire into any matter.

(8) In relation to a trade union or an employers' association whose principal office is situated in Scotland, references in this section to the appointment and to the discharge of a trustee shall be construed as including

Right to terminate membership of trade union

1–170 7. [In every contract of membership of a trade union, whether made before or after the passing of this Act, there shall be implied a term conferring a right on the member, on giving reasonable notice and complying with any reasonable conditions to terminate his membership of the union.]

AMENDMENT
   The section was substituted by TULR(A) A 1976, (c. 7), s.3(1).

Lists of trade unions and employers' associations

1–171 8.—(1) The [Certification Officer] [. . .] shall maintain a list of trade unions and a list of employers' associations containing the names of those organisations which are entitled to have their names entered therein under the following provisions of this section.

(2) The [Certification Officer] shall enter in the list of trade unions or employers' associations, as the case may be, the name of every organisation of workers or of employers which—
  (a) was on 30th September 1971 registered (whether by that or any other name) as a trade union under the Trade Union Acts 1871 to 1964; or
  (b) has since that date been formed by the amalgamation of a number of such organisations each of which was so registered; or
  (c) was immediately before the commencement of this section affiliated to the Trades Union Congress; or
  (d) was immediately before that commencement registered as a trade union under section 68(4) of the 1971 Act or as an employers' association under section 72(4) of that Act;
except an organisation which appears to him not to be a trade union or, as the case may be, employers' association within the meaning of this Act.

(3) Any organisation of workers or of employers, whenever formed, whose name is not entered in the relevant list may apply to the [Certification Officer] to have its name so entered and, subject to subsection (5) below, the [Certification Officer] shall, if satisfied that the organisation is a trade union or employers' association and that subsection (4) below has been complied with, enter the name of that organisation in the relevant list.

(4) An application under subsection (3) above shall be made in such form and manner as the [Certification Officer] may require and be accompanied by a fee of [£20] or such other fee as may be prescribed by regulations made by the Secretary of State and also by—
  (a) a copy of the rules of the organisation;
  (b) a list of its officers;
  (c) the address of its head or main office; and
  (d) the name under which it is or is to be known.

(5) The [Certification Officer] shall not under subsection (3) above enter the name of an organisation in the relevant list if that name is—
  (a) the same as a name under which another organisation was registered as a trade union under the Trade Union Acts 1871 to 1964 on

30th September 1971 or was registered at any time as a trade union or employers' association under the 1971 Act or is for the time being entered in either list; or

(b) a name so nearly resembling any such name as to be likely to deceive the public.

(6) If it appears to the [Certification Officer], whether on application made to him or otherwise, that an organisation whose name is entered in the relevant list is not a trade union or employer's association [. . .] he may remove its name from the relevant list, but shall not do so without giving the organisation notice of his intention to do so and without considering any representations made to him by the organisation during a period specified in the notice (being not less than twenty-eight days beginning with the date of the notice).

[(6A) The Certificate Officer shall remove the name of an organisation from the relevant list—
(a) if he is requested by the organisation to do so, or
(b) if he is satisfied that the organisation has ceased to exist.]

(7) [Any organisation aggrieved by the refusal of the Certification Officer to enter its name in the relevant list or by a decision of his to remove its name from that list may appeal, in accordance with [section 136(3) of the Employment Protection (Consolidation) Act 1978,] to the Employment Appeal Tribunal; and on any such appeal the Tribunal, if satisfied that the name should be or remain so entered, shall declare that fact and give directions to the Certification Officer accordingly.]

(8) [*Repealed by the Employment Protection Act* 1975 (*c.* 71).]

(9) The [Certification Officer] shall at all reasonable hours keep available for public inspection (free of charge) copies of the lists of trade unions and employers' associations, as for the time being in force, and a copy of each list shall be included in the annual report made by the [Certification Officer under paragraph 13(2) of Schedule 1 to the Employment Protection Act 1975].

(10) [The fact that the name of an organisation is included in the list of trade unions or employers' associations shall be evidence (and in Scotland sufficient evidence) that the organisation is a trade union or, as the case may be, an employers' association and on the application of the organisation] the Certification Officer shall issue it with a certificate that its name is included in the relevant list; and any document purporting to be such a certificate shall be evidence (and in Scotland sufficient evidence) that the name of the organisation is entered in the relevant list [. . .].

AMENDMENT

In this section the words "Certification Officer" were substituted by the Employment Protection Act 1975 (c. 71), s. 7(1) and Sched. 16, Pt. III, para. 1.

The words in the second set of square brackets in subsection (7) were substituted by the Employment Protection (Consolidation) Act 1978 (c. 44), Sched. 16, para. 18. All other words in square brackets were substituted by the Employment Protection Act 1975 (c. 71), Sched. 16, Pt. III.

Application of existing Acts referring to registered trade unions, employers' associations, etc.

9.—(1) An enactment passed, or an instrument made under an enactment, before the commencement of this section which refers (or is to be construed as referring) to a trade union registered under the Trade Union

Acts 1871 to 1964 or a trade union or employers' association registered under the 1971 Act, shall, on and after that commencement, have effect as if it referred to a trade union or employers' association within the meaning of this Act.

(2) Where an enactment passed, or an instrument made under an enactment, before the commencement of this section refers (or is to be construed as referring) to an organisation of workers or to an organisation of employers (within the meaning of the 1971 Act), it shall, on and after that commencement, have effect as if it referred to a trade union or an employers' association, as the case may be.

(3) Subsections (1) and (2) above shall not apply to any enactment contained in the Income and Corporation Taxes Act 1970 or any other enactment relating to income tax or corporation tax.

Duty to keep accounting records

1–173   **10.**—(1) This section applies to every trade union and every employers' association except one which consists wholly or mainly of representatives of constituent or affiliated organisations (of the description referred to in subsection (1)(*b*)(ii) or subsection (2)(*b*)(ii) of section 28 below).

(2) Every trade union and every employers' association to which this section applies shall—
   (*a*) cause to be kept proper accounting records with respect to its transactions and its assets and liabilities; and
   (*b*) establish and maintain a satisfactory system of control of its accounting records, its cash holdings and all its receipts and remittances.

(3) For the purposes of paragraph (*a*) above proper accounting records shall not be taken to be kept with respect to the matters mentioned in that paragraph if there are not kept such records as are necessary to give a true and fair view of the state of the affairs of the trade union or employers' association and to explain its transactions.

(4) Where a trade union or employers' association consists of or includes branches or sections, then—
   (*a*) any duty falling upon the union or association in relation to a branch or section under this section shall be treated as having been discharged to the extent to which a branch or section discharges that duty instead of the union or association; and
   (*b*) any duty falling upon a branch or section under this section by reason of its being a trade union or employers' association shall be treated as having been discharged to the extent to which the union or association of which it is a branch or section discharges that duty instead of the branch or section.

Duties as to annual returns, auditors and members' superannuation schemes

1–174   **11.**—(1) This section applies to every trade union and every employers' association to which section 10 above applies except a union or association which has been in existence for less than 12 months.

(2) Every trade union and every employers' association to which this section applies shall in every calendar year send the [Certification Officer] a return relating to its affairs.

(3) Every trade union and every employers' association to which this section applies shall appoint an auditor or auditors to audit the accounts contained in its annual return.

(4) Every trade union and every employers' association to which this section applies shall at the request of any person, supply him with a copy of its rules and of its most recent annual return either free of charge or on payment of a reasonable charge.

(5) The [Certification Officer] shall at all reasonable hours keep available for public inspection, either free of charge or on payment of a reasonable charge, copies of all annual returns sent to him under this section.

(6) The provisions of Part I of Schedule 2 to this Act shall have effect with respect to the annual return and to the qualifications, appointment, removal and functions of auditors of trade unions and employers' associations to which this section applies.

(7) The provisions of Part II of Schedule 2 to this Act shall have effect with respect to members' superannuation schemes maintained or to be maintained by trade unions or employers' associations to which this section applies.

(8) Where a trade union or employers' association consists of or includes branches or sections, then—

(*a*) any duty falling upon the union or association in relation to a branch or section under this section or Schedule 2 to this Act shall be treated as having been discharged to the extent to which a branch or section discharges that duty instead of the union or association; and

(*b*) any duty falling upon a branch or section under this section or Schedule 2 to this Act by reason of its being a trade union or employers' association shall be treated as having been discharged to the extent to which the union or association of which it is a branch or section discharges that duty instead of the branch or section.

AMENDMENT

The words in square brackets in this section were substituted by the Employment Protection Act 1975 (c. 71), Sched. 16, Pt. III, para. 1.

Offences

12.—(1) If a trade union or an employers' association refuses or wilfully neglects to perform a duty imposed on it by or under any of the provisions of section 10 or 11 above or Schedule 2 to this Act the trade union or employers' association shall be guilty of an offence.

(2) Subject to subsection (3) below, any offence committed by a trade union or an employers' association under subsection (1) above shall be deemed to have been also committed by—

(*a*) every officer of that trade union or employers' association who is bound by the rules of the union or association to discharge on its behalf the duty breach of which constitutes that offence; or

(*b*) if there is no such officer, every member of the general committee of management of the union or association.

(3) In any proceedings brought against an officer or member by virtue of subsection (2) above in respect of any breach of duty, it shall be a defence for him to prove that he had reasonable cause to believe, and did believe, that some other person who was competent to discharge that duty was authorised to discharge it instead of him and had discharged it or would do so.

(4) A person who wilfully alters or causes to be altered a document

88   *Trade Union and Labour Relations Act 1974*

which is required for the purpose of any of the provisions of section 10 or 11 above or Schedule 2 to this Act, with intent to falsify the document or to enable a trade union or employers' association to evade any of those provisions, shall be guilty of an offence.

(5) For every offence committed under this section the trade union, employers' association or other person guilty of the offence shall be liable on summary conviction—
- (*a*) in the case of an offence under subsection (1) above, to a fine not exceeding £100;
- (*b*) in the case of an offence under subsection (4) above, to a fine not exceeding £400.

Restrictions on legal liability and legal proceedings

Acts in contemplation or furtherance of trade disputes

1–176   13.—[(1) An Act done by a person in contemplation or furtherance of a trade dispute shall not be actionable in tort on the ground only—
- (*a*) that it induces another person to break a contract or interferes or induces any other person to interfere with its performance; or
- (*b*) that it consists in his threatening that a contract (whether one to which he is a party or not) will be broken or its performance interfered with, or that he will induce another person to break a contract or to interfere with its performance.]

(2) [*Repealed by the Employment Act* 1982 (*c.* 46) *s.*19(1), *Sched.* 4].

(3) [*Repealed by the Employment Act* 1980, *s.*17, *Sched.* 2.]

(4) An agreement or combination by two or more persons to do or procure the doing of any act in contemplation or furtherance of a trade dispute shall not be actionable in tort if the act is one which, if done without any such agreement or combination, would not be actionable in tort.

AMENDMENT
    The words in square brackets in subs. (1) were added by the Trade Union and Labour Relations (Amendment) Act 1976 (c. 7), s.3(2).

Peaceful picketing

1–177   [15.—(It shall be lawful for a person in contemplation or furtherance of a trade dispute to attend—
- (*a*) at or near his own place of work, or
- (*b*) if he is an official of a trade union, at or near the place of work of a member of that union whom he is accompanying and whom he represents.

for the purpose only of peacefully obtaining or communicating information, or peacefully persuading any person to work or abstain from working.

(2) If a person works or normally works—
- (*a*) otherwise than at any one place, or
- (*b*) at a place the location of which is such that attendance there for a purpose mentioned in subsection (1) above is impracticable,

his place of work for the purposes of that subsection shall be any premises of his employer from which he works or from which his work is administered.

(3) In the case of a worker who is not in employment [where—(*a*) his] last employment was terminated in connection with a trade dispute [or (*b*) the termination of his employment was one of the circumstances giving rise

to a trade dispute] subsection (1) above shall in relation to that dispute have effect as if any reference to his place of work were a reference to his former place of work.

(4) A person who is an official of a trade union by virtue only of having been elected or appointed to be a representative of some of the members of the union shall be regarded for the purposes of subsection (1) above as representing only those members; but otherwise an official of a trade union shall be regarded for those purposes as representing all its members.]

AMENDMENT
This section was substituted by the Employment Act 1980, s.16. The words in square brackets in subs. (3) were substituted by the Employment Act 1982, Sched. 3, para. 12.

. . . . . .

No compulsion to work
16. No court shall, whether by way of—
    (a) an order for specific performance or specific implement of a contract of employment, or
    (b) an injunction or interdict restraining a breach or threatened breach of such a contract,
compel an employee to do any work or attend at any place for the doing of any work.

Restriction on grant of ex parte injunctions and interdicts
17.—[1] Where an application for an injunction or interdict is made to a court in the absence of the party against whom the injunction or interdict is sought or any representative of his and that party claims, or in the opinion of the court would be likely to claim, that he acted in contemplation or furtherance of a trade dispute, the court shall not grant the injunction or interdict unless satisfied that all steps which in the circumstances were reasonable have been taken with a view to securing that notice of the application and an opportunity of being heard with respect to the application have been given to that party.

[(2) It is hereby declared for the avoidance of doubt that where an application is made to a court, pending the trial of an action, for an interlocutory injunction and the party against whom the injunction is sought claims that he acted in contemplation or furtherance of a trade dispute, the court shall, in exercising its discretion whether or not to grant the injunction, have regard to the likelihood of that party's succeeding at the trial of the action in establishing the matter or matters which would, under any provision of section 13, [. . .] or 15 above, afford a defence to the action.

(3) Subsection (2) above shall not extend to Scotland.]

AMENDMENT
The words in square brackets in this section were substituted by the Employment Protection Act 1975 (c. 71), Sched. 16, Pt. III, para. 6, and the words omitted in subs. (2) were repealed by the Employment Act 1982 (c. 46), s.15(a), Sched. 4.

Collective Agreements

Enforceability of collective agreements
18.—(1) Subject to subsection (3) below, any collective agreement made before 1st December 1971 or after the commencement of this section shall

be conclusively presumed not to have been intended by the parties to be a legally enforceable contract unless the agreement—
  (a) is in writing, and
  (b) contains a provision which (however expressed) states that the parties intend that the agreement shall be a legally enforceable contract.

(2) Any such agreement which satisfies the conditions in subsection (1)(a) and (b) above shall be conclusively presumed to have been intended by the parties to be a legally enforceable contract.

(3) If any such agreement is in writing and contains a provision which (however expressed) states that the parties intend that one or more parts of the agreement specified in that provision, but not the whole of the agreement, shall be a legally enforceable contract, then—
  (a) the specified part or parts shall be conclusively presumed to have been intended by the parties to be a legally enforceable contract; and
  (b) the remainder of the agreement shall be conclusively presumed not to have been intended by the parties to be such a contract, but a part of an agreement which by virtue of this paragraph is not a legally enforceable contract may be referred to for the purpose of interpreting a part of that agreement which is such a contract.

(4) Notwithstanding anything in subsections (2) and (3) above, any terms of a collective agreement (whether made before or after the commencement of this section) which prohibit or restrict the right of workers to engage in a strike or other industrial action, or have the effect of prohibiting or restricting that right, shall not form part of any contract between any worker and the person for whom he works unless the collective agreement—
  (a) is in writing; and
  (b) contains a provision expressly stating that those terms shall or may be incorporated in such a contract; and
  (c) is reasonably accessible at his place of work to the worker to whom it applies and is available for him to consult during working hours; and
  (d) is one where each trade union which is a party to the agreement is an independent trade union;
and unless the contract with that worker expressly or impliedly incorporates those terms in the contract.

(5) Subsection (4) above shall have effect notwithstanding any provision to the contrary in any agreement (including a collective agreement or a contract with any worker).

Miscellaneous

Transitional provisions for trade unions and employers' associations ceasing to be incorporated

19.—(1) The provisions of this section shall have effect in relation to a trade union or an employers' association to which they are applied by section 2(4) or 3(3) above; and in this section "the relevant date means the day on which, under section 2(4) or 3(3) above, such a trade union or employers' association ceases to be a body corporate.

(2) On the relevant date—

(a) all property vested in the trade union or in the employers' association immediately before that date shall by virtue of this paragraph (and without the execution of any instrument) vest in the trustees who, in accordance with subsection (3) below, are the appropriate trustees;

(b) all liabilities, obligations and rights of the trade union or of the employers' association subsisting immediately before that date shall, in so far as they are liabilities, obligations or rights affecting any property so vested (instead of continuing to be liabilities, obligations or rights of the union or association), become liabilities, obligations and rights of the trustees who, in accordance with subsection (3) below, are the appropriate trustees.

(3) The appropriate trustees for the purposes of subsection (2) above are—

(a) the trustees appointed in writing for the purposes of this section by or on behalf of the members of the trade union or employers' association;

(b) in a case where no such trustees are appointed, the official trustees of the trade union or employers' association.

(4) A certificate given by the official trustees of a trade union or employers' association that the persons named in the certificate are the appropriate trustees of that union or association for the purposes of subsection (2) above shall be conclusive evidence that those persons are the appropriate trustees of that union or association for those purposes; and a document which purports to be such a certificate shall be taken to be such a certificate unless the contrary is proved.

(5) In this section "official trustees", in relation to a trade union or an employers' association, means the two officers of the union or association who, on the relevant date, are the president and the general secretary of the union or association or occupy a position equivalent to that of president and general secretary respectively of a trade union or employers' association.

(6) Nothing in section 12 of the Finance Act 1895 (which requires certain Acts to be stamped as conveyances on sale) shall be taken as applying to this Act.

Power to alter certain rules of trade unions restricting the applications of funds

20.—(1) Where during the period commencing with 1st December 1970 and ending with the passing of this Act a trade union has—

(a) made or amended any rule of the union so as to preclude any particular fund belonging to or held in trust for the union from being used for financing strikes or other industrial action; and

(b) has declared in its rules that the rule or the rule as so amended shall be incapable of revocation or alteration;

then, notwithstanding the declaration, the rule so made or amended may, subject to subsection (2) below, be revoked or amended.

(2) No rule of a trade union shall be revoked or amended by virtue of subsection (1) above after the expiration of the period of four years beginning with the date of the passing of this Act; and nothing in that subsection shall be taken to authorise the amendment or revocation of a rule of a trade union otherwise than in accordance with the procedural rules of that union.

Effect of abolition of National Industrial Relations Court on pending proceedings and decisions given

1–183   21.—(1) In this section and sections 22 and 23 below—

"the Court" means the National Industrial Relations Court;

"abate", in relation to any proceedings, means that the proceedings shall be treated as discontinued and, in relation to any decision, means that the decision, so far as not enforced, shall be unenforceable;

"decision" includes a judgment, order or award and any reference to the giving of a decision shall be construed accordingly;

"pending" means pending immediately before the passing of this Act; and for the purposes of this section and those sections proceedings shall be treated as pending in the Court or an industrial tribunal until a final decision is given in those proceedings by the Court or the tribunal, as the case may be.

(2) On the passing of this Act, except in so far as provision is made by subsections (3) to (7) below for proceedings of the descriptions mentioned in those subsections—

(a) proceedings commenced in the Court before 30th April 1974 and pending in the Court shall be transferred by virtue of this paragraph to the High Court or the Court of Session;

(b) proceedings commenced in the Court on or after 30th April 1974 or any decision in those proceedings shall abate;

(c) any right of appeal against any such decision other than a right saved by section 23(1) below shall be extinguished and any appeal from any decision or any decision on any such appeal shall abate.

(3) Where a complaint has been presented to the Court under section 103 of the 1971 Act (complaints by Registrar against registered union or employers' association), then, if the complaint was presented before 30th April 1974 and is pending in the Court, the complaint shall, on the passing of this Act, be transferred by virtue of this subsection to an industrial tribunal.

(4) Where an appeal arising out of any proceedings or decision of an industrial tribunal has been instituted in the Court, then—

(a) in the case of an appeal which is pending in the Court and arose out of proceedings or a decision under the Contracts of Employment Act 1972 or the Redundancy Payments Act 1965 or on a complaint under the 1971 Act by an employee that he has been unfairly dismissed by his employer, the appeal shall on the passing of this Act be transferred by virtue of this paragraph, to the High Court or the Court of Session;

(b) in the case of an appeal of any other description, the appeal shall, if the proceedings in the industrial tribunal were commenced before 30th April 1974 and the appeal is pending in the Court, be transferred by virtue of this paragraph on the passing of this Act to the High Court or the Court of Session;

(c) in the case of an appeal of a description referred to in paragraph (b) above, where the proceedings in the industrial tribunal were commenced on or after 30th April 1974, the appeal or any decision on the appeal shall on the passing of this Act abate.

(5) Where an appeal arising out of proceedings before the Chief Registrar of Trade Unions and Employers' Associations or any assistant registrar of his has been instituted and is pending in the Court, then—

(*a*) if the decision appealed from was made under any provisions of the Trade Union Act 1913 (funds for political purposes), the appeal shall on the passing of this Act be transferred by virtue of this paragraph to the High Court or the Court of Session;

(*b*) if the appeal is by way of case stated in proceedings on a complaint under section 4 of the Trade Union (Amalgamations, etc.) Act 1964 (complaints about resolutions to amalgamate), the appeal shall on the passing of this Act be so transferred by virtue of this paragraph;

(*c*) if the appeal arises out of any other proceedings, the appeal or any decision on the appeal shall on the passing of this Act abate.

(6) Where a complaint has been transferred by an industrial tribunal to the Court by virtue of section 111 of the 1971 Act and is pending in the Court, then—

(*a*) in the case of a complaint by an employee, that he has been unfairly dismissed by his employer, the complaint shall on the passing of this Act be transferred by virtue of this paragraph back to the tribunal from which it was so transferred;

(*b*) in the case of a complaint of any other description presented before 30th April 1974, the complaint shall on the passing of this Act be transferred by virtue of this paragraph back to the tribunal from which it was so transferred;

(*c*) in the case of a complaint of a description referred to in paragraph (*b*) above presented on or after 30th April 1974, the complaint or any decision on such a complaint shall on the passing of this Act abate.

(7) Where, under any provision of the 1971 Act, proceedings have been commenced in the Court at any time with a view to the making of a reference or request to the Commission on Industrial Relations, then—

(*a*) if the proceedings are pending in the Court and no reference or request has been made in the proceedings, those proceedings shall on the passing of this Act abate;

(*b*) if a reference or request so made in those proceedings is outstanding immediately before the passing of this Act, the reference or request shall be treated as withdrawn on the passing of this Act, and subject to subsection (10) below, those proceedings shall then abate;

(*c*) any order of the Court made in proceedings resulting from a reference or request to that Commission shall cease to have effect on the passing of this Act.

(8) Where proceedings are transferred by virtue of subsection (2), (4) or (5) above the proceedings shall be transferred, in the case of proceedings in England and Wales, to the High Court and, in the case of proceedings in Scotland, to the Court of Session and may be continued there accordingly.

(9) [. . .] no appeal to the Court of Appeal shall be brought against a decision of the High Court on an appeal transferred by virtue of any provision of this section except with the leave of the High Court or the Court of Appeal.

(10) Where a reference or a request by the Court to the Commission on Industrial Relations is treated as withdrawn by virtue of subsection (7)(*b*) above, the Secretary of State may authorise the Commission to make a report of its findings and recommendations on that reference or request to those persons appearing to the Commission to be directly concerned, and to arrange for the report to be published in such manner as the Com-

mission consider appropriate; and paragraph 43(1) of Schedule 3 to the 1971 Act (disclosure of information) shall not apply to that report.

AMENDMENT
The words omitted in subs. (9) were repealed by the Administration of Justice Act 1977 (c. 38), s.32 and Sched. 5, Pt. IV.

Effect of repeals on pending proceedings and decisions given by industrial tribunals

1–184   22. Where a complaint, other than a complaint that an employee has been unfairly dismissed by his employer, has been presented to an industrial tribunal under any provision of the 1971 Act on or after 30th April 1974, then, when the repeal of that provision by this Act takes effect—
(a) the complaint or any decision on the complaint shall abate;
(b) any right of appeal against any such decision which is exercisable before that repeal takes effect shall be extinguished;
(c) any appeal from any such decision or any decision on any such appeal shall abate.

Provisions supplementary to sections 21 and 22

1–185   23.—(1) A decision given by the Court before the passing of this Act—
(a) in proceedings commenced in the Court before 30th April 1974;
(b) on an appeal instituted in the Court on or after 30th April 1974 in proceedings in which, if the appeal had been pending in the Court immediately before the passing of this Act, the appeal would have been transferred by virtue of any provision of section 21 above; or
(c) on a complaint which, if it had been pending in the Court immediately before the passing of this Act, would have been transferred back to an industrial tribunal by virtue of section 21(6) above;
may so far as not enforced be enforced after the passing of this Act as if it were a judgment of the High Court or the Court of Session, and any right of appeal from such a decision to the Court of Appeal or the Court of Session exercisable under paragraph 29 of Schedule 3 to the 1971 Act (appeals) shall continue to be exercisable, and any appeal from such a decision (whether instituted before or after the passing of this Act) shall be heard and determined accordingly, after the repeal of that paragraph by this Act takes effect.

(2) Without prejudice to section 38 of the Interpretation Act 1889 (effect of repeals) any decision given by any court or tribunal—
(a) in any proceedings (including proceedings under the 1971 Act) before the repeal by this Act of sections 153 and 154 of the 1971 Act (enforcement) takes effect, or
(b) in any proceedings transferred to any court by virtue of any provision of section 21 above;
and falling to be enforced to any extent after that repeal takes effect shall not be enforceable against property of any description against which it would not have been enforceable before that repeal takes effect by virtue of any provision of the said section 153 or 154, as the case may be.

(3) Where any right, obligation or liability has accrued or been incurred under any provision of the 1971 Act (other than a provision re-enacted in Schedule 1 to this Act) before the repeal of that provision by this Act takes effect, but no proceedings have been commenced in any court or tribunal to enforce that right, obligation or liability, no proceedings to enforce it

(directly or indirectly and by whatever means) shall be commenced in any court or tribunal after that repeal takes effect.

(4) If on an appeal from the Court after the passing of this Act the Court of Appeal would have exercised a power to order a new trial by the Court, the Court of Appeal shall order the re-hearing to be by the High Court.

Power to compensate for loss of office

24.—(1) If it appears to the Secretary of State that a person who ceases to be a member of the Commission on Industrial Relations by reason of its abolition by this Act should receive compensation for loss of office, he may pay him out of moneys provided by Parliament such sum as he may with the approval of the Minister for the Civil Service determine.   1–186

(2) If it appears to the Lord Chancellor that a person who ceases to be a member of the National Industrial Relations Court by reason of its abolition by this Act should receive compensation for loss of office, he may pay him out of moneys provided by Parliament such sum as he may with the approval of the Minister for the Civil Service determine.

Miscellaneous amendments, and transitional provisions and repeals

25.—(1) Schedule 3 to this Act shall have effect for undoing certain amendments and repeals made by the 1971 Act in certain enactments specified in that Schedule, for continuing the effect of other amendments so made and for making minor amendments and amendments consequential on other provisions of this Act in other enactments so specified.   1–187

(2) The transitional provisions in Schedule 4 shall have effect.

(3) The enactments specified in Schedule 5 are hereby repealed to the extent specified in the third column of that Schedule.

Supplementary

Regulations and orders

26.—(1) The Secretary of State may make regulations for any purpose for which regulations are authorised or required to be made under this Act.   1–188

(2) Any power to make regulations under this Act shall be exercisable by statutory instrument.

(3) A statutory instrument containing any such regulations, other than regulations required to be laid in draft before Parliament before being made, shall be subject to annulment in pursuance of a resolution of either House of Parliament.

(4) Any power to make an order under any provision of this Act shall include power to revoke or vary the order by a subsequent order under that provision.

Expenses

27. There shall be defrayed out of moneys provided by Parliament—   1–189
  (*a*) any administrative expenses incurred by the Secretary of State in consequence of the provisions of this Act; and
  (*b*) any increase attributable to the provisions of this Act in the sums payable out of moneys so provided under any other enactment.

Meaning of trade union and employers' association

1–190   **28.**—(1) In this Act, except so far as the context otherwise requires, "trade union" means an organisation (whether permanent or temporary) which either—
- (a) consists wholly or mainly of workers of one or more descriptions and is an organisation whose principal purposes include the regulation of relations between workers of that description or those descriptions and employers' associations; or
- (b) consists wholly or mainly of—
  - (i) constituent or affiliated organisations which fulfil the conditions specified in paragraph (a) above (or themselves consist wholly or mainly of constituent or affiliated organisations which fulfil those conditions), or
  - (ii) representatives of such constituent or affiliated organisations;

and in either case is an organisation whose principal purposes include the regulation of relations between workers and employers or between workers and employers' associations, or include the regulation of relations between its constituent or affiliated organisations.

(2) In this Act, except so far as the context requires, "employers' association" means an organisation (whether permanent or temporary) which either—
- (a) consists wholly or mainly of employers or individual proprietors of one or more descriptions and is an organisation whose principal purposes include the regulation of relations between employers of that description or those descriptions and workers or trade unions; or
- (b) consists wholly or mainly of—
  - (i) constituent or affiliated organisations which fulfil the conditions specified in paragraph (a) above (or themselves consist wholly or mainly of constituent or affiliated organisations which fulfil those conditions), or
  - (ii) representatives of such constituent or affiliated organisations;

and in either case is an organisation whose principal purposes include the regulation of relations between employers and workers or between employers and trade unions, or include the regulation of relations between its constituent or affiliated organisations.

Meaning of trade dispute

1–191   **29.**—(1) In this Act "trade dispute" means a dispute [between workers and their employer] [. . .] which [relates wholly or mainly to] one or more of the following, that is to say—
- (a) terms and conditions of employment, or the physical conditions in which any workers are required to work;
- (b) engagement or non-engagement, or termination of suspension of employment or the duties of employment, of one or more workers;
- (c) allocation of work or the duties of employment as between workers or groups of workers;
- (d) matters of discipline;
- (e) the membership or non-membership of a trade union on the part of a worker;
- (f) facilities for officials of trade unions; and
- (g) machinery for negotiation or consultation, and other procedures

relating to any of the foregoing matters, including the recognition by employers or employers' associations of the right of a trade union to represent workers in ay such negotiation or consultation or in the carrying out of such procedures.

(2) A dispute between a Minister of the Crown and any workers shall, notwithstanding that he is not the employer of those workers, be treated for the purposes of this Act as a dispute between [those workers and their employer] if the dispute relates—
- (a) to matters which have been referred for consideration by a joint body on which, by virtue of any provision made by or under any enactment, that Minister is represented; or
- (b) to matters which cannot be settled without that Minister exercising a power conferred on him by or under an enactment.

(3) There is a trade dispute for the purposes of this Act even though it relates to matters [occurring outside the United Kingdom, so long as the person or persons whose actions in the United Kingdom are said to be in contemplation or furtherance of a trade dispute relating to matters occurring outside the United Kingdom are likely to be affected in respect of one or more of the matters specified in subsection (1) of this section by the outcome of that dispute].

(4) [*Repealed by the Employment Act 1982, s.18(5).*]

(5) An act, threat or demand done or made by one person or organisation against another which, if resisted, would have led to a trade dispute with that other, shall, notwithstanding that because that other submits to the act or threat or accedes to the demand no dispute arises, be treated for the purposes of this Act as being done or made in contemplation of a trade dispute with that other.

(6) In this section—
"employment" includes any relationship whereby one person personally does work or performs services for another;
["worker", in relation to a dispute with an employer, means—
- (a) a worker employed by that employer; or
- (b) a person who has ceased to be employed by that employer where—
    - (i) his employment was terminated in connection with the dispute; or
    - (ii) the termination of his employment was one of the circumstances giving rise to the dispute.].

(7) [*Repealed by the Criminal Law Act 1977, (c. 45), s.65 and Sched. 13.*]

AMENDMENT

The words in square brackets in this section were substituted by the Employment Act 1982 (c. 46), s.18.

General provisions as to interpretation

30.—(1) In this Act, except so far as the context otherwise requires,—   1–192
"act" and "action" each includes omission and references to doing an act or taking action shall be construed accordingly;
["Certification Officer" means the officer appointed under section 7 of the Employment Protection Act 1975;]
"collective agreement" means any agreement or arrangement made by or on behalf of one or more trade unions and one or more

employers or employers' associations and relating to one or more of the matters mentioned in section 29(1) above;

"contract of employment" means a contract of service or of apprenticeship, whether it is express or implied and (if it is express) whether it is oral or in writing;

[...]

"employee" means an individual who has entered into or works under (or, where the employment has ceased, worked under) a contract of employment, otherwise than in police service;

["employer" (subject to subsection (2) below—
  (a) where the reference is to an employer in relation to an employee, means the person by whom the employee is (or, in a case where the employment has ceased, was) employed, and
  (b) in any other case, means a person regarded in that person's capacity as one for whom one or more workers work, or have worked or normally work or seek to work;]

"employers' association" includes a combination of employers and employers' associations;

"independent trade union" means a trade union which—
  (a) is not under the domination or control of an employer or a group of employers or of one or more employers' associations; and
  (b) is not liable to interference by an employer or any such group or association (arising out of the provision of financial or material support or by any other means whatsoever) tending towards such control [and, "in relation to a trade union", "independence" and "independent" shall be construed accordingly;]

"individual proprietor" means an individual who is the owner of an undertaking;

[...]

"1971 Act" means the Industrial Relations Act 1971;

["officer", in relation to a trade union or an employers' association includes any member of the governing body of that union or association and any trustee of any fund applicable for the purposes of that union or association;]

"official", in relation to a trade union, means any person who is an officer of the union or of a branch or section of the union or who (not being such an officer) is a person elected or appointed in accordance with the rules of the union to be a representative of its members or of some of them, including any person so elected or appointed who is an employee of the same employer as the members, or one or more of the members, whom he is to represent;

"police service" means service—
  (a) in England and Wales as a member of a police force or as a special constable;
  (b) as a constable within the meaning of the Police (Scotland) Act 1967;
  (c) as a member of any constabulary maintained by virtue of any enactment; or
  (d) in any other capacity by virtue of which a person has the powers or privileges of a constable;

[...]

"special register body" means an organisation whose name was immediately before the commencement of sections 2 and 3 above entered in the special register maintained under section 84 of the 1971 Act and which for the time being is a company registered under the Companies Act 1948 or is incorporated by charter or letters patent;

"tort", as respects Scotland, means [delict] and cognate expressions shall be construed accordingly;

"union membership agreement" means an agreement or arrangement which—
   (a) is made by or on behalf of, or otherwise exists between, one or more independent trade unions and one or more employers or employers' associations; and
   (b) relates to employees of an identifiable class; and
   (c) has the effect [in practice of requiring the employees for the time being of the class to which it relates (whether or not there is a condition to that effect in their contract of employment) to] be or become a member of the union or one of the unions which is or are parties to the agreement or arrangement or of another [specified] independent trade union; [and references in this definition to a trade union include references to a branch or section of a trade union; and a trade union is specified for the purposes of, or in relation to, a union membership agreement if it is specified in the agreement or is accepted by the parties to the agreement as being the equivalent of a union so specified].

"worker" (subject to the following provisions of this section) means an individual regarded in whichever (if any) of the following capacities is applicable to him, that is to say, as a person who works or normally works or seeks to work—
   (a) under a contract of employment; or
   (b) under any other contract (whether express or implied, and, if express, whether oral or in writing) whereby he undertakes to do or perform personally any work or services for another party to the contract who is not a professional client of his; or
   (c) in employment under or for the purposes of a government department (otherwise than as a member of the naval, military or air forces of the Crown or of any women's service administered by the Defence Council) in so far as any such employment does not fall within paragraph (a) or (b) above.

otherwise than in police service.

(2) Without prejudice to the generality of the definitions in subsection (1) of this section, in this Act—
   (a) "worker" includes an individual regarded in his capacity as one who works or normally works or seeks to work as a person providing general medical services, pharmaceutical services, general dental services or general ophthalmic services in accordance with arrangements made by an Area Health Authority [District Health Authority] or Family Practitioner Committee under [sections 29, 35, 38 or 41 of the National Health Service Act 1977] or by a Health Board under [sections 19, 25, 26 and 27 of the National Health Service (Scotland) Act 1978]; and
   (b) "employer" includes any Area Health Authority, [District Health Authority], Family Practitioner Committee or Health Board in accordance with whose arrangements a person provides or has pro-

vided or normally provides or seeks to provide any such service as aforesaid.

(3) Subject to subsection (4) below, in this Act "successor", in relation to the employer of an employee, means a person who, in consequence of a change occurring (whether by virtue of a sale or other disposition or by operation of law) in the ownership of the undertaking or of part of the undertaking for the purposes of which the employee was employed, has become the owner of that undertaking or of that part of it, as the case may be.

(4) Subsection (3) above shall have effect (subject to the necessary modifications) in relation to a case where—

(a) the person by whom an undertaking or part of an undertaking is owned immediately before a change is one of the persons by whom (whether as partners, trustees or otherwise) it is owned immediately after the change, or

(b) the persons by whom an undertaking or part of an undertaking is owned immediately before a change (whether as partners, trustees or otherwise) include the persons by whom, or include one or more of the persons by whom, it is owned immediately after the change,

as that subsection has effect where the previous owner and the new owner are wholly different persons; and any reference in this Act to a successor of an employer shall be construed accordingly.

(5) For the purposes of this Act any two employers are to be treated as associated if one is a company of which the other (directly or indirectly) has control, or if both are companies of which a third person (directly or indirectly) has control; and in this Act "associated employer" shall be construed accordingly.

[(5A) For the purposes of this Act employees are to be treated, in relation to a union membership agreement, as belonging to the same class if they have been identified as such by the parties to the agreement, and employees may be so identified by reference to any characteristics or circumstances whatsoever].

(6) For the purposes of this Act it is immaterial whether the law which (apart from this Act) governs any persons' employment is the law of the United Kingdom, or of a part of the United Kingdom, or not.

(7) Except so far as the context otherwise requires, any reference in this Act to any enactment shall be construed as a reference to that enactment as amended or extended by or under any other enactment, including this Act.

AMENDMENTS
Amendments to this section are made by the Employment Protection Act 1975 (c. 71), the Trade Union and Labour Relations (Amendment) Act 1976 (c. 7), the National Health Service Act 1977 (c. 49), the National Health Service (Scotland) Act 1978 (c. 29), the Employment Protection (Consolidation) Act 1978 (c. 44), and the Health Services Act 1980 (c. 53).

Short title, commencement and extent

1–193   31.—(1) This Act may be cited as the Trade Union and Labour Relations Act 1974.

(2) This Act, except as provided by section 1(3) above and except sections 21 to 23 above, shall come into operation on such day as the Secretary of State may appoint by order made by statutory instrument, and different days may be so appointed for different purposes.

(3) Any reference in this Act to the commencement of any provision of this Act shall be construed as a reference to the day appointed under this section for the coming into operation of that provision.

(4) An order made under this section may make such transitional provision or savings as appear to the Secretary of State to be necessary or expedient in connection with the provisions of this Act which are thereby brought (wholly or in part) into operation, including such adaptations of those provisions or of any provision of this Act then in force as appear to the Secretary of State to be necessary or expedient in consequence of the partial operation of this Act (whether before, on or after the day appointed by the order).

(5) The following provisions of this Act shall extend to Northern Ireland, that is to say, sections 4 and 19 any of any provision of Schedule 3 or 5 to this Act which amends or repeals any provision of [. . .] the Trade Union (Amalgamations, etc.) Act (Northern Ireland) 1965, the Insurance Companies Act (Northern Ireland) 1968, the Merchant Shipping Act 1970 or the Insurance Companies Amendment Act 1973 or repeals any provision of the 1971 Act which extends to Northern Ireland, but except as aforesaid this Act shall not extend there.

AMENDMENT
The words omitted in subs. (5) were repealed by the House of Commons Disqualification Act 1975 (c. 24), Sched. 3.

SCHEDULES

SCHEDULE 1

. . . . . .

Section 155 *Nominations by members of trade unions* **1–194**

31.—(1) Regulations may make provision—
    (*a*) for enabling members of trade unions who are not under sixteen years of age to nominate a person or persons to become entitled, on the death of the person making the nomination, to the whole or part of any money payable on his death out of the funds of the trade union which he is a member; and
    (*b*) for enabling any money payable out of the funds of a trade union on the death of a member of the trade union, to an amount not exceeding [£1,500], to be paid or distributed on his death (whether in accordance with such a nomination or otherwise) without letters of administration, probate of any will or confirmation.

(2) Any regulation made in accordance with sub-paragraph (1)(*a*) above—
    (*a*) may include provision as to the manner in which nominations may be made and as to the manner in which nominations may be varied or revoked, and
    (*b*) may provide, that, subject to such exceptions as may be prescribed, no nomination made by a member of a trade union shall be valid if at the date of the nomination the person nominated is an officer or employee of the trade union or is otherwise connected with the trade union in such manner as may be prescribed by the regulations.

(3) Any regulations under this section may include such incidental, transitional or supplementary provisions as the Secretary of State may consider appropriate and, in particular, any such regulations made in accordance with sub-paragraph (1)(*a*) above may include provision for securing, to such extent and subject to such conditions as may be prescribed in the regulations, that nominations made under the Trade Union Act Amendment Act 1876 shall have effect as if they have been made under the regulations and may be varied or revoked accordingly.

[(4) Sub-paragraph (1)(*b*) above shall be included among the provisions with respect to which the Treasury may make an order under section 6(1) of the Administration of Estates (Small Payments) Act 1965, substituting, for references to the amount for the time being provided for, references to such higher amount as may be specified in the order.]

102 *Trade Union and Labour Relations Act 1974*

AMENDMENT
The words in square brackets in this paragraph were substituted by the Employment Protection Act 1975, Sched. 16, Pt. III, paras. 31 and 32.

Section 161 *Restrictions on contracting out*
32.—(1) [. . .] any provision in an agreement (whether a contract of employment or not) shall be void in so far as it purports—
  (a) to exclude or limit the operation of any provision of this Act; or
  (b) [. . .]
(2) [*Repealed by the Employment Act* 1980, *Sched.* 2.]

AMENDMENTS
Sub-para. (1)(b) was repealed by the Employment Protection (Consolidation) Act 1978, s.159(3), Sched. 17. The words omitted at the beginning of sub-para. (1) were repealed by the Employment Act 1980, Sched. 2.

Section 162 *Employment under the crown*
33.—(1) Subject to the following provisions of this paragraph, the provisions of this Act shall have effect in relation to Crown employment and to workers in Crown employment as they have effect in relation to other employment and to other workers.
(2) In this paragraph (subject to sub-paragraph (4) below) "Crown employment" means employment under or for the purposes of a government department, [or any officer or body exercising on behalf of the Crown functions conferred by any enactment] otherwise than as a member of the naval, military or air forces of the Crown or of any women's service administered by the Defence Council, and "Crown employee" means a person who is for the time being in Crown employment or (when it has ceased) was in Crown employment.
(3) For the purposes of the application of the provisions of this Act in relation to Crown employment in accordance with sub-paragraph (1) above—
  (a) any reference to an employee shall be construed as a reference to a Crown employee;
  (b) any references to dismissal shall be construed as a reference to the termination of Crown employment;
  (c) [. . .]
  (d) [. . .]
  (e) any other reference to an undertaking shall be construed, in relation to a Minister of the Crown, as a reference to his functions or (as the context may require) to the department of which he is in charge, and, in relation to a government department [, officer or body] shall be construed as a reference to the functions of the department [, officer or body] or (as the context may require) to the department [, officer or body].
(4) For the purposes of this Act—
    (a) none of the bodies specified in Schedule 3 to the Redundancy Payments Act 1965 (national health service employers) shall be regarded as performing functions on behalf of the Crown, and their employees shall not be regarded as being employed under or for the purposes of a government department, and accordingly employment by any such body shall not be Crown employment within the meaning of this paragraph;
    (b) associations established for the purposes of the Auxiliary Forces Act 1953 shall be treated as if they were government departments, and accordingly employment by any such association shall be Crown employment within the meaning of this paragraph;
and for the purposes of this paragraph Crown employment does not include any employment in respect of which a certificate to which sub-paragraph (5) below applies is for the time being in force.
[(4A) [. . .]]
(5) This sub-paragraph applies to any certificate issued by or on behalf of a Minister of the Crown and certifying that employment of a description specified in the certificate, or the employment of a particular person so specified, is (or at a time specified in the certificate was) required to be excepted from sub-paragraph (1) above for the purpose of safeguarding national security; and any document purporting to be a certificate so issued shall be received in evidence and shall, unless the contrary is proved, be deemed to be such a certificate.

AMENDMENTS
The words in square brackets in this paragraph were added by the Employment Protection

Act 1975, Sched. 16, Pt. III, paras. 33 and 34. Subss. (3)(*c*)(*d*) and (4A) were repealed by the Employment Protection (Consolidation) Act 1978, s.159(3), Sched. 17.

Section 11 SCHEDULE 2

ADMINISTRATIVE PROVISIONS RELATING TO TRADE UNIONS AND EMPLOYERS' ASSOCIATIONS

PART I

ANNUAL RETURNS, AND QUALIFICATIONS, APPOINTMENT AND REMOVAL, AND FUNCTIONS, OF AUDITORS

Annual returns

1.—(1) Subject to paragraph 5 below, the annual return of a trade union or an employers' association required by section 11(1) above shall be sent to the [Certification Officer] before 1st June and shall relate to the last preceding calendar year.

(2) The annual return shall be in such form and be signed by such persons as the [Certification Officer] may require.

2. Every annual return shall contain—
   (*a*) revenue accounts indicating the income and expenditure of the trade union or employers' association for the period to which the return relates;
   (*b*) a balance sheet as at the end of that period;
   (*c*) such other accounts (if any) as the [Certification Officer] may require; and
   (*d*) a copy of the rules of the trade union or employers' association as in force at the end of that period;
and shall have attached to it a note of all changes in the officers of the union or association and of any change in the address of the head or main office of the union or association during the period to which the return relates.

3. Every revenue account, every balance sheet and every other account contained in a return in accordance with paragraph 2 above shall give a true and fair view of the matters to which it relates.

4. Every return, in addition to containing the accounts mentioned in paragraph 2 above, shall contain a copy of the report made by the auditor or auditors of the trade union or employers' association on those accounts under paragraph 18 below and such other documents relating to those accounts and such further particulars as the [Certification Officer] may require, subject in the case of the accounts contained in the return to such modifications (if any) as may be necessary to secure compliance with paragraph 3 above.

5. The [Certification Officer], if in any particular case he considers it appropriate to do so—
   (*a*) may direct that the period for which a return is to be sent to him under section 11(2) above shall be a period other than the calendar year last preceding the date on which the return is sent;
   (*b*) whether a direction under sub-paragraph (*a*) above is given or not, may direct that the date before which any such return is to be sent to him shall be such date (whether before or after 1st June) as may be specified in the direction.

Qualifications of auditors

6. Subject to paragraphs 7 to 9 below, a person shall not be qualified to be the auditor or one of the auditors of a trade union or employers' association unless he is either a member of one or more of the following bodies—
   (*a*) the Institute of Chartered Accountants in England and Wales;
   (*b*) the Institute of Chartered Accountants of Scotland;
   (*c*) the Association of Certified Accountants;
   (*d*) the Institute of Chartered Accountants in Ireland;
   (*e*) any other body of accountants established in the United Kingdom and for the time being recognised for the purposes of section 161(1)(*a*) of the Companies Act 1948 by the Secretary of State,
or a person who is for the time being authorised by the Secretary of State under section 161(1)(*b*) of that Act as being a person with similar qualifications obtained outside the United Kingdom.

7. Notwithstanding anything in paragraph 6 above, a Scottish firm may act as auditor of a trade union or employers' association if, but only if, every partner of the firm is qualified so to act.

8. A person who is not qualified under paragraph 6 above may act in respect of any accounting period as auditor of a trade union or employers' association if—

(a) it was registered under the Trade Union Acts 1871 to 1964 on 30th September 1971;
(b) he acted as its auditor in respect of the last period in relation to which it was required to make an annual return under section 16 of the Trade Union Act 1871;
(c) he has acted as its auditor in respect of every accounting period since that period; and
(d) he is for the time being authorised by the Secretary of State under section 161(1)(b) of the Companies Act 1948 otherwise than as mentioned in paragraph 6 above.

9.—(1) Two or more prsons who are not qualified under paragraph 6 above may act as auditors of a trade union or employers' association in respect of any accounting period of that union or association if—
(a) its receipts and payments in respect of its last preceding accounting period did not in the aggregate exceed £5,000;
(b) the number of its members at the end of its last preceding accounting period did not exceed 500; and
(c) the value of its assets at the end of its last preceding accounting period did not in the aggregate exceed £5,000.

(2) Where by virtue of sub-paragraph (1) above persons who are not qualified under paragraph 6 above act as auditors in respect of any accounting period of a trade union or employers' association, the [Certification Officer] may at any time (whether during that period or after it comes to an end) direct the trade union or employers' association to appoint a person who is so qualified to audit its account for that period.

(3) Regulations may—
(a) substitute for any sum or number for the time being specified in sub-paragraph (1) above such sum or number as may be specified in the regulations; and
(b) prescribe what receipts and payments sall be taken into account for the purposes of that sub-paragraph.

10.—(1) None of the following persons shall act as auditor of a trade union or employers' association, that is to say—
(a) as officer or employee of the trade union or employers' association or of any of its branches or sections;
(b) a person who is a partner of, or in the employment of, or who employs, such an officer or employee;
(c) a body corporate.

(2) References in this paragraph to an officer shall be construed as not including an auditor.

Appointment and removal of auditors

11. The rules of every trade union and every employers' association shall contain provision for the appointment and removal of auditors.

12. Notwithstanding anything in the rules of a trade union or employers' association, its auditor or auditors shall not be removed from office except by resolution passed at a general meeting of its members, or of delegates of its members.

13.—(1) Notwithstanding anything in the rules of a trade union or employers' association, a qualified auditor appointed to audit its accounts for the preceding year of account shall (subject to sub-pragraph (2) of this paragraph) be re-appointed as auditor for the current year of account unless—
(a) a resolution has been passed at a general meeting of the trade union or employers' association appointing somebody instead of him or providing expressly that he shall not be re-appointed, or
(b) he has given to the trade union or employers' association notice in writing of his unwillingness to be re-appointed; or
(c) he is ineligible for appointment as its auditor or one of its auditors for the current year of account, or
(d) he has ceased to act as its auditor or one of its auditors by reason of incapacity.

(2) Where notice is given of an intended resolution to appoint some person or persons in place of a retiring auditor and the resolution cannot be proceeded with at the meeting because of the death or incapacity of that person or perons, or because he or they are ineligible for appointment as auditor or auditors for the current year of account, the retiring auditor shall not be automatically re-appointed by virtue of this paragraph.

(3) For the purposes of this paragraph a person is ineligible for appointment as auditor of a trade union or employers' association for the current year of account if, but only if,—
(a) he would be precluded by paragraph 10 above from acting as its auditor for that year, or
(b) he is not a qualified auditor at the time when the question of his appointment falls to be considered.

(4) In this paragraph "qualified auditor", in relation to a trade union or employers' association, means a person qualified to be its auditor or one of its auditors in accordance with paragraphs 6 to 9 above, "the current year of account", in relation to the appointment of a person

as auditor, means the year of account in which the question of that appointment arises, and "the preceding year of account" means the year of account immediately preceding the current year of account.

14. Regulations may make provision as to the procedure to be followed when it is intended to move a resolution—
  (a) appointing another auditor or other auditors in place of a retiring auditor or retiring auditors of a trade union or an employers' association, or
  (b) providing expressly that a retiring auditor or auditors of a trade union or an employers' association shall not be re-appointed,

and as to the rights of auditors and members of a trade union or an employers' association in relation to such a motion.

15.—(1) Where any regulations made under paragraph 14 above require copies of any representations made by a retiring auditor to be sent out, or require any such representations to be read out at a meeting, the High Court or the Court of Session, on the application of the trade union or employers' association or of any other person, may dispense with that requirement if satisfied that the rights conferred on the retiring auditor by the regulations are being abused to secure needless publicity for defamatory matter.

(2) On any such application the High Court or the Court of Session may order the costs or expenses of the trade union or employers' association to be paid, in whole or in part, by the retiring auditor, whether he is a party to the application or not.

Auditor's right of access to books and information and right to be heard at meetings

16. Every auditor of a trade union or an employers' association—
  (a) shall have a right of access at all times to its accounting records and to all other documents relating to its affairs, and
  (b) shall be entitled to require from its officers, or the officers of any of its branches or sections, such information and explanations as he thinks necessary for the performance of his duties as auditor.

17. Every auditor of a trade union or an employers' association shall be entitled—
  (a) to attend any general meeting of its members, or of delegates of its members, and to receive all notices of and other communications relating to any general meeting which any such mmber or delegate is entitled to receive, and
  (b) to be heard at any meeting which he attends on any part of the business of the meeting which concerns him as auditor.

Auditors' reports

18. The auditor or auditors of a trade union or an employers' association shall make a report to it on the accounts of the trade union or employers' association audited by him or them and contained in its annual return.

19. The report shall state whether, in the opinion of the auditor or auditors, those accounts give a true and fair view of the matters to which they relate.

20. It shall be the duty of the auditor or auditors, in preparing a report under paragraph 18 above, to carry out such investigations as will enable him or them to form an opinion as to the following matters, that is to say—
  (a) whether the trade union or employers' association has kept proper accounting records in accordance with the requirements of section 10 above;
  (b) whether it has maintained a satisfactory system of control over its transactions in accordance with the requirements of that section; and
  (c) whether the accounts to which the report refers are in agreement with the accounting records;

and if in the opinion of the auditor or auditors the trade union or employers' association has failed to comply with section 10(2)(a) or (b) above or if the accounts to which the account relates are not in agreement with the accounting records, the auditor or auditors shall state that fact in the report.

21. If an auditor fails to obtain all the information and explanations which, to the best of his knowledge and belief, are necessary for the purposes of an audit, he shall state that fact in his report.

22. In this Part of this Schedule, "accounting period", in relation to a trade union or an employers' association, means any period in relation to which it is required under section 11(3) above to send a return to the [Certification Officer].

Part II

Members' Superannuation Schemes

Examination of superannuation schemes

23. Subject to paragraphs 2 to 31 below, every trade union and every employers' association which at the commencement of this Part of this Schedule is maintaining a members' superannuation scheme shall arrange for the scheme, as it has effect at a date not later than two years from the commencement of this Part of this Schedule, to be examined by an appropriately qualified actuary, and for the actuary to make a report to the trade union or employers' association on the results of his examination of the scheme.

24. Where a members' superannuation scheme to which paragraph 23 above applies includes provision for the maintenance of a separate fund for the purpose of the scheme, the examination under that paragraph shall include a valuation (as at the date by reference to which the examination is carried out) of the assets comprised in that fund and of the liabilities falling to be discharged out of it.

25. The report made by the actuary on the results of his examination of any such scheme—
   (a) shall state whether in his opinion the premium or contribution rates are adequate and whether the accounting or funding arrangements are suitable, and
   (b) if the scheme provides for the maintenance of a separate fund for the purposes of the scheme, shall state whether in his opinion the fund is adequate.

26. A copy of any report made by an actuary under paragraph 23 above, signed by the actuary, shall be sent to the [Certification Officer]; and it shall be the duty of the trade union or employers' association to make such arrangements under that paragraph as will enable the report to be sent to the [Certification Officer] before the end of the period of one year from the date by reference to which the actuarial examination was carried out.

27. Subject to paragraphs 30 and 31 below, no trade union or employers' association shall after the commencement of this Part of this Schedule begin to maintain a members' superannuation scheme unless, before the date on which the scheme begins to be maintained,—
   (a) the proposals for the scheme have been examined by an appropriately qualified actuary; and
   (b) a copy of a report made to the trade union or employers' association by the actuary on the results of his examination of the proposals, signed by the actuary, has been sent to the [Certification Officer];
and the provisions of paragraph 25 above shall have effect in relation to a report under this paragraph on the proposals for a scheme as they have effect in relation to a report on a scheme under paragraph 23 above.

28. A copy of any report made to a trade union or employers' association under paragraph 23 or paragraph 27 above shall, on the application of any of its members, be supplied to him free of charge.

29. Where on the application of the trade union or employers' association the [Certification Officer] is satisfied—
   (a) that a members' superannuation scheme maintained by it, as it had effect at a date not more than two years before the commencement of this Part of this Schedule, has been examined by an actuary;
   (b) that the qualifications of the actuary were adequate for the purpose of carrying out the examination; and
   (c) that the examination, and the report made by the actuary on its results, fulfil the requirements of paragraphs 24 and 25 above.
the [Certification Officer] may direct that paragraph 23 above shall have effect, in relation to that scheme, as if for the reference to two years from the commencement of this Part of this Schedule there were substituted a reference to five years from the date by reference to which that examination was carried out.

30. The [Certification Officer], on the application of a trade union or employers' association, may exempt any members' superannuation scheme which it maintains or proposes to maintain from the requirements of paragraph 23 or (as the case may be) paragraph 27 above, if he is satisfied that, by reason of the small number of members to which the scheme is or would be applicable or for any other special reasons, it is unnecessary for the scheme to be examined in accordance with those requirements.

31. The [Certification Officer] may at any time revoke any exemption granted under paragraph 30 above if it appears to him that the circumstances by reason of which the exemption was granted have ceased to exist.

Periodical re-examination of schemes

32.—(1) [Subject to paragraph 33A below] where a trade union or employers' association for the time being maintains a members' superannuation scheme, and either—

(a) the scheme has been examined in pursuance of paragraph 23 above or in pursuance of this paragraph, or
(b) the scheme itself has not been so examined but the proposals for the scheme have been examined in pursuance of paragraph 27 above, the trade union or employers' association in question shall arrange for that scheme as it has effect at each successive relevant date, to be examined by an appropriately qualified actuary, and for a report to be made to it by the actuary on the result of his examination of the scheme.

(2) Subject to the next following sub-paragraph, in this paragraph "relevant date", in relation to a members' superannuation scheme, means such date as the trade union or employers' association in question may determine, not being later than five years after the date by reference to which the last examination of the scheme, or (as the case may be) the examination of the proposals for the scheme, was carried out in accordance with paragraph 23 or paragraph 27 above or in accordance with the preceding sub-paragraph.

(3) In the case of any trade union or employers' association the [Certification Officer] may direct that, in relation to any time after the making of the direction, sub-paragraph (2) of this paragraph shall have effect as if, for the reference to five years there was substituted a reference to such shorter period as may be specified in the direction.

33. The provisions of paragraphs 24 to 26 and paragraph 28 above shall have effect in relation to the examination of a scheme under paragraph 32 above as they have effect in relation to the examination of a scheme under paragraph 23 above.

[33A. The Certification Officer, on the application of a trade union or employers' association, may exempt any members' superannuation scheme which it maintains from the requirements of paragraph 32 above if he is satisfied that, by reason of the small number of members to which the scheme is applicable or for any other special reasons, it is unnecessary for the scheme to be examined in accordance with those requirements.

33B. The Certification Officer may at any time revoke any exemption granted under paragraph 33A above if it appears to him that the circumstances by reason of which the exemption was granted have ceased to exist; and for the purposes of paragraph 32 above the relevant date next following the revocation shall be such date as the Certification Officer may direct.]

Separate fund for members' superannuation scheme

34. After the commencement of this Part of this Schedule no trade union or employers' association shall maintain a members' superannuation scheme which was not established before the commencement of this Part of this Schedule unless it maintains a separate fund for the payments of benefits in accordance with the scheme.

35. After the end of the period of five years beginning with the date on which paragraph 34 above comes into operation no trade union or employers' association shall maintain a members' superannuation scheme (whenever established) unless it maintains a separate fund for the payment of benefits in accordance with the scheme.

Interpretation of Part II

36. In this Part of this Schedule—
(a) "members' superannuation scheme" means any scheme or arrangement made by or on behalf of a trade union or employers' association (including any scheme or arrangement shown in the rules of a trade union or employers' association) in so far as it provides for benefits to be paid by way of pension (including any widows' or children's pensions or dependants' pensions) to or in respect of members or former members of the trade union or employers' association and to be so paid either out of the funds (whether the general funds or any other fund) of the trade union or employers' association or under any insurance scheme maintained out of those funds;
(b) "appropriately qualified actuary" in relation to a trade union or employers' association, means a person who is either a Fellow of the Institute of Actuaries or a Fellow of the Faculty of Actuaries or is approved by the [Certification Officer] on the application of the trade union or employers' association as a person having actuarial knowledge; and
(c) "separate fund" means a fund separate from the general fund of the trade unions or employers' association.

AMENDMENTS

In this Schedule, the words in square brackets were substituted by the Employment Protection Act 1975 (c. 71), Sched. 16, Pt. III, para. 1; except for the words in square brackets in para. 32(1) and the whole of paras. 33A and 33B, which were inserted by the Employment Act 1980 (c. 42), Sched. 1, para. 3.

1–197 Section 25

SCHEDULE 3

MISCELLANEOUS AMENDMENTS

The Conspiracy, and Protection of Property Act 1875 (c. 86)

1. In section 3 of the Conspiracy, and Protection of Property Act 1875, for the words from "an industrial dispute" to "1971" substitute the words "a trade dispute".

The Trade Union Act 1913 (c. 30)

2.—(1) The Trade Union Act 1913 shall be amended in accordance with the following provisions of this paragraph.

(2) For section 2(1), substitute as new subsections (1) and (1A) two subsections in the same terms as subsections (1) and (2) respectively of section 28 of this Act but with the insertion in the definition of "employers' association" in subsection (2), after the words "temporary) which", of the words "is unincorporated and".

(3) In sections 3 to 6, for the words substituted by Schedule 8 to the 1971 Act substitute the words contained in those sections immediately before the substitutions were effected by that Act except in the contexts specified in sub-paragraph (4) below.

(4) In sections 3(1) and 4(1) omit the words from "whether the" to "is registered or not" and in section 4(2) the words "whether registered or not".

(5) After section 6, insert—

"**Application of sections 3 to 6 to employers' associations**

6A. Sections 3 to 6 of, and the Schedule to, this Act shall apply, with the necessary modifications, in relation to unincorporated employers' associations as they apply in relation to trade unions."

(6) [*Repealed by the Employment Protection Act* 1975 (c. 71).]

The Industrial Courts Act 1919 (c. 69)

3. [*Repealed by the Employment Protection Act* 1975 (c. 71).]

The Road Haulage Wages Act 1938 (c. 44)

4. [*Repealed by the Employment Act* 1980, *Sched.* 2.]

The Industrial Assurance and Friendly Societies Act 1948 (c. 39)

5.—(1) The Industrial Assurance and Friendly Societies Act 1948 shall be amended in accordance with the following provisions of this paragraph.

(2) In section 6(1), for the words from "an organisation of workers" to "that Act" substitute the words "a trade union or an employers' association".

(3) In section 16(4), for the words substituted by the 1971 Act substitute the words "trade union and employers' association".

(4) In section 23(1) insert the following—

"(d) the expressions 'trade union' and 'employers' association' have the same meanings respectively as they have in the Trade Union and Labour Relations Act 1974".

The House of Commons Disqualification Act 1957 (c. 20)

6. [*Repealed by the House of Commons Disqualification Act* 1975 (c. 24), *Sched.* 3.]

The Insurance Companies Act 1958 (c. 72)

7. In section 1 of the Insurance Companies Act 1958, after subsection (5) insert as a new subsection (5A) in place of that inserted by Schedule 8 to the 1971 Act the following—

"(5A) Where a trade union or an employers' association carries on insurance business, this Act does not apply to it as an insurance company if the insurance business is limited to the provision for its members of provident benefits or strike benefits.

In this subsection 'trade union' and 'employers' association' have the same meanings respectively as they have in the Trade Union and Labour Relations Act 1974."

The Terms and Conditions of Employment Act 1950 (*c.* 26)
8. In section 8(2) of the Terms and Conditions of Employment Act 1959, for the words from "which is registered" to "1971, and is, or is" inserted by paragraph 2 of Schedule 7 to the 1971 Act substitute the words "being or".

The Wages Councils Act 1959 (*c.* 69)
9. [*Repealed by the Wages Councils Act* 1979 (*c.* 12), *s.*31(3), *Sched.* 7.]

The Trade Union (Amalgamations, etc.) Act 1964 (*c.* 24)
10.—(1) The Trade Union (Amalgamations, etc.) Act 1964 shall be amended in accordance with the following provisions of this paragraph.

(2) In sections 1 to 11 (and the Schedules), for the expressions "organisation to which this Act applies" or "organisation" substituted by Schedule 8 to the 1971 Act, wherever they occur, substitute the words contained in those sections (and Schedules) immediately before the substitutions were effected by that Act.

(3) In section 1, for the subsection (1A) inserted by Schedule 8 to the 1971 Act substitute—

"(1A) Subject to any express provision of this Act with respect to employers' associations, this Act shall apply, with the necessary modifications, in relation to unincorporated employers' associations as it applies in relation to trade unions."

(4) [*Repealed by the Employment Protection Act* 1975 (*c.* 71).]

(5) For section 6(2) substitute—

"(2) If the name of a trade union or employers' association is for the time being entered in the list of trade unions or employers' associations under section 4 of the Trade Union and Labour Relations Act 1974, a change of its name shall not take effect until approved by the Registrar under this Act; and the Registrar shall not approve a change of name if it appears to him that the proposed new name is the same as one entered in either list as the name of another trade union or employers' association or is a name so nearly resembling such a name as to be likely to deceive the public."

(6) [*Repealed by the Employment Protection Act* 1975 (*c.* 71).]

(7) Section 8 (which was repealed by the 1971 Act) is hereby revived.

(8) In section 9, for subsection (1) substitute—

"(1) In this Act, unless the context otherwise requires—

'amalgamating unions' and 'amalagamated union', in relation to a proposed amalgamation, mean respectively the trade unions proposing to amalgamate and the trade union which is to result from the proposed amalgamation;

'assistant registrar' means any assistant registrar of friendly societies appointed under section 1 of the Friendly Societies Act 1896;

'employers' association' has the same meaning as in the Trade Union and Labour Relations Act 1974;

'Northern Ireland union' has the meaning assigned to it by section 10 of this Act;

'the Registrar' means the Chief Registrar of Friendly Societies;

'trade union' has the same meaning as in the Trade Union and Labour Relations Act 1974;

'transferor trade union' and 'transferee trade union', in relation to a proposed transfer of engagements, mean respectively the trade union proposing to transfer its engagements and the trade union proposing to accept them."

The Trade Union (Amalgamations etc.) Act (Northern Ireland) 1965 (*c.* 2) (*N.I.*)
11. For section 9(2) of the Trade Union (Amalgamations etc.) Act (Northern Ireland) 1965 substitute—

"(2) In this Act 'Great Britain union' means a trade union or employers' association within the meaning of the Trade Union and Labour Relations Act 1974, being either—
   (*a*) a union whose name is for the time being entered in the list of trade unions or of employers' associations under section 8 of that Act; or
   (*b*) a union or association whose name is not so entered, but whose principal office is situated in England, Wales or Scotland."

The Companies Act 1967 (*c.*8)
12. In section 60(1) of the Companies Act 1967 for the paragraph (*e*) inserted by Schedule 8 to the 1971 Act substitute the following—

"(e) a trade union or employers' association (within the meaning of the Trade Union and Labour Relations Act 1974) where the insurance business carried on by the union or association is limited to the provision for its members of provident benefits or strike benefits".

The Insurance Companies Act (Northern Ireland) 1968 (c.6) (N.I.)

13.—(1) The Insurance Companies Act (Northern Ireland) 1968 shall be amended in accordance with the following provisions of this paragraph.
(2) In section 1(2)(*a*) omit the words "or trade unions".
(3) In section 1(2) after paragraph (*c*) insert—
"or
(*d*) any insurance company which is, or is deemed to be, registered under the Acts relating to trade unions or to any insurance company which is a Great Britain union if in either case the insurance business is limited to the provision for its members of provident benefits or strike benefits."
(4) In section 3(1)(*c*) omit the words "or trade unions".
(5) In section 3(1) after paragraph (*d*) insert:—
"(*e*) a body which is, or is deemed to be, registered under the Acts relating to trade unions, or is a Great Britain union and in either case limits its insurance business to the provision for its members of provident benefits or strike benefits."
(6) In section 72(1) at the appropriate place in alphabetical order insert:—
" 'Great Britain union' means a trade union or employers' association within the meaning of the Trade Union and Labour Relations Act 1974, being either—
(*a*) a union whose name is for the time being entered in the list of trade unions or of employers' associations under section 8 of that Act; or
(*b*) a union or association whose name is not so entered, but whose principal office is situated in England, Wales or Scotland."

The Merchant Shipping Act 1970 (c. 36)

14. In section 42 of the Merchant Shipping Act 1970, in subsection (2), for the words "industrial dispute" substitute the words "trade dispute (within the meaning of the Trade Union and Labour Relations Act 1974)" and omit subsection (3).

The Tribunals and Inquiries Act 1971 (c. 62)

15. [*Repealed by the Employment Protection Act 1975 (c.71).*]

The Contracts of Employment Act 1972 (c. 53)

16. [*Repealed by the Employment Protection (Consolidation) Act 1978 (c. 44).*]

The Administration of Justice (Scotland) Act 1972 (c. 59)

17. [*Repealed by the Employment Act 1982 (c. 46), Sched. 4.*]

Section 25   SCHEDULE 4

Transitional Provisions

1. [*Repealed by the Employment Protection (Consolidation) Act 1978 (c. 44).*]
2. Subject to any provision to the contrary contained in section 21 or 23 above, sections 22 to 33 of the 1971 Act (unfair dismissals) and the other provisions of that Act relating to proceedings for unfair dismissal shall, notwithstanding the repeal of that Act by this Act, continue to apply to dismissals where the effective date of termination falls before the commencement of Schedule 1 to this Act.
3. [*Repealed by the Employment Protection (Consolidation) Act 1978 (c. 44).*]
4. As respects proceedings pending in the National Industrial Relations Court immediately before the passing of this Act and transferred by section 21 above to the High Court or Court of Session, rules made by virtue of paragraph 24 of Schedule 3 to the 1971 Act (costs and expenses of parties) shall, notwithstanding the repeal of that Schedule by this Act, continue to have effect and shall with any necessary modifications, apply to the High Court and Court of Session as they applied before the passing of this Act to the National Industrial Relations Court.
5. Schedule 2 to this Act shall apply to a trade union's or employers' association's return

and accounts for 1974 or the period substituted therefor by a direction under paragraph 5 of that Schedule, notwithstanding that that Schedule was not in force for the whole of that year or period.

6.—(1) In so far as anything done or treated as done under any enactment contained in the 1971 Act, which is re-enacted, with or without amendment, in a corresponding provision of Schedule 1 or Schedule 2 to this Act, could have been done under that provision, then, subject to sub-paragraph (3) below, it shall on the commencement of that Schedule have effect as if done under that provision.

(2) In particular, sub-paragraph (1) above applies to the following things done under any such enactment, that is to say—

any complaint presented;

any application, determination, recommendation, award, order, regulations, appointment, request or report made;

any certificate, exemption or notice given.

(3) Sub-paragraph (1) above shall not apply to anything done under those provisions of the 1971 Act which continue to apply to dismissals by virtue only of paragraph 2 above.

(4) [*Repealed by the Employment Protection (Consolidation) Act 1978 (c. 44).*]

7. Any enactment or document which refers, whether specifically or by means of a general description, to an enactment contained in the 1971 Act which is re-enacted, with or without amendment, in a corresponding provision of Schedule 1 or Schedule 2 to this Act shall, except so far as the context otherwise requires, be construed as referring, or as including a reference, to that corresponding provision.

8. Nothing in this Schedule shall be construed as prejudicing section 38 of the Interpretation Act 1889 (effect of repeals).

Section 25

SCHEDULE 5

Enactments Repealed

Chapter	Short title	Extent of repeal
2 & 3 Geo. 5. c. 30.	The Trade Union Act 1913.	In sections 3 (1) and 4 (1), the words from "whether the" to "is registered or not". In section 4 (2), the words "whether registered or not".
1957 c. 20.	The House of Commons Disqualification Act 1957.	In Part II of Schedule 1, both in its application to the House of Commons of the United Kingdom and in its application to the Northern Ireland Assembly, the entries relating to the Commission on Industrial Relations and the National Industrial Relations Court. In Part III of Schedule 1, in its application to the House of Commons of the United Kingdom, the entry relating to the Chief Registrar or Assistant Registrar of Trade Unions and Employers' Associations.
1968 c. 6 (N.I.).	The Insurance Companies Act (Northern Ireland) 1968.	In section 1 (2) (*a*), the words "or trade unions". In section 3 (1) (*c*), the words "or trade unions".
1970 c. 36.	The Merchant Shipping Act 1970.	Section 42 (3).
1971 c. 72.	The Industrial Relations Act 1971.	The whole Act.
1972 c. 53.	The Contracts of Employment Act 1972.	In section 4 (2), paragraph (*a*). In section 11 (1), the definitions of "agency shop agreement" and "approved closed shop agreement".

Chapter	Short title	Extent of repeal
1972 c. 59.	The Administration of Justice (Scotland) Act 1972.	In section 3 (3), the words "described in section 124 of that Act".
1973 c. 58.	The Insurance Companies Amendment Act 1973.	Section 40. In Schedule 3, paragraph 31.

1–200

Rehabilitation of Offenders Act 1974

(1974 c.53)

An Act to rehabilitate offenders who have not been reconvicted of any serious offence for periods of years, to penalise the unauthorised disclosure of their previous convictions, to amend the law of defamation, and for purposes connected therewith.

[31st July 1974]

. . . . . .

Effect of rehabilitation

1–201   **4.**—(1) Subject to sections 7 and 8 below, a person who has become a rehabilitated person for the purposes of this Act in respect of a conviction shall be treated for all purposes in law as a person who has not committed or been charged with or prosecuted for or convicted of or sentenced for the offences which were the subject of that conviction; and, notwithstanding the provisions of any other enactment or rule of law to the contrary, but subject as aforesaid—

   (a) no evidence shall be admissible in any proceedings before a judicial authority exercising its jurisdiction or functions in Great Britain to prove that any such person has committed or been charged with or prosecuted for or convicted of or sentenced for any offence which was the subject of a spent conviction; and

   (b) a person shall not, in any such proceedings, be asked, and, if asked, shall not be required to answer, any question relating to his past which cannot be answered without acknowledging or referring to a spent conviction or spent convictions or any circumstances ancillary thereto.

(2) Subject to the provisions of any order made under subsection (4) below, where a question seeking information with respect to a person's previous convictions, offences, conduct or circumstances is put to him or to any other person otherwise than in proceedings before a judicial authority—

   (a) the question shall be treated as not relating to spent convictions or to any circumstances ancillary to spent convictions, and the answer thereto may be framed accordingly; and

   (b) the person questioned shall not be subjected to any liability or otherwise prejudiced in law by reason of any failure to acknowledge or disclose a spent conviction or any circumstances ancillary to a spent conviction in his answer to the question.

(3) Subject to the provisions of any order made under subsection (4) below,—

(a) any obligation imposed on any person by any rule of law or by the provisions of any agreement or arrangement to disclose any matter to any other person shall not extend to requiring him to disclose a spent conviction or any circumstances ancillary to a spent conviction (whether the conviction is his own or another's); and

(b) a conviction which has become spent or any circumstances ancillary thereto, or any failure to disclose a spent conviction or any such circumstances, shall not be a proper ground for dismissing or excluding a person from any office, profession, occupation or employment, or for prejudicing him in any way in any occupation or employment.

(4) The Secretary of State may by order—

    (a) make such provision as seems to him appropriate for excluding or modifying the application of either or both of paragraphs (a) and (b) of subsection (2) above in relation to questions put in such circumstances as may be specified in the order;

    (b) provide for such exceptions from the provisions of subsection (3) above as seem to him appropriate, in such cases or classes of case, and in relation to convictions of such a description, as may be specified in the order.

(5) For the purposes of this section and section 7 below any of the following are circumstances ancillary to a conviction, that is to say—

    (a) the offence or offences which were the subject of that conviction;

    (b) the conduct constituting that offence or those offences; and

    (c) any process or proceedings preliminary to that conviction, any sentence imposed in respect of that conviction, any proceedings (whether by way of appeal or otherwise) for reviewing that conviction or any such sentence, and anything done in pursuance of or undergone in compliance with any such sentence.

(6) For the purposes of this section and section 7 below "proceedings before a judicial authority" includes, in addition to proceedings before any of the ordinary courts of law, proceedings before any tribunal, body or person having power—

    (a) by virtue of any enactment, law, custom or practice;

    (b) under the rules governing any association, institution, profession, occupation or employment; or

    (c) under any provision of an agreement providing for arbitration with respect to questions arising thereunder;

to determine any question affecting the rights, privileges, obligations or liabilities of any person, or to receive evidence affecting the determination of any such question.

Social Security Pensions Act 1975

(1975, c.60)

An Act to provide for relating the rates of social security retirement pensions and certain other benefits to the earnings on which contributions have been paid; to enable employed earners to be contracted-out of full social security contributions and benefits where the requisite benefits are provided by an occupational pension; to make provision for securing that men and women are afforded equal access to occupational pension schemes; and to make other amendments in the law relating to social security (including an amendment of Part II of the Social Security Act 1975 introducing a new non-contributory benefit called "mobility allowance"); and to make other provision about occupational pensions.

[7th August 1975]

. . . . . .

Contracting-out certificates

31.—(1) Regulations shall provide for the issue by the Occupational Pensions Board to employers of contracting-out certificates specifying—
- (a) the employments which are to be treated, either generally or in relation to any specified description of earners, as contracted-out employments; and
- (b) the occupational pension schemes by reference to which those employments are to be so treated.

(2) Regulations shall also provide for the cancellation, variation or surrender of any contracting-out certificate, or the issue of an amended certificate, on any change of circumstances affecting the treatment of an employment as contracted-out employment.

(3) Subject to the provisions of this Part of this Act, an employment otherwise satisfying the conditions for inclusion in a contracting-out certificate shall be so included if and so long as the employer so elects and not otherwise; and subject to subsection (4) below an election may be so made, and an employment so included, either generally or in relation only to a particular description of earners.

(4) Except in such cases as may be prescribed, an employer shall not, in making or abstaining from making any election under this section, discriminate between different earners on any grounds other than the nature of their employment; and if the Occupational Pensions Board consider that an employer is contravening this subsection in relation to any scheme they may refuse to give effect to any election made by him in relation to that scheme or cancel any contracting-out certificate held by him in respect of that scheme.

(5) Regulations may make provision—
- (a) for regulating the manner in which an employer is to make an election with a view to the issue, variation or surrender of a contracting-out certificate;
- (b) for requiring an employer to give a notice of his intentions in respect of making or abstaining from making any such election in relation to any existing or proposed scheme—
    - (i) to employees in any employment to which the scheme applies or to which it is proposed that it should apply;
    - (ii) to any independent trade union recognised to any extent for the purpose of collective bargaining in relation to those employees;
    - (iii) to the trustees and managers of the scheme and such other persons as may be prescribed;
- (c) for requiring an employer, in connection with any such notice, to furnish such information as may beprescribed and to under-

take such consultations as may be prescribed with any such trade union as is mentioned in paragraph (*b*)(ii) above;
(*d*) for empowering the Occupational Pensions Board to refuse to give effect to any election made by an employer unless they are satisfied that he has complied with the requirements of the regulations;
(*e*) for referring to an industrial tribunal any question whether an organisation is such a trade union as is mentioned in paragraph (*b*)(ii) above or whether the requirements of the regulations as to consultation have been complied with.

(6) Regulations may enable the Occupational Pensions Board to cancel or vary a contracting-out certificate where they have reason to suppose that any employment to which it relates ought not to be treated as contracted-out employment in accordance with the certificate and the employer does not show that it ought to be so treated.

(7) Except in prescribed circumstances, no contracting-out certificate and no cancellation, variation or surrender of such a certificate shall have effect from a date earlier than that on which the certificate is issued or the cancellation, variation or surrender is made.

(8) In this section "independent trade union" has the same meaning as in the Trade Union and Labour Relations Act 1974 and "industrial tribunal" means a tribunal established under section 12 of the Industrial Training Act 1964.

[(9) A trade union shall be treated as recognised for the purpose of this section not only if it is recognised for the purpose of collective bargaining, but also if the Advisory Conciliation and Arbitration Service has made a recommendation for recognition under the Employment Protection Act 1975 and that recommendation is operative within the meaning of section 15 of that Act.]

AMENDMENT
Subs. (9) was inserted by the Employment Protection Act 1975, (c. 71) s.125, and Sched. 16, para. 17.

Sex Discrimination Act 1975

1–203

(1975 c.65)

An Act to render unlawful certain kinds of sex discrimination and discrimination on the ground of marriage, and establish a Commission with the function of working towards the elimination of such discrimination and promoting equality of opportunity between men and women generally; and for related purposes.

[12th November 1975]

PART I

DISCRIMINATION TO WHICH ACT APPLIES

Sex discrimination against women
1.—(1) A person discriminates against a woman in any circumstances

1–204

relevant for the purposes of any provision of this Act if:—
   (a) on the ground of her sex he treats her less favourably than he treats or would treat a man, or
   (b) he applies to her a requirement or condition which he applies or would apply equally to a man but—
      (i) which is such that the proportion of women who can comply with it is considerably smaller than the proportion of men who can comply with it, and
      (ii) which he cannot show to be justifiable irrespective of the sex of the person to whom it is applied, and
      (iii) which is to her detriment because she cannot comply with it.
(2) If a person treats or would treat a man differently according to the man's marital status, his treatment of a woman is for the purposes of subsection (1)(a) to be compared to his treatment of a man having the like marital status.

Sex discrimination against men

1–205 2.—(1) Section 1, and the provisions of Parts II and III relating to sex discrimination against women, are to be read as applying equally to the treatment of men, and for that purpose shall have effect with such modifications as are requisite.

(2) In the application of subsection (1) no account shall be taken of special treatment afforded to women in connection with pregnancy or childbirth.

Discrimination against married persons in employment field

1–206 3.—(1) A person discriminates against a married person of either sex in any circumstances relevant for the purposes of any provision of Part II if—
   (a) on the ground of his or her marital status he treats that person less favourably than he treats or would treat an unmarried person of the same sex, or
   (b) he applies to that person a requirement or condition which he applies or would apply equally to an unmarried person but—
      (i) which is such that the proportion of married persons who can comply with it is considerably smaller than the proportion of unmarried persons of the same sex who can comply with it, and
      (ii) which he cannot show to be justifiable irrespective of the marital status of the person to whom it is applied, and
      (iii) which is to that person's detriment because he cannot comply with it.
(2) For the purposes of subsection (1), a provision of Part II framed with reference to discrimination against women shall be treated as applying equally to the treatment of men, and for that purpose shall have effect with such modifications as are requisite.

Discrimination by way of victimisation

1–207 4.—(1) A person ("the discriminator") discriminates against another person ("the person victimised") in any circumstances relevant for the purposes of any provision of this Act if he treats the person victimised less

favourably than in those circumstances he treats or would treat other persons, and does so by reason that the person victimised has—
- (*a*) brought proceedings against the discriminator or any other person under this Act or the Equal Pay Act 1970, or
- (*b*) given evidence or information in connection with proceedings brought by any person against the discriminator or any other person under this Act or the Equal Pay Act 1970, or
- (*c*) otherwise done anything under or by reference to this Act or the Equal Pay Act 1970 in relation to the discriminator or any other person, or
- (*d*) alleged that the discriminator or any other person has committed an act which (whether or not the allegation so states) would amount to a contravention of this Act or give rise to a claim under the Equal Pay Act 1970,

or by reason that the discriminator knows the person victimised intends to do any of those things, or suspects the person victimised has done, or intends to do, any of them.

(2) Subsection (1) does not apply to treatment of a person by reason of any allegation made by him if the allegation was false and not made in good faith.

(3) For the purposes of subsection (1), a provision of Part II or III framed with reference to discrimination against women shall be treated as applying equally to the treatment of men and for that purpose shall have effect with such modifications as are requisite.

Interpretation

5.—(1) In this Act—
- (*a*) references to discrimination refer to any discrimination falling within sections 1 to 4; and
- (*b*) references to sex discrimination refer to any discrimination falling within section 1 to 2,

and related expressions shall be construed accordingly.

(2) In this Act—

"woman" includes a female of any age, and

"man" includes a male of any age.

(3) A comparison of the cases of persons of different sex or marital status under section 1(1) or 3(1) must be such that the relevant circumstances in the one case are the same, or not materially different in the other.

1–208

PART II

DISCRIMINATION IN THE EMPLOYMENT FIELD

Discrimination by Employers

Discrimination against applicants and employees

6.—(1) It is unlawful for a person, in relation to employment by him at an establishment in Great Britain, to discriminate against a woman—
- (*a*) in the arrangements he makes for the purpose of determining who should be offered that employment, or
- (*b*) in the terms on which he offers her that employment, or
- (*c*) by refusing or deliberately omitting to offer her employment.

1–209

(2) It is unlawful for a person, in the case of a woman employed by him at an establishment in Great Britain to discriminate against her—
   (a) in the way he affords her access to opportunities for promotion, transfer or training, or to any other benefits, facilities or services, or by refusing or deliberately omitting to afford her access to them, or
   (b) by dismissing her, or subjecting her to any other detriment.

(3) Except in relation to discrimination falling within section 4, subsections (1) and (2) do not apply to employment—
   (a) for the purposes of a private household, or
   (b) where the number of persons employed by the employer, added to the number employed by any associated employers of his, does not exceed five (disregarding any persons employed for the purposes of a private household).

(4) Subsections (1)(b) and (2) do not apply to provision in relation to death or retirement.

(5) Subject to section 8(3), subsection (1)(b) does not apply to any provision for the payment of money which, if the woman in question were given the employment, would be included (directly or by reference to a collective agreement or otherwise) in the contract under which she was employed.

(6) Subsection (2) does not apply to benefits consisting of the payment of money when the provision of those benefits is regulated by the woman's contract of employment.

(7) Subsection (2) does not apply to benefits, facilities or services of any description if the employer is concerned with the provision (for payment or not) of benefits, facilities or services of that description to the public, or to a section of the public comprising the woman in question, unless—
   (a) that provision differs in a material respect from the provision of the benefits, facilities or services by the employer to his employees, or
   (b) the provision of the benefits, facilities or services to the woman in question is regulated by her contract of employment, or
   (c) the benefits, facilities or services relate to training.

Exception where sex is a genuine occupational qualification

7.—(1) In relation to sex discrimination—
   (a) section 6(1)(a) or (c) does not apply to any employment where being a man is a genuine occupational qualification for the job, and
   (b) section 6(2)(a) does not apply to opportunities for promotion or transfer to, or training for, such employment.

(2) Being a man is a genuine occupational qualification for a job only where—
   (a) the essential nature of the job calls for a man for reasons of physiology (excluding physical strength or stamina) or, in dramatic performances or other entertainment, for reasons of authenticity, so that the essential nature of the job would be materially different if carried out by a woman; or
   (b) the job needs to be held by a man to preserve decency or privacy because—
      (i) it is likely to involve physical contact with men in circumstances where they might reasonably object to its being carried out by a woman, or
      (ii) the holder of the job is likely to do his work in circum-

stances where men might reasonably object to the presence of a woman because they are in a state of undress or are using sanitary facilities; or

(c) the nature or location of the establishment makes it impracticable for the holder of the job to live elsewhere than in premises provided by the employer, and—

    (i) the only such premises which are available for persons holding that kind of job are lived in, or normally lived in, by men and are not equipped with separate sleeping accommodation for women and sanitary facilities which could be used by women in privacy from men, and

    (ii) it is not reasonable to expect the employer either to equip those premises with such accommodation and facilities or to provide other premises for women; or

(d) the nature of the establishment, or of the part of it within which the work is done, requires the job to be held by a man because—

    (i) it is, or is part of, a hospital, prison or other establishment for persons requiring special care, supervision or attention, and

    (ii) those persons are all men (disregarding any woman whose presence is exceptional), and

    (iii) it is reasonable, having regard to the essential character of the establishment or that part, that the job should not be held by a woman; or

(e) the holder of the job provides individuals with personal services promoting their welfare or education, or similar personal services, and those services can most effectively be provided by a man, or

(f) the job needs to be held by a man because of restrictions imposed by the laws regulating the employment of women, or

(g) the job needs to be held by a man because it is likely to involve the performance of duties outside the United Kingdom in a country whose laws or customs are such that the duties could not, or could not effectively, be performed by a woman, or

(h) the job is one of two to be held by a married couple.

(3) Subsection (2) applies where some only of the duties of the job fall within paragraphs (a) to (g) as well as where all of them do.

(4) Paragraph (a), (b), (c), (d), (e), (f) or (g) of subsection (2) does not apply in relation to the filling of a vacancy at a time when the employer already has male employees—

(a) who are capable of carrying out the duties falling within that paragraph, and

(b) whom it would be reasonable to employ on those duties, and

(c) whose numbers are sufficient to meet the employer's likely requirements in respect of those duties without undue inconvenience.

Equal Pay Act 1970

8.—(1) In section 1 of the Equal Pay Act 1970, the following are substituted for subsections (1) to (3)—

"(1) If the terms of a contract under which a woman is employed at an establishment in Great Britain do not include (directly or by reference to a collective agreement or otherwise) an equality clause they shall be deemed to include one.

1–211

(2) An equality clause is a provision which relates to terms (whether concerned with pay or not) of a contract under which a woman is employed (the 'woman's contract'), and has the effect that—
  (a) where the woman is employed on like work with a man in the same employment—
    (i) if (apart from the equality clause) any term of the woman's contract is or becomes less favourable to the woman that a term of a similar kind in the contract under which that man is employed, that term of the woman's contract shall be treated as so modified as not to be less favourable, and
    (ii) if (apart from the equality clause) at any time the woman's contract does not include a term corresponding to a term benefiting that man included in the contract under which he is employed, the woman's contract shall be treated as including such a term;
  (b) where the woman is employed on work rated as equivalent with that of a man in the same employment—
    (i) if (apart from the equality clause) any term of the woman's contract determined by the rating of the work is or becomes less favourable to the woman than a term of a similar kind in the contract under which that man is employed, that term of the woman's contract shall be treated as so modified as not to be less favourable, and
    (ii) if (apart from the equality clause) at any time the woman's contract does not include a term corresponding to a term benefiting that man included in the contract under which he is employed and determined by the rating of the work, the woman's contract shall be treated as including such a term.
(3) An equality clause shall not operate in relation to a variation between the woman's contract and the man's contract if the employer proves that the variation is genuinely due to a material difference (other than the difference of sex) between her case and his."

(2) Section 1(1) of the Equal Pay Act 1970 (as set out in subsection (1) above) does not apply in determining for the purposes of section 6(1)(b) of this Act the terms on which employment is offered.

(3) Where a person offers a woman employment on certain terms, and if she accepted the offer then, by virtue of an equality clause, any of those terms would fall to be modified, or any additional term would fall to be included, the offer shall be taken to contravene section 6(1)(b).

(4) Where a person offers a woman employment on certain terms, and subsection (3) would apply but for the fact that, on her acceptance of the offer, section 1(3) of the Equal Pay Act 1970 (as set out in subsection (1) above) would prevent the equality clause from operating, the offer shall be taken not to contravene section 6(1)(b).

(5) An act does not contravene section 6(2) if—
  (a) it contravenes a term modified or included by virtue of an equality clause, or
  (b) it would contravene such a term but for the fact that the equality clause is prevented from operating by section 1(3) of the Equal Pay Act 1970.

(6) The Equal Pay Act 1970 is further amended as specified in Part I of Schedule 1, and accordingly has effect as set out in Part II of Schedule 1."

Discrimination against contract workers
9.—(1) This section applies to any work for a person ("the principal") which is available for doing by individuals ("contract workers") who are employed not by the principal himself but by another person, who supplies them under a contract made with the principal.

(2) It is unlawful for the principal, in relation to work to which this section applies, to discriminate against a woman who is a contract worker—
- (*a*) in the terms on which he allows her to do that work, or
- (*b*) by not allowing her to do it or continue to do it, or
- (*c*) in the way he affords her access to any benefits, facilities or services or by refusing or deliberately omitting to afford her access to them, or
- (*d*) by subjecting her to any other detriment.

(3) The principal does not contravene subsection (2)(*b*) by doing any act in relation to a woman at a time when if the work were to be done by a person taken into his employment being a man would be a genuine occupational qualification for the job.

(4) Subsection (2)(*c*) does not apply to benefits, facilities or services of any description if the principal is concerned with the provision (for payment or not) of benefits, facilities or services of that description to the public, or to a section of the public to which the woman belongs, unless that provision differs in a material respect from the provision of the benefits, facilities or services by the principal to his contract workers.

Meaning of employment at establishment in Great Britain
10.—(1) For the purposes of this Part and section 1 of the Equal Pay Act 1970 ("the relevant purposes"), employment is to be regarded as being at an establishment in Great Britain unless the employee does his work wholly or mainly outside Great Britain.

(2) Subsection (1) does not apply to—
- (*a*) employment on board a ship registered at a port of registry in Great Britain, or
- (*b*) employment on aircraft or hovercraft registered in the United Kingdom and operated by a person who has his principal place of business, or is ordinarily resident, in Great Britain;

but for the relevant purposes such employment is to be regarded as being at an establishment in Great Britain unless the employee does his work wholly outside Great Britain.

(3) In the case of employment on board a ship registered at a port of registry in Great Britain (except where the employee does his work wholly outside Great Britain, and outside any area added under subsection (5)) the ship shall for the relevant purposes be deemed to be the estblishment.

(4) Where work is not done at an establishment it shall be treated for the relevant purposes as done at the establishment from which it is done or (where it is not done from any establishment) at the establishment with which it has the closest connection.

(5) In relation to employment concerned with exploration of the sea bed or subsoil or the exploitation of their natural resources, Her Majesty may by Order in Council provide that subsections (1) and (2) shall each have

effect as if the last reference to Great Britain included any area for the time being designated under section 1(7) of the Continental Shelf Act 1964, except an area or part of an area in which the law of Northern Ireland applies.

(6) An Order in Council under subsection (5) may provide that, in relation to employment to which the Order applies, this Part and section 1 of the Equal Pay Act 1970 are to have effect with such modifications as are specified in the Order.

(7) An Order in Council under subsection (5) shall be of no effect unless a draft of the Order was laid before and approved by each House of Parliament.

Discrimination by Other Bodies

Partnerships

1–214   **11.**—(1) It is unlawful for a firm consisting of six or more partners, in relation to a position as partner in the firm, to discriminate against a woman—
    (*a*) in the arrangements they make for the purpose of determining who should be offered that position, or
    (*b*) in the terms on which they offer her that position, or
    (*c*) by refusing or deliberately omitting to offer her that position, or
    (*d*) in a case where the woman already holds that position—
        (i) in the way they afford her access to any benefits, facilities or services, or by refusing or deliberately omitting to afford her access to them, or
        (ii) by expelling her from that position, or subjecting her to any other detriment.

(2) Subsection (1) shall apply in relation to persons proposing to form themselves into a partnership as it applies in relation to a firm.

(3) Subsection (1)(*a*) and (*c*) do not apply to a position as partner where, if it were employment, being a man would be a genuine occupational qualification for the job.

(4) Subsection (1)(*b*) and (*d*) do not apply to provision made in relation to death or retirement.

(5) In the case of a limited partnership references in subsection (1) to a partner shall be construed as references to a general partner as defined in section 3 of the Limited Partnerships Act 1907.

Trade unions, etc.

1–215   **12.**—(1) This section applies to an organisation of workers, an organisation of employers, or any other organisation whose members carry on a particular profession or trade for the purposes of which the organisation exists.

(2) It is unlawful for an organisation to which this section applies, in the case of a woman who is not a member of the organisation, to discriminate against her—
    (*a*) in the terms on which it is prepared to admit her to membership, or
    (*b*) by refusing, or deliberately omitting to accept, her application for membership.

(3) It is unlawful for an organisation to which this section applies, in the

case of a woman who is a member of the organisation, to discriminate against her—
   (a) in the way it affords her access to any benefits, facilities or services, or by refusing or deliberately omitting to afford her access to them, or
   (b) by depriving her of membership, or varying the terms on which she is a member, or
   (c) by subjecting her to any other detriment.

(4) This section does not apply to provision made in relation to the death or retirement from work of a member.

Qualifying bodies

13.—(1) It is unlawful for an authority or body which can confer an authorisation or qualification which is needed for, or facilitates, engagement in a particular profession or trade to discriminate against a woman—
   (a) in the terms on which it is prepared to confer on her that authorisation or qualification, or
   (b) by refusing or deliberately omitting to grant her application for it, or
   (c) by withdrawing it from her or varying the terms on which she holds it.

(2) Where an authority or body is required by law to satisfy itself as to his good character before conferring on a person an authorisation or qualification which is needed for, or facilitates, his engagement in any profession or trade then, without prejudice to any other duty to which it is subject, that requirement shall be taken to impose on the authority or body a duty to have regard to any evidence tending to show that he, or any of his employees, or agents (whether past or present), has practised unlawful discrimination in, or in connection with, the carrying on of any profession or trade.

(3) In this section—
   (a) "authorisation or qualification" includes recognition, registration, enrolment, approval and certification,
   (b) "confer" includes renew or extend.

(4) Subsection (1) does not apply to discrimination which is rendered unlawful by section 22 or 23.

Vocational training bodies

14.—(1) It is unlawful for a person to whom this subsection applies, in the case of a woman seeking or undergoing training which would help to fit her for any employment, to discriminate against her—
   (a) in the terms on which that person affords her access to any training courses or other facilities, or
   (b) by refusing or deliberately omitting to afford her such access, or
   (c) by terminating her training.

(2) Subsection (1) applies to—
   (a) industrial training boards established under section 1 of the Industrial Training Act 1964 [or section 1 of the Industrial Training Act 1982];
   (b) the Manpower Services Commission [. . .];

1–216

1–217

(c) any association which comprises employers and has as its principal object, or one of its principal objects, affording their employees access to training facilities;

(d) any other person providing facilities for training for employment, being a person designated for the purposes of this paragraph in an order made by or on behalf of the Secretary of State.

(3) Subsection (1) does not apply to discrimination which is rendered unlawful by section 22 or 23.

AMENDMENT
The words omitted in subs. (2)(b) were repealed by the Employment and Training Act 1981, Sched. 2.

Employment agencies

1–218   **15.**—(1) It is unlawful for an employment agency to discriminate against a woman—
(a) in the terms on which the agency offers to provide any of its services, or
(b) by refusing or deliberately omitting to provide any of its services, or
(c) in the way it provides any of its services.

(2) It is unlawful for a local education authority or an education authority to do any act in the performance of its functions under section 8 of the Employment and Training Act 1973 which constitutes discrimination.

(3) References in subsection (1) to the services of an employment agency include guidance on careers and any other services related to employment.

(4) This section does not apply if the discrimination only concerns employment which the employer could lawfully refuse to offer the woman.

(5) An employment agency or local education authority or an education authority shall not be subject to any liability under this section if it proves—
(a) that it acted in reliance on a statement made to it by the employer to the effect that, by reason of the operation of subsection (4), its action would not be unlawful, and
(b) that it was reasonable for it to rely on the statement.

(6) A person who knowingly or recklessly makes a statement such as is referred to in subsection (5)(a) which in a material respect is false or misleading commits an offence, and shall be liable on summary conviction to a fine not exceeding £400.

Manpower Services Commission etc.

1–219   **16.**—[(1) It is unlawful for the Manpower Services Commission to discriminate in the provision of facilities or services under section 2 of the Employment and Training Act 1973].

(2) This section does not apply in a case where—
(a) section 14 applies, or
(b) the body is acting as an employment agency.

AMENDMENT
Subs. (1) was substituted by the Employment and Training Act 1981 (c. 57), Sched. 2.

Special Cases

Police

17.—(1) For the purposes of this Part, the holding of the office of constable shall be treated as employment—
- (*a*) by the chief officer of police as respects any act done by him in relation to a constable or that office;
- (*b*) by the police authority as respects any act done by them in relation to a constable or that office.

(2) Regulations made under section 33, 34 or 35 of the Police Act 1964 shall not treat men and women differently except—
- (*a*) as to requirements relating to height, uniform or equipment, or allowances in lieu of uniform or equipment, or
- (*b*) so far as special treatment is accorded to women in connection with pregnancy or childbirth, or
- (*c*) in relation to pensions to or in respect of special constables or police cadets.

(3) Nothing in this Part renders unlawful any discrimination between male and female constables as to matters such as are mentioned in subsection (2)(*a*).

(4) There shall be paid out of the police fund—
- (*a*) any compensation, costs or expenses awarded against a chief officer of police in any proceedings brought against him under this Act, and any costs or expenses incurred by him in any such proceedings so far as not recovered by him in the proceedings; and
- (*b*) any sum required by a chief officer of police for the settlement of any claim made against him under this Act if the settlement is approved by the police authority.

(5) Any proceedings under this Act which, by virtue of subsection (1), would lie against a chief officer of police shall be brought against the chief officer of police for the time being or, in the case of a vacancy in that office, against the person for the time being performing the functions of that office; and references in subsection (4) to the chief officer of police shall be construed accordingly.

(6) Subsections (1) and (3) apply to a police cadet and appointment as a police cadet as they apply to a constable and the office of constable.

(7) In this section—

"chief officer of police"—

    (*a*) in relation to a person appointed, or an appointment falling to be made, under a specified Act, has the same meaning as in the Police Act 1964,

    (*b*) in relation to any other person or appointment means the officer who has the direction and control of the body of constables or cadets in question;

"police authority"—

    (*a*) in relation to a person appointed, or an appointment falling to be made, under a specified Act, has the same meaning as in the Police Act 1964,

    (*b*) in relation to any other person or appointment means the authority by whom the person in question is or on appointment would be paid;

"police cadet" means any person appointed to undergo training with

a view to becoming a constable;
"police fund" in relation to a chief officer of police within paragraph (*a*) of the above definiton of that term has the same meaning as in the Police Act 1964, and in any other case means money provided by the police authority;
"specified Act" means the Metropolitan Police Act 1829, the City of London Police Act 1839 or the Police Act 1964.

(8) In the application of this section to Scotland, in subsection (7) for any reference to the Police Act 1964 there shall be substituted a reference to the Police (Scotland) Act 1967, and for the reference to sections 33, 34 and 35 of the former Act in subsection (2) there shall be substituted a reference to sections 26 and 27 of the latter Act.

Prison officers

1–221 **18.**—(1) Nothing in this Part renders unlawful any discrimination between male and female prison officers as to requirements relating to height.

(2) In section 7(2) of the Prison Act 1952 the words "and if women only are received in a prison the Governor shall be a woman" are repealed.

Ministers of religion etc.

1–222 **19.**—(1) Nothing in this Part applies to employment for purposes of an organised religion where the employment is limited to one sex so as to comply with the doctrines of the religion or avoid offending the religious susceptibilities of a significant number of its followers.

(2) Nothing in section 13 applies to an authorisation or qualification (as defined in that section) for purposes of an organised religion where the authorisation or qualification is limited to one sex so as to comply with the doctrines of the religion or avoid offending the religious susceptibilities of a significant number of its followers.

Midwives

1–223 **20.**—(1) Section 6(1) does not apply to employment as a midwife.

(2) Section 6(2)(*a*) does not apply to promotion, transfer or training as a midwife.

(3) Section 14 does not apply to training as a midwife.

(4) [*Repealed by the Nurses, Midwives and Health Visitors Act 1979, c. 36, Sched. 8.*]

(5) [*Repealed by the Nurses, Midwives and Health Visitors Act 1979, c. 36, Sched. 8.*]

Mineworkers

1–224 **21.**—(1) The following shall be substituted for section 124(1) of the Mines and Quarries Act 1954 (which provides that no female shall be employed below ground at a mine)—

"(1) No female shall be employed in a job the duties of which ordinarily require the employee to spend a significant proportion of his time below ground at a mine which is being worked"

(2) Throughout the Coal Mines Regulation Act 1908, for "workman" or "man" there is substituted "worker", and for "workmen" or "men" there is substituted "workers".

. . . . . .

Part IV

Other Unlawful Acts

Discriminatory practices

37.—(1) In this section "discriminatory practice" means the application of a requirement or condition which results in an act of discrimination which is unlawful by virtue of any provision of Part II or III taken with section 1(1)(*b*) or 3(1)(*b*) or which would be likely to result in such an act of discrimination if the persons to whom it is applied were not all of one sex.

(2) A person acts in contravention of this section if and so long as—
  (*a*) he applies a discriminatory practice, or
  (*b*) he operates practices or other arrangements which in any circumstances would call for the application by him of a discriminatory practice.

(3) Proceedings in respect of a contravention of this section shall be brought only by the Commission in accordance with sections 67 to 71.

Discriminatory advertisements

38.—(1) It is unlawful to publish or cause to be published an advertisement which indicates, or might reasonably be understood as indicating, an intention by a person to do any act which is or might be unlawful by virtue of Part II or III.

(2) Subsection (1) does not apply to an advertisement if the intended act would not in fact be unlawful.

(3) For the purposes of subsection (1), use of a job description with a sexual connotation (such as "waiter", "salesgirl", "postman" or "stewardess") shall be taken to indicate an intention to discriminate, unless the advertisement contains an indication to the contrary.

(4) The publisher of an advertisement made unlawful by subsection (1) shall not be subject to any liability under that subsection in respect of the publication of the advertisement if he proves—
  (*a*) that the advertisement was published in reliance on a statement made to him by the person who caused it to be published to the effect that, by reason of the operation of subsection (2), the publication would not be unlawful, and
  (*b*) that it was reasonable for him to rely on the statement.

(5) A person who knowingly or recklessly makes a statement such as is referred to in subsection (4) which in a material respect is false or misleading commits an offence, and shall be liable on summary conviction to a fine not exceeding £400.

Instructions to discriminate

39. It is unlawful for a person—
  (*a*) who has authority over another person, or
  (*b*) in accordance with whose wishes that other person is accustomed to act,
to instruct him to do any act which is unlawful by virtue of Part II or III, or procure or attempt to procure the doing by him of any such act.

Pressure to discriminate

1-228   40.—(1) It is unlawful to induce, or attempt to induce, a person to do any act which contravenes Part II or III by—
   (*a*) providing or offering to provide him with any benefit, or
   (*b*) subjecting or threatening to subject him to any detriment.
   (2) An offer or threat is not prevented from falling within subsection (1) because it is not made directly to the person in question, if it is made in such a way that he is likely to hear of it.

Liability of employers and principals

1-229   41.—(1) Anything done by a person in the course of his employment shall be treated for the purposes of this Act as done by his employer as well as by him, whether or not it was done with the employer's knowledge or approval.
   (2) Anything done by a person as agent for another person with the authority (whether express or implied, and whether precedent or subsequent) of that other person shall be treated for the purposes of this Act as done by that other person as well as by him.
   (3) In proceedings brought under this Act against any person in respect of an act alleged to have been done by an employee of his it shall be a defence for that person to prove that he took such steps as were reasonably practicable to prevent the employee from doing that act, or from doing in the course of his employment acts of that description.

Aiding unlawful acts

1-230   42.—(1) A person who knowingly aids another person to do an act made unlawful by this Act shall be treated for the purposes of this Act as himself doing an unlawful act of the like description.
   (2) For the purposes of subsection (1) an employee or agent for whose act the employer or principal is liable under section 41 (or would be so liable but for section 41(3)) shall be deemed to aid the doing of the act by the employer or principal.
   (3) A person does not under this section knowingly aid another to do an unlawful act if—
   (*a*) he acts in reliance on a statement made to him by that other person that, by reason of any provision of this Act, the act which he aids would be unlawful, and
   (*b*) it is reasonable for him to rely on the statement.
   (4) A person who knowingly or recklessly makes a statement such as is referred to in subsection (3)(*a*) which in a material respect is false or misleading commits an offence, and shall be liable on summary conviction to a fine not exceeding £400.

PART V

GENERAL EXCEPTIONS FROM PARTS II TO IV

Charities

1-231   43.—(1) Nothing in Parts II to IV shall—

(a) be construed as affecting a provision to which this subsection applies, or

(b) render unlawful an act which is done in order to give effect to such a provision.

(2) Subection (1) applies to a provision for conferring benefits on persons of one sex only (disregrding any benefits to persons of the opposite sex which are exceptional or are relatively insignificant), being a provision which is contained in a charitable instrument.

[(3) In this subsection "charitable instrument" means an enactment or other instrument passed or made for charitable purposes, or an enactment or other instrument so far as it relates to charitable purposes, and in Scotland includes the governing instrument of an endowment or of an educational endowment as those expressions are defined in section 135(1) of the Education (Scotland) Act 1962.

In the application of this section to England and Wales, "charitable purposes" means purposes which are exclusively charitable according to the law of England and Wales.]

. . . . . .

Discriminatory training by certain bodies

47.—(1) Nothing in Parts II to IV shall render unlawful any act done in relation to particular work by a training body in, or in connection with—

(a) affording women only, or men only, access to facilities for training which would help to fit them for that work, or

(b) encouraging women only, or men only, to take advantage of opportunities for doing that work,

where it appears to the training body that at any time within the 12 months immediately preceding the doing of the act there were no persons of the sex in question doing that work in Great Britain, or the number of persons of that sex doing the work in Great Britain was comparatively small.

(2) Where in relation to particular work it appears to a training body that although the condition for the operation of subsection (1) is not met for the whole of Great Britain it is met for an area within Great Britain, nothing in Parts II to IV shall render unlawful any act done by the training body in, or in connection with—

(a) affording persons who are of the sex in question, and who appear likely to take up that work in that area, access to facilities for training which would help to fit them for that work, or

(b) encouraging persons of that sex to take advantage of opportunities in the area for doing that work.

(3) Nothing in Parts II to IV shall render unlawful any act done by a training body in, or in connection with, affording persons access to facilities for training which would help to fit them for employment, where it appears to the training body that those persons are in special need of training by reason of the period for which they have been discharging domestic or family responsibilities to the exclusion of regular full time employment.

The discrimination in relation to which this subsection applies may result from confining the training to persons who have been discharging domestic or family responsibilities, or from the way persons are selected for training, or both.

(4) In this section "training body" means—

(a) a person mentioned in section 14(2)(a) or (b), or

(*b*) any other person being a person designated for the purposes of this section in an order made by or on behalf of the Secretary of State,

and a person may be designated under paragraph (*b*) for the purposes of subsections (1) and (2) only, or of subsection (3) only, or for all those subsections.

Other discriminatory training, etc.

1–233   **48.**—(1) Nothing in Parts II to IV shall render unlawful any act done by an employer in relation to particular work in his employment, being an act done in, or in connection with,—
   (*a*) affording his female employees only, or his male employees only, access to facilities for training which would help to fit them for that work, or
   (*b*) encouraging women only, or men only, to take advantage of opportunities for doing that work,

where at any time within the twelve months immediately preceding the doing of the act there were no persons of the sex in question among those doing that work or the number of persons of that sex doing the work was comparatively small.

(2) Nothing in section 12 shall render unlawful any act done by an organisation to which that section applies in, or in connection with,—
   (*a*) affording female members of the organisation only, or male members of the organisation only, access to facilities for training which would help to fit them for holding a post of any kind in the organisation, or
   (*b*) encouraging female members only, or male members only, to take advantage of opportunities for holding such posts in the organisation,

where at any time within the twelve months immediately preceding the doing of the act there were no persons of the sex in question among persons holding such posts in the organisation or the number of persons of that sex holding such posts was comparatively small.

(3) Nothing in Parts II to IV shall render unlawful any act done by an organisation to which section 12 applies in, or in connection with, encouraging women only, or men only, to become members of the organisation where at any time within the twelve months immediately preceding the doing of the act there were no persons of the sex in question among those members or the number of persons of that sex among the members was comparatively small.

Trade unions, etc.: elective bodies

1–234   **49.**—(1) If an organisation to which section 12 applies comprises a body the membership of which is wholly or mainly elected, nothing in section 12 shall render unlawful provision which ensures that a minimum number of persons of one sex are members of the body—
   (*a*) by reserving seats on the body for persons of that sex, or
   (*b*) by making extra seats on the body available (by election or co-option or otherwise) for persons of that sex on occasions when the number of persons of that sex in the other seats is below the minimum,

where in the opinion of the organisation the provision is in the circumstances needed to secure a reasonable lower limit to the number of members of that sex serving on the body; and nothing in Parts II to IV shall render unlawful any act done in order to give effect to such a provision.

(2) This section shall not be taken as making lawful—
- (*a*) discrimination in the arrangements for determining the persons entitled to vote in an election of members of the body, or otherwise to choose the persons to serve on the body, or
- (*b*) discrimination in any arrangements concerning membership of the organisation itself.

Indirect access to benefits, etc.

50.—(1) References in this Act to the affording by any person of access to benefits, facilities or services are not limited to benefits, facilities or services provided by that person himself, but include any means by which it is in that person's power to facilitate access to benefits, facilities or services provided by any other person (the "actual provider").

(2) Where by any provision of this Act the affording by any person of access to benefits, facilities or services in a discriminatory way is in certain circumstances prevented from being unlawful, the effect of the provision shall extend also to the liability under this Act of any actual provider.

Acts done under statutory authority

51.—(1) Nothing in Parts II to IV shall render unlawful any act done by a person if it was necessary for him to do it in order to comply with a requirement—
- (*a*) of an Act passed before this Act; or
- (*b*) of an instrument made or approved (whether before or after the passing of this Act) by or under an Act before this Act.

(2) Where an Act passed after this Act re-enacts (with or without modification) a provision of an Act passed before this Act, subsection (1) shall apply to that provision as re-enacted as if it continued to be contained in an Act passed before this Act.

Acts safeguarding national security

52.—(1) Nothing in Parts II to IV shall render unlawful an act done for the purpose of safeguarding national security.

(2) A certificate purporting to be signed by or on behalf of a Minister of the Crown and certifying that an act specified in the certificate was done for the purpose of safeguarding national security shall be conclusive evidence that it was done for that purpose.

(3) A document purporting to be a certificate such as is mentioned in subsection (2) shall be received in evidence and, unless the contrary is proved, shall be deemed to be such a certificate.

Part VI

Equal Opportunities Commission

General

Establishment and duties of Commission

53.—(1) There shall be a body of Commissioners named the Equal

Opportunities Commission, consisting of at least eight but not more than fifteen individuals each appointed by the Secretary of State on a full-time or part-time basis, which shall have the following duties—
  (a) to work towards the elimination of discrimination,
  (b) to promote equality of opportunity between men and women generally, and
  (c) to keep under review the working of this Act and the Equal Pay Act 1970 and, when they are so required by the Secretary of State or otherwise think it necessary, draw up and submit to the Secretary of State proposals for amending them.

(2) The Secretary of State shall appoint—
  (a) one of the Commissioners to be chairman of the Commission, and
  (b) either one or two of the Commissioners (as the Secretary of State thinks fit) to be deputy chairman or deputy chairmen of the Commission.

(3) The Secretary of State may by order amend subsection (1) so far as it regulates the number of Commissioners.

(4) Schedule 3 shall have effect with respect to the Commission.

Research and education

1–239   **54.**—(1) The Commission may undertake or assist (financially or otherwise) the undertaking by other persons of any research, and any educational activities, which appear to the Commission necessary or expedient for the purposes of section 53(1).

(2) The Commission may make charges for educational or other facilities or services made available by them.

Review of discriminatory provisions in health and safety legislation

1–240   **55.**—(1) Without prejudice to the generality of section 53(1), the Commission, in pursuance of the duties imposed by paragraphs (a) and (b) of that subsection—
  (a) shall keep under review the relevant statutory provisions in so far as they require men and women to be treated differently, and
  (b) if so required by the Secretary of State, make to him a report on any matter specified by him which is connected with those duties and concerns the relevant statutory provisions.

Any such report shall be made within the time specified by the Secretay of State, and the Secretary of State shall cause the report to be published.

(2) Whenever the Commission think it necessary, they shall draw up and submit to the Secretary of State proposals for amending the relevant statutory provisions.

(3) The Commission shall carry out their duties in relation to the relevant statutory provisions in consultation with the Health and Safety Commission.

(4) In this section "the relevant statutory provisions" has the meaning given by section 53 of the Health and Safety at Work etc. Act 1974.

Annual reports

1–241   **56.**—(1) As soon as practicable after the end of each calendar year the

Commission shall make to the Secretary of State a report on their activities during the year (an "annual report").

(2) Each annual report shall include a general survey of developments, during the period to which it relates, in respect of matters falling within the scope of the Commission's duties.

(3) The Secretary of State shall lay a copy of every annual report before each House of Parliament, and shall cause the report to be published.

[Codes of Practice

56A.—(1) The Commission may issue codes of practice containing such practical guidance as the Commission think fit for either or both of the following purposes, namely—
- (*a*) the elimination of discrimination in the field of employment;
- (*b*) the promotion of equality of opportunity in that field between men and women.

(2) When the Commission propose to issue a code of practice, they shall prepare and publish a draft of that code, shall consider any representations made to them about the draft and may modify the draft accordingly.

(3) In the course of preparing any draft code of practice for eventual publication under subsection (2) the Commission shall consult with—
- (*a*) such organisations or associations or organisations representative of employers or of workers; and
- (*b*) such other organisations, or bodies,

as appear to the Commission to be appropriate.

(4) If the Commission determine to proceed with the draft they shall transmit the draft to the Secretary of State who shall—
- (*a*) if he approves of it, lay it before both Houses of Parliament; and
- (*b*) if he does not approve of it, publish details of his reasons for withholding approval.

(5) If, within the period of forty days beginning with the day on which a copy of a draft code of practice is laid before each House of Parliament, or, if such copies are laid on different days, with the later of the two days, either House so resolves, no further proceedings shall be taken thereon, but without prejudice to the laying before Parliament of a new draft.

(6) In reckoning the period of forty days referred to in subsection (5), no account shall be taken of any period during which Parliament is dissolved or prorogued or during which both Houses are adjourned for more than four days.

(7) If no such resolution is passed as is referred to in subsection (5), the Commission shall issue the code in the form of the draft and the code shall come into effect on such day as the Secretary of State may by order appoint.

(8) Without prejudice to section 81(4), an order under subsection (7) may contain such transitional provisions or savings as appear to the Secretary of State to be necessary or expedient in connection with the code of practice thereby brought into operation.

(9) The Commission may from time to time revise the whole or any part of a code of practice issued under this section and issue that revised code, and subsections (2) to (8) shall apply (with appropriate modifications) to such a revised code as they apply to the first issue of a code.

(10) A failure on the part of any person to observe any provision of a

code of practice shall not of itself render him liable to any proceedings; but in any proceedings under this Act before an industrial tribunal any code of practice issued under this section shall be admissible in evidence, and if any provision of such a code appears to the tribunal to be relevant to any question arising in the proceedings it shall be taken into account in determining that question.

(11) Without prejudice to subsection (1), a code of practice issued under this section may include such practical guidance as the Commission think fit as to what steps it is reasonably practicable for employers to take for the purpose of preventing their employees from doing in the course of their employment acts made unlawful by this Act.]

AMENDMENT

This section was added by the Race Relations Act 1976 (c. 74), s.79(4), Sched. 4. It is in identical terms to the provisions for codes of practices as s.47 of the Race Relations Act 1976.

Investigations

Power to conduct formal investigations

1–243   **57.**—(1) Without prejudice to their general power to do anything requisite for the pe rformance of their duties under section 53(1), the Commission may if they think fit, and shall if required by the Secretary of State, conduct a formal investigation for any purpose connected with the carrying out of those duties.

(2) The Commission may, with the approval of the Secretary of State, appoint, on a full-time or part-time basis, one or more individuals as additional Commissioners for the purposes of a formal investigation.

(3) The Commission may nominate one or more Commissioners, with or without one or more additional Commissioners, to conduct a formal investigation on their behalf, and may delegate any of their functions in relation to the investigation to the persons so nominated.

Terms of reference

1–244   **58.**—(1) The Commission shall not embark on a formal investigation unless the requirements of this section have been complied with.

(2) Terms of reference for the investigation shall be drawn up by the Commission or, if the Commission were required by the Secretary of State to conduct the investigation, by the Secretary of State after consulting the Commission.

(3) It shall be the duty of the Commission to give general notice of the holding of the investigation unless the terms of reference confine it to activities of persons named in them, but in such a case the Commission shall in the prescribed manner give those persons notice of the holding of the investigation.

[(3A) Where the terms of reference of the investigation confine it to activities of persons named in them and the Commission in the course of it propose to investigate any act made unlawful by this Act which they believe that a person so named may have done, the Commission shall—

(a) inform that person of their belief and of their proposal to investigate the act in question; and

(b) offer him an opportunity of making oral or written representations with regard to it (or both oral and written representations if he thinks fit);

and a person so named who avails himself of an opportunity under this subsection of making oral representations may be represented—
  (i) by counsel or a solicitor; or
  (ii) by some other person of his choice, not being a person to whom the Commission object on the ground that he is unsuitable.]

(4) The Commission or, if the Commission were required by the Secretary of State to conduct the investigation, the Secretary of State after consulting the Commission may from time to time revise the terms of reference; and subsections (1) [(3) and (3A)] shall apply to the revised investigation and terms of reference as they applied to the original.

AMENDMENT
Subs. (3A) was added by the Race Relations Act 1976 (c. 74), s.79(4), Sched. 4.

Power to obtain information

59.—(1) For the purposes of a formal investigation the Commission, by a notice in the prescribed form served on him in the prescribed manner,—
  (*a*) may require any person to furnish such written information as may be described in the notice, and may specify the time at which, and the manner and form in which, the information is to be furnished;
  (*b*) may require any person to attend at such time and place as is specified in the notice and give oral information about, and produce all documents in his possession or control relating to, any matter specified in the notice.

1–245

(2) Except as provided by section 69, a notice shall be served under subsection (1) only where—
  (*a*) service of the notice was authorised by an order made by or on behalf of the Secretary of State, or
  (*b*) the terms of reference of the investigation state that the Commission believe that a person named in them may have done or may be doing acts of all or any of the following descriptions—
    (i) unlawful discriminatory acts,
    (ii) contraventions of section 37,
    (iii) contraventions of sections 38, 39 or 40, and
    (iv) acts in breach of a term modified or included by virtue of an equality clause,
  and confine the investigation to those acts.

(3) A notice under subsection (1) shall not require a person—
  (*a*) to give information, or produce any documents, which he could not be compelled to give in evidence, or produce, in civil proceedings before the High Court or the Court of Session, or
  (*b*) to attend at any place unless the necessary expenses of his journey to and from that place or tendered to him.

(4) If a person fails to comply with a notice served on him under subsection (1) or the Commission has reasonable cause to believe that he intends not to comply with it, the Commission may apply to a county court for an order requiring him to comply with it or with such directions for the like purpose as may be contained in the order; and section 84 (penalty for neglecting witness summons) of the County Courts Act 1959 shall apply to

failure without reasonable excuse to comply with any such order as it applies in the cases there provided.

(5) In the application of subsection (4) to Scotland—
- (*a*) for the reference to a county court there shall be substituted a reference to a sheriff court, and
- (*b*) for the words after "order; and" to the end of the subsection there shall be substituted the words "paragraph 73 of the First Schedule to the Sheriff Courts (Scotland) Act 1907 (power of sheriff to grant second diligence for compelling the attendances of witnesses or havers) shall apply to any such order as it applies in proceedings in the sheriff court".

(6) A person commits an offence if he—
- (*a*) wilfully alters, suppresses, conceals or destroys a document which he has been required by a notice or order under this section to produce, or
- (*b*) in complying with such a notice or order, knowingly or recklessly makes any statement which is false in a material particular,

and shall be liable on summary conviction to a fine not exceeding £400.

(7) Proceedings for an offence under subsection (6) may (without prejudice to any jurisdiction exercisable apart from this subsection) be instituted—
- (*a*) against any person at any place at which he has an office or other place of business;
- (*b*) against an individual at any place where he resides, or at which he is for the time being.

Recommendations and reports on formal investigations

1–246   60.—(1) If in the light of any of their findings in a formal investigation it appears to the Commission necessary or expedient, whether during the course of the investigation or after its conclusion,—
- (*a*) to make to any persons, with a view to promoting equality of opportunity between men and women who are affected by any of their activities, recommendations for changes in their policies or procedures, or as to any other matters, or
- (*b*) to make to the Secretary of State any recommendations, whether for changes in the law or otherwise,

the Commission shall make those recommendations accordingly.

(2) The Commission shall prepare a report of their findings in any formal investigation conducted by them.

(3) If the formal investigation is one required by the Secretary of State—
- (*a*) the Commission shall deliver the report to the Secretary of State, and
- (*b*) the Secretary of State shall cause the report to be published,

and unless required by the Secretary of State the Commission shall not publish the report.

(4) If the formal investigation is not one required by the Secretary of State, the Commission shall either publish the report, or make it available for inspection in accordance with subsection (5).

(5) Where under subsection (4) a report is to be made available for inspection, any person shall be entitled, on payment of such fee (if any) as may be determined by the Commission—

(*a*) to inspect the report during ordinary office hours and take copies of all or any part of the report, or

(*b*) to obtain from the Commission a copy, certified by the Commission to be correct, of the report.

(6) The Commission may if they think fit determine that the right conferred by subsection (5)(*a*) shall be exercisable in relation to a copy of the report instead of, or in addition to, the original.

(7) The Commission shall give general notice of the place or places where, and the times when, reports may be inspected under subsection (5).

Restriction on disclosure of information

61.—(1) No information given to the Commission by any person ("the informant") in connection with a formal investigation shall be disclosed by the Commission, or by any person who is or has been a Commissioner, additional Commissioner or employee of the Commission, except—

(*a*) on the order of any court, or

(*b*) with the informant's consent, or

(*c*) in the form of a summary or other general statement published by the Commission which does not identify the informant or any other person to whom the information relates, or

(*d*) in a report of the investigation published by the Commission or made available for inspection under section 60(5), or

(*e*) to the Commissioners, additional Commissioners or employees of the Commission, or, so far as may be necessary for the proper performance of the functions of the Commission, to other persons, or

(*f*) for the purpose of any civil proceedings under this Act to which the Commission are a party, or any criminal proceedings.

(2) Any person who discloses information in contravention of subsection (1) commits an offence and shall be liable on summary conviction to a fine not exceeding £400.

(3) In preparing any report for publication or for inspection the Commission shall exclude, so far as is consistent with their duties and the object of the report, any matter which relates to the private affairs of any individual or business interests of any person where the publication of that matter might, in the opinion of the Commission, prejudicially affect that individual or person.

Part VII

Enforcement

General

[Restriction of proceedings for breach of Act

62.—(1) Except as provided by this Act no proceedings, whether civil or criminal, shall lie against any person in respect of an act by reason that the act is unlawful by virtue of a provision of this Act.

(2) Subsection (1) does not preclude the making of an order of certiorari, mandamus or prohibition.

(3) In Scotland, subsection (1) does not preclude the exercise of the

jurisdiction of the Court of Session to entertain an application for reduction or suspension of any order or determination, or otherwise to consider the validity of any order or determination, or to require reasons for any order or determination to be stated.]

AMENDMENT
The original section was substituted by the Race Relations Act 1976 (c. 74), s.79(4) and Sched. 4, para. 3.

Enforcement in Employment Field

Jurisdiction of industrial tribunals

1–249 63.—(1) A complaint by any person ("the complainant") that another person ("the respondent")—
(a) has committed an act of discrimination against the complainant which is unlawful by virtue of Part II, or
(b) is by virtue of section 41 or 42 to be treated as having committed such an act of discrimination against the complainant,
may be presented to an industrial tribunal.

(2) Subsection (1) does not apply to a complaint under section 13(1) of an act in respect of which an appeal, or proceedings in the nature of an appeal may be brought under any enactment.

Conciliation in employment cases

1–250 64.—(1) Where a complaint has been presented to an industrial tribunal under section 63, or under section 2(1) of the Equal Pay Act 1970, and a copy of the complaint has been sent to a conciliation officer, it shall be the duty of the conciliation officer—
(a) if he is requested to do so both by the complainant and the respondent, or
(b) if, in the absence of requests by the complainant and respondent, he considers that he could act under this subsection with a reasonable prospect of success,
to endeavour to promote a settlement of the complaint without its being determined by an industrial tribunal.

(2) Where, before a complaint such as is mentioned in subsection (1) has been presented to an industrial tribunal, a request is made to a conciliation officer to make his services available in the matter by a person who, if the complaint were so presented, would be the complainant or respondent, subsection (1) shall apply as if the complaint had been so presented and a copy of it had been sent to the conciliation officer.

(3) In proceeding under subsection (1) or (2), a conciliation officer shall where appropriate have regard to the desirability of encouraging the use of other procedures available for the settlement of grievances.

(4) Anything communicated to a conciliation officer in connection with the performance of his functions under this section shall not be admissible in evidence in any proceedings before an industrial tribunal except with the consent of the person who communicated it to that officer.

Remedies on complaint under section 63

1–251 65.—(1) Where an industrial tribunal finds that a complaint presented to

it under section 63 is well-founded the tribunal shall make such of the following as it considers just and equitable—
- (a) an order declaring the rights of the complainant and the respondent in relation to the act to which the complaint relates;
- (b) an order requiring the respondent to pay the complainant compensation of an amount corresponding to any damages he could have been ordered by a county court or by a sheriff court to pay to the complainant if the complaint had fallen to be dealt with under section 66;
- (c) a recommendation that the respondent take within a specified period action appearing to the tribunal to be practicable for the purpose of obviating or reducing the adverse effect on the complainant of any act of discrimination to which the complaint relates.

(2) The amount of compensation awarded to a person under subsection (1)(b) shall not exceed the limit for the time being imposed by [section 75 of the Employment Protection (Consolidation) Act 1978].

(3) If without reasonable justification the respondent to a complaint fails to comply with a recommendation made by an industrial tribunal under subsection (1)(c), then, if they think it just and equitable to do so—
- (a) the tribunal may [subject to the limit in subsection (2)] increase the amount of compensation required to be paid to the complainant in respect of the complaint by an order made under subsection (1)(b), or
- (b) if an order under subsection (1)(b) could have been made but was not, the tribunal may make such an order.

AMENDMENT
    The words in square brackets in subs. (2) were substituted by the Employment Protection Act 1975 (c. 71), s.125 and Sched. 16, para. 18, and the Employment Protection (Consolidation) Act 1978 (c. 44), s.159(2), Sched. 16, and in subs. (3)(a) by the Race Relations Act 1976 (c. 74), s.79(4), Sched. 4.

Enforcement of Part III

Claims under Part III

66.—(1) A claim by any person ("the claimant") that another person ("the respondent")—
- (a) has committed an act of discriminating against the claimant which is unlawful by virtue of Part III, or
- (b) is by virtue of section 41 or 42 to be treated as having committed such an act of discrimination against the claimant,

may be made the subject of civil proceedings in like manner as any other claim in tort or (in Scotland) in reparation for breach of statutory duty.

(2) Proceedings under subsection (1)—
- (a) shall be brought in England and Wales only in a county court, and
- (b) shall be brought in Scotland only in a sheriff court,

but all such remedies shall be obtainable in such proceedings as, apart from this subsection [and section 62(1)], would be obtainable in the High Court or the Court of Session, as the case may be.

(3) As respects an unlawful act of discrimination falling within section 1(1)(b) (or, where this section is applied by section 65(1)(b), section 3(1)(b)) no award of damages shall be made if the respondent proves that

the requirement or condition in question was not applied with the intention of treating the claimant unfavourably on the ground of his sex or marital status as the case may be.

(4) For the avoidance of doubt it is hereby declared that damages in respect of an unlawful act of discrimination may include compensation for injury to feelings whether or not they include compensation under any other head.

(5) Civil proceedings in respect of a claim by any person that he has been discriminated against in contravention of section 22 or 23 by a body to which section 25(1) applies shall not be instituted unless the claimant has given notice of the claim to the Secretary of State and either the Secretary of State has by notice informed the claimant that the Secretary of State does not require further time to consider the matter, or the period of two months has elapsed since the claimant gave notice to the Secretary of State; but nothing in this subsection applies to a counterclaim.

[(5A) In Scotland, when any proceedings are brought under this section, in addition to the service on the defender of a copy of the summons or initial writ initiating the action a copy thereof shall be sent as soon as practicable to the Commission in a manner to be prescribed by Act of Sederunt.]

(6) For the purposes of proceedings under subsection (1)—
  (a) section 91(1) (power of judge to appoint assessors) of the County Courts Act 1959 shall apply with the omission of the words "on the application of any party", and
  (b) the remuneration of assessors appointed under the said section 91(1) shall be at such rate as may be determined by the Lord Chancellor with the approval of the Minister for the Civil Service.

(7) For the purpose of proceedings before the sheriff, provision may be made by act of sederunt for the appointment of assessors by him, and the remuneration of any assessors so appointed shall be at such rate as the Lord President of the Court of Session with the approval of the Minister for the Civil Service may determine.

(8) A county court or sheriff court shall have jurisdiction to entertain proceedings under subsection (1) with respect to an act done on a ship, aircraft or hovercraft outside its district, including such an act done outside Great Britain.

AMENDMENT
The words in square brackets were inserted by the Race Relations Act 1976 (c. 74), s.79(4), Sched. 4.

Non-Discrimination Notices

Issue of non-discrimination notice
67.—(1) This section applies to—
  (a) an unlawful discriminatory act, and
  (b) a contravention of section 37, and
  (c) a contravention of section 38, 39 or 40, and
  (d) an act in breach of a term modified or included by virtue of an equality clause.
and so applies whether or not proceedings have been brought in respect of the act.

(2) If in the course of a formal investigation the Commission become satisfied that a person is committing, or has committed, any such acts, the Commission may in the prescribed manner serve on him a notice in the prescribed form ("a non-discrimination notice") requiring him—
   (a) not to commit any such acts, and
   (b) where compliance with paragraph (a) involves changes in any of his practices or other arrangements—
      (i) to inform the Commission that he has effected those changes and what those changes are, and
      (ii) to take such steps as may be reasonably required by the notice for the purpose of affording that information to other persons concerned.

(3) A non-discrimination notice may also require the person on whom it is served to furnish the Commission with such other information as may be reasonably required by the notice in order to verify that the notice has been complied with.

(4) The notice may specify the time at which, and the manner and form in which, any information is to be furnished to the Commission, but the time at which any information is to be furnished in compliance with the notice shall not be later than five years after the notice has become final.

(5) The Commission shall not serve a non-discrimination notice in respect of any person unless they have first—
   (a) given him notice that they are minded to issue a non-discrimination notice in his case, specifying the grounds on which they contemplate doing so, and
   (b) offered him an opportunity of making oral or written representations in the matter (or both oral and written representations if he thinks fit) within a period of not less than 28 days specified in the notice, and
   (c) taken account of any representations so made by him.

(6) Subsection (2) does not apply to any acts in respect of which the Secretary of State could exercise the powers conferred on him by section 25(2) and (3); but if the Commission become aware of any such acts they shall give notice of them to the Secretary of State.

(7) Sections 59(4) shall apply to requirements under subsection (2)(b), (3) and (4) contained in a non-discrimination notice which has become final as it applies to requirements in a notice served under section 59(1).

Appeal against non-discrimination notice

68.—(1) Not later than six weeks after a non-discrimination notice is served on any person he may appeal against any requirement of the notice—
   (a) to an industrial tribunal, so far as the requirement relates to acts which are within the jurisdiction of the tribunal;
   (b) to a county court or to a sheriff court so far as the requirement relates to acts which are within the jurisdiction of the court and are not within the jurisdiction of an industrial tribunal.

(2) Where the court or tribunal considers a requirement in respect of which an appeal is brought under subsection (1) to be unreasonable because it is based on an incorrect finding of fact or for any other reason, the court or tribunal shall quash the requirement.

(3) On quashing a requirement under subsection (2) the court or tribunal

may direct that the non-discrimination notice shall be treated as if, in place of the requirement quashed, it had contained a requirement in terms specified in the direction.

(4) Subection (1) does not apply to a requirement treated as included in a non-discrimination notice by virtue of a direction under subsection (3).

Investigation as to compliance with non-discrimination notice

1–255   69.—(1) If—
(a) the terms of reference of a formal investigation state that its purpose is to determine whether any requirements of a non-discrimination notice are being or have been carried out, but section 59(2)(b) does not apply, and
(b) section 58(3) is complied with in relation to the investigation on a date ("the commencement date") not later than the expiration of the period of five years beginning when the non-discrimination notice became final,

the Commission may within the period referred to in subsection (2) serve notices under section 59(1) for the purposes of the investigation without needing to obtain the consent of the Secretary of State.

(2) The said period begins on the commencement date and ends on the later of the following dates—
(a) the date on which the period of five years mentioned in subsection (1)(b) expires;
(b) the date two years after the commencement date.

Register of non-discrimination notices

1–256   70.—(1) The Commission shall establish and maintain a register ("the register") of non-discriminate notices which have become final.

(2) Any person shall be entitled, on payment of such fee (if any) as may be determined by the Commissioner,—
(a) to inspect the register during ordinary office hours and take copies of any entry, or
(b) to obtain from the Commission a copy, certified by the Commission to be correct, of any entry in the register.

(3) The Commission may, if they think fit, determine that the right conferred by subsection (2)(a) shall be exercisable in relation to a copy of the register instead of, or in addition to, the original.

(4) The Commission shall give general notice of the place or places where, and the times when, the register or a copy of it may be inspected.

Other Enforcement by Commission

Persistent discrimination

1–257   71.—(1) If, during the period of five years beginning on the date on which either of the following became final in the case of any person, namely,—
(a) a non-discrimination notice served on him.
(b) a finding by a court or tribunal under section 63 or 66, or section 2 of the Equal Pay Act 1970, that he has done an unlawful discriminatory act or an act in breach of a term modified or included by virtue of an equality clause,

it appears to the Commission that unless restrained he is likely to do one or more acts falling within paragraph (b), or contravening section 37, the

Commission may apply to a county court for an injunction, or to the sheriff court for an order, restraining him from doing so; and the court, if satisfied that the application is well-founded, may grant the injunction or order in the terms applied for or in more limited terms.

(2) In proceedings under this section the Commission shall not allege that the person to whom the proceedings relate has done an act which is within the jurisdiction of an industrial tribunal unless a finding by an industrial tribunal that he did that act has become final.

Enforcement of ss.38 to 40

72.—(1) Proceedings in respect of a contravention of section 38, 39 or 40 shall be brought only by the Commission in accordance with the following provisions of this section.   1–258

(2) The proceedings shall be—
   (*a*)   an application for a decision whether the alleged contravention occurred, or
   (*b*)   an application under subsection (4) below,
or both.

(3) An application under subsection (2)(*a*) shall be made—
   (*a*)   in a case based on any provision of Part II, to an industrial tribunal, and
   (*b*)   in any other case to a county court or sheriff court.

(4) If it appears to the Commission—
   (*a*)   that a person has done an act which by virtue of section 38, 39 or 40 was unlawful, and
   (*b*)   that unless restrained he is likely to do further acts which by virtue of that section are unlawful,
the Commission may apply to a county court for an injunction, or to a sheriff court for an order, restraining him from doing such acts; and the court, if satisfied that the application is well-founded, may grant the injunction or [. . .] order in the terms applied for or more limited terms.

(5) In proceedings under subsection (4) the Commission shall not allege that the person to whom the proceedings relate has done an act which is unlawful under this Act and within the jurisdiction of an industrial tribunal unless a finding by an industrial tribunal that he did that act has become final.

AMENDMENT
   The word omitted in subs. (5) was repealed by the Race Relations Act 1978 (c. 74), Sched. 4, para. 6 and Sched. 5.

Preliminary action in employment cases

73.—(1) With a view to making an application under section 71(1) or 72(4) in relation to a person the Commission may present to an industrial tribunal a complaint that he has done an act within the jurisdiction of an industrial tribunal, and if the tribunal considers that the complaint is well-founded they shall make a finding to that effect and, if they think it just and equitable to do so in the case of an act contravening any provision of Part II may also (as if the complaint had been presented by the person discriminated against) make an order such as is referred to in section 65(1)(*a*), or a recommendation such as is referred to in section 65(1)(*c*), or both.   1–259

(2) Subsection (1) is without prejudice to the jurisdiction conferred by section 72(2).

(3) Any finding of an industrial tribunal under—
    (*a*) this Act, or
    (*b*) the Equal Pay Act 1970,
in respect of any act shall, if it has become final, be treated as conclusive—
    (i) by the county court or sheriff court on an application under section 71(1) or 72(4) or in proceedings on an equality clause,
    (ii) by an industrial tribunal on a complaint made by the person affected by the act under section 63 or in relation to an equality clause.

(4) In sections 71 and 72 and this section, the acts "within the jurisdiction of an industrial tribunal" are those in respect of which such jurisdiction is conferred by sections 63 and 72 and by section 2 of the Equal Pay Act 1970.

Help for Persons Suffering Discrimination

Help for aggrieved persons in obtaining information, etc.

74.—(1) With a view to helping a person ("the person aggrieved") who considers he may have been discriminated against in contravention of this Act to decide whether to institute proceedings and, if he does so, to formulate and present his case in the most effective manner, the Secretary of State shall by order prescribe—
    (*a*) forms by which the person aggrieved may question the respondent on his reasons for doing any relevant act, or on any matter which is or may be relevant;
    (*b*) forms by which the respondent may if he so wishes reply to any questions.

(2) Where the person aggrieved questions the respondent (whether in accordance with an order under subsection (1) or not)—
    (*a*) the question, and any reply by the respondent (whether in accordance with such an order or not) shall, subject to the following provisions of this section, be admissible as evidence in the proceedings;
    (*b*) if it appears to the court or tribunal that the respondent deliberately, and without reasonable excuse, omitted to reply within a reasonable period or that his reply is evasive or equivocal, the court or tribunal may draw any inference from that fact that it considers it just and equitable to draw, inluding an inference that he committed an unlawful act.

(3) The Secretary of State may by order—
    (*a*) prescribe the period within which questions must be duly served in order to be admissible under subsection (2)(*a*), and
    (*b*) prescribe the manner in which a question, and any reply by the respondent, may be duly served.

(4) Rules may enable the court entertaining a claim under section 66 to determine, before the date fixed for the hearing of the claim, whether a question or reply is admissible under this section or not.

(5) This section is without prejudice to any other enactment or rule of law regulating interlocutory and preliminary matters in proceedings before a county court, sheriff court or industrial tribunal, and has effect subject to any enactment or rule of law regulating the admissibility of evidence in such proceedings.

(6) In this section "respondent" includes a prospective respondent and "rules"—

(*a*) in relation to county court proceedings, means county court rules;
(*b*) in relation to sheriff court proceedings, means sheriff court rules.

Assistance by Commission

75.—(1) Where, in relation to proceedings or prospective proceedings either under this Act or in respect of an equality clause, an individual who is an actual or prospective complainant or claimant applies to the Commission for assistance under this section, the Commission shall consider the application and may grant it if they think fit to do so on the ground that—
   (*a*) the case raises a question of principle, or
   (*b*) it is unreasonable, having regard to the complexity of the case or the applicant's position in relation to the respondent or another person involved or any other matter, to expect the applicant to deal with the case unaided,
or by reason of any other special consideration.

(2) Assistance by the Commission under this section may include—
   (*a*) giving advice;
   (*b*) procuring or attempting to procure the settlement of any matter in dispute;
   (*c*) arranging for the giving of advice or assistance by a solicitor or counsel;
   (*d*) arranging for representation by any person including all such assistance as is usually given by a solicitor or counsel in the steps preliminary or incidental to any proceedings, or in arriving at or giving effect to a compromise to avoid or bring to an end any proceedings,
   [(*e*) any other form of assistance which the Commission may consider appropriate]
but paragraph (*d*) shall not affect the law and practice regulating the descriptions of persons who may appear in, conduct, defend and address the court in, any proceedings.

(3) In so far as expenses are incurred by the Commission in providing the applicant with assistance under this section the recovery of those expenses (as taxed or assessed in such manner as may be prescribed by rules or regulations) shall constitute a first charge for the benefit of the Commission—
   (*a*) on any costs or expenses which (whether by virtue of a judgment or order of a court or tribunal or an agreement or otherwise) are payable to the applicant by any other person in respect of the matter in connection with which the assistance is given, and
   (*b*) so far as relates to any costs or expenses, on his rights under any compromise or settlement arrived at in connection with that matter to avoid or bring to an end any proceedings.

(4) The charge conferred by subsection (3) is subject to any charge under the Legal Aid Act 1974, or any charge or obligation for payment in priority to other debts under the Legal Aid and Advice (Scotland) Acts 1967 and 1972, and is subject to any provision in any of those Acts for payment of any sum into the legal aid fund.

(5) In this section "respondent" includes a prospective respondent and "rules or regulations"—
   (*a*) in relation to county court proceeding, means county court rules;
   (*b*) in relation to sheriff court proceedings, means sheriff court rules;

(c) in relation to industrial tribunal proceedings, means regulations made under [paragraph 1 of Schedule 9 to the Employment Protection (Consolidation) Act 1978].

AMENDMENT

The words in square brackets in subs. (2)(e) were added by the Race Relations Act 1976 (c. 74), s.79(4), Sched. 4, and in subs. (5)(c) by the Employment Protection (Consolidation) Act 1978 (c. 44), s.159(2), Sched. 16.

Period within which Proceedings to be Brought

Period within which proceedings to be brought

1–262   **76.**—(1) An industrial tribunal shall not consider a complaint under section 63 unless it is presented to the tribunal before the end of the period of three months beginning when the act complained of was done.

(2) A county court or a sheriff court shall not consider a claim under section 66 unless proceedings in respect of the claim are instituted before the end of

[(a) the period of six months beginning when the act complained of was done; or

(b) in a case to which section 66(5) applies, the period of eight months so beginning.]

(3) [An industrial tribunal, county court or sheriff court shall not consider an application under section 72(2)(a) unless it is made before the end of the period of six months beginning when the act to which it relates was done; and a county court or sheriff court shall not consider an application under section 72(4) unless it is made before the end of the period of five years so beginning.]

(4) An industrial tribunal shall not consider a complaint under section 73(1) unless it is presented to the tribunal before the end of the six months beginning when the act complained of was done.

(5) A court or tribunal may nevertheless consider any such complaint, claim or application which is out of time if, in all the circumstances of the case, it considers that it is just and equitable to do so.

(6) For the purposes of this section—
   (a) where the inclusion of any term in a contract renders the making of the contract an unlawful act that act shall be treated as extending throughout the duration of the contract, and
   (b) any act extending over a period shall be treated as done at the end of that period, and
   (c) a deliberate omission shall be treated as done when the person in question decided upon it,

and in the absence of evidence establishing the contrary a person shall be taken for the purposes of this section to decide upon an omission when he does an act inconsistent with doing the omitted act or, if he has done no such inconsistent act, when the period expires within which he might reasonably have been expected to do the omitted act if it was to be done.

AMENDMENT

The words in square brackets were substituted by the Race Relations Act 1976, s.79(4), Sched. 4.

Part VIII

Supplemental

Validity and revision of contracts

77.—(1) A term of a contract is void where— 1–263
   (a) its inclusion renders the making of the contract unlawful by virtue of this Act, or
   (b) it is included in furtherance of an act rendered unlawful by this Act, or
   (c) it provides for the doing of an act which would be rendered unlawful by this Act.

(2) Subsection (1) does not apply to a term the inclusion of which constitutes, or is in furtherance of, or provides for, unlawful discrimination against a party to the contract, but the term shall be unenforceable against that party.

(3) A term in a contract which purports to exclude or limit any provision of this Act or the Equal Pay Act 1970 is unenforceable by any person in whose favour the term would operate apart from this subsection.

(4) Subsection (3) does not apply—
   (a) to a contract settling a complaint to which section 63(1) of this Act or section 2 of the Equal Pay Act 1970 applies where the contract is made with the assistance of a conciliation officer;
   (b) to a contract settling a claim to which section 66 applies.

(5) On the application of any person interested in a contract to which subsection (2) applies, a county court or sheriff court may make such order as it thinks just for removing or modifying any term made unenforceable by that subsection; but such an order shall not be made unless all persons affected have been given notice of the application (except where under rules of court notice may be dispensed with) and have been afforded an opportunity to make representations to the court.

(6) An order under subsection (5) may include provision as respects any period before the making of the order.

. . . . . .

Power to amend certain provisions of Act

80.—(1) The Secretary of State may by an order the draft of which has 1–264
been approved by each House of Parliament—
   (a) amend any of the following provisions, namely, sections 6(3), 7, 19, 20(1), (2) and (3), 31(2), 32, 34, 35 and 43 to 48 (including any such provision as amended by a previous order under this subsection);
   (b) amend or repeal any of the following provisions, namely, sections 11(4), 12(4), 33 and 49 (including any such provision as amended by a previous order under this subsection);
   (c) amend Part II, III or IV so as to render lawful an act which, apart from the amendment, would be unlawful by reason of section 6(1) or (2), 29(1), 30 or 31;
   (d) amend section 11(1) so as to alter the number of partners specified in that provision.

(2) The Secretary of State shall not lay before Parliament the draft of an

order under subsection (1) unless he has consulted the Commission about the contents of the draft.

(3) An order under subsection (1)(*c*) may make such amendments to the list of provisions given in subsection (1)(*a*) as in the opinion of the Secretary of State are expedient having regard to the contents of the order.

Orders

1–265   **81.**—(1) Any power of the Secretary of State to make orders under the provisions of this Act (except sections 14(2)(*d*), 27, 47(4)(*b*) and 59(2)) shall be exercisable by statutory instrument.

(2) An order made by the Secretary of State under the preceding provisions of this Act (except sections 14(2)(*d*), 27, 47(4)(*b*), 59(2) and 80(1)) shall be subject to annulment in pursuance of a resolution of either House of Parliament.

(3) Subsections (1) and (2) do not apply to an order under section 78 or 79, but—

(*a*) an order under section 78 which modifies an enactment, and
(*b*) any order under section 79 other than one which relates to an endowment to which [section 115 of the Education (Scotland) Act 1980] (small endowments) applies,

shall be made by statutory instrument subject to annulment in pursuance of a resolution of either House of Parliament.

(4) An order under this Act may make different provision in relation to different cases or classes of case, may exclude certain cases or classes of case, and may contain transitional provisions and savings.

(5) Any power conferred by this Act to make orders includes power (exercisable in the like manner and subject to the like conditions) to vary or revoke any order so made.

AMENDMENT

In subs. (3)(*b*), the words in square brackets were substituted by the Education (Scotland) Act 1980 (c. 44), Sched. 4.

General interpretation provisions

1–266   **82.**—(1) In this Act, unless the context otherwise requires—

"access" shall be construed in accordance with section 50;
"act" includes a deliberate omission;
"advertisement" includes every form of advertisement, whether to the public or not, and whether in a newspaper or other publication, by television or radio, by display of notices, signs, labels, showcards or goods, by distribution of samples, circulars, catalogues, price lists or other material, by exhibition of pictures, models or films, or in any other way, and references to the publishing of advertisements shall be construed accordingly;
"associated employer" shall be construed in accordance with subsection (2);
"the Commission" means the Equal Opportunities Commission;
"Commissioner" means a member of the Commission;
[. . .];
"designate" shall be construed in accordance with subsection (3);

"discrimination" and related terms shall be construed in accordance with section 5(1);

"dispose," in relation to premises, includes granting a right to occupy the premises, and any reference to acquiring premises shall be construed accordingly;

"education" includes any form of training or instruction;

"education authority" and "educational establishment" in relation to Scotland have the same meaning as they have respectively in [section 135(1) of the Education (Scotland) Act 1980];

"employment" means employment under a contract of service or of apprenticeship or a contract personally to execute any work or labour, and related expressions shall be construed accordingly;

"employment agency" means a person who, for profit or not, provides services for the purpose of finding employment for workers or supplying employers with workers;

"equality clause" has the meaning given in section 1(2) of the Equal Pay Act 1970 (as set out in section 8(1) of this Act);

"estate agent" means a person who, by way of profession or trade, provides services for the purpose of finding premises for persons seeking to acquire them or assisting in the disposal of premises;

"final" shall be construed in accordance with subsection (4);

"firm" has the meaning given by section 4 of the Partnership Act 1890;

"formal investigation" means an investigation under section 57;

"further education" has the meaning given by section 41(*a*) of the Education Act 1944 and in Scotland has the meaning given by [section 135(1) of the Education (Scotland) Act 1980];

"general notice," in relation to any person, means a notice published by him at a time and in a manner appearing to him suitable for securing that the notice is seen within a reasonable time by persons likely to be affected by it;

"genuine occupational qualification" shall be construed in accordance with section 7(2);

"Great Britain" includes such of the territorial waters of the United Kingdom as are adjacent to Great Britain;

"independent school" has the meaning given by section 114(1) of the Education Act 1944 and in Scotland has the meaning given by section 135(1) of the Education (Scotland) Act 1980];

[. . .]

"man" includes a male of any age;

"managers" has the same meaning for Scotland as in [section 135(1) of the Education (Scotland) Act 1980];

"near relative" shall be construed in accordance with subsection (5);

"non-discrimination notice" means a notice under section 67;

"notice" means a notice in writing;

"prescribed" means prescribed by regulations made by the Secretary of State by statutory instrument;

"profession" includes any vocation or occupation;

"proprietor," in relation to any school, has the meaning given by section 114(1) of the Education Act 1944 and in Scotland has the meaning given by [section 135(1) of the Education (Scotland) Act 1980];

"pupil" in Scotland includes a student of any age;

"retirement" includes retirement (whether voluntary or not) on grounds of age, length of service or incapacity;

"school" has the meaning given by section 114(1) of the Education Act 1944, and in Scotland has the meaning given by [section 135(1) of the Education (Scotland) Act 1980];

"school education" has the meaning given by [section 135(1) of the Education (Scotland) Act 1980];

"trade" includes any business;

"training" includes any form of education or instruction;

"university" includes a university college and the college, school or hall of a university;

"upper limit of compulsory school age" means, subject to section 9 of the Education Act 1962, the age that is that limit by virtue of section 35 of the Education Act 1944 and the Order in Council made under that section;

"woman" includes a female of any age.

(2) For the purposes of this Act two employers are to be treated as associated if one is a company of which the other (directly or indirectly) has control or if both are companies of which a third person (directly or indirectly) has control.

(3) Any power conferred by this Act to designate establishments or persons may be exercised either by naming them or by identifying them by reference to a class or other description.

(4) For the purposes of this Act a non-discrimination notice or a finding by a court or tribunal becomes final when an appeal against the notice or finding is dismissed, withdrawn or abandoned or when the time for appealing expires without an appeal having been brought; and for this purpose an appeal against a non-discrimination notice shall be taken to be dismissed if, notwithstanding that a requirement of the notice is quashed on appeal, a direction is given in respect of it under section 68(3).

(5) For the purposes of this Act, a person is a near relative of another if that person is the wife or husband, a parent or child, a grandparent or grandchild, or a brother or sister of the other (whether of full blood or half-blood or by affinity), and "child" includes an illegitimate child and the wife or husband of an illegitimate child.

(6) Except so far as the context otherwise requires, any reference in this Act to an enactment shall be construed as a reference to that enactment as amended by or under any other enactment, including this Act.

(7) In this Act, except where otherwise indicated—
  (*a*) a reference to a numbered Part, section or Schedule is a reference to the Part or section of, or the Schedule to, this Act so numbered, and
  (*b*) a reference in a section to a numbered subsection is a reference to the subsection of that section so numbered, and
  (*c*) a reference in a section, subsection or Schedule to a numbered paragraph is a reference to the paragraph of that section, subsection or Schedule so numbered, and
  (*d*) a reference to any provision of an Act (including this Act) includes a Schedule incorporated in the Act by that provision.

AMENDMENTS

The words omitted in subs. (1) were repealed by the Employment Protection Act 1975

(c. 71), s.125 and Sched. 18 and by the Industrial Training Act 1982 (c. 10), Sched. 4. The words in square brackets were substituted by the Education (Scotland) Act 1980 (c. 44), Sched. 4.

Transitional and commencement provisions, amendments and repeals
83.—(1) The provisions of Schedule 4 shall have effect for making transitional provision for the purposes of this Act.

(2) Parts II to VII shall come into operation on such day as the Secretary of State may by order appoint, and different days may be so appointed for different provisions and for different purposes.

(3) Subject to subsection (4)—
   (*a*) the enactments specified in Schedule 5 shall have effect subject to the amendments specified in that Schedule (being minor amendments or amendments consequential on the preceding provisions of this Act), and
   (*b*) the enactments specified in Schedule 6 are hereby repealed to the extent shown in column 3 of that Schedule.

(4) The Secretary of State shall by order provide for the coming into operation of the amendments contained in Schedule 5 and the repeals contained in Schedule 6, and those amendments and repeals shall have effect only as provided by an order so made.

(5) An order under this section may make such transitional provision as appears to the Secretary of State to be necessary or expedient in connection with the provisions thereby brought into operation, including such adaptations of those provisions, or of any provisions of this Act then in operation, as appear to the Secretary of State necessary or expedient in consequence of the partial operation of this Act.

1–267

Financial provisions
84.—(1) There shall be defrayed out of money provided by Parliament—
   (*a*) sums required by the Secretary of State for making payments under paragraphs 5 to 14 of Schedule 3, and for defraying any other expenditure falling to be made by him under or by virtue of this Act;
   (*b*) payments falling to be made under section 66(6)(*b*) or (7) in respect of the remuneration of assessors; and
   (*c*) any increase attributable to the provisions of this Act in the sums payable out of money provided by Parliament under any other Act.

1–268

Application to Crown
85.—(1) This Act applies—
   (*a*) to an act done by or for purposes of a Minister of the Crown or government department, or
   (*b*) to an act done on behalf of the Crown by a statutory body, or a person holding a statutory office,
as it applies to an act done by a private person.

(2) Parts II and IV apply to—
   (*a*) service for purposes of a Minister of the Crown or government department, other than service of a person holding a statutory office, or
   (*b*) service on behalf of the Crown for purposes of a person holding a statutory office or purposes of a statutory body,
as they apply to employment by a private person, and shall so apply as if

1–269

references to a contract of employment included references to the terms of service.

(3) Subsections (1) and (2) have effect subject to section 17.

(4) Subsections (1) and (2) do not apply in relation to service in—
    (*a*) the naval, military or air forces of the Crown, or
    (*b*) any women's service administered by the Defence Council.

(5) Nothing in this Act shall render unlawful discrimination in admission to the Army Cadet Force, Air Training Corps, Sea Cadet Corps or Combined Cadet Force, or any other cadet training corps for the time being administered by the Ministry of Defence.

(6) This Act (except section 8(1) and (6)) does not apply to employment in the case of which the employee may be required to serve in support of a force or service mentioned in subsection (4)(*a*) or (*b*).

(7) Subsection (2) of section 10 shall have effect in relation to any ship, aircraft or hovercraft belonging to or possessed by Her Majesty in right of the Government of the United Kingdom as it has effect in relation to a ship, aircraft or hovercraft mentioned in paragraph (*a*) or (*b*) of that subsection, and section 10(5) shall apply accordingly.

(8) The provisions of Parts II to IV of the Crown Proceedings Act 1947 shall apply to proceedings against the Crown under this Act as they apply to proceedings in England and Wales which by virtue of section 23 of that Act are treated for the purposes of Part II of that Act as civil proceedings by or against the Crown, except that in their application to proceedings under this Act section 20 of that Act (removal of proceedings from the county court to High Court) shall not apply.

(9) The provisions of Part V of the Crown Proceedings Act 1947 shall apply to proceedings against the Crown under this Act as they apply to proceedings in Scotland which by virtue of the said Part are treated as civil proceedings by or against the Crown, except that in their application to proceedings under this Act the proviso to section 44 of that Act (removal of proceedings from the sheriff court to the Court of Session) shall not apply.

(10) In this section "statutory body" means a body set up by or in pursuance of an enactment, and "statutory office" means an office so set up; and service "for purposes of" a Minister of the Crown or government department does not include service in any office in Schedule 2 (Ministerial offices) to the House of Commons Disqualification Act 1975 as for the time being in force.

Government appointments outside section 6

1–270   **86.**—(1) This section applies to any appointment by a Minister of the Crown or government department to an office or post where section 6 does not apply in relation to the appointment.

(2) In making the appointment, and in making the arrangements for determining who should be offered the office or post, the Minister of the Crown or government department shall not do an act which would be unlawful under section 6 if the Crown were the employer for the purposes of this Act.

Short title and extent

1–271   **87.**—(1) This Act may be cited as the Sex Discrimination Act 1975.

(2) This Act (except paragraph 16 of Schedule 3) does not extend to Northern Ireland.

SCHEDULES

. . . . .

Section 27   SCHEDULE 2   1–272

TRANSITIONAL EXEMPTION ORDERS FOR EDUCATIONAL ADMISSIONS

Public sector (England and Wales)

1.* Where [under the provisions of s.12 or 13 of the Education Act 1980 a responsible body submits to the Secretary of State], proposals for an alteration in its admissions arrangements such as is mentioned in section 27(1) of this Act the submission of those proposals shall be treated as an application for the making by the Secretary of State of a transitional exemption order, and if he thinks fit the Secretary of State may make the order accordingly.

2. [*Repealed by the Education Act* 1980 (c. 20), *Sched.* 7.]

3. Regulations under section 100 of the Education Act 1944 may provide for the submission to the Secretary of State of an application for the making by him of a transitional exemption order in relation to an establishment—

(*a*) which is designated under section 24(1), and

(*b*) in respect of which grants are payable under subsection (1)(*b*) of the said section 100, and for the making by him of the order.

4. Regulations under section 5(2) of the Local Government Act 1974 may provide for the submission to the Secretary of State of an application for the making by him of a transitional exemption order in relation to any educational establishment maintained by a local education authority and not falling within paragraphs 1 to 3, and for the making by him of the order.

Private sector (England and Wales)

5.—(1) In the case of an establishment in England or Wales not falling within paragraphs 1 to 4 the responsible body may submit to the Equal Opportunities Commission set up under Part VI an application for the making by the Commission of a transitional exemption order in relation to the establishment, and if they think fit the Commission may make the order accordingly.

(2) An application under this paragraph shall specify the transitional period proposed by the responsible body to be provided for in the order, the stages by which within that period the body proposes to move to the position where section 22(*b*) is complied with, and any other matters relevant to the terms and operation of the order applied for.

(3) The Commission shall not make an order on an application under this paragraph unless they are satisfied that the terms of the application are reasonable having regard to the nature of the premises at which the establishment is carried on, the accommodation, equipment and facilities available, and the financial resources of the responsible body.

Public and private sectors (Scotland)

6. Any application for a transitional exemption order made by the responsible body in relation to an establishment falling within paragraph 6 or 7 of the Table in section 22 shall be made to the Secretary of State, and in relation to an establishment falling within paragraphs 8, 9 and 10 of that Table shall be made to the Equal Opportunities Commission.

7. An application under paragraph 6 shall specify the transitional period proposed by the responsible body to be provided for in the order, the stages by which within that period the body proposes to move to the position where section 22(*b*) is complied with, and any other matters relevant to the terms and operation of the order applied for.

8. The Secretary of State on any application under paragraph 6 may make a transitional exemption order on such terms and conditions as he may think fit.

9. The Commission on any application under paragraph 6 may if they think fit make a transitional exemption order, but shall not make such an order unless they are satisfied that the terms of the application are reasonable having regard to the nature of the premises at which the establishment is carried on, the accommodation, equipment and facilities available, and the financial resources of the responsible body.

AMENDMENT

The words in square brackets in para. 1 of this Schedule were substituted by the Education Act 1980 (c. 20), Sched. 3.

1-273 Section 53

SCHEDULE 3

Equal Opportunities Commission

Incorporation and status

1. On the appointment by the Secretary of State of the first Commissioners, the Commission shall come into existence as a body corporate with perpetual succession and a common seal.

2.—(1) The Commission is not an emanation of the Crown, and shall not act or be treated as the servant or agent of the Crown.

(2) Accordingly—
- (a) neither the Commission nor a Commissioner or member of its staff as such is entitled to any status, immunity, privilege or exemption enjoyed by the Crown;
- (b) the Commissioners and members of the staff of the Commission as such are not civil servants; and
- (c) the Commission's property is not property of, or held on behalf of the Crown.

Tenure of office of Commissioners

3.—(1) A Commissioner shall hold and vacate his office in accordance with the terms of his appointment.

(2) A person shall not be appointed a Commissioner for more than five years.

(3) With the consent of the Commissioner concerned, the Secretary of State may alter the terms of an appointment so as to make a full-time Commissioner into a part-time Commissioner or vice versa, or for any other purpose.

(4) A Commissioner may resign by notice to the Secretary of State.

(5) The Secretary of State may terminate the appointment of a Commissioner if satisfied that—
- (a) without the consent of the Commission, he failed to attend the meetings of the Commission during a continuous period of six months beginning not earlier than nine months before the termination; or
- (b) he is an undischarged bankrupt, or has made an arrangement with his creditors, or is insolvent within the meaning of paragraph 9(2) of Schedule 3 to the Conveyancing and Feudal Reform (Scotland) Act 1970; or
- (c) he is by reason of physical or mental illness, or for any other reason, incapable of carrying out his duties.

(6) Past service as a Commissioner is no bar to re-appointment.

Tenure of office of chairman and deputy chairmen

4.—(1) The chairman and each deputy chairman shall hold and vacate his office in accordance with the terms of his appointment, and may resign by notice to the Secretary of State.

(2) The office of the chairman or a deputy chairman is vacated if he ceases to be a Commissioner.

(3) Past service as chairman or a deputy chairman is no bar to re-appointment.

Remuneration of Commissioners

5. The Secretary of State may pay, or make such payments towards the provision of, such remuneration, pensions, allowances or gratuities to or in respect of the Commissioners or any of them as, with the consent of the Minister for the Civil Service, he may determine.

6. Where a person ceases to be a Commissioner otherwise than on the expiry of his term of office, and it appears to the Secretary of State that there are special circumstances which make it right for that person to receive compensation, the Secretary of State may with the consent of the Minister for the Civil Service direct the Commission to make to that peron a payment of such amount as, with the consent of that Minister, the Secretary of State may determine.

Additional Commissioners

7.—(1) Paragraphs 2(2), 3(1) and (6), and 6 shall apply to additional Commissioners appointed under section 57(2) as they apply to Commissioners.

(2) The Commission may pay, or make such payments towards the provision of, such remuneration, pensions, allowances or gratuities to or in respect of an additional Commissioner as the Secretary of State, with the Consent of the Minister for the Civil Service, may determine.

(3) With the approval of the Secretary of State and the consent of the additional Commissioner concerned, the Commission may alter the term of an appointment of an additional

Commissioner so as to make a full-time additional Commissioner into a part-time additional Commissioner or vice versa, or for any other purpose.

(4) An additional Commissioner may resign by notice to the Commission.

(5) The Secretary of State, or the Commission acting with the approval of the Secretary of State, may terminate the appointment of an additional Commissioner if satisfied that—

    (a) without reasonable excuse he failed to carry out the duties for which he was appointed during a continuous period of three months beginning not earlier than six months before the termination; or

    (b) he is a person such as is mentioned in paragraph 3(5)(b); or

    (c) he is by reason of physical or mental illness, or for any other reason, incapable of carrying out his duties.

(6) The appointment of an additional Commissioner shall terminate at the conclusion of the investigation for which he was appointed, if not sooner.

Staff

8. The Commission may, after consultation with the Secretary of State, appoint such officers and servants as they think fit, subject to the approval of the Minister for the Civil Service as to numbers and as to remuneration and other terms and conditions of service.

9.—(1) Employment with the Commission shall be included among the kinds of employment to which a superannuation scheme under section 1 of the Superannuation Act 1972 can apply, and accordingly in Schedule 1 to that Act (in which those kinds of employment are listed) the words "Equal Opportunities Commission" shall be inserted at the appropriate place in alphabetical order.

(2) Where a person who is employed by the Commission and is by reference to that employment a participant in a scheme under section 1 of the Superannuation Act 1972 becomes a Commissioner or an additional Commissioner, the Minister for the Civil Service may determine that his service as a Commissioner or additional Commissioner shall be treated for the purposes of the scheme as service as an employee of the Commission; and his rights under the scheme shall not be affected by paragraph 5 or 7(2).

10. The Employers' Liability (Compulsory Insurance) Act 1969 shall not require insurance to be effected by the Commission.

Proceedings and business

11.—(1) Subject to the provisions of this Act, the Commission may make arrangements for the regulation of their proceedings and business, and may vary or revoke those arrangements.

(2) The arrangements may, with the approval of the Secretary of State, provide for the discharge under the general direction of the Commission of any of the Commission's functions by a committee of the Commission, or by two or more Commissioners.

(3) Anything done by or in relation to a committee, or Commissioners, in the discharge of the Commission's functions shall have the same effect as if done by or in relation to the Commission.

12. The validity of any proceedings of the Commission shall not be affected by any vacancy among the members of the Commission or by any defect in the appointment of any Commissioner or additional Commissioner.

13. The quorum for meetings of the Commission shall in the first instance be determined by a meeting of the Commission attended by not less than five Commissioners.

Finance

14. The Secretary of State shall pay to the Commission expenses incurred or to be incurred by it under paragraphs 6, 7 and 8, and, with the consent of the Minister for the Civil Service and the Treasury, shall pay to the Commission such sums as the Secretary of State thinks fit for enabling the Commission to meet other expenses.

[15.—(1) The accounting year of the Commission shall be the twelve months ending on 31st March.

(2) It shall be the duty of the Commission—

    (a) to keep proper accounts and proper records in relation to the accounts;

    (b) to prepare in respect of each accounting year a statement of accounts in such form as the Secretary of State may direct with the approval of the Treasury; and

    (c) to send copies of the statement to the Secretary of State and the Comptroller and Auditor General before the end of the month of November next following the accounting year to which the statement relates.

(3) The Comptroller and Auditor General shall examine, certify and report on each statement received by him in pursuance of this Schedule and shall lay copies of each statement and of his report before each House of Parliament.]

GENERAL NOTE
Paragraph 15 was substituted by the Race Relations Act 1976, s.79(4), Sched. 4.

Disqualification Acts

16.—(1) In Part II of Schedule 1 to the House of Commons Disqualification Act 1975 and Part II of Schedule 1 to the Northern Ireland Assembly Disqualification Act 1975 (bodies of which all members are disqualified under those Acts) there shall (at the appropriate place in alphabetical order) be inserted the following entry:—
 "The Equal Opportunities Commission.".
(2) In Part III of Schedule 1 to each of those Acts of 1975 (other disqualifying offices) there shall (at the appropriate place in alphabetical order) be inserted the following entry:—
 "Additional Commissioner of the Equal Opportunities Commission".

Section 83   SCHEDULE 4

TRANSITIONAL PROVISIONS

1. Section 12 does not apply, as respects any organisation,—
 (a) to contributions or other payments falling to be made to the organisation by its members or by persons seeking membership, or
 (b) to financial benefits accruing to members of the organisation by reason of their membership,
where the payment falls to be made, or the benefit accrues, before 1st January 1978 under rules of the organisation made before the passing of this Act.

2. Until 1st January 1978, secion 12(2) does not apply to any organisation of members of the teaching profession where at the passing of this Act—
 (a) the organisation is an incorporated company with articles of association, and
 (b) the articles of association restrict membership to persons of one sex (disregarding any minor exceptions), and
 (c) there exists another organisation within paragraphs (a) and (b) which is for persons of the opposite sex and has objects, as set out in the memorandum of association, which are substantially the same as those of the first mentioned organisation, subject only to difference consequential on the difference of sex.

3.—(1) Until a date specified by order made by the Secretary of State the courses of training to be undergone by men as a condition of the issue of certificates to them under the Midwives Act 1951 or the Midwives (Scotland) Act 1951 (as amended by section 20) must be courses approved in writing by or on behalf of the Secretary of State for the purposes of this paragraph.
 (2) [Repealed by the Nurses, Midwives and Health Visitors Act 1979, c. 36, Sched. 8.]
 (3) [Repealed by the Nurses, Midwives and Health Visitors Act 1979, c. 36, Sched. 8.]
 (4) An order under this paragraph shall be laid in draft before each House of Parliament, and section 6(1) of the Statutory Instruments Act 1946 (Parliamentary control by negative resolution of draft instruments) shall apply accordingly.

4.—(1) If the responsible body for any educational establishment which (apart from this sub-paragraph) would be required to comply with the provisions of section 22(b), and of section 25 so far as they apply to acts to which section 22(b) relates, from the commencement of those provisions, is of the opinion that it would be impracticable for it to do so, it may before that commencement apply for an order authorising discriminatory admissions during the transitional period specified in the order.
 (2) Section 27(2) to (5) and Schedule 2 shall apply for the purposes of sub-paragraph (1) as they apply in relation to transitional exemption orders.

5.—(1) Section 6 of the Equal Pay Act 1970 (as amended by paragraph 3 of Schedule 1 to this Act) shall apply as if the references to death or retirement in subsection (1A)(b) of the said section 6 included references to sums payable on marriage in pursuance of a contract of employment made before the passing of this Act, or the commutation, at any time, of the right to such sums.
 (2) In relation to service within section 1(8) of the said Act of 1970 (service of the Crown) for the reference in this paragraph to a contract of employment made before the passing of this Act there shall be substituted a reference to terms of service entered into before the passing of this Act.

Employment Protection Act 1975

(1975 c.71)

An Act to establish machinery for promoting the improvement of industrial relations; to amend the law relating to workers' rights and otherwise to amend the law relating to workers, employers, trade unions and employers' associations; to provide for the establishment and operation of a Maternity Pay Fund; to provide for the extension of the jurisdiction of industrial tribunals; to amend the law relating to entitlement to and recoupment of unemployment benefit and supplementary benefit; to amend the Employment Agencies Act 1973 as respects the exercise of licensing functions under that Act; to amend the Employment and Training Act 1973 as respects the status of bodies established, and the powers of the Secretary of State, under that Act; to amend the Health and Safety at Work etc. Act 1974 as respects the appointment of safety representatives, health and safety at work in agriculture, the status of bodies established and the disclosure of information obtained under that Act; to provide for the extension of employment legislation to certain parliamentary staff and to certain areas outside Great Britain; and for connected purposes.

[12th November 1975]

Part I

Machinery for Promoting the Improvement of Industrial Relations

Advisory, Conciliation and Arbitration Service, etc.

Advisory, Conciliation and Arbitration Service

1.—(1) There shall be a body to be known as the Advisory, Conciliation and Arbitration Service, in this Act referred to as "the Service."

(2) The Service shall be charged with the general duty of promoting the improvement of industrial relations, and in particular of encouraging the extension of collective bargaining and the development and, where necessary, reform of collective bargaining machinery.

(3) The provisions (so far as applicable) of Parts I and III of Schedule 1 to this Act shall have effect with respect to the Service.

Conciliation

2.—(1) Where a trade dispute exists or is apprehended the Service may, at the request of one or more parties to the dispute or otherwise, offer the parties to the dispute its assistance with a view to bringing a settlement.

(2) The assistance offered by the Service may be by way of conciliation or by other means, and may include the appointment of a person other than an officer or servant of the Service to offer assistance to the parties to the dispute with a view to bringing about a settlement.

(3) In exercising its functions under subsection (1) above, the Service shall have regard to the desirability of encouraging the parties to a dispute

to use any appropriate agreed procedures for negotiation or the settlement of disputes.

(4) The Service shall designate officers of the Service to perform the functions of conciliation officers under any enactment (including any provision of this Act or any Act passed after this Act) in respect of matters which are or could be the subject of proceedings before an industrial tribunal, and accordingly any reference in any such enactment to a conciliation officer is a reference to an officer designated under this subsection.

[The next paragraph is 1–288]

Arbitration

1–288 3.—(1) Where a trade dispute exists or is apprehended the Service may, at the request of one or more parties to the dispute and with the consent of all the parties to the dispute, refer all or any of the matters to which the dispute relates for settlement to the arbitration of—
> (a) one or more persons appointed by the Service for that purpose (not being an officer or servant of the Service);
> (b) the Central Arbitration Committee constituted under section 10 below.

(2) In exercising its functions under subsection (1) above, the Service shall consider the likelihood of the dispute being settled by conciliation and, where there exists appropriate agreed procedures for negotiation or the settlement of disputes, shall not refer a matter for settlement to arbitration under that subsection unless those procedures have been used and have failed to result in a settlement or unless, in the opinion of the Service, there is a special reason which justifies arbitration under that subsection as an alternative to those procedures.

(3) Where in any case more than one arbitrator is appointed under subsection (1)(a) above the Service shall appoint one of the arbitrators to act as chairman.

(4) An award by an arbitrator appointed under subsection (1)(a) above may be published if the Service so decides and all the parties consent.

(5) Part I of the Arbitration Act 1950 shall not apply to an arbitration under this section.

(6) In the application of this section to Scotland, references to an arbitrator shall be construed as references to an arbiter.

Advice

1–289 4.—(1) The Service shall, if it thinks fit, on request or otherwise, provide, without charge, to employers, employers' associations, workers and trade unions such advice as it thinks appropriate on any matter concerned with industrial relations or employment policies, including the following—
> (a) the organisation of workers or employers for the purpose of collective bargaining;
> (b) the recognition of trade unions by employers;
> (c) machinery for the negotiation of terms and conditions of employment, and for joint consultation;
> (d) procedures for avoiding and settling disputes and workers' grievances;
> (e) questions relating to communication between employers and workers;

(f) facilities for officials of trade unions;
(g) procedures relating to the termination of employment;
(h) disciplinary matters;
(i) manpower planning, labour turnover and absenteeism;
(j) recruitment, retention, promotion and vocational training of workers;
(k) payment systems, including job evaluation and equal pay.

(2) The Service may publish general advice on any matter concerned with industrial relations or employment policies, including any of the matters referred to in paragraphs (a) to (k) of subsection (1) above.

Inquiry

5.—(1) The Service may, if it thinks fit, inquire into any question relating to industrial relations generally or to industrial relations in any particular industry or in any particular undertaking or part of an undertaking.

(2) The findings of any inquiry under this section, together with any advice given by the Service in connection with those findings, may be published by the Service if—
  (a) it appears to the Service that publication is desirable for the improvement of industrial relations, either generally or in relation to the specific question inquired into; and,
  (b) after sending a draft of the findings to, and taking into account the views of, all the parties appearing to the Service to be concerned, the Service thinks fit.

1–290

Codes of Practice

6.—(1) The Service may issue Codes of Practice containing such practical guidance as the Service thinks fit for the purpose of promoting the improvement of industrial relations.

(2) Without prejudice to the generality of subsection (1) above, the Service shall, in one or more Codes of Practice, provide practical guidance on the following matters [. . .]—
  (a) the disclosure of information, in accordance with sections 17 and 18 below, by employers to trade union representatives for the purpose of collective bargaining;
  (b) the time off to be permitted by an employer—
    (i) to a trade union official in accordance with [section 27 of the Employment Protection (Consolidation) Act 1978, including guidance on the circumstances in which a trade union official is to be permitted to take time off under that section in respect of duties connected with industrial action; and]
    (ii) to a trade union member in accordance with [section 28 of the said Act of 1978, including guidance on the question whether, and the circumstances in which, a trade union member is to be permitted to take time off under that section for trade union activities connected with industrial action].

(3) When the Service proposes to issue a Code of Practice, it shall prepare and publish a draft of that Code, shall consider any representations made to it about the draft and may modify the draft accordingly.

(4) If the Service determines to proceed with the draft, it shall transmit the draft to the Secretary of State who shall—
  (a) if he approves of it, lay it before both Houses of Parliament; and

1–291

(b) if he does not approve of it, publish details of his reasons for withholding approval.

(5) In the case of a draft Code of Practice containing practical guidance on the matters referred to in paragraph (a) or (b) of subsection (2) above, if the draft is approved by resolution of each House of Parliament the Service shall issue the Code in the form of the draft and the Code shall come into effect on such day as the Secretary of State may by order appoint.

(6) In the case of a draft Code of Practice not containing such practical guidance, if, within the period of forty days beginning with the day on which a copy of the draft is laid before each House of Parliament, or, if such copies are laid on different days, with the later of the two days, either House so resolves, no further proceedings shall be taken thereon, but without prejudice to the laying before Parliament of a new draft.

(7) In reckoning the period of forty days referred to in subsection (6) above, no account shall be taken of any period during which Parliament is dissolved or prorogued or during which both Houses are adjourned for more than four days.

(8) If no such resolution is passed as is referred to in subsection (6) above, the Service shall issue the Code in the form of the draft and the Code shall come into effect on such day as the Secretary of State may by order appoint.

(9) Without prejudice to section 123(3) below, an order under subsection (5) or subsection (8) above may contain such transitional provisions or savings as appear to the Secretary of State to be necessary or expedient in connection with the Code of Practice thereby brought into operation.

(10) The Service may from time to time revise the whole or any part of a Code of Practice issued under this section and issue that revised Code, and subsections (3) to (9) above shall apply (with appropriate modifications) to such a revised Code as they apply to the first issue of a Code.

[(10A) If the Service is of the opinion that the provisions of a Code of Practice to be issued under this section will supersede the whole or part of a Code previously issued by it under this section or by the Secretary of State under section 3 of the Employment Act 1980, it shall in the new Code state that on the day on which the new Code comes into effect in pursuance of an order under subsection (5) or (8) above the old Code or a specified part of it shall cease to have effect (subject to any transitional provisions or savings made by the order).]

(11) A failure on the part of any person to observe any provision of a Code of Practice shall not of itself render him liable to any proceedings; but in any proceedings before an industrial tribunal or the Central Arbitration Committee any Code of Practice issued under this section shall be admissible in evidence, and if any provision of such a Code appears to the tribunal or Committee to be relevant to any question arising in the proceedings it shall be taken into account in determining that question.

AMENDMENT
The words in subs. (2) were substituted by the Employment Protection (Consolidation) Act 1978 (c. 44), s.159(2), Sched. 16.
Subs. (10A) was inserted by the Employment Act 1980 (c. 44), Sched. 1, para. 4.

Certification Officer

7.—(1) The Secretary of State shall, after consultation with the Service, appoint an officer to be known as the Certification Officer.

(2) The functions under the following Acts which before the commencement of this section were performed by the Chief Registrar of Friendly Societies or any assistant registrar shall become functions of the Certification Officer, that is to say,—
   (a) the Trade Union Act 1913;
   (b) the Trade Union (Amalgamations, etc.) Act 1964;
   (c) the 1974 Act.

(3) The provisions (so far as applicable) of Parts I and III of Schedule 1 to this Act shall have effect with respect to the Certification Officer.

(4) The Certification Officer may appoint one or more assistant certification officers and shall appoint an assistant certification officer for Scotland.

(5) The Certification Officer may delegate to an assistant certification officer such functions as he thinks appropriate and in particular may delegate to the assistant certification officer for Scotland such functions as he thinks appropriate in relation to organisations whose principal office is in Scotland.

(6) References in any enactment (except in subsections (4) and (5) above, this subsection, Part I and paragraph 28 of Schedule 1 to this Act and the House of Commons Disqualification Act 1975) to the Certification Officer shall be construed as including, in relation to such functions as have been delegated in accordance with subsection (5) above, references to an assistant certification officer.

Certification as independent trade union

8.—(1) A trade union whose name is entered on the list of trade unions maintained under section 8 of the 1974 Act may apply to the Certification Officer for a certificate that it is independent.

(2) An application under subsection (1) above shall be made in such form and manner as the Certification Officer may require and shall be accompanied by a fee of [£118] or such other fee as may be prescribed by regulations made by the Secretary of State.

(3) The Certification Officer shall maintain a record showing details of all applications made under subsection (1) above and shall keep it available for public inspection (free of charge) at all reasonable hours.

(4) If an application is made, or by virtue of subsection (12) below is treated as being made, by a trade union whose name is not entered on the list of trade unions maintained under section 8 of the 1974 Act, the Certification Officer shall refuse a certificate of independence and shall enter that refusal on the record maintained in accordance with subsection (3) above.

(5) In the case of an application not falling within subsection (4) above, the Certification Officer shall—
   (a) determine whether the applicant trade union is independent;
   (b) enter his decision and the date of his decision on the record maintained in accordance with subsection (3) above; and
   (c) if he determines that the trade union is independent, issue a certificate accordingly, or, if he determines that it is not, give reasons for his decision.

(6) The Certification Officer shall not make any determination under subsection (5) above whether a trade union is independent until one month after the application has been entered on the record in accordance with subsection (3) above, and before making such a determination he shall

make such inquiries as he thinks fit and shall take into account any relevant information submitted to him by any person.

(7) The Certification Officer may at any time withdraw a certificate, in accordance with subsection (8) below, if he is of the opinion that the trade union in question is no longer independent.

(8) Where the Certification Officer proposes to withdraw a certificate under subsection (7) above—
   (a) he shall notify the trade union concerned of the proposal;
   (b) subsections (3), (5) and (6) above shall apply (with appropriate modifications) to such a proposal as they apply to an application under subsection (1) above; and
   (c) the Certification Officer shall confirm or withdraw the certificate accordingly.

(9) A trade union aggrieved by the refusal of the Certification Officer to issue it with a certificate or by a decision of his to withdraw its certificate may appeal, in accordance with [section 136(3) of the Employment Protection (Consolidation) Act 1978], to the Employment Appeal Tribunal; and on any such appeal the Tribunal, if satisfied that the certificate should be issued or as the case may be should not be withdrawn, shall declare that fact and give directions to the Certification Officer accordingly.

(10) Where the name of an organisation is removed from the list of trade unions maintained under section 8 of the 1974 Act, the Certification Officer shall cancel any certificate of independence in force in respect of that organisation by entering on the record the fact that the organisation's name has been removed from the said list and that the certificate is accordingly cancelled.

(11) A certificate of independence which is in force, or, as the case may be, a refusal, withdrawal or cancellation of a certificate entered on the record, shall for all purposes be conclusive evidence that the trade union in question is, or, as the case may be, is not, independent; and a document purporting to be such a certificate or a certified copy of such an entry on the record, and to be signed by the Certification Officer or by any person authorised to act on his behalf, shall be taken to be such a certificate or a true copy of such an entry unless the contrary is proved.

(12) If in any proceedings before any court, the Employment Appeal Tribunal, the Central Arbitration Committee, the Service, or an industrial tribunal a question arises as to whether a trade union is independent and there is no certificate of independence in force and no refusal, withdrawal or cancellation of a certificate recorded in relation to that trade union—
   (a) the question shall not be decided in those proceedings, and those proceedings shall be stayed or, in Scotland, sisted until a certificate has been issued or refused by the Certification Officer; and
   (b) the body before whom the proceedings are stayed, or sisted, may refer the question as to the independence of the trade union to the Certification Officer who shall proceed in accordance with subsection (3) to (6) above as if the reference were an application by that trade union.

AMENDMENT

The words in square brackets in subs. (9) were substituted by the Employment Protection (Consolidation) Act 1978 (c. 44), s.159(2), Sched. 16.

The fee of £118 was substituted in subs. (2) by the Certification Officer (Amendment of Fees) Regulations 1981 (S.I. 1981 No. 1631).

Custody of documents

9.—(1) The Certification Officer shall take custody of all annual returns, accounts, copies of rules and other documents submitted, for the purposes of the Trade Union Acts 1871 to 1964 or the Industrial Relations Act 1971 or the 1974 Act to the Chief Registrar of Friendly Societies or any assistant registrar, or to the Registrar of Trade Unions and Employers' Associations or any assistant registrar, and which are, on the commencement of this section, in the custody of the Chief Registrar of Friendly Societies or any assistant registrar.

(2) The Certification Officer shall keep available for public inspection (either free of charge or on payment of a reasonable charge) at all reasonable hours such of the documents referred to in subsection (1) above as are, or were, available for public inspection in pursuance of any of the Acts referred to in that subsection.

1–294

Central Arbitration Committee

10.—(1) There shall be a body to be known as the Central Arbitration Committee, in this Act referred to as the "Committee".

(2) Any reference in any enactment, statutory instrument or other document to the Industrial Arbitration Board (whether by that or any other name) shall be construed as a reference to the Committee.

(3) The provisions of Part II and (so far as applicable) Parts I and III of Schedule 1 to this Act shall have effect with respect to the Committee.

1–295

. . . .

Disclosure of Information

[handwritten: S.126 EPA. → S.29]

General duty of employers to disclose information

17.—(1) For the purposes of all the stages of such collective bargaining between an employer and representatives of an independent trade union as is referred to in subsection (2) below, it shall be the duty of the employer, subject to section 18 below, to disclose to those representatives on request all such information relating to his undertaking as is in his possession, or that of any associated employer, and is both—

   (a) information without which the trade union representatives would be to a material extent impeded in carrying on with him such collective bargaining, and

   (b) information which it would be in accordance with good industrial relations practice that he should disclose to them for the purposes of collective bargaining.

(2) The collective bargaining for the purposes of which an employer must disclose information under subsection (1) above is collective bargaining about matters, and in relation to description of workers,—

   (a) in respect of which the trade union is recognised by that employer;

   (b) [. . .]

and in this section and sections 19 to 21 below "representative", in relation to a trade union, means an official or other person authorised by the trade union to carry on such collective bargaining.

(3) Where a request for information is made by trade union representatives under this section, the request shall, if the employer so requests, be in writing.

1–296

(4) In determining, for the purposes of subsection (1)(*b*) above, what would be in accordance with good industrial relations practice, regard shall be had to the relevant provisions of any Code of Practice issued by the Service under section 6 above, but not so as to exclude any other evidence of what that practice is.

(5) Where an employer is required by virtue of this section to disclose any information to trade union representatives, the disclosure of it shall, if they so request, be in writing or be confirmed in writing.

AMENDMENT
Subs. (2)(*b*) was repealed by the Employment Act 1980 (c. 42), Sched. 2.

Restrictions on general duty under s.17

1–297
18.—(1) No employer shall, by virtue of section 17 above, be required to disclose—
  (*a*) any information the disclosure of which would be against the interests of national security, or
  (*b*) any information which he could not disclose without contravening a prohibition imposed by or under an enactment, or
  (*c*) any information which has been communicated to the employer in confidence, or which the employer has otherwise obtained in consequence of the confidence reposed in him by another person, or
  (*d*) any information relating specifically to an individual, unless he has consented to its being disclosed, or
  (*e*) any information the disclosure of which would cause substantial injury to the employer' undertaking for reasons other than its effect on collective bargaining, or
  (*f*) any information obtained by the employer for the purpose of bringing, prosecuting or defending any legal proceedings;
and in formulating the provisions of any Code of Practice relating to the disclosure of information, the Service shall have regard to the provisions of this subsection.

(2) In the performance of his duty under section 17 above an employer shall not be required—
  (*a*) to produce, or allow inspection of, any document (other than a document prepared for the purpose of conveying or confirming the information) or to make a copy of or extracts from any document, or
  (*b*) to compile or assemble any information where the compilation or assembly would involve an amount of work or expenditure out of reasonable proportion to the value of the information in the conduct of collective bargaining.

Complaint of failure to disclose information

1–298
19.—(1) An independent trade union may present to the Central Arbitration Committee, in writing in such form as the Committee may require, a complaint that an employer has failed to disclose to representatives of that trade union information which he was required to disclose to them by section 17 above, or to confirm any such information in writing in accordance with subsection (5) of that section.

(2) If on receipt of such a complaint the Committee is of the opinion that the complaint is reasonably likely to be settled by conciliation, it shall refer the complaint to the Service and shall notify the trade union and employer

accordingly, whereupon the Service shall seek to promote a settlement of the matter.

(3) If the complaint is not settled or withdrawn and the Service is of the opinion that further attempts at conciliation are unlikely to result in a settlement it shall inform the Committee of its opinion.

(4) If the complaint is not referred to the Service under subsection (2) above, or, if it is so referred, on the Service informing the Committee of its opinion in accordance with subsection (3) above, the Committee shall proceed to hear and determine the complaint and shall make a declaration stating whether it finds the complaint well-founded, wholly or in part, and stating the reasons for its findings.

(5) On the hearing of a complaint under this section any person who the Committee considers has a proper interest in the complaint shall be entitled to be heard by the Committee, but a failure to accord a hearing to a person other than the trade union and employer directly concerned shall not affect the validity of any decision of the Committee in those proceedings.

(6) If the Committee finds the complaint wholly or partly well-founded, the declaration shall specify—
- (*a*) the information in respect of which the Committee finds that the complaint is well founded;
- (*b*) the date (or, if more than one, the earliest date) on which the employer refused or failed to disclose, or, as the case may be, to confirm in writing, any of the information specified under paragraph (*a*) above; and
- (*c*) a period (not being less than one week from the date of the declaration) within which the employer ought to disclose, or, as the case may be, to confirm in writing, the information specified under paragraph (*a*) above.

(7) On a hearing of a complaint under this section a certificate signed by or on behalf of a Minister of the Crown and certifying that a particular request for information could not be complied with except by disclosing information the disclosure of which would have been against the interests of national security shall be conclusive evidence of that fact: and a document which purports to be such a certificate shall be taken to be such a certificate unless the contrary is proved.

Further complaint arising from failure to disclose information

20.—(1) At any time after the expiration of the period specified in a declaration under section 19(6)(*c*) above the trade union may present to the Committee, in writing in such form as the Committee may require, a complaint (hereafter in this section and section 21 below referred to as a "further complaint") that the employer has failed to disclose, or, as the case may be, to confirm in writing, to representatives of that union information specified in the declaration under section 19(6)(*a*) above.

(2) On receipt of a further complaint the Committee shall proceed to hear and determine the complaint and shall make a declaration stating whether it finds the complaint well-founded, wholly or in part, and stating the reasons for its findings.

(3) On the hearing of a further complaint under this section any person who the Committee considers has a proper interest in the complaint shall be entitled to be heard by the Committee, but a failure to accord a hearing

to a person other than the trade union and employer directly concerned shall not affect the validity of any decision of the Committee in those proceedings.

(4) If the Committee finds the further complaint wholly or partly well-founded the declaration shall specify the information in respect of which the Committee finds that the complaint is well-founded.

Determination of claim and award

1–300

21.—(1) On or after presenting a further complaint under section 20 above, the trade union may present to the Committee, in writing, a claim in respect of one or more descriptions of employees (but not workers who are not employees) specified in the claim that their contracts should include the terms and conditions specified in the claim.

(2) The right to present a claim under subsection (1) above shall expire, or, as the case may be, a claim so presented shall be treated as withdrawn, if at any time before the Committee makes an award under this section the employer discloses, or, as the case may be, confirms in writing, to representatives of the trade union the information specified in the declaration under section 19(6)(a) or, as the case may be, section 20(4) above.

(3) If the Committee finds, or has found, the further complaint wholly or partly well-founded, it may, after hearing the parties, make an award that in respect of any description of employees specified in the claim the employer shall, from a specified date, observe either—

(a) the terms and conditions specified in the claim; or
(b) other terms and conditions which the Committee considers appropriate.

(4) The date specified in an award under subsection (3) abvoe may be a date earlier than that on which the award is made but shall not be earlier than the date specified in accordance with section 19(6)(b) above in the declaration made by the Committee on the original complaint.

(5) An award under subsection (3) above shall be made only in respect of a description of employees, and shall comprise only terms and conditions relating to matters,—

(a) in respect of which the trade union making the claim is recognised by the employer;
(b) [. . .]

(6) Any terms and conditions which by an award under this section the employer is required to observe in respect of employees of his shall have effect as part of the contract of employment of any such employee, as from the date specified in the award, except in so far as they are superseded or varied—

(a) by a subsequent award under this section;
(b) by a collective agreement between the employer and the union for the time being representing that employee; or
(c) by express or implied agreement between the employee and the employer so far as that agreement effects an improvement in any terms and the conditions having effect by virtue of the award.

(7) Where—

(a) by virtue of any enactment, other than one contained in this section, providing for minimum remuneration or terms and conditions, a contract of employment is to have effect as modified by an award, order or other instrument under that enactment; and

(b) by virtue of an award under this section any terms and conditions are to have effect as part of that contract,

that contract shall have effect in accordance with that award, order or other instrument or in accordance with the award under this section, whichever is the more favourable, in respect of any terms and conditions of that contract, to the employee.

(8) No award shall be made under this section in respect of any terms and conditions of employment which are fixed by virtue of any enactment.

AMENDMENT
  The words omitted in subs. 5(b) were repealed by the Employment Act 1980 (c. 42), Sched. 2.

. . . . . .

Financing of Maternity Pay Fund

40.—(1) In the Social Security Act 1975 for the words "appropriate allocation to the Redundancy Fund", wherever they occur, substitute the words "appropriate employment protection allocation". 1–301

(2) In section 1(1) of that Act (outline of contributory system), after the words "Redundancy Fund" insert the words "and the Maternity Pay Fund".

(3) [*Repealed by the Social Security (Miscellaneous Provisions) Act* 1977 (*c.* 5), *s.*24(6), *Sched.* 2.]

(4) In section 122(4) of that Act (power to alter contributions), after the words "the Redundancy Fund" insert the words "or the Maternity Pay Fund", and for the words "that Fund" substitute the words "either or both those Funds".

(5) In section 134 of that Act (destination of contributions etc.)—
  (a) in subsection (4), for the words "0·2 per cent." substitute the words "0·25 per cent."; and
  (b) in subsection (5)(b), for the words "that Fund" substitute the words "Redundancy Fund and the Maternity Pay Fund in such shares as the Secretary of State may, with the consent of the Treasury, determine."

(6) In Schedule 20 to that Act (glossary of expressions), at the appropriate place in alphabetical order insert in the first column the entry "Appropriate employment protection allocation" and against it in the second column insert the entry "See section 134(4).".

. . . . . .

Powers of Agricultural Wages Boards

Amendments of Agricultural Wages Acts

97.—(1) For section 3 of the Agricultural Wages Act 1948 (power to fix remuneration and holidays) there shall be substituted the section set out in Part I of Schedule 9 to this Act (which reproduces section 3 with amendments enabling the Agricultural Wages Board to fix other terms and conditions of employment as well as remuneration and holidays and to specify the date from which remuneration fixed by them is to be payable). 1–302

(2) The other provisions of that Act shall have effect subject to the

amendments set out in Part II of Schedule 9 to this Act, being minor and consequential amendments.

(3) For section 3 of the Agricultural Wages (Scotland) Act 1949 (power to fix remuneration and holidays) there shall be substituted the section set out in Part I of Schedule 10 to this Act (which reproduces section 3 with amendments enabling the Scottish Agricultural Wages Board to fix other terms and conditions of employment as well as remuneration and holidays and to specify the date from which remuneration fixed by them is to be payable).

(4) The other provisions of the said Act of 1949 shall have efect subject to the amendments set out in Part II of Schedule 10 to this Act, being minor and consequential amendments.

. . . . . .

Duty of employer to consult trade union representatives on redundancy

99.—(1) An employer proposing to dismiss as redundant an employee of a description in respect of which an independent trade union is recognised by him shall consult representatives of that trade union about the dismissal in accordance with the following provisions of this section.

(2) In this section and sections 100 and 101 below, "trade union representative" in relation to a trade union means an official or other person authorised to carry on collective bargaining with the employer in question by that trade union.

(3) The consultation required by this section shall begin at the earliest opportunity, and shall in any event begin—

(a) where the employer is proposing to dismiss as redundant 100 or more employees at one establishment within a period of 90 days or less, at least 90 days before the first of those dismissals takes effect; or

(b) where the employer is proposing to dismiss as redundant 10 or more employees at one establishment within a period of 30 days or less, [at least 30 days] before the first of those dismissals takes effect.

(4) In determining for the purpose of subsection (3) above whether an employer is proposing to dismiss as redundant 100 or more, or, as the case may be, 10 or more, employees within the periods mentioned in that subsection, no account shall be taken of employees whom he proposes to dismiss as redundant in respect of whose proposed dismissals consultation has already begun.

(5) For the purposes of the consultation required by this section the employer shall disclose in writing to trade union representatives—

(a) the reasons for his proposals;
(b) the numbers and descriptions of employees whom it is proposed to dismiss as redundant;
(c) the total number of employees of any such description employed by the employer at the establishment in question;
(d) the proposed method of selecting the employees who may be dismissed; and
(e) the proposed method of carrying out the dismissals, with due regard to any agreed procedure, including the period over which the dismissals are to take effect.

(6) The information which is to be given to trade union representatives

under this section shall be delivered to them, or sent by post to an address notified by them to the employer, or sent by post to the union at the address of its head or main office.

(7) In the course of the consultation required by this section the employer shall—
- (a) consider any representations made by the trade union representatives; and
- (b) reply to those representations and, if he rejects any of those representations, state his reasons.

(8) If in any case there are special circumstances which render it not reasonably practicable for the employer to comply with any of the requirements of subsections (3), (5) or (7) above, the employer shall take all such steps towards compliance with that requirement as are reasonably practicable in those circumstances.

(9) This section shall not be construed as conferring any rights on a trade union or an employee except as provided by section 101 to 103 below.

AMENDMENT

The words in square brackets in subs. (3)(b) were substituted by the Employment Protection (Handling of Redundancies) Variation Order 1979 (S.I. 1979 No. 958).

Duty of employer to notify Secretary of State of certain redundancies

100.—(1) An employer proposing to dismiss as redundant—
- (a) 100 or more employees at one establishment within a period of 90 days or less; or
- (b) 10 or more employees at one establishment within a period of 30 days or less,

shall notify the Secretary of State, in writing, of his proposal—
- (i) in a case falling within paragraph (a) above, at least 90 days before the first of those dismissals takes effect; and
- (ii) in a case falling within paragraph (b) above, [at least 30 days] before the first of those dismissals takes effect,

and where the notice relates to employees of any description in respect of which an independent trade union is recognised by him, he shall give a copy of the notice to representatives of that union.

(2) In determining for the purpose of subsection (1) above whether an employer is proposing to dismiss as redundant 100 or more, or, as the case may be, 10 or more, employees within the periods mentioned in that subsection, no account shall be taken of employees whom he proposes to dismiss as redundant in respect of whose proposed dismissals notice has already been given to the Secretary of State.

(3) A notice under this section shall—
- (a) be given to the Secretary of State by delivery to him or by sending it by post to him, at such address as the Secretary of State may direct in relation to the establishment where the employees proposed to be dismissed are employed;
- (b) in a case where consultation with trade union representatives is required by section 90 above, identify the trade union concerned and state the date when consultation began; and
- (c) be in such form and contain such particulars, in addition to those required by paragraph (b) above, as the Secretary of State may direct.

(4) The copy of the notice under this section which is to be given to trade

union representatives shall be delivered to them, or sent by post to an address notified by them to the employer, or sent by post to the union at the address of its head or main office.

(5) At any time after receiving a notice under this section from an employer the Secretary of State may by written notice require the employer to give him such further information as may be specified in the requirement.

(6) If in any case there are special circumstances rendering it not reasonably practicable for the employer to comply with any of the requirements of subsections (1) to (5) above, he shall take all such steps towards compliance with that requirement as are reasonably practicable in those circumstances.

AMENDMENT

The words in subs. (1)(ii) were substituted by the Employment Protection (Handling of Redundancies) Variation Order 1979 (S.I. 1979 No. 958).

Complaint by trade union and protective award

1–305   101.—(1) An appropriate trade union may present a complaint to an industrial tribunal on the ground that an employer has dismissed as redundant or is proposing to dismiss as redundant one or more employees and has not complied with any of the requirements of section 99 above.

(2) If on a complaint under this section a question arises as to the matters referred to in section 99(8) above, it shall be for the employer to show—

(a) that there were special circumstances which rendered it not reasonably practicable for him to comply with any requirement of section 99 above; and

(b) that he took all such steps towards compliance with that requirement as were reasonably practicable in those circumstances.

(3) Where the tribunal finds a complaint under subsection (1) above well-founded it shall make a declaration to that effect and may also make a protective award in accordance with subsection (4) below.

(4) A protective award is an award that in respect of such descriptions of employees as may be specified in the award, being employees who have been dismissed, or whom it is proposed to dismiss, as redundant, and in respect of whose dismissal or proposed dismissal the employer has failed to comply with any requirement of section 99 above, the employer shall pay remuneration for a protected period.

(5) The protected period under an award under subsection (4) above shall be a period beginning with the date on which the first of the dismissals to which the complaint relates takes effect, or the date of the award, whichever is the earlier, of suh length as the tribunal shall determine to be just and equitable in all the circumstances having regard to the seriousness of the employer's default in complying with any requirement of section 99 above, not exceeding—

(a) in a case falling within section 99(3)(a) above, 90 days;

(b) in a case falling within section 99(3)(b) above, [30 days]; or

(c) in any other case, 28 days.

(6) An industrial tribunal shall not consider a complaint under subsection (1) above in respect of an employer's default in relation to a dismissal or proposed dismissal unless it is presented to the tribunal before the pro-

posed dismissal takes effect or before the end of the period of three months beginning with the date on which the dismissal takes effect or within such further period as the tribunal considers reasonable in a case where it is satisfied that it was not reasonably practicable for the complaint to be presented within the period of three months.

(7) "Appropriate trade union", in relation to an employee of any description, means an independent trade union recognised by his employer in respect of that description of employee.

AMENDMENT
The words in square brackets in subs. (5)(*b*) are substituted by the Employment Protection (Handling of Redundancies) Variation Order 1979 (S.I. 1979 No. 958).

Entitlement under protective award

102.—(1) Where an industrial tribunal has made a protective award under section 101 above, every employee of a description to which the award relates shall be entitled, subject to the following provisions of this section, to be paid remuneration by his employer for the protected period specified in the award.

(2) The rate of remuneration payable under a protective award shall be a week's pay for each week of the protected period, and if remuneration falls to be calculated for a period less than one week the amount of a week's pay shall be reduced proportionately.

(3) Any payment made to an employee by an employer under his contract of employment, or by way of damages for breach of that contract, in respect of a period falling within a protected period, shall go towards discharging the employer's liability to pay remuneration under the protective award in respect of that first mentioned period, and conversely any payment of remuneration under a protective award in respect of any period shall go towards discharging any liability of the employer under, or in respect of breach of, the contract of employment in respect of that period.

(4) In respect of a period during which he is employed by the employer an employee shall not be entitled to remuneration under a protective award unless he would be entitled to be paid by the employer in respect of that period, either by virtue of his contract of employment or by virtue of [Schedule 3 to the Employment Protection (Consolidation) Act 1978] (rights of employee in period of notice), if that period fell within the period of notice required to be given by [section 49(1)].

(5) Where the employee is employed by the employer during the protected period and—
   (*a*) he is fairly dismissed by his employer for a reason other than redundancy; or
   (*b*) he unreasonably terminates the contract of employment,
then, subject to the following provisions of this section, he shall not be entitled to remuneration under the protective award in respect of any period during which but for that dismissal or termination he would have been employed.

(6) If an employer makes an employee an offer (whether in writing or not and whether before or after the ending of his employment under the previous contract) to renew his contract of employment, or to re-engage him under a new contract, so that the renewal or re-engagement would take effect before or during the protected period and either—
   (*a*) the provisions of the conract as renewed, or of the new contract, as

to the capacity and place in which he would be employed, and as to the other terms and conditions of his employment, would not differ from the corresponding provisions of the previous contract; or

(b) the first mentioned provisions would differ from those corresponding provisions, but the offer constitutes an offer of suitable employment in relation to the employee;

the provisions of subsections (7) to (11) below shall effect.

(7) If, in a case to which subsection (6) above applies, the employee unreasonably refuses that offer, then, he shall not be entitled to any remuneration under a protective award in respect of any period during which but for that refusal he would have been employed.

(8) If an employee's contract of employmnt is renewed, or he is re-engaged under a new contract of employment, in pursuance of such an offer as is referred to in subsection (6)(b) above, there shall be a trial period in relation to the contract as renewed, or the new contract (whether or not there has been a previous trial period under this section).

(9) The trial period shall begin with the ending of the employee's employment under the previous contract and end with the expiration of the period of four weeks beginning with the date on which the employee starts work under the contract as renewed, or the new contract, or such longer period as may be agreed in accordance with subsection (10) below for the purpose of retraining the employee for employment under that contract.

(10) Any such agreement shall—
   (a) be made between the employer and the employee or his representative before the employee starts work under the contract as renewed or, as the case may be, the new contract;
   (b) be in writing;
   (c) specify the date of the end of the trial period; and
   (d) specify the terms and conditions of employment which will apply in the employee's case after the end of that period.

(11) If during the trial period—
   (a) the employee, for whatever reason, terminates the contract, or gives notice to terminate it and the contract is thereafter, in consequence, terminated; or
   (b) the employer, for a reason connected with or arising out of the change to the renewed, or new, employment, terminates the contract, or gives notice to terminate it and the contract is thereafter, in consequence terminated,

then, the employee shall remain entitled under the protective award unless, in a case falling within paragraph (a) above, he acted unreasonably in terminating or giving notice to terminate the contract.

AMENDMENT
The words in square brackets in subs. (4) were substituted by the Employment Protection (Consolidation) Act 1978 (c. 44), s.159(2), Sched. 16.

Complaint by employee to industrial tribunal

103.—(1) An employee may present a complaint to an industrial tribunal on the ground that he is an employee of a description to which a protective award relates and that his employer has failed, wholly or in part, to pay him remuneration under that award.

(2) An industrial tribunal shall not entertain a complaint under subsec-

tion (1) above unless it is presented to the tribunal before the end of the period of three months beginning with the day (or, if the complaint relates to more than one day, the last of the days) in respect of which the complaint is made of failure to pay remuneration, or within such further period as the tribunal considers reasonable in a case where it is satisfied that it was not reasonably practicable for the complaint to be presented within the period of three months.

(3) Where the tribunal finds a complaint under subsection (1) above well-founded it shall order the employer to pay the complainant the amount of remuneration which it finds is due to him.

Reduction of rebate on failure to notify redundancies

104.—(1) Where an employer— 1–308
   (*a*) is under [section 104(1) of the Employment Protection (Consolidation) Act 1978] (rebates in respect of redundancy, etc., payments) entitled to any rebate in respect of a payment made to an employee dismissed by reason of redundancy; and
   (*b*) fails to give notice to the Secretary of State in accordance with section 100 above of his proposal to dismiss that employee,
the Secretary of State may, subject to subsection (2) below, reduce the amount of that rebate by such proportion (not exceeding one-tenth) as appears to the Secretary of State to be appropriate in the circumstances.

(2) No reduction of a rebate shall be made in respect of a failure to comply with section 100 above if proceedings have been instituted for an offence under section 105 below arising out of the same failure by the employer.

(3) Where the Secretary of State reduces a rebate in pursuance of this section, the employer may appeal to an industrial tribunal within the period of three months beginning with the date on which the decision of the Secretary of State is communicated to him or within such further period as the tribunal considers reasonable in a case where it is satisfied that it was not reasonably practicable for the appeal to be presented within the period of three months.

(4) Where on an appeal under this section an industrial tribunal is satisfied that a rebate which was reduced to any extent should not have been reduced, or should have been reduced by a greater or lesser proportion, the tribunal shall determine accordingly, and the Secretary of State shall comply with the determination.

AMENDMENT

The words in square brackets in subs. (1)(*a*) were substituted by the Employment Protection (Consolidation) Act 1978 (c.44), s.159(2), Sched. 16.

Offence and proceedings

105.—(1) If an employer fails to give notice to the Secretary of State in 1–309
accordance with section 100 above, he shall be liable on summary conviction to a fine not exceeding £400.

(2) Proceedings in England and Wales for an offence under subsection (1) above shall be instituted only by or with the consent of the Secretary of State or by an officer authorised for that purpose by special or general directions of the Secretary of State.

(3) An officer so authorised may, although not of counsel or a solicitor, prosecute or conduct before a magistrates' court any proceedings for such an offence.

(4) No proceedings for an offence under subsection (1) above shall be instituted in respect of a failure to comply with section 100 above if the Secretary of State has, by reason of the same failure by the employer, reduced to any extent, in accordance with section 104 above, the amount payable to the employer of any rebate.

(5) For the purposes of subsection (4) above, a certificate signed by or on behalf of the Secretary of State stating that no such reduction of a rebate has been made shall be conclusive evidence of that fact; and a document which purports to be such a certificate shall be taken to be such a certificate unless the contrary is proved.

Supplementary

106.—(1) [*Repealed by the Employment Act 1980, Sched. 2.*]

(2) For the purposes of any proceedings under this Part of this Act, the dismissal or proposed dismissal of an employee shall be presumed, unless the contrary is proved, to be by reason of redundancy.

(3) [Schedule 14 to the Employment Protection (Consolidation) Act 1978 shall apply for the calculation of a week's pay for the purposes of section 102 above, and for the purposes of Part II of that Schedule, the calculation date is—
   (*a*) in the case of an employee who was dismissed before the date on which the protective award was made, the date which by virtue of paragraph 7(1)(*k*) or (*l*) of the said Schedule 14] is the calculation date for the purpose of computing the amount of a redundancy payment in relation to that dismissal (whether or not the employee concerned is entitled to any such payment); and
   (*b*) in any other case, the date on which the protective award was made.

(4) The Secretary of State may by order vary the provisions of sections 99(3) and 100(1) above and the periods referred to in section 101(5)(*a*) to (*c*) above and may vary those provisions or periods either generally or in their application to any description of employees, but no such order shall be made which has the effect of reducing to less than 30 days the periods referred to in sections 99(3) and 100(1) as the periods which must elapse before the first of the dismissals takes effect.

(5) No order shall be made under subsection (4) above unless a draft of the order has been laid before Parliament and approved by a resolution of each House of Parliament.

AMENDMENT
   The words in square brackets in subs. (3) were substituted by the Employment Protection (Consolidation) Act 1978 (c. 44), s. 159(2), Sched. 16.

Power to adapt foregoing provisions in case of collective agreements on redundancies

107.—(1) If at any time there is in force a collective agreement which establishes—
   (*a*) arrangements for providing alternative employment for employees to whom the agreement relates if they are dismissed as redundant by an employer to whom it relates; or
   (*b*) arrangements for the handling of redundancies;

and on the application of all the parties to the agreement the Secretary of State, having regard to the provisions of the agreement, is satisfied that the arrangements are on the whole at least as favourable to those employees as the foregoing provisions of this Part of this Act, he may make an order under this section adapting, modifying or excluding any of those provisions both in their application to all or any of those employees and in their application to any other employees of any such employer.

(2) The Secretary of State shall not make an order under this section in respect of an agreement unless—
 (a) the agreement provides for procedures to be followed (whether by arbitration or otherwise) in cases where an employee to whom the agreement relates claims that an employer or other person to whom it relates has not complied with the provisions of the agreement, and that those procedures include a right to arbitration or adjudication by an independent referee or body in cases where (by reason of an equality of votes or otherwise) a decision cannot otherwise be reached; or
 (b) the agreement indicates that any such employee may present a complaint to an industrial tribunal that any such employer or other person has not complied with those provisions.

(3) An order under this section may confer on an industrial tribunal to whom a complaint is presented as mentioned in subsection (2)(b) above such powers and duties as the Secretary of State considers appropriate.

(4) Without prejudice to section 123 below, an order under this section may be varied or revoked by a subsequent order thereunder, whether in pursuance of an application made by all or any of the parties to the agreement in question or without any such application.

Part V

Miscellaneous and Supplementary Provisions

General provisions as to industrial tribunals and conciliation officers

108.—(1) The remedy of an employee for infringement of any of the rights conferred on him by any provision of this Act shall, if provision is made for a complaint or for the reference of a question to an industrial tribunal, be by way of such complaint or reference in accordance with the relevant provisions of this Act and with tribunal regulations made under [paragraph 1 of Schedule 9 to the Employment Protection (Consolidation) Act 1978,] and not otherwise.

(2)–(8) [. . .]

1–312

AMENDMENT
The words in square brackets in subs. (1) were replaced by the Employment Protection (Consolidation) Act 1978 (c. 44). Subss. (2)–(8) were repealed by the 1978 Act.

. . . . . .

Death of employee or employer

110. The provisions of Schedule 12 to this Act shall have effect in relation to the death of an employee or employer.

1–313

Disentitlement to unemployment benefit and supplementary benefit during trade dispute

1–314   **111.**—(1) In section 19(1) of the Social Security Act 1975 (disqualification for unemployment benefit where stoppage of work due to trade dispute)—

(a) in paragraph (a) the words "or financing" and the word "and", and
(b) paragraph (b),

are hereby repealed.

(2) [*Repealed by the Supplementary Benefits Act* 1976 (c. 71).]

. . . . . .

Amendments of the Employment Agencies Act 1973

1–315   **114.** The Employment Agencies Act 1973 shall have effect subject to the amendments specified in Schedule 13 to this Act, being amendments which transfer the licensing functions under that Act from local authorities to the Secretary of State.

Amendments of the Employment and Training Act 1973

1–316   **115.** The Employment and Training Act 1973 shall have effect subject to the amendments specified in Schedule 14 to this Act, being amendments which provide for the status of the bodies established under section 1(1) of that Act and enlarge the powers of the Secretary of State to make arrangements for the purpose of providing or obtaining employment.

Amendments of the Health and Safety at Work etc. Act 1974

1–317   **116.** The Health and Safety at Work etc. Act 1974 shall have effect subject to the amendments specified in Schedule 15 to this Act, being amendments which restrict the appointment of safety representatives to those appointed by recognised trade unions, remove the special provisions relating to health and safety at work in agriculture and enable certain statements to be given notwithstanding the restrictions on disclosure of information obtained under that Act.

Offences by bodies corporate

1–318   **117.**—(1) Where an offence under this Act committed by a body corporate is proved to have been committed with the consent or connivance of, or to be attributable to any neglect on the part of, any director, manager, secretary or other similar officer of the body corporate, or any person who was purporting to act in any such capacity, he as well as the body corporate shall be guilty of that offence and shall be liable to be proceeded against and punished accordingly.

(2) Where the affairs of a body corporate are managed by its members, subsection (1) above shall apply in relation to the acts and defaults of a member in connection with his functions of management as if he were a director of the body corporate.

Restrictions on contracting out

1–319   **118.**—(1) Except as provided by subsection (2) below, any provision in an agreement (whether a contract of employment or not) shall be void in so far as it purports—

(a) to exclude or limit the operation of any provision of this Act; or

(b) to preclude any person from presenting a complaint to, or bringing any proceedings under this Act before, an industrial tribunal, or for making any reference, claim, complaint or application under this Act to the Service or the Committee.

(2) Subsection (1) above shall not apply—
    (a) to any provision in a collective agreement excluding rights under [. . .] Part IV of this Act, if an order under [. . .] section 107 above is for the time being in force in respect of it;
    (b) [*Repealed by the Employment Protection (Consolidation) Act 1978 (c. 44), s.159(3), Sched. 17.*]
    (c) [*Repealed by the Employment Protection (Consolidation) Act 1978 (c. 44), s.159(3), Sched. 17.*]
    (d) to any agreement such as is referred to in section [. . .] 21(6)(b) or (c) above, [. . .] to the extent that it varies or supersedes an award under section [. . .] 21 above [. . .].

AMENDMENTS

The words omitted in subs. (2)(a) were repealed by the Employment Protection (Consolidation) Act 1978 (c. 44), s.159(3), Sched. 17. The words omitted in subs. (2)(d) were repealed by the Employment Act 1980 (c. 42), Sched. 2.

Excluded classes of employment

119.—(1) Subject to the following provisions of this section, [Part IV of this Act applies] to every employment.

(2) [*Repealed by the Employment Protection (Consolidation) Act 1978 (c.44), s.159(3), Sched. 17.*]

(3) [*Repealed by the Dock Work Regulation Act 1976 (c.79).*]

(4) The following provisions of this Act do not apply to employment as master or as a member of the crew of a fishing vessel, where the employee is not remunerated otherwise than by a share in the profits or gross earnings of the vessel, that is to say, sections [. . .] 99 and 100.

(5) the following provisions of this Act do not apply to employment where under his contract of employment the employee ordinarily works outside Great Britain, that is to say, sections [. . .] 99 and 100.

(6) For the purposes of subsection (5) above a person employed to work on board a ship registered in the United Kingdom (not being a ship registered at a port outside Great Britain) shall, unless—
    (a) the employment is wholly outside Great Britain or
    (b) he is not ordinarily resident in Great Britain,
be regarded as a person who under his contract ordinarily works in Great Britain.

(7) The following provisions of this Act do not apply to employment under a contract for a fixed term of [three months] or less or to employment under a contract made in contemplation of the performance of a specific task which is not expected to last for more than [three months] unless in either case the employee has been continuously employed for a period of more than [three months] that is to say, sections [. . .] 99 and 100.

[Section 151 of and Schedule 13 to the Employment Protection (Consolidation) Act 1978 (computation of period of continuous employment), and any provision modifying or supplementing that section or Schedule for the purposes of that Act, shall apply for the purposes of this subsection as if this subsection were contained in that Act.]

(8)–(11) [*Repealed by the Employment Protection (Consolidation) Act 1978 (c.44), s.159(3), Sched. 17.*]

(12) The following provisions of this Act do not apply to employment as a merchant seaman, that is to say, sections [. . .] 99 and 100.

(13) Subject to subsection (14) below, employment as a merchant seaman does not include employment in the fishing industary or employment on board a ship otherwise than by the owner, manager or charterer of that ship except employment as a radio officer but save as aforesaid includes employment as master or a member of the crew of any ship, as an apprentice to the sea service, and as a trainee undergoing training for the sea service, and employment in or about a ship in port by the owner, manager or charterer of the ship to do work of the kind ordinarily done by a merchant seaman on such a ship while it is in port.

(14) For the purposes of subsection (12) above as it applies in relation to sections 99 and 100, employment as a merchant seaman means employment as master or as a member of the crew of a sea-going ship, including an apprentice or trainee employed on any such ship and employment as a radio officer on such a ship.

(15) The Secretary of State may by order—
    (*a*) provide that any enactment contained in this Act which is specified in the order shall not apply to persons or to employments of such classes as may be prescribed by the order, or shall apply to persons or employments of such classes as may be prescribed by the order subject to such exceptions and modifications as may be so prescribed;
    (*b*) vary or revoke any of the provisions of subsection (1) to (14) of this section.

(16) No order under subsection (15) above shall be made unless a draft of the order has been laid before Parliament and approved by a resolution of each House of Parliament.

(17) [*Repealed by the Employment Act 1982 (c.46), Sched. 4.*]

AMENDMENTS

The amendments in square brackets were made by the Employment Protection (Consolidation) Act 1978 (c. 44), s.159(2)(3), Scheds. 16, 17, and by the Employment Act 1982 (c. 46), Sched. 2, para. 6.

. . . . . .

Application to Crown

121.—(1) Subject to the following provisions of this section, the provisions of this Act (except sections [. . .] 20, 21 [. . .] 90 to 96 and [99] to 107) shall have effect in relation to Crown employment and to persons in Crown employment as they have effect in relation to other employment and to other employees.

(2) In this section, subject to subsections (3) to (5) below, "Crown employment" means employment under or for the purposes of a government department or any officer or body excercising on behalf of the Crown functions conferred by any enactment.

(3) This section does not apply to service as a member of the naval, military or air forces of the Crown, or of any women's service administered by the Defence Council, but does apply to employment by any association established for the purposes of the Auxiliary Forces Act 1953.

(4) For the purposes of this section, Crown employment does not include any employment in respect of which there is in force a certificate issued by or on behalf of a Minister of the Crown certifying that employment of a description specified in the certificate, or the employment of a particular person so specified, is (or, at a time specified in the certificate, was) required to be excepted from this section for the purpose of safeguarding national security; and any document purporting to be a certificate so issued shall be received in evidence and shall, unless the contrary is proved, be deemed to be such a certificate.

(5) For the purposes of this Act (except sections [. . .] 90 to 96 and 105), none of the bodies referred to in [Schedule 5 to the Employment Protection (Consolidation) Act 1978] (national health service employers) shall be regarded as performing functions on behalf of the Crown, and accordingly employment by any such body shall not be Crown employment within the meaning of this section.

(6) For the purposes of the application of the provisions of this Act in relation to employment by any such body as is referred to in subsection (5) above, any reference to redundancy shall be construed as a reference to the existence of such circumstances as, in accordance with any arrangements for the time being in force as mentioned in [section 111(3) of the Employment Protection (Consolidation) Act 1978,] are treated as equivalent to redundancy in relation to such employment.

(7) For the purposes of the application of the provisions of this Act in relation to Crown employment in accordance with subsection (1) above—
- (*a*) any reference to an employee shall be construed as a reference to a person in Crown employment;
- (*b*) any reference to a contract of employment shall be construed as a reference to the terms of employment of a person in Crown employment;
- (*c*) any reference to dismissal shall be construed as a reference to the termination of Crown employment;
- (*d*) any reference to redundancy shall be construed as a reference to the existence of such circumstances as, in accordance with any arrangements for the time being in force as mentioned in section [section 111(3) of the Employment Protection (Consolidation) Act 1978,] are treated as equivalent to redundancy in relation to Crown employment;
- (*e*) the reference in section 18(1)(*e*) above to the employer's undertaking shall be construed as a reference to the national interest; and
- (*f*) any other reference to an undertaking shall be construed, in relation to a Minister of the Crown, as a reference to his functions or (as the context may require) to the department of which he is in charge and, in relation to a government department, officer or body, shall be construed as a reference to the functions of the department, officer or body or (as the context may require) to the department, officer or body.

(8) [*Repealed by the Employment Protection (Consolidation) Act* 1978 (*c.* 44), *s.*159(3), *Sched.* 17;]

180   *Employment Protection Act 1975*

AMENDMENTS

The amendments in square brackets were made by the Employment Protection (Consolidation) Act 1978 (c. 44), s.159(2) (3), Scheds. 16, 17. The amendments in the first and third set of square brackets in subs. (1), however, were made by the Employment Act 1980 (c. 42), Scheds. 1 and 2.

Application of employment legislation to House of Commons staff

1–322   **122.**—(1) The provisions of this Act [. . .] shall apply to relevant members of House of Commons staff as they apply to persons in Crown employment within the meaning of section 121 above, and accordingly for the purposes of the application of those provisions in relation to any such members—

(*a*) any reference to an employee shall be construed as a reference to any such member;

(*b*) any reference to a contract of employment shall be construed as a reference to the terms of employment of any such member;

(*c*) any reference to dismissal shall be construed as a reference to the termination of such member's employment;

(*d*) the references in [. . .] section 18(1)(*e*) above to any person's undertaking or any undertaking in which he works shall be construed as a reference to the national interest or, if the case so requires, the interests of the House of Commons; and

(*e*) any other reference to an undertaking shall be construed as a reference to the House of Commons.

(2) [The provisions of the following enactments, that is to say—

(*a*) section 1 of the Equal Pay Act 1970; and

(*b*) Parts II and IV of the Sex Discrimination Act 1975; and

(*c*) Parts II and IV of the Race Relations Act 1976]

shall apply to an act done by an employer of a relevant member of House of Commons staff and to service as such a member as they apply to an act done by, and to service for the purposes of, a Minister of the Crown or Government department, and accordingly shall so apply as if references in those provisions to a contract of employment included references to the terms of service of such a member.

(3) [*Repealed by the Employment Protection (Consolidation) Act 1978, s.159(3), Sched. 17.*]

(4) In this section "relevant member of the House of Commons staff" means any person employed in or for the purposes of the House of Commons as follows:—

(*a*) in the Department of the Clerk of that House;

(*b*) in Mr. Speaker's Department;

(*c*) in the Department of the Serjeant at Arms;

(*d*) in the Department of the Library;

(*e*) in the administration department;

(*f*) in the refreshment department.

(5) It is hereby declared that in this section "relevant member of House of Commons staff" does not include the Clerk of that House or any Clerk Assistant or the Sergeant at Arms of that House.

(6) For the purposes of the enactments applied by subsection (1) and (2) above, Mr. Speaker shall be deemed to be the employer of House of Commons staff, except that in relation to any description of members of the staff for the time being designated by Mr. Speaker a person so designated

shall be deemed to be the employer of members of that description for those purposes or, if it is so stated in the designation, such of those purposes as are so designated.

(7) Where any proceedings are brought by virtue of this section against Mr. Speaker or any person designated under subsection (6) above, the person against whom the proceedings are brought may apply to the industrial tribunal to have some other person against whom the proceedings could have been properly brought so substituted for him as a party to those proceedings.

(8) If the House of Commons resolves at any time that any provision of subsections (4) to (6) above should be amended in its application to any member of the staff of that House, Her Majesty may by Order in Council amend that provision accordingly.

(9) [*Repealed by the House of Commons (Administration) Act* 1978 (*c.* 36), *s.*5, *Sched.* 3.]

AMENDMENTS
The words in square brackets were added by the Race Relations Act 1976 (c. 74), s.79(4), Sched. 4. The words omitted were repealed by the Employment Protection (Consolidation) Act 1978 (c. 44), s.159(3), Sched. 17.

Orders, rules and regulations

123.—(1) Any power conferred by any provision of this Act to make an order (other than an Order in Council) or to make rules or regulations shall be exercisable by statutory instrument.

(2) Any statutory instrument made under any power conferred by this Act to make an Order in Council or other order or to make rules or regulations, except—

(*a*) an instrument required to be laid before Parliament in draft; and

(*b*) an order under section [. . .] 107 above or section 129 below,

shall be subject to annulment in pursuance of a resolution of either House of Parliament.

(3) Any such power shall include power to make such incidental, supplementary or transitional provisions as appear to the authority exercising the power to be necessary or expedient.

(4) Any such power to make an order shall, except in the case of an order made under Part III of this Act, include power to revoke or vary the order by a subsequent order made under that provision.

1-323

AMENDMENT
The words in subs. (2)(*b*) were omitted by the Employment Protection (Consolidation) Act 1978 (c. 44), s.159(3), Sched. 17.

Financial provisions

124.—(1) Subject to the following provisions of this section, there shall be defrayed out of moneys provided by Parliament—
  (*a*) all expenses incurred by the Secretary of State or any other Minister of the Crown or any government department in consequence of the provisions of this Act;
  (*b*) any expenses incurred by Mr. Speaker or by any person designated by him under section 122 above, in consequence of any enactment which is applied by that section; and
  (*c*) any increase attributable to the provisions of this Act in the sums payable out of moneys so provided under any other enactment.

1-324

(2)–(4) [*Repealed by the Employment Protection (Consolidation) Act 1978 (c.44), s.159(3), Sched. 17.*]

(5) There shall be paid into the Consolidated Fund any sums received by a Minister of the Crown by virtue of this Act, except sums which are expressly required to be paid into the Maternity Pay Fund, the Redundancy Fund or the National Insurance Fund.

(6) As respect any increase attributable to the provisions of this Act in the expenses which under section 135(3)(*a*) of the Social Security Act 1975 are to be paid out of moneys provided by Parliament, subsection (1)(*c*) above is without prejudice to the provision made by subsection (5) of that section for reimbursement out of the National Insurance Fund.

Minor and consequential amendments, transitional provisions and repeals

1–325   **125.**—(1) [The provisions of the 1974 Act specified in Part III of Schedule 16 to this Act] and the enactments specified in Part IV of that Schedule, shall have effect subject to the amendments so specified respectively, being minor amendments and amendments consequential on any provisions of this Act.

(2) The transitional provisions in Schedule 17 to this Act shall have effect.

(3) The enactments specified in Schedule 18 to this Act are hereby repealed to the extent specified in column 3 of that Schedule.

AMENDMENT
The words in square brackets were substituted by the Employment Protection (Consolidation) Act 1978 (c. 44), s.159(2), Sched. 16.

Interpretation

1–326   **126.**—(1) In this Act, except so far as the context otherwise requires—
"associated employer", "collective agreement", "employee", "employer", "independent trade union" and "independence" and "independent" (in relation to a trade union), "official", "successor", [. . . .], "trade union", "union membership agreement" and "worker" have the same meanings respectively as in the 1974 Act;
"business" includes a trade or profession and includes any activity carried on by a body of persons, whether corporate or unincorporate;
"collective bargaining" means negotiations relating to or connected with one or more of the matters specified in section 29(1) of the 1974 Act;
"Committee" has the meaning assigned to it by section 10 above;
"dismiss", "dismissal" and "effective date of termination" shall be construed in accordance with [section 55 of the Employment Protection (Consolidation) Act 1978];
[. . .]
[. . .]
"the 1974 Act" means the Trade Union and Labour Relations Act 1974;
"recognition" [in relation to a trade union, means the recognition of the union by an employer, or two or more associated employers, to any extent, for the purpose of collective bargaining] and cognate expressions shall be construed accordingly;
"Service" has the meaning assigned to it by section 1 above;

["trade dispute" has the meaning assigned by section 126A below;].

(2) "Employers' associations", except in Part III of this Act, has the same meaning as in the 1974 Act and in the said Part III and in any enactment thereby amended means any organisation representing employers and any association of such organisations or of employers and such organisations.

(3)–(5) [*Repealed by the Employment Protection (Consolidation) Act 1978 (c.44), s.159(3), Sched. 17.*]

(6) In this Act references to redundancy or to being redundant, in relation to an employee, are references to—
- (a) the fact that the employer has ceased, or intends to cease, to carry on the business for the purposes of which the employee is or was employed by him, or has ceased, or intends to cease, to carry on that business in the place where the employee is or was so employed, or
- (b) the fact that the requirements of that business for employees to carry out work of a particular kind, or for employees to carry out work of a particular kind in the place where he is or was so employed, have ceased or diminished or are expected to cease or diminish.

(7) In subsection (6) above "cease" means cease either permanently or temporarily and from whatsoever cause, and "diminish" has a corresponding meaning.

(8) For the purposes of this Act it is immaterial whether the law which (apart from this Act) governs any person's employment is the law of the United Kingdom, or a part of the United Kingdom, or not.

(9) Except so far as the context otherwise requires, any reference in this Act to any enactment shall be construed as a reference to that enactment as amended or extended by or under any other enactment, including this Act.

AMENDMENTS

The substitutions and repeals in this section were made by the Employment Protection (Consolidation) Act 1978 (c. 44), s. 159(2), Sched. 16, except for the amendment to the definition of "recognition," which was made by the Employment Act 1980 (c. 42), Sched. 1, para. 6, and the amendment to the definition of "trade dispute" which was made by the Employment Act 1982 (c. 46), Sched. 3, para. 13.

[Meaning of trade dispute

126A.—(1) In this Act "trade dispute" means a dispute between employers and workers, or between workers and workers, which is connected with one or more of the following, that is to say— 1–327
- (a) terms and conditions of employment, or the physical conditions in which any workers are required to work;
- (b) engagement or non-engagement, or termination or suspension of employment or the duties of employment, of one or more workers;
- (c) allocation of work or the duties of employment as between workers or groups of workers;
- (d) matters of discipline;
- (e) the membership or non-membership of a trade union on the part of a worker;
- (f) facilities for officials of trade unions: and
- (g) machinery for negotiation or consultation, and other procedures, relating to any of the foregoing matters, including the recognition

by employers or employers' associations of the right of a trade union to represent workers in any such negotiation or consultation or in the carrying out of such procedures.

(2) A dispute between a Minister of the Crown and any workers shall, notwithstanding that he is not the employer of those workers, be treated for the purposes of this Act as a dispute between an employer and those workers if the dispute relates—
- (a) to matters which have been referred for consideration by a joint body on which, by virtue of any provision made by or under any enactment, that Minister is represented; or
- (b) to matters which cannot be settled without that Minister exercising a power conferred upon him by or under an enactment.

(3) There is a trade dispute for the purposes of this Act even though it relates to matters occurring outside Great Britain [. . .].

(4) A dispute to which a trade union or employers' association is a party shall be treated for the purposes of this Act as a dispute to which workers or, as the case may be, employers are parties.

(5) An act, threat or demand done or made by one person or organisation against another which, if resisted, would have led to a trade dispute with that other, shall, notwithstanding that because that other submits to the act or threat or accedes to the demand no dispute arises, be treated for the purposes of this Act as being done or made in contemplation of a trade dispute with that other.

(6) In this section—
"employment" includes any relationship whereby one person personally does work or performs services for another;
"worker", in relation to a dispute to which an employer is a party, includes any worker even if not employed by that employer.]

AMENDMENT
This section was inserted by the Employment Act 1982 (c. 46), Sched. 3, para. 13(3).

Power to extend employment legislation
127.—(1) Her majesty may by Order in Council provide that the provisions of—
- (a) [. . .];
- (b) [the Industrial Training Act 1982]
- (c) [. . .]
- (d) [. . .]
- (e) the 1974 Act;
- (f) this Act;
- [(ff) the Employment Act 1980; and]
- [(fg) the Employment Act 1982; and]
- (g) any legislation (that is to say any enactment of the Parliament of Northern Ireland and any provision made by or under a Measure of the Northern Ireland Assembly) for the time being in force in Northern Ireland which makes provision for purposes corresponding to any of the purposes of any of the Acts mentioned [. . .] above,

shall, to such extent and for such purposes as may be specified in the Order, apply (with or without modification) to or in relation to any person in employment to which this section applies.

(2) This section applies to employment for the purposes of any activities—
  (a) in the territorial waters of the United Kingdom; or
  (b) connected with the exploration of the sea bed or subsoil or the exploitation of their natural resources in any area designated by order under section 1(7) of the Continental Shelf Act 1964.
(3) An Order in Council under subsection (1) above—
  (a) may make different provision for different cases;
  (b) may provide that all or any of the provisions of any Act mentioned in that subsection, as applied by such an Order, shall apply to individuals whether or not they are British subjects and to bodies corporate whether or not they are incorporated under the law of any part of the United Kingdom (notwithstanding that the application may affect their activities outside the United Kingdom);
  (c) may make provision for conferring jurisdiction on any court or class of court specified in the Order, or on industrial tribunals, in respect of offences, causes of action or of matters arising in connection with employment to which this section applies;
  (d) without prejudice to the generality of subsection (1) above or of paragraph (a) above, may provide that the enactments referred to in that subsection shall apply in relation to any person in employment for the purposes of such activities as are referred to in subsection (2) above in any part of the areas specified in paragraphs (a) and (b) of that subsection;
  (e) may exclude from the operation of section 3 of the Territorial Waters Jurisdiction Act 1878 (consents required for prosecutions) proceedings for offences under the enactments referred to in subsection (1) above in connection with employment to which this section applies;
  (f) may provide that such proceedings shall not be brought without such consent as may be required by the Order;
  (g) may, without prejudice to the generality of the power under subsection (1) above to modify the enactments referred to in that subsection in their application for the purposes of this section, modify or exclude the operation of [. . .] section 119 above and of any corresponding provision in any such Northern Irish legislation as is referred to in subsection (1)(g) above.
(4) Any jurisdiction conferred on any court or tribunal under this section shall be without prejudice to jurisdiction exercisable apart from this section by that or any other court or tribunal.

AMENDMENTS

The words omitted in subs. (1)(a) were repealed by the Wages Councils Act 1979 (c. 12), s. 31(3), Sched. 7. The words in subs. (1)(b) were substituted by the Industrial Training Act 1982, Sched. 3, para. 6. Para. (ff) in subs. (1) was inserted by the Employment Act 1980 (c. 42), Sched. 1, para. 7. Para. (fg) was inserted by the Employment Act 1982 (c. 46), Sched. 3, para. 13. The words omitted in subs. (1)(g) were repealed by the Employment Act 1980 (c. 42), Sched. 2.

The words omitted in subs. (3)(g) were repealed by the Employment Protection (Consolidation) Act 1978 (c. 44), s. 159(3), Sched. 17.

Northern Ireland

128.—(1) If provision is made by Northern Irish legislation (that is to say by or under a Measure of the Northern Ireland Assembly) for purposes corresponding to any of the purposes of this Act [. . .] the Secretary of State may, with the consent of the Treasury make reciprocal arrangements with the appropriate Northern Irish authority for co-ordinating the relevant provisions of this Act [. . .] with the corresponding provisions of the Northern Irish legislation, so as to secure that they operate, to such extent as may be provided by the arrangements, as a single system.

(2) [*Repealed by the Employment Protection (Consolidation) Act 1978, s. 159(3), Sched. 17.*]

(3) The Secretary of State may make regulations for giving effect in Great Britain to any such arrangements, and any such regulations may make different provision for different cases, and may provide that this Act [. . .] shall have effect in relation to persons affected by the arrangements subject to such modifications and adaptations as may be specified in the regulations, including provision—

(*a*) for securing that acts, omissions and events having any effect for the purposes of the Northern Irish legislation shall have a corresponding effect for the purposes of this Act [. . .] (but not so as to confer a right to double payment in respect of the same act, omission or event); and

(*b*) for determining, in cases where rights accrue both under this Act [. . .] and under the Northern Irish legislation, which of those rights shall be available to the person concerned.

(4) In this section "the appropriate Northern Irish authority" means such authority as may be specified in that behalf in the Northern Irish legislation.

AMENDMENT
The words omitted in square brackets were repealed by the Employment Protection (Consolidation) Act 1978 (c. 44), s.159(3), Sched. 17.

Short title, commencement and extent

1–330   **129.**—(1) This Act may be cited as the Employment Protection Act 1975.

(2) [*Repealed by the Employment Protection (Consolidation) Act 1978, s.159(3), Sched. 17.*]

(3) The other provisions of this Act shall come into operation on such day as the Secretary of State may by order appoint, and different days may be so appointed for different purposes.

(4) Any reference in this Act to the commencement of any provision of this Act shall be construed as a reference to the day appointed under this section for the coming into operation of that provision.

(5) Without prejudice to the generality of section 123(3) above, an order under this section may contain such transitional provision or savings as appear to the Lord Chancellor or, as the case may be, the Secretary of State to be necessary or expedient in connection with the provisions of this Act which are thereby brought (wholly or in part) into operation, including such adaptations of those provisions then in force as appear to the Lord Chancellor or, as the case may be, the Secretary of State to be necessary or expedient in consequence of their partial operation (whether before, on or after the day appointed by the order).

(6) Sections 127 and 128 above and any provision of this Act which amends or repeals any provision of the House of Commons Disquali-

fication Act 1975 or the Northern Ireland Assembly Disqualification Act 1975 shall extend to Northern Ireland, but except as aforesaid this Act shall not extend there.

SCHEDULES

Sections 1, 7 and 10   SCHEDULE 1   1–331

ADVISORY, CONCILIATION AND ARBITRATION SERVICE, ETC.

PART I

CONSTITUTION ETC. OF ADVISORY, CONCILIATION AND ARBITRATION SERVICE AND ITS COUNCIL

The Council

1. The Service shall be directed by a Council constituted in accordance with paragraphs 2 to 4 below and shall be a body corporate of which the corporators are the members of that Council.

2.—(1) The Council shall consist of a full-time chairman appointed by the Secretary of State and, subject to sub-paragraphs (3)(*b*) and (4) below, nine other members appointed by the Secretary of State in accordance with sub-paragraph (2) below.

(2) Before appointing the members of the Council (other than the chairman and any deputy chairman appointed as mentioned in sub-paragraph (3)(*b*) below) the Secretary of State shall—

(*a*) as to three of them, consult such organisations representing employers as he considers appropriate; and

(*b*) as to three of them, consult such organisations representing workers as he considers appropriate.

(3) The Secretary of State may appoint up to three full-time or part-time deputy chairmen of the Council who may be appointed—

(*a*) from the members appointed in accordance with sub-paragraph (2) above or sub-paragraph (4) below; or

(*b*) in addition to those members.

(4) The Secretary of State may, if he thinks fit, appoint a further two members of the Council (who shall be appointed so as to take office at the same time) and before making those appointments he shall—

(*a*) as to one of them, consult such organisations representing employers as he considers appropriate; and

(*b*) as to one of them, consult such organisations representing workers as he considers appropriate.

3.—(1) Subject to the following provisions of this paragraph, the members, chairman and any deputy chairman of the Council shall hold and vacate office in accordance with their terms of appointment.

(2) A person shall not be appointed to the Council for a term exceeding five years; but previous membership shall not affect eligibility for re-appointment.

(3) The Secretary of State may appoint persons to the Council either as full-time members or as part-time members.

(4) The Secretary of State may, with the consent of the member concerned, vary the terms of appointment of any member of the Council so as to provide for him to serve as a full-time member instead of a part-time member or, as the case may be, as a part-time member instead of as a full-time member.

(5) A member may at any time resign his membership, and the chairman and any deputy chairman mayt at any time resign his office as such, by, in each case, notice in writing addressed to the Secretary of State.

(6) A deputy chairman appointed as mentioned in paragraph 2(3)(*b*) above shall on resigning his office as deputy chairman cease to be a member of the council.

(7) If the Secretary of State is satisfied that a member—

(*a*) has been absent from meetings of the Council for a period longer than six consecutive months without the permission of the Council; or

(*b*) has become bankrupt or made an arrangement with his creditors; or

(c) is incapacitated by physical or mental illness; or
(d) is otherwise unable or unfit to discharge the functions of a member,
the Secretary of State may declare his office as a member to be vacant and shall notify the declaration in such manner as the Secretary of State thinks fit; and thereupon the office shall become vacant.

(8) In the application of sub-paragraph (7) above to Scotland for the references in paragraph (b) to a member's having become bankrupt and to a member's having made an arrangement with his creditors there shall be substituted respectively references to a member's estate having been sequestrated and to a member's having made a trust deed for behoof of his creditors or a composition contract.

(9) If the chairman ceases to be a member of the Council, or if a deputy chairman ceases to be a member of the Council, he shall cease to be chairman or, as the case may be, a deputy chairman.

4.—(1) The Council shall determine its own procedure, including the quorum necessary for its meetings.

(2) If the Secretary of State has not appointed a deputy chairman the Council may choose a member to act as chairman in the absence or incapacity of the chairman.

5. The validity of any proceedings of the Council shall not be affected by any vacancy among the members of the Council or by any defect in the appointment of any member of the Council.

Staff

6. The Service may, with the approval of the Secretary of State, appoint a secretary, such an appointment shall not be made without the consent as to terms and conditions of service of the Secretary of State, and such consent shall not be given without the approval of the Minister for the Civil Service.

7. The Service may appoint such other officers and servants as it may determine with the consent as to numbers, manner of appointment and terms and conditions of service of the Secretary of State; and such consent shall not be given without the approval of the Minister for the Civil Service.

8. The Service shall provide for the Certification Officer and the Committee the requisite staff (from among the Service's officers and servants) and the requisite accommodation, equipment and other facilities.

Supplemental

9. The Service shall maintain offices in such of the major centres of employment in Great Britain as it thinks fit for the purpose of discharging its functions under any enactment.

10.—(1) The fixing of the common seal of the Service shall be authenticated by the signature of the secretary of the Service or some other person authorised by the Service to act for that purpose.

(2) A document purporting to be duly executed under the seal of the Service shall be received in evidence and shall, unless the contrary is proved, be deemed to be so executed.

11.—(1) The functions of the Service and of its officers and servants shall be performed on behalf of the Crown, but, subject to paragraph 35 below, the Service shall not be subject to directions of any kind from any Minister of the Crown as to the manner in which it is to exercise any of its functions under any enactment.

(2) For the purposes of any civil proceedings arising out of those functions, the Crown Proceedings Act 1947 and the Crown Suits (Scotland) Act 1857 shall apply to the Service as if it were a government department within the meaning of the said Act of 1947 or, as the case may be, a public department within the meaning of the said Act of 1857.

12. Nothing in section 9 of the Statistics of Trade Act 1947 (restriction on the disclosure of information obtained under that Act) shall prevent or penalise the disclosure to the Service for the purpose of the exercise of any of its functions, of information obtained under that Act by any government department.

13.—(1) The Service shall, as soon as practicable after the end of each calendar year, make a report to the Secretary of State on its activities and the activities of the Central Arbitration Committee during that year.

(2) The Certification Officer shall, as soon as practicable after the end of each calendar year, make a report of his activities during that year to the Service and to the Secretary of State.

(3) The Secretary of State shall lay before each House of Parliament a copy of every report received by him under sub-paragraph (1) or sub-paragraph (2) above and shall arrange for it to be published.

Part II

Central Arbitration Committee

Constitution

14.—(1) The Committee shall consist of a chairman appointed by the Secretary of State after consultation with the Service and other members appointed by the Secretary of State in accordance with sub-paragraph (2) below.

(2) The members of the Committee (apart from the chairman) shall be appointed by the Secretary of State from persons nominated by the Service as experienced in industrial relations and shall include some persons whose experience is as representatives of employers and some persons whose experience is as representatives of workers.

(3) The Secretary of State may, after consultation with the Service, appoint one or more deputy chairmen of the Committee in addition to the existing members of the Committee.

15.—(1) Subject to the following provisions of this paragraph, the members, chairman and any deputy chairman of the Committee shall hold and vacate office in accordance with the terms of appointment.

(2) A person shall not be appointed to the Committee for a term exceeding five years; but previous membership shall not affect eligibility for re-appointment.

(3) The Secretary of State may, with the consent of the member concerned, vary the terms of appointment of any member of the Committee so as to provide for him to serve as a full-time member instead of a part-time member or, as the case may be, as a part-time member instead of as a full-time member.

(4) A member may at any time resign his membership, and the chairman and any deputy chairman may at any time resign his office as such, by, in each case, notice in writing addressed to the Secretary of State.

(5) If the Secretary of State is satisfied that a member—
    (*a*) has become bankrupt or made an arrangement with his creditors; or
    (*b*) is incapacitated by physical or mental illness; or
    (*c*) is otherwise unable or unfit to discharge the functions of a member,
the Secretary of State may declare his office as a member to be vacant and shall notify the declaration in such manner as the Secretary of State thinks fit; and thereupon the office shall become vacant.

(6) In the application of sub-paragraph (5) above to Scotland for the references in paragraph (*a*) to a member's having become bankrupt and to a member's having made an arrangement with his creditors there shall be substituted respectively references to a member's estate having been sequestrated and to a member's having made a trust deed for behoof of his creditors or a composition contract.

(7) If the chairman ceases to be a member of the Committee, or if a deputy chairman ceases to be a member of the Committee, he shall cease to be chairman or, as the case may be, a deputy chairman.

16.—(1) At any time when the chairman of the Committee is absent or otherwise incapable of acting, or there is a vacancy in the office of chairman, and the Committee has a deputy chairman or deputy chairmen—
    (*a*) the deputy chairman, if there is only one; or
    (*b*) if there is more than one deputy chairman, such one of them as they may agree or, in default of agreement, as the Secretary of State may direct,
may perform any of the functions of the chairman of the Committee.

(2) At any time when every person who is chairman or deputy chairman of the Committee is absent or otherwise incapable of acting, or there is no such person, such member of the Committee as the Secretary of State may direct, may perform any of the functions of the chairman of the Committee.

Proceedings

17.—(1) For the purpose of discharging any of its functions under this or any other enactment, the Committee shall, subject to sub-paragraph (2) below, consist of the chairman and such other members as the chairman may direct.

(2) The Committee may sit in two or more divisions constituted of such members as the chairman may direct, and in a division in which the chairman does not sit the functions of the chairman shall be performed by a deputy chairman.

(3) The Committee may, at the discretion of the chairman, where it appears expedient to

do so, call in the aid of one or more assessors, and may settle the matter wholly or partly with their assistance.

18. The Committee may at the discretion of the chairman sit in private where it appears expedient to do so.

19. If in any case the Committee cannot reach a unanimous decision on its award the Chairman shall decide the matter acting with the full powers of an umpire, or, in Scotland, an oversman.

20. Subject to paragraphs 17 to 19 above, the Committee shall determine its own procedure.

21. The validity of any proceedings of the Committee shall not be affected by any vacancy among the members of the Committee or by any defect in the appointment of any member of the Committee.

Awards

22. The Committee may correct in any award any clerical mistake or error arising from an accidental slip or omission.

23.—(1) If any question arises as to the interpretation of an award of the Committee, any party to the awrad may apply to the Committee for a decision on that question.

(2) The Committee shall decide the question after hearing the parties or, if the parties consent, without a hearing, and shall notify the parties of the decision.

24. Decisions of the Committee in the exercise of any of its functions conferred by any enactment shall be published.

Supplemental

25. For the purpose of assisting the Service in the discharge of its duty under paragraph 13(1) above, the Committee shall, as soon as practicable after the end of each calendar year, transmit to the Service an account of its activities during that year.

26. Part I of the Arbitration Act 1950 shall not aply to any proceedings of the Committee.

27. The functions of the Committee shall be performed on behalf of the Crown, but the Committee shall not be subject to directions of any kind from any Minister of the Crown as to the manner in which it is to exercise any of its functions under any enactment.

PART III

SUPPLEMENTARY PROVISIONS

Remuneration and allowances

1–333

28. The Service shall pay to—
    (*a*) members of the Council of the Service;
    (*b*) members of the Central Arbitration Committee; and
    (*c*) the Certification Officer and any assistant certificate officer,
such remuneration and travelling and other allowances as may be determined by the Secretary of State with the approval of the Minister for the Civil Service.

29. The Service may pay to—
    (*a*) persons appointed under section 2(2) above who are not officers or servants of the Service; and
    (*b*) arbitrators or arbiters appointed by the Service under any provision of this Act or any other enactment,
such fees and travelling and other allowances as may be determined by the Secretary of State with the approval of the Minister for the Civil Service.

Sums payable on retirement

30. The Secretary of State may pay, or make provision for paying, to, or in respect of, any holder of an office mentioned in paragraph 28 above, such pension, allowance or gratuity on the death or retirement of that office-holder as he may, with the approval of the Minister for the Civil Service, determine.

31. Where a person ceases to be the holder of an office mentioned in paragraph 28 above otherwise than on the expiry of his term of office, and it appears to the Secretary of State that

there are special circumstances which make it right for him to receive compensation, the Secretary of State may make him a payment of such amount as the Secretary of State may, with the approval of the Minister for the Civil Service, determine.

32. The Service shall pay to the Minister for the Civil Service, at such times in each accounting year as may be determined by that Minister subject to any directions of the Treasury, sums of such amounts as he may so determine for the purpose of this paragraph as being equivalent to the increase during that year of such liabilities of his as are attributable to the provision of pensions, allowances or gratuities to or in respect of persons who are or have been in the service of the Service in so far as that increase results from the service of those persons during that accounting year and to the expense to be incurred in administering those pensions, allowances or gratuities.

Expenses

33. The Secretary of State shall pay to the Service such sums as are approved by the Treasury and as he considers appropriate for the purpose of enabling the Service to perform its functions.

Accounts

34. I shall be the duty of the Service to keep proper accounts and proper records in relation to the accounts.

35.—(1) The Service shall prepare in respect of each accounting year a statement of accounts, in particular showing separately any sums disbursed to or on behalf of the Committee or the Certification Officer in consequence of the foregoing provisions of this Schedule, in such form as the Secretary of State may direct with the approval of the Treasury.

(2) The Service shall, not later than 30th November following the end of the accounting year to which the statement relates, send copies of the statement to the Secretary of State and to the Comptroller and Auditor General, and the Comptroller and Auditor General shall examine, certify and report on each such statement and shall lay copies of eahc statement and of his report before each House of Parliament.

(3) In this paragraph "accounting year" means the period of 12 months ending with 31st March in any year except that the first accounting year of the Service shall, if the Secretary of State so directs, be such period shorter or longer than 12 months (but not longer than two years) as is specified in the direction.

. . . . . .

Section 97   SCHEDULE 9   1–334

AMENDMENTS OF AGRICULTURAL WAGES ACT 1948

PART I

SECTION 3, AS SUBSTITUTED

Power of Agricultural Wages Board to fix wages, holidays and other terms and conditions

3.—(1) Subject to and in accordance with the provisions of this section, the Board shall have power, for each county for which an agricultural wages committee is established under this Act, to make an order in accordance with the provisions of Schedule 4 to this Act—
  (*a*) fixing minimum rates of wages;
  (*b*) directing holidays to be allowed;
  (*c*) fixing any other terms and conditions of employment;
for workers employed in agriculture.

(2) The power of the Board to make an order under subsection (1)(*a*) of this section fixing minimum rates of wages is a power to make an order—
  (*a*) fixing minimum rates for time work;
  (*b*) fixing minimum rates for piece work;
  (*c*) fixing minimum rates for time work, to apply in the case of workers employed on piece work, for the purpose of securing to such workers a minimum rate of remuneration on a time work basis; or
  (*d*) fixing separate minimum rates by way of pay in respect of holidays:
Provided that the minimum time rate for piece work shall not in any case be higher than

the minimum rate which, if the work were time work, would be applicable thereto by virtue of paragraph (*a*) of this subsection.

(2A) It shall be the duty of the Board to make an order under this section fixing such minimum rates of wages for time work as are referred to in paragraph (*a*) of the last preceding subsection.

(3) An order under paragraph (*b*) of subsection (1) of this section directing that a worker shall be allowed a holiday—
   (*a*) shall not be made unless both minimum rates of wages in respect of the period of the holiday and minimum rates of wages otherwise than in respect of the holiday have been or are being fixed under this section for that worker;
   (*b*) shall provide for the duration of the holiday being related to the duration of the period for which the worker has been employed or engaged to be employed by the employer who is to allow the holiday; and
   (*c*) subject as aforesaid, may make provision as to the times at which or the periods within which, and the circumstances in which, the holiday shall be allowed.

(3A) An order under this section fixing separate minimum rates of wages in respect of holidays may make provision—
   (*a*) with respect to the times at which, and the conditions subject to which, those wages shall accrue and shall become payable, and
   (*b*) for securing that any such wages which have accrued to a worker during his employment by any employer shall, in the event of his ceasing to be employed by that employer before he becomes entitled to be allowed a holiday by him, nevertheless become payable by the employer to the worker.

(4) Any such minimum rates of wages as are mentioned in subsection (2) of this section may be fixed so as to vary according as the employment is for a day, week, month or other period, or according to the number of working hours, or the conditions of the employment, or so as to provide for a differential rate in the case of employment defined by the Board as being overtime employment, whether that employment is remunerated on a time work or a piece work basis.

In the exercise of their powers under this subsection, the Board shall, so far as is reasonably practicable, secure a weekly half-holiday for workers.

(5) An order under this section shall have effect as regards any terms as to remuneration from a date specified in the order, which may be a date earlier than the date of the order but not earlier than the date on which the Board agreed on those terms prior to publishing (in accordance with Schedule 4 to this Act) the original proposals to which effect is given, with or without modifications, by the order.

(6) Any increase of wages payable by virtue of an order under this section in respect of any time before the date of the order (hereafter in this Act referred to as arrears of wages) shall be paid by the employer within a period specified in the order being—
   (*a*) in the case of a worker who is in the employment of the employer on that date, a period beginning with that date;
   (*b*) in the case of a worker who is no longer in the employment of the employer on that date a period beginning with that date or the date on which the employer receives from the worker or a person acting on his behalf a request in writing for those wages, whichever is the later.

(7) Nothing in this section shall be construed as preventing the Board fixing a minimum rate of wages so as to secure that workers employed in agriculture receive remuneration calculated by reference to periods during the currency of their employment.

Part II

Minor and Consequential Amendments

1. In section 4(1) (enforcement) after paragraph (*c*) there shall be inserted the words "or
   (*d*) to pay to any such worker arrears of wages within the period specified in the order";
and accordingly references in the provisions of that section following that paragraph and in any other provisions of the Agricultural Wages Act 1948 to wages or to the payment of wages at a rate not less than the minimum rate or the minimum rate applicable shall include references to arrears of wages or their payment, as the case may require.

2.—(1) In section 5 (permits to incapacitated persons) after subsection (2) insert the following subsection:—

"(2A) If on an application in that behalf an agricultural wages committee are satisfied that a worker employed or desiring to be employed in their county is so affected by any physical injury or mental deficiency, or any infirmity due to age or any other cause, as to make it inappropriate for any terms and conditions of employment (other than those with respect to wages and holidays) fixed by an order under this Act to apply to him, the committee shall grant him, subject to any conditions they may determine, a permit dispensing, as from the date of the application or a later date specified in the permit, with a term or condition specified in the order, and while the permit is in force and any conditions to which the permit is subject are complied with, the terms and conditions fixed by the order shall be deemed to be observed."

(2) In section 5(3) (revocation of permit) after the words "subsection (1)" in both places where they occur insert the words "or (2A)".

(3) In section 5(4) (variation of condition of permit) at the end insert the words "and, in the case of a variation caused by a change made by an order under this Act in the minimum rates of wages, that variation shall take effect from a date specified in the direction, not being earlier than the date of the change".

(4) After section 5(4) insert the following subsection:—

"(4A) Any increase of wages payable by virtue of a variation of a permit under subsection (4) of this section in respect of any time before the date of the variation shall be paid by the employer within a period specified in the order being—
  (a) in the case of a worker who is in the employment of the employer on the date on which notice of the variation is given in accordance with subsection (5) of this section, a period beginning with that date;
  (b) in the case of a worker who is no longer in the employment of the employer on the date referred to in the last preceding paragraph, a period beginning with that date or the date on which the employer receives from the worker or a person acting on his behalf a request in writing or those wages, whichever is the later".

3.—(1) In section 11(1) (void agreements) at the end add the following paragraph:—

"(c) any term or condition of a contract of employment that is inconsistent with a term or condition of employment fixed by an order of the Board under this Act or any agreement for abstaining from enforcing a term or condition so fixed".

(2) In section 11(2) (saving for more favourable agreements), at end add the words "or a term or condition of a contract of employment that is not inconsistent with a term or condition so fixed".

4.—(1) In section 12(3)(a) (inspection of records), at the end add the words "and records of terms and conditions of employment of such workers".

(2) In section 12(5) omit the words from "and in any such civil proceedings" onwards, and at the end of that subsection insert the following subsections:—

"(5A) Where it appears to an officer so appointed that a term or condition of employment fixed by order of the Board is not being complied with by an employer, the officer (if he is authorised as aforesaid) may institute, on behalf or in the name of the worker, civil proceedings in respect of the failure to comply with the term or condition.

(5B) In any civil proceedings instituted by an officer by virtue of this section the court shall, if the officer is not a party to the proceedings, have the same power to make an order for the payment of costs by the officer as if he were a party to the proceedings".

(3) In section 12, for subsection (6) (saving for ordinary right to bring proceedings) substitute the following subsection:—

"(6) Nothing in subsection (5) or (5A) of this section shall be taken to exclude the bringing otherwise than in accordance with either of those subsections of proceedings of any description mentioned in those subsections."

5. The provisions specified in column 1 of the following Table (which create offences) shall each have effect as if the maximum fine which may be imposed on summary convictions of any offence specified in that provision were a fine not exceeding the amount specified in column 3 of that Table instead of a fine not exceeding the amount specified in column 2 of that Table.

TABLE

Provision	Old maximum fine	New maximum fine
Section 4 (1) (failure to pay wages, or arrears, or allow holidays).	£20 and in addition £1 for each day on which the offence is continued after conviction.	£100 and an additional £5 for each day on which the offence is continued after conviction.
Section 6 (6) (payment of unlawful premiums).	£20.	£100.

Section 12 (7) (hindering officers (paragraph (*a*)), failure to produce documents or information (paragraph (*b*)), producing false documents (paragraph (*c*)) and furnishing false information (paragraph (*d*))).	£20.	£100 in the case of an offence under paragraph (*a*) or (*b*) and £400 in the case of an offence under paragraph (*c*) or (*d*).

6. In paragraph 6 of Schedule 4 (power to vary and revoke orders) omit the words from the beginning to "holidays".

Section 97

SCHEDULE 10

AMENDMENTS OF AGRICULTURAL WAGES (SCOTLAND) ACT 1949

PART I

SECTION 3, AS SUBSTITUTED

Power of Scottish Agricultural Wages Board to fix rates of wages and holidays

3.—(1) Subject to and in accordance with the provisions of this section, the Board shall have power to make an order in accordance with the provisions of Schedule 3 to this Act—
  (*a*) fixing minimum rates of wages;
  (*b*) directing holidays to be allowed;
  (*c*) fixing any other terms and conditions of employment
for workers employed in agriculture.

(2) The power of the Board to make an order under subsection (1)(*a*) of this section fixing minimum rates of wages is a power to make an order—
  (*a*) fixing minimum rates for time work;
  (*b*) fixing minimum rates for piece work;
  (*c*) fixing minimum rates for time work, to apply in the case of workers employed on piece work, for the purpose of securing to such workers a minimum rate of remuneration on a time work basis; or
  (*d*) fixing separate minimum rates by way of pay in respect of holidays:
Provided that the minimum time rate for piece-work shall not in any case be higher than the minimum rate which, if the work were time work, would be applicable thereto by virtue of paragraph (*a*) of this subsection.

(2A) It shall be the duty of the Board to make an order under this section fixing such minimum rates of wages for time work as are referred to in paragraph (*a*) of the last preceding subsection.

(3) An order under paragraph (*b*) of subsection (1) of this section directing that a worker shall be allowed a holiday—
  (*a*) shall not be made unless both minimum rates of wages in respect of the period of the holiday and minimum rates of wages otherwise than in respect of the holiday ahve been or are being fixed under this section for that worker;
  (*b*) shall provide for the duration of the holiday being related to the duration of the period for which the worker has been employed or engaged to be employed by the employer who is to allow the holiday; and
  (*c*) subject as aforesaid, may make provisions as to the times at which or the periods within which, and the circumstances in which, the holiday shall be allowed.

(3A) An order under this section fixing separate minimum rates of wages in respect of holidays may make provision—
  (*a*) with respect to the times at which, and the conditions subject to which, those wages shall accrue and shall become payable, and

(b) for securing that any such wages which have accrued to a worker during his employment by any employer shall, in the event of his ceasing to be employed by that employer before he becomes entitled to be allowed a holiday by him, nevertheless become payable by the employer to the worker.

(4) Any such minimum rates of wages as are mentioned in subsection (2) of this section may be fixed so as to vary according as the employment is for a day, week, month or other period, or according to the number of working hours, or the conditions of the employment or so as to provide for a differential rate in the case of employment defined by the Board as being overtime employment, whether that employment is remunerated on a time work or a piece work basis.

In the exercise of their powers under this subsection, the Board shall, so far as is reasonably practicable, secure a weekly half-holiday for workers.

(5) An order under this section shall have effect as regards any terms as to remuneration from a date specified in the order, which may be a date earlier than the date of the order but not earlier than the date on which the Board agreed on those terms prior to publishing (in accordance with Schedule 3 to this Act) the original proposals to which effect is given, with or without modifications, by the order.

(6) Any increase in wages payable by virtue of an order under this section in respect of any time before the date of the order (hereafter in this Act referred to as arrears of wages) shall be paid by the employer within a period specified in the order being—
(a) in the case of a worker who is in the employment of the employer on that date, a period beginning with that date;
(b) in the case of a worker who is no longer in the employment of the employer on that date, a period beginning with that date or the date on which the employer receives from the worker or a person acting on his behalf a request in writing for those wages, whichever is the later.

(7) Nothing in this section shall be construed as preventing the Board fixing a minimum rate of wages so as to secure that workers employed in agriculture receive remuneration calculated by reference to periods during the currency of their employment.

PART II

MINOR AND CONSEQUENTIAL AMENDMENTS

1. In section 4(1) (enforcement), after paragraph (c) there shall be inserted the words "or (d) to pay to any such worker arrears of wages within the period specified in the order;" and accordingly references in the provisions of that section following that paragraph and in any other provisions of the Agricultural Wages (Scotland) Act 1949 to wages or to the payment of wages at a rate not less than the minimum rate or the minimum rate applicable shall include references to arrears of wages or their payment, as the case may require.

2.—(1) In section 5 (permits to infirm and incapacitated persons), after subsection (2) there shall be inserted the following subsection:—

"(2A) If on an application in that behalf the Secretary of State is satisfied that a worker employed or desiring to be employed is so affected by any physical injury or mental deficiency, or any infirmity due to age or any other cause, as to make it inappropriate for any terms and conditions of employment (other than those with respect to wages and holidays) fixed by an order under this Act to apply to him, the Secretary of State shall grant him, subject to any conditions he may determine, a permit dispensing, as from the date of the application or a later date specified in the permit, with a term or condition specified in the order, and while the permit is in force and any conditions to which the permit is subject are complied with, the terms and conditions fixed by the order shall be deemed to be observed".

(2) In section 5(3) (revocation of permit), after the words "subsection (1)", in both places where they occur, there shall be inserted the words "or (2A)".

(3) In section 5(4) (variation of condition of permit),
(a) after the words "subsection (1)" there shall be inserted the words "or (2A)";
(b) at the end there shall be inserted the words "and, in the case of a variation caused by a change made by an order under this Act in the minimum rates of wages, that variation shall take effect from a date specified in the direction, not being earlier than the date of the change.".

(4) In section 5(4A), after the words "subsection (1)" there shall be inserted the words "or (2A)".

(5) After section 5(4A) there shall be inserted the following subsection:—

"(4B) Any increase of wages payable by virtue of a variation of a permit under subsection (4) of this section in respect of any time before the date of the variation shall be paid by the employer within a period specified in the order being—
> (a) in the case of a worker who is in the employment of the employer on the date on which notice of the variation is given in accordance with subsection (5) of this section a period beginning with that date;
> (b) in the case of a worker who is no longer in the employment of the employer on the date referred to in the last preceding paragraph, a period beginning with that date or the date on which the employer receives from the worker or a person acting on his behalf a request in writing for those wages, whichever is the later.".

3.—(1) In section 11(1) (void agreements), at end there shall be added the following paragraph:—

"(c) any term or condition of a contract of employment that is inconsistent with a term or condition of employment fixed by an order of the Board under this Act or any agreement for abstaining from enforcing a term or condition so fixed.".

(2) In section 11(2) (saving for more favourable agreements), at end there shall be added the words "or a term or condition of a contract of employment that is not inconsistent with a term or condition so fixed.".

4.—(1) In section 13(3)(a) (inspection of records), at end there shall be added the words "and records of terms and conditions of employment of such workers".

(2) In section 12(4), the words from "and in any such civil proceedings" onwards shall be omitted and at the end of that subsection there shall be inserted the follwing subsections:—

"(4A) Where it appears to the Secretary of State that a term or condition of employment fixed by order of the Board is not being complied with by an employer, the Secretary of State may institute, on behalf or in the name of the worker, civil proceedings in respect of the failure to comply with the term or condition.

(4B) In any civil proceedings instituted by the Secretary of State by virtue of this section the court shall, if the Secretary of State is not a party to the proceedings, have the same power to make an order for the payment of expenses by the Secretary of State as if he were a party to the proceedings.".

(3) In section 12, for subsection (5) (saving for ordinary right to bring proceedings) substitute the following subsection:—

"(5) Nothing in subsection (4) or (4A) of this section shall be taken to exclude the bringing otherwise than in accordance with either of those subsections proceedings of any description mentioned in those subsections".

5. The provisions specified in column 1 of the following Table (which create offences) shall each have effect as if the maximum fine which may be imposed on summary conviction of any offence specified in that provision were a fine not exceeding the amount specified in column 3 of that Table instead of a fine not exceeding the amount specified in column 2 of that Table.

TABLE

Provision	Old maximum fine	New maximum fine
Section 4 (1) (failure to pay wages, or arrears, or allow holidays).	£20 and in addition £1 for each day on which the offence is continued after conviction.	£100 and an additional £5 for each day on which the offence is continued after conviction.
Section 6 (6) (payment of unlawful premiums).	£20	£100
Section 12 (6) (hindering officers (paragraph (a)), failure to produce documents or information (paragraph (b)), and furnishing false information (paragraph (d))).	£20	£100 in the case of an offence under paragraph (a) or (b) and £400 in the case of an offence under paragraph (c) or (d).

6. In paragraph 6 of Schedule 3 (power to vary and revoke orders), the words from the beginning to "holidays" shall be omitted.

. . . . . .

Section 110 SCHEDULE 12

DEATH OF EMPLOYEE OR EMPLOYER

PART I

GENERAL

Introductory

1. In this Schedule "the relevant provisions" means the provisions of this Act (including this Schedule) conferring rights on employees, or connected therewith [. . .].

Institution or continuance of tribunal proceedings

2. Where an employee or employer has died tribunal proceedings arising under any of the relevant provisions may be instituted or continued by a personal representative of the deceased employee or, as the case may be, defended by a personal representative of the deceased employer.

3.—(1) If there is no personal representative of a deceased employee, tribunal proceedings arising under any of the relevant provisions (or proceedings to enforce a tribunal award made in any such proceedings) may be instituted or continued on behalf of the estate of the deceased employee by such other person as the industrial tribunal may appoint being either—
   (*a*) a person authorised by the employee to act in connection with the proceedings before the employee's death; or
   (*b*) the widower, widow, child, father, mother, brother or sister of the deceased employee, and references in this Schedule to a personal representative shall be construed as including such a person.

(2) In such a case any award made by the industrial tribunal shall be in such terms and shall be enforceable in such manner as may be provided by regulations made by the Secretary of State.

4.—(1) Subject to any specific provision of this Schedule to the contrary, in relation to an employee or employer who has died—
   (*a*) any reference in relevant provisions to the doing of anything by or in relation to an employee or employer shall be construed as including a reference to the doing of that thing by or in relation to any personal representative of the deceased employee or employer; and
   (*b*) any reference in the said provisions to a thing required or authorised to be done by or in relation to an employee or employer shall be construed as including a reference to any thing which, in accordance with any such provision as modified by this Schedule (including sub-paragraph (*a*) above), is required or authorised to be done by or in relation to any personal representative of the deceased employee or employer.

(2) Nothing in this paragraph shall prevent references in the relevant provisions to a successor of an employer from including a personal representative of a deceased employer.

Rights and liabilities accruing after death

5. Any right arising under any of the relevant provisions as modified by this Schedule shall, if it had not accrued before the death of the employee in question, nevertheless devolve as if it had so accrued.

6. Where by virtue of any of the relevant provisions as modified by this Schedule a personal representative of a deceased employer is liable to pay any amount and that liability had not accrued before the death of the employer, it shall be treated for all purposes as if it were a liability of the deceased employer which had accrued immediately before the death.

Death during protected period

7. Where an industrial tribunal makes a protective award under section 101 above and an employee of a description to which the award under section 101 above and an employee of a description to which the award relates dies during the protected period, the award shall be treated in his case as if it specified a protected period of such length as to end on the date of his death.

AMENDMENT

The words omitted in para. 1 were repealed by the Employment Protection (Consolidation) Act 1978, s.159(3), Sched. 17.

Section 114

SCHEDULE 13

AMENDMENTS OF THE EMPLOYMENT AGENCIES ACT 1973

1. In sections 1 and 2, for the words "licensing authority", wherever they occur, substitute the words "Secretary of State".

2. In section 1(2)(b) for the words from "time for appealing" to the end, substitute the words "refusal is notified to him in accordance with section 3(10) of this Act".

3.—(1) After section 2(3) insert the following subsection—

"(3A) A licence may be revoked by the Secretary of State on any of the grounds specified in subsection (3) of this section."

(2) Section 2(4) is hereby repealed.

(3) In section 2(5) omit the words "under the subsequent provisions of this Act" and for the words from "time for appealing" to the end, substitute the words "refusal is notified to him in accordance with section 3(10) of this Act".

4. For sections 3 and 4, substitute the following sections—

"Right to make repesentations

3.—(1) Where the Secretary of State proposes to refuse or to revoke a licence he shall notify the applicant for or the holder of the licence of—
   (a) the proposal and the reasons for it; and
   (b) his right under this section to make written representations relating to that proposal and the time within which that right may be exercised.

(2) A person who receives a notification of a proposal such as is mentioned in subsection (1) of this section may make written representations about it to the Secretary of State.

(3) Written representations in relation to a proposal to refuse or revoke a licence must be received by the Secretary of State within 21 days of the receipt of the notification of that proposal.

(4) If the Secretary of State receives such representations within the time specified in subsection (3) of this section, he shall consider them and—
   (a) if he decides not to proceed with the proposal, and accordingly decides to grant or not to revoke the licence, shall notify the applicant or holder of his decision;
   (b) in any other case, shall appoint a person to consider the representations on his behalf, and shall notify the applicant or holder of that appointment and of the name of the appointed person, and shall require the applicant or holder to state within 14 days whether he wishes to make oral representations to the appointed person.

(5) If a person who receives such a notification as is mentioned in subsection (4)(b) of this section expresses, within the time mentioned in that paragraph, a wish to make oral representations to the appointed person the Secretary of State shall give the former written notice of the place, date and time of hearing.

(6) A notice under subsection (5) of this section shall not specify a date for the hearing earlier than 21 days from the date of the notice, unless the person who wishes to make the representations has agreed to an earlier hearing.

(7) The appointed person shall, in accordance with the notice given under subsection (5) of this section, afford to the person who wishes to make oral representations an opportunity to do so, either in person or by any person authorised by him in that behalf.

(8) The appointed person shall consider the written representations referred to in subsection (4) of this section and any oral representations made under subsection (7) of this section, and shall make a report to the Secretary of State giving his findings of fact and his recommendations.

(9) Where representations relating to a proposal have been made under this section, the Secretary of State may make a final decision relating to that proposal only after receiving and considering the report on it of the appointed person.

(10) The Secretary of State shall notify the applicant, or holder, of his decision and the reasons for it and shall send him a copy of the appointed person's report".

5. Section 8 is hereby repealed.

6.—(1) In section 9(1) for the words "of a licensing authority duly authorised by them in that behalf" substitute the words "duly authorised in that behalf by the Secretary of State."

(2) In section 9(1)(c) for the words "licensing authority" and "their" substitute respectively the words "Secretary of State" and "his".

(3) In section 9(4)(a) sub-paragraphs (ii) and (iii) are hereby repealed, sub-paragraphs (iv) and (v) shall be renumbered as, respectively, sub-paragraphs (ii) and (iv), and after the renumbered sub-paragraph (ii) there shall be inserted the following sub-paragraph—

"(iii) by the Secretary of State, or an officer or servant appointed by, or persons exercising functions on behalf of, the Secretary of State to the person carrying on or proposing to carry on the employment agency or employment business concerned, to any person in his employment or, in the case of information relating to a person availing himself of the services of such an agency or business, to that person; or",

and in sub-paragraph (iv) (as renumbered) for the words from "on an appeal" to the end, substitute the words "under section 3(7) of this Act".

Section 115   SCHEDULE 14   **1–340**

AMENDMENTS OF THE EMPLOYMENT AND TRAINING ACT 1973

1. For section 1(7) substitute the following subsections—

"(7) The functions of the Commission and of the Agencies and of their officers and servants shall be performed on behalf of the Crown.

(8) For the purposes of any civil proceedings arising out of those functions, the Crown Proceedings Act 1947 and the Crown Suits (Scotland) Act 1857 shall apply to the Commission and the Agencies as if they were government departments within the meaning of the said Act of 1947 or, as the case may be, public departments within the meaning of the said Act of 1857."

2.—(1) In section 5(1), for the words from "providing" onwards substitute—

"(a) providing temporary employment for persons in Great Britain who are without employment;

(b) securing a temporary continuation of employment for persons in Great Britain who in his opinion would otherwise be likely to be dismissed by reason of redundancy; and

(c) obtaining employment for any description of persons in Great Britain who in his opinion would, because of their special circumstances and a high or increasing level of unemployment in Great Britain, otherwise have or be likely to have difficulty in obtaining employment;

and any such arrangements may include arrangements for the making by the Secretary of State of payments by way of grant or loan to employers or other persons in order to facilitate the carrying out of the arrangements.".

(2)–(5) [*Repealed by the Employment Subsidies Act* 1978 (*c.* 6), *s*.3(7)(*b*).]

3. After section 13(1) insert the following subsection:—

"(1A) Any reference in this Act to redundancy shall be construed as a reference to the existence of one or other of the facts specified in section 1(2)(a) and (b) of the Redundancy Payments Act 1965.".

4. In Schedule 1, after paragraph 10 insert the following paragraph:—

"10A. The Commission shall pay to the Minister for the Civil Service, at such times in each accounting year as may be determined by that Minister subject to any directions of the Treasury, sums of such amounts as he may so determine for the purposes of this paragraph as being equivalent to the increase during that year of such liabilities of his as are attributable to the provision of pensions, allowances or gratuities to or in respect of persons who are or have been in the service of the Commission in so far as that increase results from the service of those persons during that accounting year and to the expense to be incurred in administering those pensions, allowances or gratuities.".

5. In paragraph 13 of Schedule 1 for the words "or employee" substitute the words, "officer or servant".

6. The following provisions and passages are hereby repealed:—

Section 7.

In section 13(1), in the defintion of "employee" the words ", except in section 7 and Schedule 1".

Section 13(5).

In section 15(3), the references to paragraphs 5 and 13 of Schedule 3.

In Schedule 1, in paragraph 10(1) the words from "and any" to the end, paragraphs 10(2), 11, 12 and 16.

In Schedule 3, paragraphs 5 and 13.

Section 116

SCHEDULE 15

AMENDMENTS OF THE HEALTH AND SAFETY AT WORK ETC. ACT 1974

1. In section 1(2) omit the words "and agricultural health and safety regulations".
2. In section 2, omit subsection (5) and in subsection (7) for the words "subsections (4) and (5)" substitute the words 'subsection (4)".
3. After section 10(7) insert the following subsection:—

"(8) For the purposes of any civil proceedings arising out of those functions, the Crown Proceedings Act 1947 and the Crown Suits (Scotland) Act 1857 shall apply to the Commission and the Executive as if they were government departments within the meaning of the said Act of 1947 or, as the case may be, public departments within the meaning of the said Act of 1857.".

4. In section 11, in subsection (1) omit the words "except as regards matters relating exclusively to agricultureal operations", and in subsection (2) omit the words "except as aforesaid".
5. In section 14(2), omit the words from "but shall not do so" to "agricultural operations".
6. In section 15, for subsection (1) substitute—

"(1) Subject to the provisions of section 50, the Secretary of State, the Minister of Agriculture, Fisheries and Food or the Secretary of State and that Minister acting jointly shall have power to make regulations under this section for any of the general purposes of this Part (and regulations so made are in this Part referred to as "health and safety regulations").".

7. In section 16(1), omit the words "and except as regards matters relating exclusively to agricultural operations".
8. In section 18, in subsection (3) omit the words "or agricultural health and safety regulations", and in subsection (5) omit the words "the appropriate Agriculture Minister".
9. In section 28, after subsection (8) insert the following subsection—

"(9) Notwithstanding anything in subsection (7) above, a person who has obtained such information as is referred to in that subsection may furnish to a person who appears to him to be likely to be a party to any civil proceedings arising out of any accident, occurrence, situation or other matter, a written statement of relevant facts observed by him in the course of exercising any of the powers referred to in that subsection.".

10. Sections 29, 30, 31 and 32 are hereby repealed.
11. In section 33, in subsection (1)(c) omit the words "or agricultural health and safety regulations", and in subsection (4)(a) omit the words "or the appropriate Agriculture Minister".
12. In section 43, in subsection (3) omit the words "the Minister of Agriculture, Fisheries and Food" and for subsections (6) and (7) substitute—

"(6) The power to make regulations under this section shall be exercisable by the Secretary of State, the Minister of Agriculture, Fisheries and Food or the Secretary of State and that Minister acting jointly.".

13. In section 44, in subsection (1) omit the words "agricultural licences and", and in subsection (7)(a) for the words "an agricultural licence or nuclear site licence" substitute the words "a nuclear site licence".
14. In section 47, in subsection (2) omit the words "or agricultural health and safety regulations", in subsection (3) omit the words "or, as the case may be, agricultural health and safety regulations" and in subsection (5) omit the words "or, as the case may be, agricultural health and safety regulations".
15.—(1) In section 49, in subsection (1) for the words "The appropriate Minister may by regulations amend" substitute the words "Regulations made under this subsection may amend", in subsection (2) for the words "appropriate Minister" substitute the words "authority making the regulations", in subsection (3) omit the words "by the appropriate Minister" and for the words "if the appropriate Minister" substitute the words "if the authority making the regulations".

(2) For subsection (4) of that section substitute—

"(4) The power to make regulations under this section shall be exercisable by the Secretary of State, the Minister of Agriculture, Fisheries and Food or the Secretary of State and that Minister acting jointly ".

16.—(1) In section 50, for subsection (1) substitute—

"(1) Where any power to make regulations under any of the relevant statutory provisions is exercisable by the Secretary of State, the Minister of Agriculture, Fisheries and Food or both of them acting jointly that power may be exercised either so as to give effect (with or without modifications) to proposals submitted by the Commission under section 11(2)(*d*) or independently of any such proposals; but the authority who is to exercise the power shall not exercise it independently of proposals from the Commission unless he has consulted the Commission and such other bodies as appear to him to be appropriate".

(2) In subsection (2) of that section, for the words from "Secretary of State" to "preceding subsection" substitute "authority who is to exercise any such power as is mentioned in subection (1) above proposes to exercise that power".

(3) In subsection (3), for the words "to the Secretary of State" substitute the words "under section 11(2)(*d*)".

(4) Subsections (4) and (5) are hereby repealed.

17. In section 52, for subsections (3) and (4) substitute—

"(3) The power to make regulations under subsection (2) above shall be exercisable by the Secretary of State, the Minister of Agriculture, Fisheries and Food or the Secretary of State and that Minister acting jointly.".

18.—(1) In section 53, in subsection (1) omit the definitions of "agriculture", "the Agriculture Ministers", "agricultural health and safety regulations", "agricultural licence", "agricultural operation", "the appropriate Agriculture Minister", "forestry", "livestock" and "the relevant agricultural purposes" and in the definition of "the relevant statutory provisions" omit the words "and agricultural health and safety regulations".

(2) Subsections (2) to (6) of that section are hereby repealed.

19. In section 80, for subsections (4) to (6) substitute—

"(4) The power to make regulations under subsection (1) above shall be exercisable by the Secretary of State, the Minister of Agriculture, Fisheries and Food or the Secretary of State and that Minister acting jointly; but the authority who is to exercise the power shall, before exercising it, consult such bodies as appear to him to be appropriate.

(5) In this section 'the relevant statutory provisions' has the same meaning as in Part I."

20. In section 84(1)(*a*), omit the words "or 30".

21. Schedule 4 is hereby repealed.

Section 125   SCHEDULE 16   1–342

Minor and Consequential Amendments

. . . . . .

Part III

Trade Union and Labour Relations Act 1974

1. In sections 8 and 11, and in Schedule 2, for the words "Registrar of Friendly Societies" and "Registrar" wherever they occur substitute the words "Certification Officer".   1–343

2. In section 8, after subsection (6) insert the following subsection:—

"(6A) The Certification Officer shall remove the name of an organisation from the relevant list—

(*a*) if he is requested by the organisation to do so, or

(*b*) if he is satisfied that the organisation has ceased to exist".

3. For section 8(7) substitute the following subsection:—

"(7) Any organisation aggrieved by the refusal of the Certification Officer to enter its name in the relevant list or by a decision of his to remove its name from that list may appeal, in accordance with section 88(3) of the Employment Protection Act 1975, to the Employment Appeal Tribunal; and on any such appeal the Tribunal, if satisfied that the name should be or remain so entered, shall declare that fact and give directions to the Certificate Officer accordingly".

4. In section 8(9), for the words from "Chief Registrar" to the end of the subsection substitute the words "Certification Officer under paragraph 13(2) of Schedule 1 to the Employment Protection Act 1975".

5. In section 8(10), for the words from the beginning to "employers' associations" substitute the words "The fact that the name of an organisation is included in the list of trade unions or employers' associations shall be evidence (and in Scotland sufficient evidence) that the

organisation is a trade union or, as the case may be, an employers' association, and on the application of the organisation" and omit the words from "and that the organisation" to the end.

6. Renumber section 17 (restriction on grant of ex parte injunctions and interdicts) as subsection (1) of that section and at the end of that section insert the following subsections:—

"(2) It is hereby declared for the avoidance of doubt that where an application is made to a court, pending the trial of an action, for an interlocutory injunction and the party against whom the injunction is sought claims that he acted in contemplation or furtherance of a trade dispute, the court shall, in exercising its discretion whether or not to grant the injunction, have regard to the likelihood of that party's succeeding at the trial of the action in establishing the matter or matters which would, under any provision of section 13, 14(2) or 15 above, afford a defence to the action.

(3) Subsection (2) above shall not extend to Scotland."

7.—(1) In section 30(1), after the definition of "act" and "action" insert—

"Certification Officer" means the officer appointed under section 7 of the Employment Protection Act 1975;".

(2) In that subsection, after the definition of "employee" insert—

" "employer" (subject to subsection (2) below)—

(a) Where the reference is to an employer in relation to an employee, means the person by whom the employee is (or, in a case where the employment has ceased, was) employed, and

(b) in any other case, means a person regarded in that person's capacity as one for whom one or more workers work, or have worked or normally work or seek to work;".

(3) In that subsection, at the end of the definition of "independent trade union" insert "and 'in relation to a trade union' "independence" and "independent" shall be construed accordingly;".

(4) In that subsection, after the definition of "individual proprietor" insert—

"job", in relation to an employee, means the nature of the work which he is employed to do in accordance with his contract and the capacity and place in which he is so employed;".

(5) In that subsection, after the definition of "1971 Act", insert—

" "officer", in relation to a trade union or an employers' association includes any member of the governing body of that union or association and any trustee of any fund applicable for the purposes of that union or association;".

8–30. [*Repealed by the Employment Protection (Consolidation) Act 1978, s.159(3), Sched. 17.*]

31. In paragraph 31(1)(b) of Schedule 1 (nominations by members of trade unions) for the words "£500" substitute the words "£1,500".

32. In paragraph 31 of Schedule 1, for sub-paragraphs (4) and (5) substitute the following sub-paragraph:—

"(4) Sub-paragraph (1)(b) above shall be included among the provisions with respect to which the Treasury may make an order under section 6(1) of the Administration of Estates (Small Payments) Act 1965, substituting, for references to the amount for the time being provided for, references to such higher amount as may be specified in the order.".

33. In paragraph 33(2) of Schedule 1, after the words 'government department" insert the words "or any officer or body exercising on behalf of the Crown functions conferred by any enactment", and in paragraph 33(3)(e) of that Schedule, after the word "department" in the second, third and fourth places where it occurs insert the words ", officer or body".

34. [*Repealed by the Employment Protection (Consolidation) Act 1978 (c. 44), s.159(3), Sched. 17.*]

35.—(1) For the avoidance of doubt it is hereby declared that the change of name of the Industrial Court to the Industrial Arbitration Board originally effected by section 124(2) of the Industrial Relations Act 1971 and continued in force, so far as the Industrial Court Act 1919 is concerned by paragraph 3 of Schedule 3 to the 1974 Act, shall, as respects the relevant period, be taken not to have divested that body of any functions under any other enactment or any instrument notwithstanding that after the repeal by the 1974 Act of the said section 124(2) references in any such other enactment or any such instrument to the Industrial Court were no longer expressly directed to be construed as references to the Industrial Arbitration Board.

(2) In this paragraph "the relevant period" means the period beginning with 16th September 1974 (the day appointed for the coming into operation of the said Schedule 3) and ending with the repeal by this Act of Part I of the Industrial Courts Act 1919.

Part IV

Miscellaneous Amendments

House of Commons Offices Act 1846 (*c*. 77)

1. [*Repealed by the House of Commons (Administration) Act* 1978 (*c*. 36), *s*.5, *Sched*. 3.]   **1–344**

Trade Union Act 1913 (2 & 3 Geo. 5 *c*. 30)

2.—(1) The Trade Union Act 1913 shall be amended in accordance with the following provisions of this paragraph.

(2) In sections 3 to 5 for the words "Registrar of Friendly Societies" and "Registrar" wherever they occur substitute the words "Certification Officer".

(3) After section 5 insert the following section—

"**Appeals**

5A. An appeal shall lie, in accordance with section 88(2) of the Employment Protection Act 1975, to the Employment Appeal Tribunal on any question of law arising in any proceedings before or arising from any decision of the Certification Officer under section 3, 4 or 5 of this Act".

(4) For section 7 substitute—

"**Definition of Certification Officer**

7. In this Act references to the "Certification Officer" are references to the officer appointed under section 7 of the Employment Protection Act 1975".

Industrial Courts Act 1919 (*c*.69)

3.—(1) The Industrial Courts Act 1919 shall be amended in accordance with the following provisions of this paragraph.

(2) The following provisions and passages are hereby repealed:—
Sections 1, 2 and 3.
In section 4(1), the words "whether or not the dispute is reported to him under Part I of this Act".
In section 7, the words "of the Industrial Arbitration Board and".
In section 9, the words "before the Industrial Arbitration Board, before an arbitrator or".
Sections 11 and 12.

(3) [*Repealed by the Employment Act* 1982 (*c*.46), *Sched*. 4.]

(4) For section 10 substitute—

"**Employment under the Crown**

10.—(1) Subject to the following provisions of this section, the provisions of this Act shall have effect in relation to Crown employment and to workers who are Crown employees as they have effect in relation to other employment and to other workers.

(2) In this section "Crown employment" means, subject to subsection (3) of this section, employment under or for the purposes of a government department or any officer or body exercising on behalf of the Crown functions conferred by any enactment.

(3) This section does not apply to service as a member of the naval, military or air forces of the Crown or of any women's service administered by the Defence Council, but does apply to employment by any association established for the purposes of the Auxiliary Forces Act 1953.

(4) A Minister of the Crown may exempt from the provisions of this section employment of a specified description or the employment of a particular person by certificate stating that such exemption is required for the purpose of safeguarding national security; and any document purporting to be such a certificate shall, unless the contrary is proved, be deemed to be such a certificate".

Road Haulage Wages Act 1938 (c.44)

4. [Repealed by the Employment Act 1980, Sched. 2.]

Civil Aviation Act 1949 (c.67)

5. In section 15 of the Civil Aviation Act 1949 in subsection (2) for the word "Minister" substitute the words "Advisory, Conciliation and Arbitration Service", and in subsections (2) and (3) for the words "Industrial Court" and "Court" wherever they occur substitute respectively the words "Central Arbitration Committee" and "Committee."

Public Records Act 1958 (c.51)

6. In Part II of the Table at the end of paragraph 3(2) of Schedule 1 to the Public Records Act 1958, insert at the appropriate place in alphabetical order the following entry—
"Commission on Industrial Relations.".

Road Traffic Act 1960 (c.16)

7. In section 152 of the Road Traffic Act 1960,—
    (a) for subsection (2) substitute the following subsection—
        "(2) Any organisation representative of the persons engaged in the road transport industry may make representations to the Advisory, Conciliation and Arbitration Service to the effect that the wages paid to, or the conditions of employment of, any persons employed by the holder of a road service licence are not in accordance with the requirements of the foregoing subsection, and if the matter in dispute is not otherwise disposed of it shall be referred by the Service to the Central Arbitration Committee for settlement."; and
    (b) in subsections (3) and (4) for the words "Industrial Court" and "Court", wherever they occur, substitute respectively the words "Central Arbitration Committee" and "Committee".

Films Act 1960 (c.57)

8. In section 42 of the Films Act 1960 for the words "Minister of Labour" substitute the words "Advisory, Conciliation and Arbitration Service" and for the words "industrial court" and "court" wherever they occur substitute respectively the words "Central Arbitration Committee" and "Committee".

Education (Scotland) Act 1962 (c.47)

9.—(1) The Education (Scotland) Act 1962 shall be amended in accordance with the following provisions of this paragraph.
(2) In section 85, subsection (3) and, in subsection (5), the word "(3)" are hereby repealed.
(3) In section 123(2), in the proviso, the words from "and", where secondly occurring, to the end are hereby repealed.
(4) After section 123(2), insert the following subsection—
"(2A) In any scheme for any endowment, any provision which applies subsection (3) of section 85 of this Act to any certificated or registered teacher in the employment of the governing body of that endowment, or which has, in relation to such a teacher, the like effect as such a provision, shall cease to have effect".

Trade Union (Amalgamations, etc.) Act 1964 (c.24)

10.—(1) The Trade Union (Amalgamations, etc.) Act 1964 shall be amended in accordance with the following provisions of this paragraph.
(2) In sections 1, 4, 6 and 7 (and the Schedules), for the word "Registrar" wherever it occurs substitute the words "Certification Officer", and in section 9(1) after the definition of "the amalgamating unions" and "the amalgamated union" insert—
    " 'Certification Officer' means the officer appointed under section 7 of the Employment Protection Act 1975".
(3) For section 4(8) substitute the following subsection—
    "(8) An appeal shall lie, in accordance with section 88(2) of the Employment Protection

Act 1975, as the instance of the complainant or the trade union to the Employment Appeal Tribunal on any question of law arising in any proceedings before, or arising from any decision of, the Certification Officer under this section".

Remuneration of Teachers Act 1965 (c.3)

11.—(1) The Remuneration of Teachers Act 1965 shall be amended in accordance with the following provisions of this paragraph.

(2) In section 3(3) for the words "Minister of Labour" substitute the words "Advisory, Conciliation and Arbitration Service"; and references in any arrangements made by the Secretary of State under section 3(1) to the Minister of Labour shall be construed as references to the Service.

(3) In section 3(3), the words from "and, where arbitrators" to the end, and section 6(*d*) are hereby repealed.

Remuneration of Teachers (Scotland) Act 1967 (c. 36)

12.—(1) The Remuneration of Teachers (Scotland) Act 1967 shall be amended in accordance with the following provisions of this paragraph.

(2) In section 3(3) for the words "Minister of Labour" substitute the words "Advisory, Conciliation and Arbitration Service"; and references in any arrangements made by the Secretary of State under section 3(1) to the Minister of Labour shall be construed as references to the Service.

(3) In section 3(3), the words from "and, where arbiters" to the end, and section 7(*c*) are hereby repealed.

Equal Pay Act 1970 (c. 41)

13.—(1) The Equal Pay Act 1970 shall be amended in accordance with the following provisions of this paragraph.

(2) In sections 3, 4, 5, 7 and 10, for the words "Industrial Arbitration Board" (being words substituted by Part I of Schedule 1 to the Sex Discrimination Act 1975), wherever they occur, substitute the words "Central Arbitration Committee".

(3) In sections 4, 5 and 10 for the word "Board" (being a word so substituted), wherever it occurs except in the expression "Agricultural Wages Board", substitute the word "Committee".

(4) In section 3(1), for the words "Part I of the Industrial Courts Act 1919" there shall be substituted the words "section 10 of the Employment Protection Act 1975".

(3) In section 3(2), for paragraph (*b*) substitute the following paragraph—
"(*b*) if an award or determination is, or has been, made under any enactment requiring an employer to observe the collective agreement, that award or determination shall have effect by reference to the agreement as so amended."

(6) In section 4, in subsections (1) and (2), for the words "wages regulation order" wherever they occur there shall be substituted the words "order under section 11 of the Wages Council Act 1959".

(7) In section 4(1) for the words from "the Secretary of State" in the second place where they occur to the end there shall be substituted the words "it shall be the duty of the wages council or statutory joint industrial council, by a further order coming into operation not later than five months after the date of the Committee's decision, either to make those amendments in the order referred to by the Committee or otherwise to replace or amend that order so as to remove the discrimination".

(8) In section 4, after subsection (1) there shall be inserted the following subsection—
"(1A) Where a wages council or statutory joint industrial council certifies that the effect of an order under section 11 of the Wages Councils Act 1959 is only to make such amendments of a previous order as have under this section been declared by the Central Arbitration Committee to be needed, or to make such amendments as aforesaid with minor modifications or modifications of limited application, or is only to revoke and reproduce with such amendments a previous order, then the wages council or statutory joint industrial council may instead of complying with subsections (3) and (3A) of the said section 11 give notice of the proposed order in such manner as appears to the council expedient in the circumstances, and may make the order at any time after the expiration of seven days from the giving of the notice".

(9) In section 4, for subsection (2) there shall be inserted the following subsection—
"(2) An order under section 11 of the Wages Council Act 1959 shall be referred to the

Central Arbitration Committee under this section if the Secretary of State is requested so to refer it either—
   (a) by an employers' association for the time being entitled to nominate for membership of the wages council or statutory joint industrial council in question persons representing employers (or, if provision is made for any of the persons representing employers to be elected instead of nominated, then by a member or members representing employers); or
   (b) by a trade union for the time being entitled to nominate for membership of the wages council or statutory joint industrial council in question persons representing workers (or, if provision is made for any of the persons representing workers to be elected instead of nominated, then by a member or members representing workers);
or if in any case it appears to the Secretary of State that the order may be amendable under this section.".

(10) In section 4(3), after the words "12(1)" wherever they occur there shall be inserted the words "or (1A)", and for the words "11(7)" there shall be substituted the words "11(8)".

(11) Section 4(4) is hereby repealed.

Tribunals and Inquiries Act 1971 (c. 62)

14. [Repealed by the Employment Protection (Consolidation) Act 1978, s.159(3), Sched. 17.]

Independent Broadcasting Authority Act 1973 (c. 19)

15. In section 16 of the Independent Broadcasting Authority Act 1973 for the words "Secretary of State" wherever they occur substitute the words "Advisory, Conciliation and Arbitration Service" and for the words "Industrial Arbitration Board" and "Board" wherever they occur substitute respectively the words "Central Arbitration Committee" and "Committee".

House of Commons Disqualification Act 1975 (c. 24)

16.—(1) The House of Commons Disqualification Act 1975 shall be amended in accordance with the following provisions of this paragraph.

(2) In Part II of Schedule 1 (bodies of which all members are disqualified under that Act), insert, at the appropriate places in alphabetical order, the following entries:—
"The Central Arbitration Committee."
"The Council of the Advisory, Conciliation and Arbitration Service."
"The Employment Appeal Tribunal."
"The Employment Service Agency."
"The Training Services Agency."

(3) In Part III of Schedule 1 (other disqualifying offices), insert the following entry at the appropriate place in alphabetical order:—
"Certification Officer or assistant certification officer appointed under section 7 of the Employment Protection Act 1975."

Social Security Pensions Act 1975 (c. 60)

17. After section 31(8) of the Social Security Pensions Act 1975 there shall be inserted the following subsection:—
"(9) A trade union shall be treated as recognised for the purpose of this section not only if it is recognised for the purpose of collective bargaining, but also if the Advisory Conciliation and Arbitration Service has made a recommendation for recognition under the Employment Protection Act 1975 and that recommendation is operative within the meaning of section 15 of that Act."

Sex Discrimination Act 1975 (c. 65)

18.—(1) The Sex Discrimination Act 1975 shall be amended in accordance with the following provisions of this paragraph.

(2) In section 65(2), for the words "amount for the time being specified in paragraph 20(1)(b)" substitute the words "limit for the time being imposed by paragraph 20".

(3) In the Equal Pay Act 1970 as set out in Part II of Schedule 1 to the Sex Discrimination

Section 125 SCHEDULE 17

TRANSITIONAL PROVISIONS

1. Subject to any express provision made in any of the following paragraphs of this Schedule, in so far as anything done or treated as done under any enactment replaced or amended by any provision of this Act, could have been done under that provision or, as the case may be, that enactment as amended, then it shall on the commencement of that provision have effect as if done under that provision or, as the case may be, that enactment as so amended.

2. Where any action has been taken by a conciliation officer under paragraph 26(2) to (5) of Schedule 1 to the 1974 Act before the commencement of section 2 above, that action shall on the commencement of that section be treated as if it had been taken by a conciliation officer appointed under that section.

3. Any matter which immediately before the commencement of section 10(2) above stood referred to the Industrial Arbitration Board under section 2(2) of the Industrial Courts Act 1919 or section 13 of the National Health Service (Amendment) Act 1949 shall be treated as if it had been referred to the Committee by the Service under section 3(1) above.

4.—(1) The Code of Practice in effect under Part I of Schedule 1 to the 1974 Act immediately before the repeal of that Part by this Act shall remain in effect and shall be taken into account in industrial tribunal proceedings in accordance with paragraph 3 of that Schedule, notwithstanding that repeal, until it is superseded in accordance with sub-paragraph (2) below by one or more Codes of Practice issued by the Service under section 6 above.

(2) If on issuing any Code of Practice under section 6 above the Service is of the opinion that the code of practice continued in effect by sub-paragraph (1) above, or any part of that code, should cease to have effect by reason of being superseded by the provisions of the Code of Practice under section 6 above, the Service shall state in the new Code of Practice that the old code, or a specified part is so superseded and that old code, or part, shall cease to have effect on the date on which the new Code comes into effect in pursuance of an order by the Secretary of State under section 6(8) above.

(3) Without prejudice to any other power to make transitional and other supplementary or incidental provisions in an order under the said section, such an order may contain such transitional provision or savings as appear to the Secretary of State to be necessary or expedient in connection with any provisions of the code of practice under Part I of Schedule 1 to the 1974 Act which ceases to have effect on the day appointed by that order.

5.—(1) Anything done before the commencement of section 7 above by, to or in relation to the Chief Registrar of Friendly Societies or any assistant registrar under any of the Acts referred to in section 7(2) above, shall be treated on the commencement of that section as having been done by, to or in relation to the Certification Officer.

(2) In particular, sub-paragraph (1) above applies to the following things done under any such Act, that is to say,—
  any complaint presented;
  any application, determination, registration, order, entry, return, report, or requirement made;
  any certificate, approval, notice, direction or exemption given.

6. Anything done before the commencement of section 10(2) above by, to or in relation to the Industrial Arbitration Board under any enactment in which by virtue of that subsection references to the Industrial Arbitration Board (whether by that or any other name) are to be construed as references to the Central Arbitration Committee, shall be treated after the commencement of that subsection as if they had been done by, to or in relation to the Committee.

7–10. [*Repealed by the Employment Protection (Consolidation) Act 1978, s.159(3), Sched. 17.*]

11. [*Repealed by the Wages Councils Act 1979 (c. 12), s.31(3), Sched. 7.*]

12. An order under [. . .] section 3 of the Agricultural Wages Act 1948 or section 3 of the Agricultural Wages (Scotland) Act 1949 (as substituted, in each case, by this Act) which may have effect as from a date earlier than the date of the order, shall not have effect from a date earlier than the commencement of the provision of this Act effecting that substitution.

13. [*Repealed by the Employment Act 1980, Sched. 2.*]

14. Where any provision of this Act increases the penalty for an offence under any other enactment, that increase shall not have effect in relation to an offence committed before the commencement of the relevant provision.

15. The repeals effected by section 111 above—
   (a) in the case of subsection (1) of that section, shall not confer or affect any right to unemployment benefit in respect of any day before the commencement of that subsection, and
   (b) in the case of subsection (2) of that section, shall not affect the manner in which any person's requirements or resources are to be ascertained in relation to any period beginning before the commencement of that subsection.

16, 17. [*Repealed by the Employment Protection (Consolidation) Act* 1978, *s.*159(3), *Sched.* 17.]

18. Any enactment or document which refers, whether specifically or by means of a general description, to an enactment which is replaced or amended by any provision of this Act, shall, except so far as the context otherwise requires, be construed as referring or as including a reference, to that provision.

19. Nothing in this Schedule shall be construed as prejudicing section 38 of the Interpretation Act 1889 (effect of repeals).

AMENDMENT

In para. 12 the words omitted in square brackets were repealed by the Wages Councils Act 1979 (c. 12), s.31, Sched. 7.

Section 125

SCHEDULE 18

ENACTMENTS REPEALED

Chapter	Short Title	Extent of Repeal
1896 c. 30.	The Conciliation Act 1896.	The whole Act.
2 & 3 Geo. 5. c. 30.	The Trade Union Act 1913.	In section 3 (2) the words from "shall be binding" to "restrainable by injunction, and" and the words "and 'interdict' sghall be substituted for 'injunction' ".
1919 c. 69.	The Industrial Courts Act 1919.	Part I. In section 4 (1), the words "whether or not the dispute is reported to him under Part I of this Act". In section 7, the words "of the Industrial Arbitration Board and". In section 9, the words "before the Industrial Arbitration Board, before an arbitrator or". Sections 11 and 12.
1938 c. 44.	The Road Haulage Wages Act 1938.	Section 5 (5).
1948 c. 67.	The Agricultural Wages Act 1948.	In section 12 (5), the words from "and in any such civil proceedings" onwards. In Schedule 4, in paragraph 6, the words from the beginning to "holidays".
1949 c. 30.	The Agricultural Wages (Scotland) Act 1949.	In section 12 (4), the words from "and in any such civil proceedings" onwards. In Schedule 3, in paragraph 6, the words from the beginning to "holidays".
1949 c. 93.	The National Health Service (Amendment) Act 1949.	Section 13.
1958 c. 51.	The Public Records Act 1958.	In Schedule 1, in Part II of the Table at the end of paragraph 3, the entries relating to the Employment Service Agency, the Manpower Services Commission and the Training Services Agency.

Chapter	Short Title	Extent of Repeal
1959 c. 26.	The Terms and Conditions of Employment Act 1959.	The whole Act, so far as unrepealed.
1959 c. 69.	The Wages Councils Act 1959.	Section 9 (1). In section 23, the words "a commission of inquiry". In section 24, the definitions of "wages regulation order" and "wages regulation proposals". Schedule 4.
1960 c. 37.	The Payment of Wages Act 1960.	Section 2 (4) to (8). In section 4 (2), the words from "and, at or before" to the end. In section 4 (3), the words from "and, at or before" to the end. Section 7 (3). The Schedule.
1962 c. 47.	The Education (Scotland) Act 1962.	In section 85, subsection (3) and in subsection (5) the word "3". In section 123 (2), in the proviso, the words from "and", where secondly occurring, to the end.
1964 c. 24.	The Trade Union (Amalgamations, etc.) Act 1964.	In section 7 (1) (c), the words "or by any assistant registrar". In section 9, the definitions of "assistant registrar" and "Registrar".
1965 c. 3.	The Remuneration of Teachers Act 1965.	In section 3 (3), the words from "and, where arbitrators'" to the end. Section 6 (d).
1965 c. 62.	The Redundancy Payments Act 1965.	In section 5 (2) the words "(calculated in accordance with Schedule 2 to this Act)". Schedule 2. In Schedule 4, paragraphs 6 and 12. In Schedule 5, in paragraph 1 the words from "and paragraph 5" onwards; and paragraph 13.
1966 c. 20.	The Supplementary Benefit Act 1966.	In section 10 (2), in paragraph (a), the words "or financing" and the word "and" and paragraph (b).
1967 c. 36.	The Remuneration of Teachers (Scotland) Act 1967.	In section 3 (3), the words from "and, where arbiters" to the end. Section 7 (c).
1968 c. 73.	The Transport Act 1968.	Section 35 (3) (b).
1970 c. 41.	The Equal Pay Act 1970.	Section 4 (4).
1972 c. 11.	The Superannuation Act 1972.	In Schedule 1, the entries relating to the Manpower Services Commission, the Employment Service Agency and the Training Services Agency.
1973 c. 35.	The Employment Agencies Act 1973.	Section 2 (4). In section 2 (5), the words "under the subsequent provisions of this Act". Section 8. In section 9 (4) (a), sub-paragraphs (ii) and (iii). In section 13 (1), the definition of "licensing authority".
1973 c. 38.	The Social Security Act 1973.	In Schedule 27, paragraph 54.
1973 c. 50.	The Employment and Training Act 1973.	Section 7. In section 13 (1) in the definition of

Chapter	Short Title	Extent of Repeal
1974 c. 37.	The Health and Safety at Work etc. Act 1974.	"employee" the words "except in Schedule 1"; and in the definition of "employment" the words "except in section 7 and Schedule 1". Section 13 (5). In section 15 (3), the words "5" and "13". In Schedule 1, in paragraph 10 (1) the words from "and any" to the end, and paragraphs 10 (2), 11, 12 and 16. In Schedule 3, paragraphs 5 and 13. In section 1 (2) the words "and agricultural health and safety regulations". Section 2 (5). In section 11, in subsection (1), the words "except as regards matters relating exclusively to agricultural operations"; and in subsection (2), the words "except as aforesaid". In section 14 (2), the words from "but shall not do so" to "agricultural operations". In section 16 (1), the words "and except as regards matters relating exclusively to agricultural operations". In section 18, in subsection (3), the words "or agricultural health and safety regulations"; and in subsection (5), the words "the appropriate Agricultural Minister". Sections 29, 30, 31 and 32. In section 33, in subsection (1) (c), the words "or agricultural health and safety regulations"; and in subsection (4) (a), the words "or the appropriate Agricultural Minister". In section 43 (3), the words "the Minister of Agriculture, Fisheries and Food". In section 44 (1), the words "agricultural licences and". In section 47, in subsection (2), the words "or agricultural health and safety regulations"; in subsection (3), the words "or, as the case may be, agricultural health and safety regulations"; and in subsection (5) the words "or, as the case may be, agricultural health and safety regulations". In section 49 (3), the words "by the appropriate Minister". Section 50 (4) and (5). In section 53 (1), the definitions of "agriculture", "the Agriculture Ministers", "agricultural health and safety regulations", "agricultural licence", "agricultural operation", "the appropriate Agricultural Minister", "forestry", "livestock" and "the relevant agricultural purposes"; and in the definition of "the relevant statutory provisions", the words "and agricultural health and safety regulations".

Chapter	Short Title	Extent of Repeal
1974 c. 39.	The Consumer Credit Act 1974.	Section 53 (2) to (6). In section 84 (1) (*a*), the words "or 30". Schedule 4. In section 16 (3) (*b*) the words "or (*c*)".
1974 c. 52.	The Trade Union and Labour Relations Act 1974.	In section 8 (1), the words in brackets. Section 8 (8). In section 8 (10), the words from "and that the organisation" to the end. In section 30 (1), the definition of "Registrar". In Schedule 1, Part I; in paragraph 5 (3), the words "obligatory" and "in writing"; paragraph 5 (4); in paragraph 9 (1), paragraphs (*a*), (*e*) and (*f*) and in paragraph (*b*) the words "or a close relative"; paragraph 9 (4); in paragraph 17 (1), words from "or by a person" onwards; paragraphs 17 (2) and (3), 19 and 26 (1); in paragraph 26 (3) (*a*) the words "his engagement"; and paragraph 29. In Schedule 3, paragraphs 2 (6), 3, 8, 9 (4), (6) and (7), 10 (4), and (6) and 15.
1975 c. 14.	The Social Security Act 1975.	In section 19 (1), in paragraph (*a*), the words "or financing" and the word "and", and paragraph (*b*).
1975 c. 18.	The Social Security (Consequential Provisions) Act 1975.	In Schedule 2, in paragraph 19 the words "17 (3) and (4A) and ", and paragraph 20.
1975 c. 24.	The House of Commons Disqualification Act 1975.	In Part II of Schedule 1, the entry relating to the Industrial Arbitration Board. In Part III of Schedule 1, in the entry relating to members of Wages Councils and other persons appointed under the Wages Councils Act 1959, the words "or a member of a Commission of Inquiry appointed under paragraph 1 (*a*) of Schedule 4 to that Act".
1975 c. 25.	The Northern Ireland Assembly Disqualification Act 1975.	In Part II of Schedule 1, the entry relating to the Industrial Arbitration Board. In Part III of Schedule 1, in the entry relating to member of Wages Councils and other persons appointed under the Wages Council Act 1959, the words "or a member of a Commission of Inquiry appointed under paragraph 1 (*a*) of Schedule 4 to that Act".
1975 c. 65.	The Sex Discrimination Act 1975.	In section 82 (1), the definition of "conciliation officer". In Schedule 5. paragraph 4.

Race Relations Act 1976

(1976 c.74)

An Act to make fresh provision with respect to discrimination on racial grounds and relations between people of different racial groups; and to make in the Sex Discrimination Act 1975 amendments for bringing provisions in that Act relating to its administration and enforcement into conformity with the corresponding responding provisions in this Act

[22nd November 1976]

Part I

Discrimination to which Act Applies

Racial discrimination

1.—(1) A person discriminates against another in any circumstances relevant for the purposes of any provision of this Act if—
  (a) on racial grounds he treats that other less favourably than he treats or would treat other persons; or
  (b) he applies to that other a requirement or condition which he applies or would apply equally to persons not of the same racial group as that other but—
    (i) which is such that the proportion of persons of the same racial group as that other who can comply with it is considerably smaller than the proportion of persons not of that racial group who can comply with it; and
    (ii) which he cannot show to be justifiable irrespective of the colour, race, nationality or ethnic or national origins of the person to whom it is applied; and
    (iii) which is to the detriment of that other because he cannot comply with it.

(2) It is hereby declared that, for the purposes of this Act, segregating a person from other persons on racial grounds is treating him less favourably than they are treated.

Discrimination by way of victimisation

2.—(1) A person ("the discriminator") discriminates against another person ("the person victimised") in any circumstances relevant for the purposes of any provision of this Act if he treats the person victimised less favourably than in those circumstances he treats or would treat other persons, and does so by reason that the person victimised has—
  (a) brought proceedings against the discriminator or any other person under this Act; or
  (b) given evidence or information in connection with proceedings brought by any person against the discriminator or any other person under this Act; or
  (c) otherwise done anything under or by reference to this Act in relation to the discriminator or any other person; or

(*d*) alleged that the discriminator or any other person has committed an act which (whether or not the allegation so states) would amount to a contravention of this Act,

or by reason that the discriminator knows that the person victimised intends to do any of those things, or suspects that the person victimised has done, or intends to do, any of them.

(2) Subsection (1) does not apply to treatment of a person by reason of any allegation made by him if the allegation was false and not made in good faith.

Meaning of "racial grounds," "racial group," etc.

3.—(1) In this Act, unless the context otherwise requires— 1–350
"racial grounds" means any of the following grounds, namely colour, race, nationality or ethnic or national origins;
"racial group" means a group of persons defined by references to colour, race, nationality or ethnic or national origins, and references to a person's racial group refer to any racial group into which he falls.

(2) The fact that a racial group comprises two or more distinct racial groups does not prevent it from constituting a particular racial group for the purposes of this Act.

(3) In this Act—
    (*a*) references to discrimination refer to any discrimination falling within section 1 or 2; and
    (*b*) references to racial discrimination refer to any discrimination falling within section 1,
and related expressions shall be construed accordingly.

(4) A comparison of the case of a person of a particular racial group with that of a person not of that group under section 1(1) must be such that the relevant circumstances in the one case are the same, or not materially different, in the other.

PART II

DISCRIMINATION IN THE EMPLOYMENT FIELD

Discrimination by Employers

Discrimination against applicants and employees

4.—(1) It is unlawful for a person, in relation to employment by him at 1–351
an establishment in Great Britain, to discriminate against another—
    (*a*) in the arrangements he makes for the purpose of determining who should be offered that employment; or
    (*b*) in the terms on which he offers him that employment; or
    (*c*) by refusing or deliberately omitting to offer him that employment.

(2) It is unlawful for a person, in the case of a person employed by him at an establishment in Great Britain, to discriminate against that employee—
    (*a*) in the terms of employment which he affords him; or
    (*b*) in the way he affords him access to opportunities for promotion, transfer or training, or to any other benefits, facilities or services, or by refusing or deliberately omitting to afford him access to them; or

(c) by dismissing him, or subjecting him to any other detriment.

(3) Except in relation to discrimination falling within section 2, subsections (1) and (2) do not apply to employment for the purposes of a private household.

(4) Subsection (2) does not apply to benefits, facilities or services of any description if the employer is concerned with the provision (for payment or not) of benefits, facilities or services of that description to the public, or to a section of the public comprising the employee in question, unless—
- (a) that provision differs in a material respect from the provision of the benefits, facilities or services by the employer to his employees; or
- (b) the provision of the benefits, facilities or services to the employee in question is regulated by his contract of employment; or
- (c) the benefits, facilities or services relate to training.

Exceptions for genuine occupational qualifications

1-352 5.—(1) In relation to racial discrimination—
- (a) section 4(1)(a) or (c) does not apply to any employment where being of a particular racial group is a genuine occupational qualification for the job; and
- (b) section 4(2)(b) does not apply to opportunities for promotion or transfer to, or training for, such employment.

(2) Being of a particular racial group is a genuine occupational qualification for a job only where—
- (a) the job involves participation in a dramatic performance or other entertainment in a capacity for which a person of that racial group is required for reasons of authenticity; or
- (b) the job involves participation as an artist's or photographic model in the production of a work of art, visual image or sequence of visual images for which a person of that racial group is required for reasons of authenticity; or
- (c) the job involves working in a place where food or drink is (for payment or not) provided to and consumed by members of the public or a section of the public in a particular setting for which, in that job, a person of that racial group is required for reasons of authenticity; or
- (d) the holder of the job provides persons of that racial group with personal services promoting their welfare, and those services can most effectively be provided by a person of that racial group.

(3) Subsection (2) applies where some only of the duties of the job fall within paragraph (a), (b), (c) or (d) as well as where all of them do.

(4) Paragraph (a), (b), (c) or (d) of subsection (2) does not apply in relation to the filling of a vacancy at a time when the employer already has employees of the racial group in question—
- (a) who are capable of carrying out the duties falling within that paragraph; and
- (b) whom it would be reasonable to employ on those duties; and
- (c) whose numbers are sufficient to meet the employer's likely requirements in respect of those duties without undue inconvenience.

Exception for employment intended to provide training in skills to be exercised outside Great Britain

1-353 6. Nothing in section 4 shall render unlawful any act done by an employer for the benefit of a person not ordinarily resident in Great

Britain in or in connection with employing him at an establishment in Great Britain, where the purpose of that employment is to provide him with training in skills which he appears to the employer to intend to exercise wholly outside Great Britain.

Discrimination against contract workers

7.—(1) This section applies to any work for a person ("the principal") which is available for doing by individuals ("contract workers") who are employed not by the principal himself but by another person, who supplies them under a contract made with the principal.

1–354

(2) It is unlawful for the principal, in relation to work to which this section applies, to discriminate against a contract worker—
- (a) in the terms on which he allows him to do that work; or
- (b) by not allowing him to do it or continue to do it; or
- (c) in the way he affords him access to any benefits, facilities or services or by refusing or deliberately omitting to afford him access to them; or
- (d) by subjecting him to any other detriment.

(3) The principal does not contravene subsection (2)(b) by doing any act in relation to a person not of a particular racial group at a time when, if the work were to be done by a person taken into the principal's employment, being of that racial group would be a genuine occupational qualification for the job.

(4) Nothing in this section shall render unlawful any act done by the principal for the benefit of a contract worker not ordinarily resident in Great Britain in or in connection with allowing him to do work to which this section applies, where the purpose of his being allowed to do that work is to provide him with training in skills which he appears to the principal to intend to exercise wholly outside Great Britain.

(5) Subsection (2)(c) does not apply to benefits, facilities or services of any description if the principal is concerned with the provision (for payment or not) of benefits, facilities or services of that description to the public, or to a section of the public to which the contract worker in question belongs, unless that provision differs in a material respect from the provision of the benefits, facilities or services by the principal to his contract workers.

Meaning of employment at establishment in Great Britain

8.—(1) For the purposes of this Part ("the relevant purposes"), employment is to be regarded as being at an establishment in Great Britain unless the employee does his work wholly or mainly outside Great Britain.

1–355

(2) In relation to—
- (a) employment on board a ship registered at a port of registry in Great Britain; or
- (b) employment on an aircraft or hovercraft registered in the United Kingdom and operated by a person who has his principal place of business, or is ordinarily resident, in Great Britain, other than an aircraft or hovercraft while so operated in pursuance of a contract with a person who has his principal place of business, or is ordinarily resident, outside the United Kingdom,

subsection (1) shall have effect as if the words "or mainly" were omitted.

(3) In the case of employment on board a ship registered at a port of registry in Great Britain (except where the employee does his work wholly outside Great Britain) the ship shall for the relevant pupurposes be deemed to be the establishment.

(4) Where work is not done at an establishment it shall be treated for the relevant purposes as done at the establishment from which it is done or (where it is not done from any establishment) at the establishment with which it has the closest connection.

(5) In relation to employment concerned with exploration of the sea bed or subsoil or the exploitation of their natural resources, Her Majesty may by Order in Council provide that subsections (1) to (3) shall have effect as if in both subsection (1) and subsection (3) the last reference to Great Britain included any area for the time being designated under section 1(7) of the Continental Shelf Act 1964, except an area or part of an area in which the law of Northern Ireland applies.

(6) An Order in Council under subsection (5) may provide that, in relation to employment to which the Order applies, this Part is to have effect with such modifications as are specified in the Order.

(7) An Order in Council under subsection (5) shall be of no effect unless a draft of the Order has been laid before and approved by resolution of each House of Parliament.

Exception for seamen recruited abroad

1–356　　9.—(1) Nothing in section 4 shall render unlawful any act done by an employer in or in connection with employment by him on any ship in the case of a person who applied or was engaged for that employment outside Great Britain.

(2) Nothing in section 7 shall, as regards work to which that section applies, render unlawful any act done by the principal in or in connection with such work on any ship in the case of a contract worker who was engaged outside Great Britain by the person by whom he is supplied.

(3) Subsections (1) and (2) do not apply to employment or work concerned with exploration of the sea bed or subsoil or the exploitation of their natural resources in any area for the time being designated under section 1(7) of the Continental Shelf Act 1964, not being an area or part of an area in which the law of Northern Ireland applies.

(4) For the purposes of subsection (1) a person brought to Great Britain with a view to his entering into an agreement in Great Britain to be employed on any ship shall be treated as having applied for the employment outside Great Britain.

Discrimination by Other Bodies

Partnerships

1–357　　10.—(1) It is unlawful for a firm consisting of six or more partners, in relation to a position as partner in the firm, to discriminate against a person—
　　(a) in the arrangements they make for the purpose of determining who should be offered that position; or
　　(b) in the terms on which they offer him that position; or
　　(c) by refusing or deliberately omitting to offer him that position; or
　　(d) in a case where the person already holds that position—

(i) in the way they afford him access to any benefits, facilities or services, or by refusing or deliberately omitting to afford him access to them; or

(ii) by expelling him from that position, or subjecting him to any other detriment.

(2) Subsection (1) shall apply in relation to persons proposing to form themselves into a partnership as it applies in relation to a firm.

(3) Subsection (1)(*a*) and (*c*) do not apply to a position as partner where, if it were employment, being of a particular racial group would be a genuine occupational qualification for the job.

(4) In the case of a limited partnership references in this section to a partner shall be construed as references to a general partner as defined in section 3 of the Limited Partnerships Act 1907.

Trade unions, etc.

11.—(1) This section applies to an organisation of workers, an organisation of employers, or any other organisation whose members carry on a particular profession or trade for the purposes of which the organisation exists.

(2) It is unlawful for an organistion to which this section applies, in the case of a person who is not a member of the organisation, to discriminate against him—

(*a*) in the terms on which it is prepared to admit him to membership; or

(*b*) by refusing, or deliberately omitting to accept, his application for membership.

(3) It is unlawful for an organisation to which this section applies, in the case of a person who is a member of the organisation, to discriminate against him—

(*a*) in the way it affords him access to any benefits, facilities or services, or by refusing or deliberately omitting to afford him access to them; or

(*b*) by depriving him of membership, or varying the terms on which he is a member; or

(*c*) by subjecting him to any other detriment.

1–358

Qualifying bodies

12.—(1) It is unlawful for an authority or body which can confer an authorisation or qualification which is needed for, or facilitates, engagement in a particular profession or trade to discriminate against a person—

(*a*) in the terms on which it is prepared to confer on him that authorisation or qualification; or

(*b*) by refusing, or deliberately omitting to grant, his application for it; or

(*c*) by withdrawing it from him or varying the terms on which he holds it.

(2) In this section—

(*a*) "authorisation or qualification" includes recognition, registration, enrolment, approval and certification;

(*b*) "confer" includes renew or extend.

1–359

(3) Subsection (1) does not apply to discrimination which is rendered unlawful by section 17 or 18.

Vocational training bodies

1–360   13.—(1) It is unlawful for a person to whom this subsection applies, in the case of an individual seeking or undergoing training which would help to fit him for any employment, to discriminate against him—
  (*a*) in the terms of which that person affords him access to any training courses or other facilities; or
  (*b*) by refusing or deliberately omitting to afford him such access; or
  (*c*) by terminating his training.
(2) Subsection (1) applies to—
  (*a*) industrial training boards established under section 1 of the Industrial Training Act 1964 [or section 1 of the Industrial Training Act 1982].
  (*b*) the Manpower Services Commission, [. . .];
  (*c*) any association which comprises employers and has as its principal object, or one of its principal objects, affording their employees access to training facilities;
  (*d*) any other person providing facilities for training for employment, being a person designated for the purposes of this paragraph in an order made by the Secretary of State.
(3) Subsection (1) does not apply to discrimination which is rendered unlawful by section 17 or 18.

AMENDMENTS
  The words in square brackets in subs. (2)(*a*) were added by the Industrial Training Act 1982, Sched. 3, para. 7.
  The words omitted from subs. (2)(*b*) were repealed by the Employment and Training Act 1981, Sched. 2.

Employment agencies

1–361   14.—(1) It is unlawful for an employment agency to discriminate against a person—
  (*a*) in the terms on which the agency offers to provide any of its services; or
  (*b*) by refusing or deliberately omitting to provide any of its services; or
  (*c*) in the way it provides any of its services.
(2) It is unlawful for a local education authority or an education authority to do any act in the performance of its functions under section 8 of the Employment and Training Act 1973 which constitutes discrimination.
(3) References in subsection (1) to the services of an employment agency include guidance on careers and any other services related to employment.
(4) This section does not apply if the discrimination only concerns employment which the employer could lawfully refuse to offer the person in question.
(5) An employment agency or local education authority or an education authority shall not be subject to any liability under this section if it proves—
  (*a*) that it acted in reliance on a statement made to it by the employer to the effect that, by reason of the operation of subsection (4), its action would not be unlawful; and

(b) that it was reasonable for it to rely on the statement.

(6) A person who knowingly or recklessly makes a statement such as is referred to in subsection (5)(a) which in a material respect is false or misleading commits an offence, and shall be liable on summary conviction to a fine not exceeding £400.

Manpower Services Commission, etc.

15.—[(1) It is unlawful for the Manpower Services Commission to discriminate in the provision of facilities or services under section 2 of the Employment and Training Act 1973].

(2) This section does not apply in a case where—
    (a) section 13 applies; or
    (b) the body is acting as an employment agency.

Police

Police

16.—(1) For the purposes of this Part, the holding of the office of constable shall be treated as employment—
    (a) by the chief officer of police as respects any act done by him in relation to a constable or that office;
    (b) by the police authority as respects any act done by them in relation to a constable or that office.

(2) There shall be paid out of the police fund—
    (a) any compensation, costs or expenses awarded against a chief officer of police in any proceedings brought against him under this Act, and any costs or expenses incurred by him in any such proceedings so far as not recovered by him in the proceedings; and
    (b) any sum required by a chief officer of police for the settlement of any claim made against him under this Act if the settlement is approved by the police authority.

(3) Any proceedings under this Act which, by virtue of subsection (1), would lie against a chief officer of police shall be brought against the chief officer of police for the time being or, in the case of a vacancy in that office, against the person for the time being performing the functions of that office; and references in subsection (2) to the chief officer of police shall be construed accordingly.

(4) Subsection (1) applies to a police cadet and appointment as a police cadet as it applies to a constable and the office of constable.

(5) In this section—
"chief officer of police"—
    (a) in relation to a person appointed, or an appointment falling to be made, under a specified Act, has the same meaning as in the Police Act,
    (b) in relation to any other person or appointment, means the officer who has the direction and control of the body of constables or cadets in question;
"the Police Act" means, for England and Wales, the Police Act 1964 or, for Scotland, the Police (Scotland) Act 1967;
"police authority"—
    (a) in relation to a person appointed, or an appointment falling

to be made, under a specified Act, has the same meaning as in the Police Act,

(b) in relation to any other person or appointment, means the authority by whom the person in question is or on appointment would be paid;

"police cadet" means any person appointed to undergo training with a view to becoming a constable;

"police fund" in relation to a chief officer of police within paragraph (a) of the above definition of that term has the same meaning as in the Police Act, and in any other case means money provided by the police authority;

"specified Act" means the Metropolitan Police Act 1829, the City of London Police Act 1839 or the Police Act.

. . . . . .

PART IV

OTHER UNLAWFUL ACTS

Discriminatory practices

1–364   **28.**—(1) In this section "discriminatory practice" means the application of a requirement or condition which results in an act of discrimination which is unlawful by virtue of any provision of Part II or III taken with section 1(1)(b), or which would be likely to result in such an act of discrimination if the persons to whom it is applied included persons of any particular racial group as regards which there has been no occasion for applying it.

(2) A person acts in contravention of this section if and so long as—
(a) he applies a discriminatory practice; or
(b) he operates practices or other arrangements which in any circumstances would call for the application by him of a discriminatory practice.

(3) Proceedings in respect of a contravention of this section shall be brought only by the Commission in accordance with sections 58 to 62.

Discriminatory advertisements

1–365   **29.**—(1) It is unlawful to publish or to cause to be published an advertisement which indicates, or might reasonably be understood as indicating, an intention by a person to do an act of discrimination, whether the doing of that act by him would be lawful or, by virtue of Part II or III, unlawful.

(2) Subsection (1) does not apply to an advertisement—
(a) if the intended act would be lawful by virtue of any of sections 5, 6, 7(3) and (4), 10(3), 26, 34(2)(b), 35 to 39 and 41; or
(b) if the advertisement relates to the services of an employment agency (within the meaning of section 14(1)) and the intended act only concerns employment which the employer could by virtue of section 5, 6 or 7(3) or (4) lawfully refuse to offer to persons against whom the advertisement indicates an intention to discriminate.

(3) Subsection (1) does not apply to an advertisement which indicates that persons of any class defined otherwise than by reference to colour, race or ethnic or national origins are required for employment outside Great Britain.

(4) The publisher of an advertisement made unlawful by subsection (1) shall not be subject to any liability under that subsection in respect of the publication of the advertisement if he proves—
- (*a*) that the advertisement was published in reliance on a statement made to him by the person who caused it to be published to the effect that, by reason of the operation of subsection (2) or (3), the publication would not be unlawful; and
- (*b*) that it was reasonable for him to rely on the statement.

(5) A person who knowingly or recklessly makes a statement such as is mentioned in subsection (4)(*a*) which in a material respect is false or misleading commits an offence, and shall be liable on summary conviction to a fine not exceeding £400.

Instructions to discriminate

30. It is unlawful for a person—   1–366
- (*a*) who has authority over another person; or
- (*b*) in accordance with whose wishes that other person is accustomed to act,

to instruct him to do any act which is unlawful by virtue of Part II or III, or procure or attempt to procure the doing by him of any such act.

Pressure to discriminate

31.—(1) It is unlawful to induce, or attempt to induce, a person to do any act which contravenes Part II or III.   1–367

(2) An attempted inducement is not prevented from falling within subsection (1) because it is not made directly to the person in question, if it is made in such a way that he is likely to hear of it.

Liability of employers and principals

32.—(1) Anything done by a person in the course of his employment shall be treated for the purposes of this Act (except as regards offences thereunder) as done by his employer as well as by him, whether or not it was done with the employer's knowledge or approval.   1–368

(2) Anything done by a person as agent for another person with the authority (whether express or implied, and whether precedent or subsequent) of that other person shall be treated for the purposes of this Act (except as regards offences thereunder) as done by that other person as well as by him.

(3) In proceedings brought under this Act against any person in respect of an act alleged to have been done by an employee of his it shall be a defence for that person to prove that he took such steps as were reasonably practicable to prevent the employee from doing that act, or from doing in the course of his employment acts of that description.

Aiding unlawful acts

33.—(1) A person who knowingly aids another person to do an act made unlawful by this Act shall be treated for the purposes of this Act as himself doing an unlawful act of the like description.   1–369

(2) For the purposes of subsection (1) an employee or agent for whose

act the employer or principal is liable under section 32 (or would be so liable but for section 32(3)) shall be deemed to aid the doing of the act by the employer or principal.

(3) A person does not under this section knowingly aid another to do an unlawful act if—
 (a) he acts in relaince on a statement made to him by that other person that, by reason of any provision of this Act, the act which he aids would not be unlawful; and
 (b) it is reasonable for him to rely on the statement.

(4) A person who knowingly or recklessly makes a statement such as is mentioned in subsection (3)(a) which in a material respect is false or misleading commits an offence, and shall be liable on summary conviction to a fine not exceeding £400.

Charities

34.—(1) A provision which is contained in a charitable instrument (whenever that instrument took or takes effect) and which provides for conferring benefits on persons of a class defined by reference to colour shall have effect for all purposes as if it provided for conferring the like benefits—
 (a) on persons of the class which results if the restriction by reference to colour is disregarded; or
 (b) where the original class is defined by reference to colour only, on persons generally;
but nothing in this subsection shall be taken to alter the effect of any provision as regards any time before the coming into operation of this subsection.

(2) Nothing in Parts II to IV shall—
 (a) be construed as affecting a provision to which this subsection applies; or
 (b) render unalwful an act which is done in order to give effect to such a provision.

(3) Subsection (2) applies to any provision which is contained in a charitable instrument (whenever that instrument took or takes effect) and which provides for conferring benefits on persons of a class defined otherwise than by reference to colour (including a class resulting from the operation of subsection (1)).

(4) In this section "charitable instrument" means an enactment or other instrument passed or made for charitable purposes, or an enactment or other instrument so far as it relates to charitable purposes, and in Scotland includes the governing instrument of an endowment or of an educational endowment as those expressions are defined in section 135(1) of the Education (Scotland) Act 1962.

In the application of this section to England and Wales, "charitable purposes" means purposes which are exclusively charitable according to the law of England and Wales.

PART VI

GENERAL EXCEPTIONS FROM PARTS II TO IV

Special needs of racial groupos in regard to education, training or welfare

35. Nothing in Parts II to IV shall render unlawful any act done in affording persons of a particular racial group access to facilities or services to meet the special needs of persons of that group in regard to their education, training or welfare, or any ancillary benefits.

Provision of education or training for persons not ordinarily resident in Great Britain
36. Nothing in Parts II to IV shall render unalwful any act done by a person for the benefit of persons not ordinarily resident in Great Britain in affording them access to facilities for education or training or any ancillary benefits, where it appears to him that the persons in question do not intend to remain in Great Britain after their period of education or training there.

1–371

Discriminatory training by certain bodies
37.—(1) Nothing in Parts II to IV shall render unlawful any act done in relation to particular work by a training body in or in connection with—
  (a) affording only persons of a particular racial group access to facilities for training which would help to fit them for that work; or;
  (b) encouraging only persons of a particular racial group to take advantage of opportunities for doing that work,
where it appears to the training body that any time within the twelve months immediately preceding the doing of the act—
  (i) there were no persons of that group among those doing that work in Great Britain; or
  (ii) the proportion of persons of that group among those doing that work in Great Britain was small in comparison with the proportion of persons of that group among the population of Great Britain.
(2) Where in relation to particular work it appears to a training body that although the condition for the operation of subsection (1) is not met for the whole of Great Britain it is met for an area within Great Britain, nothing in Parts II to IV shall render unlawful any act done by the training body in or in connection with—
  (a) affording pesons who are of the racial group in question, and who appear likely to take up that work in that area, access to facilities for training which would help to fit them for that work; or
  (b) encouraging persons of that group to take advantage of opportunities in the area for doing that work.
(3) In this section "training body" means—
  (a) a person mentioned in section 13(2)(a) or (b); or
  (b) any other person being a person designated for the purposes of this section in an order made by the Secretary of State.

1–372

Other discriminatory training etc.
38.—(1) Nothing in Parts II to IV shall render unlawful any act done by an employer in relation to particular work in his employment at a particular establishment in Great Britain, being an act done in or in connection with—
  (a) affording only those of his employees working at that establishment who are of a particular racial group access to facilities for training which would help to fit them for that work; or
  (b) encouraging only persons of a particular racial group to take advantage of opportunities for doing that work at that establishment,

1–373

where any of the conditions in subsection (2) was satisfied at any time within the twelve months immediately preceding the doing of the act.

(2) Those conditions are—
   (a) that there are no persons of the racial group in question among those doing that work at that establishment; or
   (b) that the proportion of persons of that group among those doing that work at that establishment is small in comparison with the proportion of persons of that group—
      (i) among all those employed by that employer there; or
      (ii) among the population of the area from which that employer normally recruits persons for work in his employment at that establishment.

(3) Nothing in section 11 shall render unlawful any act done by an organisation to which that section applies in or in connection with—
   (a) affording only members of the organisation who are of a particular racial group access to facilities for training which would help to fit them for holding a post of any kind in the organisation; or
   (b) encouraging only members of the organisation who are of a particular racial group to take advantage of opportunities for holding such posts in the organisation,
where either of the conditions in subsection (4) was satisfied at any time within the twelve months immediately preceding the doing of the act.

(4) Those conditions are—
   (a) that there are no persons of the racial group in question among persons holding such posts in that organisation; or
   (b) that the proportion of persons of that group among those holding such posts in that organisation is small in comparison with the proportion of persons of that group among the members of the organisation.

(1) Nothing in Parts II to IV shall render unlawful any act done by an organisation to which section 11 applies in or in connection with encouraging only persons of a particular racial group to become members of the organisation where at any time within the twelve months immediately preceding the doing of the act—
   (a) no persons of that group were members of the organisation; or
   (b) the proportion of persons of that group among members of the organisation was small in comparison with the proportion of persons of that group among those eligible for membership of the organisation.

(6) Section 8 (meaning of employment at establishment in Great Britain) shall apply for the purposes of this section as if this section were contained in Part II.

. . . . . .

Indirect access to benefits etc.

1–374   **40.**—(1) References in this Act to the affording by any person of access to benefits or services are not limited to benefits, facilities or services provided by that person himself, but include any means by which it is in that person's power to facilitate access to benefits, facilities or services provided by any other person (the "actual provider").

(2) Where by any provision of this Act the affording by any person of

access to benefits, facilities or services in a discriminatory way is in certain circumstances prevented from being unlawful, the effect of the provision shall extend also to the liability under this Act of any actual provider.

Acts done under statutory authority, etc.

41.—(1) Nothing in Parts II to IV shall render unlawful any act of discrimination done—
   (*a*) in pursuance of any enactment or Order in Council; or
   (*b*) in pursuance of any instrument made under any enactment by a Minister of the Crown; or
   (*c*) in order to comply with any condition or requirement imposed by a Minister of the Crown (whether before or after the passing of this Act) by virtue of any enactment

References in this subsection to an enactment, Order in Council or instrument include an enactment, Order in Council or instrument passed or made after the passing of this Act.

(2) Nothing in Parts II to IV shall render unlawful any act whereby a person discriminates against another on the basis of that other's nationality or place of ordinary residence or the length of time for which he has been present or resident in or outside the United Kingdom or an area within the United Kingdom, if that act is done—
   (*a*) in pursuance of any arrangements made (whether before or after the passing of this Act) by or with the approval of, or for the time being approved by, a Minister of the Crown; or
   (*b*) in order to comply with any condition imposed (whether before or after the passing of this Act) by a Minister of the Crown.

Acts safeguarding national security

42. Nothing in Parts II to IV shall render unlawful an act done for the purpose of safeguarding national security.

PART VII

THE COMMISSION FOR RACIAL EQUALITY

General

Establishment and duties of Commission

43.—(1) There shall be a body of Commissioners named the Commission for Racial Equality consisting of at least eight but not more than fifteen individuals each appointed by the Secretary of State on a full-time or part-time basis, which shall have the following duties—
   (*a*) to work towards the elimination of discrimination;
   (*b*) to promote equality of opportunity, and good relations, between persons of different racial groups generally; and
   (*c*) to keep under review the working of this Act and, when they are so required by the Secretary of State or otherwise think it necessary, draw up and submit to the Secretary of State proposals for amending it.

(2) The Secretary of State shall appoint—
   (a) one of the Commissioners to be chairman of the Commission; and
   (b) either one or more of the Commissioners (as the Secretary of State thinks fit) to be deputy chairman or deputy chairmen of the Commission.

(3) The Secretary of State may by order amend subsection (1) so far as it regulates the number of Commissioners.

(4) Schedule 1 shall have effect with respect to the Commission.

(5) The Race Relations Board and the Community Relations Commission are hereby abolished.

Assistance to organisations

1–378 44.—(1) The Commission may give financial or other assistance to any organisation appearing to the Commission to be concerned with the promotion of equality of opportunity, and good relations, between persons of different racial groups, but shall not give any such financial assistance out of money provided (through the Secretary of State) by Parliament except with the approval of the Secretary of State given with the consent of the Treasury.

(2) Except in so far as other arrangements for their discharge are made and approved under paragraph 13 of Schedule 1—
   (a) the Commission's functions under subsection (1); and
   (b) other functions of the Commission in relation to matter connected with the giving of such financial or other assistance as is mentioned in that subsection,
shall be discharged under the general direction of the Commission by a committee of the Commission consisting of at least three but not more than five Commissioners, of whom one shall be the deputy chairman or one of the deputy chairmen of the Commission.

Research and education

1–379 45.–(1) The Commission may undertake or assist (financially or otherwise) the undertaking by other persons of any research, and any educational activities, which appear to the Commission necessary or expedient for the purposes of section 43(1).

(2) The Commission may make charges for educational or other facilities or services made available by them.

Annual reports

1–380 46.—(1) As soon as practicable after the end of each calendar year the Commission shall make to the Secretary of State a report on their activities during the year (an "annual report").

(2) Each annual report shall include a general survey of developments, during the period to which it relates, in respect of matters falling within the scope of the Commission's functions.

(3) The Secretary of State shall lay a copy of every annual report before each House of Parliament, and shall cause the report to be published.

Codes of practice

Codes of practice

1–381 47 —(1) The Commission may issue codes of practice containing such

practical guidance as the Commission think fit for either or both of the following purposes, namely—
> (*a*) the elimination of discrimination in the field of employment;
> (*b*) the promotion of equality of opportunity in that field between persons of different racial groups.

(2) When the Commission propose to issue a code of practice, they shall prepare and publish a draft of that code, shall consider any representations made to them about the draft and may modify the draft accordingly.

(3) In the course of preparing any draft code of practice for eventual publication under subsection (2) the Commission shall consult with—
> (*a*) such organisations or associations of organisations representative of employers or of workers; and
> (*b*) such other organisations, or bodies,

as appear to the Commission to be appropriate.

(4) If the Commission determine to proceed with the draft, they shall transmit the draft to the Secretary of State who shall—
> (*a*) if he approves of it, lay it before both Houses of Parliament; and
> (*b*) if he does not approve of it, publish details of his reasons for withholding approval.

(5) If, within the period of forty days beginning with the day on which a copy of a draft code of practice is laid before each House of Parliament, or, if such copies are laid on different days, with the later of the two days, either House so resolves, no further proceedings shall be taken thereon, but without prejudice to the laying before Parliament of a new draft.

(6) In reckoning the period of forty days referred to in subsection (5), no account shall be taken of any period during which Parliament is dissolved or prorogued or during which both Houses are adjourned for more than four days.

(7) If no such resolution is passed as is referred to in subsection (5), the Commission shall issue the code in the form of the draft and the code shall come into effect on such day as the Secretary of State may by order appoint.

(8) Without prejudice to section 74(3), an order under subsection (7) may contain such transitional provisions or savings as appear to the Secretary of State to be necessary or expedient in connection with the code of practice thereby brought into operation.

(9) The Commission may from time to time revise the whole or any part of a code of practice issued under this section and issue that revised code, and subsections (2) to (8) shall apply (with appropriate modifications) to such a revised code as they apply to the first issue of a code.

(10) A failure on the part of any person to observe any provision of a code of practice shall not of itself render him liable to any proceedings; but in any proceedings under this Act before an industrial tribunal any code of practice issued under this section shall be admissible in evidence, and if any provision of such a code appears to the tribunal to be relevant to any question arising in the proceedings it shall be taken into account in determining that question.

(11) Without prejudice to subsection (1), a code of practice issued under this section may include such practical guidance as the Commission think fit as to what steps it is reasonably practicable for employers to take for the purpose of preventing their employees from doing in the course of their employment acts made unlawful by this Act.

Investigations

Power to conduct formal investigations

1-382   48.—(1) Without prejudice to their general power to do anything requisite for the performance of their duties under section 43(1), the Commission may if they think fit, and shall if required by the Secretary of State, conduct a formal investigation for any purpose connected with the carrying out of those duties.

(2) The Commission may, with the approval of the Secretary of State, appoint, on a full-time or part-time basis, one or more individuals as additional Commissioners for the purposes of a formal investigation.

(3) The Commission may nominate one or more Commissioners, with or without one or more additional Commissioners, to conduct a formal investigation on their behalf, and may delegate any of their functions in relation to the investigation to the persons so nominated.

Terms of reference

1-383   49.—(1) The Commission shall not embark on a formal investigation unless the requirements of this section have been complied with.

(2) Terms of reference for the investigation shall be drawn up by the Commission or, if the Commission were required by the Secretary of State to conduct the investigation, by the Secretary of State after consulting the Commission.

(3) It shall be the duty of the Commission to give general notice of the holding of the investigation unless the terms of reference confine it to activities of persons named in them, but in such a case the Commission shall in the prescribed manner give those persons notice of the holding of the investigation.

(4) Where the terms of reference of the investigation confine it to activities of persons named in them and the Commission in the course of it propose to investigate any act made unlawful by this Act which they believe that a person so named may have done, the Commission shall—

   (a) inform that person of their belief and of their proposal to investigate the act in question; and
   (b) offer him an opportunity of making oral or written representations with regard to it (or both oral and written representations if he thinks fit);

and a person so named who avails himself of an opportunity under this subsection of making oral representations may be represented—

   (i) by counsel or a solicitor; or
   (ii) by some other person of his choice, not being a person to whom the Commission object on the ground that he is unsuitable.

(5) The Commission or, if the Commission were required by the Secretary of State to conduct the investigation, the Secretary of State after consulting the Commission may from time to time revise the terms of reference; and subsections (1), (3) and (4) shall apply to the revised investigation and terms of reference as they applied to the original.

Power to obtain information

1-384   50.—(1) For the purposes of a formal investigation the Commission, by a notice in the prescribed form served on him in the prescribed manner—

   (a) may require any person to furnish such written informaton as may

be described in the notice, and may specify the time at which, and the manner and form in which, the information is to be furnished;
  (b) may require any person to attend at such time and place as is specified in the notice and give oral information about, and produce all documents in his possession or control relating to, any matter specified in the notice.

(2) Except as provided by section 60, a notice shall be served under subsection (1) only where—
  (a) service of the notice was authorised by an order made by the Secretary of State; or
  (b) the terms of reference of the investigation state that the Commission believe that a person named in them may have done or may be doing acts of all or any of the following descriptions—
      (i) unlawful discriminatory acts;
      (ii) contraventions of section 28; and
      (iii) contraventions of sections 29, 30 or 31,
  and confine the investigation to those acts.

(3) A notice under subsection (1) shall not require a person—
  (a) to give information, or produce any documents, which he could not be compelled to give in evidence, or produce, in civil proceedings before the High Court or the Court of Session; or
  (b) to attend at any place unless the necessary expenses of his journey to and from that place are paid or tendered to him.

(4) If a person fails to comply with a notice served on him under subsection (1) or the Commission have reasonable cause to believe that he intends not to comply with it, the Commission may apply to a county court or, in Scotland, a sheriff court for an order requiring him to comply with it or with such directions for the like purpose as may be contained in the order.

(5) Section 84 of the County Courts Act 1959 (penalty for neglecting witness summons) shall apply to failure without reasonable excuse to comply with an order of a county court under subsection (4) as it applies in the cases provided in the said section 84; and in paragraph 73 of Schedule 1 to the Sheriff Courts (Scotland) Act 1907 (power of sheriff to grant second diligence for compelling the attendance of witnesses or havers) shall apply to an order of a sheriff court under subsection (4) as it applies in proceedings in the sheriff court.

(6) A person commits an offence if he—
  (a) wilfully alters, suppresses, conceals or destroys a document which he has been required by a notice or order under this section to produce; or
  (b) in complying with such a notice or order, knowingly or recklessly makes any statement which is false in a material particular,
and shall be liable on summary conviction to a fine not exceeding £400.

(7) Proceedings for an offence under subsection (6) may (without prejudice to any jurisdiction exercisable apart from this subsection) be instituted—
  (a) against any person at any place at which he has an office or other place of business;
  (b) against an individual at any place where he resides, or at which he is for the time being.

Recommendations and reports on formal investigations

1–385 51.—(1) If in the light of any of their findings in a formal investigation it appears to the Commission necessary or expedient, whether during the course of the investigation or after its conclusion—
   (a) to make to any person, with a view to promoting equality of opportunity between persons of different racial groups who are affected by any of his activities, recommendations for changes in his policies or procedures, or as to any other matters; or
   (b) to make to the Secretary of State any recommendations, whether for changes in the law or otherwise,
the Commission shall make those recommendations accordingly.

(2) The Commission shall prepare a report of their findings in any formal investigation conducted by them.

(3) If the formal investigation is one required by the Secretary of State—
   (a) the Commission shall deliver the report to the Secretary of State; and
   (b) the Secretary of State shall cause the report to be published,
and, unless required by the Secretary of State, the Commission shall not publish the report.

(4) If the formal investigation is not one required by the Secretary of State, the Commission shall either publish the report, or make it available for inspection in accordance with subsection (5).

(5) Where under subsection (4) a report is to be made available for inspection, any person shall be entitled, on payment of such fee (if any) as may be determined by the Commission—
   (a) to inspect the report during ordinary office hours and take copies of all or any part of the report; or
   (b) to obtain from the Commission a copy, certified by the Commission to be correct, of the report.

(6) The Commission may, if they think fit, determine that the right conferred by subsection (5)(a) shall be exercisable in relation to a copy of the report instead of, or in addition to, the original.

(7) The Commission shall give general notice of the place or places where, and the times when, reports may be inspected under subsection (5).

Restriction on disclosure of information

1–386 52.—(1) No information given to the Commission by any person ("the informant") in connection with a formal investigation shall be disclosed by the Commission, or by any person who is or has been a Commissioner, additional Commissioner or employee of the Commission, except—
   (a) on the order of any court; or
   (b) with the informant's consent; or
   (c) in the form of a summary or other general statement published by the Commission which does not identify the informant or any other person to whom the information relates; or
   (d) in a report of the investigation published by the Commission or made available for inspection under section 51(5); or
   (e) to the Commissioners, additional Commissioners or employees of the Commission, or, so far as may be necessary for the proper performance of the functions of the Commission, to other persons; or
   (f) for the purpose of any civil proceedings under this Act to which the Commission are a party, or any criminal proceedings.

(2) Any person who discloses information in contravention of subsection (1) commits an offence and shall be liable on summary conviction to a fine not exceeding £400.

(3) In preparing any report for publication or for inspection the Commission shall exclude, so far as is consistent with their duties and the object of the report, any matter which relates to the private affairs of any individual or the business interests of any person where the publication of that matter might, in the opinion of the Commission, prejudicially affect that individual or person.

Part VIII

Enforcement

General

Restriction of proceedings for breach of Act

53.—(1) Except as provided by this Act no proceedings, whether civil or criminal, shall lie against any person in respect of an act by reason that the act is unlawful by virtue of a provision of this Act.

(2) Subsection (1) does not preclude the making of an order of certiorari, mandamus or prohibition.

(3) In Scotland, subsection (1) does not preclude the exercise of the jurisdiction of the Court of Session to entertain an application for reduction or suspension of any order or determination or otherwise to consider the validity of any order or determination, or to require reasons for any order or determination to be stated.

Enforcement in Employment Field

Jurisdiction of industrial tribunals

54.—(1) A complaint by any person ("the complainant") that another person ("the respondent")—
   (a) has committed an act of discrimination against the complainant which is unlawful by virtue of Part II; or
   (b) is by virtue of section 32 or 33 to be treated as having committed such an act of discrimination against the complainant,
may be presented to an industrial tribunal.

(2) Subsection (1) does not apply to a complaint under section 12(1) of an act in respect of which an appeal, or proceedings in the nature of an appeal, may be brought under any enactment, or to a complaint to which section 75(8) applies.

Conciliation in employment cases

55.—(1) Where a complaint has been presented to an industrial tribunal under section 54 and a copy of the complaint has been sent to a conciliation officer, it shall be the duty of the conciliation officer—
   (a) if he is requested to do so both by the complainant and by the respondent; or
   (b) if, in the absence of requests by the complainant and the respon-

dent, he considers that he could act under this subsection with a reasonable prospect of success,

to endeavour to promote a settlement of the complaint without its being determined by an industrial tribunal.

(2) Where, before a complaint such as is mentioned in subsection (1) has been prsented to an industrial tribunal, a request is made to a conciliation officer to make his services available in the matter by a person who, if the complaint were so presented, would be the complainant or respondent, subsection (1) shall apply as if the complaint had been so presented and a copy of it had been sent to the conciliation officer.

(3) In proceeding under subsection (1) or (2), a conciliation officer shall where appropriate have regard to the desirability of encouraging the use of other procedures available for the settlement of grievances.

(4) Anything communicated to a conciliation officer in connection with the performance of his functions under this section shall not be admissible in evidence in any proceedings before an industrial tribunal except with the consent of the person who communicated it to that officer.

Remedies on complaint under s.54

56.—(1) Where an industrial tribunal finds that a complaint presented to it under section 54 is well-founded, the tribunal shall make such of the following as it considers just and equitable—
   (a) an order declaring the rights of the complainant and the respondent in relation to the act to which the complaint relates;
   (b) an order requiring the respondent to pay to the complainant compensation of an amount corresponding to any damages he could have been ordered by a county court or by a sheriff court to pay to the complainant if the complaint had fallen to be dealt with under section 57;
   (c) a recommendation that the respondent take within a specified period action appearing to the tribunal to be practicable for the purpose of obviating or reducing the adverse effect on the complainant of any act of discrimination to which the complaint relates.

(2) The amount of compensation awarded to a person under subsection (1)(b) shall not exceed the limit for the time being imposed by [section 75 of the Employment Protection (Consolidation) Act 1978].

(3) Where compensation falls to be awarded in respect of any act both under the Sex Discrimination Act 1975 and this Act, the aggregate of the following amounts of compensation awarded by an industrial tribunal, that is to say—
   (a) any compensation awarded under the said Act of 1975; and
   (b) any compensation awarded under subsection (1)(b),
shall not exceed the limit refered to in subsection (2).

(4) If without reasonable justification the respondent to a complaint fails to comply with a recommendation made by an industrial tribunal under subsection (1)(c), then, if it thinks it just and equitable to do so—
   (a) the tribunal may (subject to the limit in subsection (2)) increase the amount of compensation required to be paid to the complainant in respect of the complaint by an order made under subsection (1)(b); or
   (b) if an order under subsection (1)(b) could have been made but was not, the tribunal may make such an order.

AMENDMENT

The words in square brackets in subs. (2) were substituted by the Employment Protection (Consolidation) Act 1978 (c. 44), s.159(2), Sched. 16.

. . . . . .

Non-Discrimination Notices

Issue of non-discrimination notice

58.—(1) This section applies to—
  (*a*) an unlawful discriminatory act; and
  (*b*) an act contravening section 28; and
  (*c*) an act contravening section 29, 30 or 31,
and so applies whether or not proceedings have been brought in respect of the act.

(2) If in the course of a formal investigation the Commission become satisfied that a person is committing, or has committed, any such acts, the Commission may in the prescribed manner serve on him a notice in the prescribed form ("a non-discrimination notice") requiring him—
  (*a*) not to commit any such acts; and
  (*b*) where compliance with paragraph (*a*) involves changes in any of his practices or other arrangements—
    (i) to inform the Commission that he has effected those changes and what those changes are; and
    (ii) to take such steps as may be reasonably required by the notice for the purpose of affording that information to other persons concerned.

(3) A non-discrimination notice may also require the person on whom it is served to furnish the Commission with such other information as may be reasonably required by the notice in order to verify that the notice has been complied with.

(4) The notice may specify the time at which, and the manner and form in which, any information is to be furnished to the Commission, but the time at which any information is to be furnished in compliance with the notice shall not be later than five years after the notice has become final.

(5) The Commission shall not serve a non-discrimination notice in respect of any person unless they have first—
  (*a*) given him notice that they are minded to issue a non-discrimination notice in his case, specifying the grounds on which they contemplate doing so; and
  (*b*) offered him an opportunity of making oral or written representations in the matter (or both oral and written representations if he 'thinks fit) within a period of not less than 28 days specified in the notice; and
  (*c*) taken account of any representation so made by him.

(6) Subsection (2) does not apply to any acts in respect of which the Secretary of State could exercise the powers conferred on him by section 19(2) and (3); but if the Commission become aware of any such acts they shall give notice of them to the Secretary of State.

(7) Section 50(4) shall apply to requirements under subsection (2)(*b*), (3) and (4) contained in a non-discrimination notice which has become final as it applies to requirements in a notice served under section 50(1).

Appeal against non-discrimination notice

1–392   **59.**—(1) Not later than six weeks after a non-discrimination notice is served on any person he may appeal against any requiremnt of the notice—
  (*a*) to an industrial tribunal, so far as the requirement relates to acts which are within the jurisdiction of the tribunal;
  (*b*) to a designated county court or a sheriff court, so far as the requirement relates to acts which are within the jurisdiction of the court and are not within the jurisdiction of an industrial tribunal.

(2) Where the tribunal or court considers a requirement in respect of which an appeal is brought under subsection (1) to be unreasonable because it is based on an incorrect finding of fact or for any other reason, the tribunal or court shall quash the requirement.

(3) On quashing a requirement under subsection (2) the tribunal or court may direct that the non-discrimination notice shall be treated as if, in place of the requirement quashed, it had contained a requirement in terms specified in the direction.

(4) Subsection (1) does not apply to a requirement treated as included in a non-discrimination notice by virtue of a direction under subsection (3).

Investigation as to compliance with non-discrimination notice

1–393   **60.**—(1) If—
  (*a*) the terms of reference of a formal investigation state that its purpose is to determine whether any requirements of a non-discrimination notice are being or have been carried out, but section 50(2)(*b*) does not apply; and
  (*b*) section 49(3) is complied with in relation to the investigation on a date ("the commencement date") not later than the expiration of the period of five years beginning when the non-discrimination notice became final,

the Commission may within the period referred to in subsection (2) serve notices under section 50(1) for the purpoion notice became final.

the Commission may within the period referred to in subsection (2) serve notices under section 50(1) for the purposes of the investigation without needing to obtain the consent of the Secretary of State.

(2) The said period begins on the commencement date and ends on the later of the following dates—
  (*a*) the date on which the period of five years mentioned in subsection (1)(*b*) rooses of the investigation without needing to obtain the consent of the Secretary of State.

(2) The said period begins on the commencemnt date and ends on the later of the following dates—
  (*a*) the date on which the period of five years mentioned in subsection (1)(*b*) expires;
  (*b*) the date two years after the commencement date.

Register of non-discrimination notices

1–394   **61.**—(1) The Commission shall establish and maintain a register ("the register") of non-discrimination notices which have become final.

(2) Any person shall be entitled, on payment of such fee (if any) as may be determined by the Commission—

(a) to inspect the register during ordinary office hours and take copies of any entry; or

(b) to obtain from the Commission a copy, certified by the Commission to be correct, of any entry in the register.

(3) The Commission may, if they think fit, determine that the right conferred by subsection (2)(a) shall be exercisable in relation to a copy of the register instead of, or in addition to, the original.

(4) The Commission shall give general notice of the place or places where, and the times when, the register or a copy of it may be inspected.

Other Enforcement by Commission

Persistent discrimination

62.—(1) If, during the period of five years beginning on the date on which any of the following became final in the case of any person, namely—

(a) a non-discrimination notice served on him; or

(b) a finding by a tribunal or court under section 54 or 57; that he has done an unlawful discriminatory act; or

(c) a finding by a court in proceedings under section 19 or 20 of the Race Relations Act 1968 that he has done an act which was unlawful by virtue of any provision of Part I of that Act,

it appears to the Commission that unless restrained he is likely to do one or more acts falling within paragraph (b), or contravening section 28, the Commission may apply to a designated county court for an injunction, or to a sheriff court for an order, restraining him from doing so; and the court, if satisfied that the application is well-founded, may grant the injunction or order in the terms applied for or in more limited terms.

(2) In proceedings under this section the Commission shall not allege that the person to whom the proceedings relate has done an act falling within subsection (1)(b) or contravening section 28 which is within the jurisdiction of an industrial tribunal unless a finding by an industrial tribunal that he did that act has become final.

Enforcement of ss.29 to 31

63.—(1) Proceedings in respect of a contravention of section 29, 30 or 31 shall be brought only by the Commission in accordance with the following provisions of this section.

(2) The proceedings shall be—

(a) an application for a decision whether the alleged contravention occurred; or

(b) an application under subsection (4),

or both.

(3) An application under subsection (2)(a) shall be made—

(a) in a case based on any provision of Part II, to an industrial tribunal; and

(b) in any other case, to a designated county court or a sheriff court.

(4) If it appears to the Commission—

(a) that a person has done an act which by virtue of section 29, 30 or 31 was unlawful; and

(b) that unless restrained he is likely to do further acts which by virtue of that section are unlawful,

the Commission may apply to a designated county court for an injunction, or to a sheriff court for an order, restraining him from doing such acts; and the court, if satisfied that the application is well-founded, may grant the injunction or order in the terms applied for or more limited terms.

(5) In proceedings under subsection (4) the Commission shall not allege that the person to whom the proceedings relate has done an act which is unlawful under this Act and within the jurisdiction of an industrial tribunal unless a finding by an industrial tribunal that he did that act has become final.

Preliminary action in employment cases

1–397
64.—(1) With a view to making an application under section 62(1) or 63(4) in relation to a person the Commission may present to an industrial tribunal a complaint that he has done an act within the jurisdiction of an industrial tribunal, and if the tribunal considers that the complaintl is well-founded it shall make a finding to that effect and, if it thinks it just and equitable to do so in the case of an act contravening any provision of Part II may also (as if the complaint had been presented by the person discriminated against) make an order such as is referred to in section 56(1)(*a*), or a recommendation such as is referred to in section 56(1)(*c*), or both.

(2) Subsection (1) is without prejudice to the jurisdiction conferred by section 63(2).

(3) In sections 62 and 63 and this section, the acts "within the jurisdiction of an industrial tribunal" are those in respect of which such jurisdiction is conferred by sections 54 and 63.

Help for Persons Suffering Discrimination

Help for aggrieved persons in obtaining information, etc.

1–398
65.—(1) With a view to helping a person ("the person aggrieved") who considers he may have been discriminated against in contravention of this Act to decide whether to institute proceedings and, if he does so, to formulate and present his case in the most effective manner, the Secretary of State shall by order prescribe—
  (*a*) forms by which the person aggrieved may question the respondent on his reasons for doing any relevant act, or on any other matter which is or may be relevant; and
  (*b*) forms by which the respondent may if he so wishes reply to any questions.

(2) Where the person aggrieved questions the respondent (whether in accordance with an order under subsection (1) or not)—
  (*a*) the question, and any reply by the respondent (whether in accordance with such an order or not) shall, subject to the following provisions of this section, be admissible as evidence in the proceedings;
  (*b*) if it appears to the court or tribunal that the respondent deliberately, and without reasonable excuse, omitted to reply within a reasonable period or that his reply is evasive or equivocal, the court or tribunal may draw any inference from that fact that it considers it just and equitable to draw, including an inference that he committed an unlawful act.

(3) The Secretary of State may by order—

(a) prescribe the period wthin which questions must be duly served in order to be admissible under subsection (2)(a); and

(b) prescribe the manner in which a question, and any reply by the respondent, may be duly served.

(4) Rules may enable the court entertaining a claim under section 57 to determine, before the date fixed for the hearing of the claim, whether a question or reply is admissible under this section or not.

(5) This section is without prejudice to any other enactment or rule of law regulating interlocutory and preliminary matters in proceedings before a county court, sheriff court or industrial tribunal, and has effect subject to any enactment or rule of law regulating the admissibility of evidence in such proceedings.

(6) In this section "respondent" includes a prospective respondent and "rules"—

(a) in relation to county court proceedings, means county court rules;

(b) in relation to sheriff court proceedings, means sheriff court rules.

Assistance by Commission

66.—(1) Where, in relation to proceedings or prospective proceedings under this Act, an individual who is an actual or prospective complainant or claimant applies to the Commission for assistance under this section, the Commission shall consider the application and may grant it if they think fit to do so—

(a) on the ground that the case raises a question of principle; or

(b) on the ground that it is unreasonable, having regard to the complexity of the case, or to the applicant's position in relation to the respondent or another person involved, or to any other matter, to expect the applicant to deal with the case unaided; or

(c) by reason of any other special consideration.

(2) Assistance by the Commission under this section may include—

(a) giving advice;

(b) procuring or attempting to procure the settlement of any matter in dispute;

(c) arranging for the giving of advice or assistance by a solicitor or counsel;

(d) arranging for representation by any person, including all such assistance as is usually given by a solicitor or counsel in the steps preliminary or incidental to any proceedings, or in arriving at or giving effect to a compromise to avoid or bring to an end any proceedings;

(e) any other form of assistance which the Commission may consider appropriate,

but paragraph (d) shall not affect the law and practice regulating the descriptions of persons who may appear in, conduct, defend, and address the court in, any proceedings.

(3) Where under subsection (1) an application for assistance under this section is made in writing, the Commission shall, within the period of two months beginning when the application is received—

(a) consider the application after making such enquiries as they think fit; and

(b) decide whether or not to grant it; and

(c) inform the applicant of their decision, stating whether or not assistance under this section is to be provided by the Commission and, if so, what form it will take.

(4) If, in a case where subsection (3) applies, the Commission within the period of two months there mentioned give notice to the applicant that, in relation to his application—

(a) the period of two months allowed them by that subsection is by virtue of the notice extended to three months; and

(b) the reference to two months in section 68(3) is by virtue of the notice to be read as a reference to three months,

subsection (3) and section 68(3) shall have effect accordingly.

(5) In so far as expenses are incurred by the Commission in providing the applicant with assistance under this section, the recovery of those expenses (as taxed or assessed in such manner as may be prescribed by rules or regulations) shall constitute a first charge for the benefit of the Commission—

(a) on any costs or expenses which (whether by virtue of a judgment or order of a court or tribunal or an agreement or otherwise) are payable to the applicant by any other person in respect of the matter in connection with which the assistance is given; and

(b) so far as relates to any costs or expenses, on his rights under any compromise or settlement arrived at in connection with that matter to avoid or bring to an end any proceedings.

(6) The charge conferred by subsection (5) is subject to any charge under the Legal Aid Act 1974, or any charge or obligation for payment in priority to other debts under the Legal Aid and Advice (Scotland) Acts 1967 and 1972, and is subject to any provision in any of those Acts for payment of any sum into the legal aid fund.

(7) In this section "respondent" includes a prospective respondent and "rules or regulations"—

(a) in relation to county court proceedings, means county court rules;

(b) in relation to sheriff court proceedings, means sheriff court rules;

(c) in relation to industrial tribunal proceedings, means regulations made under [paragraph 1 of Schedule 9 to the Employment Protection (Consolidation) Act 1978].

AMENDMENT

The words in square brackets were substituted by the Employment Protection (Consolidation) Act 1978 (c. 44), s.159(2), Sched. 16.

. . . . . .

Period within which Proceedings to be Brought

Period within which proceedings to be brought

68.—(1) An industrial tribunal shall not consider a complaint under section 54 unless it is presented to the tribunal before the end of the period of three months beginning when the act complained of was done.

(2) A county court or a sheriff court shall not consider a claim under section 57 unless proceedings in respect of the claim are instituted before the end of—

(a) the period of six months beginning when the act complained of was done; or

(b) in a case to which section 57(5) applies, the period of eight months so beginning.

(3) Where, in relation to proceedings or prospective proceedings by way of a claim under section 57, an application for assistance under section 66 is made to the Commission before the end of the period of six or, as the case may be, eight months mentioned in paragraph (a) or (b) of subsection (2), the period allowed by that paragraph for instituting proceedings in respect of the claim shall be extended by two months.

(4) An industrial tribunal, county court or sheriff court shall not consider an application under section 63(2)(a) unless it is made before the end of the period of six months beginning when the act to which it relates was done; and a county court or sheriff court shall not consider an application under section 63(4) unless it is made before the end of the period of five years so beginning.

(5) An industrial tribunal shall not consider a complaint under section 64(1) unless it is presented to the tribunal before the end of the period of six months beginning when the act complained of was done.

(6) A court or tribunal may nevertheless consider any such complaint, claim or application which is out of time if, in all the circumstances of the case, it considers that it is just and equitable to do so.

(7) For the purposes of this section—
  (a) when the inclusion of any term in a contract renders the making of the contract an unlawful act, that act shall be treated as extending throughout the duration of the contract; and
  (b) any act extending over a period shall be treated as done at the end of that period; and
  (c) a deliberate omission shall be treated as done when the person in question decided upon it;

and in the absence of evidence establishing the contrary a person shall be taken for the purposes of this section to decide upon an omission when he does an act inconsistent with doing the omitted act or, if he has done no such inconsistent act, when the period expires within which he might reasonably have been expected to do the omitted act if it was to be done.

Evidence

Evidence

69.—(1) Any finding by a court under section 19 or 20 of the Race Relations Act 1968, or by a court or industrial tribunal under this Act, in respect of any act shall, if it has become final, be treated as conclusive in any proceedings under this Act.

(2) In any proceedings under this Act a certificate signed by or on behalf of a Minister of the Crown and certifying—
  (a) that any arrangements or conditions specified in the certificate were made, approved or imposed by a Minister of the Crown and were in operation at a time or throughout a period so specified; or
  (b) that an act specified in the certificate was done for the purpose of safeguarding national security,
shall be conclusive evidence of the matters certified.

(3) A document purporting to be a certificate such as is mentioned in

subsection (2) shall be received in evidence and, unless the contrary is proved, shall be deemed to be such a certificate.

. . . . . .

Part X

Supplemental

Local authorities: general statutory duty

1–402   71. Without prejudice to their obligation to comply with any other provision of this Act, it shall be the duty of every local authority to make appropriate arrangements with a view to securing that their various functions are carried out with due regard to the need—
   (a) to eliminate unlawful racial discrimination; and
   (b) to promote equality of opportunity, and good relations, between persons of different racial groups.

Validity and revision of contracts

1–403   72.—(1) A term of a contract is void where—
   (a) its inclusion renders the making of the contract unlawful by virtue of this Act; or
   (b) it is included in furtherance of an act rendered unlawful by this Act; or
   (c) it provides for the doing of an act which would be rendered unlawful by this Act.
   (2) Subsection (1) does not apply to a term the inclusion of which constitutes, or is in furtherance of, or provides for, unlawful discrimination against a party to the contract, but the term shall be unenforceable against the party.
   (3) A term in a contract which purports to exclude or limit any provision of this Act is unenforceable by any person in whose favour the term would operate apart from this subsection.
   (4) Subsection (3) does not apply—
   (a) to a contract settling a complaint to which section 54(1) applies where the contract is made with the assistance of a conciliation officer; or
   (b) to a contract settling a claim to which section 57 applies.
   (5) On the application of any person interested in a contract to which subsection (2) applies, a designated county court or a sheriff court may make such order as it thinks just for removing or modifying any term made unenforceable by that subsection; but such an order shall not be made unless all persons affected have been given notice of the application (except where under rules of court notice may be dispensed with) and have been afforded an opportunity to make representations to the court.
   (6) An order under subsection (5) may include provision as respects any period before the making of the order.

Power to amend certain provisions of Act

1–404   73.—(1) The Secretary of State may by an order the draft of which has been approved by each House of Parliament—

(a) amend or repeal section 9 (including that section as amended by a previous order under this subsection);
(b) amend Part II, III or IV so as to render lawful an act which, apart from the amendment, would be unlawful by reason of section 4(1) or (2), 20(1), 21, 24 or 25;
(c) amend section 10(1) or 25(1)(a) so as to alter the number of partners or members specified in that provision.

(2) The Secretary of State shall not lay before Parliament the draft of an order under subsection (1) unless he has consulted the Commission about the contents of the draft.

Orders and regulations

74.—(1) Any power of a Minister of the Crown to make orders or regulations under the provisions of this Act (except sections 13(2)(d), 37(3)(b) and 50(2)(a)) shall be exercisable by statutory instrument.

(2) An order made by a Minister of the Crown under the preceding provisions of this Act (except sections 13(2)(d), 37(3)(b), 50(2)(a) and 73(1)), and any regulations made under section 75(5)(a), shall be subject to annulment in pursuance of a resolution of either House of Parliament.

(3) An order under this Act may make different provision in relation to different cases or classes of case, may exclude certain cases or classes of case, and may contain transitional provisions and savings.

(4) Any power conferred by this Act to make orders includes power (exercisable in the like manner and subject to the like conditions) to vary or revoke any order so made.

(5) Any document purporting to be an order made by the Secretary of State under section 13(2)(d), 37(3)(b) or 50(2)(a) and to be signed by him or on his behalf shall be received in evidence, and shall, unless the contrary is proved, be deemed to be made by him.

Application to Crown, etc.

75.—(1) This Act applies—
(a) to an act done by or for purposes of a Minister of the Crown or government department; or
(b) to an act done on behalf of the Crown by a statutory body, or a person holding a statutory office,

as it applies to an act done by a private person.

(2) Parts II and IV apply to—
(a) service for purposes of a Minister of the Crown or government department, other than service of a person holding a statutory office; or
(b) service on behalf of the Crown for purposes of a person holding a statutory office or purposes of a statutory body; or
(c) service in the armed forces,

as they apply to employment by a private person, and shall so apply as if references to a contract of employment included references to the terms of service.

(3) Subsections (1) and (2) have effect subject to section 16.

(4) Subsection (2) of section 8 and subsection (4) of section 27 shall have effect in relation to any ship, aircraft or hovercraft belonging to or possessed by Her Majesty in right of the Government of the United Kingdom

as it has effect in relation to a ship, aircraft or hovercraft such as is mentioned in paragraph (*a*) or (*b*) of the subsection in question; and section 8(3) shall apply accordingly.

(5) Nothing in this Act shall—
- (*a*) invalidate any rules (whether made before or after the passing of this Act) restricting employment in the service of the Crown or by any public body prescribed for the purposes of this subsection by regulations made by the Minister for the Civil Service to persons of particular birth, nationality, descent or residence; or
- (*b*) render unlawful the publication, display or implementation of any such rules, or the publication of advertisements stating the gist of any such rules.

In this subsection "employment" includes service of any kind, and "public body" means a body of persons, whether corporate or unincorporate, carrying on a service or undertaking of a public nature.

(6) The provisions of Parts II to IV of the Crown Proceedings Act 1947 shall apply to proceedings against the Crown under this Act as they apply to proceedings in England and Wales which by virtue of section 23 of that Act are treated for the purposes of Part II of that Act as civil proceedings by or against the Crown, except that in their application to proceedings under this Act section 20 of that Act (removal of proceedings from county court to High Court) shall not apply.

(7) The provisions of Part V of the Crown Proceedings Act 1947 shall apply to proceedings against the Crown under this Act as they apply to proceedings in Scotland which by virtue of the said Part are treated as civil proceedings by or against the Crown, except that in their application to proceedings under this Act the proviso to section 44 of that Act (removal of proceedings from the sheriff court to the Court of Session) shall not apply.

(8) This subsection applies to any complaint by a person ("the complainant") that another person—
- (*a*) has committed an act of discrimination against the complainant which is unlawful by virtue of section 4; or
- (*b*) is by virtue of section 32 or 33 to be treated as having committed such an act of discrimination against the complainant,

if at the time when the act complained of was done the complainant was serving in the armed forces and the discrimination in question relates to his service in those forces.

(9) Section 54(1) shall not apply to a complaint to which subsection (8) applies, but any such complaint may be made, and if made shall be dealt with, in accordance with whichever of the following provisions for the redress of complaints is appropriate, namely section 130 of the Naval Discipline Act 1957, section 180 or 181 of the Army Act 1955 or section 180 or 181 of the Air Force Act 1955.

(10) In this section—
- (*a*) "the armed forces" means any of the naval, military or air forces of the Crown (including any women's service administered by the Defence Council);
- (*b*) "statutory body" means a body set up by or in purusance of an enactment, and "statutory office" means an office so set up; and
- (*c*) service "for purposes of" a Minister of the Crown or government department does not include service in any office in

Schedule 2 (Ministerial offices) to the House of Commons Disqualification Act 1975 as for the time being in force.

Government appointments outside s.4

76.—(1) This section applies to any appointment by a Minister of the Crown or government department to an office or post where section 4 does not apply in relation to the appointment.

(2) In making the appointment, and in making the arrangements for determining who should be offered the office or post, the Minister of the Crown or government department shall not do an act which would be unlawful under section 4 if the Crown were the employer for the purposes of this Act.

Financial provisions

77. There shall be defrayed out of money provided by Parliament—
   (*a*) sums required by the Secretary of State for making payments under paragraph 5 or 16 of Schedule 1 or paragraph 12 of Schedule 2, and for defraying any other expenditure falling to be made by him under or by virtue of this Act;
   (*b*) any expenses incurred by the Secretary of State with the consent of the Treasury in undertaking, or financially assisting the undertaking by other persons of, research into any matter connected with relations between persons of different racial groups;
   (*c*) payments falling to be made under section 67(5) in respect of the remuneration of assessors; and
   (*d*) any increase attributable to the provisions of this Act in the sums payable out of money provided by Parliament under any other Act.

General interpretation provisions

78.—(1) In this Act, unless the context otherwise requires—
   "access" shall be construed in accordance with section 40;
   "act" includes a deliberate omission;
   "advertisement" includes every form of advertisement or notice, whether to the public or not, and whether in a newspaper or other publication, by television or radio, by display of notices, signs, labels, showcards or goods, by distribution of samples, circulars, catalogues, price lists or other material, by exhibition of pictures, models or films, or in any other way, and references to the publishing of advertisements shall be construed accordingly;
   "the Commission" means the Commission for Racial Equality;
   "Commissioner" means a member of the Commission;
   "designated county court" has the meaning given by section 67(1);
   "discrimination" and related terms shall be construed in accordance with section 3(3).
   "dispose", in relation to premises, includes granting a right to occupy the premises, and any reference to acquiring premises shall be construed accordingly;
   "education" includes any form of training or instruction;
   "education authority" and "educational establishment" have for Scot-

land the same meaning as they have respectively in [section 135(1) of the Education (Scotland) Act 1980];

"employment" means employment under a contract of service or of apprenticeship or a contract personally to execute any work or labour, and related expressions shall be construed accordingly;

"employment agency" means a person who, for profit or not, provides services for the purpose of finding employment for workers or supplying employers with workers;

"estate agent" means a person who, by way of profession or trade, provides services for the purpose of finding premises for persons seeking to acquire them or assisting in the disposal of premises;

"final" shall be construed in accordance with subsection (4);

"firm" has the meaning given by section 4 of the Partnership Act 1890;

"formal investigation" means an investigation under section 48;

"further education" has for England and Wales the meaning given by section 41(*a*) of the Education Act 1944, and for Scotland the meaning given by [section 135(1) of the Education (Scotland) Act 1980];

"general notice", in relation to any person, means a notice published by him at a time and in a manner appearing to him suitable for securing that the notice is seen within a reasonable time by persons likely to be affected by it;

"genuine occupational qualification" shall be construed in accordance with section 5;

"Great Britain" includes such of the territorial waters of the United Kingdom as are adjacent to Great Britain;

"independent school" has for England and Wales the meaning given by section 114(1) of the Education Act 1944, and for Scotland the meaning given by [section 135(1) of the Education (Scotland) Act 1980];

[. . .]

"managers" has for Scotland the same meaning as in [section 135(1) of the Education (Scotland) Act 1980];

"Minister of the Crown" includes the Treasury and the Defence Council;

"nationality" includes citizenship;

"near relative" shall be construed in accordance with subsection (5);

"non-discrimination notice" means a notice under section 58;

"notice" means a notice in writing;

"prescribed" means prescribed by regulations made by the Secretary of State;

"profession" includes any vocation or occupation;

"proprietor", in relation to a school, has for England and Wales the meaning given by section 114(1) of the Education Act 1944, and for Scotland the meaning given by [section 135(1) of the Education (Scotland) Act 1980];

"pupil" in Scotland includes a student of any age;

"racial grounds" and "racial group" have the meaning given by section 8(1);

"school" has for England and Wales the meaning given by section 114(1) of the Education Act 1944, and for Scotland the meaning given by [section 135(1) of the Education (Scotland) Act 1980];

"school education" has for Scotland the meaning given by [section 135(1) of the Education (Scotland) Act 1980];
"trade" includes any business;
"training" includes any form of education or instruction;
"university" includes a university college and the college, school or hall of a university;
"upper limit of compulsory school age" for England and Wales means, subject to section 9 of the Education Act 1962, the age that is that limit by virtue of section 35 of the Education Act 1944 and the Order in Council made under that section.

(2) It is hereby declared that in this Act "premises", unless the context otherwise requires, includes land of any description.

(3) Any power conferred by this Act to designate establishments or persons may be exercised either by naming them or by identifying them by reference to a class or other description.

(4) For the purposes of this Act a non-discrimination notice or a finding by a court or tribunal becomes final when an appeal against the notice or finding is dismissed, withdrawn or abandoned or when the time for appealing expires without an appeal having been brought; and for this purpose an appeal against a non-discrimination notice shall be taken to be dismissed if, notwithstanding that a requirement of the notice is quashed on appeal, a direction is given in respect of it under section 59(3).

(5) For the purposes of this Act a person is a near relative of another if that person is the wife or husband, a parent or child, a grandparent or grandchild, or a brother or sister of the other (whether of full blood or half blood or by affinity), and "child" includes an illegitimate child and the wife or husband of an illegitimate child.

(6) Except so far as the context otherwise requires, any reference in this Act to an enactment shall be construed as a reference to that enactment as amended by or under any other enactment, including this Act.

(7) In this Act, except where otherwise indicated—
  (a) a reference to a numbered Part, section or Schedule is a reference to the Part or section of, or the Schedule to, this Act so numbered; and
  (b) a reference in a section to a numbered subsection is a reference to the subsection of that section so numbered; and
  (c) a reference in a section, subsection or Schedule to a numbered paragraph is a reference to the paragraph of that section, subsection or Schedule so numbered; and
  (d) a reference to any provision of an Act (including this Act) includes a Schedule incorporated in the Act by that provision.

AMENDMENTS

The words in square brackets in subs. (1) were substituted by the Education (Scotland) Act 1980 (c. 44), Sched. 4. The words omitted were repealed by the Industrial Training Act 1982 (c. 10), Sched. 4.

Transitional and commencement provisions, amendments and repeals

79.—(1) The provisions of Schedule 2 shall have effect for making transitional provision for the purposes of this Act.

(2) This Act shall come into operation on such day as the Secretary of

State may by order appoint, and different days may be so appointed for different provisions and for different purposes.

(3) The enactments specified in Schedule 3 shall have effect subject to the amendments specified in that Schedule (being minor amendments or amendments consequential on the preceding provisions of this Act).

(4) The Sex Discrimination Act 1975 shall have effect subject to the amendments specified in Schedule 4, being amendments for bringing provisions in that Act relating to its administration and enforcement into conformity with the corresponding provisions in this Act.

(5) Subject to the provisions of Schedule 2, the enactments specified in Schedule 5 are hereby repealed to the extent shown in column 3 of that Schedule.

(6) Section 5 of the Public Order Act 1936 shall continue to have effect as substituted by section 7 of the Race Relations Act 1965, notwithstanding the repeal of the said section 7 by this Act.

(7) An order under this section may make such transitional provision as appears to the Secretary of State to be necessary or expedient in connection with the provisions thereby brought into operation, including such adaptations of those provisions, or of any provisions of this Act then in operation, as appear to the Secretary of State necessary or expedient in consequence of the partial operation of this Act.

Short title and extent

1–411   80.—(1) This Act may be cited as the Race Relations Act 1976.

(2) This Act, except so far as it amends or repeals any provision of the House of Commons Disqualification Act 1975 or the Northern Ireland Assembly Disqualification Act 1975, does not extend to Northern Ireland.

SCHEDULES

1–412   Section 43   SCHEDULE 1

THE COMMISSION FOR RACIAL EQUALITY

Incorporation and status

1. On the appointment by the Secretary of State of the first Commissioners, the Commissioners shall come into existence as a body corporate.

2.—(1) The Commission is not an emanation of the Crown, and shall not act or be treated as the servant or agent of the Crown.

(2) Accordingly—
   (a) neither the Commission nor a Commissioner or member of its staff as such is entitled to any status, immunity, privilege or exemption enjoyed by the Crown;
   (b) the Commissioners and members of the staff of the Commission as such are not civil servants; and
   (c) the Commission's property is not property of, or held on behalf of, the Crown

Tenure of office of Commissioners

3.—(1) A Commissioner shall hold and vacate his office in accordance with the terms of his appointment.

(2) A person shall not be appointed a Commissioner for more than five years.

(3) With the consent of the Commissioner concerned, the Secretary of State may alter the terms of an appointment so as to make a full-time Commissioner into a part-time Commissioner or vice-versa, or for any other purpose.

(4) A Commissioner may resign by notice to the Secretary of State.

(5) The Secretary of State may terminate the appointment of a Commissioner if satisfied that—

(a) without the consent of the Commission, he failed to attend the meetings of the Commission during a continuous period of six months beginning not earlier than nine months before the termination; or
(b) he is an undischarged bankrupt, or has made an arrangement with his creditors, or is insolvent within the meaning of paragraph 9(2) of Schedule 3 to the Conveyancing and Feudal Reform (Scotland) Act 1970; or
(c) he is by reason of physical or mental illness, or for any other reason, incapable of carrying out his duties.

(6) Past service as a Commissioner is no bar to re-appointment.

Tenure of office of chairman and deputy chairman

4.—(1) The chairman and each deputy chairman shall hold and vacate his office in accordance with the terms of his appointment, and may resign by notice to the Secretary of State.

(2) The office of the chairman or a deputy chairman is vacated if he ceases to be a Commissioner.

(3) Past service as chairman or a deputy chairman is no bar to re-appointment.

Remuneration of Commissioners

5. The Secretary of State may pay, or make such payments towards the provision of, such remuneration, pensions, allowances or gratuities to or in respect of the Commissioners or any of them as, with the consent of the Minister for the Civil Service, he may determine.

6. Where a person ceases to be a Commissioner otherwise than on the expiry of his term of office, and it appears to the Secretary of State that there are special circumstances which make it right for that person to receive compensation, the Secretary of State may, with the consent of the Minister for the Civil Service, direct the Commission to make to that person a payment of such amount as, with the consent of that Minister, the Secretary of State may determine.

Additional Commissioners

7.—(1) Paragraphs 2(2), 3(1) and (6), and 6 shall apply to additional Commissioners appointed under section 48(2) as they apply to Commissioners.

(2) The Commissioners may pay, or make such payments towards the provision of, such remuneration, pensions, allowances or gratuities to or in respect of an additional Commissioner as the Secretary of State, with the consent of the Minister for the Civil Service, may determine.

(3) With the approval of the Secretary of State and the consent of the additional Commissioner concerned, the Commission may alter the terms of an appointment of an additional Commissioner so as to make a full-time additional Commissioner into a part-time additional Commissioner or vice-versa, or for any other purpose.

(4) An additional Commissioner may resign by notice to the Commission.

(5) The Secretary of State, or the Commission acting with the approval of the Secretary of State, may terminate the appointment of an additional Commissioner if satisfied that—
(a) without reasonable excuse he failed to carry out the duties for which he was appointed during a continuous period of three months beginning not earlier than six months before the termination; or
(b) he is a person such as is mentioned in paragraph 3(5)(b); or
(c) he is by reason of physical or mental illness, or for any other reason, incapable of carrying out his duties.

(6) The appointment of an additional Commissioner shall terminate at the conclusion of the investigation for which he was appointed, if not sooner.

Staff

8. The Commission may, after consultation with the Secretary of State, appoint such officers and servants as they think fit, subject to the approval of the Minister for the Civil Service as to numbers and as to remuneration and other terms and conditions of service.

9.(1) Employment with Commission shall be included among the kinds of employment to which a superannuation scheme under section 1 of the Superannuation Act 1972 can apply, and accordingly in Schedule 1 to that Act (in which those kinds of employment are listed) the words "Commission for Racial Equality" shall be inserted after the words "Commission on Industrial Relations."

(2) Where a person who is employed by the Commission and is by reference to that employment a participant in a scheme under section 1 of the Superannuation Act 1972 becomes a

Commissioner or an additional Commissioner, the Minister for the Civil Service may determine that his service as a Commissioner or additional Commissioner shall be treated for the purposes of the scheme as service as an employee of the Commission.

10.—(1) In this paragraph—
"the new Commission" means the Commission for Racial Equality;
"present Commission employee" means a person who immediately before the repeal date is employed by the Community Relations Commission;
"private pension scheme" means a scheme for the payment of pensions, allowances or gratuities other than one made under section 1 of the Superannuation Act 1972;
"the repeal date" means the date on which the repeal of the Race Relations Act 1968 by this Act takes effect.

(2) If a present Commission employee enters the employment of the new Commission on the repeal date and on so doing elects to be covered for his service in that employment by a private pension scheme in which he was a participant in respect of his service in the employment of the Community Relations Commission, the new Commission may make such payments towards the provision of benefits to or in respect of him under that scheme (or any other private pension scheme replacing it) as may be determined by the new Commission with the consent of the Secretary of State given with the approval of the Minister for the Civil Service; and it shall be the duty of the new Commission and those Ministers in the exercise of their functions under this sub-paragraph to ensure that his rights under the scheme do not become less advantageous than they were when he entered the employment of the new Commission.

(3) Where a person who is employed by the new Commission and is in respect of that employment a participant in a private pension scheme becomes a Commissioner or an additional Commissioner, his service as a Commissioner or additional Commissioner may be treated for the purposes of the scheme as service as an employee of the new Commission.

11. The Employers' Liability (Compulsory Insurance) Act 1969 shall not require insurance to be effected by the Commission.

Advisory committees

12. The Commission may, with the approval of the Secretary of State, appoint advisory committees for the purpose of such of their functions as they think fit.

Proceedings and business

13.—(1) Subject to the provisions of this Act—
(a) the Commission shall discharge their functions in accordance with arrangements made by the Commission and approved by the Secretary of State; and
(b) arrangments so made and approved may provide for the discharge under the general direction of the Commission of any of the Commission's functions by a committee of the Commission, or by two or more Commissioners.

(2) Anything done by or in relation to a Committee of the Commission or Commissioners in the discharge of the Commission's functions shall have the same effect as if done by or in relation to the Commission.

14. The validity of any proceedings of te Commission shall not be affected by any vacancy among the members of the Commission or by any defect in the appointment of any Commissioner or additional Commissioner.

15. The quorum for meetings of the Commission shall in the first instance be determined by a meeting of the Commission attended by not less than five Commissioners.

Finance

16. The Secretary of State shall pay to the Commission expenses incurred or to be incurred by them under paragraph 6, 7, 8 or 10 of this Schedule or paragraph 7 of Schedule 2, and with the consent of the Minister for the Civil Service and the Treasury, shall pay to the Commission such sums as the Secretary of State thinks fit for enabling the Commission to meet other expenses.

17.—(1) The accounting year of the Commission shall be the twelve months ending on 31st March.
(2) It shall be the duty of the Commission—
(a) to keep proper accounts and proper records in relation to the accounts;
(b) to prepare in respect of each accounting year a statement of accounts in such form as the Secretary of State may direct with the approval of the Treasury; and
(c) to send copies of the statement to the Secretary of State and the Comptroller and

Auditor General before the end of the month of November next following the accounting year to which the statement relates.

(3) The Comptroller and Auditor General shall examine, certify and report on each statement received by him in pursuance of this Schedule and shall lay copies of each statement and of his report before each House of Parliament.

Disqualification Acts

18.—(1) In Part II of Schedule 1 to the House of Commons Disqualification Act 1975 and Part II of Schedule 1 to the Northern Ireland Assembly Disqualification Act 1975 (bodies of which all members are disqualified under those Acts), there shall (at the appropriate place in alphabetical order) be inserted the following entry:—

"The Commission for Racial Equality".

(2) In Part III of Schedule 1 to each of those Acts of 1975 (other disqualifying offices) there shall (at the appropriate place in alphabetical order) be inserted the following entry:—

"Additional Commissioner of the Commission for Racial Equality".

Section 79   SCHEDULE 2

TRANSITIONAL PROVISIONS

Interpretation

1. In this Schedule—

"the 1968 Act" means the Race Relations Act 1968;

"the repeal date" means the date on which the repeal of the 1968 Act by this Act takes effect;

"the Board" means the Race Relations Board.

Enforcement

2. The repeal of the 1968 Act shall not—
   (*a*) invalidate any injunction or order granted or made under section 21 or 23 of that Act which is in force immediately before the repeal date; or
   (*b*) remove from any court any jurisdiction which, but for that repeal, it would have in relation to any such injunction or order.

3. Any proceedings under section 19 or 20 of the 1968 Act which are pending immediately before the repeal date may be continued on and after that date by the Commission as if that Act had not been repealed and the Commission were the Board.

4.—(1) Where a complaint such as is mentioned in section 15(1) or 16(1) of the 1968 Act was made but not disposed of before the repeal date, the relevant provisions of the 1968 Act shall, notwithstanding their repeal, continue to apply in relation to the complaint and the act complained of, but as if anything falling to be done in that connection by or in relation to the Bard or a conciliation committee fell to be done by or in relation to the Commission or, in so far as the Commission may so direct, a committee appointed for that purpose by the Commission.

(2) For the purposes of this paragraph the relevant provisions of the 1968 Act are—
   (*a*) for a complaint such as is mentioned in section 15(1) of that Act, sections 15, 18 to 24 and 27 to 29 of that Act;
   (*b*) for a complaint such as is mentioned in section 16(1) of that Act, section 16(1) of, Schedule 2 to, and sections 18 to 24 and 27 to 29 of, that Act.

5. Where a complaint such as is mentioned in section 15(1) or 16(1) of the 1968 Act could have been, but was not, made before the repeal date in respect of an act done before that date, the relevant provisions of the 1968 Act (within the meaning of paragraph 4) shall, notwithstanding their repeal, continue to apply in relation to that act and any such complaint made in respect of it, but as if anything falling to be done in that connection by or in relation to the Board or a conciliation committee fell to be done as mentioned in paragraph 4(1).

6.—(1) Where—
   (*a*) an investigation under subsection (1) of section 17 of the 1968 Act was begun but not completed before the repeal date; or
   (*b*) a matter was before that date referred for investigation under that subsection but was at that date still awaiting investigation; or
   (*c*) an investigation under that subsection having been completed before that date, some action arising out of the investigation would have fallen to be taken or continued under the 1968 Act on or after that date if that Act had not been repealed,

the relevant provisions of the 1968 Act shall, notwithstanding their repeal, continue to apply in relation to the investigation and its subject-matter, but as if anything falling to be done in that connection by or in relation to the Board or a conciliation committee fell to be done as mentioned in paragraph 4(1).

(2) For the purposes of this paragraph the relevant provisions of the 1968 Act are section 17(1) of, Schedule 3 to, and sections 18 to 24 and 27 to 29 of, that Act.

7. The Commission—
    (*a*) may pay to members of any committee appointed by the Commission for the purposes of paragraph 4, 5 or 6 travelling or other allowances in accordance with such scales as may be approved by the Secretary of State with the consent of the Treasury, and may defray any other expenses of such a committee to such amount as may be so approved; and
    (*b*) shall pay to any assessors appointed by the Commission under section 18 of the 1968 Act such remuneration and allowances as the Commission may, with the consent of the Treasury and after consultation with the Secretary of State, determine.

8.—(1) An order under section 19 of the 1968 Act appointing a county court to have jurisdiction under, and assigning to it a district for the purposes of, that section, or providing for the discontinuance of any jurisdiction of a county court for those purposes, shall, so far as it is in force immediately before the repeal date, have effect with the necessary modifications as if made under section 67(1) for the purposes of this Act.

In its application on or after the repeal date by virtue of paragraph 3, 4, 5 or 6, section 19 of the 1968 Act shall have effect as if—
    (*a*) subsections (3) to (5) were omitted; and
    (*b*) any reference to, or to the district assigned to, a county court appointed to have jurisdiction thereunder were a reference to, or to the district of, a designated county court;

and section 67(6) shall apply in relation to proceedings under that section in its application as aforesaid as if they were proceedings under this Act.

Regulations under s.27(9) of 1968 Act

9. Any regulations under section 27(9) of the 1968 Act shall, so far as they are in force immediately before the repeal date, have effect as if made under section 75(5).

Property, rights and liabilities of Race Relations Board and Community Relations Commission

10.—(1) On the repeal date all property, rights and liabilities which immediately before that date were property, rights and liabilities of the Board or of the Community Relations Commission shall vest in the Commission for Racial Equality by virtue of this paragraph and without further assurance.

(2) Section 12 of the Finance Act 1895 (which requires Acts to be stamped as conveyances on sale in certain cases) shall not apply to any transfer of property effected by this paragraph.

(3) Any damages recovered by the Commission for Racial Equality on or after the repeal date by virtue of an award made under section 22 of the 1968 Act shall be accounted for by the Commission to the person in respect of whom they were awarded.

Staff

11.—(1) In this and the following paragraph "present employee" means a person who immediately before the repeal date is employed by the Board or the Community Relations Commission.

(2) This sub-paragraph applies to any present employee—
    (*a*) who is employed by the Commission as from the repeal date; or
    (*b*) who was offered employment with the Commission as from that date on terms which, taken as a whole, are not less favourable than those on which he was employed at the time of the offer, but unreasonably refused the offer.

(3) For the purposes of [Part VI of the Employment Protection (Consolidation) Act 1978] and any scheme under section 1 of the Superannuation Act 1972 a present employee to whom sub-paragraph (2) above applies shall not be treated as having been dismissed by reason of, or retired on, redundancy on his ceasing to be employed by the Board or the Community Relations Commission (as the case may be).

(4) For the purposes of—
    [(*a*) the Employment Protection (Consolidation) Act 1978 except Part VI of that Act;]
    (*b*) [. . .]
    (*c*) the Employment Protection Act 1975; and

(*d*) any scheme under section 1 of the Superannuation Act 1972,
there shall be deemed to have been no break at the repeal date in the employment of a present employee who as from that date is employed by the Commission.

(5) Any liability to pay a redundancy payment under the Redundancy Payments Act 1965 to an employee of the Community Relations Commission which arises on the repeal date and which, if it had so arisen without that Commission ceasing to exist, would have arisen as a liability of that Commission, shall instead be a liability of the Secretary of State.

12. Where a present employee whose employment immediately before the repeal date is with the Community Relations Commission is not employed by the Commission for Racial Equality as from that date and is not within paragraph 11(2)(*b*), the Secretary of State may, with the consent of the Minister for the Civil Service, make to him as compensation for his loss of employment (whether or not he is entitled to a redundancy payment in respect thereof) a payment of such amount as, with the consent of that Minister, the Secretary of State may determine.

13. Any dispute arising under paragraph 11 as to whether or not—
   (*a*) the terms of employment offered to a person are, taken as a whole, less favourable than those on which he was employed at the time when an offer of employment with the Commission was made to him; or
   (*b*) a person's refusal of an offer of employment with the Commission was unreasonable,

shall be referred to and determined by an industrial tribunal.

AMENDMENT

The words in square brackets in para. 11 were substituted by the Employment Protection (Consolidation) Act 1978, s.159(2), Sched. 16; sub-para. (4)(*b*) is repealed.

Patents Act 1977

(1977 c.37)

An Act to establish a new law of patents applicable to future patents and applications for patents, to amend the law of patents applicable to existing patents and applications for patents; to give effect to certain international conventions on patents; and for connected purposes.

[29th July 1977]

. . . . . .

Employees' Inventions

Right to employees' inventions

39.—(1) Notwithstanding anything in any rule of law, an invention made by an employee shall, as between him and his employer, be taken to belong to his employer for the purposes of this Act and all other purposes if—
   (*a*) it was made in the course of the normal duties of the employee or in the course of duties falling outside his normal duties, but specifically assigned to him, and the circumstances in either case were such that an invention might reasonably be expected to result from the carrying out of his duties; or
   (*b*) the invention was made in the course of the duties of the employee and, at the time of making the invention, because of the nature of his duties and the particular responsibilities arising from the nature of his duties he had a special obligation to further the interests of the employer's undertaking.

(2) Any other invention made by an employee shall, as between him and his employer, be taken for those purposes to belong to the employee.

Compensation of employees for certain inventions

1–416 40.—(1) Where it appears to the court or the comptroller on an application made by an employee within the prescribed period that the employee has made an invention belonging to the employer for which a patent has been granted, that the patent is (having regard among other things to the size and nature of the employer's undertaking) of outstanding benefit to the employer and that by reason of those facts it is just that the employee should be awarded compensation to be paid by the employer, the court or the comptroller may award him such compensation of an amount determined under section 41 below.

(2) Where it appears to the court or the comptroller on an application made by an employee within the prescribed period that—
   (a) a patent has been granted for an invention made by and belonging to the employee;
   (b) his rights in the invention, or in any patent or application for a patent for the invention, have since the appointed day been assigned to the employer or an exclusive licence under the patent or application has since the appointed day been granted to the employer;
   (c) the benefit derived by the employee from the contract of assignment, assignation or grant or any ancillary contract ("the relevant contract") is inadequate in relation to the benefit derived by the employer from the patent; and
   (d) by reason those facts it is just that the employee should be awarded compensation to be paid by the employer in addition to the benefit derived from the relevant contract;
the court or the comptroller may award him such compensation of an amount determined under section 41 below.

(3) Subsections (1) and (2) above shall not apply to the invention of an employee where a relevant collective agreement provides for the payment of compensation in respect of inventions of the same description as that invention to employees of the same description as that employee.

(4) Subsection (2) above shall have effect notwithstanding anything in the relevant contract or any agreement applicable to the invention (other than any such collective agreement).

(5) If it appears to the comptroller on an application under this section that the application involves matters which would more properly be determined by the court, he may decline to deal with it.

(6) In this section—
   "the prescribed period", in relation to proceedings before the court, means the period prescribed by rules of court, and
   "relevant collective agreement" means a collective agreement within the meaning of the Trade Union and Labour Relations Act 1974, made by or on behalf of a trade union to which the employee belongs, and by the employer or an employer's association to which the employer belongs which is in force at the time of the making of the invention.

(7) References in this section to an invention belonging to an employer

or employee are references to it so belonging as between the employer and the employee.

Amount of compensation

41.—(1) An award of compensation to an employee under section 40(1) or (2) above in relation to a patent for an invention shall be such as will secure for the employee a fair share (having regard to all the circumstances) of the benefit which the employer has derived, or may reasonably be expected to derive, from the patent or from the assignment, assignation or grant to a person connected with the employer of the property or any right in the invention or the property in, or any right in or under, an application for that patent.

(2) For the purposes of subsection (1) above the amount of any benefit derived or expected to be derived by an employer from the assignment, assignation or grant of—
  (a) the property in, or any right in or under, a patent for the invention or an application for such a patent; or
  (b) the property or any right in the invention;
to a person connected with him shall be taken to be the amount which could reasonably be expected to be so derived by the employer if that person had not been connected with him.

(3) Where the Crown or a Research Council in its capacity as employer assigns or grants the property in, or any right in or under, an invention, patent or application for a patent to a body having among its functions that of developing or exploiting inventions resulting from public research and does so for no consideration or only a nominal consideration, any benefit derived from the invention, patent or application by that body shall be treated for the purposes of the foregoing provisions of this section as so derived by the Crown or, as the case may be, Research Council.

In this subsection "Research Council" means a body which is a Research Council for the purposes of the Science and Technology Act 1965.

(4) In determining the fair share of the benefit to be secured for an employee in respect of a patent for an invention which has always belonged to an employer, the court or the comptroller shall, among the things, take the following matters into account, that is to say—
  (a) the nature of the employee's duties, his remuneration and the other advantages he derives or has derived from his employment or has derived in relation to the invention under this Act;
  (b) the effort and skill which the employee has devoted to making the invention;
  (c) the effort and skill which any other person has devoted to making the invention jointly with the employee concerned, and the advice and other assistance contributed by any other employee who is not a joint inventor of the invention; and
  (d) the contribution made by the employer to the making, developing and working of the invention by the provision of advice, facilities and other assistance, by the provision of opportunities and by his managerial and commercial skill and activities.

(5) In determining the fair share of the benefit to be secured for an employee in respect of a patent for an invention which originally belonged to him, the court or the comptroller shall, among other things, take the following matters into account, that is to say—

(a) any conditions in a licence or licences granted under this Act or otherwise in respect of the invention or the patent;

(b) the extent to which the invention was made jointly by the employee with any other person; and

(c) the contribution made by the employer to the making, developing and working of the invention as mentioned in subsection (4)(d) above.

(6) Any order for the payment of compensation under section 40 above may be an order for the payment of a lump sum or for periodical payment, or both.

(7) Without prejudice to section 32 of the Interpretation Act 1889 (which provides that a statutory power may in general he exercised from time to time), the refusal of the court or the comptroller to make any such order on an application made by an employee under section 40 above shall not prevent a further application being made under that section by him or any successor in title of his.

(8) Where the court or the comptroller has made any such order, the court or he may on the application of either the employer or the employee vary or discharge it or suspend any provision of the order and revive any provision so suspended, and section 40(5) above shall apply to the application as it applies to an application under that section.

(9) In England and Wales any sums awarded by the comptroller under section 40 above shall, if a county court so orders, be recoverable by execution issued from the county court or otherwise, as if they were payable under an order of that court.

(10) In Scotland an order made under section 40 above by the comptroller for the payment of any sums may be enforced in like manner as a recorded decree arbitral.

(11) In Northern Ireland an order made under section 40 above by the comptroller for the payment of any sums may be enforced as if it were a money judgment.

Enforceability of contracts relating to employees' inventions

1–418   42.—(1) This section applies to any contract (whenever made) relating to inventions made by an employee, being a contract entered into by him—

(a) with the employer (alone or with another); or

(b) with some other person at the request of the employer or in pursuance of the employee's contract of employment.

(2) Any term in a contract to which this section applies which diminishes the employee's rights in inventions of any description made by him after the appointed day and the date of the contract, or in or under patents for those inventions or applications for such patents, shall be unenforceable against him to the extent that it diminishes his rights in an invention of that description so made, or in or under a patent for such an invention or an application for any such patent.

(3) Subsection (2) above shall not be construed as derogating from any duty of confidentiality owed to his employer by an employee by virtue of any rule of law or otherwise.

(4) This section applies to any arrangement made with a Crown employee by or on behalf of the Crown as his employer as it applies to any contract made between an employee and an employer other than the

Crown, and for the purposes of this section "Crown employee" means a person employed under or for the purposes of a government department or any officer or body exercising on behalf of the Crown functions conferred by any enactment.

Supplementary

43.—(1) Sections 39 to 42 above shall not apply to an invention made before the appointed day.

1–419

(2) Sections 39 to 42 above shall not apply to an invention made by an employee unless at the time he made the invention one of the following conditions was satisfied in his case, that is to say—
   (*a*) he was mainly employed in the United Kingdom; or
   (*b*) he was not mainly employed anywhere or his place of employment could not be determined, but his employer had a place of business in the United Kingdom to which the employee was attached, whether or not he was also attached elsewhere.

(3) In sections 39 to 42 above and this section, except so far as the context otherwise requires, references to the making of an invention by an employee are references to his making it alone or jointly with any other person, but do not include references to his merely contributing advice or other assistance in the making of an invention by another employee.

(4) Any references in sections 40 to 42 above to a patent and to a patent being granted are respectively references to a patent or other protection and to its being granted whether under the law of the United Kingdom or the law in force in any other country or under any treaty or international convention.

(5) For the purposes of sections 40 and 41 above the benefit derived or expected to be derived by an employer from a patent shall, where he dies before any award is made under section 40 above in respect of the patent, include any benefit derived or expected to be derived from the patent by his personal representatives or by any person in whom it was vested by their assent.

(6) Where an employee dies before an award is made under section 40 above in respect of a patented invention made by him, his personal representatives or their successors in title may exercise his right to make or proceed with an application for compensation under subsection (1) or (2) of that section.

(7) In sections 40 and 41 above and this section "benefit" means benefit in money or money's worth.

(8) Section 533 of the Income and Corporation Taxes Act 1970 (definition of connected persons) shall apply for determining for the purposes of section 41(2) above whether one person is connected with another as it applies for determining that question for the purposes of the Tax Acts.

Criminal Law Act 1977
(1977 c. 45)

Part I

Conspiracy

The offence of conspiracy

1.—(1) Subject to the following provisions of this Part of this Act, if a person agrees with any other person or persons that a course of conduct shall be pursued which will necessarily amount to or involve the commission of any offence or offences by one or more of the parties to the agreement if the agreement is carried out in accordance with their intentions, he is guilty of conspiracy to commit the offence or offences in question.

(2) Where liability for any offence may be incurred without knowledge on the part of the person committing it of any particular fact or circumstance necessary for the commission of the offence, a person shall nevertheless not be guilty of conspiracy to commit that offence by virtue of subsection (1) above unless he and at least one other party to the agreement intend or know that the fact or circumstance shall or will exist at the time when the conduct constituting the offence is to take place.

(3) Where in pursuance of any agreement the acts in question in relation to any offence are to be done in contemplation or furtherance of a trade dispute (within the meaning of the Trade Union and Labour Relations Act 1974) that offence shall be disregarded for the purposes of subsection (1) above provided that it is a summary offence which is not punishable with imprisonment.

(4) In this Part of this Act "offence" means an offence triable in England and Wales, except that it includes murder notwithstanding that the murder in question would not be so triable if committed in accordance with the intentions of the parties to the agreement.

Exemptions from liability for conspiracy

2.—(1) A person shall not by virtue of section 1 above be guilty of conspiracy to commit any offence if he is an intended victim of that offence.

(2) A person shall not by virtue of section 1 above be guilty of conspiracy to commit any offence or offences if the only other person or persons with whom he agrees are (both initially and at all times during the currency of the agreement) persons of any one or more of the following descriptions, that is to say—
  (a) his spouse;
  (b) a person under the age of criminal responsibility; and
  (c) an intended victim of that offence or of each of those offences.

(3) A person is under the age of criminal responsibility for the purposes of subsection (2)(b) above so long as it is conclusively presumed, by virtue of section 50 of the Children and Young Persons Act 1933, that he cannot be guilty of any offence.

Penalties for conspiracy

3.—(1) A person guilty by virtue of section 1 above of conspiracy to commit any offence or offences shall be liable on conviction on indictment—
  (a) in a case falling within subsection (2) or (3) below, to imprisonment for a term related in accordance with that subsection to the gravity

of the offence or offences in question (referred to below in this section as the relevant offence or offences); and

(*b*) in any other case, to a fine.

Paragraph (*b*) above shall not be taken as prejudicing the application of section 30(1) of the Powers of Criminal Courts Act 1973 (general power of court to fine offender convicted on indictment) in a case falling within subsection (2) or (3) below.

(2) Where the relevant offence or any of the relevant offences is an offence of any of the following descriptions, that is to say—
- (*a*) murder, or any other offence the sentence for which is fixed by law;
- (*b*) an offence for which a sentence extending to imprisonment for life is provided; or
- (*c*) an indictable offence punishable with imprisonment for which no maximum term of imprisonment is provided,

the person convicted shall be liable for imprisonment for life.

(3) Where in a case other than one to which subsection (2) above applies the relevant offence or any of the relevant offences is punishable with imprisonment, the person convicted shall be liable to imprisonment for a term not exceeding the maximum term provided for that offence or (where more than one such offence is in question) for any one of those offences (taking the longer or the longest term as the limit for the purposes of this section where the terms provided differ).

In the case of an offence triable either way the references above in this subsection to the maximum term provided for that offence are references to the maximum term so provided on conviction on indictment.

Restrictions on the institution of proceedings for conspiracy

4.—(1) Subject to subsection (2) below proceedings under section 1 above for conspiracy to commit any offence or offences shall not be instituted against any person except by or with the consent of the Director of Public Prosecutions if the offence or (as the case may be) each of the offences in question is a summary offence.

(2) In relation to the institution of proceedings under section 1 above for conspiracy to commit—
- (*a*) an offence which is subject to a prohibition by or under any enactment on the institution of proceedings otherwise than by, or on behalf or with the consent of, the Attorney General, or
- (*b*) two or more offences of which at least one is subject to such a prohibition,

subsection (1) above shall have effect with the substitution of a reference to the Attorney General for the reference to the Director of Public Prosecutions.

(3) Any prohibition by or under any enactment on the institution of proceedings for any offence which is not a summary offence otherwise than by, or on behalf or with the consent of, the Director of Public Prosecutions or any other person shall apply also in relation to proceedings under section 1 above for conspiracy to commit that offence.

(4) Where—
- (*a*) an offence has been committed in pursuance of any agreement; and
- (*b*) proceedings may not be instituted for that offence because any

258 *Criminal Law Act 1977*

time limit applicable to the institution of any such proceedings has expired,

proceedings under section 1 above for conspiracy to commit that offence shall not be instituted against any person on the basis of that agreement.

Abolitions, savings, transitional provisions, consequential amendment and repeals

1–425   5.—(1) Subject to the following provisions of this section, the offence of conspiracy at common law is hereby abolished.

(2) Subsection (1) above shall not affect the offence of conspiracy at common law so far as relates to conspiracy to defraud, and section 1 above shall not apply in any case where the agreement in question amounts to a conspiracy to defraud at common law.

(3) Subsection (1) above shall not affect the offence of conspiracy at common law if and in so far as it may be committed by entering into an agreement to engage in conduct which—
   (*a*) tends to corrupt public morals or outrages public decency; but
   (*b*) would not amount to or involve the commission of an offence if carried out by a single person otherwise than in pursuance of an agreement.

(4) Subsection (1) above shall not affect—
   (*a*) any proceedings commenced before the time when this Part of this Act comes into force;
   (*b*) any proceedings commenced after that time against a person charged with the same conspiracy as that charged in any proceedings commenced before that time; or
   (*c*) any proceedings commenced after that time in respect of a trespass committed before that time;
but a person convicted of conspiracy to trespass in any proceedings brought by virtue of paragraph (*c*) above shall not in respect of that conviction be liable to imprisonment for a term exceeding six months.

(5) Sections 1 and 2 above shall apply to things done before as well as to things done after the time when this Part of this Act comes into force, but in the application of section 3 above to a case were the agreement in question was entered into before that time—
   (*a*) subsection (2) shall be read without the reference to murder in paragraph (*a*); and
   (*b*) any murder intended under the agreement shall be treated as an offence for which a maximum term of imprisonment of ten years is provided.

(6) The rules laid down by sections 1 and 2 above shall apply for determining whether a person is guilty of an offence of conspiracy under any enactment other than section 1 above, but conduct which is an offence under any such other enactment shall not also be an offence under section 1 above.

(7) Incitement and attempt to commit the offence of conspiracy (whether the conspiracy incited or attempted would be an offence at common law or under section 1 above or any other enactment) shall cease to be offences.

(8) The fact that the person or persons who, so far as appears from the indictment on which any person has been convicted of conspiracy, were the only other parties to the agreement on which his conviction was based have

been acquitted of conspiracy by reference to that agreement (whether after being tried with the person convicted or separately) shall not be a ground for quashing his conviction unless under all the circumstances of the case his conviction is inconsistent with the acquittal of the other person in question.

(9) Any rule of law or practice inconsistent with the provisions of subsection (8) above is hereby abolished.

(10) In section 4 of the Offences against the Person Act 1861—
- (a) the words preceding "whosoever" shall cease to have effect; and
- (b) for the words from "be kept" to "years" there shall be substituted the words "imprisonment for life".

(11) Section 3 of the Conspiracy and Protection of Property Act 1875 shall cease to have effect.

. . . . . .

State Immunity Act 1978

(1978 c.33)

. . . . . .

Contracts of employment

4.—(1) A State is not immune as respects proceedings relating to a contract of employment between the State and an individual where the contract was made in the United Kingdom or the work is to be wholly or partly performed there.

(2) Subject to subsections (3) and (4) below, this section does not apply if—
- (a) at the time when the proceedings are brought the individual is a national of the State concerned; or
- (b) at the time when the contract was made the individual was neither a national of the United Kingdom nor habitually resident there; or
- (c) the parties to the contract have otherwise agreed in writing.

(3) Where the work is for an office, agency or establishment maintained by the State in the United Kingdom for commercial purposes, subsection (2)(a) and (b) above do not exclude the application of this section unless the individual was, at the time when the contract was made, habitually resident in that State.

(4) Subsection (2)(c) above does not exclude the application of this section where the law of the United Kingdom requires the proceedings to be brought before a court of the United Kingdom.

(5) In subsection (2)(b) above "national of the United Kingdom" means a citizen of the United Kingdom and Colonies, a person who is a British subject by virtue of section 2, 13 or 16 of the British Nationality Act 1948 or by virtue of the British Nationality Act 1965, a British protected person within the meaning of the said Act of 1948 or a citizen of Southern Rhodesia.

(6) In this section "proceedings relating to a contract of employment"

includes proceedings between the parties to such a contract in respect of any statutory rights or duties to which they are entitled or subject as employer or employee.

1–427 # Employment Protection (Consolidation) Act 1978

(1978 c.44)

An Act to consolidate certain enactments relating to rights of employees arising out of their employment; and certain enactments relating to the insolvency of employers; to industrial tribunals; to recoupment of certain benefits; to conciliation officers; and to the Employment Appeal Tribunal.

[31st July 1978]

PART I

PARTICULARS OF TERMS OF EMPLOYMENT

Written Particulars of Terms of Employment

Written particulars of terms of employment

1–428   1.—(1) Not later than thirteen weeks after [the beginning of an employee's employment] with an employer, the employer shall give to the employee a written statement in accordance with the following provisions of this section.
  (2) An employer shall in a statement under this section—
    (a) identify the parties;
    (b) specify the date when the employment began;
    [(c) specify the date on which the employee's period of continuous employment began (taking into account any employment with a previous employer which counts towards that period).]
  (3) A statement under this section shall contain the following particulars of the terms of employment as at a specified date not more than one week before the statement is given, that is to say—
    (a) the scale or rate of remuneration, or the method of calculating remuneration,
    (b) the intervals at which remuneration is paid (that is, whether weekly or monthly or by some other period),
    (c) any terms and conditions relating to hours of work (including any terms and conditions relating to normal working hours),
    (d) any terms and conditions relating to—
      (i) entitlement to holidays, including public holidays, and holiday pay (the particulars given being sufficient to enable the employee's entitlement, including any entitlement to accrued holiday pay on the termination of employment, to be precisely calculated),
      (ii) incapacity for work due to sickness or injury, including any provision for sick pay,

(iii) pensions and pension schemes,
  (e) the length of notice which the employee is obliged to give and entitled to receive to determine his contract of employment, and
  (f) the title of the job which the employee is employed to do;
Provided that paragraph (d)(iii) shall not apply to the employees of any body or authority if the employees' pension rights depend on the terms of a pension scheme established under any provision contained in or having effect under an Act of Parliament and the body or authority are required by any such provision to give to new employees information concerning their pension rights, or concerning the determination of questions affecting their pension rights.

(4) Subject to subsection (5), every statement given to an employee under this section shall include a note—
  (a) specifying any disciplinary rules applicable to the employee, or referring to a document which is reasonably accessible to the employee and which specifies such rules;
  (b) specifying, by description or otherwise—
    (i) a person to whom the employee can apply if he is dissatisfied with any disciplinary decision relating to him; and
    (ii) a person to whom the employee can apply for the purpose of seeking redress of any grievance relating to his employment, and the manner in which any such application should be made;
  (c) where there are further steps consequent upon any such application, explaining those steps or referring to a document which is reasonably accessible to the employee and which explains them; and
  (d) stating whether a contracting-out certificate is in force for the employment in respect of which the statement is given.

(5) The provisions of paragraphs (a) to (c) of subsection (4) shall not apply to rules, disciplinary decisions, grievances or procedures relating to health or safety at work.

(6) The definition of week given by section 158(1) does not apply for the purposes of this section.

AMENDMENT
The words in square brackets in subss. (1) and (2) were substituted by the Employment Act 1982 (c.46), Sched. 2, para. 8.

Supplementary provisions relating to statements under s.1

2.—(1) If there are no particulars to be entered under any of the heads of paragraph (d) of subsection (3) of section 1, or under any of the other provisions of section 1(2) and (3), that fact shall be stated.

(2) If the contract is for a fixed term, the statement given under section 1 shall state the date when the contract expires.

(3) A statement given under section 1 may, for all or any of the particulars to be given by the statement, refer the employee to some document which the employee has reasonable opportunities of reading in the course of his employment or which is made reasonably accessible to him in some other way.

[(4) No statement need be given under section 1 where—
  (a) the employee's terms of employment are the same as those of earlier employment with the same employer in respect of which a statement under that section and any information subsequently required under section 4 was duly given, and

1–429

(b) that earlier employment ended not more than six months before the beginning of the employment in question;
but without prejudice to the operation of subsection (1) of section 4 if there is subsequently a change in the terms of employment.]

AMENDMENT
Subs. (4) was substituted by the Employment Act 1982 (c.46), Sched. 2, para. 8(2).

. . . . . .

Changes in terms of employment

4.—(1) If after the date to which a statement given under section 1 relates there is a change in the terms of employment to be included, or referred to, in that statement the employer shall, not more than one month after the change, inform the employee of the nature of the change by a written statement and, if he does not leave a copy of the statement with the employee, shall preserve the statement and ensure that the employee has reasonable opportunities of reading it in the course of his employment, or that it is made reasonably accessible to him in some other way.

(2) A statement given under subsection (1) may, for all or any of the particulars to be given by the statement, refer the employee to some document which the employee has reasonable opportunities of reading in the course of his employment, or which is made reasonably accessible to him in some other way.

(3) If, in referring in the statement given under section 1 or under subsection (1) of this section to any such document, the employer indicates to the employee that future changes in the terms of which the particulars are given in the document will be entered up in the document (or recorded by some other means for the information of persons referring to the document), the employer need not under subsection (1) inform the employee of any such change if it is duly entered up or recorded not later than one month after the change is made.

(4) Where, after an employer has given to an employee a written statement in accordance with section 1—
  (a) the name of the employer (whether an individual or a body corporate or partnership) is changed, without any change in the identity of the employer, or
  (b) the identity of the employer is changed, in such circumstances that, [. . .] the continuity of the employee's period of employment is not broken,
and (in either case) the change does not involve any change in the terms (other than the names of the parties) included or referred to in the statement, then, the person who, immediately after the change, is the employer shall not be required to give to the employee a statement in accordance with section 1, but, subject to subsection (5), the change shall be treated as a change falling within subsection (1) of this section.

(5) A written statement under this section which informs an employee of such a change in his terms of employment as is referred to in subsection (4)(b) shall specify the date on which the employee's [period of continuous employment] began.

AMENDMENT
The words omitted from subs. 4(b) were repealed by the Employment Act 1982 (c. 46),

Sched. 4; and the words in square brackets in subs. (5) were substituted by *ibid.*, Sched. 2, para. 8(3).

Exclusion of certain contracts in writing

5. Sections 1 and 4 shall not apply to an employee if and so long as the following conditions are fulfilled in relation to him, that is to say—

    (*a*) the employee's contract of employment is a contract which has been reduced to writing in one or more documents and which contains express terms affording the particulars to be given under each of the paragraphs in subsection (3) of section 1, and under each head of paragraph (*d*) of that subsection;

    (*b*) there has been given to the employee a copy of the contract (with any variations made from time to time), or he has reasonable opportunities of reading such a copy in the course of his employment, or such a copy is made reasonably accessible to him in some other way; and

    (*c*) such a note as is mentioned in section 1(4) has been given to the employee or he has reasonable opportunities of reading such a note in the course of his employment or such a note is made reasonably accessible to him in some other way:

[. . .]

1–431

AMENDMENT

The proviso to this section was repealed by the Employment Act 1982 (c. 46), Sched. 4.

[Employees becoming or ceasing to be excluded from ss.1 to 4

5A.—(1) Sections 1 to 4 shall apply to an employee who at any time comes or ceases to come within the exceptions from those sections provided for by section 5, 141, 144, 145 or 146(4) to (7), or under section 149, as if his employment with his employer terminated or began at that time.

(2) Subsection (1) of section 1 shall apply to an employee who ceases to come within the exception provided by section 5 with the substitution for the words "thirteen weeks" of the words "one month".

(3) The fact that section 1 is directed to apply to an employee as if his employment began on his ceasing to come within one of the exceptions referred to in subsection (1) shall not affect the obligation under subsection (2)(*b*) of that section to specify the date on which his employment actually began.]

1–432

AMENDMENT

This section was inserted by the Employment Act 1982 (c. 46), Sched. 2, para. 8(4).

Power of Secretary of State to require further particulars

6. The Secretary of State may by order provide that section 1 shall have effect as if such further particulars as may be specified in the order were included in the particulars to be included in a statement under that section, and, for that purpose, the order may include such provisions amending section 1(1), (2) and (3) as appear to the Secretary of State to be expedient.

1–433

. . . . . .

Itemised Pay Statements

Right to itemised pay statement

1–434   8. Every employee shall have the right to be given by his employer at or before the time at which any payment of wages or salary is made to him an itemised pay statement, in writing, containing the following particulars, that is to say—
  (a) the gross amount of the wages or salary;
  (b) the amounts of any variable and, subject to section 9, any fixed deductions from that gross amount and the purposes for which they are made;
  (c) the net amount of wages or salary payable; and
  (d) where different parts of the net amount are paid in different ways, the amount and method of payment of each part-payment.

Standing statement of fixed deductions

1–435   9.—(1) A pay statement given in accordance with section 8 need not contain separate particulars of a fixed deduction if it contains instead an aggregate amount of fixed deductions, including that deduction, and the employer has given to the employee, at or before the time at which that pay statement is given, a standing statement of fixed deductions, in writing, which contains the following particulars of each deduction comprised in that aggregate amount, that is to say—
  (a) the amount of the deduction;
  (b) the intervals at which the deduction is to be made; and
  (c) the purpose for which it is made,
and which, in accordance with subsection (4), is effective at the date on which the pay statement is given.

   (2) A standing statement of fixed deductions may be amended, whether by addition of a new deduction or by a change in the particulars or cancellation of an existing deduction, by notice in writing, containing particulars of the amendment, given by the employer to the employee.

   (3) An employer who has given to an employee a standing statement of fixed deductions shall, within the period of twelve months beginning with the date on which the first standing statement was given and at intervals of not more than twelve months thereafter, re-issue it in a consolidated form incorporating any amendments notified in accordance with subsection (2).

   (4) A standing statement of fixed deductions shall become effective, for the purposes of subsection (1), on the date on which it is given to the employee and shall cease to have effect on the expiration of the period of twelve months beginning with that date, or, where it is re-issued in accordance with subsection (3), the expiration of the period of twelve months beginning with the date on which it was last re-issued.

Power to amend ss.8 and 9

1–436   10. The Secretary of State may by order—
  (a) vary the provisions of sections 8 and 9 as to the particulars which must be included in a pay statement or a standing statement of fixed deductions by adding items to or removing items from the particulars listed in those sections or by amending any such particulars; and
  (b) vary the provisions of section 9(3) and (4) so as to shorten or

extend the periods of twelve months referred to in those subsections, or those periods as varied from time to time under this section.

Enforcement of Rights under Part I

Reference to industrial tribunals

11.—(1) Where an employer does not give an employee a statement as required by section 1 or 4(1) or 8, the employee may require a reference to be made to an industrial tribunal to determine what particulars ought to have been included or referred to in a statement so as to comply with the requirements of the relevant section.

(2) Where—
- (*a*) a statement purporting to be a statement under section 1 or 4(1), or
- (*b*) a pay statement, or a standing statement of fixed deductions, purporting to comply with section 8 or 9(1),

has been given to an employee, and a question arises as to the particulars which ought to have been included or referred to in the statement so as to comply with the requirements of this Part, either the employer or the employee may require that question to be referred to and determined by an industrial tribunal.

(3) Where a statement under section 1 or 4(1) given by an employer to an employee contains such an indication as is mentioned in section 4(3), and
- (*a*) any particulars purporting to be particulars of a change to which that indication relates are entered up or recorded in accordance with that indication, and
- (*b*) a question arises as to the particulars which ought to have been so entered up or recorded,

either the employer or the employee may require that question to be referred to and determined by an industrial tribunal.

(4) In this section, a question as to the particulars which ought to have been included—
- (*a*) in a pay statement, or in a standing statement of fixed deductions, does not include a question solely as to the accuracy of an amount stated in any such particulars;
- (*b*) in a note under section 1(4), does not include any question whether the employment is, has been or will be contracted-out employment for the purposes of Part III of the Social Security Pensions Act 1975.

(5) Where, on a reference under subsection (1), an industrial tribunal determines particulars as being those which ought to have been included or referred to in a statement given under section 1 or 4(1) the employer shall be deemed to have given to the employee a statement in which those particulars were included, or referred to, as specified in the decision of the tribunal.

(6) On determining a reference under subsection (2)(*a*), an industrial tribunal may either confirm the particulars as included or referred to in the statement given by the employer, or may amend those particulars, or may substitute other particulars for them, as the tribunal may determine to be appropriate; and the statement shall be deemed to have been given by the employer to the employee in accordance with the decision of the tribunal.

(7) On determining a reference under subsection (3), an industrial tribunal may either confirm the particulars to which the reference relates, or may amend those particulars or may substitute other particulars for them, as the tribunal may determine to be appropriate; and particulars of the change to which the reference relates shall be deemed to have been entered up or recorded in accordance with the decision of the tribunal.

(8) Where on a reference under this section an industrial tribunal finds that an employer has failed to give an employee any pay statement in accordance with section 8 or that a pay statement or standing statement of fixed deductions does not, in relation to a deduction, contain the particulars required to be included in that statement by that section or section 9(1)—
- (a) the tribunal shall make a declaration to that effect; and
- (b) where the tribunal further finds that any unnotified deductions have been made from the pay of the employee during the period of thirteen weeks immediately preceding the date of the application for the reference (whether or not the deductions were made in breach of the contract of employment), the tribunal may order the employer to pay the employee a sum not exceeding the aggregate of the unnotified deductions so made.

In this subsection "unnotified deduction" means a deduction made without the employer giving the employee, in any pay statement or standing statement of fixed deductions, the particulars of that deduction required by section 8 or 9(1).

(9) An industrial tribunal shall not entertain a reference under this section in a case where the employment to which the reference relates has ceased unless an application requiring the reference to be made was made before the end of the period of three months beginning with the date on which the employment ceased.

Part II

Rights Arising in Course of Employment

Guarantee Payments

Right to guarantee payment

1–438   12.—(1) Where an employee throughout a day during any part of which he would normally be required to work in accordance with his contract of employment is not provided with work by his employer by reason of—
- (a) a diminution in the requirements of the employer's business for work of the kind which the employee is employed to do, or
- (b) any other occurrence affecting the normal working of the employer's business in relation to work of the kind which the employee is employed to do,

he shall, subject to the following provisions of this Act, be entitled to be paid by his employer a payment, referred to in this Act as a guarantee payment, in respect of that day, and in this section and sections 13 and 16—
- (i) such a day is referred to as a "workless day", and
- (ii) "workless period" has a corresponding meaning.

(2) In this section and sections 13 to 17, "day" means the period of twenty-four hours from midnight to midnight, and where a period of

employment begun on any day extends over midnight into the following day, or would normally so extend, then—
- (a) if the employment before midnight is, or would normally be, of longer duration than that after midnight, that period of employment shall be treated as falling wholly on the first day; and
- (b) in any other case, that period of employment shall be treated as falling wholly on the second day.

General exclusions from right under s.12

[**13.**—(1) An employee shall not be entitled to a guarantee payment unless he has been continuously employed for a period of not less than one month ending with the day before that in respect of which the guarantee payment is claimed.

(2) An employee who is employed—
- (a) under a contract for a fixed term of three months or less, or
- (b) under a contract made in contemplation of the performance of a specific task which is not expected to last for more than three months,

shall not be entitled to a guarantee payment unless he has been continuously employed for a period of more than three months ending with the day before that in respect of which the guarantee payment is claimed.]

[(3)] An employee shall not be entitled to a guarantee payment in respect of a workless day if the failure to provide him with work occurs in consequence of a [strike, lockout or other industrial action] involving any employee of his employer or of an associated employer.

[(4)] An employee shall not be entitled to a guarantee payment in respect of a workless day if—
- (a) his employer has offered to provide alternative work for that day which is suitable in all the circumstances whether or not work which the employee is under his contract employed to perform, and the employee has unreasonably refused that offer; or
- (b) he does not comply with reasonable requirements imposed by his employer with a view to ensuring that his services are available.

AMENDMENT

Subss. (1) and (2) were inserted, and subss. (3) and (4) renumbered, by the Employment Act 1982 (c. 46), Sched. 2. The words in square brackets in subs. (3) were substituted by *ibid.*, Sched. 3, para. 15.

Calculation of guarantee payment

14.—(1) Subject to the limits set by section 15, the amount of a guarantee payment payable to an employee in respect of any day shall be the sum produced by multiplying the number of normal working hours on that day by the guaranteed hourly rate, and, accordingly, no guarantee payment shall be payable to an employee in whose case there are no normal working hours on the day in question.

(2) Subject to subsection (3), the guaranteed hourly rate in relation to an employee shall be the amount of one week's pay divided by—
- (a) the number of normal working hours in a week for that employee when employed under the contract of employment in force; or
- (b) where the number of such normal working hours differs from week

to week or over a longer period, the average number of such hours calculated by dividing by twelve the total number of the employee's normal working hours during the period of twelve weeks ending with the last complete week before the day in respect of which the guarantee payment is payable; or

(c) in a case falling within paragraph (b) but where the employee has not been employed for a sufficient period to enable the calculation to be made under that paragraph, a number which fairly represents the number of normal working hours in a week having regard to such of the following considerations as are appropriate in the circumstances, that is to say—

(i) the average number of normal working hours in a week which the employee could expect in accordance with the terms of his contract;

(ii) the average number of such hours of other employees engaged in relevant comparable employment with the same employer.

(3) If in any case an employee's contract has been varied, or a new contract has been entered into, in connection with a period of short-time working, subsection (2) shall have effect as if for the reference to the day in respect of which the guarantee payment is payable there was substituted a reference to the last day on which the original contract was in force.

Limits on amount of and entitlement to guarantee payment

1–441 15.—(1) The amount of a guarantee payment payable to an employee in respect of any day shall not exceed [£9.15].

(2) An employee shall not be entitled to guarantee payments in respect of more than the specified number of days in [any period of three months].

(3) The specified number of days for the purposes of subsection (2) shall be, subject to subsection (4),—

(a) the number of days, not exceeding five, on which the employee normally works in a week under the contract of employment in force on the day in respect of which the guarantee payment is claimed; or

(b) where that number of days varies from week to week or over a longer period, the average number of such days, not exceeding five, calculated by dividing by twelve the total number of such days during the period of twelve weeks ending with the last complete week before the day in respect of which the guarantee payment is claimed, and rounding up the resulting figure to the next whole number; or

(c) in a case falling within paragraph (b) but where the employee has not been employed for a sufficient period to enable the calculation to be made under that paragraph, a number which fairly represents the number of the employee's normal working days in a week, not exceeding five, having regard to such of the following considerations as are appropriate in the circumstances, that is to say,—

(i) the average number of normal working days in a week which the employee could expect in accordance with the terms of his contract;

(ii) The average number of such days of other employees engaged in relevant comparable employment with the same employer.

(4) If in any case an employee's contract has been varied, or a new contract has been entered into, in connection with a period of short-time working, subsection (3) shall have effect as if for the references to the day in respect of which the guarantee payment is claimed there were substituted references to the last day on which the original contract was in force.

(5) The Secretary of State may vary any of the limits referred to in this section, and may in particular vary the [length of the period] referred to in subsection (2), after a review under section 148, by order made in accordance with that section.

AMENDMENTS
The figure in square brackets in subs. (1) was substituted by Employment Protection (Variation of Limits) Order 1982 (S.I. 1982 No. 77). The words in square brackets in subs. (2) were substituted by the Employment Act 1980 (c. 42), s.14(1). The words in square brackets in subs. (5) were substituted by *ibid.*, Sched. 1, para. 8.

Supplementary provisions relating to guarantee payments

16.—(1) Subject to subsection (2), a right to a guarantee payment shall not affect any right of an employee in relation to remuneration under his contract of employment (in this section referred to as "contractual remuneration").   **1–442**

(2) Any contractual remuneration paid to an employee in respect of a workless day shall go towards discharging any liability of the employer to pay a guarantee payment in respect of that day, and conversely any guarantee payment in respect of a day shall go towards discharging any liability of the employer to pay contractual remuneration in respect of that day.

(3) For the purposes of subsection (2), contractual remuneration shall be treated as paid in respect of a workless day—
  (*a*) where it is expressed to be calculated or payable by reference to that day or any part of that day, to the extent that it is so expressed; and
  (*b*) in any other case, to the extent that it represents guaranteed remuneration, rather than remuneration for work actually done, and is referable to that day when apportioned rateably between that day and any other workless period falling within the period in respect of which the remuneration is paid.

(4) The Secretary of State may by order provide that in relation to any description of employees the provisions of sections 12(2), 14 and 15(3) (as originally enacted or as varied under section 15(5)) and of subsections (1) to (3), and, so far as they apply for the purposes of those provisions, the provisions of Schedule 14 shall have effect subject to such modifications and adaptations as may be prescribed by the order.

Complaint to industrial tribunal

17.—(1) An employee may present a complaint to an industrial tribunal that his employer has failed to pay the whole or any part of a guarantee payment to which the employee is entitled.   **1–443**

(2) An industrial tribunal shall not entertain a complaint relating to a guarantee payment in respect of any day unless the complaint is presented to the tribunal before the end of the period of three months beginning with that day or within such further period as the tribunal considers reasonable in a case where it is satisfied that it was not reasonably practicable for the complaint to be presented within the period of three months.

(3) Where an industrial tribunal finds a complaint under subsection (1)

well-founded, the tribunal shall order the employer to pay the complainant the amount of guarantee payment which it finds is due to him.

Exemption orders

1–444   **18.**—(1) If at any time there is in force a collective agreement, or a wages order, whereby employees to whom the agreement or order relates have a right to guaranteed remuneration and on the application of all the parties to the agreement or, as the case may be, of the council or Board making the order, the appropriate Minister, having regard to the provisions of the agreement or order, is satisfied that section 12 should not apply to those employees, he may make an order under this section excluding those employees from the operation of that section.

(2) In subsection (1), a wages order means an order made under any of the following provisions, that is to say—

(*a*) [section 14 of the Wages Councils Act 1979];
(*b*) section 3 of the Agricultural Wages Act 1948;
(*c*) section 3 of the Agricultural Wages (Scotland) Act 1949.

(3) In subsection (1), "the appropriate Minister" means—

(*a*) as respects a collective agreement or such an order as is referred to in subsection (2)(*a*) or (*c*), the Secretary of State;
(*b*) as respects such an order as is referred to in subsection (2)(*b*), the Minister of Agriculture, Fisheries and Food.

(4) The Secretary of State shall not make an order under this section in respect of an agreement unless—

(*a*) the agreement provides for procedures to be followed (whether by arbitration or otherwise) in cases where an employee claims that his employer has failed to pay the whole or any part of any guaranteed remuneration to which the employee is entitled under the agreement, and that those procedures include a right to arbitration or adjudication by an independent referee or body in cases where (by reason of an equality of votes or otherwise) a decision cannot otherwise be reached; or
(*b*) the agreement indicates that an employee to whom the agreement relates may present a complaint to an industrial tribunal that his employer has failed to pay the whole or any part of any guaranteed remuneration to which the employee is entitled under the agreement;

and where an order under this section is in force in respect of such an agreement as is described in paragraph (*b*) an industrial tribunal shall have jurisdiction over such a complaint as if it were a complaint falling within section 17.

(5) Without prejudice to section 154(4), an order under this section may be varied or revoked by a subsequent order thereunder, whether in pursuance of an application made by all or any of the parties to the agreement in question, or, as the case may be, by the council or Board which made the order in question, or without any such application.

AMENDMENT
   The words in subs. (2)(*a*) were substituted by the Wages Councils Act 1979 (c.12), s.31, Sched. 6, para. 6.

Suspension from Work on Medical Grounds

Right to remuneration on suspension on medical grounds

1–445   **19.**—(1) An employee who is suspended from work by his employer on

medical grounds in consequence of—
  (a) any requirement imposed by or under any provision of any enactment or of any instrument made under any enactment, or
  (b) any recommendation in any provisions of a code of practice issued or approved under section 16 of the Health and Safety at Work etc. Act 1974,
which is a provision for the time being specified in Schedule 1 shall, subject to the following provisions of this Act, be entitled to be paid by his employer remuneration while he is so suspended for a period not exceeding twenty-six weeks.

(2) For the purposes of this section and sections 20 to 22 and 61, an employee shall be regarded as suspended from work only if, and so long as, he continues to be employed by his employer, but is not provided with work or does not perform the work he normally performed before the suspension.

(3) The Secretary of State may by order add provisions to or remove provisions from the list of specified provisions in Schedule 1.

General exclusions from right under s.19
20.—[(1) An employee shall not be entitled to remuneration under section 19 unless he has been continuously employed for a period of not less than one month ending with the day before that on which the suspension begins.

(2) An employee who is employed—
  (a) under a contract for a fixed term of three months or less, or
  (b) under a contract made in contemplation of the performance of a specific task which is not expected to last for more than three months,
shall not be entitled to remuneration under section 19 unless he has been continuously employed for a period of more than three months ending with the day before that on which the suspension begins.]

[(3)] An employee shall not be entitled to remuneration under section 19 in respect of any period during which he is incapable of work by reason of disease or bodily or mental disablement.

[(4)] An employee shall not be entitled to remuneration under section 19 in respect of any period during which—
  (a) his employer has offered to provide him with suitable alternative work, whether or not work which the employee is under his contract, or was under the contract in force before the suspension, employed to perform, and the employee has unreasonably refused to perform that work; or
  (b) he does not comply with reasonable requirements imposed by his employer with a view to ensuring that his services are available.

1–446

AMENDMENT
Subss. (1) and (2) were inserted, and subss. (3) and (4) renumbered, by the Employment Act 1982 (c.46), Sched. 2.

Calculation of remuneration
21.—(1) The amount of remuneration payable by an employer to an employee under section 19 shall be a week's pay in respect of each week

1–447

272 Employment Protection (Consolidation) Act 1978

of the period of suspension referred to in subsection (1) of that section, and if in any week remuneration is payable in respect only of part of that week the amount of a week's pay shall be reduced proportionately.

(2) Subject to subsection (3), a right to remuneration under section 19 shall not affect any right of an employee in relation to remuneration under his contract of employment (in this section referred to as "contractual remuneration").

(3) Any contractual remuneration paid by an employer to an employee in respect of any period shall go towards discharging the employer's liability under section 19 in respect of that period, and conversely any payment of remuneration in discharge of an employer's liability under section 19 in respect of any period shall go towards discharging any obligation of the employer to pay contractual remuneration in respect of that period.

Complaint to industrial tribunal

1–448   22.—(1) An employee may present a complaint to an industrial tribunal that his employer has failed to pay the whole or any part of remuneration to which the employee is entitled under section 19.

(2) An industrial tribunal shall not entertain a complaint relating to remuneration under section 19 in respect of any day unless the complaint is presented to the tribunal before the end of the period of three months beginning with that day, or within such further period as the tribunal considers reasonable in a case where it is satisfied that it was not reasonably practicable for the complaint to be presented within the period of three months.

(3) Where an industrial tribunal finds a complaint under subsection (1) well-founded the tribunal shall order the employer to pay the complainant the amount of remuneration which it finds is due to him.

Trade Union Membership and Activities

Trade union membership and activities

1–449   23.—(1) Subject to the following provisions of this section, every employee shall have the right not to have action (short of dismissal) taken against him as an individual by his employer for the purpose of—
   (a) preventing or deterring him from being or seeking to become a member of an independent trade union, or penalising him for doing so; or
   (b) preventing or deterring him from taking part in the activities of an independent trade union at any appropriate time, or penalising him for doing so; or
   (c) compelling him to be or become a member of [any trade union or of a particular trade union or of one of a number of particular trade unions] [. . .].

[(1A) Every employee shall also have the right not to have action (short of dismissal) taken against him for the purpose of enforcing a requirement (whether or not imposed by his contract of employment or in writing) that, in the event of his failure to become or his ceasing to remain a member of any trade union or of a particular trade union or of one of a number of particular trade unions, he must make one or more payments.

(1B) For the purposes of this section, any deduction made by an employer from the remuneration payable to an employee of his in respect of that employee's employment shall, if the deduction is attributable to the employee's failure to become or his ceasing to remain a member of any trade union or of a particular trade union or of one of a number of particular trade unions, be treated as if it were action (short of dismissal) taken against the employee for the purpose of enforcing a requirement of a kind mentioned in subsection (1A).].

(2) In this section "appropriate time", in relation to an employee taking part in any activities of a trade union, means time which either—

(a) is outside his working hours, or
(b) is a time within his working hours at which, in accordance with arrangements agreed with, or consent given by his employer, it is permissible for him to take part in those activities;

and in this subsection "working hours", in relation to an employee, means any time when, in accordance with his contract of employment, he is required to be at work.

[(2A) Where it is the practice, in accordance with a union membership agreement, for the employees of any class of an employer to belong to a specified independent trade union, or to one of a number of specified independent trade unions, then—

(a) subject to subsection (2B), the right conferred on employees of that class by virtue of subsection (1)(b) in relation to a union's activities shall extend to activities on the employer's premises only if the union is a specified union; and
(b) employees of that class shall not have the right conferred by virtue of subsection (1)(c) [or (1A)] except in respect of action which, if it amounted to dismissal from employment to which section 54 applies, would be regarded as unfair by reason of [section 58].

[(2B) A union membership agreement having effect in relation to the employees of any class of an employer shall be disregarded for the purposes of the application of subsection (2A)(a) to those employees unless the agreement has, for the purposes of section 58(3)(c), been approved in relation to them in accordance with section 58A through a ballot held within the period of five years ending with the date on which the action in question occurred.]

(3)–(6) [*Repealed by the Employment Act* 1980, *s*.15(3), *Sched.* 2.]

(7) In this section, unless the context otherwise requires, references to a trade union include references to a branch or section of a trade union.

AMENDMENTS

The words omitted in para. (c) of subs. (1) were repealed by the Employment Act 1980 (c. 42), s.15(1). The words in square brackets were substituted by the Employment Act 1982 (c. 46), s.10(4).

Subs. (2A) was inserted by s.15(2) of the Employment Act 1980 (c. 42). Subss. (1A), (1B) and (2B) were inserted by the Employment Act 1982 (c. 46), s.10(2) and (3).

Complaint to industrial tribunal

24.—(1) An employee may present a complaint to an industrial tribunal on the ground that action has been taken against him by his employer in contravention of section 23.

(2) An industrial tribunal shall not entertain a complaint under subsection (1) unless it is presented to the tribunal before the end of the period

1–450

of three months beginning with the date on which there occurred the action complained of, or where that action is part of a series of similar actions, the last of those actions, or within such further period as the tribunal considers reasonable in a case where it is satisfied that it was not reasonably practicable for the complaint to be presented within the period of three months.

(3) Where the tribunal finds the complaint well-founded it shall make a declaration to that effect and may make an award of compensation, calculated in accordance with section 26, to be paid by the employer to the employee in respect of the action complained of.

Supplementary provisions relating to complaints under s.24

1–451   **25.**—(1) On a complaint under section 24 it shall be for the employer to show—
   (a) the purpose for which action was taken against the complainant;
   (b) [. . .]

(2) In determining on a complaint under section 24, any question as to whether action was taken by the complainant's employer or the purpose for which it was taken, no account shall be taken of any pressure which, by calling, organising, procuring or financing a strike or other industrial action, or threatening to do so, was exercised on the employer to take the action complained of, and that question shall be determined as if no such pressure had been exercised.

AMENDMENT
   Para. (b) of subs. (1) was repealed by the Employment Act 1980 (c. 42), s.15(3), Sched. 2.

Assessment of compensation on a complaint under s.24

1–452   **26.**—(1) The amount of the compensation awarded by a tribunal on a complaint under section 24 shall be such amount as the tribunal considers just and equitable in all the circumstances having regard to the infringement of the complainant's right under section 23 by the employer's action complained of and to any loss sustained by the complainant which is attributable to that action.

(2) The said loss shall be taken to include—
   (a) any expenses reasonably incurred by the complainant in consequence of the action complained of, and
   (b) loss of any benefit which he might reasonably be expected to have had but for that action.

(3) In ascertaining the said loss the tribunal shall apply the same rule concerning the duty of a person to mitigate his loss as applies to damages recoverable under the common law of England and Wales or of Scotland, as the case may be.

(4) In determining the amount of compensation to be awarded under subsection (1), no account shall be taken of any pressure as is referred to in section 25(2), and that question shall be determined as if no such pressure had been exercised.

(5) Where the tribunal finds that the action complained of was to any extent caused or contributed to by any action of the complainant it shall reduce the amount of the compensation by such proportion as it considers just and equitable having regard to that finding.

[Awards against third parties

1–453   **26A.**—(1) Where—

(a) a complaint is presented to an industrial tribunal under section 24 on the ground that action has been taken against the complainant by his employer for the purpose of compelling him to be or become a member of any trade union or of a particular trade union or of one of a number of particular trade unions, and

(b) either the employer or the complainant claims in proceedings before the tribunal that the employer was induced to take the action by pressure which a trade union or other person exercised on the employer by calling, organising, procuring or financing a strike or other industrial action, or by threatening to do so,

the employer or the complainant may request the tribunal to direct that the person who he claims exercised the pressure be joined, or in Scotland sisted, as a party to the proceedings.

(2) A request under subsection (1) shall be granted if it is made before the hearing of the complaint begins, but may be refused if it is made after that time; and no such request may be made after the tribunal has made a declaration under section 24(3).

(3) Where a person has been joined, or in Scotland sisted, as a party to proceedings before an industrial tribunal by virtue of subsection (1), and the tribunal—

(a) makes an award of compensation, but
(b) finds that the claim mentioned in subsection (1) is well-founded,

the award may be made against that person instead of against the employer, or partly against that person and partly against the employer, as the tribunal may consider just and equitable in the circumstances.]

AMENDMENT
This section was substituted by the Employment Act 1982 (c. 46), s.11.

Time Off Work

Time off for carrying out trade union duties

27.—(1) An employer shall permit an employee of his who is an official of an independent trade union recognised by him to take time off, subject to and in accordance with subsection (2), during the employee's working hours for the purpose of enabling him—

(a) to carry out those duties of his as such an official which are concerned with industrial relations between his employer and any associated employer, and their employees; or
(b) to undergo training in aspects of industrial relations which is—
    (i) relevant to the carrying out of those duties; and
    (ii) approved by the Trades Union Congress or by the independent trade union of which he is an official.

(2) The amount of time off which an employee is to be permitted to take under this section and the purposes for which, the occasions on which and any conditions subject to which time off may be so taken are those that are reasonable in all the circumstances having regard to any relevant provisions of a Code of Practice issued by the Advisory, Conciliation and Arbitration Service under section 6 of the Employment Protection Act 1975.

(3) An employer who permits an employee to take time off under this section for any purpose shall, subject to the following provisions of this section, pay him for the time taken off for that purpose in accordance with the permission—
  (a) where the employee's remuneration for the work he would ordinarily have been doing during that time does not vary with the amount of work done, as if he had worked at that work for the whole of that time;
  (b) where the employee's remuneration for that work varies with the amount of work done, an amount calculated by reference to the average hourly earnings for that work.

(4) The average hourly earnings referred to in subsection (3)(b) shall be the average hourly earnings of the employee concerned or, if no fair estimate can be made of those earnings, the average hourly earnings for work of that description of persons in comparable employment with the same employer or, if there are no such persons, a figure of average hourly earnings which is reasonable in the circumstances.

(5) Subject to subsection (6), a right to be paid any amount under subsection (3) shall not affect any right of an employee in relation to remuneration under his contract of employment (in this section referred to as "contractual remuneration").

(6) Any contractual remuneration paid to an employee in respect of a period of time off to which subsection (1) applies shall go towards discharging any liability of the employer under subsection (3) in respect of that period, and conversely any payment of any amount under subsection (3) in respect of a period shall go towards discharging any liability of the employer to pay contractual remuneration in respect of that period.

(7) An employee who is an official of an independent trade union recognised by his employer may present a complaint to an industrial tribunal that his employer has failed to permit him to take time off as required by this section or to pay him the whole or part of any amount so required to be paid.

Time off for trade union activities

28.—(1) An employer shall permit an employee of his who is a member of an appropriate trade union to take time off, subject to and in accordance with subsection (3), during the employee's working hours for the purpose of taking part in any trade union activity to which this section applies.

(2) In this section "appropriate trade union", in relation to an employee of any description, means an independent trade union which is recognised by his employer in respect of that description of employee, and the trade union activities to which this section applies are—
  (a) any activities of an appropriate trade union of which the employee is a member; and
  (b) any activities, whether or not falling within paragraph (a), in relation to which the employee is acting as a representative of such a union,
excluding activities which themselves consist of industrial action whether or not in contemplation or furtherance of a trade dispute.

(3) The amount of time off which an employee is to be permitted to take under this section and the purposes for which, the occasions on which and any conditions subject to which time off may be so taken are those that are reasonable in all the circumstances having regard to any relevant provi-

sions of a Code of Practice issued by the Advisory, Conciliation and Arbitration Service under section 6 of the Employment Protection Act 1975.

(4) An employee who is a member of an independent trade union recognised by his employer may present a complaint to an industrial tribunal that his employer has failed to permit him to take time off as required by this section.

Time off for public duties

29.—(1) An employer shall permit an employee of his who is—   1–456
- (*a*) a justice of the peace;
- (*b*) a member of a local authority;
- (*c*) a member of any statutory tribunal;
- (*d*) a member of, in England and Wales, a Regional Health Authority [an Area Health Authority or a District] Health Authority or, in Scotland, a Health Board;
- (*e*) a member of, in England and Wales, the managing or governing body of an educational establishment maintained by a local education authority, or, in Scotland, a school or college council or the governing body of a central institution or a college of education; or
- (*f*) a member of, in England and Wales, a water authority or, in Scotland, river purification board,

to take time off, subject to and in accordance with subsection (4), during the employee's working hours for the purposes of performing any of the duties of his office or, as the case may be, his duties as such a member.

(2) In subsection (1)—
- (*a*) "local authority" in relation to England and Wales includes the Common Council of the City of London but otherwise has the same meaning as in the Local Government Act 1972, and in relation to Scotland has the same meaning as in the Local Government (Scotland) Act 1973;
- (*b*) "Regional Health Authority," "Area Health Authority" [and District Health Authority] have the same meaning as in the National Health Service Act 1977, and "Health Board" has the same meaning as in the National Health Service (Scotland) Act 1972;
- (*c*) "local education authority" means the authority designated by section 192(1) of the Local Government Act 1972, "school or college council" means a body appointed under section 125(1) of the Local Government (Scotland) Act 1973, and "central institution" and "college of education" have the meanings assigned to them by section 145(10) and (14) respectively of the Education (Scotland) Act 1962; and
- (*d*) "river purification board" means a board established under section 135 of the Local Government (Scotland) Act 1973.

(3) For the purposes of subsection (1) the duties of a member of a body referred to in paragraphs (*b*) to (*f*) of that subsection are:—
- (*a*) attendance at a meeting of the body or one of its committees or sub-committees;
- (*b*) the doing of any other thing approved by the body, or anything of a class so approved, for the purpose of the discharge of the functions of the body or of any of its committees or sub-committees.

(4) The amount of time off which an employee is to be permitted to take under this section and the occasions on which and any conditions subject to which time off may be so taken are those that are reasonable in all the circumstances having regard, in particular, to the following:—
   (a) how much time off is required for the performance of the duties of the office or as a member of the body in question, and how much time off is required for the performance of the particular duty;
   (b) how much time off the employee has already been permitted under this section or section 27 and 28;
   (c) the circumstances of the employer's business and the effect of the employee's absence on the running of that business.
(5) The Secretary of State may by order—
   (a) modify the provisions of subsection (1) by adding any office or body to, or removing any office or body from, that subsection or by altering the description of any office or body in that subsection; and
   (b) modify the provisions of subsection (3).
(6) An employee may present a complaint to an industrial tribunal that his employer has failed to permit him to take time off as required by this section.

AMENDMENT
The words in square brackets in subss. (1)(d) and (2)(b) were substituted or inserted by the Health Services Act 1980 (c.53), Sched. 1, para. 84.

Provisions as to industrial tribunals

1–457 30.—(1) An industrial tribunal shall not consider—
   (a) a complaint under section 27, 28 or 29 that an employer has failed to permit an employee to take time off; or
   (b) a complaint under section 27 that an employer has failed to pay an employee the whole or part of any amount required to be paid under that section;
unless it is presented within three months of the date when the failure occurred or within such further period as the tribunal considers reasonable in a case where it is satisfied that it was not reasonably practicable for the complaint to be presented within the period of three months.

(2) Where an industrial tribunal finds any complaint mentioned in subsection (1)(a) well-founded, the tribunal shall make a declaration to that effect and may make an award of compensation to be paid by the employer to the employee which shall be of such amount as the tribunal considers just and equitable in all the circumstances having regard to the employer's default in failing to permit time off to be taken by the employee and to any loss sustained by the employee which is attributable to the matters complained of.

(3) Where on a complaint under section 27 an industrial tribunal finds that the employer has failed to pay the employee the whole or part of the amount required to be paid under that section, the tribunal shall order the employer to pay the employee the amount which it finds due to him.

Time off to look for work or make arrangements for training

1–458 31.—(1) An employee who is given notice of dismissal by reason of redundancy shall, subject to the following provisions of this section, be entitled before the expiration of his notice to be allowed by his employer reasonable time off during the employee's working hours in order to look for new employment to make arrangements for training for future employment.

(2) An employee shall not be entitled to time off under this section unless, on whichever is the later of the following dates, that is to say,—
  (a) the date on which the notice is due to expire; or
  (b) the date on which it would expire were it the notice required to be given by section 49(1),
he will have been or, as the case may be, would have been continuously employed for a period of two years or more.

(3) An employee who is allowed time off during his working hours under subsection (1) shall, subject to the following provisions of this section, be entitled to be paid remuneration by his employer for the period of absence at the appropriate hourly rate.

(4) The appropriate hourly rate in relation to an employee shall be the amount of one week's pay dividend by—
  (a) the number of normal working hours in a week for that employee when employed under the contract of employment in force on the day when notice was given; or
  (b) where the number of such normal working hours differs from week to week or over a longer period, the average number of such hours calculated by dividing by twelve the total number of the employee's normal working hours during the period of twelve weeks ending with the last complete week before the day on which notice was given.

(5) If an employer unreasonably refuses to allow an employee time off from work under this section, the employee shall, subject to subsection (9), be entitled to be paid an amount equal to the remuneration to which he would have been entitled under subsection (3) if he had been allowed the time off.

(6) An employee may present a complaint to an industrial tribunal on the ground that his employer has unreasonably refused to allow him time off under this section or has failed to pay the whole or any part of any amount to which the employee is entitled under subsection (3) or (5).

(7) An industrial tribunal shall not entertain a complaint under subsection (6) unless it is presented to the tribunal within the period of three months beginning with the day on which it is alleged that the time off should have been allowed, or within such further period as the tribunal considers reasonable in a case where it is satisfied that it was not reasonably practicable for the complaint to be presented within the period of three months.

(8) If on a complaint under subsection (6) the tribunal finds the grounds of the complaint well-founded it shall make a declaration to that effect and shall order the employer to pay to the employee the amount which it finds due to him.

(9) The amount—
  (a) of an employer's liability to pay remuneration under subsection (3); or
  (b) which may be ordered by a tribunal to be paid by an employer under subsection (8),
or, where both paragraphs (a) and (b) are applicable, the aggregate

amount of the liabilities referred to in those paragraphs, shall not exceed, in respect of the notice period of any employee, two-fifths of week's pay of that employee.

(10) Subject to subsection (11), a right to any amount under subsection (3) or (5) shall not affect any right of an employee in relation to remuneration under the contract of employment (in this section referred to as "contractual remuneration").

(11) Any contractual remuneration paid to an employee in respect of a period when he takes time off for the purposes referred to in subsection (1) shall go towards discharging any liability of the employer to pay remuneration under subsection (3) in respect of that period, and conversely any payment of remuneration under subsection (3) in respect of a period shall go towards discharging any liability of the employer to pay contractual remuneration in respect of that period.

[Time off for ante-natal care

31A.—(1) An employee who is pregnant and who has, on the advice of a registered medical practitioner, registered midwife or registered health visitor, made an appointment to attend at any place for the purpose of receiving ante-natal care shall, subject to the following provisions of this section, have the right not to be unreasonably refused time off during her working hours to enable her to keep the appointment.

(2) Subject to subsection (3), an employer shall not be required by virtue of this section to permit an employee to take time off to keep an appointment unless, if he requests her to do so, she produces for his inspection—

 (*a*) a certificate from a registered medical practitioner, registered midwife or registered health visitor stating that the employee is pregnant, and
 (*b*) an appointment card or some other document showing that the appointment has been made.

(3) Subsection (2) shall not apply where the employee's appointment is the first appointment during her pregnancy for which she seeks permission to take time off in accordance with subsection (1).

(4) An employee who is permitted to take time off during her working hours in accordance with subsection (1) shall be entitled to be paid remuneration by her employer for the period of absence at the appropriate hourly rate.

(5) The appropriate hourly rate in relation to an employee shall be the amount of one week's pay divided by—

 (*a*) the number of normal working hours in a week for that employee when employed under the contract of employment in force on the day when the time off is taken; or
 (*b*) where the number of such normal working hours differs from week to week or over a longer period, the average number of such hours calculated by dividing by twelve the total number of the employee's normal working hours during the period of twelve weeks ending with the last complete week before the day on which the time off is taken; or
 (*c*) in a case falling within paragraph (*b*) but where the employee has not been employed for a sufficient period to enable the calculation to be made under that paragraph, a number which fairly represents

the number of normal working hours in a week having regard to such of the following considerations as are appropriate in the circumstances, that is to say,—

(i) the average number of normal working hours in a week which the employee could expect in accordance with the terms of her contract;

(ii) the average number of such hours of other employees engaged in relevant comparable employment with the same employer.

(6) An employee may present a complaint to an industrial tribunal that her employer has unreasonably refused her time off as required by this section or that he has failed to pay her the whole or part of any amount to which she is entitled under subsection (4).

(7) An industrial tribunal shall not entertain a complaint under subsection (6) unless it is presented within the period of three months beginning with the day of the appointment concerned, or within such further period as the tribunal considers reasonable in a case where it is satisfied that it was not reasonably practicable for the complaint to be presented within the period of three months.

(8) Where on a complaint under subsection (6) the tribunal finds the complaint well-founded it shall make a declaration to that effect; and

   (a) if the complaint is that the employer has unreasonably refused the employee time off, the tribunal shall order the employer to pay to the employee an amount equal to the remuneration to which she would have been entitled under subsection (4) if the time off had not been refused; and

   (b) if the complaint is that the employer has failed to pay the employee the whole or part of any amount to which she is entitled under subsection (4), the tribunal shall order the employer to pay to the employee the amount which it finds due to her.

(9) Subject to subsection (10), a right to any amount under subsection (4) shall not affect any right of an employee in relation to remuneration under her contract of employment (in this section referred to as "contractual remuneration").

(10) Any contractual remuneration paid to an employee in respect of a period of time off under this section shall go towards discharging any liability of the employer to pay remuneration under subsection (4) in respect of that period, and conversely any payment of remuneration under subsection (4) in respect of a period shall go towards discharging any liability of the employer to pay contractual remuneration in respect of that period.

(11) Until the coming into operation of section 10 of the Nurses, Midwives and Health Visitors Act 1979, this section shall have effect as if for any reference to a registered midwife or registered health visitor there was substituted a reference to a certified midwife.]

AMENDMENT
This section was inserted by the Employment Act 1980 (c. 42), s.13.

Provisions supplementary to ss.27 to 31

32.—(1) For the purposes of sections 27 to 31A—

   (a) a trade union shall be treated as recognised [. . .] if it is recognised for the purposes of collective bargaining, [. . .] and

   (b) the working hours of an employee shall be taken to be any time when, in accordance with his contract of employment, he is required to be at work.

(2) In subsection (1)—
"collective bargaining" means negotiations related to or connected with one or more of the matters specified in section 29(1) of the Trade Union and Labour Relations Act 1974;
"recognised" means recognised by an employer, or two or more associated employers, to any extent for the purposes of collective bargaining.

AMENDMENT
The words omitted in subs. (1)(a) were repealed by the Employment Act 1980 (c. 42), Sched. 2.

PART III

MATERNITY

General Provisions

Rights of employee in connection with pregnancy and confinement

1–461   33.—(1) An employee who is absent from work wholly or partly because of pregnancy or confinement shall, subject to the following provisions of this Act,—
   (a) be entitled to be paid by her employer a sum to be known as maternity pay; and
   (b) be entitled to return to work.
(2) Schedule 2 shall have effect for the purpose of supplementing the following provisions of this Act in relation to an employee's right to return to work.
(3) An employee shall be entitled to the rights referred to in subsection (1) whether or not a contract of employment subsists during the period of her absence but, subject to subsection (4), she shall not be so entitled unless—
   (a) she continues to be employed by her employer (whether or not she is at work) until immediately before the beginning of the eleventh week before the expected week of confinement;
   (b) she has at the beginning of that eleventh week been continuously employed for a period of not less than two years;
   [(c) in the case of the right to maternity pay, she informs her employer (in writing if he so requests) at least twenty-one days before her absence begins or, if that is not reasonably practicable, as soon as reasonably practicable, that she will be (or is) absent from work wholly or partly because of pregnancy or confinement; and
   (d) in the case of the right to return, she informs her employer in writing at least twenty-one days before her absence begins or, if that is not reasonably practicable, as soon as reasonably practicable,—
      (i) that she will be (or is) absent from work wholly or partly because of pregnancy or confinement,
      (ii) that she intends to return to work with her employer, and
      (iii) of the expected week of confinement or, if the confinement has occurred, the date of confinement.]

[(3A) Where not earlier than forty-nine days after the beginning of the expected week of confinement (or the date of confinement) notified under subsection (3)(*d*) an employee is requested in accordance with subsection (3B) by her employer or a successor of his to give him written confirmation that she intends to return to work, she shall not be entitled to the right to return unless she gives that confirmation within fourteen days of receiving the request or, if that is not reasonably practicable, as soon as reasonably practicable.

(3B) A request under subsection (3A) shall be made in writing and shall be accompanied by a written statement of the effect of that subsection.]

(4) An employee who has been dismissed by her employer for a reason falling within section 60(1)(*a*) or (*b*) and has not been re-engaged in accordance with that section, shall be entitled to the rights referred to in subsection (1) of this section notwithstanding that she has thereby ceased to be employed before the beginning of the eleventh week before the expected week of confinement if, but for that dismissal, she would at the beginning of that eleventh week have been continuously employed for a period of not less than two years, but she shall not be entitled to the right to return unless she informs her employer (in writing if he so requests), before or as soon as reasonably practicable after the dismissal takes effect, that she intends to return to work with him.

In this subsection "dismiss" and "dismissal" have the same meaning as they have for the purposes of Part V.

(5) An employee shall not be entitled to either of the rights referred to in subsection (1) unless, if requested to do so by her employer, she produces for his inspection a certificate from a registered medical practitioner or a certified midwife stating the expected week of her confinement.

(6) The Secretary of State may by order vary the periods of two years referred to in subsections (3) and (4), or those periods as varied from time to time under this subsection, but no such order shall be made unless a draft of the order has been laid before Parliament and approved by resolution of each House of Parliament.

AMENDMENT

Paras. (*c*) and (*d*) in subs. (3) were substituted, and subss. (3A) and (3B) inserted, by the Employment Act 1980 (c. 42), s.11.

Maternity Pay

Maternity pay

34.—(1) Maternity pay shall be paid in respect of a period not exceeding, or periods not exceeding in the aggregate, six weeks during which the employee is absent from work wholly or partly because of pregnancy or confinement (in this section and sections 35 and 36 referred to as the payment or payment periods).   1–462

(2) An employee shall not be entitled to maternity pay for any absence before the beginning of the eleventh week before the expected week of confinement, and her payment period or payment periods shall be the first six weeks of absence starting on or falling after the beginning of that eleventh week.

(3) The Secretary of State may by order vary the periods of six weeks referred to in subsections (1) and (2), or those periods as varied from time

to time under this subsection, but no such order shall be made unless a draft of the order has been laid before Parliament and approved by resolution of each House of Parliament.

(4) Where an employee gives her employer the information required by section 33(3)(c) or produces any certificate requested under section 33(5) after the beginning of the payment period or the first of the payments periods, she shall not be entitled to maternity pay for any part of that period until she gives him that information or certificate, but on giving him the information or, as the case may be, producing the certificate, she shall be entitled to be paid in respect of that part of the period or periods which fell before the giving of the information or the production of the certificate.

Calculation of maternity pay

1–463   35.—(1) The amount of maternity pay to which an employee is entitled as respects any week shall be nine-tenths of a week's pay reduced by the amount of maternity allowance payable for the week under Part I of Schedule 4 to the Social Security Act 1975, whether or not the employee in question is entitled to the whole or any part of that allowance.

(2) Maternity pay shall accrue due to an employee from day to day and in calculating the amount of maternity pay payable for any day—
   (a) there shall be disregarded Sunday or such other day in each week as may be prescribed in relation to that employee under section 22(10) of the Social Security Act 1975 for the purpose of calculating the daily rate of maternity allowance under that Act; and
   (b) the amount payable for any other day shall be taken as one-sixth of the amount of the maternity pay for the week in which the day falls.

(3) Subject to subsection (4), a right to maternity pay shall not affect any right of an employee in relation to remuneration under any contract of employment (in this section referred to as "contractual remuneration").

(4) Any contractual remuneration paid to an employee in respect of a day within a payment period shall go towards discharging any liability of the employer to pay maternity pay in respect of that day, and conversely any matenity pay paid in respect of a day shall go towards discharging any liability of the employer to pay contractual remuneration in respect of that day.

Complaint to industrial tribunal

1–464   36.—(1) A complaint may be presented to an industrial tribunal by an employee against her employer that he has failed to pay her the whole or any part of the maternity pay to which she is entitled.

(2) An industrial tribunal shall not entertain a complaint under subsection (1) unless it is presented to the tribunal before the end of the period of three months beginning with the last day of the payment period or, as the case may be, the last of the payment periods, or within such further period as the tribunal considers reasonable in a case where it is satisfied that it was not reasonably practicable for the complaint to be presented within the period of three months.

(3) Where an industrial tribunal finds a complaint under subsection (1) well-founded, the tribunal shall order the employer to pay the complainant the amount of maternity pay which it finds is due to her.

Maternity Pay Fund

1–465   37.—(1) The Secretary of State shall continue to have the control and management of the Maternity Pay Fund established under section 39 of the Employment Protection Act 1975, and payments shall be made out of that fund in accordance with the following provisions of this Part and section 156(1).

(2) The Secretary of State shall prepare accounts of the Maternity Pay Fund in such form as the Treasury may direct and shall send them to the Comptroller and Auditor General not later than the end of the month of November following the end of the financial year to which the accounts relate; and the Comptroller and the Auditor General shall examine and certify every such account and shall lay copies thereof, together with his report thereon, before Parliament.

(3) Any money in the Maternity Pay Fund may from time to time be paid over to the National Debt Commissioners and invested by them, in accordance with such directions as may be given by the Treasury, in any such manner as may be specified by an order of the Treasury for the time being in force under section 22(1) of the National Savings Bank Act 1971.

Advances out of National Loans Fund

38.—(1) Subject to the provisions of subsections (2) to (4), the Treasury may from time to time advance out of the National Loans Fund to the Secretary of State for the purposes of the Maternity Pay Fund such sums as the Secretary of State may request; and any sums advanced to the Secretary of State under this section shall be paid into the Maternity Pay Fund.

1–466

(2) The aggregate amount outstanding by way of principal in respect of sums advanced to the Secretary of State under subsection (1) shall not at any time exceed £4 million, or such larger sum, not exceeding £10 million, as the Secretary of State may by order made with the consent of the Treasury determine.

(3) No order under subsection (2) shall be made unless a draft of the order has been laid before Parliament and approved by resolution of each House of Parliament.

(4) Any sums advanced to the Secretary o State under subsection (1) shall be re-paid by the Secretary of State out of the Maternity Pay Fund into the National Loans Fund in such manner and at such times, and with interest thereon at such rate, as the Treasury may direct.

Maternity pay rebate

39.—(1) Subject to any regulations made under this section, the Secretary of State shall pay out of the Maternity Pay Fund to every employer who makes a claim under this section and who, being liable to pay, has paid maternity pay to an employee, an amount equal to the full amount of maternity pay so paid (in this section and sections 42 and 43 referred to as a "maternity pay rebate").

1–467

(2) The Secretary of State may if he thinks fit, and if he is satisfied that it would be just and equitable to do so having regard to all the relevant circumstances, pay such a rebate to an employer who makes a claim under this section and who has paid maternity pay to an employee in circumstances in which, by reason of the time limit provided for in section 36(2) a complaint by the employee has been dismissed, or would not be entertained, by an industrial tribunal.

(3) For the purposes of subsections (1) and (2), a payment of contractual

remuneration by an employer shall be treated as a payment of maternity pay to the extent that, by virtue of section 35(4),—
(a) it extinguishes the employer's liability to pay maternity pay; or
(b) in a case falling within subsection (2), it would extinguish that liability if a complaint by the employee were not time-barred as described in that subsection.

(4) The Secretary of State shall make provision by regulations as to the making of claims for maternity pay rebates under this section and such regulations may in particular—
(a) require a claim to be made within such time limit as may be prescribed; and
(b) require a claim to be supported by such evidence as may be prescribed.

Payments to employees out of Maternity Pay Fund

1–468   40.—(1) Where an employee claims that her employer is liable to pay her maternity pay and—
(a) that she has taken all reasonable steps (other than proceedings to enforce a tribunal award) to recover payment from the employer; or
(b) that her employer is insolvent (as defined in section 127 for the purposes of section 122 to 126);
and that the whole or part of the maternity pay remains unpaid, the employee may apply to the Secretary of State under this section.

(2) If the Secretary of State is satisfied that the claim is well-founded the Secretary of State shall pay the employee out of the Maternity Pay Fund the amount of the maternity pay which appears to the Secretary of State to be unpaid.

(3) A payment made by the Secretary of State to an employee under this section shall, for the purpose of discharging any liability of the employer to the employee, be treated as if it had been made by the employer.

Unreasonable default by employer

1–469   41.—(1) Where the Secretary of State makes a payment to an employee in respect of unpaid maternity pay in a case falling within section 40(1)(a) and it appears to the Secretary of State that the employer's default in payment was without reasonable excuse, the Secretary of State may recover from the employer such amount as the Secretary of State considers appropriate, not exceeding the amount of maternity pay which the employer failed to pay.

(2) Where a sum is recovered by the Secretary of State by virtue of this section that sum shall be paid into the Maternity Pay Fund.

Supplementary provisions relating to employer's insolvency

1–470   42.—(1) Where the Secretary of State makes a payment to an employee under section 122 (which provides for payments out of the Redundancy Fund in respect of certain debts where an employer is insolvent) and that payment, in whole or in part, represents arrears of pay, then, in ascertaining for the purpose of section 40 the amount of any unpaid maternity pay, section 35(4) shall apply as if the arrears of pay in question had been duly paid by the employer to the employee in accordance with the contract of employment.

(2) Where the Secretary of State makes a payment to an employee out of the Redundancy Fund under section 122 which, if it had been made by

the employer to the employee, would have attracted a maternity pay rebate from the Maternity Pay Fund in accordance with section 39, then, the Secretary of State shall make payment out of the Maternity Pay Fund into the Redundancy Fund of an amount corresponding to the amount of rebate which would have been so payable.

Complaints and appeals to industrial tribunal

43.—(1) A person who has—
    (*a*) made a claim for a maternity pay rebate under section 39, in a case to which subsection (1) of that section applies; or
    (*b*) applied for a payment under section 40,
may, subject to subsection (5), present a complaint to an industrial tribunal that—
    (i) the Secretary of State has failed to make any such payment; or
    (ii) any such payment made by the Secretary of State is less than the amount which should have been paid.

(2) Where an industrial tribunal finds that the Secretary of State ought to make any such payment or further payment, it shall make a declaration to that effect and shall also declare the amount of any such payment which it finds the Secretary of State ought to make.

(3) An employer who has made a claim for a maternity pay rebate under section 39, in a case to which subsection (2) of that section applies, may, subject to subsection (5), appeal to an industrial tribunal on the ground that—
    (*a*) the Secretary of State has refused to pay a maternity pay rebate; or
    (*b*) any rebate paid by the Secretary of State is less than the amount which should have been paid,
and if on any such appeal the tribunal is satisfied that it is just and equitable having regard to all the relevant circumstances that a maternity pay rebate should be paid or, as the case may be, finds that a further payment by way of rebate should be made, the tribunal shall determine accordingly, and the Secretary of State shall comply with the determination.

(4) Where the Secretary of State determines that an amount is recoverable from an employer under section 41, the employer may, subject to subsection (5), appeal to an industrial tribunal; and if on any such appeal the tribunal is satisfied that no amount should be recovered from the employer, or that a lesser or greater amount should be recovered (but in any case not exceeding the amount of maternity pay which the employer failed to pay) the tribunal shall determine accordingly and the amount, if any, so determined shall be the amount recoverable from the employer by the Secretary of State.

(5) An industrial tribunal shall not entertain a complaint or appeal under this section unless it is presented to the tribunal within the period of three months beginning with the date on which the relevant decision of the Secretary of State was communicated to the complainant or appellant or within such further period as the tribunal considers reasonable in a case where it is satisfied that it was not reasonably practicable for the complaint or appeal to be presented within the period of three months.

Provisions as to information

44.—(1) Where an application is made to the Secretary of State by an employee under section 40, the Secretary of State may require—
    (*a*) the employer to provide him with such information as the Secretary

of State may reasonably require for the purpose of determining whether the employee's application is well-founded; and

(b) any person having the custody or control of any relevant records or other documents to produce for examination on behalf of the Secretary of State any such document in that person's custody or under his control which is of such a description as the Secretary of State may require.

(2) Any such requirement shall be made by a notice in writing given to the person on whom the requirement is imposed and may be varied or revoked by a subsequent notice so given.

(3) If a person refuses or wilfully neglects to furnish any information or produce any document which he has been required to furnish or produce by a notice under this section he shall be liable on summary conviction to a fine not exceeding £100.

(4) If any person in making a claim under section 39 or an application under section 40 or in purporting to comply with a requirement of a notice under this section knowingly or recklessly makes any false statement he shall be liable on summary conviction to a fine not exceeding £400.

Right to Return to Work

Right to return to work

1–473   **45.**—(1) The right to return to work of an employee who has been absent from work wholly or partly because of pregnancy or confinement is, subject to the following provisions of this Act, a right to return to work with her original employer, or, where appropriate, his successor, at any time before the end of the period of twenty-nine weeks beginning with the week in which the date of confinement falls, in the job in which she was employed under the original contract of employment and on terms and conditions not less favourable than those which would have been applicable to her if she had not been so absent.

(2) In subsection (1) "terms and conditions not less favourable than those which would have been applicable to her if she had not been so absent" means, as regards seniority, pension rights and other similar rights, that the period or periods of employment prior to the employee's absence shall be regarded as continuous with her employment following that absence.

(3) If an employee is entitled to return to work in accordance with subsection (1), but it is not practicable by reason of redundancy for the employer to permit her so to return to work she shall be entitled, where there is a suitable vacancy, to be offered alternative employment with her employer (or his successor), or an associated employer, under a new contract of employment complying with subsection (4).

(4) The new contract of employment must be such that—
(a) the work to be done under the contract is of a kind which is both suitable in relation to the employee and appropriate for her to do in the circumstances; and
(b) the provisions of the new contract as to the capacity and place in which she is to be employed and as to the other terms and conditions of her employment are not substantially less favourable to her than if she had returned to work in accordance with subsection (1).

Enforcement of rights under s.45

46. The remedies of an employee for infringement of either of the rights mentioned in section 45 are those conferred by or by virtue of the provisions of sections 47, 56 and 86 and Schedule 2.

Exercise of right to return to work

47.—(1) An employee shall exercise her right to return to work by [giving written notice to] the employer (who may be her original employer or a successor of that employer) at least [twenty-one] days before the day on which she proposes to return of her proposal to return on that day (in this section referred to as the "notified day of return").

(2) An employer may postpone an employee's return to work until a date not more than four weeks after the notified day of return if he notifies her before that day that for specified reasons he is postponing her return until that date, and accordingly she will be entitled to return to work with him on that date.

(3) Subject to subsection (4), an employee may—
   (a) postpone her return to work until a date not exceeding four weeks from the notified day of return, notwithstanding that that date falls after the end of the period of twenty-nine weeks mentioned in section 45(1); and
   (b) where no day of return has been notified to the employer, extend the time during which she may exercise her right to return in accordance with subsection (1), so that she returns to work not later than four weeks from the expiration of the said period of twenty-nine weeks;
if before the notified day of return or, as the case may be, the expiration of the period of twenty-nine weeks she gives the employer a certificate from a registered medical practitioner stating that by reason of disease or bodily or mental disablement she will be incapable of work on the notified day of return or the expiration of that period, as the case may be.

(4) Where an employee has once exercised a right of postponement or extension under subsection (3)(a) or (b), she will not again be entitled to exercise a right of postponement or extension under that subsection in connection with the same return to work.

(5) If an employee has notified a day of return but there is an interruption of work (whether due to industrial action or some other reason) which renders it unreasonable to expect the employee to return to work on the notified day of return, she may instead return to work when work resumes after the interruption or as soon as reasonably practicable thereafter.

(6) If no day of return has been notified and there is an interruption of work (whether due to industrial action or some other reason) which renders it unreasonable to expect the employee to return to work before the expiration of the period of twenty-nine weeks referred to in section 45(1), or which appears likely to have that effect, and in consequence the employee does not notify a day of return, the employee may exercise her right to return in accordance with subsection (1) so that she returns to work at any time before the end of the period of [twenty-eight] days from the end of the interruption notwithstanding that she returns to work outside the said period of twenty-nine weeks,

(7) Where the employee has either—

(a) exercised the right under subsection (3)(b) to extend the period during which she may exercise her right to return; or
(b) refrained from notifying the day of return in the circumstances described in subsection (6),

the other of those subsections shall apply as if for the reference to the expiration of the period of twenty-nine weeks there were substituted a reference to the expiration of the further period of four weeks or, as the case may be, of the period of [twenty-eight] days from the end of the interruption of work.

(8) Where—
(a) an employee's return is postponed under subsection (2) or (3)(a), or
(b) the employee returns to work on a day later than the notified day of return in the circumstances described in subsection (5).

then, subject to subsection (4), references in those subsections and in sections 56 and 86 and Schedule 2 to the notified day of return shall be construed as references to the day to which the return is postponed or, as the case may be, that later day.

AMENDMENTS

The words in square brackets in subss. (1), (6) and (7) were substituted by the Employment Act 1980 (c. 42), s.11(3).

Contractual right to return to work

1–476   **48.**—(1) An employee who has a right both under the Act and under a contract of employment, or otherwise, to return to work, may not exercise the two rights separately but may in returning to work take advantage of whichever right is, in any particular respect, the more favourable.

(2) The provisions of sections 45, 46, 47, 56 and 86 and paragraphs 1 to 4 and 6 of Schedule 2 shall apply, subject to any modifications necessary to give effect to any more favourable contractual terms, to the exercise of the composite right described in subsection (1) as they apply to the exercise of the right to return conferred solely by this Part.

PART IV

TERMINATION OF EMPLOYMENT

Rights of employer and employee to a minimum period of notice

1–477   **49.**—(1) The notice required to be given by an employer to terminate the contract of employment of a person who has been continuously employed for [one month] or more—
(a) shall be not less than one week's notice if his period of continuous employment is less than two years;
(b) shall be not less that one week's notice for each year of continuous employment if his period of continuous employment is two years or more but less than twelve years; and
(c) shall be not less than twelve weeks' notice if his period of continuous employment is twelve years or more.

(2) The notice required to be given by an employee who has been continuously employed for [one month] or more to terminate his contract of employment shall be not less than one week.

(3) Any provision for shorter notice in any contract of employment with a person who has been continuously employed for [one month] or more shall have effect subject to the foregoing subsections, but this section shall not be taken to prevent either party from waiving his right to notice on any occasion, or from accepting a payment in lieu of notice.

(4) Any contract of employment of a person who has been continuously employed for [three months] or more which is a contract for a term certain of [one month] or less shall have effect as if it were for an indefinite period and, accordingly, subsections (1) and (2) shall apply to the contract.

[(4A) Subsections (1) and (2) do not apply to a contract made in contemplation of the performance of a specific task which is not expected to last for more than three months unless the employee has been continuously employed for a period of more than three months.]

(5) It is hereby declared that this section does not affect any right of either party to treat the contract as terminable without notice by reason of such conduct by the other party as would have enabled him so to treat it before the passing of this Act.

(6) The definition of week given by section 153(1) does not apply for the purposes of this section.

AMENDMENTS
The words in square brackets in subss. (1)–(4) were substituted, and subs. (4A) was added, by the Employment Act 1982 (c. 46), Sched. 2, para. 3.

Rights of employee in period of notice

50.—(1) If an employer gives notice to terminate the contract of employment of a person who has been continuously employed for [one month] or more, the provisions of Schedule 3 shall have effect as respects the liability of the employer for the period of notice required by section 49(1).

(2) If an employee who has been continuously employed for [one month] or more gives notice to terminate his contract of employment, the provisions of Schedule 3 shall have effect as respects the liability of the employer for the period of notice required by section 49(2).

(3) This section shall not apply in relation to a notice given by the employer or the employee if the notice to be given by the employer to terminate the contract must be at least one week more than the notice required by section 49(1).

1–478

AMENDMENTS
The words in square brackets in subss. (1) and (2) were substituted by the Employment Act 1982 (c.46), Sched. 2, para. 3.

Measure of damages in proceedings against employers

51. If an employer fails to give the notice required by section 49, the rights conferred by section 50 (with Schedule 3) shall be taken into account in assessing his liability for breach of the contract.

1–479

Statutory contracts

52. Sections 49 and 50 shall apply in relation to a contract all or any of the terms of which are terms which take effect by virtue of any provision contained in or having effect under an Act of Parliament, whether public

1–480

or local, as they apply in relation to any other contract; and the reference in this section to an Act of Parliament includes, subject to any express provision to the contrary, an Act passed after this Act.

Written statement of reasons for dismissal

1–481   **53.**—(1) An employee shall be entitled—
(a) if he is given by his employer notice of termination of his contract of employment;
(b) if his contract of employment is terminated by his employer without notice; or
(c) if, where he is employed under a contract for a fixed term, that term expires without being renewed under the same contract,
to be provided by his employer, on request, within fourteen days of that request, with a written statement giving particulars of the reasons for his dismissal.

(2) An employee shall not be entitled to a written statement under subsection (1) unless on the effective date of termination he has been, or will have been, continuously employed for a period of [six months ending with that date.]

(3) A written statement provided under this section shall be admissible in evidence in any proceedings.

(4) A complaint may be presented to an industrial tribunal by an employee against his employer on the ground that the employer unreasonably refused to provide a written statement under subsection (1) or that the particulars of reasons given in purported compliance with that subsection are inadequate or untrue, and if the tribunal finds the complaint well-founded—
(a) it may make a declaration as to what it finds the employer's reasons were for dismissing the employee; and
(b) it shall make an award that the employer pay to the employee a sum equal to the amount of two weeks' pay.

(5) An industrial tribunal shall not entertain a complaint under this section relating to the reasons for a dismissal unless it is presented to the tribunal at such a time that the tribunal would, in accordance with section 67(2) or (4), entertain a complaint of unfair dismissal in respect of that dismissal presented at the same time.

AMENDMENT
The words in square brackets in subs. (2) were substituted by the Employment Act 1982 (c.46), Sched. 2, para. 4.

Right not to be Unfairly Dismissed

Right of employee not to be unfairly dismissed

1–482   **54.**—(1) In every employment to which this section applies every employee shall have the right not to be unfairly dismissed by his employer.
(2) This section applies to every employment except in so far as its application is excluded by or under any provision of this Part or by section 141 to 149.

Meaning of Unfair Dismissal

Meaning of "dismissal"

1–483   **55.**—(1) In this Part, except as respects a case to which section 56 applies, "dismissal" and "dismiss" shall be construed in accordance with the following provisions of this section.

(2) Subject to subsection (3), an employee shall be treated as dismissed by his employer if, but only if,—
   (a) the contract under which he is employed by the employer is terminated by the employer, whether it is so terminated by notice or without notice, or
   (b) where under that contract he is employed for a fixed term, that term expires without being renewed under the same contract, or
   (c) the employee terminates that contract, with or without notice, in circumstances such that he is entitled to terminate it without notice by reason of the employer's conduct.

(3) Where an employer gives notice to an employee to terminate his contract of employment and, at a time within the period of that notice, the employee gives notice to the employer to terminate the contract of employment on a date earlier than the date on which the employer's notice is due to expire, the employee shall for the purposes of this Part be taken to be dismissed by his employer, and the reasons for the dismissal shall be taken to be the reasons for which the employer's notice is given.

(4) In this Part "the effective date of termination"—
   (a) in relation to an employee whose contract of employment is terminated by notice, whether given by his employer or by the employee, means the date on which that notice expires;
   (b) in relation to an employee whose contract of employment is terminated without notice, means the date on which the termination takes effect; and
   (c) in relation to an employee who is employed under a contract for a fixed term, where that term expires without being renewed under the same contract, means the date on which that term expires.

[(5) Where the contract of employment is terminated by the employer and the notice required by section 49 to be given by an employer would, if duly given on the material date, expire on a date later than the effective date of termination (as defined by subsection (4)) then, for the purposes of sections 53(2), 64(1)(a), 64A and 73(3) and paragraph 8(3) of Schedule 14, the later date shall be treated as the effective date of termination in relation to the dismissal.

(6) Where the contract of employment is terminated by the employee and—
   (a) the material date does not fall during a period of notice given by the employer to terminate that contract; and
   (b) had the contract been terminated not by the employee but by notice given on the material date by the employer, that notice would have been required by section 49 to expire on a date later than the effective date of termination (as defined by subsection (4)),
then, for the purposes of section 64(1)(a), 64A and 73(3) and paragraph 8(3) of Schedule 14, the later date shall be treated as the effective date of termination in relation to the dismissal.

(7) "Material date" means—
   (a) in subsection (5), the date when notice of termination was given

by the employer of (where no notice was given) the date when the contract of employment was terminated by the employer; and

(b) in subsection (6), the date when notice of termination was given by the employee or (where no notice was given) the date when the contract of employment was terminated by the employee.].

AMENDMENT
Subss. (5)–(7) were substituted by the Employment Act 1982, Sched. 3, para. 1.

Failure to permit woman to return to work after confinement treated as dismissal

1–484 **56.** Where an employee is entitled to return to work and has exercised her right to return in accordance with section 47 but is not permitted to return to work, then [subject to section 56A] she shall be treated for the purposes of this Part as if she had been employed until the notified day of return, and, if she would not otherwise be so treated, as having been continuously employed until that day, and as if she had been dismissed with effect from that day for the reason for which she was not permitted to return.

AMENDMENT
The words in square brackets were inserted by the Employment Act 1980, Sched. 1, para. 11.

[Exclusion of s.56 in certain cases

1–485 **56A.**—(1) Section 56 shall not apply in relation to an employee if—
(a) immediately before her absence began the number of employees employed by her employer, added to the number employed by any associated employer of his, did not exceed five, and
(b) it is not reasonably practicable for the employer (who may be the same employer or a successor of his) to permit her to return to work in accordance with section 45(1), or for him or an associated employer to offer her employment under a contract of employment satisfying the conditions specified in subsection (3).

(2) Section 56 shall not apply in relation to an employee if—
(a) it is not reasonably practicable for a reason other than redundancy for the employer (who may be the same employer or a successor of his) to permit her to return to work in accordance with section 45(1), and
(b) he or an associated employer offers her employment under a contract of employment satisfying the conditions specified in subsection (3), and
(c) she accepts or unreasonably refuses that offer.

(3) The conditions referred to in subsections (1) and (2) are—
(a) that the work to be done under the contract is of a kind which is both suitable in relation to the employee and appropriate for her to do in the circumstances; and
(b) that the provisions of the contract as to the capacity and place in which she is to be employed and as to the other terms and conditions of her employment are not substantially less favour-

able to her than if she had returned to work in accordance with section 45(1).

(4) Where on a complaint of unfair dismissal any question arises as to whether the operation of section 56 nis excluded by subsection (1) or (2), it shall be for the employer to show that the provisions of that subsection were satisfied in relation to the complaint.]

AMENDMENT

This section was inserted by the Employment Act 1980 (c. 42), s.12.

General provisions relating to fairness of dismissal

57.—(1) In determining for the purposes of this Part whether the dismissal of an employee was fair or unfair, it shall be for the employer to show—
 (a) what was the reason (or, if there was more than one, the principal reason) for the dismissal, and
 (b) that it was a reason falling within subsection (2) or some other substantial reason of a kind such as to justify the dismissal of an employee holding the position which that employee held.

(2) In subsection (1)(b) the reference to a reason falling within this subsection is a reference to a reason which—
 (a) related to the capability or qualifications of the employee for performing work of the kind which he was employed by the employer to do, or
 (b) related to the conduct of the employee, or
 (c) was that the employee was redundant, or
 (d) was that the employee could not continue to work in the position which he held without contravention (either on his part or on that of his employer) of a duty or restriction imposed by or under an enactment.

(3) Where the employer has fulfilled the requirements of subsection (1), then, subject to section 58 to 62, the determination of the question whether the dismissal was fair or unfair, having regard to the reason shown by the employer, shall depend on whether [in the circumstances (including the size and administrative resources of the employer's undertaking) the employer acted reasonably or unreasonably in treating it as a sufficient reason for dismissing the employee; and that question shall be determined in accordance with equity and the substantial merits of the case].

(4) In this section, in relation to an employee,—
 (a) "capability" means capability assessed by reference to skill, aptitude, health or any other physical or mental quality;
 (b) "qualifications" means any degree, diploma or other academic, technical or professional qualification relevant to the position which the employee held.

AMENDMENT

The words in square brackets in subs. (3) were substituted by the Employment Act 1980 (c. 42), s.6.

[Dismissal relating to trade union membership

58.—(1) Subject to subsection (3), the dismissal of an employee by an

employer shall be regarded for the purposes of this Part as having been unfair if the reason for it (or, if more than one, the principal reason) was that the employee—
- (*a*) was, or proposed to become, a member of an independent trade union, or
- (*b*) had taken part, or proposed to take part, in the activities of an independent trade union at an appropriate time, or
- (*c*) was not a member of any trade union, or of a particular trade union, or of one of a number of particular trade unions, or had refused or proposed to refuse to become or remain a member.

(2) In subsection (1) "an appropriate time", in relation to an employee taking part in the activities of a trade union, means a time which either—
- (*a*) is outside his working hours, or
- (*b*) is a time within his working hours at which, in accordance with arrangements agreed with or consent given by his employer, it is permissible for him to take part in those activities;

and in this subsection "working hours", in relation to employee, means any time when, in accordance with his contract of employment, he is required to be at work.

(3) Subject to the following provisions of this section, the dismissal of an employee by an employer shall be regarded for the purposes of this Part as having been fair if—
- (*a*) it is the practice, in accordance with a union membership agreement, for employees of the employer who are of the same class as the dismissed employee to belong to a specified independent trade union, or to one of a number of specified independent trade unions; and
- (*b*) the reason (or, if more than one, the principal reason) for the dismissal was that the employee was not, or had refused or proposed to refuse to become or remain, a member of a union in accordance with the agreement; and
- (*c*) the union membership agreement had been approved in relation to employees of that class in accordance with section 58A through a ballot held within the period of five years ending with the time of dismissal.

(4) Subsection (3) shall not apply if the employee genuinely objects on grounds of conscience or other deeply-held personal conviction to being a member of any trade union whatsoever or of a particular trade union.

(5) Subsection (3) shall not apply if the employee—
- (*a*) has been among those employees of the employer who belong to the class to which the union membership agreement relates since before the agreement had the effect of requiring them to be or become members of a trade union, and
- (*b*) has not at any time while the agreement had that effect been a member of a trade union in accordance with the agreement.

(6) Subsection (3) shall not apply if—
- (*a*) the union membership agreement took effect after 14th August 1980 in relation to the employees of the employer who are of the same class as the dismissed employee, and
- (*b*) the employee was entitled to vote in the ballot through which the agreement was approved in accordance with section 58A or, if there have been two or more such ballots, in the first of them, and

(c) the employee has not at any time since the day on which that ballot was held been a member of a trade union in accordance with the agreement.

(7) Subsection (3) shall not apply if the dismissal was from employment in respect of which, at the time of dismissal, either—
- (a) there was in force a declaration made on a complaint presented by the employee under section 4 of the Employment Act 1980 (unreasonable exclusion or expulsion from trade union), or
- (b) proceedings on such a complaint were pending before an industrial tribunal,

unless the employee has at any time during the period beginning with the date of the complaint under section 4 and ending with the effective date of termination been, or failed through his own fault to become, a member of a trade union in accordance with the union membership agreement.

(8) In any case where neither subsection (4) nor subsection (7) has the effect of displacing subsection (3) and the employee—
- (a) holds qualifications which are relevant to the employment in question,
- (b) is subject to a written code which governs the conduct of those persons who hold those qualifications, and
- (c) has—
    - (i) been expelled from a trade union for refusing to take part in a strike or other industrial action, or
    - (ii) refused to become or remain a member of a trade union,

subsection (3) shall not apply if the reason (or, if more than one, the principal reason for his refusal was, in a case falling within paragraph (c)(i), that his taking the action in question would be in breach of the code or, in a case falling within paragraph (c)(ii), that if he became, or as the case may be remained, a member he would be required to take part in a strike, or other industrial action, which would be in breach of that code.

(9) For the purposes of subsection (3)(c) and (6)(c), where votes in a ballot may be cast on more than one day, the ballot shall be treated as held on the last of those days.

(10) For the purpose of subsections (3) and (7) the reference to the time of the dismissal shall, in a case where the dismissal was with notice, be construed as a reference to the time when the notice was given.

(11) For the purposes of subsection (7) an employee shall be taken to have failed through his own fault to become a member of a trade union only if the tribunal is satisfied that the fact that he is not a member is attributable to his failure to apply (or re-apply) for membership or to his failure to accept an offer of membership.

(12) Where the employer of any employees changes in such circumstances that the employees' period of continuous employment is not broken, this section and section 58A shall have effect as if any reference to the employees of any class of the later employer included a reference to the employees of that class of the former employer.

(13) Where the reason, or one of the reasons, for the dismissal of an employee was—
- (a) his refusal, or proposed refusal, to comply with a requirement (whether or not imposed by his contract of employment or in writing) that, in the event of his failure to become or his ceasing to remain a member of any trade union or of a particular trade union

or of one of a number of particular trade unions, he must make one or more payments; or

(b) his objection, or proposed objection, (however expressed) to the operation of a provision (whether or not forming part of his contract of employment or in writing) under which, in the event mentioned in paragraph (a), his employer is entitled to deduct one or more sums from the remuneration payable to him in respect of his employment;

that reason shall be treated as falling within subsections (1)(c) and (3)(b).

(14) References in this section and section 58A to a trade union include references to a branch or section of a trade union, unless the context otherwise requires.

Ballots as to union membership agreements

1–488 58A.—(1) Subject to the following provisions of this section, a union membership agreement shall be taken for the purposes of section 58(3)(c) to have been approved in relation to the employees of any class of an employer if a ballot has been held on the question whether the agreement should apply in relation to them and either—
   (a) not less than 80 per cent. of those entitled to vote, or
   (b) not less than 85 per cent. of those who voted,
voted in favour of the agreement's application.

(2) Subsection (1)(b) shall not apply if the agreement—
   (a) has not previously been approved in accordance with this section in relation to the employer's employees of the class in question, and
   (b) came into force in relation to them after 14th August 1980.

(3) The persons entitled to vote in a ballot under this section, in relation to the application of a union membership agreement to the employees of any class of an employer, shall be all those employees who belong to that class and who—
   (a) in the case of a ballot in which votes may only be cast on one day, are in the employment of the employer on that day; or
   (b) in any other case, are in that employment on the qualifying day.

(4) "Qualifying day" means the day specified as such by the person conducting the ballot; but no day shall be specified which—
   (a) falls after the last of the days on which votes may be cast in the ballot; or
   (b) is so long before that date as to be unreasonable in relation to that ballot.

(5) A ballot under this section shall be so conducted as to secure that, so far as reasonably practicable, all those entitled to vote—
   (a) have an opportunity of voting, and of doing so in secret; and
   (b) in a case which does not fall within subsection (3)(a), know, before they cast their votes, which day has been specified as the qualifying day.

(6) In determining for the purposes of subsection (3) whether a person belongs to a class of employees, any restriction of the class by reference to membership (or objection to membership) of a trade union shall be disregarded.

(7) An agreement shall not be taken for the purposes of section 58(3)(c) to have been approved through a ballot of the employees of any class of

an employer if since it was held another ballot of those employees has been held under this section and both—
  (a) less than 80 per cent. of those entitled to vote, and
  (b) less than 85 per cent. of those who voted.
voted in favour of the agreement's application.

(8) Subsection (7) shall not affect the determination in any case of the question whether the condition in subsection (2)(a) is satisfied.]

AMENDMENT
  Ss.58 and 58A were substituted by the Employment Act 1982 (c.46), s.3.

Dismissal on ground of redundancy

59. Where the reason or principal reason for the dismissal of an employee was that he was redundant, but it is shown that the circumstances constituting the redundancy applied equally to one or more other employees in the same undertaking who held positions similar to that held by him and who have not been dismissed by the employer, and either—
  (a) that the reason (or, if more than one, the principal reason) for which he was selected for dismissal was [one of those specified in section 58(1)]; or
  (b) that he was selected for dismissal in contravention of a customary arrangement or agreed procedure relating to redundancy and there were no special reasons justifying a departure from that arrangement or procedure in his case,
then, for the purposes of this Part, the dismissal shall be regarded as unfair.

AMENDMENT
  The words in square brackets in para (a) were substituted by the Employment Act 1982 (c. 46), Sched. 3, para. 17.

Dismissal on ground of pregnancy

60.—(1) An employee shall be treated for the purposes of this Part as unfairly dismissed if the reason or principal reason for her dismissal is that she is pregnant or is any other reason connected with her pregnancy, except one of the following reasons—
  (a) that at the effective date of termination she is or will have become, because of her pregnancy, incapable of adequately doing the work which she is employed to do;
  (b) that, because of her pregnancy, she cannot or will not be able to continue after that date to do that work without contravention (either by her or her employer) of a duty or restriction imposed by or under any enactment.

(2) An employee shall be treated for the purposes of this Part as unfairly dismissed if her employer dismisses her for a reason mentioned in subsection (1)(a) or (b), but neither he nor any successor of his, where there is a suitable available vacancy, makes her an offer before or on the effective date of termination to engage her under a new contract of employment complying with subsection (3).

(3) The new contract of employment must—
  (a) take effect immediately on the ending of employment under the previous contract, or, where that employment ends on a Friday, Saturday or Sunday, on or before the next Monday after that Friday, Saturday or Sunday;

(*b*) be such that the work to be done under the contract is of a kind which is both suitable in relation to the employee and appropriate for her to do in the circumstances; and

(*c*) be such that the provisions of the new contract as to the capacity and place in which she is to be employed and as to the other terms and conditions of her employment are not substantially less favourable to her than the corresponding provisions of the previous contract.

(4) On a complaint of unfair dismissal on the ground of failure to offer to engage an employee as mentioned in subsection (2), it shall be for the employer to show that he or a successor made an offer to engage her in compliance with subsections (2) and (3) or, as the case may be, that there was no suitable available vacancy for her.

(5) Section 55(3) shall not apply in a case where an employer gives notice to an employee to terminate her contract of employment for a reason mentioned in subsection (1)(*a*) or (*b*).

Dismissal of replacement

1–491   61.—(1) Where an employer—

(*a*) on engaging an employee informs the employee in writing that his employment will be terminated on the return to work of another employee who is, or will be, absent wholly or partly because of pregnancy or confinement; and

(*b*) dismisses the first-mentioned employee in order to make it possible to give work to the other employee;

then, for the purposes of section 57(1)(*b*), but without prejudice to the application of section 57(3), the dismissal shall be regarded as having been for a substantial reason of a kind such as to justify the dismissal of an employee holding the position which that employee held.

(2) Where an employer—

(*a*) on engaging an employee informs the employee in writing that his employment will be terminated on the end of a suspension such as is referred to in section 19 of another employee; and

(*b*) dismisses the first-mentioned employee in order to make it possible to allow the other employee to resume his original work;

then, for the purposes of section 57(1)(*b*), but without prejudice to the application of section 57(3), the dismissal shall be regarded as having been for a substantial reason of a kind such as to justify the dismissal of an employee holding the position which that employee held.

Dismissal in connection with a lock-out, strike or other industrial action

1–492   62.—(1) The provisions of this section shall have effect in relation to an employee [(the "complainant")] who claims that he has been unfairly dismissed by his employer where at the date of dismissal—

(*a*) the employer was conducting or instituting a lock-out, or

(*b*) the [complainant] was taking part in a strike or other industrial action.

(2) In such a case an industrial tribunal shall not determine whether the dismissal was fair or unfair unless it is shown—

(*a*) that one or more relevant employees of the same employer have not been dismissed, or [(b) that any such employee has, before the expiry of the period of three months beginning with that employee's date of dismissal, has been offered re-engagement and that the complainant has not been offered re-engagement.]

(3) Where it is shown that the condition referred to in paragraph (b) of subsection (2) is fulfilled, the provisions of sections 57 to 60 shall have effect as if in those sections for any reference to the reason or principal reason for which the [complainant] was dismissed there were substituted a reference to the reason or principal reason for which he has not been offered re-engagement.

(4) In this section—
    (a) "date of dismissal" means—
        (i) where the employee's contract of employment was terminated by notice, the date on which the employer's notice was given, and
        (ii) in any other case, the effective date of termination;
    (b) "relevant employees" means—
        (i) in relation to a lock-out, employees who were directly interested in the [. . .] dispute in contemplation or furtherance of which the lock-out occurred, and
        [(ii) in relation to a strike or other industrial action, those employees at the establishment who were taking part in the action at the complainant's date of dismissal;
"establishment", in sub-paragraph (ii), meaning that establishment of the employer at or from which the complainant works; and]
    (c) any reference to an offer of re-engagement is a reference to an offer (made either by the original employer or by a successor of that employer or an associated employer) to re-engage an employee, either in the job which he held immediately before the date of dismissal or in a different job which would be reasonably suitable in his case.

AMENDMENT
    The words in square brackets in this section were substituted by the Employment Act 1982 (c. 46), s.9(2)–(4).

Pressure on employer to dismiss unfairly

63. In determining, for the purposes of this Part any question as to the reason, or principal reason, for which an employee was dismissed or any question whether the reason or principal reason for which an employee was dismissed was a reason fulfilling the requirements of section 57(1)(b) or whether the employer acted reasonably in treating it as a sufficient reason for dismissing him,—
    (a) no account shall be taken of any pressure which, by calling, organising, procuring or financing a strike or other industrial action, or threatening to do so, was exercised on the employer to dismiss the employee, and
    (b) any such question shall be determined as if no such pressure had been exercised.

1–493

Exclusion of Section 54

Qualifying period and upper age limit

64.—(1) Subject to subsection (3), section 54 does not apply to the dis-

1–494

missal of an employee from any employment if the employee—
- (a) was not continuously employed for a period of not less than [one year] ending with the effective date of termination, or
- (b) on or before the effective date of termination attained the age which, in the undertaking in which he was employed, was the normal retiring age for an employee holding the position which he held, or, if a man, attained the age of sixty-five, or, if a woman, attained the age of sixty.

(2) If an employee is dismissed by reason of any such requirement or recommendation as is referred to in section 19(1), subsection (1)(a) shall have effect in relation to that dismissal as if for the words [one year] there were substituted ["one month"].

(3) Subsection (1) shall not apply to the dismissal of an employee if it is shown that the reason (or, if more than one, the principal reason) for the dismissal was [one of those specified in section 58(1).]

AMENDMENT

The words in square brackets were substituted by the Employment Act 1982 (c. 46), Sched. 2, para. 5, and Sched. 3, para. 19.

[Extended qualifying period where no more than twenty employees

64A.—(1) Subject to subsection (2), section 54 does not apply to the dismissal of an employee from any employment if—
- (a) the period (ending with the effective date of termination) during which the employee was continuously employed did not exceed two years; and
- (b) at no time during that period did the number of employees employed by the employer for the time being of the dismissed employee, added to the number employed by an associated employer, exceed twenty;

(2) Subsection (1) shall not apply to the dismissal of an employee by reason of any such requirement or recommendation as is referred to in section 19(1), or if it is shown that the reason (or, if more than one, the principal reason) for the dismissal was [one of those specified in section 58(1)]].

AMENDMENT

This section was inserted by the Employment Act 1980, s.8(1). The final words were substituted by the Employment Act 1982, Sched. 3, para. 20.

Exclusion in respect of dismissal procedures agreement

65.—(1) An application may be made jointly to the Secretary of State by all the parties to a dismissal procedures agreement to make an order designating that agreement for the purposes of this section.

(2) On any such application the Secretary of State may make such an order if he is satisfied—
- (a) that every trade union which is a party to the dismissal procedures agreement is an independent trade union;
- (b) that the agreement provides for procedures to be followed in cases

where an employee claims that he has been, or is in the course of being, unfairly dismissed;
(c) that those procedures are available without discrimination to all employees falling within any description to which the agreement applies;
(d) that the remedies provided by the agreement in respect of unfair dismissal are on the whole as beneficial as (but not necessarily identical with) those provided in respect of unfair dismissal by this Part;
(e) that the procedures provided by the agreement include a right to arbitration or adjudication by an independent referee, or by a tribunal or other independent body, in cases where (by reason of an equality of votes or for any other reason) a decision cannot otherwise be reached; and
(f) that the provisions of the agreement are such that it can be determined with reasonable certainty whether a particular employee is one to whom the agreement applies or not.

(3) Where a dismissal procedures agreement is designated by an order under this section which is for the time being in force, the provisions of that agreement relating to dismissal shall have effect in substitution for any rights under section 54; and accordingly that section shall not apply to the dismissal of an employee from any employment if it is employment to which, and he is an employee to whom, those provisions of the agreement apply.

(4) Subsection (3) shall not apply to the right not to be unfairly dismissed for any reason mentioned in subsection (1) or (2) of section 60.

Revocation of exclusion order under s.65

66.—(1) [. . .]   1–497

(2) If [at any time when an order under section 65 is in force in respect of a dismissal procedures agreement the Secretary of State is satisfied, whether on an application by any of the parties to the agreement or otherwise,] either—
   (a) that it is the desire of all the parties to the dismissal procedures agreement that the order should be revoked, or
   (b) that the agreement has ceased to fulfil all the conditions specified in section 65(2),
the Secretary of State shall revoke the order by a further order made under this section.

(3) Any order made under this section may contain such transitional provisions as appear to the Secretary of State to be appropriate in the circumstances, and, in particular, may direct—
   (a) that, notwithstanding section 65(3), an employee shall not be excluded from his rights under section 54 where the effective date of termination falls within a transitional period which is specified in the order and is a period ending with the date on which the order under this section takes effect and shall have an extended time for presenting a complaint under section 67 in respect of a dismissal where the effective date of termination falls within that period, and
   (b) that in determining any complaint of unfair dismissal presented by an employee to whom the dismissal procedures agreement applies, where the effective date of termination falls within that transitional

period, an industrial tribunal shall have regard to such considerations (in addition to those specified in this Part and paragraph 2 of Schedule 9) as may be specified in the order.

AMENDMENTS
Subs. (1) was repealed by the Employment Act 1980 (c. 42), Sched. 1, para. 13 and Sched. 2. The words in square brackets in subs. (2) were substituted by *ibid.*

Remedies for Unfair Dismissal

Complaint to industrial tribunal

1–498   67.—(1) A complaint may be presented to an industrial tribunal against an employer by any person (in this Part referred to as the complainant) that he was unfairly dismissed by the employer.

(2) Subject to subsection (4), an industrial tribunal shall not consider a complaint under this section unless it is presented to the tribunal before the end of the period of three months beginning with the effective date of termination or within such further period as the tribunal considers reasonable in a case where it is satisfied that it was not reasonably practicable for the complaint to be presented before the end of the period of three months.

[(3) Subsection (2) shall apply in relation to a complaint to which section 62(3) applies as if—
   (a) for the references to three months there were substituted, in each case, a reference to six months; and
   (b) as if for the reference to the effective date of termination there were substituted a reference to the complainant's date of dismissal (within the meaning of section 62(4).)]

(4) An industrial tribunal shall consider a complaint under this section if, where the dismissal is with notice, the complaint is presented after the notice is given notwithstanding that it is presented before the effective date of termination and in relation to such a complaint the provisions of this Act, so far as they relate to unfair dismissal, shall have effect—
   (a) as if references to a complaint by a person that he was unfairly dismissed by his employer included references to a complaint by a person that his employer has given him notice in such circumstances that he will be unfairly dismissed when the notice expires;
   (b) as if references to reinstatement included references to the withdrawal of the notice by the employer;
   (c) as if references to the effective date of termination included references to the date which would be the effective date of termination on the expiry of the notice; and
   (d) as if references to an employee ceasing to be employed included references to an employee having been given notice of dismissal.

AMENDMENT
Subs. (3) was substituted by the Employment Act 1982 (c. 46), s.9(5).

Remedies for unfair dismissal

1–499   68.—(1) Where on a complaint under section 67 an industrial tribunal finds that the grounds of the complaint are well-founded, it shall explain to the complainant what orders for reinstatement or re-engagement may be made under section 69 and in what circumstances they may be made and shall ask him whether he wished the tribunal to make such an order, and if he does express such a wish the tribunal may make an order under section 69.

(2) If on a complaint under section 67 the tribunal finds that the grounds of the complaint are well-founded and no order is made under section 69, the tribunal shall make an award of compensation for unfair dismissal, calculated in accordance with [sections 72 to 76] to be paid by the employer to the employee.

AMENDMENT
The words in square brackets in subs. (2) were substituted by the Employment Act 1982 (c. 46), Sched. 3, para. 21.

Order for reinstatement or re-engagement

69.—(1) An order under this section may be an order for reinstatement (in accordance with subsections (2) and (3)) or an order for re-engagement (in accordance with subsection (4)), as the industrial tribunal may decide, and in the latter case may be on such terms as the tribunal may decide.

(2) An order for reinstatement is an order that the employer shall treat the complainant in all respects as if he had not been dismissed, and on making such an order the tribunal shall specify—
   (*a*) any amount payable by the employer in respect of any benefit which the complainant might reasonably be expected to have had but for the dismissal, including arrears of pay, for the period between the date of termination of employment and the date of reinstatement;
   (*b*) any rights and privileges, including seniority and pension rights, which must be restored to the employee; and
   (*c*) the date by which the order must be complied with.

(3) Without prejudice to the generality of subsection (2), if the complainant would have benefited from an improvement in his terms and conditions of employment had he not been dismissed, an order for reinstatement shall require him to be treated as if he had benefited from that improvement from the date on which he would have done so but for being dismissed.

(4) An order for re-engagement is an order that the complainant be engaged by the employer, or by a successor of the employer or by an associated employer, in employment comparable to that from which he was dismissed or other suitable employment, and on making such an order the tribunal shall specify the terms on which re-engagement is to take place including—
   (*a*) the identity of the employer;
   (*b*) the nature of the employment;
   (*c*) the remuneration for the employment;
   (*d*) any amount payable by the employer in respect of any benefit which the complainant might reasonably be expected to have had but for the dismissal, including arrears of pay, for the period between the date of termination of employment and the date of re-engagement;
   (*e*) any rights and privileges, including seniority and pension rights, which must be restored to the employee; and
   (*f*) the date by which the order must be complied with.

(5) In exercising its discretion under this section the tribunal shall first consider whether to make an order for reinstatement and in so doing shall take into account the following consideration, that is to say—

(a) whether the complainant wishes to be reinstated;
(b) whether it is practicable for the employer to comply with an order for reinstatement;
(c) where the complainant caused or contributed to some extent to the dismissal, whether it would be just to order his reinstatement.

(6) If the tribunal decides not to make an order for reinstatement it shall then consider whether to make an order for re-engagement and if so on what terms; and in so doing the tribunal shall take into account the following considerations, that is to say—
(a) any wish expressed by the complainant as to the nature of the order to be made;
(b) whether it is practicable for the employer or, as the case may be, a successor or associated employer to comply with an order for re-engagement;
(c) where the complainant caused or contributed to some extent to the dismissal, whether it would be just to order his re-engagement and if so on what terms;

and except in a case where the tribunal takes into account contributory fault under paragraph (c) it shall, if it orders re-engagement, do so on terms which are, so far as is reasonably practicable, as favourable as an order for reinstatement.

Supplementary provisions relating to s.69

1–501   70.—(1) Where in any case an employer has engaged a permanent replacement for a dismissed employee, the tribunal shall not take that fact into account in determining, for the purposes of subsection 5(b) or (6)(b) of section 69, whether it is practicable to comply with an order for reinstatement or re-engagement unless the employer shows—
(a) that it was not practicable for him to arrange for the dismissed employee's work to be done without engaging a permanent replacement; or
(b) that he engaged the replacement after the lapse of a reasonable period, without having heard from the dismissed employee that he wished to be reinstated or re-engaged, and that when the employer engaged the replacement it was no longer reasonable for him to arrange for the dismissed employee's work to be done except by a permanent replacement.

(2) In calculating for the purpose of subsection (2)(a) or 4(d) of section 69 any amount payable by the employer, the tribunal shall take into account, so as to reduce the employer's liability, any sums received by the complainant in respect of the period between the date of termination of employment and the date of reinstatement or re-engagement by way of—
(a) wages in lieu of notice or ex gratia payments paid by the employer;
(b) remuneration paid in respect of employment with another employer;

and such other benefits as the tribunal thinks appropriate in the circumstances.

Enforcement of s.69 order and compensation

1–502   71.—(1) If an order under section 69 is made and the complainant is reinstated or, as the case may be, re-engaged but the terms of the order are not fully complied with, then, subject to section 75, an industrial tribunal shall make an award of compensation, to be paid by the employer to the employee, of such amount as the tribunal thinks fit having regard to the loss sustained by the complainant in consequence of the failure to comply fully with the terms of the order.

(2) Subject to subsection (1), if an order under section 69 is made but the complainant is not reinstated or, as the case may be, re-engaged in accordance with the order—
  (a) the tribunal shall make an award of compensation for unfair dismissal, calculated in accordance with [sections 72 to 76] to be paid by the employer to the employee; and
  (b) [except in a case in which the dismissal is to be regarded as unfair by virtue of section 58 or 59(a) or in which] the employer satisfies the tribunal that it was not practicable to comply with the order, the tribunal shall make an additional award of compensation to be paid by the employer to the employee of an amount—
    (i) where the dismissal is of a description referred to in subsection (3), not less than twenty-six nor more than fifty-two weeks' pay, or
    (ii) in any other case, not less than thirteen nor more than twenty-six weeks' pay.

(3) The descriptions of dismissal in respect of which an employer may incur a higher additional award in accordance with subsection (2)(b)(i) are the following, that is to say,—
  (a) [Repealed by the Employment Act 1982 (c. 46), Sched. 4,]
  (b) a dismissal which is an act of discrimination within the meaning of the Sex Discrimination Act 1975 which is unlawful by virtue of that Act;
  (c) a dismissal which is an act of discrimination within the meaning of the Race Relations Act 1976 which is unlawful by virtue of that Act.

(4) Where in any case an employer has engaged a permanent replacement for a dismissed employee the tribunal shall not take that fact into account in determining, for the purposes of subsection (2)(b) whether it was practicable to comply with the order for reinstatement or re-engagement unless the employer shows that it was not practicable for him to arrange for the dismissed employee's work to be done without engaging a permanent replacement.

(5) Where in any case an industrial tribunal makes an award of compensation for unfair dismissal, calculated in accordance with [sections 72 to 76] and the tribunal finds that the complainant has unreasonably prevented an order under section 69 from being complied with, it shall, without prejudice to the generality of section 74(4), take that conduct into account as a failure on the part of the complainant to mitigate his loss.

AMENDMENT
  The words in square brackets in subss. 2, 3 and 5 were substituted by the Employment Act 1982 (c. 46), s.5(1), Sched.3, para.22.

Amount of Compensation

[Compensation for unfair dismissal

72. Where a tribunal makes an award of compensation for unfair dismissal under section 68(2) or 71(2) the award shall consist of— 1–503
  (a) a basic award (calculated in accordance with section 73), and

(b) a compensatory award (calculated in accordance with section 74), and
(c) where the dismissal is to be regarded as unfair by virtue of section 58 or 59(a), a special award (calculated in accordance with section 75A);

but paragraph (c) shall not apply unless the complainant requested the tribunal to make an order under section 69, and shall not in any event apply in a case within section 73(2).]

AMENDMENT

This section was substituted by the Employment Act 1982 (c.46), s.5(2).

[Reduction of compensation: matters to be disregarded

1-504   72A.—(1) This section applies in any case where a tribunal makes an award of compensation for unfair dismissal under section 68(2) or 71(2)(a) and the dismissal is to be regarded as unfair by virtue of section 58 or 59(a).

(2) In such a case the tribunal, in considering whether it would be just and equitable to reduce, or further reduce, the amount of any part of the award, shall disregard any conduct or action of the complainant in so far as it constitutes—
(a) a breach, or proposed breach, of any requirement falling within subsection (3);
(b) a refusal, or proposed refusal, to comply with a requirement of a kind mentioned in section 58(13)(a); or
(c) an objection, or proposed objection, (however expressed) to the operation of a provision of a kind mentioned in section 58(13)(b).

(3) A requirement falls within this subsection if it is imposed on the complainant in question by or under any arrangement or contract of employment or other agreement and requires him—
(a) to be or become a member of any trade union or of a particular trade union or of one of a number of particular trade unions;
(b) to cease to be, or refrain from becoming, a member of any trade union or of a particular trade union or of one of a number of particular trade unions; or
(c) not to take part in the activities of any trade union or of a particular trade union or of one of a number of particular trade unions.]

AMENDMENT

This section was inserted by the Employment Act 1982, (c. 46), s.6.

Calculation of basic award

1-505   73.—(1) The amount of the basic award shall be the amount calculated in accordance with subsections (3) to (6), subject to—
(a) subsection (2) of this section (which provides for an award of two weeks' pay in certain redundancy cases);
(b) [Repealed by the Employment Act 1982 (c. 46), Sched. 4]
[(ba) subsection (7A) (which provides for the amount of the award to be reduced where the employee has unreasonably refused an offer of reinstatement);
(bb) subsection (7B) (which provides for the amount of the award to be reduced because of the employee's conduct)];

(c) [...]
(d) subsection (9) (which provides for the amount of the award to be reduced where the employee received a payment in respect of redundancy); and
(e) section 76 (which prohibits compensation being awarded under this Part and under the Sex Discrimination Act 1975 or the Race Relations Act 1976 in respect of the same matter).

(2) The amount of the basic award shall be two weeks' pay where the tribunal finds that the reason or principal reason for the dismissal of the employee was that he was redundant and the employee—
(a) by virtue of section 82(5) or (6) is not, or if he were otherwise entitled would not be, entitled to a redundancy payment; or
(b) by virtue of the operation of section 84(1) is not treated as dismissed for the purposes of Part VI.

(3) The amount of the basic award shall be calculated by reference to the period, ending with the effective date of termination, during which the employee has been continuously employed, by starting at the end of that period and reckoning backwards the numbers of years of employment falling within that period, and allowing—
(a) one and a half weeks' pay for each such year of employment [...] in which the employee was not below the age of forty-one;
[(b) one week's pay for each year of employment not falling within paragraph (a) [...] in which the employee was not below the age of twenty-two; and
(c) half a week's pay for each year of employment not falling within either of paragraphs (a) and (b).]

(4) Where, in reckoning the number of years of employment in accordance with subsection (3), twenty years of employment have been reckoned no account shall be taken of any year of employment earlier than those twenty years.

(4A) Where the dismissal is to be regarded as unfair by virtue of section 58 or 59(a), the amount of the basic award (before any reduction under the following provisions of this section) shall not be less than £2,000.

(4B) The Secretary of State may by order increase or further increase the minimum award provided for by subsection (4A), but no order shall be made under this subsection unless a draft of the order has been laid before Parliament and approved by a resolution of each House of Parliament.]

(5) Where in the case of an employee the effective date of termination is after the specified anniversary the amount of the basic award calculated in accordance with subsections (3) and (4) shall be reduced by the appropriate fraction.

(6) In subsection (5) "the specified anniversary" in relation to a man means the sixty-fourth anniversary of the day of his birth, and in relation to a woman means the fifty-ninth anniversary of the day of her birth, and "the appropriate fraction" means the fraction of which—
(a) the numerator is the number of whole months reckoned from the specified anniversary in the period beginning with that anniversary and ending with the effective date of termination; and
(b) the denominator is twelve.

(7) [*Repealed by the Employment Act* 1982 (c. 46), *s*.4(2), *Sched.* 4.]

[(7A) Where the tribunal finds that the complainant has unreasonably refused an offer by the employer which if accepted would have the effect of reinstating the complainant in his employment in all respects as if he had not been dismissed, the tribunal shall reduce or further reduce the amount of the basic award to such extent as it considers just and equitable having regard to that finding.

(7B) Where the tribunal considers that any conduct of the complainant before the dismissal (or, where the dismissal was with notice, before the notice was given), [. . .], was such that it would be just and equitable to reduce or further reduce the amount of the basic award to any extent, the tribunal shall reduce or further reduce that amount accordingly.]

[(7C) Subsection (7B) shall not apply where the reason or principal reason for the dismissal was that the employee was redundant unless the dismissal is to be regarded as unfair by virtue of section 59(*a*), and in that event shall apply only to so much of the basic award as is payable because of subsection (4A).]

(8) [. . .]

(9) The amount of the basic award shall be reduced or, as the case may be, be further reduced, by the amount of any redundancy payment awarded by the tribunal under Part VI in respect of the same dismissal or of any payment made by the employer to the employee on the ground that the dismissal was by reason of redundancy, whether in pursuance of Part VI or otherwise.

AMENDMENTS

Paras. (*ba*) and (*bb*) in subs. (1) were added, and paras. (*b*) and (*c*) in subs. (3)(substituted, by the Employment Act 1980 (c. 42), s.9. Subss. (7A) and (7B) were added by *ibid.*; and para. (1)(*c*) and subs. (8) ceased to have effect as a result of *ibid.*, s.9, Sched. 2. The words omitted from subs. (3)(*a*) and (*b*) and from subs. (7B) were repealed by the Employment Act 1982 (c. 46), Scheds. 2 and 4. Subss. 4A, 4B and 7C were inserted by *ibid.*, s.4(2).

Calculation of compensatory award

74.—(1) Subject to sections 75 and 76, the amount of the compensatory award shall be such amount as the tribunal considers just and equitable in all the circumstances having regard to the loss sustained by the complainant in consequence of the dismissal in so far as that loss is attributable to action taken by the employer.

(2) The said loss shall be taken to include—
   (*a*) any expenses reasonably incurred by the complainant in consequence of the dismissal, and
   (*b*) subject to subsection (3), loss of any benefit which he might reasonably be expected to have had but for the dismissal.

(3) The said loss, in respect of any loss of any entitlement or potential entitlement to, or expectation of, a payment on account of dismissal by reason of redundancy, whether in pursuance of Part VI or otherwise, shall include only the loss referable to the amount, if any, by which the amount of that payment would have exceeded the amount of a basic award (apart from any reduction under [section 73(7A) to (9)]) in respect of the same dismissal.

(4) In ascertaining the said loss the tribunal shall apply the same rule concerning the duty of a person to mitigate his loss as applies to damages recoverable under the common law of England and Wales or of Scotland, as the case may be.

(5) In determining, for the purposes of subsection (1), how far any loss

sustained by the complainant was attributable to action taken by the employer no account shall be taken of any pressure which, by calling, organising, procuring or financing a strike or other industrial action, or threatening to do so, was exercised on the employer to dismiss the employee, and that question shall be determined as if no such pressure had been exercised.

(6) Where the tribunal finds that the dismissal was to any extent caused or contributed to by any action of the complainant it shall reduce the amount of the compensatory award by such proportion as it considers just and equitable having regard to that finding.

(7) If the amount of any payment made by the employer to the employee on the ground that the dismissal was by reason of redundancy, whether in pursuance of Part VI or otherwise, exceeds the amount of the basic award which would be payable but for section 73(9) that excess shall go to reduce the amount of the compensatory award.

Limit on compensation

75.—(1) The amount of compensation awarded to a person under section 71(1) or of a compensatory award to a person calculated in accordance with section 74 shall not exceed [£7,500].   1–507

(2) The Secretary of State may by order increase the said limit of £5,200 or that limit as from time to time increased under this subsection, but no such order shall be made unless a draft of the order has been laid before Parliament and approved by a resolution of each House of Parliament.

(3) It is hereby declared for the avoidance of doubt that the limit imposed by this section applies to the amount which the industrial tribunal would, apart from this section, otherwise award in respect of the subject matter of the complant after taking into account any payment made by the respondent to the complainant in respect of that matter and any reduction in the amount of the award required by any enactment or rule of law.

AMENDMENT
The figure in square brackets was substituted by the Unfair Dismissal (Increase of Compensatory Limit) Order 1982 (S.I. 1982 No. 1868).

[Calculation of special award]

75A.—(1) Subject to the following provisions of this section, the amount of the special award shall be—   1–508

(*a*) one week's pay multiplied by 104, or
(*b*) £10,000,

whichever is the greater, but shall not exceed £20,000.

(2) If the award of compensation is made under section 71(2)(*a*) then, unless the employer satisfies the tribunal that it was not practicable to comply with the preceding order under section 69, the amount of the special award shall be increased to—

(*a*) one week's pay multiplied by 156, or
(*b*) £15,000.

whichever is the greater, but subject to the following provisions of this section.

(3) In a case where the amount of the basic award is reduced under section 73(5), the amount of the special award shall be reduced by the same fraction.

(4) Where the tribunal considers that any conduct of the complainant

before the dismissal (or, where the dismissal was with notice, before the notice was given) was such that it would be just and equitable to reduce or further reduce the amount of the special award to any extent, the tribunal shall reduce or further reduce that amount accordingly.

(5) Where the tribunal finds that the complainant has unreasonably—
- (a) prevented an order under section 69 from being complied with; or
- (b) refused an offer by the employer (made otherwise than in compliance with such an order) which if accepted would have the effect of reinstating the complainant in his employment in all respects as if he had not been dismissed;

the tribunal shall reduce or further reduce the amount of the special award to such extent as it considers just and equitable having regard to that finding.

(6) Where the employer has engaged a permanent replacement for the complainant, the tribunal shall not take that fact into account in determining, for the purposes of subsection (2), whether it was practicable to comply with an order under section 69 unless the employer shows that it was not practicable for him to arrange for the complainant's work to be done without engaging a permanent replacement.

(7) The Secretary of State may by order increase any of the sums of £10,000, £20,000 and £15,000 specified in subsections (1) and (2), or any of those sums as from time to time increased under this subsection, but no such order shall be made unless a draft of the order has been laid before Parliament and approved by a resolution of each House of Parliament.]

AMENDMENT
This section was inserted by the Employment Act 1982 (c. 46), s.5(3).

Compensation for act which is both sex or racial discrimination (or both) and unfair dismissal

1–509   76.—(1) Where compensation falls to be awarded in respect of any act both under the provisions of this Act, relating to unfair dismissal and under one or both of the following Acts, namely the Sex Discrimination Act 1975 and the Race Relations Act 1976, an industrial tribunal shall not award compensation under any one of those two or, as the case may be, three Acts in respect of any loss or other matter which is or has been taken into account under the other or any other of them by the tribunal or another industrial tribunal in awarding compensation on the same or another complaint in respect of that act.

(2) Without prejudice to section 75 (whether as enacted or as applied by section 65 of the Sex Discrimination Act 1975 or section 56 of the Race Relations Act 1976) in a case to which subsection (1) applies, the aggregate of the following amounts of compensation awarded by an industrial tribunal, that is to say—
- (a) any compensation awarded under the said Act of 1975; and
- (b) any compensation awarded under the said Act 1976; and
- (c) any compensation awarded under section 71(1) or, as the case may be, which is calculated in accordance with section 74;

shall not exceed the limit for the time being imposed by section 75.

[Awards against third parties

1–510   76A.—(1) If in proceedings before an industrial tribunal on a complaint

against an employer under section 67 either the employer or the complainant claims—
  (a) that the employer was induced to dismiss the complainant by pressure which a trade union or other person exercised on the employer by calling, organising, procuring or financing a strike or other industrial action, or by threatening to do so, and
  (b) that the pressure was exercised because the complainant was not a member of any trade union or of a particular trade union or of one of a number of particular trade unions,
the employer or the complainant may request the tribunal to direct that the person who he claims exercised the pressure be joined, or in Scotland sisted, as a party to the proceedings.

(2) A request under subsection (1) shall be granted if it is made before the hearing of the complaint begins, but may be refused if it is made after that time; and no such request may be made after the tribunal has made an award under section 68(2) or an order under section 69.

(3) Where a person has been joined, or in Scotland sisted, as a party to proceedings before an industrial tribunal by virtue of subsection (1) and the tribunal—
  (a) makes an award of compensation under section 68(2) or 71(2)(a) or (b), but
  (b) finds that the claim mentioned in subsection (1) is well founded,
the award may be made against the person instead of against the employer, or partly against that person and partly against the employer, as the tribunal may consider just and equitable in the circumstances.]

AMENDMENT
  This section was substituted by the Employment Act 1982 (c.46), s.7.

. . . . . .

Interim relief

Interim relief pending determination of complaint of unfair dismissal

77.—[(1) An employee who presents a complaint to an industrial tribunal under section 67 alleging that the dismissal is to be regarded as unfair by virtue of section 58 may apply to the tribunal for an order under the following provisions of this section.]

(2) An industrial tribunal shall not entertain an application under this section unless—
  (a) it is presented to the tribunal before the end of the period of seven days immediately following the effective date of termination (whether before, on or after that date); and
  (b) [in a case in which the employee relies on section 58(1)(a) or (b)] before the end of that period there is also so presented a certificate in writing signed by an authorised official of the independent trade union of which the employee was or had proposed to become a member stating that on the date of the dismissal the employee was or had proposed to become a member of the union and that there appear to be reasonable grounds for supposing that the reason for his dismissal (or, if more than one, the principal reason) was one alleged in the complaint.

(3) An industrial tribunal shall determine an application under this section as soon as practicable after receiving the application and [(where appropriate)] the relevant certificate, but shall, [give at the appropriate time—
    (a) to the employer; and
    (b) in the case of a section 76A request made at least three days before the date of the hearing, to the person to whom the request relates;
a copy of the application and certificate (if any) together with notice of the date, time and place of the hearing.

(3A) In subsection (3)—
    "appropriate time" means—
        (a) in relation to paragraph (a), not later than seven days before the date of the hearing;
        (b) in relation to paragraph (b), as soon as reasonably practicable; and
    "section 76A request" means a request made under section 76A(1) for the tribunal to direct a person to be joined or sisted as a party to the proceedings.]

(4) An industrial tribunal shall not exercise any power it has of postponing the hearing in the case of an application under this section except where the tribunal is satisfied that special circumstances exist which justify it in doing so.

(5) If on hearing an application under this section it appears to an industrial tribunal that it is likely that on determining the complaint to which the application relates the tribunal will find that the complainant [is by virtue of section 58 to be regarded as having been unfairly dismissed] the tribunal shall announce its findings and explain to both parties (if present) what powers the tribunal may exercise on an application under this section and in what circumstances it may exercise them, and shall ask the employer (if present) whether he is willing, pending the determination or settlement of the complaint—
    (a) to reinstate the employee, that is to say, to treat the employee in all respects as if he had not been dismissed; or
    (b) if not, to re-engage him in another job on terms and conditions not less favourable than those which would have been applicable to him if he had not been dismissed.

(6) In subsection (5) "terms and conditions not less favourable than those which would have been applicable to him if he had not been dismissed" means, as regards seniority, pension rights and other similar rights, that the period prior to the dismissal shall be regarded as continuous with his employment following the dismissal.

(7) If the employer states that he is willing to reinstate the employee, the tribunal shall make an order to that effect.

(8) If the employer states that he is willing to re-engage the employee in another job and specifies the terms and conditions on which he is willing to do so, the tribunal shall ask the employee whether he is willing to accept the job on those terms and conditions, and—
    (a) if the employee is willing to accept the job on those terms and conditions, the tribunal shall make an order to that effect; and
    (b) if the employee is unwilling to accept the job on those terms and conditions, then, if the tribunal is of the opinion that the refusal is reasonable, the tribunal shall make an order for the continuation of

his contract of employment, but otherwise the tribunal shall make no order under this section.

(9) If, on the hearing of an application under this section, the employer fails to attend before the tribunal or he states that he is unwilling either to reinstate the employee or re-engage him as mentioned in subsection (5), the tribunal shall make an order for the continuation of the employee's contract of employment.

(10) In this section—

[. . .];

"authorised official", in relation to a trade union, means an official of the union authorised by the union to act for the purposes of this section;

and any reference to the date of dismissal is a reference—

(a) where the employee's contract of employment was terminated by notice (whether given by his employer or by him), to the date on which the employer's notice was given; and

(b) in any other case, to the effective date of termination.

(11) A document purporting to be an authorisation of an official by a trade union to act for the purposes of this section and to be signed on behalf of the union shall be taken to be such an authorisation unless the contrary is proved, and a document purporting to be a certificate signed by such an official shall be taken to be signed by him unless the contrary is proved.

AMENDMENTS

The words in square brackets were substituted by the Employment Act 1982 (c. 46), s.8, and Sched. 3, para. 24. The definition of "appropriate time" in subs. (10) was repealed by the Employment Act 1982, Sched. 4.

Orders for continuation of contract of employment

78.—(1) An order for the continuation of a contract of employment under section 77 shall be an order that the contract of employment, if it has been terminated, shall continue in force as if it had not been terminated and if not, shall on its termination, continue in force, in either case until the determination or settlement of the complaint and only for the purposes of pay or any other benefit derived from the employment, seniority, pension rights and other similar matters and for the purpose of determining for any purpose the period for which the employee has been continuously employed.

1–512

(2) Where the tribunal makes any such order it shall specify is the order the amount which is to be paid by the employer to the employee by way of pay in respect of each normal pay period or part of any such period falling between the date of the dismissal and the determination or settlement of the complaint and, subject to subsection (5), the amount so specified shall be that which the employee could reasonably have been expected to earn during that period or part, and shall be paid, in the case of a payment for any such period falling wholly or partly after the order, on the normal pay day for that period and, in the case of a payment for any past period, within a time so specified.

(3) If an amount is payable by way of pay in pursuance of any such order in respect only of part of a normal pay period the amount shall be calculated by reference to the whole period and be reduced proportionately.

(4) Any payment made to an employee by an employer under his contract of employment, or by way of damages for breach of that contract, in respect of any normal pay period or part of any such period shall go towards discharging the employer's liability in respect of that period under subsection (2), and conversely any payment under subsection (2) in respect of any period shall go towards discharging any liability of the employer under, or in respect of breach of, the contract of employment in respect of that period.

(5) If an employee, on or after being dismissed by his employer, receives a lump sum which, or part of which, is in lieu of wages but is not referable to any normal pay period, the tribunal shall take the payment into account in determining the amount of pay to be payable in pursuance of any such order.

(6) For the purposes of this section the amount which an employee could reasonably have been expected to earn, his normal pay period and the normal pay for each such period shall be determined as if he had not been dismissed.

Supplementary provisions relating to interim relief

79.—(1) At any time between the making of an order by an industrial tribunal under section 77 and the determination or settlement of the complaint to which it relates, the employer or the employee may apply to the tribunal for the revocation or variation of the order on the ground of a relevant change of circumstances since the making of the order, and that section shall apply to the application as it applies to an application for an order under that section except that—

(a) no certificate need be presented to the tribunal under subsection (2)(b), and no copy of the certificate need be given to the employer under subsection (3), of that section; and

(b) in the case of an application by an employer; for the reference in the said subsection (3) to the employer there shall be substituted a reference to the employee.

(2) If on the application of an employee an industrial tribunal is satisfied that the employer has not complied with the terms of an order for the reinstatement or re-engagement of the employee under section 77(7) or (8),—

(a) the tribunal shall make an order for the continuation of the employee's contract of employment and section 78 shall apply to an order under this subsection as it applies to an order for the continuation of a contract of employment under section 77; and

(b) the tribunal shall also order the employer to pay the employee such compensation as the tribunal considers just and equitable in all the circumstances having regard to the infringement of the employee's right to be reinstated or re-engaged in pursuance of the order under section 77(7) or (8) and to any loss suffered by the employee in consequence of the non-compliance.

(3) If on the application of an employee an industrial tribunal is satisfied that the employer has not complied with the terms of an order for the continuation of a contract of employment, then—

(a) if the non-compliance consists of a failure to pay an amount by way of pay specified in the order, the tribunal shall determine the amount of pay owed by the employer to the employee on the date of the determination, and, if on that date the tribunal also determines the employee's complaint that he has been unfairly dismissed by his employer, the tribunal shall specify that amount separately from any other sum awarded to the employee; and

(b) in any other case, the tribunal shall order the employer to pay the employee such compensation as the tribunal considers just and equitable in all the circumstances having regard to any loss suffered by the employee in consequence of the non-compliance.

Teachers in Aided Schools

Teacher in aided school dismissed on requirement of local education authority

80.—(1) Where a teacher in an aided school is dismissed by the governors [. . .] of the school in pursuance of a requirement of the local education authority under paragraph (*a*) of the proviso to section 24(2) of the Education Act 1944, this Part shall have effect in relation to the dismissal as if— 1–514

(*a*) the local education authority had at all material times been the teacher's employer, and

(*b*) the local education authority had dismissed him, and the reason or principal reason for which they did so had been the reason or principal reason for which they required his dismissal.

(2) For the purposes of a complaint under section 67 as applied by this section—

(*a*) section 71(2)(*b*) shall have effect as if for the words "not practicable to comply" there were substituted the words "not practicable for the local education authority to permit compliance"; and

(*b*) section 74(5) shall have effect as if any reference to the employer were a reference to the local education authority.

AMENDMENT

The words omitted from subs. (1) were repealed by the Education Act 1980 (c.20); Sched. 1.

Right to Redundancy Payment

General provisions as to right to redundancy payment

81.—(1) Where an employee who has been continuously employed for the requisite period— 1–515

(*a*) is dismissed by his employer by reason of redundancy, or

(*b*) is laid off or kept on short-time to the extent specified in subsection (1) of section 88 and complies with the requirements of that section,

then, subject to the following provisions of this Act, the employer shall be liable to pay to him a sum (in this Act referred to as a "redundancy payment") calculated in accordance with Schedules 4, 13 and 14.

(2) For the purposes of this Act an employee who is dismissed shall be taken to be dismissed by reason of redundancy if the dismissal is attributable wholly or mainly to—

(*a*) the fact that his employer has ceased, or intends to cease, to carry on the business for the purposes of which the employee was employed by him, or has ceased, or intends to cease, to carry on that business in the place where the employee was so employed, or

(b) the fact that the requirements of that business for employees to carry out work of a particular kind, or for employees to carry out work of a particular kind in the place where he was so employed, have ceased or diminished or are expected to cease or diminish.

For the purposes of this subsection, the business of the employer together with the business or businesses of his associated employers shall be treated as one unless either of the conditions specified in this subsection would be satisfied without so treating those businesses.

[(2A) For the purposes of subsection (2) the activities carried on by a local education authority with respect to the schools maintained by it and the activities carried on by the governors of those schools shall be treated as one business unless either of the conditions specified in subsection (2) would be satisfied without so treating them.]

(3) In subsection (2), "cease" means cease either permanently or temporarily and from whatsoever cause, and "diminish" has a corresponding meaning.

(4) For the purposes of subsection (1), the requisite period is the period of two years ending with the relevant date [. . .].

AMENDMENTS

The words omitted from subs. (4) were repealed by the Employment Act 1982 (c. 46), Scheds. 2 and 4. Subs. (2A) was inserted by *ibid.*, Sched. 3.

General exclusions from right to redundancy payment

82.—(1) An employee shall not be entitled to a redundancy payment if immediately before the relevant date the employee—

(a) if a man, has attained the age of sixty-five, or
(b) if a woman, has attained the age of sixty.

(2) Except as provided by section 92, an employee shall not be entitled to a redundancy payment by reason of dismissal where his employer, being entitled to terminate his contract of employment without notice by reason of the employee's conduct, terminates it either—

(a) without notice, or
(b) by giving shorter notice than that which, in the absence of such conduct, the employer would be required to give to terminate the contract, or
(c) by giving notice (not being such shorter notice as is mentioned in paragraph (b)) which includes, or is accompanied by, a statement in writing that the employer would, by reason of the employee's conduct, be entitled to terminate the contract without notice.

(3) If an employer makes an employee an offer (whether in writing or not) before the ending of his employment under the previous contract to renew his contract of employment, or to re-engage him under a new contract of employment, so that the renewal or re-engagement would take effect either immediately on the ending of his employment under the previous contract or after an interval of nor more than four weeks thereafter, the provisions of subsections (5) and (6) shall have effect.

(4) For the purposes of the application of subsection (3) to a contract under which the employment ends on a Friday, Saturday or Sunday—

(a) the renewal or re-engagement shall be treated as taking effect immediately on the ending of the employment under the previous contract if it takes effect on or before the next Monday after that Friday, Saturday or Sunday; and

(b) the interval of four weeks shall be calculated as if the employment had ended on that Monday.

(5) If an employer makes an employee such an offer as is referred to in subsection (3) and either—
  (a) the provisions of the contract as renewed, or of the new contract, as to the capacity and place in which he would be employed, and as to the other terms and conditions of his employment, would not differ from the corresponding provisions of the previous contract; or
  (b) the first-mentioned provisions would differ (wholly or in part) from those corresponding provisions, but the offer constitutes an offer of suitable employment in relation to the employee;
and in either case the employee unreasonably refuses that offer, he shall not be entitled to a redundancy payment by reason of his dismissal.

(6) If an employee's contract of employment is renewed, or he is re-engaged under a new contract of employment, in pursuance of such an offer as is referred to in subsection (3), and the provisions of the contract as renewed, or of the new contract, as to the capacity and place in which he is employed, and as to the other terms and conditions of his employment, differ (wholly or in part) from the corresponding provisions of the previous contract but the employment is suitable in relation to the employee, and during the trial period referred to in section 84 the employee unreasonably terminates the contract, or unreasonably gives notice to terminate it and the contract is thereafter, in consequence, terminated, he shall not be entitled to a redundancy payment by reason of his dismissal from employment under the previous contract.

(7) Any reference in this section to re-engagement by the employer shall be construed as including a reference to re-engagement by the employer or by any associated employer, and any reference in this section to an offer made by the employer shall be construed as including a reference to an offer made by an associated employer.

Dismissal by employer

83.—(1) In this Part, except as respects a case to which section 86 applies "dismiss" and "dismissal" shall, subject to sections 84, 85 and 93, be construed in accordance with subsection (2).

(2) An employee shall be treated as dismissed by his employer if, but only if,—
  (a) the contract under which he is employed by the employer is terminated by the employer, whether it is so terminated by notice or without notice, or
  (b) where under that contract he is employed for a fixed term, that term expires without being renewed under the same contract, or
  (c) the employee terminates that contract with or without notice, in circumstances (not falling within section 92(4) such that he is entitled to terminate it without notice by reason of the employer's conduct.

Renewal of contract or re-engagement

84.—(1) If an employee's contract of employment is renewed, or he is re-engaged under a new contract of employment in pursuance of an offer (whether in writing or not) made by his employer before the ending of his employment under the previous contract, and the renewal or re-engagement takes effect either immediately on the ending of that employment or after an interval of not more than four weeks thereafter, then, subejct to subsections (3) to (6), the employee shall not be regarded as having been dismissed by his employer by reason of the ending of his employment under the previous contract.

(2) For the purposes of the application of subsection (1) to a contract under which the employment ends on a Friday, Saturday or Sunday—
- (*a*) the renewal or re-engagement shall be treated as taking effect immediately on the ending of the employment if it takes effect on or before the Monday after that Friday, Saturday or Sunday, and
- (*b*) the interval of four weeks referred to in that subsection shall be calculated as if the employment had ended on that Monday.

(3) If, in a case to which subsection (1) applies, the provisions of the contract as renewed, or of the new contract, as to the capacity and place in which the employee is employed, and as to the other terms and conditions of his employment, differ (wholly or in part) from the corresponding provisions of the previous contract, there shall be a trial period in relation to the contract as renewed, or the new contract (whether or not there has been a previous trial under this section).

(4) The trial period shall begin with the ending of the employee's employment under the previous contract and end with the expiration of the period of four weeks beginning with the date on which the employee starts work under the contract as renewed, or the new contract, or such longer period as may be agreed in accordance with the next following subsection for the purposes of retraining the employee for employment under that contract.

(5) Any such agreement shall—
- (*a*) be made between the employer and the employee or his representative before the employee starts work under the contract as renewed or, as the case may be, the new contract;
- (*b*) be in writing;
- (*c*) specify the date of the end of the trial period; and
- (*d*) specify the terms and conditions of employment which will apply in the employee's case after the end of that period.

(6) If during the trial period—
- (*a*) the employee, for whatever reason, terminates the contract, or gives notice to terminate it and the contract is thereafter, in consequence, terminated; or
- (*b*) the employer, for a reason connected with or arising out of the change to the renewed, or new, employment, terminates the contract, or gives notice to terminate it and the contract is thereafter, in consequence, terminated,

then, unless the employee's contract of employment is again renewed, or he is again re-engaged under a new contract of employment, in circumstances such that subsection (1) again applies, he shall be treated as having been dismissed on the date on which his employment under the previous contract or, if there has been more than one trial period, the original contract ended for the reason for which he was then dismissed or would have been dismissed had the offer (or original offer) of renewed, or new, employment not been made, or, as the case may be, for the reason which resulted in that offer being made.

(7) Any reference in this section to re-engagement by the employer shall be construed as including a reference to re-engagement by the employer or by any associated employer, and any reference in this section to an offer made by the employer shall be construed as including a reference to an offer made by an associated employer.

Employee anticipating expiry of employer's notice
    85.—(1) The provisions of this section shall have effect where—   1–519
      (*a*) an employer gives notice to an employee to terminate his contract of employment, and
      (*b*) at a time within the obligatory period of that notice, the employee gives notice in writing to the employer to terminate the contract of employment on a date earlier than the date on which the employer's notice is due to expire.

(2) Subject to the following provisions of this section, in the circumstances specified in subsection (1) the employee shall, for the purposes of this Part, be taken to be dismissed by his employer.

(3) If, before the employer's notice is due to expire, the employer gives him notice in writing—
      (*a*) requiring him to withdraw his notice terminating the contract of employment as mentioned in subsection (1)(*b*) and to continue in the employment until the date on which the employer's notice expires, and
      (*b*) stating that, unless he does so, the employer will contest any liability to pay to him a redundancy payment in respect of the termination of his contract of employment,

but the employee does not comply with the requirements of that notice, the employee shall not be entitled to a redundancy payment by virtue of subsection (2) except as provided by subsection (4).

(4) Where, in the circumstances specified in subsection (1), the employer has given notice to the employee under subsection (3), and on a reference to a tribunal it appears to the tribunal, having regard both to the reasons for which the employee seeks to leave the employment and those for which the employer requires him to continue in it, to be just and equitable that the employee should receive the whole or part of any redundancy payment to which he would have been entitled apart from subsection (3), the tribunal may determine that the employer shall be liable to pay to the employee—
      (*a*) the whole of the redundancy payment to which the employee would have been so entitled, or
      (*b*) such part of that redundancy payment as the tribunal thinks fit.

(5) In this section—
      (*a*) if the actual period of the employer's notice (that is to say, the period beginning at the time when the notice is given and ending at the time when it expires) is equal to the minimum period which (whether by virtue of any enactment or otherwise) is required to be given by the employer to terminate the contract of employment, "the obligatory period", in relation to that notice, means the actual period of the notice;
      (*b*) in any other case, "the obligatory period", in relation to an

employer's notice, means that period which, being equal to the minimum period referred to in paragraph (*a*), expires at the time when the employer's notice expires.

Failure to permit woman to return to work after confinement treated as dismissal

1–520   **86.** Where an employee is entitled to return to work and has exercised her right to return in accordance with section 47 but is not permitted to return to work, then she shall be treated for the purposes of the provisions of this Part as if she had been employed until the notified day of return, and, if she would not otherwise be so treated, as having been continuously employed until that day, and as if she had been dismissed with effect from that day for the reason for which she was not permitted to return.

Lay-off and short-time

1–521   **87.**—(1) Where an employee is employed under a contract on such terms and conditions that his remuneration thereunder depends on his being provided by the employer with work of the kind which he is employed to do, he shall, for the purposes of this Part, be taken to be laid off for any week in respect of which, by reason that the employer does not provide such work for him, he is not entitled to any remuneration under the contract.

(2) Where by reason of a diminution in the work provided for an employee by his employer (being work of a kind which under his contract the employee is employed to do) the employee's remuneration for any week is less than half a week's pay, he shall for the purposes of this Part be taken to be kept on short-time for that week.

Right to redundancy payment by reason of lay-off or short-time

1–522   **88.**—(1) An employee shall not be entitled to a redundancy payment by reason of being laid off or kept on short-time unless he gives notice in writing to his employer indicating (in whatsoever terms) his intention to claim a redundancy payment in respect of lay-off or short-time (in this Act referred to as a "notice of intention to claim") and, before the service of that notice, either—
   (*a*) he has been laid off or kept on short-time for four or more consecutive weeks of which the last before the service of the notice ended on the date of service thereof or ended not more than four weeks before that date, or
   (*b*) he has been laid off or kept on short-time for a series of six or more weeks (of which not more than three were consecutive) within a period of thirteen weeks, where the last week of the series before the service of the notice ended on the date of service thereof or ended not more than four weeks before that date.

(2) Where an employee has given notice of intention to claim,—
   (*a*) he shall not be entitled to a redundancy payment in pursuance of that notice unless he terminates his contract of employment by a week's notice which (whether given before or after or at the same time as the notice of intention to claim) is given before the end of the period allowed for the purposes of this paragraph (as specified in subsection (5) of section 89), and

(b) he shall not be entitled to a redundancy payment in pursuance of the notice of intention to claim if he is dismissed by his employer (but without prejudice to any right to a redundancy payment by reason of the dismissal):

Provided that, if the employee is required by his contract of employment to give more than a week's notice to terminate the contract, the reference in paragraph (a) to a week's notice shall be construed as a reference to the minimum notice which he is so required to give.

(3) Subject to subsection (4), an employee shall not be entitled to a redundancy payment in pursuance of a notice of intention to claim if, on the date of service of that notice, it was reasonably to be expected that the employee (if he continued to be employed by the same employer) would, not later than four weeks after that date, enter upon a period of employment of not less than thirteen weeks during which he would not be laid off or kept on short-time for any week.

(4) Subsection (3) shall not apply unless, within seven days after the service of the notice of intention to claim, the employer gives to the employee notice in writing that he will contest any liability to pay to him a redundancy payment in pursuance of the notice of intention to claim.

Supplementary provisions relating to redundancy payments in respect of lay-off or short-time

89.—(1) If, in a case where, an employee gives notice of intention to claim and the employer gives notice under section 88(4) (in this section referred to as a "counter-notice"), the employee continues or has continued, during the next four weeks after the date of service of the notice of intention to claim, to be employed by the same employer, and he is or has been laid off or kept on short-time for each of those weeks, it shall be conclusively presumed that the condition specified in subsection (3) of section 88 was not fulfilled.

(2) For the purposes of both subsection (1) of section 88 and subsection (1) of this section, it is immaterial whether a series of weeks (whether it is four weeks, or four or more weeks, or six or more weeks) consists wholly of weeks for which the employee is laid off or wholly of weeks for which he is kept on short-time of partly of the one and partly of the other.

(3) For the purposes mentioned in subsection (2), no account shall be taken of any week for which an employee is laid off or kept on short-time where the lay-off or short-time is wholly or mainly attributable to a strike or a lock-out (within the meaning of paragraph 24 of Schedule 13) whether the strike or lock-out is in the trade or industry in which the employee is employed or not and whether it is in Great Britain or elsewhere.

(4) Where the employer gives a counter-notice within seven days after the service of a notice of intention to claim, and does not withdraw the counter-notice by a subsequent notice in writing, the employee shall not be entitled to a redundancy payment in pursuance of the notice of intention to claim except in accordance with a decision of an industrial tribunal.

(5) The period allowed for the purposes of subsection (2)(a) of section 88 is as follows, that is to say—
  (a) if the employer does not give a counter-notice within seven days after the service of the notice of intention to claim, that period is three weeks after the end of those seven days;
  (b) if the employer gives a counter-notice within those seven days, but

withdraws it by a subsequent notice in writing, that period is three weeks after the service of the notice of withdrawal;

(c) if the employer gives a counter-notice within those seven days and does not so withdraw it, and a question as to the right of the employee to a redundancy payment in pursuance of the notice of intention to claim is referred to a tribunal that period is three weeks after the tribunal has notified to the employee its decision on that reference.

(6) For the purposes of paragraph (c) of subsection (5) no account shall be taken of any appeal against the decision of the tribunal, or of any requirement to the tribunal to state a case for the opinion of the High Court or the Court of Session, or of any proceedings or decision in consequence of such an appeal or requirement.

The relevant date

90.—(1) Subject to the following provisions of this section, for the purposes of the provisions of this Act so far as they relate to redundancy payments, "the relevant date", in relation to the dismissal of an employee—

(a) where his contract of employment is terminated by notice, whether given by his employer or by the employee, means the date on which that notice expires;

(b) where his contract of employment is terminated without notice, means the date on which the termination takes effect;

(c) where he is employed under a contract for a fixed term and that term expires as mentioned in subsection (2)(b) of section 83, means the date on which that term expires;

(d) where he is treated, by virtue of subsection (6) of section 84, as having been dismissed on the termination of his employment under a previous contract, means—

(i) for the purposes of section 101, the date which is the relevant date as defined by paragraph (a), (b) or (c) in relation to the renewed, or new, contract, or, where there has been more than one trial period under section 84, the last such contract; and

(ii) for the purposes of any other provision, the date which is the relevant date as defined by paragraph (a), (b) or (c) in relation to the previous contract, or, where there has been more than one trial period under section 84, the original contract; and

(e) where he is taken to be dismissed by virtue of section 85(2), means the date on which the employee's notice to terminate his contract of employment expires.

(2) "The relevant date", in relation to a notice of intention to claim or a right to a redundancy payment in pursuance of such a notice,—

(a) in a case falling within paragraph (a) of subsection (1) of section 88, means the date on which the last of the four or more consecutive weeks before the service of the notice came to an end, and

(b) in a case falling within paragraph (b) of that subsection means the date on which the last of the series of six or more weeks before the service of the notice came to an end.

(3) Where the notice required to be given by an employer to terminate a contract of employment by section 49(1) would, if duly given when notice of termination was given by the employer, or (where no notice was given) when the contract of employment was terminated by the employer, expire

on a date later than the relevant date as defined by subsection (1), then for the purposes of section 81(4) and paragraph 1 of Schedule 4 and paragraph 8(4) of Schedule 14, that later date shall be treated as the relevant date in relation to the dismissal.

Reference of questions to tribunal

91.—(1) Any question arising under this Part as to the right of an employee to a redundancy payment, or as to the amount of a redundancy payment, shall be referred to and determined by an industrial tribunal.

(2) For the purposes of any such reference, an employee who has been dismissed by his employer shall, unless the contrary is proved, be presumed to have been so dismissed by reason of redundancy.

(3) In relation to lay-off or short-time, the questions which may be referred to and determined by an industrial tribunal, as mentioned in subsection (1), shall include any question whether an employee will become entitled to a redundancy payment if he is not dismissed by his employer and he terminates his contract of employment as mentioned in subsection (2)(*a*) of section 88; and any such question shall for the purposes of this Part be taken to be a question as to the right of the employee to a redundancy payment.

Special provisions as to termination of contract in cases of misconduct or industrial dispute

92.—(1) Where at any such time as is mentioned in subsection (2), an employee who—
  (*a*) has been given notice by his employer to terminate his contract of employment, or
  (*b*) has given notice to his employer under subsection (1) of section 88,
takes part in a strike, in such circumstances that the employer is entitled, by reason of his taking part in the strike, to treat the contract of employment as terminable without notice, and the employer for that reason terminates the contract as mentioned in subsection (2) of section 82, that subsection shall not apply to that termination of the contract.

(2) The times referred to in subsection (1) are—
  (*a*) in a case falling within paragraph (*a*) of that subsection any time within the obligatory period of the employer's notice (as defined by section 85(5)), and
  (*b*) in a case falling within paragraph (*b*) of subsection (1), any time after the service of the notice mentioned in that paragraph.

(3) Where at any such time as is mentioned in subsection (2) an employee's contract of employment, otherwise than by reason of his taking part in a strike, is terminated by his employer in the circumstances specified in subsection (2) of section 82, and is so terminated as mentioned therein, and on a reference to an industrial tribunal it appears to the tribunal, in the circumstances of the case, to be just and equitable that the employee should receive the whole or part of any redundancy payment to which he would have been entitled apart from section 82(2), the tribunal may determine that the employer shall be liable to pay to the employee—
  (*a*) the whole of the redundancy payment to which the employee would have been so entitled, or
  (*b*) such part of that redundancy payment as the tribunal thinks fit.

(4) Where an employee terminates his contract of employment without notice, being entitled to do so by reason of a lock-out by his employer, section 83(2)(c) shall not apply to that termination of the contract.

(5) In this section "strike" and "lock-out" each has the meaning given by paragraph 24 of Schedule 13.

Implied or constructive termination of contract

93.—(1) Where in accordance with any enactment or rule of law—
   (a) any act on the part of an employer, or
   (b) any event affecting an employer (including, in the case of an individual, his death),

operates so as to terminate a contract under which an employee is employed by him, that act or event shall for the purposes of this Part be treated as a termination of the contract by the employer, if apart from this subsection it would not constitute a termination of the contract by him and, in particular, the provisions of sections 83, 84 and 90 shall apply accordingly.

(2) Where subsection (1) applies, and the employee's contract of employment is not renewed and he is not re-engaged under a new contract of employment, so as to be treated by virtue of section 84(1), as not having been dismissed, he shall, without prejudice to section 84(6), be taken for the purposes of this Part to be dismissed by reason of redundancy if the circumstances in which his contract is not so renewed and he is not so re-engaged are wholly or mainly attributable to one or other of the facts specified in paragraphs (a) and (b) of section 81(2).

(3) For the purposes of subsection (2), section 81(2)(a), in so far as it relates to the employer ceasing or intending to cease to carry on the business, shall be construed as if the reference to the employer included a reference to any person to whom, in consequence of the act or event in question, power to dispose of the business has passed.

(4) In this section, any reference to section 84(1) includes a reference to that subsection as applied by section 94(2) or as so applied and (where appropriate) modified by section 95(2), and where section 84(1), renewal of or re-engagement under a contract of employment shall be construed as including references to renewal of or re-engagement in employment otherwise than under a contract of employment.

Change of ownership of business

94.—(1) The provisions of this section shall have effect where—
   (a) a change occurs (whether by virtue of a sale or other disposition or by operation of law) in the ownership of a business for the purposes of which a person is employed, or of a part of such a business, and
   (b) in connection with that change the person by whom the employee is employed immediately before the change occurs (in this section referred to as "the previous owner") terminates the employee's contract of employment, whether by notice or without notice.

(2) If, by agreement with the employee, the person who immediately after the change occurs is the owner of the business, or of the part of the business in question, as the case may be (in this section referred to as "the new owner"), renews the employee's contract of employment (with the substitution of the new owner for the previous owner) or re-engages him under a new contract of employment, sections 84 and 90 shall have effect

as if the renewal or re-engagement had been a renewal or re-engagement by the previous owner (without any substitution of the new owner for the previous owner).

(3) If the new owner offers to renew the employee's contract of employment (with the substitution of the new owner for the previous owner) or to re-engage him under a new contract of employment, subsections (3) to (6) of section 82 shall have effect, subject to subsection (4), in relation to that offer as they would have had effect in relation to the like offer made by the previous owner.

(4) For the purposes of the operation, in accordance with subsection (3), of subsections (3) to (6) of section 82 in relation to an offer made by the new owner—
- (*a*) the offer shall not be treated as one whereby the provisions of the contract as renewed, or of the new contract, as the case may be, would differ from the corresponding provisions of the contract as in force immediately before the dismissal by reason only that the new owner would be substituted for the previous owner as the employer, and
- (*b*) no account shall be taken of that substitution in determining whether the refusal of the offer was unreasonable or, as the case may be, whether the employee acted reasonably in terminating the renewed, or new, employment during the trial period referred to in section 84.

(5) The preceding provisions of this section shall have effect (subject to the necessary modifications) in relation to a case where—
- (*a*) the person by whom a business, or part of a business, is owned immediately before a change is one of the persons by whom (whether as partners, trustees or otherwise) it is owned immediately after the change, or
- (*b*) the persons by whom a business, or part of a business, is owned immediately before a change (whether as partners, trustees or otherwise) include a person by whom, or include one or more of the persons by whom, it is owned immediately after the change,

as those provisions have effect where the previous owner and the new owner are wholly different persons.

(6) Sections 82(7) and 84(7) shall not apply in any case to which this section applies.

(7) Nothing in this section shall be construed as requiring any variation of a contract of employment by agreement between the parties to be treated as constituting a termination of the contract.

Transfer to Crown employment

95.—(1) Section 94 shall apply to a transfer of functions from a person not acting on behalf of the Crown (in this section referred to as the transferor) to a government department or any other officer or body exercising functions on behalf of the Crown (in this section referred to as the transferee) as that section applies to a transfer of a business, but with the substitution for references to the previous owner and new owner of references to the transferor and transferee respectively.

(2) In so far as the renewal or re-engagement of the employee by the transferee is in employment otherwise than under a contract of employment—
- (*a*) references in section 94 (and in sections 82(4) to (6), 84 and 90 as

they apply by virtue of that section) to a contract of employment or to the terms of such a contract shall be construed as references to employment otherwise than under such a contract and to the terms of such employment; and

(b) references in subsection (4) of sections 94, as modified by subsection (1) of this section, to the substitution of the transferee for the transferor shall be construed as references to the substitution of employment by the transferee otherwise than under a contract of employment for employment by the transferor under such a contract.

Exemption orders

1–530   **96.**—(1) If at any time there is in force an agreement between one or more employers or organisations of employers and one or more trade unions representing employees, whereby employees to whom the agreement applies have a right in certain circumstances to payments on the termination of their contracts of employment, and, on the application of all the parties to the agreement, the Secretary of State, having regard to the provisions of the agreement, is satisfied that section 81 should not apply to those employees, he may make an order under this section in respect of that agreement.

(2) The Secretary of State shall not make an order under this section in respect of an agreement unless the agreement indicates (in whatsoever terms) the willingness of the parties to it to submit to an industrial tribunal such questions as are mentioned in paragraph (b) of subsection (3).

(3) Where an order under this section is in force in respect of an agreement—

(a) section 81 shall not have effect in relation to any employee who immediately before the relevant date is an employee to whom the agreement applies, but

(b) section 91 shall have effect in relation to any question arising under the agreement as to the right of an employee to a payment on the termination of his employment, or as to the amount of such a payment, as if the payment were a redundancy payment and the question arose under this Part.

(4) Any order under this section may be revoked by a subsequent order thereunder, whether in pursuance of an application made by all or any of the parties to the agreement in question or without any such application.

. . . . . .

Exclusion or reduction of redundancy payment on account of pension rights

1–531   **98.**—(1) The Secretary of State shall by regulations make provision for excluding the right to a redundancy payment, or reducing the amount of any redundancy payment, in such cases as may be prescribed by the regulations, being cases in which an employee has (whether by virtue of any statutory provision or otherwise) a right or claim (whether legally enforceable or not) to a periodical payment or lump sum by way of pension, gratuity or superannuation allowance which is to be paid by reference to his employment by a particular employer and is to be paid, or to begin to be paid, at the time when he leaves that employment or within such period thereafter as may be prescribed by the regulations.

(2) Provision shall be made by any such regulations for securing that the

right to a redundancy payment shall not be excluded, and that the amount of a redundancy payment shall not be reduced, by reason of any right or claim to a periodical payment or lump sum, in so far as that payment or lump sum represents such compensation as is mentioned in section 118(1) and is payable under a statutory provision, whether made or passed before, on or after the passing of this Act.

(3) In relation to any case where, under section 85 or 92 or 110, an industrial tribunal determines that an employer is liable to pay part (but not the whole) of a redundancy payment, any reference in this section to a redundancy payment, or to the amount of a redundancy payment, shall be construed as a reference to that part of the redundancy payment, or to the amount of that part, as the case may be.

Public offices, etc.

99.—(1) Without prejudice to any exemption or immunity of the Crown, section 81 shall not apply to any person in respect of any employment which—

    (*a*) is employment in a public office for the purposes of section 38 of the Superannuation Act 1965, or

    (*b*) whether by virtue of that Act or otherwise, is treated for the purposes of pensions and other superannuation benefits as service in the civil service of the State, or

    (*c*) is employed by any such body as is specified in Schedule 5.

(2) Without prejudice to any exemption or immunity of the Crown, section 81 shall not apply to any person in respect of his employment in any capacity under the Government of an overseas territory (as defined by section 114).

1–532

Domestic servants

100.—(1) For the purposes of the application of the provisions of this Part to an employee who is employed as a domestic servant in a private household, those provisions (except section 94) shall apply as if the household were a business and the maintenance of the household were the carrying on of that business by the employer.

(2) [. . .] section 81 shall not apply to any person in respect of employment as a domestic servant in a private household, where the employer is the father, mother, grandfather, grandmother, stepfather, son, daughter, grandson, grand-daughter, stepson, stepdaughter, brother, sister, half-brother, or half-sister of the employee.

1–533

AMENDMENT

    The words omitted from subs. (2) were repealed by the Employment Act 1982 (c. 46), Sched. 4.

Claims for redundancy payments

101.—(1) Notwithstanding anything in the preceding provisions of this Part, an employee shall not be entitled to a redundancy payment unless, before the end of the period of six months beginning with the relevant date—

    (*a*) the payment has been agreed and paid, or

1–534

(b) the employee has made a claim for the payment by notice in writing given to the employer, or
(c) a question as to the right of the employee to the payment, or as to the amount of the payment, has been referred to an industrial tribunal, or
(d) a complaint relating to his dismissal has been presented by the employee under section 67.

(2) An employee shall not by virtue of subsection (1) lose his right to a redundancy payment if, during the period of six months immediately following the period mentioned in that subsection, the employee—
(a) makes such a claim as is referred to in paragraph (b) of that subsection,
(b) refers to a tribunal such as is referred to in paragraph (c) of that subsection, or
(c) makes such a complaint as is referred to in paragraph (d) of that subsection,

and it appears to the tribunal to be just and equitable that the employee should receive a redundancy payment having regard to the reason shown by the employee for his failure to take any such step as is referred to in paragraph (a), (b) or (c) of this subsection within the period mentioned in subsection (1), and to all the other relevant circumstances.

Written particulars of redundancy payment

1–535
102.—(1) On making any redundancy payment, otherwise than in pursuance of a decision of a tribunal which specifies the amount of the payment to be made, the employer shall give to the employee a written statement indicating how the amount of the payment has been calculated.

(2) Any employer who without reasonable excuse fails to comply with subsection (1) shall be guilty of an offence and liable on summary conviction to a fine not exceeding £20.

(3) If an employer fails to comply with the requirements of subsection (1), then (without prejudice to any proceedings for an offence under subsection (2)) the employee may by notice in writing to the employer require him to give to the employee a written statement complying with those requirements within such period (not being less than one week beginning with the day on which the notice is given) as may be specified in the notice; and if the employer without reasonable excuse fails to comply with the notice he shall be guilty of an offence under this subsection and liable on summary conviction—
(a) if it is his first conviction of an offence under this subsection, to a fine not exceeding £20, or
(b) in any other case, to a fine not exceeding £100.

Redundancy Fund

Establishment and maintenance of fund

1–536
103.—(1) The Secretary of State shall continue to have the control and management of the Redundancy Fund established under section 26 of the Redundancy Payments Act 1965 (in this Part referred to as "the fund"), and payments shall be made out of the fund in accordance with the provisions of sections 104 to 109 and 156 and Part VII.

(2) The Secretary of State shall prepare accounts of the fund in such form as the Treasury may direct, and shall send them to the Comptroller and Auditor General not later than the end of the month of November following the end of the financial year to which the accounts relate; and the Comptroller and Auditor General shall examine and certify the accounts and shall lay copies thereof, together with his report thereon, before Parliament.

(3) Any moneys forming part of the fund may from time to time be paid over to the National Debt Commissioners and by them invested, in accordance with such directions as may be given by the Treasury, in such manner as may be specified by an order of the Treasury for the time being in force under section 22(1) of the National Savings Bank Act 1971.

Redundancy rebates

104.—(1) Subject to the provisions of this section, the Secretary of State shall make a payment (in this Part referred to as a "redundancy rebate") out of the fund to any employer who—
- (*a*) is liable under the foregoing provisions of this Part to pay, and has paid, a redundancy payment to an employee, or
- (*b*) under an agreement in respect of which an order is in force under section 96, is liable to make, and has made, a payment to an employee on the termination of his contract of employment, or
- (*c*) by virtue of any award made by the Central Arbitration Committee as mentioned in section 97(2) in relation to an agreement in respect of which such an order is in force, is liable to make, and has made, a payment to an employee on the termination of his contract of employment.

(2) No redundancy rebate shall be payable by virtue of this section in a case falling within paragraph (*b*) or paragraph (*c*) of subsection (1) if the employee's right to the payment referred to in that paragraph arises by virtue of a [period of continuous employment] (computed in accordance with the provisions of the agreement in question) which is less than [two years].

(3) The Secretary of State may if he thinks fit pay a redundancy rebate to an employer who has paid an employee a redundancy payment in circumstances in which, owing to section 101, the employee had no right to, and the employer had no liability for, the payment, if the Secretary of State is satisfied that it would be just and equitable to do so having regard to all the relevant circumstances.

(4) The amount of any redundancy rebate shall (subject to subsection (7)) be calculated in accordance with Schedule 6.

(5) The Secretary of State shall make provision by regulations as to the making of claims for redundancy rebates; and any such regulations may in particular—
- (*a*) require any claim for a redundancy rebate to be made at or before a time prescribed by the regulations;
- (*b*) in such cases as may be so prescribed, require prior notice that such a claim may arise to be given at or before a time so prescribed, so however that, where the claim would relate to an employer's payment in respect of dismissal, the regulations shall not require the notice to be given more than four weeks before the date on which the termination of the contract of employment takes effect; and
- (*c*) for the purpose of determining the right of any person to, and the

amount of, any redundancy rebate, require a person at any time when he makes a claim or gives prior notice as mentioned in paragraph (*a*) or paragraph (*b*) to provide such evidence and such other information, and to produce for examination on behalf of the Secretary of State documents in his custody or under his control of such descriptions, as may be determined in accordance with the regulations.

(6) In relation to any case where, under section 85 or 92 or 110, an industrial tribunal determines that an employer is liable to pay part (but not the whole) of a redundancy payment, the reference in subsection (1)(*a*) to a redundancy payment shall be construed as a reference to that part of the redundancy payment.

(7) If any employer who, in accordance with subsection (1), would be entitled to a redundancy rebate fails to give prior notice as required by any such regulations in accordance with paragraph (*b*) of subsection (5) and it appears to the Secretary of State that he has so failed without reasonable excuse, the Secretary of State may, subject to section 108, reduce the amount of the rebate by such proportion (not exceeding one-tenth) as appears to the Secretary of State to be appropriate in the circumstances.

(8) Any person who—
- (*a*) in providing any information required by regulations under this section, makes a statement which he knows to be false in a material particular, or recklessly makes a statement which is false in a material particular, or
- (*b*) produces for examination in accordance with any such regulations a document which to his knowledge has been wilfully falsified,

shall be guilty of an offence.

(9) A person guilty of an offence under subsection (8) shall be liable on summary conviction to a fine not exceeding the prescribed sum or to imprisonment for a term not exceeding three months or both, or on conviction on indictment to a fine or to imprisonment for a term not exceeding two years or both.

(10) In subsection (9) above "the prescribed sum" means—
- (*a*) in England and Wales, the prescribed sum within the meaning of section 28 of the Criminal Law Act 1977 (that is to say, £1,000 or another sum fixed by order under section 61 of that Act to take account of changes in the value of money);
- (*b*) in Scotland, the prescribed sum within the meaning of section 289B of the Criminal Procedure (Scotland) Act 1975 (that is to say, £1,000 or another sum fixed by an order made under section 289D of that Act for that purpose).

AMENDMENT
The words in square brackets in subs. (2) were substituted by the Employment Act 1982 (c. 46), Sched. 2, para. 6.

Payments out of fund to employers in other cases

105.—(1) The Secretary of State may make payments out of the fund to employers in respect of employees to whom this section applies.

(2) This section applies to employees to whom, by virtue of section 144(2), 145 or 149, section 81 does not apply.

(3) The Secretary of State may determine the classes of employees to

whom this section applies in respect of whom payments are to be made by virtue of this section, and, with the approval of the Treasury, may determine the amounts of the payments which may be so made in respect of any class of such employees.

(4) The payments made to an employer by virtue of this section shall not, in respect of any period, exceed the amount appearing to the Secretary of State to be equal to the amount paid into the fund from the appropriate employment protection allocation (under section 134 of the Social Security Act 1975) from all secondary Class 1 contributions paid by that employer under Part I of that Act.

Payments out of fund to employees

106.—(1) Where an employee claims that his employer is liable to pay to him an employer's payment, and either—
  (a) that the employee has taken all reasonable steps (other than legal proceedings) to recover the payment from the employer and that the employer has refused or failed to pay it, or has paid part of it and has refused or failed to pay the balance, or
  (b) that the employer is insolvent and that the whole or part of the payment remains unpaid,
the employee may apply to the Secretary of State for a payment under this section.

(2) If on an application under this section the Secretary of State is satisfied—
  (a) that the employee is entitled to the employer's payment;
  (b) that either of the conditions specified in subsection (1) is fulfilled; and
  (c) that, in a case where the employer's payment is such a payment as is mentioned in paragraph (b) or paragraph (c) of section 104(1), the employee's right to the payment arises by virtue of a [period of continuous employment] (computed in accordance with the provisions of the agreement in question) which is not less than [two years],
the Secretary of State shall pay to the employee out of the fund a sum calculated in accordance with Schedule 7, reduced by so much (if any) of the employer's payment as has been paid.

(3) Where the Secretary of State pays a sum to an employee in respect of an employer's payment—
  (a) all rights and remedies of the employee with respect to the employer's payment, or (if the Secretary of State has paid only part of it) all his rights and remedies with respect to that part of the employer's payment, shall be transferred to and vest in the Secretary of State; and
  (b) any decision of an industrial tribunal requiring the employer's payment to be paid to the employee shall have effect as if it required that payment, or, as the case may be, that part of it which the Secretary of State has paid, to be paid to the Secretary of State;
and any moneys recovered by the Secretary of State by virtue of this subsection shall be paid into the fund.

(4) Where the Secretary of State pays a sum under this section in respect of an employer's payment, then (subject to the following provisions of this subsection) section 104 shall apply as if that sum had been paid by the

1–539

employer to the employee on account of that payment; but if, in a case falling within paragraph (*a*) of subsection (1), it appears to the Secretary of State that the refusal or failure of the employer to pay the employer's payment, or part of it, as the case may be, was without reasonable excuse, the Secretary of State may, subject to section 108, withhold any redundancy rebate to which the employer would otherwise be entitled in respect of the employer's payment, or may reduce the amount of any such rebate to such extent as the Secretary of State considers appropriate.

(5) For the purposes of this section an employer shall be taken to be insolvent if—

(*a*) he has become bankrupt or has made a composition or arrangement with his creditors or a receiving order is made against him;

(*b*) he has died and an order has been made under section 130 of the Bankruptcy Act 1914 for the administration of his estate according to the law of bankruptcy, or by virtue of an order of the court his is being administered in accordance with the rules set out in Part I of Schedule 1 to the Administration of Estates Act 1925; or

(*c*) where the employer is a company, a winding-up order has been made with respect to it or a resolution for voluntary winding-up has been passed with respect to it, or a receiver or manager of its undertaking has been duly appointed, or possession has been taken, by or on behalf of the holders of any debentures secured by a floating charge, of any property of the company comprised in or subject to the charge.

(6) In the application of this section to Scotland, for paragraphs (*a*), (*b*) and (*c*) of subsection (5) there shall be substituted the following paragraphs:—

(*a*) an award of sequestration has been made on his estate, or he has executed a trust deed for his creditors or entered into a composition contract;

(*b*) he has died and a judicial factor appointed under section 163 of the Bankruptcy (Scotland) Act 1913 is required by the provisions of that section to divide his insolvent estate among his creditors; or

(*c*) where the employer is a company, a winding-up order has been made or a resolution for voluntary winding-up is passed with respect to it or a receiver of its undertaking is duly appointed.

(7) In this section "legal proceedings" does not include any proceedings before an industrial tribunal, but includes any proceedings to enforce a decision or award of an industrial tribunal.

AMENDMENT

The words in square brackets in subs. (2)(*c*) were substituted by the Employment Act 1982 (c. 46), Sched. 2, para. 6.

Supplementary provisions relating to applications under s.106

107.—(1) Where an employee makes an application to the Secretary of State under section 106, the Secretary of State may, by notice in writing given to the employer, require the employer to provide the Secretary of State with such information, and to produce for examination on behalf of the Secretary of State documents in his custody or under his control of such descriptions, as the Secretary of State may reasonably require for the purpose of determining whether the application is well-founded.

(2) If any person on whom a notice is served under this section fails with-

out reasonable excuse to comply with a requirement imposed by the notice, he shall be guilty of an offence and liable on summary conviction to a fine not exceeding £100.

(3) Any person who—
   (a) in providing any information required by a notice under this section, makes a statement which he knows to be false in a material particular, or recklessly makes a statement which is false in a material particular, or
   (b) produces for examination in accordance with any such notice a document which to his knowledge has been wilfully falsified,

shall be guilty of an offence under this subsection.

(4) A person guilty of an offence under subsection (3) shall be liable on summary conviction to a fine not exceeding the prescribed sum or to imprisonment for a term not exceeding three months or both, or on conviction on indictment to a fine or to imprisonment for a term not exceeding two years or both.

(5) In subsection (4) above "the prescribed sum" means—
   (a) in England and Wales, the prescribed sum within the meaning of section 28 of the Criminal Law Act 1977 (that is to say, £1,000 or another sum fixed by order under section 61 of that Act to take account of changes in the value of money);
   (b) in Scotland, the prescribed sum within the meaning of section 289B of the Criminal Procedure (Scotland) Act 1975 (that is to say, £1,000 or another sum fixed by an order made under section 289D of that Act for that purpose).

References and appeals to tribunal relating to payments out of fund

108.—(1) Subsections (2) and (3) shall have effect where—
   (a) a claim is made for a redundancy rebate on the grounds that an employer is liable to pay, and has paid, an employer's payment, or prior notice that such a claim may arise is given in accordance with regulations made under section 104(5)(b), or
   (b) an application is made to the Secretary of State for a payment under section 106, where it is claimed that an employer is liable to pay an employer's payment.

(2) Where any such claim or application is made or such prior notice is given, there shall be referred to an industrial tribunal—
   (a) any question as to the liability of the employer to pay the employer's payment;
   (b) in a case falling within paragraph (a) of subsection (1), any question as to the amount of the rebate payable in accordance with Schedule 6;
   (c) in a case falling within paragraph (b) of subsection (1), any question as to the amount of the sum payable in accordance with Schedule 7.

(3) For the purposes of any reference under subsection (2), an employee who has been dismissed by his employer shall, unless the contrary is proved, be presumed to have been so dismissed by reason of redundancy.

(4) Where, in any case to which section 104(3) applies, the Secretary of State refuses to pay a redundancy rebate, the employer may appeal to an industrial tribunal; and if on any such appeal the tribunal is satisfied that it is just and equitable having regard to all the relevant circumstances that

336   *Employment Protection (Consolidation) Act 1978*

a redundancy rebate should be paid, the tribunal shall determine accordingly, and the Secretary of State shall comply with any such determination of a tribunal.

(5) In any case where the Secretary of State withholds, or reduces the amount of, a redundancy rebate in pursuance of section 104(7) or section 106(4), the employer may appeal to an industrial tribunal; and if on any such appeal the tribunal is satisfied—
- (*a*) in a case where the rebate was withheld, that it should be paid in full, or should be reduced instead of being withheld, or
- (*b*) in a case where the rebate was reduced, that it should not be reduced, or should be reduced by a smaller or larger proportion than that which the Secretary of State has applied,

the tribunal shall determine accordingly, and the Secretary of State shall comply with any such determination.

Financial provisions relating to the fund

1–542   **109.**—(1) Subject to the following provisions of this section, the Treasury may from time to time advance out of the National Loans Fund to the Secretary of State for the purposes of the fund such sums as the Secretary of State may request; and any sums advanced to the Secretary of State under this section shall be paid into the fund.

(2) The aggregate amount outstanding by way of principal in respect of sums advanced to the Secretary of State under this section shall not at any time exceed [£300 million] [. . .].

(3) Any sums advanced to the Secretary of State under this section shall be repaid by the Secretary of State out of the fund into the National Loans Fund in such manner and at such times, and with interest thereon at such rate, as the Treasury may direct.

(4) An order shall not be made under this section unless a draft of the order has been laid before Parliament and approved by resolution of each House of Parliament.

AMENDMENT
    The figures in square brackets in subs. (2) were substituted by the Redundancy Fund (Advances out of the National Loans Fund) Order 1981 (S.I. 1981 No. 1744).

Miscellaneous and Supplemental

Strike during currency of employer's notice to terminate contract

1–543   **110.**—(1) The provisions of this section shall have effect where, after an employer has given notice to an employee to terminate his contract of employment (in this section referred to as a "notice of termination")—
- (*a*) the employee begins to take part in a strike of employees of the employer, and
- (*b*) the employer serves on him a notice in writing (in this section referred to as a "notice of extension") requesting him to agree to extend the contract of employment beyond the time of expiry by an additional period comprising as many available days as the number of working days lost by striking (in this section referred to as "the proposed period of extension").

(2) A notice of extension shall indicate the reasons for which the employer makes the request contained in the notice, and shall state that unless either—

(a) the employee complies with the request, or

(b) the employer is satisfied that, in consequence of sickness, injury or otherwise, he is unable to comply with it, or that (notwithstanding that he is able to comply with it) in the circumstances it is reasonable for him not to do so,

the employer will contest any liability to pay him a redundancy payment in respect of the dismissal effected by the notice of termination.

(3) For the purposes of this section an employee shall be taken to comply with the request contained in a notice of extension if, but only if, on each available day within the proposed period of extension, he attends at his proper or usual place of work and is ready and willing to work, whether he has signified his agreement to the request in any other way or not.

(4) Where an employee on whom a notice of extension has been served—

(a) complies with the request contained in the notice, or

(b) does not comply with it, but attends at his proper or usual place of work and is ready and willing to work on one or more (but not all) of the available days within the proposed period of extension,

the notice of termination shall have effect, and shall be deemed at all material times to have had effect, as if the period specified in it had (in a case falling within paragraph (a)) been extended beyond the time of expiry by an additional period equal to the proposed period of extension or (in a case falling within paragraph (b)) had been extended beyond the time of expiry up to the end of the day (or, if more than one, the last of the days) on which he so attends and is ready and willing to work; and section 50 and Schedule 3 shall apply accordingly as if the period of notice required by section 49 were extended to a corresponding extent.

(5) Subject to subsection (6), if an employee on whom a notice of extension is served in pursuance of subsection (1) does not comply with the request contained in the notice, he shall not be entitled to a redundancy payment by reason of the dismissal effected by the notice of termination, unless the employer agrees to pay such a payment to him notwithstanding that the request has not been complied with.

(6) Where a notice of extension has been served, and on a reference to an industrial tribunal it appears to the tribunal that the employee has not complied with the request contained in the notice and the employer has not agreed to pay a redundancy payment in respect of the dismissal in question, but that the employee was unable to comply with the request, or it was reasonable for him not to comply with it, as mentioned in subsection (2)(b) the tribunal may determine that the employer shall be liable to pay to the employee—

(a) the whole of any redundancy payment to which the employee would have been entitled apart from subsection (5), or

(b) such part of any such redundancy payment as the tribunal thinks fit.

(7) The service of a notice of extension, and any extension, by virtue of subsection (4) of the period specified in a notice of termination,—

(a) shall not affect any right either of the employer or of the employee to terminate the contract of employment (whether before, at or after the time of expiry) by a further notice or without notice, and

(b) shall not affect the operation of sections 81 to 102 in relation to any such termination of the contract of employment.

(8) In this section any reference to the number of working days lost by

striking is a reference to the number of working days in the period beginning with the date of service of the notice of termination and ending with the time of expiry which are days on which the employee in question takes part in a strike of employees of the employer.

(9) In this section, "strike" has the meaning given by paragraph 24 of Schedule 13, "time of expiry", in relation to a notice of termination, "working day", in relation to an employee, means a day on which, in accordance with his contract of employment, he is normally required to work, "available day", in relation to an employee, means a working day beginning at or after the time of expiry which is a day on which he is not taking part in a strike of employees of the employer, and "available day within the proposed period of extension" means an available day which begins before the end of that period.

Payments equivalent to redundancy rebates of civil servants, etc.

111.—(1) The provisions of this section shall have effect with respect to employment of any of the following descriptions, that is to say—
   (*a*) any such employment as is mentioned in paragraph (*a*), paragraph (*b*) or paragraph (*c*) of subsection (1) of section 99 whether as originally enacted or as modified by any order under section 149(1);
   (*b*) any employment remunerated out of the revenue of the Duchy of Lancaster or the Duchy of Cornwall;
   (*c*) any employment remunerated out of the Queen's Civil List;
   (*d*) any employment remunerated out of Her Majesty's Privy Purse.

(2) Where the Secretary of State is satisfied that a payment has been, or will be, made in respect of the termination of any person's employment of any description specified in subsection (1), and that the payment has been, or will be, so made to or in respect of him—
   (*a*) in accordance with the Superannuation Act 1965, as that Act continues to have effect by virtue of section 23(1) of the Superannuation Act 1972,
   (*b*) in accordance with any provision of a scheme made under section 1 of the Superannuation Act 1972, or
   (*c*) in accordance with any such arrangements as are mentioned in subsection (3),
the Secretary of State shall pay the appropriate sum out of the fund to the appropriate fund or authority.

(3) The arrangements referred to in paragraph (*c*) of subsection (2) are any arrangements made with the approval of the Minister for the Civil Service for securing that payments by way of compensation for loss of any such employment as is mentioned in subsection (1) will be made—
   (*a*) in circumstances which in the opinion of the Minister for the Civil Service correspond (subject to the appropriate modifications) to those in which a right to a redundancy payment would have accrued if section 81 had applied, and
   (*b*) on a scale which in the opinion of the Minister for the Civil Service, taking into account any sums which are payable as mentioned in subsection (2)(*a*) or (*b*) to or in respect of the person losing the employment in question, corresponds (subject to the appropriate modifications) to that on which a redundancy payment would have been payable if section 81 had applied.

(4) For the purposes of subsection (2) the appropriate sum is the sum appearing to the Secretary of State to be equal to the amount of the redundancy rebate which would have been payable under section 104 if such a right as is mentioned in paragraph (*a*) of subsection (3) had accrued, and such a redundancy payment as is mentioned in paragraph (*b*) of subsection (3) had been payable and had been paid.

(5) Any accounts prepared by the Secretary of State under section 103(2) shall show as a separate item the aggregate amount of sums paid under subsection (2) during the period to which the accounts relate.

(6) In this section "the appropriate fund or authority"—
- (*a*) in relation to employment of any description falling within paragraph 7 of subsection (1) of section 39 of the Superannuation Act 1965 (whether as originally enacted or as modified by any order under that section), means the fund out of which, or the body out of whose revenues, the employment is remunerated;
- (*b*) in relation to any employment remunerated out of the revenues of the Duchy of Lancaster, means the Chancellor of the Duchy, and, in relation to any employment remunerated out of the revenues of the Duchy of Cornwall, means such person as the Duke of Cornwall, or the possessor for the time being of the Duchy of Cornwall, appoints;
- (*c*) in relation to any employment remunerated out of the Queen's Civil List or out of Her Majesty's Privy Purse, means the Civil List or the Privy Purse, as the case may be; and
- (*d*) in any other case, means the Consolidated Fund.

References to tribunal relating to equivalent payments

112.—(1) This section applies to any such payment as is mentioned in subsection (3) of section 111 which is payable in accordance with any such arrangements as are mentioned in that subsection.

(2) Where the terms and conditions (whether constituting a contract of employment or not) on which any person is employed in any such employment as is mentioned in subsection (1) of section 111 include provision—
- (*a*) for the making of any payment to which this section applies, and
- (*b*) for referring to a tribunal any such question as is mentioned in the following provisions of this subsection,

any question as to the right of any person to such a payment in respect of that employment, or as to the amount of such a payment shall be referred to and determined by an industrial tribunal.

1–545

Employment under Government of overseas territory

113.—(1) Where the Secretary of State is satisfied that, in accordance with any such arrangements as are mentioned in subsection (3), a payment has been, or will be, made in respect of the termination of a person's employment in any capacity under the Government of an overseas territory (in this section referred to as "the relevant Government"), and that in respect of the whole or part of the period during which that person was in that employment, employer's contributions were paid in respect of him, the Secretary of State shall pay the appropriate sum out of the fund to such other fund or authority as may be designated in that behalf by the relevant Government.

(2) The reference in subsection (1) to employer's contributions is a reference to secondary Class 1 contributions paid in respect of the person in

1–546

question by persons who were in relation to him secondary Class 1 contributors by virtue of section 4(4)(a) of the Social Security Act 1975, and in relation to any period before 6th April 1975, to employer's contributions within the meaning of the National Insurance Act 1965.

(3) The arrangements referred to in subsection (1) are any arrangements made by or on behalf of the relevant Government for securing that payments by way of compensation for loss of employment in the capacity in question will be made—
  (a) in circumstances which in the opinion of the Secretary of State correspond (subject to the appropriate modifications) to those in which a right to a redundancy payment would have accrued if section 81 had applied, and
  (b) on a scale which in the opinion of the Secretary of State corresponds (subject to the appropriate modifications) to that on which a redundancy payment would have been payable if that section had applied.

(4) For the purposes of subsection (1) the appropriate sum (subject to subsection (5)) is the sum appearing to the Secretary of State to be equal to the amount of the redundancy rebate which would have been payable under section 104 if such a right as is mentioned in paragraph (a) of subsection (3) had accrued, and such a redundancy payment as is mentioned in paragraph (b) of that subsection had been payable and had been paid.

(5) Where it appears to the Secretary of State that such contributions as are mentioned in subsection (1) were paid in respect of part (but not the whole) of the period of employment in question, the rebate which would have been payable as mentioned in subsection (4) shall be calculated as if the employment had been limited to that part of the period.

(6) Any accounts prepared by the Secretary of State under section 103(2) shall show as a separate item the aggregate amount of sums paid under subsection (1) during the period to which the accounts relate.

Meaning of "Government of overseas territory"

114.—(1) In this Part "overseas territory" means any territory or country outside the United Kingdom; and any reference to the Government of an overseas territory includes a reference to a Government constituted for two or more overseas territories and to any authority established for the purpose of providing or administering services which are common to, or relate to matters of common interest to, two or more such territories.

Application of Part VI to employment not under contract of employment

115.—(1) This section applies to employment of any description which—
  (a) is not employment under a contract of service or of apprenticeship, and
  (b) is not employment of any description falling within paragraphs (a) to (d) of section 111(1),

but is employment such that secondary Class 1 contributions are payable under Part I of the Social Security Act 1975 in respect of persons engaged therein.

(2) The Secretary of State may by regulations under this section provide that, subject to such exceptions and modifications as may be prescribed by the regulations, this Part and the provisions of this Act supplementary thereto shall have effect in relation to any such employment of a description to which this section applies as may be so prescribed as if—

(a) it were employment under a contract of employment, and
(b) any person engaged in employment of that description were an employee, and
(c) such person as may be determined by or under the regulations were his employer.

(3) Without prejudice to the generality of subsection (2), regulations made under this section may provide that section 105 shall apply to persons engaged in any such employment of a description to which this section applies as may be prescribed by the regulations, as if those persons were employees to whom that section applies.

Provision for treating termination of certain employments by statute as equivalent to dismissal

116.—(1) The Secretary of State may by regulations under this section provide that, subject to such exceptions and modifications as may be prescribed by the regulations, the provisions of this Part shall have effect in relation to any person who, by virtue of any statutory provisions,— 1–549
(a) is transferred to, and becomes a member of, a body specified in those provisions, but
(b) at a time so specified ceases to be a member of that body unless before that time certain conditions so specified have been fulfilled,
as if the cessation of his membership of that body by virtue of those provisions were dismissal by his employer by reason of redundancy.

(2) The power conferred by subsection (1) shall be exercisable whether membership of the body in question constitutes employment within the meaning of section 153 or not; and, where that membership does not constitute such employment, that power may be exercised in addition to any power exercisable by virtue of section 115.

Employees paid by person other than employer

117.—(1) This section applies to any employee whose remuneration is, by virtue of any statutory provision, payable to him by a person other than his employer. 1–550

(2) For the purposes of the operation, in relation to employees to whom this section applies, of the provisions of this Part and Schedule 13 specified in column 1 of Schedule 8, any reference to the employer which is specified in column 2 of Schedule 8 shall be construed as a reference to the person responsible for paying the remuneration.

(3) In relation to employees to whom this section applies, section 119 shall have effect as if—
(a) any reference in subsection (1) or subsection (2) of that section to a notice required or authorised to be given by or to an employer included a reference to a notice which, by virtue of subsection (2), is required or authorised to be given by or to the person responsible for paying the remuneration;
(b) in relation to a notice required or authorised to be given to that person, any reference to the employer in paragraph (a) or paragraph (b) of subsection (2) of that section were a reference to that person; and
(c) the reference to the employer in subsection (5) of that section included a reference to that person.

(4) In this section and in Schedule 8, "the person responsible for paying

the remuneration" means the person by whom the remuneration is payable as mentioned in subsection (1).

Statutory compensation schemes

1–551   118.—(1) This section applies to any statutory provision which was in force immediately before 6th December 1965, whereby the holders of such situations, places or employments as are specified in that provision are, or may become, entitled to compensation for loss of employment, or for loss or diminution of emoluments or of pension rights, in consequence of the operation of any other statutory provision referred to therein.

(2) The Secretary of State may make provision by regulations for securing that where apart from this section a person is entitled to compensation under a statutory provision to which this section applies, and the circumstances are such that he is also entitled to a redundancy payment, the amount of the redundancy payment shall be set off against the compensation to which he would be entitled apart from this section; and any statutory provision to which any such regulations apply shall have effect subject to the regulations.

Provisions as to notices

1–552   119.—(1) Any notice which under this Part is required or authorised to be given by an employer to an employee may be given by being delivered to the employee, or left for him at his usual or last-known place of residence, or sent by post addressed to him at that place.

(2) Any notice which under this Part is required or authorised to be given by an employee to an employer may be given either by the employee himself or by a person authorised by him to act on his behalf, and, whether given by or on behalf of the employee,—
  (*a*) may be given by being delivered to the employer, or sent by post addressed to him at the place where the employee is or was employed by him, or
  (*b*) if arrangements in that behalf have been made by the employer, may be given by being delivered to a person designated by the employer in pursuance of the arrangements, or left for such a person at a place so designated, or sent by post to such a person at an address so designated.

(3) In the preceding provisions of this section, any reference to the delivery of a notice shall, in relation to a notice which is not required by this Part to be in writing, be construed as including a reference to the oral communication of the notice.

(4) Any notice which, in accordance with any provision of this section, is left for a person at a place referred to in that provision shall, unless the contrary is proved, be presumed to have been received by him on the day on which it was left there.

(5) Nothing in subsection (1) or subsection (2) shall be construed as affecting the capacity of an employer to act by a servant or agent for the purposes of any provision of this Part, including either of those subsections.

Offences

1–553   120.—(1) Where an offence under this Part committed by a body corporate is proved to have been committed with the consent or connivance of, or to be attributable to any neglect on the part of, any director, manager, secretary or other similar officer of the body corporate or any person who was purporting to act in any such capacity, he as well as the body corporate shall be guilty of that offence and shall be liable to be proceeded against and punished accordingly.

(2) In this section "director", in relation to a body corporate established by or under any enactment for the purpose of carrying on under national ownership any industry or part of an industry or undertaking, being a body corporate whose affairs are managed by its members, means a member of that body corporate.

PART VII

INSOLVENCY OF EMPLOYER

Priority of certain debts on insolvency

121.—(1) An amount to which this section applies shall be treated for the purposes of—
   (a) section 33 of the Bankruptcy Act 1914;
   (b) section 118 of the Bankruptcy (Scotland) Act 1913; and
   (c) section 319 of the Companies Act 1948;
as if it were wages payable by the employer to the employee in respect of the period for which it is payable.

(2) This section applies to any amount owed by an employer to an employee in respect of—
   (a) a guarantee payment;
   (b) remuneration on suspension on medical grounds under section 19;
   (c) any payment for time off under section 27(3) [31(3) or 31A(4)];
   (d) remuneration under a protective award made under section 101 of the Employment Protection Act 1975.

1-554

AMENDMENT
The section numbers in square brackets in subs. (2)(c) were substituted by the Employment Act 1980 (c. 42), Sched. 1, para. 15.

Employee's rights on insolvency of employer

122.—(1) If on an application made to him in writing by an employee the Secretary of State is satisfied—
   (a) that the employer of that employee has become insolvent; and
   (b) that on the relevant date the employee was entitled to be paid the whole or part of any debt to which this section applies,
the Secretary of State shall, subject to the provisions of this section, pay the employee out of the Redundancy Fund the amount to which in the opinion of the Secretary of State the employee is entitled in respect of that debt.

1-555

[(2) In this section the "relevant date", in relation to a debt, means whichever is the latest of—
   (a) the date on which the employer became insolvent;
   (b) the date of the termination of the employee's employment; or
   (c) where the debt falls within section 12(2)(d) or subsection (3)(d), the date on which the award was made.]

(3) This section applies to the following debts:—

[(a) any arrears of pay in respect of one or more (but not more than eight) weeks;]

(b) any amount which the employer is liable to pay the employee for the period of notice required by section 49(1) or (2) or for any failure of the employer to give the period of notice required by section 49(1);

[(c) any holiday pay—
   (i) in respect of a period or periods of holiday not exceeding six weeks in all; and
   (ii) to which the employee became entitled during the twelve months ending with the relevant date.]

(d) any basic award of compensation for unfair dismissal (within the meaning of section 72);

(e) any reasonable sum by way of reimbursement of the whole or part of any fee or premium paid by an apprentice or articled clerk.

(4) For the purposes of subsection (3)(a), any such amount as is referred to in section 121(2) shall be treated as if it were arrears of pay.

(5) The total amount payable to an employee in respect of any debt mentioned in subsection (3), where the amount of that debt is referable to a period of time, shall not exceed [£135] in respect of any one week or, in respect of a shorter period, an amount bearing the same proportion to [£135] to that shorter period bears to a week.

(6) The Secretary of State may vary the limit referred to in subsection (5) after a review under section 148, by order made in accordance with that section.

(7) A sum shall be taken to be reasonable for the purposes of subsection (3)(e) in a case where a trustee in bankruptcy or liquidator has been or is required to be appointed if it is admitted to be reasonable by the trustee in bankruptcy or liquidator under section 34 of the Bankruptcy Act 1914 (preferential claims of apprentices and articled clerks), whether as originally enacted or as applied to the winding up of a company by section 317 of the Companies Act 1948.

(8) Subsection (7) shall not apply to Scotland, but in Scotland a sum shall be taken to be reasonable for the purposes of subsection (3)(e) in a case where a trustee in bankruptcy or liquidator has been or is required to be appointed if it is admitted by the trustee in bankruptcy or the liquidator for the purposes of the bankruptcy or winding up.

(9) The provisions of subsections (10) and (11) shall apply in a case where one of the following officers (hereinafter in this section referred to as the "relevant officer") has been or is required to be appointed in connection with the employer's insolvency, that is to say, a trustee in bankruptcy, a liquidator, a receiver or manager, or a trustee under a composition or arrangement between the employer and his creditors or under a trust deed for his creditors executed by the employer; and in this subsection "liquidator" and "receiver" include the Official Receiver in his capacity as a provisional liquidator or interim receiver.

(10) Subject to subsection (11), the Secretary of State shall not in such a case make any payment under this section in respect of any debt until he has received a statement from the relevant officer of the amount of that debt which appears to have been owed to the employee on the relevant

date and to remain unpaid; and the relevant officer shall, on request by the Secretary of State, provide him, as soon as reasonably practicable, with such a statement.

(11) Where—
   (a) [the application for a payment under this section has been] received by the Secretary of State, but no such payment has been made;
   (b) the Secretary of State is satisfied that a payment under this section should be made; and
   (c) it appears to the Secretary of State that there is likely to be [unreasonable] delay before he receives a statement about the debt in question,

then, the Secretary of State may, if the applicant so requests or, if the Secretary of State thinks fit, without such a request, make a payment under this section, notwithstanding that no such statement has been received.

AMENDMENT
The figures in square brackets in subs. (5) were substituted by the Employment Protection (Variation of Limits) Order 1982 (S.I. 1982 No. 77). All words in square brackets were substituted by the Employment Act 1982 (c. 46), Sched. 3, paras. 3–5.

Payment of unpaid contributions to occupational pension scheme
123.—(1) If, on application made to him in writing by the persons competent to act in respect of an occupational pension scheme, the Secretary of State is satisfied that an employer has become insolvent and that at the time that he did so there remained unpaid relevant contributions falling to be paid by him to the scheme, the Secretary of State shall, subject to the provisions of this section, pay into the resources of the scheme out of the Redundancy Fund the sum which in his opinion is payable in respect of the unpaid relevant contributions.

1–556

(2) In this section "relevant contributions" means contributions falling to be paid by an employer in accordance with an occupational pension scheme, either on his own account or on behalf of an employee; and for the purposes of this section a contribution of any amount shall not be treated as falling to be paid on behalf of an employee unless a sum equal to that amount has been deducted from the pay of the employee by way of a contribution from him.

(3) The sum payable under this section in respect of unpaid contributions of an employer on his own account to an occupational pension scheme shall be at least of the following amounts—
   (a) the balance of relevant contributions remaining unpaid on the date when he became insolvent and payable by the employer on his own account to the scheme in respect of the twelve months immediately preceding that date;
   (b) the amount certified by an actuary to be necessary for the purpose of meeting the liability of the scheme on dissolution to pay the benefits provided by the scheme to or in respect of the employees of the employer;
   (c) an amount equal to ten per cent. of the total amount of remuneration paid or payable to those employees in respect of the twelve months immediately preceding the date on which the employer became insolvent.

(4) For the purposes of subsection (3)(c), "remuneration" includes holi-

day pay, maternity pay and any such payment as is referred to in section 121(2).

(5) Any sum payable under this section in respect of unpaid contributions on behalf of an employee shall not exceed the amount deducted from the pay of the employee in respect of the employee's contributions to the occupational pension scheme during the twelve months immediately preceding the date on which the employer became insolvent.

(6) The provisions of subsections (7) to (9) shall apply in a case where one of the following officers (hereafter in this section referred to as the "relevant officer") has been or is required to be appointed in connection with the employer's insolvency, that is to say, a trustee in bankruptcy, a liquidator, a receiver or manager, or a trustee under a composition or arrangement between the employer and his creditors or under a trust deed for his creditors executed by the employer; and in this subsection "liquidator" and "receiver" include the Official Receiver in his capacity as a provisional liquidator or interim receiver.

(7) Subject to subsection (9), the Secretary of State shall not in such a case make any payment under this section in respect of unpaid relevant contributions until he has received a statement from the relevant officer of the amount of relevant contributions which appear to have been unpaid on the date on which the employer became insolvent and to remain unpaid; and the relevant officer shall, on request by the Secretary of State provide him, as soon as reasonably practicable, with such a statement.

(8) Subject to subsection (9), an amount shall be taken to be payable, paid or deducted as mentioned in subsection (3)(*a*) or (*c*) or subsection (5), only if it is so certified by the relevant officer.

(9) Where—
  (*a*) [the application for a payment under this section has been] received by the Secretary of State, but no such payment has been made;
  (*b*) the Secretary of State is satisfied that a payment under this section should be made; and
  (*c*) it appears to the Secretary of State that there is likely to be [unreasonable] delay before he receives a statement or certificate about the contributions in question,
then, the Secretary of State may, if the applicants so request or, if the Secretary of State thinks fit, without such a request, make a payment under this section, notwithstanding that no such statement or certificate has been received.

AMENDMENT
The words in square brackets in subs. (9) were substituted by the Employment Act 1982 (c. 46), Sched. 3, para. 5.

Complaint to industrial tribunal

124.—(1) A person who has applied for a payment under section 122 may, within the period of three months beginning with the date on which the decision of the Secretary of State on that application was communicated to him or, if that is not reasonably practicable, within such further period as is reasonable, present a complaint to an industrial tribunal that—
  (*a*) the Secretary of State has failed to make any such payment; or
  (*b*) any such payment made by the Secretary of State is less than the amount which should have been paid.

(2) Any persons who are competent to act in respect of an occupational pension scheme and who have applied for a payment to be made under section 123 into the resources of the scheme may, within the period of three months beginning with the date on which the decision of the Secretary of State on that application was communicated to them, or, if that is not reasonably practicable, within such further period as is reasonable, present a complaint to an industrial tribunal that—
    (*a*) the Secretary of State has failed to make any such payment; or
    (*b*) any such payment made by him is less than the amount which should have been paid.

(3) Where an industrial tribunal finds that the Secretary of State ought to make a payment under section 122 or 123, it shall make a declaration to that effect and shall also declare the amount of any such payment which it finds the Secretary of State ought to make.

Transfer to Secretary of State of rights and remedies

125.—(1) Where, in pursuance of section 122, the Secretary of State makes any payment to an employee in respect of any debt to which that section applies—

    (*a*) any rights and remedies of the employee in respect of that debt (or, if the Secretary of State has paid only part of it, in respect of that part) shall, on the making of the payment, become rights and remedies of the Secretary of State; and

    (*b*) any decision of an industrial tribunal requiring an employer to pay that debt to the employee shall have the effect that the debt or, as the case may be, that part of it which the Secretary of State has paid, is to be paid to the Secretary of State.

1–558

(2) There shall be included among the rights and remedies which become rights and remedies of the Secretary of State in accordance with subsection (1)(*a*) any right to be paid in priority to other creditors of the employer in accordance with—
    (*a*) section 33 of the Bankruptcy Act 1914;
    (*b*) section 118 of the Bankruptcy (Scotland) Act 1913; and
    (*c*) section 319 of the Companies Act 1948,
and the Secretary of State shall be entitled to be so paid in priority to any other unsatisfied claim of the employee; and in computing for the purposes of any of those provisions any limit on the amount of sums to be so paid any sums paid to the Secretary of State shall be treated as if they had been paid to the employee.

(3) Where in pursuance of section 123 the Secretary of State makes any payment into the resources of an occupational pension scheme in respect of any contributions to the scheme, any rights and remedies in respect of those contributions belonging to the persons competent to act in respect of the scheme shall, on the making of the payment, become rights and remedies of the Secretary of State.

(4) Any sum recovered by the Secretary of State in exercising any right or pursuing any remedy which is his by virtue of this section shall be paid into the Redundancy Fund.

Power of Secretary of State to obtain information in connection with application

126.—(1) Where an application is made to the Secretary of State under section 122 or 123 in respect of a debt owed, or contributions to an occupa-

1–559

tional pension scheme falling to be made, by an employer, the Secretary of State may require—
  (a) the employer to provide him with such information as the Secretary of State may reasonably require for the purpose of determining whether the application is well-founded; and
  (b) any person having the custody or control of any relevant records or other documents to produce for examination on behalf of the Secretary of State any such document in that person's custody or under his control which is of such a description as the Secretary of State may require.

(2) Any such requirement shall be made by notice in writing given to the person on whom the requirement is imposed and may be varied or revoked by a subsequent notice so given.

(3) If a person refuses or wilfully neglects to furnish any information or produce any document which he has been required to furnish or produce by a notice under this section he shall be liable on summary conviction to a fine not exceeding £100.

(4) If a person, in purporting to comply with a requirement of a notice under this section, knowingly or recklessly makes any false statement he shall be liable on summary conviction to a fine not exceeding £400.

Interpretation of ss.122 to 126

1–560   **127.**—(1) For the purposes of sections 122 to 126, an employer shall be taken to be solvent if, but only if, in England and Wales,—
  (a) he becomes bankrupt or makes a composition or arrangement with his creditors or a receiving order is made against him;
  (b) he has died and an order is made under section 130 of the Bankruptcy Act 1914 for the administration of his estate according to the law of bankruptcy, or by virtue of an order of the court his estate is being administered in accordance with rules set out in Part I of Schedule I to the Administration of Estates Act 1925; or
  (c) where the employer is a company, a winding up order is made or a resolution for voluntary winding up is passed with respect to it, or a receiver or manager of its undertaking is duly appointed, or possession is taken, by or on behalf of the holders of any debentures secured by a floating charge, of any property of the company comprised in or subject to the charge.

(2) For the purposes of sections 122 to 126, an employer shall be taken to be insolvent if, but only if, in Scotland—
  (a) an award of sequestration is made on his estate or he executes a trust deed for his creditors or enters into a composition contract;
  (b) he has died and a judicial factor appointed under section 163 of the Bankruptcy (Scotland) Act 1913 is required by that section to divide his insolvent estate among his creditors; or
  (c) where the employer is a company, a winding-up order is made or a resolution for voluntary winding up is passed with respect to it or a receiver of its undertaking is duly appointed.

(3) In sections 122 to 126—
  "holiday pay" means—
    (a) pay in respect of a holiday actually taken; or
    (b) any accrued holiday pay which under the employee's contract of

employment would in the ordinary course have become payable to him in respect of the period of a holiday if his employment with the employer had continued until he became entitled to a holiday;

"occupational pension scheme" means any scheme or arrangement which provides or is capable of providing, in relation to employees in any description of employment, benefits (in the form of pensions or otherwise) payable to or in respect of any such employees on the termination of their employment or on their death or retirement;

and any reference in those sections to the resources of such a scheme is a reference to the funds out of which the benefits provided by the scheme are from time to time payable.

Part VIII

Resolution of Disputes Relating to Employment

Industrial Tribunals

Industrial tribunals

128.—(1) The Secretary of State may by regulations make provision for the establishment of tribunals, to be known as industrial tribunals, to exercise the jurisdiction conferred on them by or under this Act or any other Act, whether passed before or after this Act.

(2) Regulations made wholly or partly under section 12 of the Industrial Training Act 1964 and in force immediately before the date on which this section comes into force shall, so far as so made, continue to have effect as if they had been made under subsection (1), and tribunals established in accordance with such regulations shall continue to be known as industrial tribunals.

(3) Schedule 9, which makes provision, among other things, with respect to proceedings before industrial tribunals, shall have effect.

(4) Complaints, references [applications] and appeals to industrial tribunals shall be made in accordance with regulations made under paragraph 1 of Schedule 9.

1–561

Amendment
The word in square brackets in subs. (4) was inserted by the Employment Act 1980 (c. 42), Sched. 1, para. 16.

Remedy for infringement of certain rights under this Act

129. The remedy of an employee for infringement of any of the rights conferred on him by sections 8 and 53 and Parts II, III, V and VII shall, if provision is made for a complaint or for the reference of a question to an industrial tribunal, be by way of such complaint or reference and not otherwise.

1–562

Jurisdiction of referees to be exercised by tribunals

130.—(1) There shall be referred to and determined by an industrial tribunal any question which by any statutory provision is directed (in whatsoever terms) to be determined by a referee or board of referees constituted

1–563

under any of the statutory provisions specified in Schedule 10 or which is so directed to be determined in the absence of agreement to the contrary.

(2) The transfer of any jurisdiction by this section shall not affect the principles on which any question is to be determined or the persons on whom the determination is binding, or any provision which requires particular matters to be expressly dealt with or embodied in the determination, or which relates to evidence.

Power to confer jurisdiction on industrial tribunals in respect of damages, etc., for breach of contract of employment

1–564   **131.**—(1) The appropriate Minister may by order provide that on any claim to which this section applies or any such claim of a description specified in the order, being in either case a claim satisfying the relevant condition or conditions mentioned in subsection (3), proceedings for the recovery of damages or any other sum, except damages or a sum due in respect of personal injuries, may be brought before an industrial tribunal.

(2) Subject to subsection (3), this section applies to any of the following claims, that is to say—
   (*a*) a claim for damages for breach of a contract of employment or any other contract connected with employment;
   (*b*) a claim for a sum due under such a contract;
   (*c*) a claim for the recovey of a sum in pursuance of any enactment relating to the terms or performance of such a contract;
being in each case a claim such that a court in England and Wales or Scotland, as the case may be, would under the law for the time being in force have jurisdiction to hear and determine an action in respect of the claim.

(3) An order under this section may make provision with respect to any such claim only if it satisfies either of the following conditions, that is to say—
   (*a*) it arises or is outstanding on the termination of the employee's employment; or
   (*b*) it arises in circumstances which also give rise to proceedings already or simultaneously brought before an industrial tribunal otherwise than by virtue of this section;
or, if the order so provides, it satisfies both those conditions.

(4) Where on proceedings under this section an industrial tribunal finds that the whole or part of a sum claimed in the proceedings is due, the tribunal shall order the respondent to the proceedings to pay the amount which it finds due.

(5) Without prejudice to section 154(3), an order under this section may include provisions—
   (*a*) as to the manner in which and time within which proceedings are to be brought by virtue of this section; and
   (*b*) modifying any other enactment.

(6) Any jurisdiction conferred on an industrial tribunal by virtue of this section in respect of any claim shall be exercisable concurrently with any court in England and Wales or in Scotland, as the case may be, which has jurisdiction to hear and determine an action in respect of the claim.

(7) In this section—
   "appropriate Minister", as respects a claim in respect of which an action could be heard and determined in England and Wales,

means the Lord Chancellor and, as respects a claim in respect of which an action could be heard and determined by a court in Scotland, means the Secretary of State;

"personal injuries" includes any disease and any impairment of a person's physical or mental condition;

and any reference to breach of a contract includes a reference to breach of—
(a) a term implied in a contract by or under any enactment or otherwise;
(b) a term of a contract as modified by or under any enactment or otherwise; and
(c) a term which, although not contained in a contract, is incorporated in the contract by another term of the contract.

(8) No order shall be made under this section unless a draft of the order has been laid before Parliament and approved by resolution of each House of Parliament.

Recoupment of Certain Benefits

Recoupment of unemployment benefit and supplementary benefit

132.—(1) This section applies to payments which are the subject of proceedings before industrial tribunals, and which are— 1–565
(a) payments of wages or compensation for loss of wages; or
(b) payments, by employers to employees, under Part II, III or V or section 53 or in pursuance of an award under section 103 of the Employment Protection Act 1975; or
(c) payments, by employers to employees, of a nature similar to, or for a purpose corresponding to the purpose of, such payments as are mentioned in pargraph (b);
and to payments of remuneration in pursuance of a protective award under section 101 of the said Act of 1975.

(2) The Secretary of State may by regulations make provision with respect to payments to which this section applies for all or any of the following purposes—
(a) enabling the Secretary of State to recover from an employer, by way of total or partial recoupment of unemployment benefit or supplementary benefit, a sum not exceeding the amount of the prescribed element of the monetary award or, in the case of a protective award, the amount of the remuneration;
(b) requiring or authorising the tribunal to order the payment of such a sum, by way of total or partial recoupment of either benefit, to the Secretary of State instead of to the employee;
(c) requiring the tribunal to order the payment to the employee of only the excess of the prescribed element of the monetary award over the amount of any unemployment benefit or supplementary benefit shown to the tribunal to have been paid to the employee, and enabling the Secretary of State to recover from the employer, by way of total or partial recoupment of the benefit, a sum not exceeding that amount.

(3) Without prejudice to subsection (2), regulations under that subsection may—

(a) be so framed as to apply to all payments to which this section applies or one or more classes of those payments, and so as to apply both to unemployment benefit and supplementary benefit or only to one of those benefits;
(b) confer powers and impose duties on industrial tribunals, on [a benefit officer within the meaning of the Supplementary Benefits Act 1976] and on insurance officers and other persons;
(c) impose, on an employer to whom a monetary award or protective award relates, a duty to furnish particulars connected with the award and to suspend payments in pursuance of the award during any period prescribed by the regulations;
(d) provide for an employer who pays a sum to the Secretary of State in pursuance of this section to be relieved from any liability to pay the sum to another person;
(e) confer on an employee who is aggrieved by any decision of [a benefit officer within the meaning of the Supplementary Benefits Act 1976] as to the total or partial recoupment of supplementary benefit in pursuance of the regulations (including any decision as to the amount of benefit) a right to appeal against the decision to an Appeal Tribunal constituted in accordance with the Supplementary Benefits Act 1976 and for that purpose apply section [15(3) and (4) and regulations under section 2(1A) of that Act] with or without modifications;
(f) provide for the proof in proceedings before industrial tribunals (whether by certificate or in any other manner) of any amount of unemployment benefit or supplementary benefit paid to an employee; and
(g) make different provision for different cases.

(4) Where in pursuance of any regulations under subsection (2) a sum has been recovered by or paid to the Secretary of State by way of total or partial recoupment of unemployment benefit or supplementary benefit—

(a) section 119(1) [(2) and (2A)] of the Social Security Act 1975 (repayment of benefit revised on review) shall not apply to the unemployment benefit recouped; and
[(b) no sum shall be recoverable under the Supplementary Benefits Act 1976, and no abatement, payment or reduction shall be made under section 12(1), (2) or (3) of that Act, by reference to the supplementary benefit recouped.]

(5) Any amount found to have been duly recovered by or paid to the Secretary of State in pursuance of regulations under subsection (2) by way of total or partial recoupment of unemployment benefit shall be paid into the National Insurance Fund.

(6) In this section—

"monetary award" means the amount which is awarded or ordered to be paid, to the employee by the tribunal or would be so awarded or ordered apart from any provision of regulations under this section;

"the prescribed element", in relation to any monetary award, means so much of that award as is attributable to such matters as may be prescribed by regulations under subsection (2);

"supplementary benefit" has the same meaning as in the Supplementary Benefits Act 1976; and "unemployment benefit" means unemployment benefit under the Social Security Act 1975.

AMENDMENTS

The words in square brackets in subs. (3)(*b*) and (*e*) were substituted by the Social Security Act 1980 (c. 30), Sched. 4, para. 13. Subs. (4)(*b*) was substituted by *ibid*. The words in square brackets in subs. (4)(*a*) were substituted by the Social Security Act 1979 (c. 18), s.21(4), Sched. 3.

Conciliation Officers

General provisions as to conciliation officers

133.—(1) The provisions of subsections (2) to (6) shall have effect in relation to industrial tribunal proceedings, or claims which could be the subject tribunal proceedings,—

1–566

(*a*) arising out of a contravention, or alleged contravention, of any of the following provisions of this Act, that is to say, sections 8, 12, 19, 23, 27, 28, 29, 31, [31A] 33 and 53; or

(*b*) arising out of a contravention, or alleged contravention, of section 99 or 102 of the Employment Protection Act 1975 or of a provision of any other Act specified by an order under subsection (7) as one to which this paragraph applies; or

(*c*) which are proceedings or claims in respect of which an industrial tribunal has jurisdiction by virtue of an order under section 131; [or

(*d*) arising out of a contravention, or alleged contravention, of section 4 of the Employment Act 1980].

(2) Where a complaint has been presented to an industrial tribunal, and a copy of it has been sent to a conciliation officer, it shall be the duty of the conciliation officer—

(*a*) if he is requested to do so by the complainant and by the person against whom the complaint is presented, or

(*b*) if, in the absence of any such request, the conciliation officer considers that he could act under this subsection with a reasonable prospect of success,

to endeavour to promote a settlement of the complaint without its being determined by an industrial tribunal.

(3) Where at any time—

(*a*) a person claims that action has been taken in respect of which a complaint could be presented by him to an industrial tribunal, but

(*b*) before any complaint relating to that action has been presented by him,

a request is made to a conciliation officer (whether by that person or by the person against whom the complaint could be made) to make his services available to them, the conciliation officer shall act in accordance with subsection (2) as if a complaint has been presented to an industrial tribunal.

(4) Subsections (2) and (3) shall apply, with appropriate modifications, to the presentation of a claim and the reference of a question to an industrial tribunal as they apply to the presentation of a complaint.

(5) In proceeding under subsection (2) or (3) a conciliation officer shall, where appropriate, have regard to the desirability of encouraging the use of other procedures available for the settlement of grievances.

(6) Anything communicated to a conciliation officer in connection with

the performance of his functions under this section shall not be admissible in evidence in any proceedings before an industrial tribunal, except with the consent of the person who communicated it to that officer.

(7) The Secretary of State may by order—
 (a) direct that further provisions of this Act be added to the list in subsection (1)(a);
 (b) specify a provision of any other Act as one to which subsection (1)(b) applies.

AMENDMENT
The words in square brackets in subs. (1) were inserted by the Employment Act 1980, Sched. 1, para. 17.

Functions of conciliation officers on complaint under s.67

134.—(1) Where a complaint has been presented to an industrial tribunal under section 67 by a person (in this section referred to as the complainant) and a copy of it has been sent to a conciliation officer, it shall be the duty of the conciliation officer—
 (a) if he is requested to do so by the complainant and by the employer against whom it was presented, or
 (b) if, in the absence of any such request, the conciliation officer considers that he could act under this section with a reasonable prospect of success,
to endeavour to promote a settlement of the complaint without its being determined by an industrial tribunal.

(2) For the purpose of promoting such a settlement, in a case where the complainant has ceased to be employed by the employer against whom the complaint was made—
 (a) the conciliation officer shall in particular seek to promote the reinstatement or re-engagement of the complainant by the employer, or by a successor of the employer or by an associated employer, on terms appearing to the conciliation officer to be equitable; but
 (b) where the complainant does not wish to be reinstated or re-engaged, or where reinstatement or re-engagement is not practicable, and the parties desire the conciliation officer to act under this section, he shall seek to promote agreement between them as to a sum by way of compensation to be paid by the employer to the complainant.

[(3) Where—
 (a) a person claims that action has been taken in respect of which a complaint could be presented by him under section 67, and
 (b) before any complaint relating to that action has been so presented, a request is made to a conciliation officer (whether by that person or by the employer) to make his services available to them,
the conciliation officer shall act in accordance with subsections (1) and (2) above as if a complaint had been presented.]

(4) In proceeding under subsections (1) to (3), a conciliation officer shall where appropriate have regard to the desirability of encouraging the use of other procedures available for the settlement of grievances.

(5) Anything communicated to a conciliation officer in connection with the performance of his functions under this section shall not be admissible

in evidence in any proceedings before an industrial tribunal, except with the consent of the person who communicated it to that officer.

AMENDMENT
Subs. (3) was substituted by the Employment Act 1980, Sched. 1, para. 18.

Employment Appeal Tribunal

Employment Appeal Tribunal

135.—(1) The Employment Appeal Tribunal established under section 87 of the Employment Protection Act 1975 shall continue in existence by that name [. . .].

(2) The Employment Appeal Tribunal (in this Act referred to as "the Appeal Tribunal") shall consist of—
   (a) such number of judges as may be nominated from time to time by the Lord Chancellor from among the judges (other than the Lord Chancellor) of the High Court and the Court of Appeal;
   (b) at least one judge of the Court of Session nominated from time to time by the Lord President of that Court; and
   (c) such number of other members as may be appointed from time to time by Her Majesty on the joint recommendation of the Lord Chancellor and the Secretary of State.

(3) The members of the Appeal Tribunal appointed under subsection (2)(c) shall be persons who appear to the Lord Chancellor and the Secretary of State to have special knowledge or experience of industrial relations, either as representatives of employers or as representatives of workers (within the meaning of the Trade Union and Labour Relations Act 1974).

(4) The Lord Chancellor shall, after consultation with the Lord President of the Court of Session, appoint one of the judges nominated under subsection (2) to be President of the Appeal Tribunal.

(5) No judge shall be nominated a member of the Appeal Tribunal except with his consent.

(6) The provisions of Schedule 11 shall have effect with respect to the Appeal Tribunal and proceedings before the Tribunal.

1–568

AMENDMENT
The words omitted from subs. (1) were repealed by the Employment Protection Act 1980, Sched. 2.

Appeals to Tribunal from industrial tribunals and Certification Officer

136.—(1) An appeal shall lie to the Appeal Tribunal on a question of law arising from any decision of, or arising in any proceedings before, an industrial tribunal under, or by virtue of, the following Acts—
   (a) the Equal Pay Act 1970;
   (b) the Sex Discrimination Act 1975;
   (c) the Employment Protection Act 1975;
   (d) the Race Relations Act 1976;
   (e) this Act.

(2) The Appeal Tribunal shall hear appeals on questions of law arising in any proceedings before, or arising from any decision of, the Certificate Officer under the following enactments—

1–569

(a) sections 3, 4 and 5 of the Trade Union Act 1913;
(b) section 4 of the Trade Union (Amalgamations, etc.) Act 1964.

(3) The Appeal Tribunal shall hear appeals on questions of fact or law arising in any proceedings before, or arising from any decision of, the Certification Officer under the following enactments—

(a) section 8 of the Trade Union and Labour Relations Act 1974;
(b) section 8 of the Employment Protection Act 1975.

(4) Without prejudice to section 13 of the Administration of Justice Act 1960 (appeal in case of contempt of court), an appeal shall lie on any question of law from any decision or order of the Appeal Tribunal with the leave of the Tribunal or of the Court of Appeal or, as the case may be, the Court of Session,—

(a) in the case of proceedings in England and Wales, to the Court of Appeal;
(b) in the case of proceedings in Scotland, to the Court of Session.

(5) No appeal shall lie except to the Appeal Tribunal from any decision of an industrial tribunal under the Acts listed in subsection (1) [or under section 2, 4 or 5 of the Employment Act 1980] or from any decision under the enactments listed in subsections (2) and (3) of the Certification Officer appointed under section 7 of the Employment Protection Act 1975.

AMENDMENT
The words in square brackets in subs. (5) were inserted by the Employment Act 1980, Sched. 1, para. 19.

PART IX

MISCELLANEOUS AND SUPPLEMENTAL

Extension of employment protection legislation

Power to extend employment protection legislation

1–570   **137.**—(1) Her Majesty may by Order in Council provide that—
(a) the provisions of this Act; and
(b) any legislation (that is to say any enactment of the Parliament of Northern Ireland and any provision made by or under a Measure of the Northern Ireland Assembly) for the time being in force in Northern Ireland which makes provision for purposes corresponding to any of the purposes of this Act,

shall, to such extent and for such purposes as may be specified in the Order, apply (with or without modification) to or in relation to any person in employment to which this section applies.

(2) This section applies to employment for the purposes of any activities—

(a) in the territorial waters of the United Kingdom; or
(b) connected with the exploration of the sea bed or subsoil or the exploitation of their natural resources in any area designated by order under section 1(7) of the Continental Shelf Act 1964; or
(c) connected with the exploration or exploitation, in a foreign sector of the continental shelf, of a cross-boundary petroleum field.

(3) An Order in Council under subsection (1)—

(a) may make different provision for different cases;
(b) may provide that all or any of the enactments referred to in subsection (1), as applied by such an Order, shall apply to individuals whether or not they are British subjects and to bodies corporate whether or not they are incorporated under the law of any part of the United Kingdom (notwithstanding that the application may affect their activities outside the United Kingdom);
(c) may make provision for conferring jurisdiction on any court or class of court specified in the Order, or on industrial tribunals, in respect of offences, causes of action or other matters arising in connection with employment to which this section applies;
(d) without prejudice to the generality of subsection (1) or of paragraph (a), may provide that the enactments referred to in subsection (1), as applied by the Order, shall apply in relation to any person in employment for the purposes of such activities as are referred to in subsection (2) in any part of the areas specified in paragraphs (a) and (b) of that subsection;
(e) may exclude from the operation of section 3 of the Territorial Waters Jurisdiction Act 1878 (consents required for prosecutions) proceedings for offences under the enactments referred to in subsection (1) in connection with employment to which this section applies;
(f) may provide that such proceedings shall not be brought without such consent as may be required by the Order;
(g) may, without prejudice to the generality of the power under subsection (1) to modify the enactments referred to in that subsection in their application for the purposes of this section, modify or exclude the operation of sections 141 and 144 or paragraph 14 of Schedule 13 or of any corresponding provision in any such Northern Irish legislation as is referred to in subsection (1)(b).

(4) Any jurisdiction conferred on any court or tribunal under this section shall be without prejudice to jurisdiction exercisable apart from this section by that or any other court or tribunal.

(5) In subsection (2) above—

"cross-boundary petroleum field" means a petroleum field that extends across the boundary between a designated area and a foreign sector of the continental shelf;

"foreign sector of the continental shelf" means an area which is outside the territorial waters of any State and within which rights are exercisable by a State other than the United Kingdom with respect to the sea bed and subsoil and their natural resources;

"petroleum field" means a geological structure identified as an oil or gas field by the Order in Council concerned.

Crown Employment

Application of Act to Crown employment

138.—(1) Subject to the following provisions of this section, Parts I (so far as it relates to itemised pay statements), II, III (except section 44), V, VII and this Part and section 53 shall have effect in relation to Crown employment and to persons in Crown employment as they have effect in relation to other employment and to other employees.

(2) In this section, subject to subsections (3) to (5), "Crown employment" means employment under or for the purposes of a government department or any officer or body exercising on behalf of the Crown functions conferred by any enactment.

(3) This section does not apply to service as a member of the naval, military or air forces of the Crown, or of any women's service administered by the Defence Council, but does apply to employment by any association established for the purposes of the Auxiliary Forces Act 1953.

(4) For the purposes of this section, Crown employment does not include any employment in respect of which there is in force a certificate issued by or on behalf of a Minister of the Crown certifying that employment of a description specified in the certificate, or the employment of a particular person so specified, is (or, at a time specified in the certificate, was) required to be excepted from this section for the purpose of safeguarding national security; and any document purporting to be a certificate so issued shall be received in evidence and shall, unless the contrary is proved, be deemed to be such a certificate.

(5) For the purposes of Parts I (so far as it relates to itemised pay statements), II, III (except section 44(3) and (4)), V, VII (except section 126(3) and (4), VIII and this Part and section 53, none of the bodies referred to in Schedule 5 shall be regarded as perfoming functions on behalf of the Crown and accordingly employment by any such body shall not be Crown employment within the meaning of this section.

(6) For the purposes of the application of the provision of this Act in relation to employment by any such body as is referred to in subsection (5), any reference to redundancy shall be construed as a reference to the existence of such circumstances as, in accordance with any arrangements for the time being in force as mentioned in section 111(3), are treated as equivalent to redundancy in relation to such employment.

(7) For the purposes of the application of the provisions of this Act in relation to Crown employment in accordance with subsection (1)—

(a) any reference to an employee shall be construed as a reference to a person in Crown employment;

(b) any reference to a contract of employment shall be construed as a reference to the terms of employment of a person in Crown employment;

(c) any reference to dismissal shall be construed as a reference to the termination of Crown employment;

(d) any reference to redundancy shall be construed as a reference to the existence of such circumstances as, in accordance with any arrangements for the time being in force as mentioned in section 111(3), are treated as equivalent to redundancy in relation to Crown employment;

(e) the reference in paragraph 1(5)(c) of Schedule 9 to a person's undertaking or any undertaking in which he works shall be construed as a reference to the national interest; and

(f) any other reference to an undertaking shall be construed, in relation to a Minister of the Crown, as a reference to his functions or (as the context may require) to the department of which he is in charge and, in relation to a government department, officer or body, shall be construed as a reference to the functions of the department, officer or body or (as the context may require) to the department, officer or body.

(8) Where the terms of employment of a person in Crown employment restrict his right to take part in—
(*a*) certain political activities; or
(*b*) activities which may conflict with his official functions,
nothing in section 29 shall require him to be allowed time off work for public duties connected with any such actictivies.

House of Commons Staff

Provisions as to House of Commons staff

139.—(1) The provisions of Parts I (so far as it relates to itemised pay statements), II, III (except section 44), V and VIII, and this Part and section 53 shall apply to relevant members of House of Commons staff as they apply to persons in Crown employment within the meaning of section 138 and accordingly for the purposes of the application of those provisions in relation to any such members—
(*a*) any reference to an employee shall be construed as a reference to any such member;
(*b*) any reference to a contract of employment shall be construed as including a reference to the terms of employment of any such member;
(*c*) any reference to dismissal shall be construed as including a reference to the termination of any such member's employment;
(*d*) the reference in paragraph 1(5)(*c*) of Schedule 9 to a person's undertaking or any undertaking in which he works shall be construed, as a reference to the national interest or, if the case so requires, the interests of the House of Commons; and
(*e*) any other reference to an undertaking shall be construed as a reference to the House of Commons.

(2) Nothing in any rule of law or the law or practice of Parliament shall prevent a relevant member of the House of Commons staff from bringing a civil employment claim before the court or from bringing before an industrial tribunal proceedings of any description which could be brought before such a tribunal by any person who is not such a member.

(3) In this section—
"relevant member of the House of Commons staff" means—
(*a*) any person appointed by the House of Commons Commission (in this section referred to as the Commission) or employed in the refreshment department; and
(*b*) any member of Mr. Speaker's personal staff;
"civil employment claim" means a claim arising out of or relating to a contract of employment or any other contract connected with employment, or a claim in tort arising in connection with a person's employment; and
"the court" means the High Court or the county court.

(4) It is hereby declared that for the purposes of the enactments applied by subsection (1) and of Part VI (where applicable to relevant members of House of Commons staff) and for the purposes of any civil employment claim—

(a) the Commission is the employer of staff appointed by the Commission; and

(b) Mr. Speaker is the employer of his personal staff and of any person employed in the refreshment department and not falling within paragraph (a);

but the foregoing provision shall have effect subject to subsection (5).

(5) The Commission or, as the case may be, Mr. Speaker may designate for all or any of the purposes mentioned in subsection (4)—

(a) any description of staff other than Mr. Speaker's personal staff; and

(b) in relation to staff so designated, any person;

and where a person is so designated he, instead of the Commission or Mr. Speaker, shall be deemed for the purposes to which the designation relates to be the employer of the persons in relation to whom he is so designated.

(6) Where any proceedings are brought by virtue of this section against the Commission or Mr. Speaker or any person designated under subsection (5), the person against whom the proceedings are brought may apply to the court or the industrial tribunal, as the case may be, to have some or other person against whom the proceedings could at the time of the application be properly brought substituted for him as a party to those proceedings.

(7) For the purposes mentioned in subsection (4) a person's employment in or for the purposes of the House of Commons shall not, provided he continues to be employed in such employment, be treated as terminated by reason only of a change (whether effected before or after the passing of the House of Commons (Administration) Act 1978, and whether effected by virtue of that Act or otherwise) in his employer and (provided he so continues) his first appointment to such employment shall be deemed after the change to have been made by his employer for the time being, and accordingly—

(a) he shall be treated for the purposes so mentioned as being continuously employed by that employer from the commencement of such employment until its termination; and

(b) anything done by or in relation to his employer for the time being in respect of such employment before the change shall be so treated as having been done by or in relation to the person who is his employer for the time being after the change.

(8) In subsection (7) "employer for the time being", in relation to a person who has ceased to be employed in or for the purposes of the House of Commons, means the person who was his employer immediately before he ceased to be so employed, except that where some other person would have been his employer for the time being if he had not ceased to be so employed, it means that other person.

(9) If the House of Commons resolves at any time that any provision of subsections (3) to (6) should be amended in its application to any member of the staff of that House, Her Majesty may by Order in Council amend that provision accordingly.

Contracting Out of Provisions of Act

Restrictions on contracting out

140.—(1) Except as provided by the following provisions of this section, any provision in an agreement (whether a contract of employment or not) shall be void in so far as it purports—

(*a*) to exclude or limit the operation of any provision of this Act; or
(*b*) to preclude any person from presenting a complaint to, or bringing any proceedings under this Act before, an industrial tribunal.

(2) Subsection (1) shall not apply—
  (*a*) to any provision in a collective agreement excluding rights under section 12 if an order under section 18 is for the time being in force in respect of it;
  (*b*) [. . .]
  (*c*) to any provision in a dismissal procedures agreement excluding rights under section 54 if that provision is not to have effect unless an order under section 65 is for the time being in force in respect of it;
  (*d*) to any agreement to refrain from presenting a complaint under section 67, where in compliance with a request under section 134(3) a conciliation officer has taken action in accordance with that subsection;
  (*e*) to any agreement to refrain from proceeding with a complaint presented under section 67 where a conciliation officer has taken action in accordance with section 134(1) and (2);
  (*f*) to any provision in an agreement if an order under section 96 is for the time being in force in respect of it;
  (*g*) to any agreement to refrain from instituting or continuing any proceedings before an industrial tribunal where a conciliation officer has taken action in accordance with section 133(2) or (3);
  (*h*) to any provision of an agreement relating to dismissal from employment such as is mentioned in section 12(1) or (2).

AMENDMENT
Subs. (2)(*b*) was repealed by the Employment Act 1980, Sched. 1, para. 20, Sched. 2.

Excluded Classes of Employment

Employment outside Great Britain

141.—(1) Sections 1 to 4 and 49 to 51 do not apply in relation to employment during any period when the employee is engaged in work wholly or mainly outside Great Britain unless the employee ordinarily works in Great Britain and the work outside Great Britain is for the same employer.

(2) Sections 8 and 53 and Parts II, III, V and VII do not apply to employment where under his contract of employment the employee ordinarily works outside Great Britain.

(3) An employee shall not be entitled to a redundancy payment if on the relevant date he is outside Great Britain, unless under his contract of employment he ordinarily worked in Great Britain.

(4) An employee who under his contract of employment ordinarily works outside Great Britain shall not be entitled to a redundancy payment unless on the relevant date he is in Great Britain in accordance with instructions given to him by his employer.

(5) For the purpose of subsection (2), a person employed to work on board a ship registered in the United Kingdom (not being a ship registered at a port outside Great Britain) shall, unless—
  (*a*) the employment is wholly outside Great Britain, or
  (*b*) he is not ordinarily resident in Great Britain,

Contracts for a fixed term ✱ S.54

1-575   **142.**—(1) Section 54 does not apply to dismissal from employment under a contract for a fixed term of [one year] or more, where the dismissal consists only of the expiry of that term without its being renewed, if before the term so expires the employee has agreed in writing to exclude any claim in respect of rights under that section in relation to that contract.

(2) An employee employed under a contract of employment for a fixed term of two years or more entered into after 5th December 1965 shall not be entitled to a redundancy payment in respect of the expiry of that term without its being renewed (whether by the employer or by an associated employer of his), if before the term so expires he has agreed in writing to exclude any right to a redundancy payment in that event.

(3) Such an agreement as is mentioned in subsection (1) or (2) may be contained either in the contract itself or in a separate agreement.

(4) where an agreement under subsection (2) is made during the currency of a fixed term, and that term is renewed, the agreement under that subsection shall not be construed as applying to the term as renewed, but without prejudice to the making of a further agreement under that subsection in relation to the term so renewed.

AMENDMENT
    The words in square brackets in subs. (1) were substituted by the Employment Act 1980 (c. 40), s.8(2).

. . . . . .

Mariners

1-576   **144.**—(1) Sections 1 to 6 and 49 to 51 do not apply to—
    (a) a person employed as a master of or a seaman on a sea-going British ship having a gross registered tonnage of eighty tons or more, including a person ordinarily employed as a seaman who is employed in or about such a ship in port by the owner or charterer of the ship to do work of a kind ordinarily done by a seaman on such a ship while it is in port; or
    (b) a person employed as a skipper of or a seaman on a fishing boat for the time being required to be registered under section 373 of the Merchant Shipping Act 1894.

(2) Sections 8 and 53 and Parts II, III and V to VII do not apply to employment as master or as a member of the crew of a fishing vessel where the employee is remunerated only by a share in the profits or gross earnings of the vessel.

(3) Section 141(3) and (4) do not apply to an employee, and section 142(2) does not apply to a contract of employment, if the employee is employed as a master or seaman in a British ship and is ordinarily resident in Great Britain.

(4) Sections 8, 29, 31, 122 and 123 do not apply to employment as a merchant seaman.

(5) Employment as a merchant seaman does not include employment in the fishing industry or employment on board a ship otherwise than by the owner, manager or charterer of that ship except employment as a radio officer, but, save as aforesaid, it includes employment as master or a mem-

ber of the crew of any ship and as a trainee undergoing training for the sea service, and employment in or about a ship in port by the owner, manager or charterer of the ship to do work of the kind ordinarily done by a merchant seaman on a ship while it is in port.

Dock workers

145.—(1) Sections 1 to 6 and 49 to 51 do not apply to any registered dock worker except when engaged in work which is not dock work.

(2) Sections 12, 19, 31, 53, 54, 122 and 123 do not apply to employment as a registered dock worker other than employment by virtue of which the employee is wholly or mainly engaged in work which is not dock work.

(3) Subject to subsection (4), section 81 does not apply to any person in respect of his employment as a registered dock worker, unless it is employment by virtue of which he is wholly or mainly engaged in work which is not dock work.

(4) Subsection (3) does not apply where—
- (*a*) the person became a registered dock worker in consequence of having been employed on work which became classified;
- (*b*) at the date of the termination of his employment he has been continuously employed since a time before that work was classified; and
- (*c*) as a result of the termination he ceases to be a registered dock worker,

and, for the purposes of this subsection, Schedule 13 shall have effect subject to the provisions of the new Scheme.

(5) In this section—

"classified" means classified as dock work for the purposes of the new Scheme by an order under section 11 of the Dock Work Regulation Act 1976;

"dock work", in relation to a dock worker registered under the 1967 Scheme, means the same as in that Scheme and in relation to one registered under the new Scheme means any work which, by reference to what it is or where it is done, is classified;

"registered" means registered under the 1967 Scheme or under the new Scheme, and in relation to a worker who is registered under the Scheme, means registered in a main register thereunder, and not in an extension register;

"the 1967 Scheme" means the Scheme made under the Dock Workers (Regulation of Employment) Act 1946 and set out, as varied, in Schedule 2 to the Dock Workers (Regulation of Employment) (Amendment) Order 1967;

"the new Scheme" means the Scheme made and in force under section 4 of the Dock Work Regulation Act 1976.

Miscellaneous classes of employment

146.—(1) [*Repealed by the Employment Act* 1982 (*c*.46), *Scheds.* 3 *and* 4.]

(2) Parts II, III, V and VII and sections 8, 9, 53 and 86 do not apply to employment under a contract of employment in police service or to persons engaged in such employment.

(3) in subsection (2), "police service" means service—
- (*a*) as a member of any constabulary maintained by virtue of any enactment, or

(b) in any other capacity by virtue of which a person has the powers or privileges of a constable.

(4) Subject to subsections (5), (6) and (7), the following provisions of this Act (which confer rights which do not depend upon an employee having a qualifying period of continuous employment) do not apply to employment under a contract which normally involves employment for less than sixteen hours weekly, that is to say, sections [1, 4,] 8, 27, 28 and 29.

(5) If the employee's relations with his employer cease to be governed by a contract which normally involves work for sixteen hours or more weekly and become governed by a contract, which normally involves employment for eight hours or more, but less than sixteen hours, weekly, the employee shall nevertheless for a period of twenty-six weeks, computed in accordance with subsection (6), be treated for the purposes of subsection (4) as if his contract normally involved employment for sixteen hours or more weekly.

(6) In computing the said period of twenty-six weeks no account shall be taken of any week—
(a) during which the employee is in fact employed for sixteen hours or more;
(b) during which the employee takes part in a strike (as defined by paragraph 24 of Schedule 13) or is absent from work because of a lockout (as so defined) by his employer; or
(c) during which there is no contract of employment but which, by virtue of paragraph 9(1) of Schedule 13, counts in computing a period of continuous employment.

(7) an employee whose relations with his employer are governed by a contract of employment which normally involves employment for eight hours or more, but less than sixteen hours, weekly shall nevertheless, if he has been continuously employed for a period of five years or more be treated for the purposes of subsection (4) as if his contract normally involved employment for sixteen hours or more weekly.

[(8) References in subsection (4) to (7) to weeks are to weeks within the meaning of Schedule 13.]

AMENDMENT
The figures in square brackets in subs. (4), and subs. (8) were inserted by the Employment Act 1982 (c.46), Sched. 2, para. 8(5).

. . . . . .

Supplementary Provisions

Review of limits
148.—(1) the Secretary of State shall in each calendar year review—
(a) the limits referred to in section 15;
(b) the limit referred to in section 122(5); and
(c) the limits imposed by paragraph 8(1) of Schedule 14 on the amount of a week's pay for the purposes of those provisions;
and shall determine whether any of those limits should be varied.

(2) In making a review under this section the Secretary of State shall consider—
(a) the general level of earnings obtaining in Great Britain at the time of the review;
(b) the national economic situation as a whole; and

(c) such other matters as he thinks relevant.

(3) If on a review under this section the Secretary of State determines that, having regard to the considerations mentioned in subsection (2), any of those limits should be varied, he shall prepare and lay before each House of Parliament the draft of an order giving effect to his decision.

(4) Where a draft of an order under this section is approved by resolution of each House of Parliament the Secretary of State shall make an order in the form of the draft.

(5) If, following the completion of an annual review under this section, the Secretary of State determines that any of the limits referred to in subsection (1) shall not be varied, he shall lay before each House of Parliament a report containing a statement of his reasons for that determination.

(6) The Secretary of State may at any time, in addition to the annual review provided for in subsection (1), conduct a further review of the limits mentioned in subsection (1), so as to determine whether any of those limits should be varied, and subsections (2) to (4) shall apply to such a review as if it were a review under subsection (1).

General power to amend Act
149.—(1) Subject to the following provisions of this section, the Secretary of State may by order
   (a) provide that any enactment contained in this Act which is specified in the order shall not apply to persons or to employments of such classes as may be prescribed in the order.
   (b) provide that any such enactment shall apply to persons or employment of such classes as may be prescribed in the order subject, except in relation to section 54 (but without prejudice to paragraph (a)), to such exceptions and modifications as may be so prescribed;
   (c) vary, or exclude the operation of, any of the following provisions of this Act, that is to say, sections [13(2), 20(2), 49(4A)] 64(1), [64A(1)] 99, 141(2) and (5), [. . .], 144(1), (2), (4) and (5), 145(1), (2) and (3) and 146 [. . .] (4) to (7);
   (d) add to, vary or delete any of the provisions of Schedule 5.

(2) Subsection (1) does not apply to the following provisions of this Act, namely, sections [. . .] 52, 55, 57, 58, [58A] 59, 62, 63, 65, 66, 67, [73(4B), 75, 75A(7)] 80, 103, to 120, 128, 134, 141(1), [142(1) and 151] and Schedules 3, 9, and 13, and, in addition, paragraph (b) of subsection (1) does not apply to sections 1 to 6 and 49 to 51 [. . .].

(3) the provisions of this section are without prejudice to any other power of the Secretary of State to amend, vary or repeal any provision of this Act or to extend or restrict its operation in relation to any person or employment.

(4) No order under subsection (1) shall be made unless a draft of the order has been laid before Parliament and approved by a resolution of each House of Parliament.

1–580

AMENDMENT
   The figures in square brackets in subss. (1)(c) and (2) were inserted by the Employment Act 1980 (c. 42), Sched. 1, para. 21 and by the Employment Act 1982 (c. 46), Sched. 2, para. 9(1) and Sched. 3, para. 24. The words omitted from these subsections were repealed by the Employment Act 1982 (c. 46), Sched. 4.

Death of employee or employer
150. Schedule 12 shall have effect for the purpose of supplementing and

1–581

modifying the provisions of Part I (so far as it relates to itemised pay statements), section 53 and Parts II, III, and V to VII as respects the death of an employee or employer.

[Computation of period of continuous employment

151.—(1) References in any provision of this Act to a period of continuous employment are, except where provision is expressly made to the contrary, to a period computed in accordance with the provisions of this section and Schedule 13; and in any such provision which refers to a period of continuous employment expressed in months or years a month means a calendar month and a year means a year of twelve calendar months.

(2) In computing an employee's period of continuous employment any question arising as to—
  (*a*) whether the employee's employment is of a kind counting towards a period of continuous employment, or
  (*b*) whether periods (consecutive or otherwise) are to be treated as forming a single period of continuous employment,
shall be determined in accordance with Schedule 13 (that is to say, week by week), but the length of an employee's period of employment shall be computed in months and years of twelve months in accordance with the following rules.

(3) Subject to the following provisions of this section, an employee's period of continuous employment for the purposes of any provision of this Act begins with the day on which he starts work and ends with the day by reference to which the length of his period of continuous employment falls to be ascertained for the purposes of the provision in question.

(4) For the purposes of section 81 and Schedule 4 an employee's period of continuous employment shall be treated as beginning on his eighteenth birthday if that date is later than the starting date referred to in subsection (3).

(5) If an employee's period of continuous employment includes one or more periods which, by virtue of any provision of Schedule 13, do not count in computing the length of the period but do not break continuity, the beginning of the period shall be treated as postponed by the number of days falling within that intervening period or, as the case may be, by the aggregate number of days falling within those periods.

(6) The number of days falling within such an intervening period is—
  (*a*) in the case of a period to which paragraph 14(3) of Schedule 13 applies, seven days for each week within that sub-paragraph;
  (*b*) in the case of a period to which paragraph 15(2) or (4) of that Schedule applies, the number of days between the last working day before the strike or lock-out and the day on which work was resumed;
  (*c*) in the case of a period to which paragraph 16(1) of that Schedule applies, the number of days between the employee's last day of employment before service under Part I of the National Service Act 1948 and the day on which he resumed employment in accordance with Part II of that Act.]

AMENDMENT
This section was substituted by the Employment Act 1982 (c.46), Sched. 2, para. 7.

Calculation of normal working hours and a week's pay

152. Schedule 14 shall have effect for the purposes of this Act for calculating the normal working hours and the amount of a week's pay of any employee.

1–583

Interpretation

153.—(1) In this Act, except so far as the context otherwise requires—

1–584

"act" and "action" each includes omission and references to doing an act or taking action shall be construed accordingly;

"business" includes a trade or profession and includes any activity carried on by a body or persons, whether corporate or unincorporate; [. . .];

"collective agreement" has the meaning given by section 30(1) of the Trade Union and Labour Relations Act 1974;

"confinement" means the birth of a living child or the birth of a child whether living or dead after twenty-eight weeks of pregnancy;

"contract of employment" means a contract of service or apprenticeship, whether express or implied, and (if it is express) whether it is oral or in writing;

"dismissal procedures agreement" means an agreement in writing with respect to procedures relating to dismissal made by or on behalf of one or more independent trade unions and one or more employers or employers' associations;

"effective date of termination" has the meaning given by section 55(4) [to (6)].

"employee" means an individual who has entered into or works under (or, where the employment has ceased, worked under) a contract of employment;

"employer", in relation to an employee, means the person by whom the employee is (or, in a case where the employment has ceased, was) employed;

"employers' association" has the same meaning as it has for the purposes of the Trade Union and Labour Relations Act 1974;

"employer's payment" means a payment falling within paragraph (*a*), (*b*) or (*c*) of section 104(1);

"employment", except for the purposes of sections 111 to 115, means employment under a contract of employment;

"expected week of confinement" means the week, beginning with midnight between Saturday and Sunday, in which it is expected that confinement will take place;

"government department", except in section 138 and paragraph 19 of Schedule 13, includes a Minister of the Crown;

"guarantee payment" has the meaning given by section 12(1); [. . .];

"independent trade union" means a trade union which—

> (*a*) is not under the domination or control of an employer or a group of employers or of one or more employers' associations; and
>
> (*b*) is not liable to interference by an employer or any such group or association (arising out of the provision of financial or material support or by any other means whatsoever) tending towards such control;

and, in relation to a trade union, "independent" and "independence" shall be construed accordingly;

"job", in relation to an employee, means the nature of the work which he is employed to do in accordance with his contract and the capacity and place in which he is so employed;

"maternity pay" has the meaning given by section 33(1);

"Maternity Pay Fund" means the fund referred to in section 37;

"maternity pay rebate" has the meaning given by section 39;

"notice of intention to claim" has the meaning given by section 88;

"notified day of return" has the meaning given by section 47(1) and (8);

"official", in relation to a trade union, has the meaning given by section 30(1) of the Trade Union and Labour Relations Act 1974;

"original contract of employment", in relation to an employee who is absent from work wholly or partly because of pregnancy or confinement, means the contract under which she worked immediately before the beginning of her absence or, if she entered into that contract during her pregnancy by virtue of section 60(2) or otherwise by reason of her pregnancy, the contract under which she was employed immediately before she entered into the later contract or, if there was more than one later contract, the first of the later contracts;

"position", in relation to an employee, means the following matters taken as a whole, that is to say, his status as an employee, the nature of his work and his terms and conditions of employment;

"Redundancy Fund" means the fund referred to in section 103;

"redundancy payment" has the meaning given by section 81 (1);

"redundancy rebate" has the meaning given by section 104;

"relevant date", for the purposes of the provisions of this Act which relate to redundancy payments, has the meaning given by section 90;

"renewal" includes extension, and any reference to renewing a contract or a fixed term shall be construed accordingly;

"statutory provision" means a provision, whether of a general or a special nature, contained in, or in any document made or issued under, any Act, whether of a general or special nature;

"successor" has the meaning given by section 30(3) and (4) of the Trade Union and Labour Relations Act 1974;

"trade dispute" has the meaning given by section 29 of the said Act of 1974;

"trade union" has the meaning given by section 28 of the said Act of 1974;

"union membership agreement" has the meaning given by section 30(1) of the said Act of 1974 and "employees", in relation thereto, has the meaning given by section 30(5A) of that Act;

"week" means, in relation to an employee whose remuneration is calculated weekly by a week ending with a day other than Saturday, a week ending with that other day, and in relation to any other employee, a week ending with Saturday.

(2) References in this Act to dismissed by reason of redundancy, and to cognate expressions, shall be construed in accordance with section 81.

(3) In sections 33, 47, 56, 61 and 86 and Schedule 2, except where the

context otherwise requires, "to return to work" means to return to work in accordance with section 45(1), and cognate expressions shall be construed accordingly.

(4) For the purposes of this Act, any two employers are to be treated as associated if one is a company of which the other (directly or indirectly) has control, or if both are companies of which a third person (directly or indirectly) has control; and the expression "associated employer" shall be construed accordingly.

(5) For the purposes of this Act it is immaterial whether the law which (apart from this Act) governs any person's employment is the law of the United Kingdom, or of a part of the United Kingdom, or not.

(6) In this Act, except where otherwise indicated—
- (a) a reference to a numbered Part, section or Schedule is a reference to the Part or section of, or the Schedule to, this Act so numbered, and
- (b) a reference in a section to a numbered subsection is a reference to the subsection of that section so numbered, and
- (c) a reference in a section, subsection or Schedule to a numbered paragraph is a reference to the paragraph of that section, subsection or Schedule so numbered, and
- (d) a reference to any provision of an Act (including this Act) includes a Schedule incorporated in the Act by that provision.

(7) Except so far as the context otherwise requires, any reference in this Act to an enactment shall be construed as a reference to that enactment as amended or extended by or under any other enactment, including this Act.

AMENDMENTS

The definition of "certified midwife" in subs. (1) was repealed by the Nurses, Midwives and Health Visitors Act 1979 (c. 36), Sched. 8. The definition of "inadmissible reason" was repealed by the Employment Act 1982 (c. 46), Sched. 4.

Orders, rules and regulations

154.—(1) Any power conferred by any provision of this Act to make an order (other than an Order in Council [. . .]) or to make rules or regulations shall be exercisable by statutory instrument.

(2) Any statutory instrument made under any power conferred by this Act to make an Order in Council or other order or to make rules or regulations, except—
- (a) an instrument required to be laid before Parliament in draft; and
- (b) an order under section 18,

shall be subject to annulment in pursuance of a resolution of either House of Parliament.

(3) Any power conferred by this Act which is exercisable by statutory instrument shall include power to make such incidental, supplementary or transitional provisions as appear to the authority exercising the power to be necessary or expedient.

(4) An order made by statutory instrument under any provision of this Act may be revoked or varied by a subsequent order made under that provision.

This subsection does not apply to an order under [section 65, 66 or 96].

AMENDMENT
The words omitted in subs. (1) were repealed, and the words in square brackets in subs. (4) were substituted, by the Employment Act 1980 (c. 42), Sched. 1, para. 22.

Offences by bodies corporate

1–586   **155.**—(1) Where an offence under section 44 or 126 committed by a body corporate is proved to have been committed with the consent or connivance of, or to be attributable to any neglect on the part of, any director, manager, secretary or other similar officer of the body corporate, or any person who was purporting to act in any such capacity, he as well as the body corporate shall be guilty of that offence and shall be liable to be proceeded against and punished accordingly.

(2) Where the affairs of a body corporate are managed by its members, subsection (1) shall apply in relation to the acts and defaults of a member in connection with his functions of management as if he were a director of the body corporate.

Payments into the Consolidated Fund

1–587   **156.**—(1) There shall be paid out of the Maternity Pay Fund into the Consolidated Fund sums equal to the amount of any expenses incurred by the Secretary of State in exercising his functions under this Act relating to maternity pay.

(2) There shall be paid out of the Redundancy Fund into the Consolidated Fund sums equal to the amount of any expenses incurred—
  (*a*) by the Secretary of State in consequence of Part VI, except expenses incurred in the payment of sums in accordance with any such arrangements as are mentioned in section 111(3);
  (*b*) by the Secretary of State (or by persons acting on his behalf) in exercising his functions under sections 122 to 126.

(3) There shall be paid out of the Redundancy Fund into the Consolidated Fund such sums as the Secretary of State may estimate in accordance with directions given by the Treasury to be the amount of any expenses incurred by any government department other than the Secretary of State in consequence of the provisions of sections 103 to 109.

Northern Ireland

1–587/   **157.**—(1) If provision is made by Northern Ireland legislation (that is to say by or under a Measure of the Northern Ireland Assembly) for purposes corresponding to any of the purposes of this Act, except [sections 1 to 6] and 49 to 51, the Secretary of State may, with the consent of the Treasury, make reciprocal arrangements with the appropriate Northern Irish authority for co-ordinating the relevant provisions of this Act with the corresponding provisions of the Northern Irish legislation, so as to secure that they operate, to such extent as may be provided by the arrangements, as a single system.

(2) For the purpose of giving effect to any such arrangements the Secretary of State shall have power, in conjunction with the appropriate Northern Irish authority—
  (*a*) where the arrangements relate to the provisions of this Act relating to maternity pay, to make any necessary financial adjustments between the Maternity Pay Fund and any fund established under Northern Irish legislation; and

(b) where the arrangements relate to Part VI or to sections 122 to 126, to make any necessary financial adjustments between the Redundancy Fund and the Northern Ireland Redundancy Fund.

(3) The Secretary of State may make regulations for giving effect in Great Britain to any such arrangements, and any such regulations may make different provision for different cases, and may provide that the relevant provisions of this Act shall have effect in relation to persons affected by the arrangements subject to such modifications and adaptations as may be specified in the regulations, including provision—
- (a) for securing that acts, omissions and events having any effect for the purposes of the Northern Irish legislation shall have a corresponding effect for the purposes of this Act (but not so as to confer a right to double payment in respect of the same act, omission or event); and
- (b) for determining, in cases where rights accrue both under this Act and under the Northern Irish legislation, which of those rights shall be available to the person concerned.

(4) In this section "the appropriate Northern Irish authority" means such authority as may be specified in that behalf in the Northern Irish legislation.

The Isle of Man
158.—(1) If an Act of Tynwald is passed for purposes similar to the purposes of Part VI, the Secretary of State may, with the consent of the Treasury, make reciprocal arrangements with the appropriate Isle of Man authority for co-ordinating the provisions of Part VI with the corresponding provisions of the Act of Tynwald so as to secure that they operate, to such extent as may be provided by the arrangements, as a single system.

(2) For the purpose of giving effect to any such arrangements, the Secretary of State shall have power, in conjunction with the appropriate Isle of Man authority, to make any necessary financial adjustments between the Redundancy Fund and any fund established under the Act of Tynwald.

(3) The Secretary of State may make regulations for giving effect in Great Britain to any such arrangements, and any such regulations may provide that Part VI shall have effect in relation to persons affected by the arrangements subject to such modifications and adaptations as may be specified in the regulations, including provision—
- (a) for securing that acts, omissions and events having effect for the purposes of the Act of Tynwald shall have a corresponding effect for the purposes of Part VI (but not so as to confer a right to double payment in respect of the same act, omission or event); and
- (b) for determining, in cases where rights accrue both under this Act and under the Act of Tynwald, which of those rights shall be available to the person concerned.

(4) In this section "the appropriate Isle of Man authority" means such authority as may be specified in that behalf in an Act of Tynwald.

Transitional provisions, savings, consequential amendments and repeals
159.—(1) The transitional provisions and savings in Schedule 15 shall have effect but nothing in that Schedule shall be construed as prejudicing section 38 of the Interpretation Act 1889 (effect or repeals).

(2) The enactments specified in Schedule 16 shall have effect subject to the amendments specified in that Schedule.

372   *Employment Protection (Consolidation) Act 1978*

(3) The enactments specified in the first column of Schedule 17 are hereby repealed to the extent specified in column 3 of that Schedule.

Citation, commencement and extent

1–590   160.—(1) This Act may be cited as the Employment Protection (Consolidation) Act 1978.

(2) This Act, except section 139(2) to (9) and the repeals in section 122 of the Employment Protection Act 1975 provided for in Schedule 17 to this Act, shall come into force on 1st November 1978, and section 139(2) to (9) and those repeals shall come into force on 1st January 1979.

(3) This Act, except sections 137 and 157 and paragraphs 12 and 28 of Schedule 16, shall not extend to Northern Ireland.

SCHEDULES

1–591 Section 19   SCHEDULE 1

PROVISIONS LEADING TO SUSPENSION ON MEDICAL GROUNDS

1–6. [*Removed by S.I. 1980 No. 1581.*]		
7. The Indiarubber Regulations 1922.	S.R. & O. 1922 No. 329	Reg. 12.
8. The Chemical Works Regulations 1922.	S.R. & O. 1922 No. 731	Reg. 30.
9–12. [*Removed by S.I. 1980 No. 1581.*]		
13. The Ionising Radiations (Unsealed Radioactive Substances) Regulations 1968.	S.I. 1968 No. 780	. . . Regs. 12 and 33.
14. The Ionising Radiations (Sealed Sources) Regulations 1969.	S.I. 1969 No. 808	. . . Regs. 11 and 30.
15. The Radioactive Substances (Road Transport Workers) (Great Britain) Regulations 1970.	S.I. 1970 No. 1827.	. . . Reg. 14.
[The Radioactive Substances (Road Transport Workers) (Great Britain) (Amendment) Regulations 1975.	S.I. 1975 No. 1522	
The Control of Lead at Work Regulations 1980.	S.I. 1980 No. 1248	. . . Reg. 16]

AMENDMENT

The provisions in square brackets were added to the list by the Employment Protection (Medical Suspension) Order 1980 (S.I. 1980 No. 1581).

1–592 Section 33   SCHEDULE 2

SUPPLEMENTARY PROVISIONS RELATING TO MATERNITY

PART I

UNFAIR DISMISSAL

Introductory

1. References in this Part to provisions of this Act relating to unfair dismissal are references to those provisions as they apply by virtue of section 56.

Adaptation of unfair dismissal provisions

2.—(1) Section 57 shall have effect as if for subsection (3) there were substituted the following subsection:—

"(3) Where the employer has fulfilled the requirements of subsection (1), then, subject to section 58(1), 59, 60 and 62, the determination of the question whether the dismissal was fair or unfair having regard to the reason shown by the employer, shall depend on whether [in the circumstances (including the size and administrative resources of the employer's undertaking) the employer would have been acting reasonably or unreasonably in treating it as a sufficient reason for dismissing the employee if she had not been absent from work; and that question shall be determined in accordance with equity and the substantial merits of the case].

(2) If in the circumstances described in section 45(3) no offer is made of such alternative employment as is referred to in that subsection, then the dismissal which by virtue of section 56 treated as taking place shall, notwithstanding anything in section 57 or 58, be treated as an unfair dismissal for the purposes of Part V of this Act.

(3) The following references shall be construed as references to the notified day of return, that is to say—
   (*a*) references in Part V of this Act to the effective date of termination;
   (*b*) references in sections 69 and 70 to the date of termination of employment.

(4) The following provisions of this Act shall not apply, that is to say, sections 55, [58(3) to (12)] [58A], 64(1), 65, 66, 73(5) and (6), 141(2), 142(1), 144(2) and 145(2)] paragraph 11(1) of Schedule 13, paragraphs 7(1)(*f*) to (*i*) and (2) and 8(3) of Schedule 14 and paragraph 10 of Schedule 15.

(5) For the purposes of Part II of Schedule 14 as it applies for the calculation of a week's pay for the purposes of section 71 or 73, the calculation date is the last day on which the employee worked under the original contract of employment.

PART II

REDUNDANCY PAYMENTS

Introductory

3. References in this Part to provisions of this Act relating to redundancy are references to those provisions as they apply by virtue of section 86.

1–593

Adaptation of redundancy payments provisions

4.—(1) References in Part VI of this Act shall be adapted as follows, that is to say—
   (*a*) references to the relevant date, wherever they occur, shall be construed, except where the context otherwise requires, as references to the notified day of return;
   (*b*) references in sections 82(4) and 84(1) to a renewal or re-engagement taking effect immediately on the ending of employment under the previous contract or after an interval of not more than four weeks thereafter, shall be construed as references to a renewal or re-engagement taking effect on the notified day of return or not more than four weeks after that day; and
   (*c*) references in section 84(3) to the provisions of the previous contract shall be construed as references to the provisions of the original contract of employment.

(2) Nothing in section 86 shall prevent an employee from being treated, by reason of the operation of section 84(1), as not having been dismissed for the purposes of Part VI of this Act.

(3) The following provisions of this Act shall not apply, that is to say, sections 81(1)(*b*), 82(1) and (2), 83(1) and (2), 85, 87 to 89, 90(3), 92, 93, 96, 110, 144(2) [. . .] and 150, paragraph 4 of Schedule 4, Schedule 12 and paragraphs 7(1)(*j*) and (*k*) and 8(4) of Schedule 14.

(4) For the purposes of Part II of Schedule 14 as it applies for the calculation of a week's pay for the purposes of Schedule 4, the calculation date is the last day on which the employee worked under the original contract of employment.

Prior redundancy

5. If, in proceedings arising out of a failure to permit an employee to return to work, the employer shows—
   (*a*) that the reason for the failure is that the employee is redundant; and
   (*b*) that the employee was dismissed or, had she continued to be employed by him, would have been dismissed, by reason of redundancy during her absence on a day earlier than

the notified day of return and falling after the beginning of the eleventh week before the expected week of confinement,
then, for the purposes of Part VI of this Act the employee—
  (i) shall not be treated as having been dismissed with effect from the notified day of return; but
  (ii) shall, if she would not otherwise be so treated, be treated as having been continuously employed until that earlier day and as having been dismissed by reason of redundancy with effect from that day.

PART III

GENERAL

Dismissal during period of absence

1–594 6.—(1) This paragraph applies to the dismissal of an employee who is under this Act entitled to return to work and whose contract of employment continues to subsist during the period of her absence but who is dismissed by her employer during that period after the beginning of the eleventh week before the expected week of confinement.

(2) For the purposes of sub-paragraph (1), an employee shall not be taken to be dismissed during the period of her absence if the dismissal occurs in the course of the employee's attempting to return to work in accordance with her contract in circumstances in which section 48 applies.

(3) In the application of Part V of this Act to a dismissal to which this paragraph applies, the following provisions shall not apply, that is to say, sections [58(3) to (12)] [58A], 64, 65, 66, 141(2), 144(2), and 145].

(4) Any such dismissal shall not affect the employee's right to return to work, but—
  (a) compensation in any unfair dismissal proceedings arising out of that dismissal shall be assessed without regard to the employee's right to return; and
  (b) that right shall be exercisable only on her repaying any redundancy payment or compensation for unfair dismissal paid in respect of that dismissal, if the employer requests such repayment.

Power to amend or modify

7.—(1) The Secretary of State may by order amend the provisions of this Schedule and section 48 or modify the application of those provisions to any description of case.

(2) No order under this paragraph shall be made unless a draft of the order has been laid before Parliament and approved by a resolution of each House of Parliament.

AMENDMENTS
The numbers in square brackets in paras. 2(4) and 6(3) were inserted by the Employment Act 1980 (c. 42), Sched. 1, para. 24 and by the Employment Act 1982 (c. 46), Sched. 3, para. 27. The numbers omitted from para. 4(3) were repealed by the Employment Act 1982 (c.46), Sched. 4.

1–595 Section 50   SCHEDULE 3

RIGHTS OF EMPLOYEE IN PERIOD OF NOTICE

Preliminary

1. In this Schedule the "period of notice" means the period of notice required by section 49(1) or, as the case may be, section 49(2).

Employments for which there are normal working hours

2.—(1) If an employee has normal working hours under the contract of employment in force during the period of notice, and if during any part of those normal working hours—
  (a) the employee is ready and willing to work but no work is provided for him by his employer; or
  (b) the employee is incapable of work because of sickness or injury; or

(c) the employee is absent from work in accordance with the terms of his employment relating to holidays,

then the employer shall be liable to pay the employee for the part of normal working hours covered by paragraphs (*a*), (*b*) and (*c*) a sum not less than the amount of remuneration for that part of normal working hours calculated at the average hourly rate of remuneration produced by dividing a week's pay by the number of normal working hours.

(2) Any payment made to the employee by his employer in respect of the relevant part of the period of notice whether by way of sick pay, holiday pay or otherwise, shall go towards meeting the employers' liability under this paragraph.

(3) Where notice was given by the employee, the employer's liability under this paragraph shall not arise unless and until the employee leaves the service of the employer in pursuance of the notice.

Employments for which there are no normal working hours

3.—(1) If an employee does not have normal working hours under the contract of employment in force in the period of notice the employer shall be liable to pay the employee for each week of the period of notice a sum not less than a week's pay.

(2) Subject to sub-paragraph (3), the employer's obligation under this paragraph shall be conditional on the employee being ready and willing to do work of a reasonable nature and amount to earn a week's pay.

(3) Sub-paragraph (2) shall not apply—
  (*a*) in respect of any period during which the employee is incapable of work because of sickness or injury, or
  (*b* in respect of any period during which the employee is absent from work in accordance with the terms of his employment relating to holidays,
and any payment made to an employee by his employer in respect of such a period, whether by way of sick pay, holiday pay or otherwise, shall be taken into account for the purposes of this paragraph as if it were remuneration paid by the employer in respect of that period.

(4) Where the notice was given by the employee, the employer's liability under this paragraph shall not arise unless and until the employee leaves the service of the employer in pursuance of the notice.

Sickness or industrial injury benefit

4.—(1) The following provisions of this paragraph shall have effect where the arrangements in force relating to the employment are such that—
  (*a*) payments by way of sick pay are made by the employer to employees to whom the arrangements apply, in cases where any such employees are incapable of work because of sickness or injury, and
  (*b*) in calculating any payment so made to any such employee an amount representing, or treated as representing, sickness benefit or industrial injury benefit is taken into account, whether by way of deduction or by way of calculating the payment as a supplement to that amount.

(2) If during any part of the period of notice the employee is incapable of work because of sickness or injury, and—
  (*a*) one or more payments, by way of sick pay are made to him by the employer in respect of that part of the period of notice, and
  (*b*) in calculating any such payment such an amount as is referred to in sub-paragraph (1)(*b*) is taken into account as therein mentioned,
then for the purposes of this Schedule the amount so taken into account shall be treated as having been paid by the employer to the employee by way of sick pay in respect of that part of that period, and shall go towards meeting the liability of the employer under paragraph 2 or paragraph 3 accordingly.

Absence on leave granted at request of employee

5. The employer shall not be liable under the foregoing provisions of this Schedule to make any payment in respect of a period during which the employee is absent from work with the leave of the employer granted at the request of the employee (including any period of time off taken in accordance with section 27, 28, 29 [31 or 31A]).

Notice given before a strike

6. No payment shall be due under this Schedule in consequence of a notice to terminate a contract given by an employee if, after the notice is given and on or before the termination of the contract, the employee takes part in a strike of employees of the employer.

In this paragraph "strike" has the meaning given by paragraph 24 of Schedule 13.

Termination of employment during period of notice

7.—(1) If, during the period of notice, the employer breaks the contract of employment, payments received under this Schedule in respect of the part of the period after the breach shall go towards mitigating the damages recoverable by the employee for loss of earnings in that part of the period of notice.

(2) If, during the period of notice, the employee breaks the contract and the employer rightfully treats the breach as terminating the contract, no payment shall be due to the employee under this Schedule in respect of the part of the period of notice falling after the termination of the contract.

AMENDMENT

The figures in square brackets in para. 5 were substituted by the Employment Act 1980 (c. 42), Sched. 1, para. 25.

1–596 Section 81

SCHEDULE 4

CALCULATION OF REDUNDANCY PAYMENTS

1. The amount of a redundancy payment to which an employee is entitled in any case shall, subject to the following provisions of this Schedule, be calculated by reference to the period, ending with the relevant date, during which he has been continuously employed.

2. Subject to paragraphs 3 and 4, the amount of the redundancy payment shall be calculated by reference to the period specified in paragraph 1 by starting at the end of that period and reckoning backwards the number of years of employment falling within that period, and allowing—
   (a) one and a half weeks' pay for each such year of employment [. . .] in which the employee was not below the age of forty-one;
   (b) one week's pay for each such year of employment (not falling within the preceding sub-paragraph) [. . .] in which the employee was not below the age of twenty-two; and
   (c) half a week's pay for each such year of employment not falling within either of the preceding sub-paragraphs.

3. Where, in reckoning the number of years of employment in accordance with paragraph 2, twenty years of employment have been reckoned, no account shall be taken of any year of employment earlier than those twenty years.

4.—(1) Where in the case of an employee the relevant date is after the specified anniversary, the amount of the redundancy payment, calculated in accordance with the preceding provisions of this Schedule, shall be reduced by the appropriate fraction.

(2) In this paragraph "the specified anniversary", in relation to a man, means the sixty-fourth anniversary of the day of his birth, and, in relation to a woman, means the fifty-ninth anniversary of the day of her birth, and "the appropriate fraction" means the fraction of which—
   (a) the numerator is the number of whole months, reckoned from the specified anniversary, in the period beginning with that anniversary and ending with the relevant date, and
   (b) the denominator is twelve.

5. For the purposes of any provision contained in Part VI whereby an industrial tribunal may determine that an employer shall be liable to pay to an employee either—
   (a) the whole of the redundancy payment to which the employee would have been entitled apart from another provision therein mentioned, or
   (b) such part of that redundancy payment as the tribunal thinks fit,
the preceding provisions of this Schedule shall apply as if in those provisions any reference to the amount of a redundancy payment were a reference to the amount of the redundancy payment to which the employee would have been so entitled.

6. The preceding provisions of this Schedule shall have effect without prejudice to the

operation of any regulations made under section 98 whereby the amount of a redundancy payment, or part of a redundancy payment, may be reduced.

7. [*Repealed by the Employment Act* 1982 *(c.46), Sched.* 4].

AMENDMENT

The words omitted from para. 2(*a*) and (*b*) were repealed by the Employment Act 1982 (c.46), Sched. 4.

Section 99   SCHEDULE 5   1–597

NATIONAL HEALTH SERVICE EMPLOYERS

1. A Regional Health Authority, Area Health Authority [District Health Authority], special health authority, Health Board of the Common Services Agency for the Scottish Health Service.
2. The Dental Estimates Board.
3. Any joint committee constituted under section 13(8) of the National Health Service (Scotland) Act 1972.
4. The Public Health Laboratory Service Board.

AMENDMENT

The words in square brackets in para. 1 were added by the Health Services Act 1980 (c.53), Sched. 1, para. 85.

Section 104   SCHEDULE 6   1–598

CALCULATION OF REDUNDANCY REBATES

PART I

REBATES IN RESPECT OF REDUNDANCY PAYMENTS

1. Subject to sections 104(7) and 108 and to the following provisions of this Part, the amount of any redundancy rebate payable in respect of a redundancy payment shall be calculated by taking the number of years of employment by reference to which the redundancy payment falls to be calculated in accordance with Schedule 4 and allowing—
   (*a*) 123/200 of one week's pay for each year of employment falling within sub-paragraph (*a*) of paragraph 2 of that Schedule;
   (*b*) 41/100 of one week's pay for each year of employment falling within sub-paragraph (*b*) of that paragraph; and
   (*c*) 41/200 of one week's pay for each year of employment falling within sub-paragraph (*c*) of that paragraph.

2. Where the amount of the redundancy payment, calculated in accordance with paragraphs 1, 2 and 3 of Schedule 4, is reduced by virtue of paragraph 4 of that Schedule, the amount of the rebate shall be 41/100 of the amount of the redundancy payment as so reduced.

3.—(1) The provisions of this paragraph shall have effect in relation to any case where—
   (*a*) under section 85, 92 or 110 an industrial tribunal is empowered to determine that an employer shall be liable to pay to an employee either the whole or part of the redundancy payment to which the employee would have been entitled apart from another provision therein mentioned, and
   (*b*) the tribunal determines that the employer shall be liable to pay part (but not the whole) of that redundancy payment.

(2) There shall be ascertained what proportion that part of the redundancy payment bears to the whole of it (in this paragraph referred to as "the relevant proportion").

(3) There shall also be ascertained what, in accordance with the preceding provisions of this Part, would have been the amount of the redundancy rebate payable in respect of that redundancy payment if the employer had been liable to pay the whole of it.

(4) Subject to paragraph 4, the amount of the rebate payable in that case shall then be an amount equal to the relevant proportion of the amount referred to in sub-paragraph (3).

4. Where the amount of a redundancy payment or part of a redundancy payment is reduced in accordance with regulations made under section 98,—
   (*a*) the proportion by which it is so reduced shall be ascertained, and

(b) the amount of any redundancy rebate calculated by reference to that payment shall be reduced by that proportion.

Part II

Rebates in Respect of Other Payments

Introductory

1–599 5. The provisions of this Part shall have effect for the purpose of calculating the amount of any redundancy rebate payable in respect of an employer's payment which is not a redundancy payment or part of a redundancy payment (in this Part referred to as "the agreed payment").

6. In this Part "the agreement", in relation to the agreed payment, means the agreement referred to in paragraph (b) or paragraph (c) of section 104(1) by reference to which that payment is payable; and "the relevant provisions of the agreement" means those provisions of the agreement which relate to either of the following matters, that is to say—
   (a) the circumstances in which the continuity of an employee's period of employment is to be treated as broken, and
   (b) the weeks which are to count in computing a period of employment.

7. In this Part any reference to the amount of the relevant redundancy payment, in relation to the agreed payment, shall be construed as a reference to the amount of the redundancy payment which the employer would have been liable to pay to the employee if—
   (a) the order referred to in paragraph (b) of subsection (1) of section 104, or (as the case may be) the order and the award referred to in paragraph (c) of that subsection, had not been made;
   (b) the circumstances in which the agreed payment is payable had been such that the employer was liable to pay a redundancy payment to the employee in those circumstances;
   (c) in relation to that redundancy payment, the relevant date had been the date on which the termination of the employee's contract of employment is treated for the purposes of the agreement as having taken effect; and
   (d) in so far as the relevant provisions of the agreement are inconsistent with the provisions of Schedule 13 as to the matters referred to in sub-paragraphs (a) and (b) of paragraph 6, those provisions of the agreement were substituted for those provisions of that Schedule;

and "the assumed conditions" means the conditions specified in sub-paragraphs (a) to (d) of this paragraph.

Method of calculation

8. Subject to sections 104(7) and 108, and to the following provisions of this Part, the amount of any redundancy rebate payable in respect of the agreed payment shall be an amount calculated as follows, that is to say, by taking the number of years of employment by reference to which the amount of the relevant redundancy payment would fall to be calculated in accordance with Schedule 4 (as that Schedule would have applied if the assumed conditions were fulfilled), and allowing—
   (a) 123/200 of one week's pay for each such year of employment falling within sub-paragraph (a) of paragraph 2 of that Schedule;
   (b) 41/100 of one week's pay for each such year of employment falling within sub-paragraph (b) of that paragraph; and
   (c) 41/200 of one week's pay for each such year of employment falling within sub-paragraph (c) of that paragraph.

9. For the purposes of paragraph 8, Schedule 13 shall have effect as if paragraphs 11(2), 12 and 14 were omitted.

10. Where the amount of the agreed payment is less than the amount of the relevant redundancy payment—
   (a) the proportion which it bears to the amount of the relevant redundancy payment shall be ascertained, and
   (b) the amount of the rebate shall (except as provided by the next following paragraph) be that proportion of the amount calculated in accordance with the preceding provisions of this Part of this Schedule.

11. Where the amount of the relevant redundancy calculated in accordance with paragraphs 1, 2 and 3 of Schedule 4 would (if the assumed conditions were fulfilled) have been reduced by virtue of paragraph 4 of that Schedule, the amount of the rebate shall be 41/100 of the amount of the relevant redundancy payment as so reduced.

Savings

12.—(1) This Schedule shall have effect in relation to redundancy rebates of a kind in sub-paragraph (2), as if—
  (a) in paragraphs 1 and 8, for the reference to 123/200, 41/100 and 41/200 there were substituted a reference to $\frac{3}{4}, \frac{1}{2}$ and $\frac{1}{4}$ respectively, and
  (b) in paragraphs 2 and 11 for each reference to 41/100 there were substituted a reference to $\frac{1}{2}$.
(2) The redundancy rebates referred to in sub-paragraph (1) are—
    (a) any rebate payable in respect of the whole or part of a redundancy payment in relation to which the relevant date is or would but for the operation of section 90(3) be earlier than 14th August 1977;
    (b) any rebate payable in respect of a payment to an employee on the termination of his contract of employment which is paid—
        (i) in pursuance of an agreement in respect of which an order under section 96 is in operation;
        (ii) [. . .]
where, under the agreement in question, the employee's contract is treated for the purposes of the agreement as having been terminated on a date earlier than 14th August 1977.

Power to modify paragraphs 1, 2, 8 and 11

13.—(1) The Secretary of State may from time to time by order modify this Schedule—
  (a) by substituting for the free fractions of a week's pay for the time being specified in sub-paragraphs (a), (b) and (c) of paragraphs 1 and 8 one of the other sets of three fractions specified in the following Table; and
  (b) by substituting for the fractions specified in paragraphs 2 and 11 for the purpose of calculating the amount of the rebates in respect of reduced payments the like fraction as, by virtue of paragraph (a) is substituted for the fraction in paragraphs 1(b) and 8(b).

TABLE

	Fraction in paragraphs 1 (a) and 8 (a)	Fraction in paragraphs 1 (b), 2, 8 (b) and 11	Fraction in paragraphs 1 (c) and 8 (c)
1	21/40	7/20	7/40
2	123/200	41/100	41/200
3	27/40	9/20	9/40
4	3/4	1/2	1/4
5	33/40	11/20	11/40
6	9/10	3/5	3/10
7	39/40	13/20	13/40
8	21/20	7/10	7/20
9	9/8	3/4	3/8
10	6/5	4/5	2/5

In this Table—
  (a) the three fractions specified in paragraph 2 are those which at the passing of this Act, are specified in sub-paragraphs (a), (b) and (c) of paragraphs 1 and 8;
  (b) the second of the fractions specified in paragraph 2 is the fraction which, at the passing of this Act, is specified in paragraphs 2 and 11.
(2) No order shall be made under sub-paragraph (1) unless a draft thereof has been laid before and approved by a resolution of each House of Parliament.

AMENDMENT
  In para. 12, sub-para (2)(b)(ii) was repealed by the Employment Act 1980 (c. 42), Sched. 2.

1–600 Section 106 SCHEDULE 7

CALCULATION OF PAYMENTS TO EMPLOYEES OUT OF REDUNDANCY FUND

1.—(1) Where the employer's payment is a redundancy payment, the sum referred to in section 106(2) is a sum equal to the amount of that payment.

(2) Where, in a case falling within section 104(6), the employer's payment is part of a redundancy payment, the sum referred to in section 106(2) is a sum equal to the amount of that part of the payment.

2.—(1) The provisions of this paragraph shall have effect for the purpose of determining the sum referred to in section 106(2) in relation to an employer's payment which is not a redundancy payment or part of a redundancy payment.

(2) Paragraphs 6 and 7 of Schedule 6 shall have effect for the purposes of this paragraph as they have effect for the purposes of Part II of that Schedule; and in the application of those paragraphs in accordance with this sub-paragraph the employer's payment in relation to which the sum referred to in section 106(2) falls to be determined shall be taken to be the agreed payment.

(3) In relation to any such employer's payment, the sum in question shall be a sum equal to—

(a) the amount of the employer's payment, or
(b) the amount of the relevant redundancy payment,

whichever is the less.

1–601 Section 117 SCHEDULE 8

EMPLOYEES PAID BY VIRTUE OF STATUTORY PROVISION BY PERSON OTHER THAN EMPLOYER

Provision of Act	Reference to be construed as reference to the person responsible for paying the remuneration
Section 81 (1)	The second reference to the employer.
Section 85 (3)	The reference to the employer in paragraph (b).
Section 85 (4)	The last reference to the employer.
Section 88 (4)	The reference to the employer.
Section 89 (1)	The first reference to the employer.
Section 89 (4) and (5)	The references to the employer.

1–602 Section 128 SCHEDULE 9

INDUSTRIAL TRIBUNALS

Regulations as to tribunal procedure

1.—(1) The Secretary of State may by regulations (in this Schedule referred to as "the regulations") make such provision as appears to him to be necessary or expedient with respect to proceedings before industrial tribunals.

(2) The regulations may in particular include provision—
 (a) for determining by which tribunal any appeal, question [application] or complaint is to be determined;
 (b) for enabling an industrial tribunal to hear and determine proceedings brought by virtue of section 131 concurrently with proceedings brought before the tribunal otherwise than by virtue of that section;
 (c) for treating the Secretary of State (either generally or in such circumstances as may be prescribed by the regulations) as a party to any proceedings before an industrial tribunal, where he would not otherwise be a party to them, and entitling him to appear and be heard accordingly;
 (d) for requiring persons to attend to give evidence and produce documents, and for authorising the administration of oaths to witnesses;
 (e) for granting to any person such discovery or inspection of documents or right to

further particulars as might be granted by a county court in England and Wales or, in Scotland, for granting by the sheriff;

(f) for prescribing the procedure to be followed on any appeal, reference or complaint or other proceedings before an industrial tribunal, including provisions as to the persons entitled to appear and to be heard on behalf of parties to such proceedings, and provisions for enabling an industrial tribunal to review its decisions, and revoke or vary its orders and awards, in such circumstances as may be determined in accordance with the regulations;

(g) for the appointment of one or more assessors for the purposes of any proceedings before an industrial tribunal, where the proceedings are brought under an enactment which provides for one or more assessors to be appointed.

[(ga) for authorising an industrial tribunal to require persons to furnish information and produce documents to a person required for the purposes of section 2A(1)(b) of the Equal Pay Act 1970 to prepare a report;]

(h) for the award of costs or expenses, including any allowances payable under paragraph 10 other than allowances payable to members of industrial tribunals or assessors;

(i) for taxing or otherwise settling any such costs or expenses (and, in particular, in England and Wales, for enabling such costs to be taxed in the county court); and

(j) for the registration and proof of decisions, orders and awards of industrial tribunals.

(3) In relation to proceedings on complaints under section 67 or any other enactment in relation to which there is provision for conciliation, the regulations shall include provision—

(a) for requiring a copy of any such complaint, and a copy of any notice relating to it which is lodged by or on behalf of the employer against whom the complaint is made, to be sent to a conciliation officer.

(b) for securing that the complainant and the employer against whom the complaint is made are notified that the services of a conciliation officer are available to them; and

(c) for postponing the hearing of any such complaint for such period as may be determined in accordance with the regulations for the purpose of giving an opportunity for the complaint to be settled by way of conciliation and withdrawn.

(4) In relation to proceedings under section 67—

(a) where the employee has expressed a wish to be reinstated or re-engaged which has been communicated to the employer at least seven days before the hearing of the complaint; or

(b) where the proceedings arise out of the employer's failure to permit the employee to return to work after an absence due to pregnancy or confinement,

regulations shall include provision for requiring the employer to pay the costs or expenses of any postponement or adjournment of the hearing caused by his failure, without a special reason, to adduce reasonable evidence as to the availability of the job from which the complainant was dismissed, or, as the case may be, which she held before her absence or of comparable or suitable employment.

(5) Without prejudice to paragraph 2, the regulations may enable an industrial tribunal to sit in private for the purpose of hearing evidence which in the opinion of the tribunal relates to matters of such a nature that it would be against the interests of national security to allow the evidence to be given in public or of hearing evidence from any person which in the opinion of the tribunal is likely to consist of—

(a) information which he could not disclose without contravening a prohibition imposed by or under any enactment; or

(b) any information which has been communicated to him in confidence, or which he has otherwise obtained in consequence of the confidence reposed in him by another person; or

(c) information the disclosure of which would, for reasons other than its effect on negotiations with respect to any of the matters mentioned in section 29(1) of the Trade Union and Labour Relations Act 1974 (matters to which trade disputes relate) cause substantial injury to any undertaking of his or in which he works.

(6) The regulations may include provision authorising or requiring an industrial tribunal, in circumstances specified in the regulations, to send notice or a copy of any document so specified relating to any proceedings before the tribunal, or of any decision, order or award of the tribunal, to any government department or other person or body so specified.

(7) Any person who without reasonable excuse fails to comply with any requirement imposed by the regulations by virtue of sub-paragraph (2)(d) [or (ga)] or any requirement with respect to the discovery, recovery or inspection of documents so imposed by virtue of sub-paragraph (2)(e) shall be liable on summary conviction to a fine not exceeding £100.

National security

2.—(1) If on a complaint under section 24 or 67 it is shown that the action complained of was taken for the purpose of safeguarding national security, the industrial tribunal shall dismiss the complaint.

(2) A certificate purporting to be signed by or on behalf of a Minister of the Crown, and certifying that the action specified in the certificate was taken for the purpose of safeguarding national security, shall for the purposes of sub-paragraph (1) be conclusive evidence of that fact.

Payment of certain sums into Redundancy Fund

3. Any sum recovered by the Secretary of State in pursuance of any such award as is mentioned in paragraph 1(2)(*h*) where the award was made in proceedings in pursuance of Part VI of this Act shall be paid into the Redundancy Fund.

Exclusion of Arbitration Act 1950

4. The Arbitration Act 1950 shall not apply to any proceedings before an industrial tribunal.

Presumption as to dismissal for redundancy

5. Where in accordance with the regulations an industrial tribunal determines in the same proceedings—
   (*a*) a question referred to it under sections 81 to 102, and
   (*b*) a complaint presented under section 67,
section 91(2) shall not have effect for the purposes of the proceedings in so far as they relate to the complaint under section 67.

Right of appearance

6. Any person may appear before an industrial tribunal in person or be represented by counsel or by a solicitor or by a representative of a trade union or an employers' association or by any other person whom he desires to represent him.

[Interest on sums awarded

6A.—(1) The Secretary of State may by order made with the approval of the Treasury provide that sums payable in pursuance of decisions of industrial tribunals shall carry interest at such rate and between such times as may be prescribed by the order.

(2) Any interest due by virtue of such an order shall be recoverable as a sum payable in pursuance of the decision.

(3) The power conferred by sub-paragraph (1) includes power—
   (*a*) to specify cases or circumstances in which interest shall not be payable;
   (*b*) to provide that interest shall be payable only on sums exceeding a specified amount or falling between specified amounts;
   (*c*) to make provision for the manner in which and the periods by reference to which interest is to be calculated and paid;
   (*d*) to provide that any enactment shall or shall not apply in relation to interest payable by virtue of an order under sub-paragraph (1) or shall apply to it with such modifications as may be specified in the order;
   (*e*) to make provision for cases where sums are payable in pursuance of decisions or awards made on appeal from industrial tribunals;
   (*f*) to make such incidental or supplemental provision as the Secretary of State considers necessary.

(4) Without prejudice to the generality of sub-paragraph (3), an order under sub-paragraph (1) may provide that the rate of interest shall be the rate specified in section 17 of the Judgments Act 1838 as that enactment has effect from time to time.]

Recovery of sums awarded

7.—(1) Any sum payable in pursuance of a decision of an industrial tribunal in England or Wales which has been registered in accordance with the regulations shall, if a county court so orders, be recoverable by execution issued from the county court or otherwise as if it were payable under an order of that court.

(2) [Any order for the payment of any sum made by an industrial tribunal in Scotland (or any copy of such an order certified by the Secretary of the Tribunals) may be enforced in like manner as an extract registered decree arbitral bearing a warrant for execution issued by the Sheriff Court of any Sheriffdom in Scotland.]

(3) In this paragraph any reference to a decision or order of an industrial tribunal—

(a) does not include a decision or order which, on being reviewed, has been revoked by the tribunal, and

(b) in relation to a decision or order which, on being reviewed, has been varied by the tribunal, shall be construed as a reference to the decision or order as so varied.

Constitution of tribunals for certain cases

8. An industrial tribunal hearing an application under section 77 or 79 may consist of a President of Industrial Tribunals, the chairman of the tribunal or a member of a panel of chairmen of such tribunals for the time being nominated by a President to hear such applications.

Remuneration for presidents and full-time chairmen of industrial tribunals

9. The Secretary of State may pay such remuneration as he may with the consent of the Minister for the Civil Service determine to the President of the Industrial Tribunals (England and Wales), the President of the Industrial Tribunals (Scotland) and any person who is a member on a full-time basis of a panel of chairmen of tribunals which is appointed in accordance with regulations under subsection (1) of section 128.

Remuneration etc. for members of industrial tribunals and for assessors and other persons

10. The Secretary of State may pay to members of industrial tribunals and to any assessors appointed for the purposes of proceedings before industrial tribunals [and to any persons required for the purposes of section 2A(1)(b) of the Equal Pay Act 1970 to prepare reports] such fees and allowances as he may with the consent of the Minister for the Civil Service determine and may pay to any other persons such allowances as he may with the consent of that Minister determine for the purposes of, or in connection with, their attendance at industrial tribunals.

Pensions for full-time presidents or chairmen of industrial tribunals

11.—(1) The Secretary of State may from time to time make to the Minister for the Civil Service, as respects any holder on a full-time basis of any of the following offices established by regulations under section 128 who is remunerated, apart from any allowances, on an annual basis, namely—

(a) President of the Industrial Tribunals (England and Wales);

(b) President of the Industrial Tribunals (Scotland);

(c) member of a panel of chairmen so established,

a recommendation that the Minister shall pay to that holder (hereafter in this paragraph referred to as "the pensioner") out of moneys provided by Parliament an annual sum by way of superannuation allowance calculated in accordance with sub-paragraph (3).

(2) No such allowance shall be payable unless—

(a) the pensioner is at the time of his retirement over the age of seventy-two or, where he retires after fifteen years' service, over the age of sixty-five; or

(b) the Secretary of State is satisfied by means of a medical certificate that at the time of the pensioner's retirement the pensioner is, by reason of infirmity of mind or body, incapable of discharging the duties of his office and that the incapacity is likely to be permanent.

(3) The said annual sum shall be a sum not exceeding such proportion of the pensioner's last annual remuneration (apart from any allowances) as in the following Table corresponds with the number of the pensioner's completed years of relevant service.

(4) In this paragraph the expression "relevant service" means service on a full-time basis as holder of any of the offices referred to in sub-paragraph (1) (including such service remunerated otherwise than on an annual basis) or service in any such other capacity under the

TABLE

Years of service	Fraction of remuneration
Less than 5	six-fortieths
5	ten-fortieths
6	eleven-fortieths
7	twelve-fortieths
8	thirteen-fortieths
9	fourteen-fortieths
10	fifteen-fortieths
11	sixteen-fortieths
12	seventeen-fortieths
13	eighteen-fortieths
14	nineteen-fortieths
15 or more	twenty-fortieths

Crown as may be prescribed by regulations made by the Minister for the Civil Service; and regulations under this sub-paragraph—
    (a) may be made generally or subject to specified exceptions or in relation to specified cases or classes of case and may make different provision for different cases or classes of cases; and
    (b) may provide that in calculating relevant service either the whole of a person's prescribed service of any description shall be taken into account or such part thereof only as may be determined by or under the regulations.
    (5) The decision of the Minister shall be final on any question arising as to—
        (a) the amount of any superannuation allowance under sub-paragraph (1); or
        (b) the reckoning of any service for the purpose of calculating such an allowance.
    (6) Sections 2 to 8 of the Administration of Justice (Pensions) Act 1950 (which provide for the payment of lump sums on retirement or death and of widows' and children's pensions in the case of persons eligible for pensions for service in any of the capacities listed in Schedule 1 to that Act) shall have effect as if—
    (a) the capacity of holder on a full-time basis of any of the offices referred to in sub-paragraph (1) were listed in the said Schedule 1; and
    (b) in relation to that capacity the expression "relevant service" in the said sections 2 to 8 had the meaning assigned by sub-paragraph (4); and
    (c) in relation to such a holder of such an office, any reference in the said section 2 to his last annual salary were a reference to his last annual remuneration apart from allowances.
    (7) Where the rate of the superannuation allowance payable to any person under sub-paragraph (1) is or would be increased by virtue of regulations made under sub-paragraph (4) in respect of relevant service in some capacity other than as holder of one of the offices referred to in sub-paragraph (1), and a pension payable to him wholly in respect of service in that other capacity would have been paid and borne otherwise than out of moneys provided by Parliament, any pension benefits paid to or in respect of him as having been the holder of such an office shall, to such extent as the Minister for the Civil Service may determine, having regard to the relative length of service and rate of remuneration in each capacity, be paid and borne in like manner as that in which a pension payable to him wholly in respect of service in that other capacity would have been paid and borne.
    (8) In this paragraph the expression "pension" includes any superannuation or other retiring allowance or gratuity, and the expression "pensionable" shall be construed accordingly, and the expression "pension benefits" includes benefits payable to or in respect of the pensioner by virtue of sub-paragraph (6).

AMENDMENTS

The word in square brackets in para. 1(2)(a) was inserted by the Employment Act 1980 (c. 42), Sched. 1, para. 26. The words in square brackets in paras. 1(2)(ga) and 1(7) were inserted by the Equal Pay (Amendment) Regulations 1983. Para. 7(2) was substituted by the Employment Act 1980 (c. 42), para. 27.

Para. (6A) was inserted by the Employment Act 1982 (c. 46), Sched. 3, para. 7.

The words in square brackets in para. 10 were inserted by the Equal Pay (Amendment) Regulations 1983.

Section 130 SCHEDULE 10

STATUTORY PROVISIONS RELATING TO REFEREES AND BOARDS OF REFEREES

1. Regulations under section 37 of the Coal Industry Nationalisation Act 1946.
2. Regulations under section 67 of the National Insurance Act 1946.
3. Regulations under section 68 of the National Health Service Act 1946, and orders under section 11(9) or section 31(5) of that Act.
4. Regulations under section 67 of the National Health Service (Scotland) Act 1947.
5. Regulations under Schedule 5 to the Fire Services Act 1947.
6. Regulations under section 101 of the Transport Act 1947.
7. Subsections (3) and (5) of section 54 of the Electricity Act 1947, and regulations under section 27 of the Electricity Act 1957.
8. Regulations under section 140 of the Local Government Act 1948, and such regulations as applied by any local Act, whether passed before or after this Act.
9. Regulations under subsection (1) or subsection (2) of section 60 of the National Assistance Act 1948.
10. Rules under section 3 of the Superannuation (Miscellaneous Provisions) Act 1948.
11. Subsections (3) and (5) of section 58 of the Gas Act 1948, and regulations under section 60 of that Act.
12. Subsection (4) of section 6 of the Commonwealth Telegraphs Act 1949 and regulations under that section.
13. Regulations under section 25 of the Prevention of Damage by Pests Act 1949.
14. Regulations under section 42 of the Justices of the Peace Act 1949.
15. Regulations under section 27 or section 28 of the Transport Act 1953.
16. Regulations under section 24 of the Iron and Steel Act 1953.
17. Regulations under section 12 of the Electricity Reorganisation (Scotland) Act 1954.
18. Orders under section 23 of the Local Government Act 1958 and regulations under section 60 of that Act.
19. Regulations under section 1 of the Water Officers Compensation Act 1960.
20. Regulations under section 18(6) of the Land Drainage Act 1961.
21. Subsection (6) of section 74 of the Transport Act 1962 and orders under that section, regulations under section 81 of that Act, and paragraph 17(3) of Schedule 7 to that Act.
22. Orders under section 84 of the London Government Act 1963 and regulations under section 85 of that Act.
23. Regulations under section 106 of the Water Resources Act 1963.

Section 135 SCHEDULE 11

EMPLOYMENT APPEAL TRIBUNAL

PART I

PROVISIONS AS TO MEMBERSHIP, SITTINGS, PROCEEDINGS AND POWERS

Tenure of office of appointed members of Appeal Tribunal

1. Subject to paragraphs 2 and 3, a member of the Appeal Tribunal appointed by Her Majesty under section 135(2)(*c*) (in this Schedule referred to as an "appointed member") shall hold and vacate office as such member in accordance with the terms of his appointment.

2. An appointed member may at any time resign his membership by notice in writing addressed to the Lord Chancellor and the Secretary of State.

3.—(1) If the Lord Chancellor, after consultation with the Secretary of State, is satisfied that an appointed member—
   (*a*) has been absent from sittings of the Appeal Tribunal for a period longer than six consecutive months without the permission of the President of the Tribunal; or
   (*b*) has become bankrupt or made an arrangement with his creditors; or
   (*c*) is incapacitated by physical or mental illness; or
   (*d*) is otherwise unable or unfit to discharge the functions of a member;
the Lord Chancellor may declare his office as a member to be vacant and shall notify the declaration in such manner as the Lord Chancellor thinks fit; and thereupon the office shall become vacant.

(2) In the application of this paragraph to Scotland for the references in sub-paragraph (1)(b) to a member's having become bankrupt and to a member's having made an arrangement with his creditors there shall be substituted respectively references to a member's estate having been sequestrated and to a member's having made a trust deed for behoof of his creditors or a composition contract.

Temporary membership of Appeal Tribunal

4. At any time when the office of President of the Appeal Tribunal is vacant, or the person holding that office is temporarily absent or otherwise unable to act as President of the Tribunal, the Lord Chancellor may nominate another judge nominated under section 135(2)(a) to act temporarily in his place.

5. At any time when a judge of the Appeal Tribunal nominated by the Lord Chancellor is temporarily absent or otherwise unable to act as a judge of that Tribunal, the Lord Chancellor may nominate another person who is qualified to be nominated under section 135(2)(a) to act temporarily in his place.

6. At any time when a judge of the Appeal Tribunal nominated by the Lord President of the Court of Session is temporarily absent or otherwise unable to act as a judge of the Appeal Tribunal, the Lord President may nominate another judge of the Court of Session to act temporarily in his place.

7. At any time when an appointed member is temporarily absent or otherwise unable to act as a member of the Appeal Tribunal, the Lord Chancellor and the Secretary of State may jointly appoint a person appearing to them to have the qualifications for appointment as such a member to act temporarily in his place.

8.—(1) At any time when it appears to the Lord Chancellor that it is expedient to do so in order to facilitate in England and Wales the disposal of business in the Appeal Tribunal, he may appoint a qualified person to be a temporary additional judge of the Tribunal during such period or on such occasions as the Lord Chancellor thinks fit.

(2) In this paragraph "qualified person" means a person qualified for appointment as a puisne judge of the High Court under section [10 of the Supreme Court Act 1981] or any person who has held office as a judge of the Court of Appeal or of the High Court.

9. A person appointed to act temporarily in place of the President or any other member of the Appeal Tribunal shall, when so acting, have all the functions of the person in whose place he acts.

10. A person appointed to be a temporary additional judge of the Appeal Tribunal shall have all the functions of a judge nominated under section 135 (2)(a).

11. No judge shall be nominated under paragraph 5 or 6 except with his consent.

Organisation and sittings of Appeal Tribunal

12. The Appeal Tribunal shall be a superior court of record and shall have an official seal which shall be judicially noticed.

13. The Appeal Tribunal shall have a central office in London.

14. The Appeal Tribunal may sit at any time and in any place in Great Britain.

15. The Appeal Tribunal may sit, in accordance with directions given by the President of the Tribunal, either as a single tribunal or in two or more divisions concurrently.

16. With the consent of the parties to any proceedings before the Appeal Tribunal, the proceedings may be heard by a judge and one appointed member, but, in default of such consent, any proceedings before the Tribunal shall be heard by a judge and either two or four appointed members, so that in either case there are equal numbers of persons whose experience is as representatives of employers and whose experience is as representatives of workers.

Rules

17.—(1) The Lord Chancellor, after consultation with the Lord President of the Court of Session, shall make rules with respect to proceedings before the Appeal Tribunal.

(2) Subject to those rules, the Tribunal shall have power to regulate its own procedure.

18. Without prejudice to the generality of paragraph 17 the rules may include provision—
  (a) with respect to the manner in which an appeal may be brought and the time within which it may be brought;
  [(aa) with respect to the manner in which an application to the Appeal Tribunal under section 5 of the Employment Act 1980 may be made];
  (b) for requiring persons to attend to give evidence and produce documents, and for authorising the administration of oaths to witnesses;
  (c) enabling the Appeal Tribunal to sit in private for the purpose of hearing evidence

to hear which an industrial tribunal may sit in private by virtue of paragraph 1 of Schedule 9.

[(d) for the registration and proof of any award made on an application to the Appeal Tribunal under section 5 of the Employment Act 1980].

[(e) for interlocutory proceedings to be dealt with otherwise than in accordance with paragraph 16.].

19.—(1) Without prejudice to the generality of paragraph 17 the rules may empower the Appeal Tribunal to order a party to any proceedings before the Tribunal to pay to any other party to the proceedings the whole or part of the costs or expenses incurred by that other party in connection with the proceedings, where in the opinion of the Tribunal—

(a) the proceedings were unnecessary, improper or vexatious, or

(b) there has been unreasonable delay or other unreasonable conduct in bringing or conducting the proceedings.

(2) Except as provided by sub-paragraph (1), the rules shall not enable the Appeal Tribunal to order the payment of costs or expenses by any party to proceedings before the Tribunal.

20. Any person may appear before the Appeal Tribunal in person or be represented by counsel or by a solicitor or by a representative of a trade union or an employers' association or by any other person whom he desires to represent him.

Powers of Tribunal

21.—(1) For the purpose of disposing of an appeal the Appeal Tribunal may exercise any powers of the body or officer from whom the appeal was brought or may remit the case to that body or officer.

(2) Any decision or award of the Appeal Tribunal on an appeal shall have the same effect and may be enforced in the same manner as a decision or award of a body or officer from whom the appeal was brought.

[21A.—(1) Any sum payable in England and Wales in pursuance of an award of the Appeal Tribunal under section 5 of the Employment Act 1980 which has been registered in accordance with the rules shall, if a county court so orders, be recoverable by execution issued from the county court or otherwise as if it were payable under an order of that court.

(2) Any order by the Appeal Tribunal for the payment in Scotland of any sum in pursuance of such an award (or any copy of such an order certified by the Secretary of the Tribunals) may be enforced in like manner as an extract registered decree arbitral bearing a warrant for execution issued by the Sheriff Court of any Sheriffdom in Scotland.]

[(3) Any sum payable in pursuance of an award of the Appeal Tribunal under section 5 of the Employment Act 1980 shall be treated as if it were a sum payable in pursuance of a decision of an industrial tribunal for the purposes of paragraph 6A of Schedule 9 (interest on industrial tribunal awards).]

22.—(1) The Appeal Tribunal shall, in relation to the attendance and examination of witnesses, the production and inspection of documents and all other matters incidental to its jurisdiction, have the like powers, rights, privileges and authority—

(a) in England and Wales, as the High Court,

(b) in Scotland, as the Court of Session.

(2) No person shall be punished for contempt of the Tribunal except by, or with the consent of, a judge.

23.—(1) In relation to any fine imposed by the Appeal Tribunal for contempt of the Tribunal [sections 31 and 32 of the Powers of Criminal Courts Act 1973 (powers of Crown Court in relation to fines and forfeited recognisances)] shall have effect as if any reference to the Crown Court included a reference to the Tribunal.

(2) A magistrates' court shall not remit the whole or any part of a fine imposed by the Appeal Tribunal except with the consent of a judge who is a member of the Tribunal.

(3) This paragraph does not extend to Scotland.

Staff

24. The Secretary of State may appoint such officers and servants of the Appeal Tribunal as he may determine, subject to the approval of the Minister for the Civil Service as to numbers and as to terms and conditions of service.

Part II

Supplementary

Remuneration and allowances

25. The Secretary of State shall pay the appointed members of the Appeal Tribunal, the persons appointed to act temporarily as appointed members, and the officers and servants of the Tribunal such remuneration and such travelling and other allowances as he may with the approval of the Minister for the Civil Service determine.

26. A person appointed to be a temporary additional judge of the Appeal Tribunal shall be paid such remuneration and allowances as the Lord Chancellor may, with the approval of the Minister for the Civil Service, determine.

Pensions, etc.

27. If the Secretary of State determines, with the approval of the Minister for the Civil Service, that this paragraph shall apply in the case of an appointed member, the Secretary of State shall pay such pension, allowance or gratuity to or in respect of that member on his retirement or death or make that member such payments towards the provision of such a pension, allowance or gratuity as the Secretary of State may with the like approval determine.

28. Where a person ceases to be an appointed member otherwise than on his retirement or death and it appears to the Secretary of State that there are special circumstances which make it right for him to receive compensation, the Secretary of State may make him a payment of such amount as the Secretary of State may, with the approval of the Minister for the Civil Service, determine.

AMENDMENTS

Paras. 18(*aa*), (*d*) and 21A were inserted by the Employment Act 1980 (c. 42), Sched. 1, paras. 28, 29. The words in square brackets in para. 23(1) were substituted by *ibid.*, para. 30.

Para. 18(*e*) was inserted by the Employment Act 1982 (c. 46), Sched. 3, para. 8; and subpara. 21A(3) was inserted by *ibid.*, para. 9.

Section 150   SCHEDULE 12

DEATH OF EMPLOYEE OR EMPLOYER

PART I

GENERAL

Introductory

1. In this Schedule "the relevant provisions" means Part I (so far as it relates to itemised pay statements), section 53 and Parts II, III, V, VI and VII of this Act and this Schedule.

Institution or continuance of tribunal proceedings

2. Where an employee or employer has died, tribunal proceedings arising under any of the relevant provisions may be instituted or continued by a personal representative of the deceased employee or, as the case may be, defended by a personal representative of the deceased employer.

3.—(1) If there is no personal representative of a deceased employee, tribunal proceedings arising under any of the relevant provisions (or proceedings to enforce a tribunal award made in any such proceedings) may be instituted or continued on behalf of the estate of the deceased employee by such person as the industrial tribunal may appoint being either—

(*a*) a person authorised by the employee to act in connection with the proceedings before the employee's death; or

(*b*) the widower, widow, child, father, mother, brother or sister of the deceased employee, and references in this Schedule to a personal representative shall be construed as including such a person.

(2) In such a case any award made by the industrial tribunal shall be in such terms and shall be enforceable in such manner as may be provided by regulation made by the Secretary of State.

4.—(1) Subject to any specific provision of this Schedule to the contrary, in relation to an employee or employer who has died—

(a) any reference in the relevant provisions to the doing of anything by or in relation to an employee or an employer shall be construed as including a reference to the doing of that thing by or in relation to any personal representative of the deceased employee or employer; and

(b) any reference in the said provisions to a thing required or authorised to be done by or in relation to an employee or employer shall be construed as including a reference to any thing which, in accordance with any such provision as modified by this Schedule (including sub-paragraph (a)), is required or authorised to be done by or in relation to any personal representative of the deceased employee or employer.

(2) Nothing in this paragraph shall prevent references in the relevant provisions to a successor of an employer from including a personal representative of a deceased employer.

Rights and liabilities accruing after death

5. Any right arising under any of the relevant provisions as modified by this Schedule shall, if it had not accrued before the death of the employee in question, nevertheless devolve as if it had so accrued.

6. Where by virtue of any of the relevant provisions as modified by this Schedule a personal representative of a deceased employer is liable to pay any amount and that liability had not accrued before the death of the employer, it shall be treated for all purposes as if it were a liability of the deceased employer which had accrued immediately before his death.

PART II

UNFAIR DISMISSAL

Introductory

7. In this Part of this Schedule "the unfair dismissal provisions" means Part V of this Act and this Schedule.

Death during notice period

8. Where an employer has given notice to an employee to terminate his contract of employment and before that termination the employee or the employer dies, the unfair dismissal provisions shall apply as if the contract had been duly terminated by the employer by notice expiring on the date of the death.

[9. Where—
   (a) the employee's contract of employment has been terminated; and
   (b) by virtue of subsection (5) or (6) of section 55 a date later than the effective date of termination as defined in subsection (4) of that section is to be treated as the effective date of termination for the purposes of certain of the unfair dismissal provisions; and
   (c) before that later date the employer or the employee dies;
subsection (5) or, as the case may be, (6) shall have effect as if the notice referred to in that section as required by section 49 would have expired on the date of the death.].

Remedies for unfair dismissal

10. Where an employee has died, then, unless an order for reinstatement or re-engagement has already been made, section 69 shall not apply; and accordingly if the industrial tribunal finds that the grounds of the complaint are well-founded the case shall be treated as falling within secton 68(2) as a case in which no order is made under section 69.

11. If an order for reinstatement or re-engagement has been made and the employee dies before the order is complied with—
   (a) if the employer has before the death refused to reinstate or re-engage the employee in accordance with the order, section 71(2) and (3) shall apply and an award shall be made under section 71(2)(b) unless the employer satisfies the tribunal that it was not practicable at the time of the refusal to comply with the order;
   ((b) if there has been no such refusal, section 71(1) shall apply if the employer fails to comply with any ancillary terms of the order which remains capable of fulfilment after the employee's death as it would apply to such a failure to comply fully with the terms of an order where the employee had been reinstated or re-engaged.

PART III

REDUNDANCY PAYMENTS: DEATH OF EMPLOYER

Introductory

12. The provisions of this Part shall have effect in relation to an employee where his employer (in this Part referred to as "the deceased employer") dies.

13. Section 94 shall not apply to any change whereby the ownership of the business, for the purposes of which the employee was employed by the deceased employer, passes to a personal representative of the deceased employer.

Dismissal

14. Where by virtue of subsection (1) of section 93 the death of the deceased employer is to be treated for the purposes of Part VI of this Act as a termination by him of the contract of employment, section 84 shall have effect subject to the following modifications:—
    (*a*) for subsection (1) there shall be substituted the following subsection—
        "(1) If an employee's contract of employment is renewed, or he is re-engaged under a new contract of employment, by a personal representative of the deceased employer and the renewal or re-engagement takes effect not later than eight weeks after the death of the deceased employer, then, subject to subsections (3) and (6), the employee shall not be regarded as having been dismissed by reason of the ending of his employment under the previous contract";
    (*b*) in subsection (2), paragraph (*a*) shall be omitted and in paragraph (*b*) for the words "four weeks" there shall be substituted the words "eight weeks";
    (*c*) in subsections (5) and (6), references to the employer shall be construed as references to the personal representative of the deceased employer.
15. Where by reason of the death of the deceased employer the employee is treated for the purposes of Part VI of this Act as having been dismissed by him, section 82 shall have effect subject to the following modifications—
    (*a*) for subsection (3) there shall be substituted the following subsection—
        "(3) If a personal representative of the deceased employer makes an employee an offer (whether in writing or not) to renew his contract of employment, or to re-engage him under a new contract of employment, so that the renewal or re-engagement would take effect not later than eight weeks after the death of the deceased employer the provisions of subsections (5) and (6) shall have effect";
    (*b*) in subsection (4), paragraph (*a*) shall be omitted and in paragraph (*b*) for the words "four weeks" there shall be subtituted the words "eight weeks";
    (*c*) in subsection (5), the reference to the employer shall be construed as a reference to the personal representative of the deceased employer.
16. For the purposes of section 82 as modified by paragraph 15—
    (*a*) an offer shall not be treated as one whereby the provisions of the contract as renewed, or of the new contract, as the case may be, would differ from the corresponding provisions of the contract as in force immediately before the death of the deceased employer by reason only that the personal representative would be substituted as the employer for the deceased employer, and
    (*b*) no account shall be taken of that substitution in determining whether the refusal of the offer was reasonable, or, as the case may be, whether the employee acted reasonably in terminating the renewed, or new, employment during the trial period referred to in section 84.

Lay-off and short-time

17. Where the employee has before the death of the deceased employer been laid off or kept on short-time for one or more weeks, but has not given to the deceased employer notice of intention to claim, then if after the death of the deceased employer—
    (*a*) his contract of employment is renewed, or he is re-engaged under a new contract by a personal representative of the deceased employer, and
    (*b*) after the renewal or re-engagement, he is laid off or kept on short-time for one or more weeks by the personal representative of the deceased employer,
the provisions of sections 88 and 89 shall apply as if the week in which the deceased employer died and the first week of the employee's employment by the personal representative were consecutive weeks, and any reference in those sections to four weeks or thirteen weeks shall be construed accordingly.
18. The provisions of paragraph 19 or (as the case may be) paragraph 20 shall have effect, where the employee has given to the deceased employer notice of intention to claim, and—
    (*a*) the deceased employer has died before the end of the next four weeks after the service of that notice, and

(b) the employee has not terminated the contract of employment by notice expiring before the death of the deceased employer.

19. If in the circumstances specified in paragraph 18 the employee's contract of employment is not renewed by a personal representative of the deceased employer before the end of the next four weeks after the service of the notice of intention to claim, and he is not re-engaged under a new contract by such a personal representative before the end of those four weeks, section 88(1) and (2) and (in relation to subsection (1) of that section) section 89(2) and (3) shall apply as if—

(a) the deceased employer had not died, and
(b) the employee had terminated the contract of employment by a week's notice (or, if under the contract he is required to give more than a week's notice to terminate the contract, he had terminated it by the minimum notice which he is so required to give) expiring at the end of those four weeks,

but sections 88(3) and (4) and 89(1) and (4) shall not apply.

20.—(1) The provisions of this paragraph shall have effect where, in the circumstances specified in paragraph 18, the employee's contract of employment is renewed by a personal representative of the deceased employer before the end of the next four weeks after the service of the notice of intention to claim, or he is re-engaged under a new contract by such a personal representative before the end of those four weeks, and—

(a) he was laid off or kept on a short-time by the deceased employer for one or more of those weeks, and
(b) he is laid off or kept on short-time by the personal representative for the week, or for the next two or more weeks, following the renewal or re-engagement.

(2) Where the conditions specified in sub-paragraph (1) are fulfilled, sections 88 and 89 shall apply as if—

(a) all the weeks for which the employee was laid off or kept on short-time as mentioned in sub-paragraph (1) were consecutive weeks during which he was employed (but laid off or kept on short-time) by the same employer, and
(b) each of the periods specified in paragraphs (a) and (b) of subsection (5) of section 89 were extended by any week or weeks any part of which was after the death of the deceased employer and before the date on which the renewal or re-engagement took effect.

Continuity of period of employment

21. For the purposes of this application, in accordance with section 100(1), of any provisions of Part VI of this Act in relation to an employee who was employed as a domestic servant in a private household, any reference to a personal representative in—

(a) this Part of this Schedule, or
(b) paragraph 17 of Schedule 13,

shall be construed as including a reference to any person to whom, otherwise than in pursuance of a sale or other disposition for valuable consideration, the management of the household has passed in consequence of the death of the deceased employer.

PART IV

REDUNDANCY PAYMENTS: DEATH OF EMPLOYEE

22.—(1) Where an employer has given notice to an employee to terminate his contract of employment, and before that notice expires the employee dies, the provisions of Part VI of this Act shall apply as if the contract had been duly terminated by the employer by notice expiring on the date of the employee's death.

(2) Where the employee's contract of employment has been terminated by the employer and by virtue of section 90(3) a date later than the relevant date as defined by subsection (1) of that section is to be treated as the relevant date for the purposes of certain provisions of Part VI of this Act, and before that later date the employee dies, section 90(3) shall have effect as if the notice referred to in that subsection as required to be given by an employer would have expired on the employee's death.

23.—(1) Where an employer has given notice to an employee to terminate his contract of employment, and has offered to renew his contract of employment, or to re-engage him under a new contract, then if—

(a) the employee dies without having either accepted or refused the offer, and
(b) the offer has not been withdrawn before his death,

section 82 shall apply as if for the words "the employee unreasonably refuses" there were substituted the words "it would have been unreasonable on the part of the employee to refuse".

(2) Where an employee's contract of employment has been renewed, or he has been re-engaged under a new contract of employment, and during the trial period the employee dies without having terminated or having given notice to terminate the contract, subsection (6) of that section shall apply as if for the words from "and during the trial period" to "terminated" there were substituted the words "and it would have been unreasonable for the employee, during the trial period referred to in section 84, to terminate or give notice to terminate the contract".

24. Where an employee's contract of employment has been renewed, or he has been re-engaged under a new contract of employment, and during the trial period he gives notice to terminate the contract but dies before the expiry of that notice, sections 82(6) and 84(6)(*a*) shall have effect as if the notice had expired and the contract had thereby been terminated on the date of the employee's death.

25.—(1) Where, in the circumstances specified in paragraphs (*a*) and (*b*) of subsection (1) of section 85, the employee dies before the notice given by him under paragraph (*b*) of that subsection is due to expire and before the employer has given him notice under subsection (3) of that section, subsection (4) of that section shall apply as if the employer had given him such notice and he had not complied with it.

(2) Where, in the said circumstances, the employee dies before his notice given under section 85(1)(*b*) is due to expire but after the employer has given him notice under subsection (3) of section 85, subsections (3) and (4) of that section shall apply as if the circumstances were that the employee had not died, but did not comply with the last-mentioned notice.

26.—(1) Where an employee has given notice of intention to claim and dies before he has given notice to terminate his contract of employment and before the period allowed for the purposes of subsection (2)(*a*) of section 88 has expired the said subsection (2)(*a*) shall not apply.

(2) Where an employee, who has given notice of intention to claim, dies within seven days after the service of that notice, and before the employer has given a counter-notice, the provisions of sections 88 and 89 shall apply as if the employer had given a counter-notice within those seven days.

(3) In this paragraph "counter-notice" has the same meaning as in section 89(1).

27.—(1) In relation to the making of a claim by a personal representative of a deceased employee who dies before the end of the period of six months beginning with the relevant date, subsection (1) of section 101 shall apply with the substitution for the words "six months", of the words "one year".

(2) In relation to the making of a claim by a personal representative of a deceased employee who dies after the end of the period of six months beginning with the relevant date and before the end of the following period of six months, subsection (2) of section 101 shall apply with the substitution for the words "six months", of the words "one year".

28. In relation to any case where, under any provision contained in Part VI of this Act as modified by this Schedule, an industrial tribunal has power to determine that an employer shall be liable to pay to a personal representative of a deceased employee either—

(*a*) the whole of a redundancy payment to which he would have been entitled apart from another provision therein mentioned, or

(*b*) such part of such a redundancy payment as the tribunal thinks fit,

any reference in paragraph 5 to a right shall be construed as including a reference to any right to receive the whole or part of a redundancy payment if the tribunal determines that the employer shall be liable to pay it.

AMENDMENT

Para. 9 was substituted by the Employment Act 1982 (c. 46), Sched. 3, para. 28.

Section 151   SCHEDULE 13

COMPUTATION OF PERIOD OF EMPLOYMENT

[*Preliminary*]

1.—(1) Except so far as otherwise provided by the following provisions of this Schedule, a week which does not count under paragraphs 3 to 12 breaks the continuity of the period of employment.

(2) The provisions of this Schedule apply, subject to paragraph 14, to a period of employ-

ment notwithstanding that during that period the employee was engaged in work wholly or mainly outside Great Britain, or was excluded by or under this Act from any right conferred by this Act.

(3) A person's employment during any period shall, unless the contrary is shown, be presumed to have been continuous.]

Normal working weeks

3. Any week in which the employee is employed for sixteen hours or more shall count in computing a period of employment.

Employment governed by contract

4. Any week during the whole or part of which the employee's relations with the employer are governed by a contract of employment which normally involves employment for sixteen hours or more weekly shall count in computing a period of employment.

5.—(1) If the employee's relations with his employer cease to be governed by a contract which normally involves work for sixteen hours or more weekly and become governed by a contract which normally involves employment for eight hours or more, but less than sixteen hours, weekly and, but for that change, the later weeks would count in computing a period of employment, then those later weeks shall count in computing a period of employment or, as the case may be, shall not break the continuity of a period of employment, notwithstanding that change.

(2) Not more than twenty-six weeks shall count under this paragraph between any two periods falling under paragraph 4, and in computing the said figure of twenty-six weeks no account shall be taken of any week which counts in computing a period of employment, or does not break the continuity of a period of employment, otherwise than by virtue of this paragraph.

6.—(1) An employee whose relations with his employer are governed, or have been from time to time governed, by a contract of employment which normally involves employment for eight hours or more, but less than sixteen hours, weekly shall nevertheless, if he satisfies the condition referred to in sub-paragraph (2), be treated for the purposes of this Schedule (apart from this paragraph) as if his contract normally involved employment for sixteen hours or more weekly, and had at all times at which there was a contract during the period of employment of five years or more referred to in sub-paragraph (2) normally involved employment for sixteen hours or more weekly.

(2) Sub-paragraph (1) shall apply if the employee, on the date by reference to which the length of any period of employment falls to be ascertained in accordance with the provisions of this Schedule, has been continuously employed within the meaning of sub-paragraph (3) for a period of five years or more.

(3) In computing for the purposes of sub-paragraph (2) an employee's period of employment, the provisions of this Schedule (apart from this paragraph) shall apply but as if, in paragraphs 3 and 4, for the words "sixteen hours" wherever they occur, there were substituted the words "eight hours".

7.—(1) If an employee has, at any time during the relevant period of employment, been continuously employed for a period which qualifies him for any right which requires a qualifying period of continuous employment computed in accordance with this Schedule, then he shall be regarded for the purposes of qualifying for that right as continuing to satisfy that requirement until the condition referred to in sub-paragraph (3) occurs.

(2) In this paragraph the relevant period of employment means the period of employment ending on the date by reference to which the length of any period of employment falls to be ascertained which would be continuous (in accordance with the provisions of this Schedule) if at all relevant times the employee's relations with the employer had been governed by a contract of employment which normally involved employment for sixteen hours or more weekly.

(3) The condition which defeats the operation of sub-paragraph (1) is that in a week subsequent to the time at which the employee qualified as referred to in that sub-paragraph—
   (a) his relations with his employer are governed by a contract of employment which normally involves employment for less than eight hours weekly; and
   (b) he is employed in that week for less than sixteen hours.

(4) If, in a case in which an employee is entitled to any right by virtue of sub-paragraph (1), it is necessary for the purpose of ascertaining the amount of his entitlement to determine for what period he has been continuously employed, he shall be regarded for that purpose as having been continuously employed throughout the relevant period.

[*Power to amend paragraphs 3 to 7 by order*]
8.—(1) The Secretary of State may by order—
   (*a*) amend paragraphs 3 to 7 so as to substitute for each of the references to sixteen hours a reference to such other number of hours less than sixteen as may be specified in the order; and
   (*b*) amend paragraphs 6 and 7 so as to substitute for each of the references to eight hours a reference to such other number of hours less than eight as may be specified in the order.
(2) No order under this paragraph shall be made unless a draft of the order has been laid before Parliament and approved by a resolution of each House of Parliament.
(3) The provisions of any order under this paragraph shall apply to periods before the order takes effect as they apply to later periods.]

Periods in which there is no contract of employment
9.—(1) If in any week the employee is, for the whole or part of the week—
   (*a*) incapable of work in consequence of sickness or injury, or
   (*b*) absent from work on account of a temporary cessation of work, or
   (*c*) absent from work in circumstances such that, by arrangement or custom, he is regarded as continuing in the employment of his employer for all or any purposes, or
   (*d*) absent from work wholly or partly because of pregnancy or confinement,
that week shall, notwithstanding that it does not fall under paragraph 3, 4 or 5, count as a period of employment.
(2) Not more than twenty-six weeks shall count under paragraph (*a*) or, subject to paragraph 10, under paragraph (*d*) of sub-paragraph (1) between any periods falling under paragraph 3, 4 or 5.

Maternity
10. If an employee returns to work in accordance with [section 45(1) or in pursuance of an offer made in the circumstances described in section 56A(2)] after a period of absence from work wholly or partly occasioned by pregnancy or confinement, every week during that period shall count in computing a period of employment, notwithstanding that it does not fall under paragraph 3, 4 or 5.

Intervals in employment where section 55(5) or 84(1) or 90(3) applies
11.—(1) In ascertaining, for the purposes of section 64(1)(*a*) [64A(1)] and of section 73(3), the period for which an employee has been continuously employed, where by virtue of section 55(5) [or, as the case may be, (6)] a date is treated as the effective date of termination which is later than the effective date of termination as defined by section 55(4), the period of the interval between those two dates shall count as a period of employment notwithstanding that it does not otherwise count under this Schedule.
(2) Where by virtue of section 84(1) an employee is treated as not having been dismissed by reason of a renewal or re-engagement taking effect after an interval, then, in determining for the purposes of section 81(1) or Schedule 4 whether he has been continuously employed for the requisite period, the period of that interval shall count as a period of employment except in so far as it is to be disregarded under paragraphs 12 to 14 (notwithstanding that it does not otherwise count under this Schedule).
(3) Where by virtue of section 90(3) a date is to be treated as the relevant date for the purposes of section 81(4) which is later than the relevant date as defined by section 90(1), then in determining for the purposes of section 81(1) or Schedule 4 whether the employee has been continuously employed for the requisite period, the period of the interval between those two dates shall count as a period of employment except in so far as it is to be disregarded under paragraphs 12 to 14 (notwithstanding that it does not otherwise count under this Schedule).

Payment of previous redundancy payment or equivalent payment
12.—(1) Where the conditions mentioned in sub-paragraph (2)(*a*) or (2)(*b*) are fulfilled in relation to a person, then in determining, for the purposes of section 81(1) or Schedule 4, whether at any subsequent time he has been continuously employed for the requisite period, or for what period he has been continuously employed, the continuity of the period of employment shall be treated as having been broken—
   (*a*) in so far as the employment was under a contract of employment, at the date which was the relevant date in relation to the payment mentioned in sub-paragraph (2)(*a*) or, as the case may be, sub-paragraph (2)(*b*); or
   (*b*) in so far as the employment was otherwise than under a contract of employment, at the

date which would have been the relevant date in relation to that payment had the employment been under a contract of employment,
and accordingly no account shall be taken of any time before that date.

(2) Sub-paragraph (1) has effect—
   (a) where—
      (i) a redundancy payment is paid to an employee, whether in respect of dismissal or in respect of lay-off or short-time; and
      (ii) the contract of employment under which he was employed (in this section referred to as "the previous contract") is renewed, whether by the same or another employer, or he is re-engaged under a new contract of employment, whether by the same or another employer; and
      (iii) the circumstances of the renewal or re-engagement are such that, in determining for the purposes of section 81(1) or Schedule 4 whether at any subsequent time he has been continuously employed for the requisite period, or for what period he has been continuously employed, the continuity of his period of employment would, apart from this paragraph, be treated as not having been broken by the termination of the previous contract and the renewal or re-engagement; or
   (b) where—
      (i) a payment has been made, whether in respect of the termination of any person's employment or in respect of lay-off or short-time, either in accordance with any provisions of a scheme under section 1 of the Superannuation Act 1972 or in accordance with any such arrangements as are mentioned in section 111(3); and
      (ii) he commences new, or renewed, employment; and
      (iii) the circumstances of the commencement of the new, or renewed, employment are such that, in determining for the purposes of section 81(1) or Schedule 4 whether at any subsequent time he has been continuously employed for the requisite period, or for what period he has been continuously employed, the continuity of his period of employment would, apart from this paragraph, be treated as not having been broken by the termination of the previous employment and the commencement of the new, or renewed, employment.

(3) For the purposes of this paragraph, a redundancy payment shall be treated as having been paid if—
   (a) the whole of the payment has been paid to the employee by the employer, or, in a case where a tribunal has determined that the employer is liable to pay part (but not the whole) of the redundancy payment, that part of the redundancy payment has been paid in full to the employee by the employer; or
   (b) the Secretary of State has paid a sum to the employee in respect of the redundancy payment under section 106.

. . . . . .

Redundancy payments: employment wholly or partly abroad

14.—(1) In computing in relation to an employee the period specified in section 81(4) or the period specified in paragraph 1 of Schedule 4, a week of employment shall not count if—
   (a) the employee was employed outside Great Britain during the whole or part of that week, and
   (b) he was not during that week, or during the corresponding contribution week,—
      (i) where the week is a week of employment after 1st June 1976 an employed earner for the purposes of the Social Security Act 1975 in respect of whom a secondary Class 1 contribution was payable under that Act; or
      (ii) where the week is a week of employment after 6th April 1975 and before 1st June 1976, an employed earner for the purposes of the Social Security Act 1975; or
      (iii) where the week is a week of employment before 6th April 1975, an employee in respect of whom an employer's contribution was payable in respect of the corresponding contribution week;
   whether or not the contribution mentioned in paragraph (i) or (iii) of this sub-paragraph was in fact paid.

(2) For the purposes of the application of sub-paragraph (1) to a week of employment where the corresponding contribution week began before 5th July 1948, an employer's contribution shall be treated as payable as mentioned in sub-paragraph (1) if such a contribution

would have been so payable if the statutory provisions relating to national insurance which were in force on 5th July 1948 had been in force in that contribution week.

(3) Where by virtue of sub-paragraph (1) a week of employment does not count in computing such a period as is mentioned in that sub-paragraph, the continuity of that period shall not be broken by reason only that that week of employment does not count in computing that period.

(4) Any question arising under this paragraph whether—
   (*a*) an employer's contribution was or would have been payable, as mentioned in sub-paragraph (1) or (2), or
   (*b*) a person was an employed earner for the purposes of the Social Security Act 1975 and if so whether a secondary Class 1 contribution was payable in respect of him under that Act,

shall be determined by the Secretary of State; and any legislation (including regulations) as to the determination of questions which under that Act the Secretary of State is empowered to determine (including provisions as to the reference of questions for decision, or as to appeals, to the High Court or the Court of Session) shall apply to the determination of any question by the Secretary of State under this paragraph.

(5) In this paragraph "employer's contribution" has the same meaning as in the National Insurance Act 1965, and "corresponding contribution week", in relation to a week of employment, means a contribution week (within the meaning of the said Act of 1965) of which so much as falls within the period beginning with midnight between Sunday and Monday and ending with Saturday also falls within that week of employment.

(6) The provisions of this paragraph shall not apply in relation to a person who is employed as a master or seaman in a British ship and is ordinarily resident in Great Britain.

Industrial disputes

15.—(1) A week shall not count under paragraph 3, 4, 5, 9 or 10 if in that week, or any part of that week, the employee takes part in a strike.

(2) The continuity of an employee's period of employment is not broken by a week which does not count under this Schedule, and which begins after 5th July 1964 if in that week, or any part of that week, the employee takes part in a strike.

(3) Sub-paragraph (2) applies whether or not the week would, apart from sub-paragraph (1), have counted under this Schedule.

(4) The continuity of the period of employment is not broken by a week which begins after 5th July 1964 and which does not count under this Schedule, if in that week, or any part of that week, the employee is absent from work because of a lock-out by the employer.

Reinstatement after service with the armed forces, etc.

16.—(1) If a person who is entitled to apply to his former employer under Part II of the National Service Act 1948 (reinstatement in civil employment) enters the employment of that employer not later than the end of the six month period mentioned in section 35(2)(*b*) of that Act, his previous period of employment with that employer (or if there was more than one such period, the last of those periods) and the period of employment beginning in the said period of six months shall be treated as continuous.

(2) The reference in this paragraph to Part II of the National Service Act 1948 includes a reference to that Part of that Act as amended, applied or extended by any other Act passed before or after this Act.

Change of employer

17.—(1) Subject to this paragraph and [paragraphs 18 and 18A], the foregoing provisions of this Schedule relate only to employment by the one employer.

(2) If a trade or business or an undertaking (whether or not it be an undertaking established by or under an Act of Parliament) is transferred from one person to another, the period of employment of an employee in the trade or business or undertaking at the time of the transfer shall count as a period of employment with the transferee, and the transfer shall not break the continuity of the period of employment.

(3) If by or under an Act of Parliament, whether public or local and whether passed before or after this Act, a contract of employment between any body corporate and an employee is modified and some other body corporate is substituted as the employer, the employee's period of employment at the time when the modification takes effect shall count as a period of employment with the second-mentioned body corporate, and the change of employer shall not break the continuity of the period of employment.

(4) If on the death of an employer the employee is taken into the employment of the personal representatives or trustees of the deceased, the employee's period of employment at the

time of the death shall count as a period of employment with the employer's personal representatives or trustees, and the death shall not break the continuity of the period of employment.

(5) If there is a change in the partners, personal representatives or trustees who employ any person, the employee's period of employment at the time of the change shall count as a period of employment with the partners, personal representatives or trustees after the change, and the change shall not break the continuity of the period of employment.

18. If an employee of an employer is taken into the employment of another employer who, at the time when the employee enters his employment is an associated employer of the first-mentioned employer, the employee's period of employment at that time shall count as a period of employment with the second-mentioned employer and the change of employer shall not break the continuity of the period of employment.

[18A.—(1) If an employee of one of the employers described in sub-paragraph (2) is taken into the employment of another of those employers, his period of employment at the time of the change of employer shall count as a period of employment with the second employer and the change shall not break the continuity of the period of employment.

(2) The employers referred to in sub-paragraph (1) are the governors of the schools maintained by a local education authority and that authority.]

Crown employment

19.—(1) Subject to the following provisions of this paragraph, the provisions of this Schedule shall have effect (for the purpose of computing an employee's period of employment, but not for any other purpose) in relation to Crown employment and to persons in Crown employment as they have effect in relation to other employment and to other employees, and accordingly, except where the context otherwise requires, references to an employer shall be construed as including a reference to the Crown.

(2) In this paragraph, subject to sub-paragraph (3), "Crown employment" means employment under or for the purposes of a government department or any officer or body exercising on behalf of the Crown functions conferred by any enactment.

(3) This paragraph does not apply to service as a member of the naval, military or air forces of the Crown, or of any women's service administered by the Defence Council, but does apply to employment by any association established for the purposes of the Auxiliary Forces Act 1953.

(4) In so far as a person in Crown employment is employed otherwise than under a contract of employment, references in this Schedule to an employee's relations with his employer being governed by a contract of employment which normally involves employment for a certain number of hours weekly shall be modified accordingly.

(5) The reference in paragraph 17(2) to an undertaking shall be construed as including a reference to any function of (as the case may require) a Minister of the Crown, a government department, or any other officer or body performing functions on behalf of the Crown.

Reinstatement or re-engagement of dismissed employee

20.—(1) Regulations made by the Secretary of State may make provision—
   (a) for preserving the continuity of a person's period of employment for the purposes of this Schedule or for the purposes of this Schedule as applied by or under any other enactment specified in the regulations, or
   (b) for modifying or excluding the operation of paragraph 12 subject to the recovery of any such payment as is mentioned in sub-paragraph (2) of that paragraph,
in cases where, in consequence of action to which sub-paragraph (2) applies, a dismissed employee is reinstated or re-engaged by his employer or by a successor or associated employer of that employer.

(2) This sub-paragraph applies to any action taken in relation to the dismissal of an employee which consists—
   (a) of the presentation by him of a complaint under section 67, or
   (b) of his making a claim in accordance with a dismissal procedures agreement designated by an order under section 65, or
   (c) of any action taken by a conciliation officer under section 134(3).

Employment before the commencement of Act

21. Save as otherwise expressly provided, the provisions of this Schedule apply to periods before it comes into force as they apply to later periods.

22. If, in any week beginning before 6th July 1964, the employee was, for the whole or any part of the week, absent from work—
   (a) because he was taking part in a strike, or

(b) because of a lock-out by the employer,
the week shall count as a period of employment.

23. Without prejudice to the foregoing provisions of this Schedule, any week which counted as a period of employment in the computation of a period of employment in accordance with the Contracts of Employment Act 1972 whether for the purposes of that Act, the Redundancy Payments Act 1965, the Trade Union and Labour Relations Act 1974 or the Employment Protection Act 1975, shall count as a period of employment for the purposes of this Act, and any week which did not break the continuity of a person's employment for the purposes of those Acts shall not break the continuity of a period of employment for the purposes of this Act.

Interpretation

24.—(1) In this Schedule, unless the context otherwise requires,—
"lock-out" means the closing of a place of employment, or the suspension of work, or the refusal by an employer to continue to employ any number of persons employed by him in consequence of a dispute, done with a view to compelling those persons, or to aid another employer in compelling persons employed by him, to accept terms or conditions of or affecting employment;
"strike" means the cessation of work by a body of persons employed acting in combination, or a concerted refusal or a refusal under a common understanding of any number of persons employed to continue to work for an employer in consequence of a dispute, done as a means of compelling their employer or any person or body of persons employed, or to aid other employees in compelling their employer or any person or body of persons employed, to accept or not to accept terms or conditions of or affecting employment;
"week" means a week ending with Saturday.

(2) For the purposes of this Schedule the hours of employment of an employee who is required by the terms of his employment to live on the premises where he works shall be the hours during which he is on duty or during which his services may be required.

AMENDMENTS

The words in square brackets in paras. 10 and 11 were inserted by the Employment Act 1980 (c. 42), Sched. 1, paras. 31, 32. Paras. 1 and 8 were substituted by the Employment Act 1982 (c. 46), Sched. 2, para. 7; and para. 18A was inserted by *ibid.*, Sched. 3, para. 2.

Section 152   SCHEDULE 14

CALCULATION OF NORMAL WORKING HOURS AND A WEEK'S PAY

PART I

NORMAL WORKING HOURS

1. For the purposes of this Schedule the cases where there are normal working hours include cases where the employee is entitled to overtime pay when employed for more than a fixed number of hours in a week or other period, and, subject to paragraph 2, in those cases that fixed number of hours shall be the normal working hours.

2. If in such a case—
   (*a*) the contract of employment fixes the number, or the minimum number, of hours of employment in the said week or other period (whether or not it also provides for the reduction of that number or minimum in certain circumstances), and
   (*b*) that number or minimum number of hours exceeds the number of hours without overtime,
that number or minimum number of hours (and not the number of hours without overtime) shall be the normal working hours.

PART II

A WEEK'S PAY

Employments for which there are normal working hours

3.—(1) This paragraph and paragraph 4 shall apply if there are normal working hours for an employee when employed under the contract of employment in force on this calculation date.

(2) Subject to paragraph 4, if an employee's remuneration for employment in normal working hours, whether by the hour or week or other period, does not vary with the amount of work done in the period, the amount of a week's pay shall be the amount payable by the employer under the contract of employment in force on the calculation date if the employee works throughout his normal working hours in a week.

(3) Subject to paragraph 4, if sub-paragraph (2) does not apply, the amount of a week's pay shall be the amount of remuneration for the number of normal working hours in a week calculated at the average hourly rate of remuneration payable by the employer to the employee in respect of the period of twelve weeks—

(*a*) where the calculation date is the last day of a week, ending with that week;

(*b*) in any other case, ending with the last complete week before the calculation date.

(4) References in this paragraph to remuneration varying with the amount of work done include references to remuneration which may include any commission or similar payment which varies in amount.

4.—(1) This paragraph shall apply if there are normal working hours for an employee when employed under the contract of employment in force on the calculation date, and he is required under that contract to work during those hours on days of the week or at times of the day which differ from week to week or over a longer period so that the remuneration payable for, or apportionable to, any week varies according to the incidence of the said days or times.

(2) The amount of a week's pay shall be the amount of remuneration for the average weekly number of normal working hours (calculated in accordance with sub-paragraph (3)) at the average hourly rate of remuneration (calculated in accordance with sub-paragraph (4)).

(3) The average number of weekly hours shall be calculated by dividing by twelve the total number of the employee's normal working hours during the period of twelve weeks—

(*a*) where the calculation date is the last day of a week, ending with that week;

(*b*) in any other case, ending with the last complete week before the calculation date.

(4) The average hourly rate of remuneration shall be the average hourly rate of remuneration payable by the employer to the employee in respect of the period of twelve weeks—

(*a*) where the calculation date is the last day of a week, ending with that week;

(*b*) in any other case, ending with the last complete week before the calculation date.

5.—(1) For the purpose of paragraphs 3 and 4, in arriving at the average hourly rate of remuneration only the hours when the employee was working, and only the remuneration payable for, or apportionable to, those hours of work, shall be brought in; and if for any of the twelve weeks mentioned in either of those paragraphs no such remuneration was payable by the employer to the employee, account shall be taken of remuneration in earlier weeks so as to bring the number of weeks of which account is taken up to twelve.

(2) Where, in arriving at the said hourly rate of remuneration, account has to be taken of remuneration payable for, or apportionable to, work done in hours other than normal working hours, and the amount of that remuneration was greater than it would have been if the work had been done in normal working hours, account shall be taken of that remuneration as if—

(*a*) the work had been done in normal working hours and

(*b*) the amount of that remuneration had been reduced accordingly.

(3) For the purpose of the application of sub-paragraph (2) to a case falling within paragraph 2, sub-paragraph (2) shall be construed as if for the words "had been done in normal working hours," in each place where those words occur, there were substituted the words "had been done in normal working hours falling within the number of hours without overtime."

Employments for which there are no normal working hours

6.—(1) This paragraph shall apply if there are no normal working hours for an employee when employed under the contract of employment in force on the calculation date.

(2) The amount of a week's pay shall be the amount of the employee's average weekly remuneration in the period of twelve weeks—

(*a*) where the calculation date is the last day of a week, ending with that week;

(*b*) in any other case, ending with the last complete week before the calculation date.

(3) In arriving at the said average weekly rate of remuneration no account shall be taken of a week in which no remuneration was payable by the employer to the employee and remuneration in earlier weeks shall be brought in so as to bring the number of weeks of which account is taken up to twelve.

The calculation date

7.—(1) For the purposes of this Part, the calculation date is,—

(a) where the calculation is for the purposes of section 14, the day in respect of which the guarantee payment is payable, or, where an employee's contract has been varied, or a new contract entered into, in connection with a period of short-time working, the last day on which the original contract was in force;

(b) where the calculation is for the purposes of section 21, the day before that on which the suspension referred to in section 19(1) begins;

(c) where the calculation is for the purposes of section 31, the day on which the employer's notice was given;

[(cc) where the calculation is for the purposes of section 31A, the day of the appointment concerned;]

(d) where the calculation is for the purposes of section 35, the last day on which the employee worked under the contract of employment in force immediately before the beginning of her absence;

(e) where the calculation is for the purposes of Schedule 3, the day immediately preceding the first day of the period of notice required by section 49(1) or, as the case may be, section 49(2);

(f) where the calculation is for the purposes of section 53 or 71(2)(b) and the dismissal was with notice, the date on which the employer's notice was given;

(g) where the calculation is for the purposes of section 53 or 71(2)(b) but sub-paragraph (f) does not apply, the effective date of termination;

(h) where the calculation is for the purposes of section 73 and by virtue of section 55(5) [or, as the case may be, (6)] a date is to be treated as the effective date of termination for the purposes of section 73(3) which is later than the effective date of termination as defined by section 55(4), the effective date of termination as defined by section 55(4);

(i) where the calculation is for the purposes of section 73 but [neither subsection (5) nor subsection (6) of section 55 applies] in relation to the date of termination, the date on which notice would have been given had the conditions referred to in sub-paragraph (2) been fulfilled (whether those conditions were in fact fulfilled or not);

(j) where the calculation is for the purposes of section 87(2), the day immediately preceding the first of the four or, as the case may be, the six weeks referred to in section 88(1);

(k) where the calculation is for the purposes of Schedule 4 and by virtue of section 90(3) a date is to be treated as the relevant date for the purposes of certain provisions of this Act which is later than the relevant date as defined by section 90(1), the relevant date as defined by section 90(1);

(l) where the calculation is for the purposes of Schedule 4 but sub-paragraph (k) does not apply, the date on which notice would have been given had the conditions referred to in sub-paragraph (2) been fulfilled (whether those conditions were in fact fulfilled or not).

(2) The conditions referred to in sub-paragraphs (1)(i) and (l) are that the contract was terminable by notice and was terminated by the employer giving such notice as is required to terminate that contract by section 49 and that the notice expired on the effective date of termination or on the relevant date, as the case may be.

Maximum amount of week's pay for certain purposes

8.—(1) Notwithstanding the preceding provisions of this Schedule, the amount of a week's pay for the purpose of calculating—

(a) an additional award of compensation (within the meaning of section 71(2)(b)) shall not exceed [£135],

(b) a basic award of compensation (within the meaning of section 72) shall not exceed [£135];

(c) a redundancy payment shall not exceed [£135].

(2) The Secretary of State may after a review under section 148 vary the limit referred to in sub-paragraph 1(a) or (b) or (c) by an order made in accordance with that section.

(3) Without prejudice to the generality of the power to make transitional provision in an order under section 148, such an order may provide that it shall apply in the case of a dismissal in relation to which the effective date of termination for the purposes of this sub-paragraph, as defined by section 55(5) [or, as the case may be, (6)] falls after the order comes into oper-

ation, notwithstanding that the effective date of termination, as defined by section 55(4), for the purposes of other provisions of this Act falls before the order comes into operation.

(4) Without prejudice to the generality of the power to make transitional provision in an order under section 148, such an order may provide that it shall apply in the case of a dismissal in relation to which the relevant date for the purposes of this sub-paragraph falls after the order comes into operation, notwithstanding that the relevant date for the purposes of other provisions of this Act falls before the order comes into operation.

Supplemental

9. In any case in which an employee has not been employed for a sufficient period to enable a calculation to be made under any of the foregoing provisions of this Part, the amount of a week's pay shall be an amount which fairly represents a week's pay; and in determining that amount the tribunal shall apply as nearly as may be such of the foregoing provisions of this Part as it considers appropriate, and may have regard to such of the following considerations as it thinks fit, that is to say—
   (*a*) any remuneration received by the employee in respect of the employment in question;
   (*b*) the amount offered to the employee as remuneration in respect of the employment in question;
   (*c*) the remuneration received by other persons engaged in relevant comparable employment with the same employer;
   (*d*) the remuneration received by other persons engaged in relevant comparable employment with other employers.

10. In arriving at an average hourly rate or average weekly rate of remuneration under this Part account shall be taken of work for a former employer within the period for which the average is to be taken if, by virtue of Schedule 13, a period of employment with the former employer counts as part of the employee's continuous period of employment with the later employer.

11. Where under this Part account is to be taken of remuneration or other payments for a period which does not coincide with the periods for which the remuneration or other payments are calculated, then the remuneration or other payments shall be apportioned in such manner as may be just.

12. The Secretary of State may by regulations provide that in prescribed cases the amount of a week's pay shall be calculated in such manner as the regulations may prescribe.

AMENDMENTS

In para. 7(1), sub-para. (*cc*) was inserted by the Employment Act 1980 (c. 42), Sched. 1, para. 33.

The figures in square brackets in para. 8 were substituted by the Employment Protection (Variation of Limits) Order 1982 (S.I. 1982 No. 77).

Section 159   SCHEDULE 15   1–613

TRANSITIONAL PROVISIONS AND SAVINGS

General

1. So far as anything done or treated as done under or for the purposes of any enactment repealed by this Act could have done under a corresponding provision of this Act it shall not be invalidated by the repeal but shall have effect as if done under or for the purposes of that provision.

2. Where any period of time specified in an enactment repealed by this Act is current immediately before the corresponding provision of this Act comes into force, this Act shall have effect as if the corresponding provisions had been in force when that period began to run.

3. Nothing in this Act shall affect the enactments repealed by this Act in their operation in relation to offences committed before the commencement of this Act.

4. Any reference in an enactment or document, whether express or implied, to—
   (*a*) an enactment which is re-enacted in a corresponding provision of this Act;
   (*b*) an enactment replaced or amended by a provision of the Employment Protection Act 1975 which is re-enacted in a corresponding provision of this Act;
   (*c*) an enactment in the Industrial Relations Act 1971 which was re-enacted with or without amendment in a corresponding provision in Schedule 1 to the Trade Union and Labour Relations Act 1974 and that corresponding provision is re-enacted by a corresponding provision of this Act;

shall, except so far as the context otherwise requires, be construed as, or as including, a reference to the corresponding provision of this Act.

5. Paragraphs 1 to 4 have effect subject to the following provisions of this Schedule.

Guarantee payments

6. Section 15(1) shall have effect in relation to any day before 1st February 1978 as if for "£6.60" there were substituted "6."

Maternity pay

7. No employee is entitled to receive maternity pay in respect of a payment period or payment periods beginning before 6th April 1977.

Termination of employment

8. Sections 49 and 50 apply in relation to any contract made before the commencement of this Act.

Unfair dismissal

9.—(1) The repeal by this Act of the provisions relating to unfair dismissals of the Employment Protection Act 1975, of Schedule 1 to the Trade Union and Labour Relations Act 1974 and of the Trade Union and Labour Relations (Amendment) Act 1976 shall not have effect in relation to dismissals where the effective date of termination is earlier than 1st October 1976 and, accordingly, those provisions shall continue to apply to such dismissals as they applied thereto before this Act came into force.

(2) Without prejudice to the generality of sub-paragraph (1), the provisions of paragraphs 17(2) and (3) and 19 of Schedule 1 to the said Act of 1974 shall, notwithstanding the repeal of those provisions by the Employment Protection Act 1975, continue to apply to dismissals where the effective date of termination falls before 1st June 1976.

(3) Where the notice required to be given by an employer to terminate a contract of employment by section 49(1) would, if duly given when notice of termination was given by the employer, or (where no notice was given) when the contract of employment was terminated by the employer, expire on a date later then the effective date of termination as defined by section 55(4), that later date shall be treated as the effective date of termination for the purposes of sub-paragraphs (1) and (2).

10.—(1) Section 54 does not apply to a dismissal from employment under a contract for a fixed term of two years or more, where the contract was made before 28th February 1972 and is not a contract of apprenticeship, and the dismissal consists only of the expiry of that term without its being renewed.

(2) Sub-paragraph (1) in its application to an employee treated as unfairly dismissed by virtue of subsection (1) or (2) of section 60 shall have effect as if for the reference to 28th February 1972 there were substituted a reference to 1st June 1976.

Redundancy

11.—(1) The repeal by this Act of any provision of the Redundancy Payments Act 1965 and of any enactment amending that Act shall not have effect in relation to dismissal, and to lay-off and short-time where the relevant date falls before 1st June 1976, and, accordingly, a person's entitlement to or the computation of a redundancy payment or the reference of questions to industrial tribunals concerning such entitlement or computation in cases where the relevant date falls before 1st June 1976 shall continue to be determined as if this Act were not in force.

(2) Where the notice required to be given by an employer to terminate a contract of employment by section 49 would, if duly given when notice of termination was given by the employer, or (where no notice was given) when the contract of employment was terminated by the employer, expire on a date later than the relevant date as defined by section 90(1), that later date shall be treated as the relevant date for the purposes of sub-paragraph (1).

12. Section 81 shall not apply to an employee who immediately before the relevant date (within the meaning of section 90) is employed under a contract of employment for a fixed term of two years or more, if that contract was made before 6th December 1965 and is not a contract of apprenticeship.

13. Sections 104 and 107 shall have effect in relation to an offence committed before 17th July 1978 as if—

(*a*) for each reference to the prescribed sum in subsection (9) of section 104 and subsection (4) of section 107 there were substituted a reference to £100, and

(b) subsection (10) of section 104 and subsection (5) of section 107 were omitted.

. . . . . .

Insolvency

15.—(1) Subject to sub-paragraph (2), the provisions of sections 122 and 123 shall apply in relation to an employer who becomes insolvent (within the meaning of section 127) after 19th April 1976, and shall in such a case apply to any debts mentioned in section 122 and to any unpaid relevant contribution (within the meaning of section 123), whether falling due before or after that date.

(2) Section 122 shall have effect in relation to any case where the employer became insolvent before 1st February 1978 as if for each reference to £100 there were substituted a reference to £80.

Calculation of a week's pay

16. Paragraph 8 of Schedule 14 shall have effect—
   (a) for the purpose of calculating an additional award of compensation in any case where the date by which the order for re-instatement or re-engagement was required to be complied with fell before 1st February 1978;
   (b) for the purpose of calculating a basic award of compensation in any case where the effective date of determination (as defined by subsection (5) of section 55 or, if the case is not within that subsection, by subsection (4) of that section) fell before 1st February, 1978;
   (c) in relation to a claim for a redundancy payment, where the relevant date fell before 1st February 1978;
as if for each reference to £100 were substituted a reference to £80.

Computation of period of continuous employment

17. For the purposes of the computation of a period of continuous employment falling to be made before 1st February 1977—
   (a) paragraphs 3 and 4 of Schedule 13 shall have effect as if for the word "sixteen" there were substituted the word "twenty-one," and
   (b) paragraphs 5, 6 and 7 of that schedule shall not apply.

Legal proceedings

18. Notwithstanding the repeal of any enactment by this Act, the Employment Appeal Tribunal and the industrial tribunals may continue to exercise the jurisdiction conferred on them by or under any enactment which is repealed by this Act with respect to matters arising out of or in connection with the repealed enactments.

House of Commons staff

19. Section 122 of the Employment Protection Act 1975 shall, until 1st January 1979, have effect as if it applied the enactments which are mentioned in subsection (1) of section 139 of this Act to relevant members of the House of Commons staff (within the meaning of the said section 122).

AMENDMENT
Para. 14 was repealed by the Health and Social Services and Social Security Adjudications Act 1983 (c. 41), s.30, Sched. 10, Pt. I.

Section 159   SCHEDULE 16

CONSEQUENTIAL AMENDMENTS

House of Commons Offices Act 1846 (9 & 10 Vict. c. 77)

1. In section 5 of the House of Commons Offices Act 1846, after the words "Employment

Protection Act 1975" there are inserted the words "the Employment Protection (Consolidation) Act 1978."

Trade Union Act 1913 (2 & 3 Geo. 5. c. 30)
2. In section 5A of the Trade Union Act 1913, for the words "section 88(2) of the Employment Protection Act 1975" there are substituted the words "section 136(2) of the Employment Protection (Consolidation) Act 1978."

Iron and Steel Act 1949 (12, 13 & 14 Geo. 6. c. 72)
3.—(1) In section 40 of the Iron and Steel Act 1949, in subsection (3), for the words from "a tribunal" to the end there are substituted the words "an industrial tribunal."

(2) In section 41 of the said Act of 1949, in subsection (3), for the words from "a tribunal" to the end are substituted the words "an industrial tribunal."

Industrial Training Act 1964 (c. 16)
[Repealed by the Industrial Training Act 1982, Sched. 4.]

Trade Unions (Amalgamations, etc.) Act 1964 (c. 24)
5. In section 4(8) of the Trade Union (Amalgamations, etc.) Act 1964, for the words "section 88(2) of the Employment Protection Act 1975" there are substituted the words "section 136(2) of the Employment Protection (Consolidation) Act 1978."

Transport Act 1968 (c. 73)
6. In section 135(4)(*b*) of the Transport Act 1968, for the words from "a tribunal" to the end there are substituted the words "an industrial tribunal."

Transport (London) Act 1969 (c. 35)
7.—(1) In section 37(4)(*b*) of the Transport (London) Act 1969, for the words from "a tribunal" to the end there are substituted the words "an industrial tribunal."

(2) In paragraph 6 of Schedule 2 to the said Act of 1969, for the words "paragraph 10(3) of Schedule 1 to the Contracts of Employment Act 1963 and section 8(2) of the Redundancy Payments Act 1965, for the purposes of those Acts" there are substituted the words "section 151(1) of and paragraph 17(3) of Schedule 13 to the Employment Protection (Consolidation) Act 1978, for the purposes of that Act."

Post Office Act 1969 (c. 48)
8. In paragraph 33 of Schedule 9 to the Post Office Act 1969—
   (*a*) in sub-paragraph (1) for the words "sections 1 and 2 of the Contracts of Employment Act 1963, Schedule 1" there are substituted the words "sections 49 and 50 and Part VI of the Employment Protection (Consolidation) Act 1978, Schedule 13"; for the words "the said Act of 1963" there are substituted the words "the said Act of 1978"; and for the words "twenty-one hours" there are substituted the words "sixteen hours";
   (*b*) in sub-paragraph (2), for the words "Schedule 1 to the said Act of 1963" there are substituted the words "Schedule 13 to the said Act of 1978";
   (*c*) in sub-paragraph (3), for the words "7 of Schedule 2 to the said Act of 1963" there are substituted the words "10 of Schedule 14 to the said Act of 1978" and for the words from "paragraph 10" to the end there are substituted the words "Schedule 13 to that Act shall be construed as a reference to that Schedule as it has effect by virtue of sub-paragraph (1) above.";
   (*d*) in sub-paragraph (4), for the words "the said Act of 1963" and "Schedule 1" there are substituted respectively the words "the said Act of 1978" and "Schedule 13";
   (*e*) at the end there is added the following sub-paragraph—
      "(6) This paragraph applies notwithstanding the provisions of section 99 of the Employment Protection (Consolidation) Act 1978."

Income and Corporation Taxes Act 1970 (c. 10)
9.—(1) In section 412(6) of the Income and Corporation Taxes Act 1970, for the words "section 32 of the Redundancy Payments Act 1965" there are substituted the words "section 106 of the Employment Protection (Consolidation) Act 1978."

(2) In section 412(7) of the said Act of 1970—
   (*a*) for the words "Part II of the Redundancy Payments Act 1965" there are substituted the words "the Employment Protection (Consolidation) Act 1978";

(b) for the words "section 30(2) of the Redundancy Payments Act 1965" there are substituted the words "section 104(2) of the Employment Protection (Consolidation) Act 1978";
(c) for the words "Schedule 5 to the Redundancy Payments Act 1965" there are substituted the words "Schedule 6 to the Employment Protection (Consolidation) Act 1978";
(d) for the words "Redundancy Payments Act 1965" in paragraph (c) of the said section 412(7), there are substituted the words "the Employment Protection (Consolidation) Act 1978."

Atomic Energy Authority Act 1971 (*c.* 11)

10.—(1) In subsection (1) of section 10 of the Atomic Energy Authority Act 1971, for the words "section 22 of the Redundancy Payments Act 1965" there are substituted the words "section 93 of the Employment Protection (Consolidation) Act 1978."

(2) In subsection (2) of the said section 10—
  (a) for the words "section 4 of the Contracts of Employment Act 1963" there are substituted the words "sections 1 to 4 of the Employment Protection (Consolidation) Act 1978";
  (b) for the words "subsection (8) of that section," in both places where they occur, there are substituted the words "section 5 of the said Act of 1978";
  (c) for the words "the said section 4" there are substituted the words "the said sections 1 to 4."

(3) In subsection (3) of the said section 10—
  (a) for the words "Section 4A(1) of the Contracts of Employment Act 1963" there are substituted the words "Section 11 of the Employment Protection (Consolidation) Act 1978";
  (b) for the words "section 4" there are substituted the words "sections 1 to 4."

(4) In subsection (4) of the said section 10—
  (a) for the words from the beginning to "Redundancy Payments Act 1965" there are substituted the words "For the purposes of Schedule 13 to the said Act of 1978 (computation of period of employment)";
  (b) for the words "paragraph 10" there are substituted the words "paragraph 17."

Tribunals and Inquiries Act 1971 (*c.* 62)

11. In section 13 of the Tribunals and Inquiries Act 1971, the following subsection is inserted after subsection (1)—

"(1A) Subsection (1) of this section shall not apply in relation to proceedings before industrial tribunals which arise under or by virtue of any of the enactments mentioned in section 136(1) of the Employment Protection (Consolidation) Act 1978."

Civil Aviation Act 1971 (*c.* 75)

12.—(1) In paragraph 1 of Schedule 9 to the Civil Aviation Act 1971—
  (a) in sub-paragraph (1) for the words "sections 1 and 2 of the Contracts of Employment Act 1963, Schedule 1" there are substituted the words "sections 49 and 50 and Part VI of the Employment Protection (Consolidation) Act 1978, Schedule 13," for the words "the said Act of 1963" there are substituted the words "the said Act of 1978"; and for the words "twenty-one hours" there are substituted the words "sixteen hours";
  (b) in sub-paragraph (2), for the words "Schedule 1 to the said Act of 1963" there are substituted the words "Schedule 13 to the said Act of 1978."
  (c) in sub-paragraph (3), for the words "7 of Schedule 2 to the said Act of 1963" there are substituted the words "10 of Schedule 14 to the said Act of 1978" and for the words from "paragraph 10" to the end there are substituted the words "Schedule 13 to that Act shall be construed as a reference to that Schedule as it has effect by virtue of sub-paragraph (1) above";
  (d) in sub-paragraph (4), for the words "the said Act of 1963" and "Schedule 1" there are substituted respectively the words "the said Act of 1978" and "Schedule 13";
  (e) at the end there is added the following sub-paragraph—
    "(6) This paragraph applies notwithstanding the provisions of section 99 of the Employment Protection (Consolidation) Act 1978."".

(2) In paragraph 4 of the said Schedule 9—
   (a) for the words "paragraph 10(2) of Schedule 1 to the Contracts of Employment Act 1963 and section 13(1) of the Redundancy Payments Act 1965" there are substituted the words "section 94(1) of and paragraph 17(2) of Schedule 13 to the Employment Protection (Consolidation) Act 1978";
   (b) for the words "the said section 13(1)" there are substituted the words "the said section 94(1)";
   (c) for the words from "the said Act of 1963" to "Act of 1965" there are substituted the words "the said paragraph 17(2) and the references to the said section 94(1)," and after the words "a reference" there are inserted the words "to paragraph 10(2) of Schedule 1."

Transport Holding Company Act 1972 (c. 14)
13.—(1) In section 2(3)(c) of the Transport Holding Company Act 1972, for the words from "a tribunal" to the end there are substituted the words "an industrial tribunal."
(2) In section 2(7) of the said Act of 1972, for the words "a tribunal established under section 12 of the Industrial Training Act 1964" there are substituted the words "an industrial tribunal."

Finance Act 1972 (c. 41)
14. In paragraph 1(b) of Part V of Schedule 12 to the Finance Act 1972, for the words "Redundancy Payments Act 1965" there are substituted the words "Employment Protection (Consolidation) Act 1978."

British Library Act 1973 (c. 54)
15. In paragraph 13(3)(a) of the Schedule to the British Library Act 1972, for the words "the Acts of 1963 and 1965" there are substituted the words "the Employment Protection (Consolidation) Act 1978."

Gas Act 1972 (c. 60)
16. In Section 36(5) of the Gas Act 1972, for the words from "a tribunal" to the end there are substituted the words "an industrial tribunal."

Health and Safety at Work etc. Act 1974 (c. 37)
17. The following subsection is inserted in section 80 of the Health and Safety at Work etc. Act 1974 after subsection (2)—
(2A) Subsection (1) above shall apply to provisions in the Employment Protection (Consolidation) Act 1978 which re-enact provisions previously contained in the Redundancy Payments Act 1965, the Contracts of Employment Act 1972 or the Trade Union and Labour Relations Act 1974 as it applies to provisions contained in Acts passed before or in the same Session as this Act."

Trade Union and Labour Relations Act 1974 (c. 52)
18. In section 8(7) of the Trade Union and Labour Relations Act 1974, for the words "section 88(3) of the Employment Protection Act 1975" there are substituted the words "section 136(3) of the Employment Protection (Consolidation) Act 1978."

Social Security Act 1975 (c. 14)
19.—(1) In section 114 of the Social Security Act 1975, the following subsection is inserted after subsection (2)—
   "(2A) It is hereby declared for the avoidance of doubt that the power to make regulations under subsection (1) above includes power to make regulations for the determination of any question arising as to the total or partial recoupment of unemployment benefit in pursuance of regulations under section 132 of the Employment Protection (Consolidation) Act 1978 (including any decision as to the amount of benefit."
(2) In subsection 139 of the said Act of 1975, after subsection (2) there is inserted the following subsection—
   "(2A) Subsection (1) above does not apply to regulations made under this Act and contained in a statutory instrument which states that the regulations provide only

that a day in respect of which there is payable a particular description of any payment to which section 132 of the Employment Protection (Consolidation) Act 1978 (recoupment of unemployment and supplementary benefits) applies shall not be treated as a day of unemployment for the purposes of entitlement to unemployment benefit."

Sex Discrimination Act 1975 (*c.* 65)

20.—(1) In section 65(2) of the Sex Discrimination Act 1975, for the words "paragraph 20 of Schedule 1 to the Trade Union and Labour Relations Act 1974" there are substituted the words "section 75 of the Employment Protection (Consolidation) Act 1978."

(2) In section 75(5)(*c*) of the said Act of 1975 for the words "paragraph 21 of Schedule 1 to the Trade Union and Labour Relations Act 1974." there are substituted the words "paragraph 1 of Schedule 9 to the Employment Protection (Consolidation) Act 1978."

Scottish Development Agency Act 1975 (*c.* 69)

21. In paragraph 6 of Schedule 3 to the Scottish Development Agency Act 1975, for sub-paragraphs (*a*), (*b*) and (*c*) there are substituted the words "the Employment Protection (Consolidation) Act 1978."

Welsh Development Agency Act 1975 (*c.* 79)

22. In paragraph 7 of Schedule 2 to the Welsh Development Agency Act 1975, for sub-paragraphs (*a*), (*b*) and (*c*) there are substituted the words "the Employment Protection (Consolidation) Act 1978."

Employment Protection Act 1975 (*c.* 71)

23.—(1) The Employment Protection Act 1975 shall be amended in accordance with the following provisions of this paragraph.

(2) In section 6(2)—
- (*a*) the words from "in relation to" to "that is to say" shall be omitted;
- (*b*) for the words "section 57 below; and" there are substituted the words "section 27 of the Employment Protection (Consolidation) Act 1978, including guidance on the circumstances in which a trade union official is to be permitted to take time off under that section in respect of duties connected with industrial action; and";
- (*c*) for the words "section 58 below" there are substituted the words "section 28 of the said Act of 1978, including guidance on the question whether, and the circumstances in which, a trade union member is to be permitted to take time off under that section for trade union activities connected with industrial action".

(3) In section 8(9), for the words "section 88(3) below" there are substituted the words "section 136(3) of the Employment Protection (Consolidation) Act 1978".

(4) In section 102(4), for the words "Schedule 2 to the Contracts of Employment Act 1972" there are substituted the words "Schedule 3 to the Employment Protection (Consolidation) Act 1978", and for the words "section 1(1)" there are substituted the words "section 49(1)".

(5) In section 104(1)(*a*), for the words "section 30(1) of the Redundancy Payments Act 1965" there are substituted the words "section 104(1) of the Employment Protection (Consolidation) Act 1978".

(6) In section 106(3), for the words from the beginning to "Redundancy Payments Act 1965" there are substituted the words "Schedule 14 to the Employment Protection (Consolidation) Act 1978 shall apply for the calculation of a week's pay for the purposes of section 102 above, and, for the purposes of Part II of that Schedule, the calculation date is—
- (*a*) in the case of an employee who was dismissed before the date on which the protective award was made, the date which by virtue of paragraph 7(1)(*k*) or (*l*) of the said Schedule 14".

(7) In section 108(1), for the words "paragraph 21 of Schedule 1 to the 1974 Act" there are substituted the words "paragraph 1 of Schedule 9 to the Employment Protection (Consolidation) Act 1978".

(8) In section 119(1), for the words "Parts II and IV of this Act apply" there are substituted the words "Part IV of this Act applies".

(9) [*Repealed by the Employment Act* 1982 (*c.*46), *Sched.* 4].

(10) In section 121(5), for the words "Schedule 3 to the Redundancy Payments Act 1965"

there are substituted the words "Schedule 5 to the Employment Protection (Consolidation) Act 1978".

(11) In section 121(6) and (7), for the words "section 41(3) of the Redundancy Payments Act 1965" there are substituted the words "section III (3) of the Employment Protection (Consolidation) Act 1978".

(12) In section 125(1) for the words from the beginning to "Part III of that Schedule" there are substituted the words "The provisions of the 1974 Act specified in Part III of Schedule 16 to this Act".

(13) In section 126(1), for the words "paragraph 5 of Schedule 1 to the 1974 Act" there are substituted the words "section 55 of the Employment Protection (Consolidation) Act 1978".

New Towns (Amendment) Act 1976 (c. 68)

24. In section 13 of the New Towns (Amendment) Act 1976—
 (a) in subsection (5), for the words "Schedule 1 to the Contracts of Employment Act 1972" there are substituted the words "Schedule 13 to the Employment Protection (Consolidation) Act 1978";
 (b) in subsection (6), for the words "section 13 of the Redundancy Payments Act 1965" there are substituted the words "section 94 of the Employment Protection (Consolidation) Act 1978."

Race Relations Act 1976 (c. 74)

25.—(1) The Race Relations Act 1976 shall be amended in accordance with the following provisions of this paragraph.

(2) In section 56(2) for the words "paragraph 20 of Schedule 1 to the Trade Union and Labour Relations Act 1974" there are substituted the words "section 75 of the Employment Protection (Consolidation) Act 1978."

(3) In section 66(7) for the words "paragraph 21 of Schedule 1 to the Trade Union and Labour Relations Act 1974" there are substituted the words "paragraph 1 of Schedule 9 to the Employment Protection (Consolidation) Act 1978."

(4) In paragraph 11 of Schedule 2—
 (a) In sub-paragraph (3) for the words "the Redundancy Payments Act 1965" there are substituted the words "Part VI of the Employment Protection (Consolidation) Act 1978";
 (b) for sub-paragraph (4)(a) and (b) there is substituted the following paragraph—
  "(a) the Employment Protection (Consolidation) Act 1978 except Part VI of that Act."

Development of Rural Wales Act 1976 (c. 75)

26. In both paragraph 6 of Schedule 2 and paragraph 6 of Schedule 6 to the Development of Rural Wales Act 1976, for sub-paragraphs (a), (b) and (c) there are substituted the words "the Employment Protection (Consolidation) Act 1978."

Dock Work Regulation Act 1976 (c. 79)

27.—(1) In section 14(7) of the Dock Work Regulation Act 1976 for the words "subsections (1), (5) and (6) above" there are substituted the words "subsection (6) above."

(2) In paragraph 17(1) of Schedule 1 to the said Act of 1976, for the words "Schedule 1 to the Contracts of Employment Act 1972" there are substituted the words "Schedule 13 to the Employment Protection (Consolidation) Act 1978."

Aircraft and Shipbuilding Industries Act 1977 (c. 3)

28. In both section 49(10) and section 50(3)(b) of the Aircraft and Shipbuilding Industries Act 1977, for the words "a tribunal established under section 12 of the Industrial Training Act 1964 or, as the case may require" there are substituted the words "an industrial tribunal or, as the case may require, a tribunal established under."

Social Security (Miscellaneous Provisions) Act 1977 (c. 5)

29. In section 18 of the Social Security (Miscellaneous Provisions) Act 1977—
 (a) in subsection (1)(c), for "Act 1975" there shall be substituted "(Consolidation) Act 1975";
 (b) in subsection (2)(a), for the words "section 43 of the Employment Protection Act 1975" there are substituted the words "section 40 of the Employment Protection (Consolidation) Act 1978";

1978 c.44 409

 (c) in subsection (2)(b), for "64(3)(a)" and "45(1)" there are substituted "122(3)(a)" and "42(1)" respectively;
 (d) in subsection (2)(e), for the words "that Act" there are substituted the words "the Employment Protection Act 1975."

New Towns (Scotland) Act 1977 (c. 16)
30. In section 3 of the New Towns (Scotland) Act 1977 for paragraphs (a), (b) and (c) there are substituted the words "Parts I, IV, V and VI of the Employment Protection (Consolidation) Act 1978."

Housing (Homeless Persons) Act 1977 (c. 48)
31. In section 14(4) of the Housing (Homeless Persons) Act 1977—
 (a) in paragraph (a), for the words "section 13 of the Redundancy Payments Act 1965" there are substituted the words "section 94 of the Employment Protection (Consolidation) Act 1978";
 (b) in paragraph (b), for the words "Schedule 1 to the Contracts of Employment Act 1972" there are substituted the words "Schedule 13 to the said Act of 1978," and the words "sections 1 and 2 of" shall cease to have effect.

National Health Service Act 1977 (c. 49)
32. In paragraph 13(1)(b) of Schedule 14 to the National Health Service Act 1977, the reference to paragraph 106 of Schedule 4 to the National Health Service Reorganisation Act 1973 shall cease to have effect, and, accordingly, for that reference to paragraph 106 there is substituted a reference to paragraph 107 of the said Schedule 4.

. . . . . .

House of Commons (Administration) Act 1978 (c. 36)
34. In paragraph 1 of Schedule 2 to the House of Commons (Administration) Act 1978, after the words "the Employment Protection Act 1975" there are inserted the words "and section 139 of the Employment Protection (Consolidation) Act 1978."

AMENDMENT
Para. 19(2) of this Schedule has been repealed by the Social Security Act 1980, Sched. 5, Pt. II, from a date to be appointed.

Section 159   SCHEDULE 17   1–615

REPEALS

Chapter	Short title	Extent of repeal
1964 c. 16.	Industrial Training Act 1964	Section 12 (2B), (3) and (4).
1965 c. 62.	Redundancy Payments Act 1965.	Sections 1 to 26. Sections 30 to 44. Sections 46 to 55 except section 55 (6)(b). Sections 56 to 58. In section 59, subsection (2) and in subsection (3) the words "except the last preceding section". Schedules 1 to 9.
1967 c. 17.	Iron and Steel Act 1967.	In section 31, in subsection (3), paragraph (c) and all the words following paragraph (c), and subsections (4) (b) and (6).
1967 c. 28.	Superannuation (Miscellaneous Provisions) Act 1967.	Section 9.
1968 c. 13.	National Loans Act 1968.	In Schedule 1, the paragraph relating to the Redundancy Payments Act 1965.

Chapter	Short Title	Extent of Repeal
1969 c. 8.	Redundancy Rebates Act 1969.	The whole Act.
1969 c. 48.	Post Office Act 1969.	In Schedule 9, paragraph 34.
1970 c. 41.	Equal Pay Act 1970.	Section 2 (7).
1971 c. 75.	Civil Aviation Act 1971.	In Schedule 9, paragraph 2.
1972 c. 11.	Superannuation Act 1972.	In Schedule 6, paragraphs 54 and 55.
1972 c. 53.	Contracts of Employment Act 1972.	The whole Act.
1972 c. 54.	British Library Act 1972.	In paragraphs 13 (2) of the Schedule, the definition of "the Act of 1963".
1972 c. 58.	National Health Service (Scotland) Act 1972.	In Schedule 6, paragraph 130.
1973 c. 32.	National Health Service Reorganisation Act 1973.	In Schedule 4, paragraph 106.
1973 c. 38.	Social Security Act 1973.	In Schedule 27, paragraphs 54 to 59.
1973 c. 50.	Employment and Training Act 1973.	In Schedule 2 in Part I, paragraph 15.
1974 c. 52.	Trade Union and Labour Relations Act 1974.	In section 1 (2), paragraphs (b) and (c) and, in paragraph (d), the references to section 146, 148, 149, 150 and 151 of the 1971 Act. In section 30 (1), the definitions of "dismissal procedures agreement", "position" and "job". In Schedule 1, paragraphs 4 to 16, 17 (1), 18, 20 to 27 and 30, in paragraph 32, sub-paragraphs (1) (b) and (2) (b) to (e) and, in paragraph 33, subparagraphs (3) (c) and (d) and (4A). In Schedule 3, paragraph 16. In Schedule 4, paragraphs 1, 3 and 6 (4).
1975 c. 18.	Social Security (Consequential Provisions) Act 1975.	In Schedule 2, paragraphs 19 to 23.
1975 c. 60.	Social Security Pensions Act 1975.	Section 30 (5).
1975 c. 71.	Employment Protection Act 1975.	Part II except section 40. Section 108 (2) to (8). Section 109. Section 112. In section 118 (2), in paragraph (a) the words "section 22 above or" and "section 28 or, as the case may be," and paragraphs (b) and (c). In section 119— subsection (2); in subsection (3) the figures from "22" to "70"; in subsection (4) the figures from "22" to "81"; in subsection (5), the figuires from "22" to "81"; in subsection (7) the figures "22" and "29"; subsections (8) to (11); in subsection (12) the figures from "59" to "81"; Section 120. In section 121— in subsection (1), the reference to sections 47 and 63 to 69;

Chapter	Short title	Extent of repeal
		in subsection (5), the reference to sections 47 (3) and (4) and 68 (3) and (4);
		subsection (8).
		In section 122 (1), the words "Schedule 1 to the Contracts of Employment Act 1972 and Parts I and II of Schedule 1 to the 1974 Act"; and in paragraph (*d*), the words "paragraph" 21 (5) (*c*) of Schedule 1 to the 1974 Act and".
		In section 122, subsection (3), in subsection (4) the definition of "civil employment claim" and in subsection (5) the words from "and of the Redundancy" to "employment claim".
		In section 123 (2) (*b*) the words "28 or".
		In section 124, subsection (2) to (4).
		In section 126—
		in subsection (1), the definitions of "guarantee payment" and 'maternity pay";
		subsections (3) and (5).
		In section 127—
		in subsection (1), paragraphs (*c*) and (*d*);
		in subsection (3) (*g*), the words from "the following" to "also of ".
		In section 128—
		in subsection (1), the words "or of the 1974 Act so far as it relates to unfair dismissal" and "and the 1974 Act";
		subsection (2);
		in subsection (3), the words "and the relevant provisions of the 1974 Act" in both places where they occur, and the words "or the relevant provisions of the 1974 Act".
		Section 129 (2).
		Schedules 2 to 6.
		In Schedule 12—
		in paragraph 1, the words from "and" to the end;
		paragraphs 8 to 12.
		In Schedule 16—
		Parts I and II;
		in Part III, paragraphs 8 to 30 and 34;
		in Part IV, paragraph 14.
		In Schedule 17, paragraphs 7 to 10, 16 and 17.
1976 c. 7.	Trade Union and Labour Relations (Amendment) Act 1976.	Section 1 (*e*). Section 3 (5) and (6).
1976 c. 68.	New Towns (Amendment) Act 1976.	In section 13 (5), the words "sections 1 and 2 of".
1976 c. 71.	Supplementary Benefits Act 1976.	In Schedule 7, paragraph 40.
1976 c. 74.	Race Relations Act 1976.	In Schedule 3, paragraphs 1 (2), (3) and (4).
1976 c. 79.	Dock Work Regulations Act 1976.	In section 14, subsections (1) to (5) and in subsection (6), paragraph (*a*) and so

Chapter	Short title	Extent of repeal
		much of paragraph (*b*) as relates to section 22, 29, 61, 64, 65 and 70 of the Employment Protection Act 1975. In Schedule 1, paragraph 17 (2).
1977 c. 5.	Social Security (Miscellaneous Provisions) Act 1977.	Section 16.
1977 c. 22.	Redundancy Rebates Act 1977.	The whole Act.
1977 c. 38.	Administration of Justice Act 1977.	Section 6. Section 32 (11).
1977 c. 48.	Housing (Homeless Persons) Act 1977.	In section 14 (4) (*b*), the words "sections 1 and 2 of".

1–616

Wages Councils Act 1979

(1979 c. 12)

An Act to consolidate the enactments relating to wages councils and statutory joint industrial councils.

[22nd March 1979]

PART I

WAGES COUNCILS

Establishment of wages councils

1–617   **1.**—(1) Subject to the provisions of this Part of this Act, the Secretary of State may by order establish a wages council to perform, in relation to the workers described in the order and their employers, the functions specified in relation to wages councils in the subsequent provisions of this Part of this Act.

(2) An order establishing a wages council may be made by the Secretary of State either—
  (*a*) if he is of opinion that no adequate machinery exists for the effective regulation of the remuneration of the workers described in the order and that, having regard to the remuneration existing among those workers, or any of them, it is expedient that such a council should be established; or
  (*b*) if he thinks fit, to give effect to a recommendation of the Advisory, Conciliation and Arbitration Service ("the Service") made on the reference to it, in accordance with section 2 below, of an application made in accordance therewith for the establishment of a wages council; or
  (*c*) if he thinks fit, to give effect to the recommendation of the Service made in a case where the Secretary of State, being of opinion that no adequate machinery exists for the effective regulation of the remuneration of any workers or the existing machinery is likely to cease to exist or be adequate for that purpose and a reasonable standard of remuneration among those workers will not be maintained, refers to the Service the question whether a wages council should be

established with respect to any of those workers and their employers.

(3) Schedule 1 to this Act shall have effect with respect to the making of orders establishing wages councils.

(4) Schedule 2 to this Act shall have effect with respect to the constitution, officers and proceedings of wages councils.

Applications for wages council orders

2.—(1) An application for the establishment of a wages council with respect to any workers and their employers may be made to the Secretary of State either—
  (*a*) by a joint industrial council, conciliation board or other similar body constituted by organisations representative respectively of those workers and their employers; or
  (*b*) jointly by any organisation of workers and any organisation of employers which claim to be organisations that habitually take part in the settlement of remuneration and conditions of employment for those workers;
on the ground, in either case, that the existing machinery for the settlement of remuneration and conditions of employment for those workers is likely to cease to exist or be adequate for that purpose.

(2) Where such an application as aforesaid is made to him, the Secretary of State—
  (*a*) subject to subsection (3) below, if he is satisfied that there are sufficient grounds to justify the reference of the application to the Service, and in the case of an application under paragraph (*b*) of subsection (1) above, that the claim of the organisations habitually to take part in the settlement of remuneration and conditions of employment for those workers is well-founded, shall refer the application to the Service to inquire into and report on the application;
  (*b*) if he is not so satisfied shall notify the applicants to that effect, in which case no further steps shall be taken on the application unless and until he is so satisfied by fresh facts brought to his notice:
Provided that before taking either of the said courses, the Secretary of State may require the applicants to furnish such information, if any, in relation to the application as he considers necessary.

(3) If, on considering an application under subsection (1) above, it appears to the Secretary of State either—
  (*a*) that there is a joint industrial council, conciliation board or other similar body constituted by organisations of workers and organisations of employers, being a council, board or body which would or might be affected by the establishment of a wages council in pursuance of the application; or
  (*b*) that there are organisations of workers and organisations of employers representative respectively of workers other than workers to whom the application relates and their employers, who would or might be affected by the establishment of a wages council as aforesaid;
being a council, board or body, or, as the case may be, organisations, which are parties to joint voluntary machinery for the settlement of remuneration and conditions of employment but are not parties to the

application for a wages council, the Secretary of State shall, before deciding to refer the application to the Service give notice of the application to that council, board or body or, as the case may be, to those organisations, shall consider any observations in writing which may be submitted to him by them within such period as he may direct, not being less than one month from the date of the notice, and, if he decides to refer the application to the Service, shall transmit a copy of the observations to the Service.

(4) If, before an application is referred to the Service, it is withdrawn by the applicants, no further proceedings shall be had thereon.

Proceedings on references as to establishment of wages councils

1–619   3.—(1) Where the Secretary of State makes any such reference as is mentioned in paragraph (*b*) or (*c*) of subsection (2) of section 1 above, it shall be the duty of the Service to consider not only the subject matter of the reference but also any other question or matter which, in the opinion of the Service, is relevant thereto, and in particular to consider whether there are any other workers (being workers who, in the opinion of the Service, are engaged in work which is complementary, subsidiary or closely allied to the work performed by the workers specified in the reference or any of them) whose position should be dealt with together with that of the workers, or some of the workers, specified as aforesaid; and in relation to any such reference, any reference in this Part of this Act to the workers with whom the Service is concerned shall be construed as a reference to the workers specified as aforesaid and any such other workers as aforesaid.

(2) If the Service is of opinion with respect to the workers with whom it is concerned or any of those workers whose position should, in the opinion of the Service, be separately dealt with—

    (*a*) that there exists machinery set up by agreement between organisations representing workers and employers respectively which is, or can be made by improvements which it is practicable to secure, adequate for regulating the remuneration and conditions of employment of those workers; and

    (*b*) that there is no reason to believe that that machinery is likely to cease to exist or be adequate for that purpose,

the Service shall report to the Secretary of State accordingly and may include in its report any suggestions which it may think fit to make as to the improvement of that machinery.

(3) Where any such suggestions are so included, the Secretary of State shall take such steps as appear to him to be expedient and practicable to secure the improvements in question.

(4) If the Service is of opinion with respect to the workers with whom it is concerned or any of those workers whose position should, in the opinion of the Service, be separately dealt with—

    (*a*) that machinery for regulating the remuneration and conditions of employment of those workers is not, and cannot be made by any improvements which it is practicable to secure, adequate for that purpose, or does not exist; or

    (*b*) that the existing machinery is likely to cease to exist or be adequate for that purpose,

and that as a result a reasonable standard of remuneration among those workers is not being or will not be maintained, the Service may make a report to the Secretary of State embodying a recommendation for the establishment of a wages council in respect of those workers and their employers.

(5) In considering for the purposes of section 1 above whether any machinery is, or is likely to remain, adequate for regulating the remuneration and conditions of employment of any workers, the Service shall consider not only what matters are capable of being dealt with by that machinery, but also to what extent those matters are covered by the agreements or awards arrived at or given thereunder, and to what extent the practice is, or is likely to be, in accordance with those agreements or awards.

Abolition of, or variation of field of operation of, wages councils

4.—(1) The Secretary of State may at any time abolish a wages council by order made—
   (a) to give effect to an application in that behalf made to him in accordance with section 5 below, or
   (b) without any such application, subject however to the provisions of section 6 below.

1–620

(2) The Secretary of State may at any time by order vary the field of operation of a wages council.

(3) The power of the Secretary of State to make an order under this section varying the field of operation of a wages council shall include power to vary that field by excluding from it any employers to whom there for the time being applies, as members of an organisation named in the order, an agreement, to which the organisation or any other organisation of which it is a member or on which it is represented, is a party, regulating remuneration or other terms or conditions of employment of their employees.

(4) Any organisation so named shall if it has not already done so furnish the Secretary of State with a list of its members and shall from time to time, and also if so required by the Secretary of State, furnish him with particulars of any changes in their membership which have occurred since the list was furnished or, as the case may be, when particulars were last furnished to him.

(5) An order under this section abolishing or varying the field of operation of one or more wages councils may include provision for the establishment of one or more wages councils operating in relation to all or any of the workers in relation to whom the first mentioned council or councils would have operated but for the order, and such other workers, if any, as may be specified in the order.

(6) Where an order of the Secretary of State under this section directs that any workers shall be excluded from the field of operation of one wages council and brought within the field of operation of another, the order may provide that anything done by, or to give effect to proposals made by, the first-mentioned council shall have effect in relation to those workers as if it had been done by, or to give effect to proposals made by, the second-mentioned council and may make such further provision as appears to the Secretary of State to be expedient in connection with the transition.

(7) Where an order of the Secretary of State under this section directs that a wages council shall be abolished or shall cease to operate in relation to any workers, then, save as is otherwise provided by the order, anything done by, or to give effect to proposals made by the wages council shall, except as respects things previously done or omitted to be done, cease to

have effect or, as the case may be, cease to have effect in relation to the workers in relation to whom the council ceases to operate.

(8) Schedule 1 to this Act shall have effect with respect to the making of orders under this section.

Applications for abolition of wages councils

1–621   5.—(1) An application such as is mentioned in paragraph (*a*) of subsection (1) of section 4 above may be made to the Secretary of State either—
  (*a*) by a joint industrial council, conciliation board or other similar body constituted by organisations of workers and organisations of employers which represent respectively substantial proportions of the workers and employers with respect to whom that wages council operates; or
  (*b*) jointly by organisations of workers and organisations of employers which represent respectively substantial proportions of the workers and employers aforesaid; or
  (*b*) by any organisation of workers which represents a substantial proportion of the workers with respect to whom that wages council operates.

(2) The grounds on which any such application may be made are that the existence of a wages council is no longer necessary for the purpose of maintaining a reasonable standard of remuneration for the workers with respect to whom that wages council operates.

References to the Service as to variation or revocation of wages council orders

1–622   6.—(1) The Secretary of State—
  (*a*) shall in any case where an application for the abolition of a wages council has been made to him under section 5 above and he does not thereupon proceed to the making of an order giving effect to the application,
  (*b*) may in any other case where he is considering whether to exercise his power under section 4 above to abolish or vary the field of operation of a wages council;
refer to the Service the question whether the council should be abolished or, as the case may be, its field of operation varied.

(2) On a reference under this section of a question as to the abolition of a wages council the Service, if of the opinion that it is expedient to do so, may make a report to the Secretary of State recommending—
  (i) the abolition of the wages council to which the reference relates, or
  (ii) the narrowing of the field of operation of the council,
and (in either case), if the Service is of the opinion that it is expedient as aforesaid, also recommending the transfer of workers to the field of operation of another wages council, whether already existing or to be established.

(3) On a reference under this section as to the variation of the field of operation of a wages council the Service may make a report to the Secretary of State recommending any such variation (including the transfer of workers to the field of operation of any other wages council, whether already existing or to be established) which appears to the Service desirable in all the circumstances.

Supplemental provisions

7.—(1) On any reference under this Part of this Act to the Service, the Service shall make all such investigations as appear to it to be necessary and shall publish in the prescribed manner a notice stating the questions which it is its duty to consider by virtue of the reference and further stating that it will consider representations with respect thereto made to it in writing within such period as may be specified in the notice, not being less than forty days from the date of the publication thereof; and it shall consider any representations made to it within that period and then make such further inquiries as it considers necessary including, so far as it considers necessary, the hearing of oral evidence.

(2) Any power conferred by this Part of this Act on the Secretary of State to make an order giving effect to a recommendation of the Service shall be construed as including power to make an order giving effect to that recommendation with such modifications as he thinks fit, being modifications which, in his opinion, do not effect important alterations in the character of the recommendations.

(3) Where the Secretary of State receives any report from the Service he may, if he thinks fit, refer the report back to the Service and the Service shall thereupon reconsider it having regard to any observations made by him and shall make a further report, and the like proceedings shall be had on any such further report as in the case of an original report.

(4) The Secretary of State shall publish every report made to him by the Service under this Part of this Act:

Provided that where he refers a report back to the Service, he shall not be bound to publish it until he publishes the further report of the Service.

Advisory committees

8.—(1) A wages council may request the Secretary of State to appoint a committee for any of the workers within the field of operation of the council and the Secretary of State shall appoint a committee accordingly, and the council may refer to it for a report and recommendations on any matter relating to those workers which the council thinks it expedient so to refer.

(2) Schedule 3 to this Act shall have effect with respect to committees appointed under this section.

General duty of wages councils to consider references by government departments

9.—(1) A wages council shall consider, as occasion requires, any matter referred to it by the Secretary of State or any government department with reference to the industrial conditions prevailing as respects the workers and employers in relation to whom it operates, and shall make a report upon the matter to the Secretary of State or, as the case may be, to that department.

(2) A wages council may, if it thinks it expedient so to do, make of its own motion a recommendation to the Secretary of State or any government department with reference to the said conditions and, where such a recommendation is so made, the Secretary of State or, as the case may be, that department, shall forthwith take it into consideration.

Part II

Statutory Joint Industrial Councils

Conversion of wages councils to statutory joint industrial councils

1–626   **10.**—(1) The Secretary of State may by order made in accordance with the following provisions of this section provide that a wages council shall become a statutory joint industrial councils by the provisions of Part III of this Act.

(2) The Secretary of State may make an order under this section with respect to a wages council—
  (a) on an application made to him by the employers' association or trade union nominated in relation to the council or by that association and union jointly; or
  (b) without an application under paragraph (a) above, but after consultation with the employers' association and trade unions so nominated.

(3) An order under this section shall not be made on an application by an employers' association or trade union alone unless the Secretary of State has consulted every employers' association and trade union nominated in relation to the wages council in question and (whether so nominated or not) all organisations of employers and workers which in his opinion represent a substantial proportion of employers and workers respectively in relation to whom that council operates.

(4) The Secretary of State shall before making an order under this section refer the question whether he should do so to the Service, and the Service shall inquire into it and report on that question.

(5) Part I of Schedule 4 to this Act shall have effect with respect to the constitution, officers and proceedings of statutory joint industrial councils and Part II of that Schedule shall have effect with respect to the transition of a wages council to a statutory joint industrial council.

Disputes between employers' and workers' representatives

1–627   **11.**—(1) If in the opinion of either the persons appointed to represent employers or the persons appointed to represent workers on a statutory joint industrial council, a dispute has arisen on any question and cannot be settled by the members of the council, those persons may request the Service to attempt to bring about a settlement of the dispute and the Service shall attempt to do so accordingly.

(2) If the Service is unable to bring about a settlement of any such dispute, the Service shall refer the dispute for settlement to the arbitration of—
  (a) one or more persons appointed by the Service for that purpose (not being an officer or servant of the Service); or
  (b) the Central Arbitration Committee.

(3) Where more than one arbitrator is appointed under subsection (2)(a) above, the Service shall appoint one of the arbitrators to act as chairman.

(4) Any determination of the arbitrator, arbitrators or Committee on a dispute referred to him, them or it under this section shall be final and binding on the statutory joint industrial council and its members, and the council shall make an order under section 14 below or take any steps which may be necessary to give effect to the determination.

(5) Part I of the Arbitration Act 1950 shall not apply to an arbitration under this section.

(6) In the application of this section to Scotland, references to an arbitrator shall be construed as references to an arbiter.

Abolition of statutory joint industrial councils

12.—(1) If the Secretary of State is of the opinion that, in the event of the abolition of a statutory joint industrial council, adequate machinery would be established for the effective regulation of the remuneration and other terms and conditions of employment of the workers within the council's field of operation and is likely thereafter to be maintained, he may by order abolish the council.

(2) An order under this section may be made on the application of the statutory joint industrial council concerned or without such an application, but shall not be made without such an application unless the Secretary of State has consulted the council.

(3) The Secretary of State shall before making an order under this section refer the questions whether he should do so to the Service, and the Service shall inquire into it and report on that question.

(4) Where an order under this section abolishes a statutory joint industrial council, then, save as is otherwise provided by the order, anything done by the council shall, except as respects things previously done or omitted to be done, cease to have effect.

Supplemental provisions

13.—(1) In sections 10 to 12 above "nominated", in relation to an employers' association or trade union, means, an association or union for the time being nominated under paragraph 1(2) of Schedule 2 to this Act to appoint persons to represent employers or workers on the wages council in question.

(2) Schedule 1 to this Act shall apply in relation to an order under section 10 above providing that a wages council shall become a statutory joint industrial council and in relation to an order under section 12 above abolishing a statutory joint industrial council.

Part III

Orders Regulating Terms and Conditions of Employment

Power to fix terms and conditions of employment

14.—(1) A wages council or a statutory joint industrial council may make an order, subject to and in accordance with the provisions of this section,—

(*a*) fixing the remuneration,
(*b*) requiring holidays to be allowed,
(*c*) fixing any other terms and conditions,

for all or any of the workers in relation to whom the council operates.

(2) An order under this section requiring a holiday to be allowed for a worker—

(a) shall not be made unless both holiday remuneration in respect of the period of the holiday and remuneration other than holiday remuneration have been or are being fixed under this Part of this Act for that worker;

(b) shall provide for the duration of the holiday being related to the duration of the period for which the worker has been employed or engaged to be employed by the employer who is to allow the holiday; and

(c) subject as aforesaid, may make provision as to the times at which or the periods within which, and the circumstances in which, the holiday shall be allowed.

(3) Any order under this section fixing holiday remuneration may contain provisions—

(a) as to the times at which, and the conditions subject to which, that remuneration shall accrue and shall become payable, and

(b) for securing that any such remuneration which has accrued due to a worker during his employment by any employer shall, in the event of his ceasing to be employed by that employer before he becomes entitled to be allowed a holiday by him, nevertheless become payable by the employer to the worker.

(4) Before making an order under this section the council shall make such investigations as it thinks fit and shall—

(a) publish in the prescribed manner notice of the council's proposals with respect to any new terms and conditions of employment (that is to say, any terms and conditions of employment differing from any then in force by virtue of an order made under this section); and

(b) give the prescribed notice for the purpose of informing, so far as practicable, all persons affected by the proposals, stating the place where copies of the proposals may be obtained and the period (which shall not be less than fourteen days from the date of publication of the notice) within which written representations with respect to the proposals may be sent to the council.

(5) After considering any written representations made with respect to any such proposals within the said period and making such further inquiries as the council considers necessary, or if no such representations are made within that period, after the expiration of that period, the council may make an order—

(a) giving effect to the proposals; or

(b) giving effect to them with such modifications as the council thinks fit having regard to any such representations;

but if it appears to the council that, having regard to the nature of any proposed modifications, an opportunity should be given to persons concerned to consider the modifications, the council shall again publish the proposals and give notice under subsection (4) above, and that subsection and this subsection shall apply accordingly.

(6) Subsections (4) and (5) above have effect subject to the provisions of subsection (1A) of section 4 of the Equal Pay Act 1970.

(7) An order under this section shall have effect as regards any terms as to remuneration as from a date specified in the order, which may be a date earlier than the date of the order but not earlier than the date on which the council agreed on those terms prior to publishing the original proposals to which effect is given, with or without modifications, by the order; but

where any such order fixing workers' remuneration applies to any worker who is paid wages at intervals not exceeding seven days and the date so specified does not correspond with the beginning of the period for which the wages are paid (hereafter in this section referred to as a wages period), the order shall, as respects that worker, have effect as from the beginning of the next wages period following the date specified in the order.

(8) Any increase in remuneration payable by virtue of an order under this section in respect of any time before the date of the order shall be paid by the employer within a period specified in the order, being—
- (a) in the case of a worker who is in the employment of the employer on the date of the order, a period beginning with that date;
- (b) in the case of a worker who is no longer in the employment of which the employer receives from the worker or a person acting on his behalf a request in writing for the remuneration;

but if, in the case of a worker falling within paragraph (a) of this subsection who is paid wages at intervals not exceeding seven days, pay day (the day on which wages are normally paid to him) for any wages period falling wholly or partly within the period so specified occurs within seven days from the end of that specified period, any such remuneration shall be paid not later than pay day.

(9) As soon as a council has made an order under this section it shall give the prescribed notice of the making and contents of the order and shall then and subsequently give such notice of other prescribed matters affecting its operation for the purpose of informing, so far as practicable, all persons who will be affected by it.

(10) An order under this section may make different provisions for different cases and may amend or revoke previous orders under this section.

(11) A document purporting to be a copy of an order made by a council under this section and to be signed by the secretary of the council shall be taken to be a true copy of the order unless the contrary is proved.

(12) An order under this section shall not prejudice any rights conferred on any worker by or under any other enactment.

Effect and enforcement of orders under section 14

15.—(1) If a contract between a worker to whom an order under section 14 above applies and his employer provides for the payment of less remuneration than the statutory minimum remuneration, it shall have effect as if the statutory minimum remuneration were substituted for the remuneration provided for in the contract, and if any such contract provides for the payment of any holiday remuneration at times or subject to conditions other than those specified in the order, it shall have effect as if the times or conditions specified in the order were substituted for those provided for in the contract.

(2) If any such contract fixes terms and conditions other than those relating to remuneration or wages which are less favourable than the corresponding terms and conditions specified in an order under section 14 above it shall have effect as if the corresponding terms and conditions were substituted for those fixed by the contract.

(3) If an employer fails—
- (a) to pay a worker to whom an order under section 14 above applies remuneration not less than the statutory minimum remuneration; or

(b) to pay him arrears of remuneration before the expiration of the period specified in the order; or
(c) to pay him holiday remuneration at the times and subject to the conditions specified in the order; or
(d) to allow to any such worker the holidays fixed by the order;

he shall for each offence be liable on summary conviction to a fine not exceeding £100.

(4) Where proceedings are brought under subsection (3) above in respect of an offence consisting of a failure to pay remuneration not less than the statutory minimum remuneration, or to pay arrears of remuneration, and the employer or any other person charged as a person to whose act or default the offence was due is found guilty of the offence, then, subject to subsection (5) below,—
(a) evidence may be given of any failure on the part of the employer to pay any such remuneration or arrears during the two years ending with the date of the offence to any worker employed by him; and
(b) on proof of the failure, the court may order the employer to pay such sum as is found by the court to represent the difference between the amount of any such remuneration or arrears which ought to have been paid during that period to any such worker, if the provisions of this Part of this Act had been complied with, and the amount actually so paid.

(5) Evidence of any failure to pay any such remuneration or arrears may be given under subsection (4) above only if—
(a) the employer or any other person charged as aforesaid has been convicted of the offence consisting of the failure; and
(b) notice of intention to adduce such evidence has been served with the summons or warrant.

(6) The powers given by this section for the recovery of sums due from an employer to a worker shall not be in derogation of any right to recover such sums by civil proceedings.

(7) In the application of this section to Scotland—
(a) in subsection (4), the words "or any other person charged as a person to whose act or default the offence was due" shall be omitted; and
(b) in subsection (5), in paragraph (a) the words "or any other person charged as aforesaid" shall be omitted, and in paragraph (b) for the words "summons or warrant" there shall be substituted the word "complaint."

Permits to infirm and incapacitated persons

16.—(1) If, as respects any worker employed or desiring to be employed in such circumstances that an order under section 14 above applies or will apply to him, the council which made the order is satisfied, on application being made to it for a permit under this section either by the worker or the employer or a prospective employer, that the worker is affected by infirmity or physical incapacity which renders him incapable of earning the statutory minimum remuneration or makes it inappropriate for other terms and conditions fixed by the order to apply to him, it may, if it thinks fit, grant, subject to any conditions it may determine, a permit authorising his employment at less than the statutory minimum remuneration or dispensing with a term or condition specified in the permit; and while the permit is in force the remuneration authorised by the permit shall, if the conditions specified in the permit are complied with, be deemed to be the statutory minimum remuneration, or, as the case may be, the terms and conditions fixed by the order shall be deemed to be observed.

(2) Where an employer employs any worker in reliance on any document purporting to be a permit granted under subsection (1) above authorising the employment of that worker at less than the statutory minimum remuneration, or dispensing with a term or condition specified in the permit, then, if the employer has notified the council in question that, relying on that document, he is employing or proposing to employ that worker at a specified remuneration or without compliance with any such term or condition, the document shall, notwithstanding that it is not or is no longer a valid permit relating to that worker, be deemed, subject to the terms thereof and as respects only any period after the notification, to be such a permit until notice to the contrary is received by the employer from the council.

Computation of remuneration

17.—(1) Subject to the provisions of this Part of this Act, any reference therein to remuneration shall be construed as a reference to the amount obtained or to be obtained in cash by the worker from his employer after allowing for the worker's necessary expenditure, if any, in connection with his employment, and clear of all deductions in respect of any matters whatsoever, except any reduction lawfully made—   **1–633**

(a) under the Income Tax Acts, the enactments relating to social security or any enactment requiring or authorising deductions to be made for the purposes of a superannuation scheme;

(b) at the request in writing of the worker, either for the purposes of a superannuation scheme or a thrift scheme or for any purpose in the carrying out of which the employer has no beneficial financial interest, whether directly or indirectly; or

(c) in pursuance of, or in accordance with, such a contract in that behalf as is mentioned in section 1, 2 or 3 of the Truck Act 1896 and in accordance with the provisions of that section.

(2) Notwithstanding subsection (1) above, orders under section 14 above may contain provisions authorising specified benefits or advantages, being benefits or advantages provided, in pursuance of the terms and conditions of the employment of workers, by the employer or by some other person under arrangements with the employer or by some other person under arrangements with the employer ad not being benefits or advantages the provision of which is illegal by virtue of the Truck Acts 1831 to 1940, or of any other enactment, to be reckoned as payment of wages by the employer in lieu of payment in cash, and defining the value at which any such benefits or advantages are to be reckoned.

(3) If any payment is made by a worker in respect of any benefit or advantage provided as mentioned in the foregoing subsection, then,—

(a) if the benefit or advantage is authorised by virtue of that subsection to be reckoned as therein mentioned, the amount of the payment shall be deducted from the defined value for the purposes of the reckoning;

(b) if the benefit or advantage is authorised by virtue of that subsection to be reckoned as therein mentioned, any excess of the amount of the payment over the defined value shall be treated for the purposes of subsection (1) above as if it had been a deduction not being one of the excepted deductions therein mentioned;

(c) if the benefit or advantage is specified in an order under section 14 above as one which has been taken into account in fixing the statutory minimum remuneration, the whole of the payment shall be treated for the purposes of subsection (1) above as if it had been a deduction not being one of the excepted deductions therein mentioned.

(4) Nothing in this section shall be construed as authorising the making of any deduction, or the giving of remuneration in any manner, which is illegal by virtue of the Truck Acts 1831 to 1940, or of any other enactment.

Apportionment of remuneration

18. Where for any period a worker receives remuneration for work for part of which he is entitled to statutory minimum remuneration at one or more time rates and for the remainder of which no statutory minimum remuneration is fixed, the amount of the remuneration which is to be attributed to the work for which he is entitled to statutory minimum remuneration shall, if not apparent from the terms of the contract between the employer and the worker, be deemed for the purposes of this Part of this Act to be the amount which bears to the total amount of the remuneration the same proportion as the time spent on the part of the work for which he is entitled to statutory minimum remuneration bears to the time spent on the whole of the work.

Employers not to receive premiums

19.—(1) Where a worker to whom an order under section 14 above applies is an apprentice or learner, it shall not be lawful for his employer to receive directly or indirectly from him, or on his behalf or on his account, and payment by way of premium:

Provided that nothing in this section shall apply to any such payment duly made in pursuance of any instrument of apprenticeship not later than four weeks after the commencement of the apprenticeship or to any such payment made at any time if duly made in pursuance of any instrument of apprenticeship approved for the purpose of this proviso by a wages council or by a statutory joint industrial council.

(2) If any employer acts in contravention of this section, he shall be liable on summary conviction in respect of each offence to a fine not exceeding £100, and the court may, in addition to imposing a fine, order him to repay to the worker or other person by whom the payment was made the sum improperly received by way of premium.

Records and notices

20.—(1) The employer of any workers to whom an order under section 14 above applies shall keep such records as are necessary to show whether or not the provisions of this Part and Part IV of this Act are being complied with as respects them, and the records shall be retained by the employer for three years.

(2) The employer of any workers shall post in the prescribed manner such notices as may be prescribed for the purpose of informing them of any proposal or order under section 14 above affecting them, and, if it is so prescribed, shall give notice in any other prescribed manner to the said

workers of the said matters and of such other matters, if any, as may be prescribed.

(3) If an employer fails to comply with any of the requirements of this section he shall be liable on summary conviction to a fine not exceeding £100.

Part IV

Miscellaneous

Offences and Enforcement

Criminal liability of agent and superior employer, and special defence open to employer

21.—(1) Where the immediate employer of any worker is himself in the employment of some other person and that worker is employed on the premises of that other person, that other person shall for the purposes of Part III and this Part of this Act be deemed to be the employer of that worker jointly with the immediate employer.

1–637

(2) Where an employer is charged with an offence under Part III or this Part of this Act, he shall be entitled, upon information duly laid by him and on giving to the prosecution not less than three days' notice in writing of his intention, to have any other person to whose act or default he alleges that the offence in question was due brought before the court at the time appointed for the hearing of the charge; and if, after the commission of the offence has been proved, the employer provides that the offence was due to the act or the default of that other person, that other person may be convicted of the offence, and, if the employer further proves that he has used all due diligence to secure that the provisions of Part III and this Part of this Act and any relevant regulation or order made thereunder are complied with, he shall be acquitted of the offence.

(3) Where a defendant seeks to avail himself of the provisions of subsection (2) above—
  (a) the prosecution, as well as the person whom the defendant charges with the offence, shall have the right to cross-examine him if he gives evidence and any witnesses called by him in support of his pleas and to call rebutting evidence;
  (b) the court may make such order as it thinks fit for the payment of costs by any party to the proceedings to any other party thereto.

(4) Where it appears to an officer acting for the purposes of Part III and this Part of this Act that an offence has been committed in respect of which proceedings might be taken under this Act against an employer, and the officer is reasonably satisfied that the offence of which complaint is made was due to an act or default of some other person and that the employer could establish a defence under subsection (2) above, the officer may cause proceedings to be taken against that other person without first causing proceedings to be taken against the employer.

In any such proceedings the defendant may be charged with and, on proof that the offence was due to his act or default, be convicted of, the offence with which the employer might have been charged.

(5) Subsections (2) to (4) above shall not apply to Scotland, but—
  (a) where an offence for which an employer is, under this Act,

liable to a fine was due to an act or default of an agent of the employer or other person, then, whether proceedings are or are not taken against the employer, then agent or other person may be charged with and convicted of the offence, and shall be liable on conviction to the same punishment as might have been inflicted on the employer if he had been convicted of the offence;

(b) where an employer who is charged with an offence under this Act proves to the satisfaction of the court that he has used due diligence to secure compliance with the provisions of Part III and this Part of this Act and any relevant regulation or order made thereunder and that the offence was due to the act or default of some other person, he shall be acquitted of the offence.

Officers

1–638   **22.**—(1) The Secretary of State, with the approval of the Minister for the Civil Service as to numbers and salaries, may appoint officers to act for the purposes of Part III and this Part of this Act, and may, in lieu of or in addition to appointing any officers under this section, arrange with any government department that officers of that department shall act for the said purposes.

(2) Every officer acting for the purposes of Part III and this Part of this Act shall be furnished by the Secretary of State with a certificate of his appointment or authority so to act, and, when so acting, shall, if so required by any person affected, produce the certificate to him.

(3) An officer acting for the purposes of Part III and this Part of this Act shall have power for the performance of his duties—

(a) to require the production of wages sheets or other records of wages kept by an employer, and records of payments made to homeworkers by persons giving out work, and any other such records as are required by this Act to be kept by employers, and to inspect and examine those sheets or records and copy any material part thereof;

(b) to require the production of any licence or certificate granted under the Transport Act 1968, and of any records kept in pursuance of Part VI of the Transport Act 1968 or of the applicable Community rules within the meaning of the said Part VI, and to examine any such licence, certificate or records and copy it or them or any material part thereof;

(c) to require any person giving out work and any homeworker to give any information which it is in his power to give with respect to the names and addresses of the persons to whom the work is given out or from whom the work is received, as the case may be, and with respect to the payments to be made for the work;

(d) at all reasonable times to enter any premises at which any employer to whom an order under section 14 above applies carries on his business (including any place used, in connection with that business, for giving out work to homeworkers and any premises which the officer has reasonable cause to believe to be used by or by arrangement with the employer to provide living accommodation for workers);

(e) to inspect and copy any material of any list of homeworkers kept by an employer or person giving out work to homeworkers;

(f) to examine, either alone or in the presence of any other person, as he thinks fit, with respect to any matters under Part III or this Part of this Act, any person whom he has reasonable cause to believe to be or to have been a worker to whom an order under section 14 above applies or applied or the employer of any such person or a servant or agent of the employer employed in the employer's business, and to require every such person to be so examined, and to sign a declaration of the truth of the matters in respect of which he is so examined;

Provided that no person shall be required under paragraph (f) above to give information tending to criminate himself or, in the case of a person who is married, his or her wife or husband.

(4) In England or Wales, an officer acting for the purposes of Part III and this Part of this Act may institute proceedings for any offence under this Act and may, although not of counsel or a solicitor, conduct any such proceedings:

Provided that an officer may not conduct proceedings for an offence under section 24 below unless he instituted those proceedings.

(5) An officer acting for the purposes of Part III and this Part of this Act who is authorised in that behalf by general or special directions of the Secretary of State may, if it appears to him that a sum is due from an employer to a worker on account of the payment to him of remuneration less than the statutory minimum remuneration, institute on behalf of and in the name of that worker civil proceedings for the recovery of that sum and in any such proceedings the court may make an order for the payment of costs by the officer as if he were a party to the proceedings.

The power given by this subsection for the recovery of sums due from an employer to a worker shall not be in derogation of any right of the worker to recover suh sums by civil proceedings.

(6) Any person who obstructs an officer acting for the purposes of Part III and this Part of this Act in the exercise of any power conferred by this section, or fails to comply with any requirement of such an officer made in the exercise of any such power, he shall be liable on summary conviction to a fine not exceeding £100:

Provided that it shall be a defence for a person charged under this subsection with failing to comply with a requirement to prove that it was not reasonably practicable to comply therewith.

Penalties for false entries in records, producing false records or giving false information

23. If any person makes or causes to be made or knowingly allows to be made any entry in a record required by this Act to be kept by employers, which he knows to be false in a material particular, or for purposes connected with Part III or the preceding provisions of this Part of this Act produces, or furnishes, or causes or knowingly allows to be produced or furnished, any wages sheet, record, list or information which he knows to be false in a material particular, he shall be liable on summary conviction to a fine not exceeding £400 or to imprisonment for a term not exceeding three months, or to both such fine and such imprisonment.

1–639

Power to obtain information

24.—(1) The Secretary of State may, for the purpose of, or in connection with the enforcement of, an order under section 14 above, by notice in

1–640

writing require an employer within the field of operation of a council making such an order to furnish such information as may be specified or described in the notice.

(2) A notice under this section may specify the way in which, and the time within which, it is to be complied with, and may be varied or revoked by a subsequent notice so given.

(3) If a person refuses or wilfully neglects to furnish any information which he has been required to furnish by a notice under subsection (i) above, he shall be liable on summary conviction to a fine not exceeding £100.

(4) If a person, in purporting to comply with a requirement of a notice under subsection (1) above, knowingly or recklessly makes any false statement he shall be liable on summary conviction to a fine not exceeding £400.

(5) Section 21 above shall not apply in relation to an offence under this section.

(6) Where an offence under this section committed by a body corporate is proved to have been committed with the consent or connivance of, or to be attributable to any neglect on the part of, any director, manager, secretary or other similar officer of the body corporate, or any person who was purporting to act in any such capacity, he as well as the body corporate shall be guilty of that offence and shall be liable to be proceeded against and punished accordingly.

(7) Where the affairs of the body corporate are managed by its members, subsection (6) above shall apply in relation to the acts and defaults of a member in connection with his functions of management as if he were a director of the body corporate.

Central Co-ordinating Committees

Central co-ordinating committees

1–641   25.—(1) The Secretary of State may, if he thinks fit to do so, by order establish a central co-ordinating committee in relation to any two or more wages councils or statutory joint industrial councils, or wages councils and statutory joint industrial councils, or abolish, or vary the field of operation of, any central co-ordinating committee so established:

Provided that, except where subsection (2) or (3) below applies, the Secretary of State shall, before making any such order, consult the wages councils or statutory joint industrial councils, or, as the case may be, the wages councils and the statutory joint industrial councils, concerned.

(2) Where the Service makes a recommendation for the establishment of a wages council or statutory joint industrial council it may include in its report a recommendation for the establishment, in relation to any council established in accordance with the recommendation and any other council (including a council proposed to be established by another recommendation embodied in the same report), of a central co-ordinating committee, or for the variation of the field of operation of an existing central co-ordinating committee so that it operates also in connection with any council established in accordance with the recommendation.

(3) Where the Service makes a recommendation for the abolition of a wages council or statutory joint industrial council, it may include in its report a recommendation for the variation of the field of operation of an existing central co-ordinating committee so that it no longer operates in

relation to the council to be abolished, or a recommendation for the abolition of any central co-ordinating committee theretofore operating in relation to the council to be abolished.

(4) The Secretary of State may by order give effect to a recommendation made under subsection (2) or (3) above.

(5) It shall be the duty of any central co-ordinating committee from time to time—
- (*a*) to consider whether the field of operation of the councils in relation to which it is established is properly divided as between the councils and to report thereon to the Secretary of State;
- (*b*) to make recommendations to the councils with respect to the principles to be allowed by them in the exercise of their powers under this Act;
- (*c*) to consider any question referred to it by the Secretary of State or by the councils or any two or more of them, and to report thereon to the Secretary of State, or to the councils which referred the question, as the case may be.

(6) Schedule 2 to this Act shall have effect with respect to the constitution, officers and proceedings of central co-ordinating committees.

Reports on Regulation of Terms and Conditions of Employment

Reports by Service on regulation of terms and conditions of employment

26. The Service shall, if requested to do so by the Secretary of State—   **1–642**
- (*a*) inquire into and report on the development by agreement of machinery for the regulation of the remuneration and terms and conditions of employment of workers within the field of operation of a wages council or statutory joint industrial council and the question whether, in order to maintain a reasonable standard of remuneration and terms and conditions of employment of those workers, it is necessary to regulate their remuneration and other terms and conditions of employment by means of orders under section 14 above;
- (*b*) inquire into and report on the operation generally of this Act;
- (*c*) publish a report made under paragraph (*a*) or (*b*) above.

Power to Extend Wages Councils Legislation

Extension of this Act and N.I. legislation

27.—(1) Her Majesty may by Order in Council provide that—   **1–643**
- (*a*) the provisions of this Act, and
- (*b*) the provisions of any legislation (that is to say any enactment of the Parliament of Northern Ireland and any provision made by or under a Measure of the Northern Ireland Assembly) for the time being in force in Northern Ireland which makes provision for purposes corresponding to any of the purposes of the provisions of this Act,

shall, to such extent and for such purposes as may be specified in the Order, apply (with or without modification) to or in relation to any person in employment to which this section applies.

(2) This section applies to employment for the purposes of any activities—
- (*a*) in the territorial waters of the United Kingdom; or

(b) connected with the exploration of the sea bed or subsoil or the exploitation of their natural resources in any designated area; or
(c) connected with the exploration or exploitation, in a foreign sector of the continental shelf, of a cross-boundary petroleum field.

(3) An Order in Council under subsection (1) above—
   (a) may make different provision for different cases;
   (b) may provide that all or any of the provisions of any Act mentioned in that subsection, as applied by such an Order, shall apply to individuals whether or not they are British subjects and to bodies corporate whether or not they are incorporated under the law of any part of the United Kingdom (notwithstanding that the application may affect their activities outside the United Kingdom);
   (c) may make provision for conferring jurisdiction on any court or class of court specified in the Order, or on industrial tribunals, in respect of offences, causes of action or other matters arising in connection with employment to which this section applies;
   (d) without prejudice to the generality of subsection (1) above or of paragraph (a) above, may provide that the enactments referred to in that subsection ahall apply in relation to any person in employment for the purposes of such activities as are referred to in subsection (2) above in any part of the areas specified in paragraphs (a) and (b) of that subsection;
   (e) may exclude from the operation of section 3 of the Territorial Waters Jurisdiction Act 1878 (consents required for prosecutions) proceedings for offences under the enactments referred to in subsection (1) above in connection with employment to which this section applies;
   (f) may provide that such proceedings shall not be brought without such consent as may be required by the Order.

(4) Any jurisdiction conferred on any court or tribunal under this section shall be without prejudice to jurisdiction exercisable apart from this section by that or any other court or tribunal.

(5) In this section—
   "cross-boundary petroleum field" means a petroleum field that extends across the boundary between a designated area and a foreign sector of the continental shelf;
   "designated area" means an area designated under section 1(7) of the Continental Shelf Act 1964;
   "foreign sector of the continental shelf" means an area which is outside the territorial waters of any State and within which rights are exercisable by a State other than the United Kingdom with respect to the sea bed and subsoil and their natural resources;
   "petroleum field" means a geological structure identified as an oil or gas field by the Order in Council concerned.

Supplemental

Interpretation

1-644 **28.** In this Act—
   "employers' association" means any organisation representing

employers and any association of such organisations or of employers and such organisations;

"homeworkers" means a person who contracts with a person, for the purposes of that person's business, for the execution of work to be done in a place not under the control or management of the person with whom he contracts, and who does not normally make use of the services of more than two persons in the carrying out of contracts for the execution of work with statutory minimum remuneration;

"organisation", in relation to workers, means a trade union and, in relation to employers, means an employers' association;

"prescribed" means prescribed by regulations made by the Secretary of State;

"the Service" means the Advisory, Conciliation and Arbitration Service;

"statutory joint industrial council" means a council established by an order made under section 10 above;

"statutory minimum remuneration" means remuneration (including holiday remuneration) fixed by an order made under section 14 above;

"statutory provision" means a provision contained in or having effect under any enactment;

"superannuation scheme" means any enactment, rules, deed or other instrument, providing for the payment of annuities or lump sums to the persons with respect to whom the instrument has effect on their retirement at a specified age or on becoming incapacitated at some earlier age, or to the personal representatives or the widows, relatives or dependants of such persons on their death or otherwise, whether with or without any further or other benefits;

"thrift scheme" means any arrangement for savings, for providing money for holidays or for other purposes, under which a worker is entitled to receive in cash sums equal to or greater than the aggregate of any sums deducted from his remuneration or paid by him for the purposes of the scheme;

"time rate" means a rate where the amount of the remuneration is to be calculated by reference to the actual number of hours worked;

"trade union" has the meaning given by section 28 of the Trade Union and Labour Relations Act 1974;

"wages council" means a wages council established by an order under section 1 above;

"worker" means any person—
  (*a*) who has entered into or works under a contract with an employer (whether express or implied, and, if express, whether oral or in writing) whether it be a contract of service or of apprenticeship or any other contract whereby he undertakes to do or perform personally any work or services for another party to the contract who is not a professional client of his; or
  (*b*) whether or not he falls within the foregoing provision, who is a homeworker;
  but does not include any person who is employed casually and otherwise than for the purposes of the business of the employer or other party to the contract;

"work with statutory minimum remuneration" means work of a description for which, when executed by a worker, statutory minimum remuneration is provided under Part III of this Act.

Orders and regulations

1–645   29.—(1) The Secretary of State may make regulations for prescribing anything which by this Act is authorised or required to be prescribed.

(2) Any power to make orders or regulations conferred on the Secretary of State by this Act shall be exercisable by statutory instrument.

(3) Any statutory instrument containing any order of the Secretary of State made under Part I or II of this Act or regulations made under any of the provisions of this Act shall (together, in the case of an order, with any report of the Service relating thereto) be laid before Parliament after being made, and shall be subject to annulment in pursuance of a resolution of either House of Parliament.

(4) Any power conferred by this Act to prescribes the manner in which anything is to be published shall include power to prescribe the date which is to be taken for the purposes of this Act as the date of publication.

Expenses

1–646   30. The expenses of the Secretary of State in carrying this Act into effect, and any expenses authorised by the Secretary of State wih the consent of the Treasury to be incurred by a wages council, the Service, or a central co-ordinating committee established under this Act by order of the Secretary of State, shall be defrayed out of moneys provided by Parliament.

Transitional provisions, amendments and repeals

1–647   31.—(1) The transitional provisions and savings in Schedule 5 to this Act shall have effect, but nothing in that Schedule shall be construed as prejudicing section 16 of the Interpretation Act 1978 (effect of repeals).

(2) The enactments specified in Schedule 6 to this Act shall have effect subject to the amendments specified in that Schedule.

(3) The enactments specified in the first column of Schedule 7 to this Act are hereby repealed to the extent specified in the third column of that Schedule.

Short title, commencement and extent

1–648   32.—(1) This Act may be cited as the Wages Councils Act 1979.

(2) This Act shall come into force on the expiry of the period of one month beginning with the date on which it is passed.

(3) This Act, except section 27, paragraphs 4 and 5 of Schedule 6 and the repeal of section 127(1)(*a*) of the Employment Protection Act 1975 provided for in Schedule 7, shall not extend to Northern Ireland.

SCHEDULES

1–649   Sections 1, 4 and 13   SCHEDULE 1

ORDERS RELATING TO WAGES COUNCILS AND STATUTORY JOINT INDUSTRIAL COUNCILS

1. In this Schedule, except in so far as the context otherwise requires, "order" means an order, whether made in pursuance of the recommendation of the Service or not, under section 1, 4, 10 or 12 of this Act.

2. Before making an order, the Secretary of State shall publish, in the prescribed manner, notice of his intention to make the order, specifying a place where copies of a draft thereof may be obtained and the time (which shall not be less than forty days from the date of the publication) within which any objection made with respect to the draft order must be sent to him.

3. In relation to the making of an order under section 4 of this Act in pursuance of an application made in accordance with section 5(1)(c) of this Act, paragraph 2 above shall have effect as if, before the words "shall publish," there were inserted the words "after consultation with the wages council concerned and with all such organisations of employers as in his opinion represent a substantial proportion of employers with respect to whom the wages council operates."

4. Every objection made with respect to the draft order must be in writing, and must state—
   (a) the specific grounds of objection, and
   (b) the omissions, additions or modifications asked for,
and the Secretary of State shall consider any such objection made by or on behalf of any person appearing to him to be affected, being an objection sent to him within the time specified in the notice, but shall not be bound to consider any other objection.

5.—(1) If there is no objection which the Secretary of State is required by paragraph 4 above to consider or if, after considering any such objection, he is of the opinion that it satisfies one of the following conditions, that is to say—
   (a) in the case of an order to be made in pursuance of a recommendation of the Service, the objection was made to the Service and was expressly dealt with in the report embodying the recommendations; or
   (b) in the case of such an order as is referred to in paragraph (a) above, the objection is one the subject-matter of which was considered by the Service and was expressly dealt with in that report or is such that a further inquiry into that subject-matter would serve no useful purpose; or
   (c) in any case, the objection will be met by a modification which he proposes to make under this paragraph, or is frivolous,
he may make the order either in the terms of the draft, or subject to such modifications, if any, as he thinks fit, being modifications which, in his opinion, do not effect important alterations in the character of the draft order as published.

(2) The Secretary of State shall not form an opinion as to any matter mentioned in paragraph (b) of sub-paragraph (1) above without consulting the Service.

6. Where the Secretary of State does not proceed under paragraph 5 above, he may, if he thinks fit, either—
   (a) amend the draft order, in which case all the provisions of this Schedule shall have effect in relation to the amended draft order as they have effect in relation to an original draft order; or
   (b) refer the draft order to the Service for inquiry and report, in which case he shall consider the report of the Service and may then, if he thinks fit, make an order either in the terms of the draft or with such modifications as he thinks fit.

7.—(1) Where any objection is made to the Secretary of State and, under sub-paragraph (b) of paragraph 6 above, he refers the draft order to the Service, the Secretary of State shall notify to the Service the objections which he wishes the Service to take into account, and the questions which it is the duty of the Service to consider and report on by virtue of the reference shall be all questions affecting the draft order which arise on or in connection with the objections so notified.

(2) The Secretary of State shall include in the objections which he notifies to the Service all the objections which, under paragraph 4 above, he is himself required to consider, other than any objections which he thinks fit to exclude, in the case of an order in pursuance of a recommendation of the Service, on the ground that, in his opinion, they were made to the Service and were expressly dealt with in the report embodying the recommendation or, in any case, on the ground that they are in the Secretary of State's opinion frivolous.

8.—(1) Where any of the councils affected by an order under section 4 or 12 of this Act is one of the councils in relation to which a central co-ordinating committee has been established under section 25 of this Act, the Secretary of State, before making the order, shall consult that committee and take into consideration any observations which it may make to him within fourteen days from the date on which he consults it.

(2) Where an order under section 4 of this Act directs that a wages council shall cease to operate in relation to any workers, and that another existing wages council shall operate in relation to them, but save as aforesaid, does not affect the field of operation of any wages council, paragraphs 2 to 7 above shall not apply but before making the order the Secretary of State shall consult the councils concerned.

(3) On the reference under sub-paragraph (*b*) of paragraph 6 above of a draft order for the abolition, or variation of the field of operation, of a wages council, subsection (2), or, as the case may be, (3) of section 6 of this Act shall apply as it would apply to the like reference under that section; and the power of the Secretary of State under the sub-paragraph (*b*) to modify the draft in making an order shall include power to make any alterations necessary to give effect to a recommendation of the Service, with or without modifications.

9. An order shall come into operation on the date on which it is first issued by Her Majesty's Stationery Office or on such later date as is specified in the order.

1–650 Sections 1 and 25 SCHEDULE 2

CONSTITUTION, OFFICES AND PROCEEDINGS OF WAGES COUNCILS AND CO-ORDINATING COMMITTEES

1.—(1) A wages council or, subject to paragraph 2 below, a central co-ordinating committee shall consist of—
  (*a*) not more than three persons appointed by the Secretary of State as being independent persons;
  (*b*) such number of persons appointed to represent employers and workers on the council or committee as falls within the limits for the time being specified for the purposes of this paragraph by the Secretary of State.

(2) Subject to sub-paragraphs (4) and (5) below, the persons appointed under sub-paragraph (1) above to represent employers shall be appointed by one or more employers' associations for the time being nominated for that purpose by the Secretary of State and those so appointed to represent workers shall be appointed by one or more trade unions so nominated.

(3) A nominated employers' association or trade union shall on making such an appointment inform the secretary of the wages council or central co-ordinating committee, in writing, of that appointment.

(4) If the nominated employers' association or the nominated trade union are unable to agree on such an appointment, they shall consult the Secretary of State who may make the appointment on their behalf.

(5) If it appears to the Secretary of State that an insufficient number of persons has been appointed to represent either employers or workers on a wages council or central co-ordinating committee he may, after consultation with such persons or organisations as he thinks fit, himself appoint such number of persons for the purpose as will secure a sufficiency of representatives of employers or workers, as the case may be, on the council or committee.

(6) Of the independent persons appointed under sub-paragraph (1)(*a*) above, one shall be appointed by the Secretary of State to act as chairman, and another may be appointed by the Secretary of State to act as chairman in the absence of the chairman.

2.—(1) A central co-ordinating committee operating in relation only to two or more statutory joint industrial councils shall consist of equal numbers of persons appointed by one or more employers' associations to represent employers on the committee and of persons appointed by one or more trade unions to represent workers on the committee.

(2) Any such committee shall elect a chairman and deputy chairman from among its members.

3. The Secretary of State may on the application of a wages council or central co-ordinating committee make such change in the number of members or the machinery for appointing them as is necessary or expedient in the circumstances.

4. The Secretary of State may appoint a secretary and such other officers as he thinks fit of a wages council or central co-ordinating committee.

5. The proceedings of a wages council or central co-ordinating committee shall not be invalidated by reason of any vacancy therein or by any defect in the appointment of a member.

6.—(1) A wages council or central co-ordinating committee may delegate any of its functions, other than the power to make orders under section 14 of this Act, to a committee or sub-committee consisting of such number of members of the council as the council or committee thinks fit.

(2) The number of members representing employers and the number of members representing workers on a committee of a council or any such sub-committee shall be equal.

7. The Secretary of State may make regulations as to the meetings and procedure of a wages council or central co-ordinating committee and of any committee or, as the case may be, sub-committee thereof, including regulations as to the quorum and the method of voting, but, subject to the provisions of this Act and to any regulations so made, a wages council or central co-ordinating committee and any committee or, as the case may be, sub-committee thereof may regulate its procedure in such manner as it thinks fit.

8.—(1) A number of a wages council or central co-ordinating committee shall hold and vacate office in accordance with the terms of his appointment, but the period for which he is to hold office, shall, without prejudice to his re-appointment, not exceed five years.

(2) Where the term for which the members of a wages council or central co-ordinating committee were appointed comes to an end before their successors are appointed, those members shall, except so far as the Secretary of State or, as the case may be, the appointing body otherwise directs, continue in office until the new appointments take effect.

9. There may be paid to the members of a wages council or central co-ordinating committee appointed under paragraph 1(*a*) above such remuneration, and to any member of any such council or committee such travelling and other allowances, as the Secretary of State may, with the consent of the Minister for the Civil Service, determine, and all such remuneration and allowances shall be defrayed as part of the expenses of the Secretary of State in carrying this Act into effect.

Section 8   SCHEDULE 3   1–651

PROVISIONS AS TO ADVISORY COMMITTEES

1.—(1) Any committee appointed by the Secretary of State at the request of a wages council shall consist of—
(*a*) a chairman chosen as being an independent person;
(*b*) persons who appear to the Secretary of State to represent the employers in relation to whom the committee will operate; and
(*c*) persons who appear to the Secretary of State to represent the workers in relation to whom the committee will operate.

(2) On any such committee the persons appointed under head (*b*), and the persons appointed under head (*c*), of sub-paragraph (1) above shall be equal in number.

2.—(1) The appointment of a member to any such committee as aforesaid shall be for such terms as may be determined by the Secretary of State before his appointment and shall be subject to such conditions as may be so determined.

(2) Where the term for which the members of an advisory committee were appointed comes to an end before the Secretary of State has appointed the persons who are to serve as members of the committee after the expiration of that term, they shall, except so far as the Secretary of State otherwise directs, continue in office until the new appointments take effect.

3. There may be paid to the chairman of any such committees as aforesaid such fees, and to any member of any such committee such travelling and other allowances, as the Secretary of State may, with the consent of the Minister for the Civil Service, determine, and all such fees and allowances shall be defrayed out of moneys provided by Parliament.

Section 10   SCHEDULE 4   1–652

STATUTORY JOINT INDUSTRIAL COUNCILS

PART I

CONSTITUTION, ETC.

1.—(1) A statutory joint industrial council (hereafter in this Part of this Schedule referred to as a council) shall consist of equal numbers (being numbers within the limits specified by the Secretary of State) of persons appointed by a nominated employers' association to represent employers on the council and of persons appointed by a nominated trade union to represent workers on the council.

(2) A nominated employers' association or trade union shall on making such an appointment inform the secretary of the council, in writing, of that appointment.

2.—(1) On the conversion of a wages council to a statutory joint industrial council—
(*a*) the limits as to the number of persons to be appointed to represent employers and workers on that wages council which are immediately before the date on which that council becomes a statutory joint industrial council for the time being specified by the Secretary of State, shall continue, subject to sub-paragraph (2) below, to be the limits in relation to that statutory joint industrial council; and
(*b*) an employers' association or trade union which immediately before the date on which that wages council becomes a statutory joint industrial council is for the time being

nominated by the Secretary of State for the purpose of appointing persons to represent employers or workers on that wages council, shall continue, subject to sub-paragraph (2) below, to be so nominated in relation to that statutory joint industrial council.

(2) The Secretary of State may, on the application of a statutory joint industrial council, make such changes in the number of members of the council or in the machinery for appointing them as are necessary or expedient in the circumstances.

3. A council shall elect a chairman and deputy chairman from among its members.

4. The proceedings of a council shall not be invalidated by reason of any vacancy among its members or by any defect in the appointment of a member.

5.—(1) A council may delegate any of its functions, other than the power to make orders under section 14 of this Act, to a committee consisting of such number of members of the council as the council thinks fit.

(2) The number of members representing employers and the number of members representing workers on a committee of a council shall be equal.

6. A council may regulate its own procedure.

7.—(1) A member of a council shall hold and vacate office in accordance with the terms of his appointment, but the period for which he is to hold office shall, without prejudice to his re-appointment, not exceed five years.

(2) Where the term for which the members of a council were appointed comes to an end before their successors are appointed, those members shall, except so far as the appointing body otherwise directs, continue in office until the new appointments take effect.

8. The Secretary of State may pay to the members of a council such travelling and other allowances, including allowances for loss of remunerative time, as the Secretary of State may, with the consent of the Minister for the Civil Service, determine.

9. The expenses of a statutory joint industrial council, to such an extent as may be approved by the Secretary of State with the consent of the Treasury, shall be paid by the Secretary of State.

10. The Secretary of State may appoint a secretary and such other officers of a council as he thinks fit.

PART II

TRANSITIONAL PROVISIONS

11. Any of the following things done by, to or in relation to a wages council, that is to say—
any order made under section 14 of this Act;
any proposals published in relation to making of such an order, any notice published and representations made with respect thereto;
any permit issued under section 16 of this Act;
any approval given under the proviso to section 19(1) of this Act;
shall as from the date when that council becomes a statutory joint industrial council be treated as having been done by, to or in relation to the latter council.

12. The persons who immediately before the date on which a wages council becomes a statutory joint industrial council are the members of the wages council appointed by an employers' association or trade union shall, subject to paragraph 2(2) above, become and continue to be members of the statutory joint industrial council as if they had been appointed under paragraph 1 above.

13. The persons who immediately before the date on which a wages council becomes a statutory joint industrial council are the secretary and officers of the wages council shall on that date become the secretary and officers of the statutory joint industrial council.

Section 31   SCHEDULE 5

TRANSITIONAL PROVISIONS

1. The repeals effected by this Act shall not affect any right of a worker to recover sums from his employer on account of the payment to the worker of remuneration less than the statutory minimum remuneration, or the power of an officer of the Secretary of State to institute on behalf of and in the name of the worker civil proceedings for the enforcement of that right or the power of the court in such proceedings to make an order for the payment of costs by the officer.

2. A member of a wages council or central co-ordinating committee who, immediately before the commencement of this Act, is by virtue of paragraph 11(3) of Schedule 17 to the

Employment Protection Act 1975 treated as having been appointed by a nominated employers' association or trade union shall continue to be so treated.

3. Any refrence in any enactment or document made before the passing of the Wages Councils Act 1945 (28th March 1945), other than an enactment repealed by that Act, to a trade board shall be construed as including a reference to a wages council.

Section 31　　　　　　　　　SCHEDULE 6　　　　　　　　　1–654

CONSEQUENTIAL AMENDMENTS

Post Office Act 1969 (*c.*48)

1. In section 81(1) of the Post Office 1969, for the words "the Wages Councils Act 1959" there are substituted the words "Wages Councils Act 1979."

Equal Pay Act 1970 (*c.*41)

2. In section 4 of the Equal Pay Act 1970—
    (*a*) in subsections (1), (1A), and (2), for the words "section 11 of the Wages Councils Act 1959," in each place where they occur, there are substituted the words "section 14 of the Wages Councils Act 1979"; and
    (*b*) in subsection (1A), for the words "subsections (3) and (3A) of the said section 11" there are substituted the words "subsections (4) and (5) of the said section 14"; and
    (*c*) in subsection (3), for the words "section 12(1) or (1A) of the Wages Councils Act 1959"; "in section 12(1) or (1A)" and "section 11(8)" there are substituted the words "section 15(1) or (2) of the Wages Councils Act 1979"; "in section 15(1) or (2)" and "section 14(12)" respectively.

Attachment of Earnings Act 1971 (*c.*32)

3. In Schedule 3 to the Attachment of Earnings Act 1971, in paragraph 3(*c*), for the words "Wages Councils Act 1959" there are substituted the words "Wages Councils Act 1979."

House of Commons Disqualification Act 1975 (*c.*24)

4. In Part III of Schedule 1 to the House of Commons Disqualification Act 1975, in the first entry relating to wages councils, for the words "paragraph 1(*a*) of Schedule 2 to the Wages Councils Act 1959 or Chairman of a Committee appointed under paragraph (1)(*a*) of Schedule 3 to that Act" there are substituted the words "paragraph 1(1)(*a*) of Schedule 2 to the Wages Councils Act 1979 or chairman of a committee appointed under paragraph 1(1)(*a*) of Schedule 3 to that Act."

Northern Ireland Assembly Disqualification Act 1975 (*c.*25)

5. In Part III of Schedule 1 to the Northern Ireland Assembly Disqualification Act 1975, in the first entry relating to wages councils, for the words "paragraph 1(*a*) of Schedule 2 to the Wages Councils Act 1959 or Chairman of a Committee appointed under paragraph 1(1)(*a*) of Schedule 3 to that Act" there are substituted the words "paragraph 1(1)(*a*() of Schedule 2 to the Wages Councils Act 1979 or chairman or a committee appointed under paragraph 1(1)(*a*) of Schedule 3 to that Act."

Employment Protection (Consolidation) Act 1978 (*c.*44)

6. In section 18(2) of the Employment Protection (Consolidation) Act 1978 for paragraph (*a*) there is substituted the following paragraph—
    "(*a*) section 14 of the Wages Councils Act 1979;"

Section 31　　　　　　　　　SCHEDULE 7　　　　　　　　　1–655

REPEALS

Chapter	Short title	Extent of repeal
7 & 8 Eliz. 2 c. 69.	Wages Councils Act 1959.	The whole Act.
1968 c. 64.	Civil Evidence Act 1968.	In the Schedule, the paragraph relating to the Wages Council Act 1959.

Chapter	Short title	Extent of repeal
1968 c. 73.	Transport Act 1968.	In Schedule 11, the paragraph relating to the Wages Councils Act 1959.
1972 c. 68.	European Communities Act 1972.	In Schedule 4, in paragraph 9 (4), the words "and in section 19 (3) (*b*) of the Wages Councils Act 1959".
1973 c. 38.	Social Security Act 1973.	In Schedule 27, paragraph 21.
1974 c. 52.	Trade Union and Labour Relations Act 1974.	In Schedule 3, paragraph 9.
1975 c. 71.	Employment Protection Act 1975.	Sections 89 to 96. In section 127 (1), paragraph (*a*). Schedules 7 and 8. In Schedule 17, paragraph 11 and, in paragraph 12, the words "section 11 of the Wages Councils Act 1959".
1976 c. 3.	Road Traffic (Drivers' Ages and Hours of Work) Act 1976.	In section 2 (3), the words "section 19 (3) (*b*) of the Wages Councils Act 1959".

1-656

Companies Act 1980

(1980 c.22)

An Act to amend the law relating to companies.

[1st May 1980]

. . . . . .

Part IV

Duties of Directors and Conflicts of Interests

Duty in Relation to Employees

Directors to have regard to interests of employees

1-657   **46.**—(1) The matters to which the directors of a company are to have regard in the performance of their functions shall include the interests of the company's employees in general as well as the interests of its members.

(2) Accordingly, the duty imposed by subsection (1) above on the directors of a company is owed by them to the company (and the company alone) and is enforceable in the same way as any other fiduciary duty owed to a company by its directors.

Particular Transactions Giving Rise to a Conflict of Interest

Contracts of employment of directors

1-658   **47.**—(1) Subject to subsection (6) below, a company shall not incorporate in any agreement a term to which this section applies unless the term is first approved by a resolution of the company in general meeting and, in the case of a director of a holding company, by a resolution of that company in general meeting.

(2) This section applies to any term by which a director's employment with the company of which he is the director or, where he is the director

of a holding company, his employment within the group is to continue, or may be continued, otherwise than at the instance of the company (whether under the original agreement or under a new agreement entered into in pursuance of the original agreement), for a period exceeding five years during which the employment—
  (a) cannot be terminated by the company by notice; or
  (b) can be so terminated only in specified circumstances.
(3) In any case where—
  (a) a person is or is to be employed with a company under an agreement which cannot be terminated by the company by notice or can be so terminated only in specified circumstances; and
  (b) more than six months before the expiration of the period for which he is or is to be so employed, the company enters into a further agreement (otherwise than in pursuance of a right conferred by or by virtue of the original agreement on the other party thereto) under which he is to be employed with the company or, where he is a director of a holding company, within the group.
subsection (2) above shall apply as if to the period for which he is to be employed under that further agreement there were added a further period equal to the unexpired period of the original agreement.

(4) A resolution of a company approving a term to which this section applies shall not be passed at a general meeting of the company unless a written memorandum setting out the proposed agreement incorporating the term is available for inspection, by members of the company both—
  (a) at the registered office of the company for not less than the period of 15 days ending with the date of the meeting; and
  (b) at the meeting itself.

(5) A term incorporated in an agreement in contravention of this section shall to the extent that it contravenes this section be void; and that agreement and in a case where subsection (3) above applies the original agreement shall be deemed to contain a term entitling the company to terminate it at any time by the giving of reasonable notice.

(6) No approval is required to be given under this section by any body corporate unless it is a company within the meaning of the 1948 Act or registered under Part VIII of that Act or if it is, for the purposes of section 150 of that Act, a wholly owned subsidiary of any body corporate, wherever incorporated.

(7) In this section—
  (a) "employment" includes employment under a contract for services; and
  (b) "group", in relation to a director of a holding company, means the group which consists of that company and its subsidiaries.

. . . . . .

Disclosure of Transactions Involving Directors and Others

Substantial contracts, etc., with directors and others to be disclosed in accounts

54.—(1) Subject to subsections (5) and (6) and to section 58 below, group accounts prepared by a holding company in accordance with the requirements of section 1 of the 1976 Act in respect of a financial year (the

1–659

"relevant period") ending on or after the appointed day shall contain the particulars specified in section 55 below of—
  (*a*) any transaction or arrangement of a kind described in section 49 above entered into by the company or by a subsidiary of the company for a person who at any time during the relevant period was a director of the company [or its holding company] or was connected wth such a director;
  (*b*) an agreement by the company or by a subsidiary of the company to enter into any such transaction or arrangement for a person who at any time during the relevant period was a director of the company [or its holding company] or was connected with such a director; and
  (*c*) any other transaction or arrangement with the company or with a subsidiary of the company in which a person who at any time during the relevant period was a director of the company [or its holding company] had, directly or indirectly, a material interest.

(2) Subject as aforesaid, accounts so prepared by any company other than a holding company in respect of a financial year (the "relevant period") ending on or after the appointed day shall contain the particulars specified in section 55 below of—
  (*a*) any transaction or arrangement of a kind described in section 49 above entered into by the company for a person who at any time during the relevant period was a director of the company or of its holding company or was connected with such a director;
  (*b*) an agreement by the company to enter into any such transaction or arrangement for a person who at any time during the relevant period was a director of the company or of its holding company or was connected with such a director; and
  (*c*) any other transaction or arrangement with the company in which a person who at any time during the relevant period was a director of the company or of its holding company had, directly or indirectly, a material interest.

[2A) Particulars which are required by subsection (1) or (2) above to be contained in any accounts shall be given by way of notes to those accounts.]

(3) Where by virtue of section 150(2) of the 1948 Act a company does not produce group accounts in relation to any financial year, subsection (1) above shall have effect in relation to the company and that financial year as if the word "group" were omitted.

(4) For the purposes of subsections (1)(*c*) and 2(*c*) above—
  (*a*) a transaction or arrangement between a company and a director of the company or of its holding company or a person connected with such a director shall (if it would not otherwise be so treated) be treated as a transaction, arrangement or agreement in which that director is interested; and
  (*b*) an interest in such a transaction or arrangement is not material if in the opinion of the majority of the directors (other than that director) of the company which is preparing the accounts in question it is not material (but without prejudice to the question whether or not such an interest in material in any case where those directors have not considered the matter).

(5) Subsections (1) and (2) above do not apply, for the purposes of any accounts prepared by any company which is, or is the holding company of, a recognised bank, in relation to a transaction or arrangement of a kind

described in section 49 above, or an agreement to enter into such a transaction or arrangement, to which that recognised bank is a party.

(6) Subsections (1) and (2) above do not apply in relation to the following transactions and arrangements—
- (*a*) a transaction, arrangement or agreement between one company and another in which a director of the firt or of its subsidiary or holding company is interested only by virtue of his being a director of the other;
- (*b*) a contract of service between a company and one of its directors or a director of its holding company [or between a director of a company and any of that company's subsidiaries];
- (*c*) a transaction, arrangement or agreement which was not entered into during the relevant period for the accounts in question [and] which did not subsist at any time during that period;
- (*d*) a transaction, arrangement or agreement which was made before the appointed day and which does not subsist on or after that day.

(7) Subsections (1) and (2) above apply whether or not—
- (*a*) the transaction or arrangement was prohibited by section 49 above;
- (*b*) the person for whom it was made was a director of the company or was connected with a director of the company at the time it was made;
- (*c*) in the case of a transaction or arrangement made by a company which at any time during a relevant period is a subsidiary of another company, it was a subsidiary of that other company at the time the transaction or arrangement was made.

AMENDMENTS

In subss. (1) and (6) the words in square brackets were inserted or substituted by the Companies Act 1981 (c. 62), s.119 and Sched. 3.

Subs. (2A) is added by *ibid*.

Extension of s.26 of 1967 Act

. . . . . .

61.—(1) In subsection (1) of section 26 of the 1967 Act (disclosure of director's service contract with company) the following paragraph shall be inserted after paragraph (*b*)—

"(*c*) in the case of each director who is employed under a contract of service with a subsidiary of the company, a copy of that contract or, if it is not in writing, a written memorandum setting out the terms of that contract;"

(2) The following subsection shall be inserted after subsection (3) ofthat section—

"(3A) Subsection (1) above shall not apply in relation to a director's contract of service with the company or with a subsidiary of the company if that contract required him to work wholly or mainly outside the United Kingdom, but the company shall keep a memorandum—
- (*a*) in the case of a contract of service with the company, setting out the name of the director and the provisions of the contract relating to its duration;

1–660

(b) in the case of a contract of service with a subsidiary of the company, setting out the name of the director, the name and place of incorporation of the subsidiary and the provisions of the contract relating to its duration,

at the same place as copies and the memorandums are kept by the company in pursuance of subsection (1) above."

(3) Each reference in subsections (4), (5) and (7) of that section to subsection (1) shall be construed as including a reference to subsection (3A) of that section; the reference in subsection (7) of that section to a contract of service with a company shall be construed as including a contract of service with a subsidiary of a company; and in subsection (8) of that section, paragraph (*a*) shall cease to have effect.

. . . . . .

Shadow directors

63.—(1) Subject to subsections (2) and (5) below, a person in accordance with whose directions or instructions the directors of a company are accustomed to act ("a shadow director") shall be treated for the purposes of this Part of this Act as a director of the company unless the directors are accustomed so to act by reason only that they do so on advice given by him in a professional capacity.

(2) A shadow director shall not be guilty of an offence under section 57(6) above by virtue only of subsection (1) above.

(3) Section 199 of the 1948 Act (disclosure by a director of a company of his interests in a contract, transaction or arrangement with the company) shall apply in relation to a shadow director of a company as it applies in relation to a director of a company, except that the shadow director shall declare his interest, not at a meeting of the directors, but by a notice in writing to the directors which is either—
    (*a*) a specific notice given before the date of the meeting at which, if he had been a director, the declaration would be required by subsection (2) of that section to be made; or
    (*b*) a notice which under subsection (3) of that section (general notices) falls to be treated as a sufficient declaration of that interest or would fall to be so treated apart from the proviso;
and section 145 of that Act (minutes of proceedings of meetings) shall have effect as if the declaration had been made at the meeting in question and had accordingly formed part of the proceedings at that meeting.

(4) A shadow director of a company shall be treated for the purposes of section 26 of the 1967 Act (director's service contracts, etc., to be open to inspection by a company's members) as a director of the company.

(5) A body corporate shall not be treated as the director of any of its subsidiary companies by reason only of subsection (1) above.

. . . . . .

Part VI

Miscellaneous and General

Interests of Employees and Members

Power of company to provide for employees on cessation or transfer of business

74.—(1) The powers of a company shall, if they would not otherwise do so, be deemed to include power to make the following provision for the benefit of the persons employed or formerly employed by the company or any of its subsidiaries, that is to say, provision in connection with the cessation or the transfer to any person of the whole or part of the undertaking of that company or that subsidiary.

(2) The power conferred by subsection (1) above to make any such provision may be exercised notwithstanding that its exercise is not in the best interests of the company.

(3) The power which a company may exercise by virtue only of subsection (1) above shall only be exercised by the company if sanctioned—
 (*a*) in a case not falling within paragraph (*b*) or (*c*) below, by an ordinary resolution of the company; or
 (*b*) if so authorised by the memorandum or articles, a resolution of the directors; or
 (*c*) if the memorandum or articles require the exercise of the power to be sanctioned by a resolution of the company of some other description for which more than a simple majority of the members voting is necessary, with the sanction of a resolution of that description;

(4) On the winding up of a company (whether by the court or a voluntary winding up) the liquidator may, subject in the case of a winding up by the court to section 245(3) of the 1948 Act as applied by subsection (7) below, make any payment which the company has, before the commencement of the winding up, decided to make under subsection (3) above.

(5) The power which a company may exercise by virtue only of subsection (1) above may be exercised by the liquidator after the winding up of the company has commenced if, after the company's liabilities have been fully satisfied and provision has been made for the costs of the winding up, the exercise of that power has been sanctioned by such a resolution of the company as would be required of the company itself by subsection (3) above before that commencement if paragraph (*b*) of that subsection were omitted and any other requirement applicable to its exercise by the company has been met.

(6) Any payment which may be made by a company under this section may—
 (*a*) in the case of a payment made before the commencement of any winding up of the company, be made out of profits of the company which are available for dividend; and
 (*b*) in the case of any other payment, be made out of the assets of the company which are available to the members on its winding up.

(7) On a winding up by the court section 245(3) of the 1948 Act (powers of the liquidator to be subject to the control of the court on winding up by the court) shall apply to the exercise by the liquidator of his powers under subsection (4) or (5) above as it applies to the exercise of his powers under that section.

(8) Subsections (4) and (5) above shall have effect notwithstanding anything in any rule of law or in section 302 of the 1948 Act (property of company after satisfaction of liabilities to be distributed among members).

. . . . . .

Interpretation

87.—(1) In this Act, except so far as the context otherwise requires,—

"accounting reference period" has the meaning given by section 2 of the 1976 Act;

"appointed day" has the meaning given by section 90(3) below;

"the appropriate rate," in relation to interest, means five per cent. per annum or such other rate as may be specified by order made by the Secretary of State by statutory instrument;

"balance sheet date" in relation to a balance sheet, means the date as at which the balance sheet was prepared;

"called-up share capital," in relation to a company, means so much of its share capital as equals the aggregate amount of the calls made on its shares, whether or not those calls have been paid, together with any share capital paid up without being called and any share capital to be paid on a specified future date under any articles, the terms of allotments of the relevant shares or any other arrangements for payment of those shares, and "uncalled share capital" shall be construed accordingly;

"[the Companies Acts" means the Companies Acts 1948 to 1981;]

"conditional sale agreement" has the same meaning as in the Consumer Credit Act 1974;

"employees' share scheme" means a scheme for encouraging or facilitating the holding of shares or debentures in a company by or for the benefit of—

(a) the bona fide employees or former employees of the company, the company's subsidiary or holding company or a subsidiary of the company's holding company; or

(b) the wives, husbands, widows, widowers or children or stepchildren under the age of 18 of such employees or former employees;

"hire-purchase agreement" has the same meaning as in the Consumer Credit Act 1974;

"the 1948 Act," "the 1967 Act" and "the 1976 Act" mean the Companies Act 1948, the Companies Act 1967 and the Companies Act 1976 respectively;

"non-cash asset" means any property or interest in property other than cash (including foreign currency);

"old public company" has the meaning given by section 8 above;

"re-registration period" has the meaning given by section 9 above;

"the statutory maximum" means—

(a) in England and Wales the prescribed sum within the meaning of section 28 of the Criminal Law Act 1977 (that is to say, £1,000 or another sum fixed by order under section 61 of that Act to take account of changes in the value of money); and

(b) in Scotland, the prescribed sum within the meaning of section 289B of the Criminal Procedure (Scotland) Act 1975 (that is to say £1,000 or another sum fixed by order under section 289D of that Act for that purpose);

"transitional period" means the period of 18 months from the appointed day in question.

(2) In relation to an allotment of shares in a company, the shares shall be taken for the purposes of the Companies Act to be allotted when a per-

son acquires the unconditional rights to be included in the company's register of members in respect of those shares.

(3) For the purposes of the Companies Acts—
- (*a*) a share in a company shall be taken to have been paid up (as to its nominal value or any premium on it) in cash or allotted for cash if the consideration for the allotment or the payment up is cash received by the company or is a cheque received by the company in good faith which the directors have no reason for suspecting will not be paid or is the release of a liability of the company for a liquidated sum or is an undertaking to pay cash to the company at a future date; and
- (*b*) in relation to the allotment or payment up of any shares in a company, references in the Companies Acts, except in section 17 of this Act, to consideration other than cash and to the payment up of shares and premiums on shares otherwise than in cash include references to the payment of, or an undertaking to pay, cash to any person other than the company;

and for the purposes of determining whether a share is or is to be alloted for cash or paid up in cash, "cash" includes foreign currency.

(4) For the purposes of this Act—
- [(*a*) any references to a balance sheet or to a profit and loss account shall include any note to the accounts in question giving information which is required by any provision of the Companies Acts and required by any provision of the Companies Acts and required or allowed by any such provision to be given in a note to a company's accounts;]
- (*b*) any reference to the transfer or acquisition of a non-cash asset includes a reference to the creation or extinction of an estate or interest in, or a right over, any property and also a reference to the discharge or any person's liability, other than a liability for a liquidated sum; and
- (*c*) the net assets of a company are the aggregate of its assets less the aggregate of its liabilities;

and in paragraph (*c*) above "liabilities" includes any provision [for liabilities or charges (within the meaning of paragraph 88 of Schedule 8 to the 1948 Act).]

(5) Expressions used in this Act and the 1948 Act have the same meanings in this Act as they have in that Act.

(6) Any order under this section specifying a rate of interest shall be subject to annulment in pursuance of a resolution of either House of Parliament.

(7) Any reference in the Companies Act 1948 to 1976 or any Act passed before this Act to an enactment which is amended by this Act shall unless the context otherwise requires, be construed as referring to that enactment as so amended.

AMENDMENT

In subs. (1) the definition of "the Companies Act" is substituted by the Companies Act 1981 (c. 62), s.119 and Sched. 3.

In subs (4) words in square brackets are substituted by *ibid.*

Employment Act 1980

(1980 c.42)

An Act to provide for payments out of public funds towards trade unions' expenditure in respect of ballots, and for the issue by the Secretary of State of Codes of Practice for the improvement of industrial relations; to make provision in respect of exclusion or expulsion from trade unions and otherwise to amend the law relating to workers, employers, trade unions and employers' associations; to repeal section 1A of the Trade Union and Labour Relations Act 1974; and for connected purposes.

[1st August 1980]

Trade Union Ballots and Codes of Practice

Payments in respect of secret ballots

1.—(1) The Secretary of State may by regulations make a scheme (below called "the scheme") providing for payments by the Certification Officer towards expenditure incurred by independent trade unions in respect of such ballots to which this section applies as may be prescribed by the scheme.

(2) This section applies to a ballot if the purpose of the question to be voted upon (or if there is more than one such question, the purpose of any of them) falls within the purposes mentioned in subsection (3) below.

(3) The purposes referred to in subsection (2) above are—

  (*a*) obtaining a decision or ascertaining the views of members of a trade union as to the calling or ending of a strike or other industrial action;

  (*b*) carrying out an election provided for by the rules of a trade union;

  (*c*) electing a worker who is a member of a trade union to be a representative of other members also employed by his employer;

  (*d*) amending the rules of a trade union;

  (*e*) obtaining a decision in accordance with the Trade Union (Amalgamations, etc.) Act 1964 on a resolution to approve an instrument of amalgamation or transfer;

  [obtaining a decision or ascertaining the views of members of a trade union as to the acceptance or rejection of a proposal made by an employer in relation to the contractual terms and conditions upon which or the other incidents of the relationship whereby a person works or provides services for the employer.]

and such other purposes as the Secretary of State may by order specify.

(4) The scheme may include provision for payments to be made towards expenditure incurred by an independent trade union in respect of arrangements to hold a ballot which is not proceeded with but which, if it had been held, would have been a ballot to which this section applies.

(5) The circumstances in which and the conditions subject to which payments may be made under the scheme, and the amounts of the payments, shall be such as may be prescribed by or determined in accordance with the scheme; and the scheme shall include provision for restricting the cases in which payments are made to cases in which the ballot is so conducted as to secure, so far as reasonably practicable, that those voting may do so in secret.

(6) The Secretary of State shall out of money provided by Parliament pay to the Certification Officer such sums as he may require for making payments under the scheme.

(7) Any power to make regulations or orders under this section shall be exercisable by statutory instrument; and—
- (a) a statutory instrument containing regulations under this section shall be subject to annulment in pursuance of a resolution of either House of Parliament;
- (b) no order shall be made under this section unless a draft of it has been laid before and approved by resolution of each House of Parliament.

(8) Expressions used in this section and in the 1974 Act have the same meanings in this section as in that Act.

Secret ballots on employer's premises

2.—(1) Subject to subsection (3) below, where an independent trade union proposes that a relevant ballot be held and requests an employer to permit premises of his to be used for the purpose of giving workers employed by him who are members of the union a convenient opportunity of voting, the employer shall, so far as reasonably practicable, comply with the request.

(2) A ballot is a relevant ballot for the purposes of this section if—
- (a) as respects the purpose of the question (or one of the questions) to be voted upon, the ballot satisfies the requirements of a scheme under section 1 of this Act, and
- (b) the proposals for the conduct of the ballot are such as to secure, so far as reasonably practicable, that those voting may do so in secret.

(3) Subsection (1) above shall not apply where, at the time the request is made,—
- (a) the union is not recognised by the employer to any extent for the purpose of collective bargaining, or
- (b) the number of workers employed by the employer, added to the number employed by any associated employer, does not exceed twenty.

(4) A trade union may present a complaint to an industrial tribunal that it has made a request in accordance with subsection (1) above and that it was reasonably practicable for the employee to comply with it, but that he has failed to do so.

(5) An industrial tribunal shall not entertain a complaint under this section unless it is presented to the tribunal before the end of the period of three months beginning with the date of the failure, or within such further period as the tribunal considers reasonable in a case where it is satisfied that it was not reasonably practicable for the complaint to be presented before the end of the period of three months.

(6) Where a tribunal finds that a complaint under this section is well-founded, the tribunal shall make a declaration to that effect, and may make an award of compensation to be paid by the employer to the union which shall be of such amount as the tribunal considers just and equitable in all the circumstances having regard to the employer's default in failing to comply with the request and to any expenses incurred by the union in consequence of the failure.

(7) An appeal shall lie to the Employment Appeal Tribunal on a question of law arising from any decision of, or arising in proceedings before, an industrial tribunal under this section.

(8) The remedy of a trade union for failure to comply with a request made in accordance with subsection (1) above shall be by way of a complaint under this section and not otherwise.

(9) Expressions used in this section and in the 1974 Act have the same meanings in this section as in that Act.

Issue by Secretary of State of Codes of Practice

1–667   3.—(1) The Secretary of State may issue Codes of Practice containing such practical guidance as he thinks fit for the purpose of promoting the improvement of industrial relations.

(2) The Secretary of State shall after consultation with the Advisory, Conciliation and Arbitration Service (whether carried out before or after the passing of this Act) prepare and publish a draft of any Code of Practice that he proposes to issue under this section.

(3) The Secretary of State shall consider any representations made to him about a draft prepared under subsection (2) above and may modify the draft accordingly.

(4) If the Secretary of State determines to proceed with the draft he shall lay it before both Houses of Parliament and, if it is approved by resolution of each House, shall issue the Code in the form of the draft.

(5) A Code of Practice issued under this section shall come into operation on such day as the Secretary of State may by order appoint; and an order under this subsection—

    (*a*) may contain such transitional provisions or savings as appear to the Secretary of State to be necessary or expedient;

    (*b*) shall be made by statutory instrument, which shall be subject to annulment in pursuance of a resolution of either House of Parliament.

(6) The Secretary of State may from time to time revise the whole or any part of a Code of Practice issued under this section and issue that revised Code, and subsections (2) to (5) above shall apply to such a revised Code as they apply to the first issue of a Code.

(7) If the Secretary of State is of the opinion that the provisions of a Code of Practice to be issued under this section will supersede the whole or part of a Code previously issued by him under this section or by the Advisory, Conciliation and Arbitration Service under section 6 of the 1975 Act or having effect by virtue of paragraph 4 of Schedule 17 to that Act, he shall in the new Code state that on the day on which the new Code comes into operation in pursuance of an order under subsection (5) above the old Code or a specified part of it shall cease to have effect (subject to any transitional provisions or savings made by the order).

(8) A failure on the part of any person to observe any provision of a Code of Practice issued under this section shall not of itself render him liable to any proceedings; but in any proceedings before a court or industrial tribunal or the Central Arbitration Committee—

    (*a*) any such Code shall be admissible in evidence, and

    (*b*) any provision of the Code which appears to the court, tribunal or Committee to be relevant to any question arising in the proceedings shall be taken into account in determining that question.

Exclusion from Trade Union Membership

Unreasonable exclusion or expulsion from trade union

4.—(1) This section applies to employment by an employer with respect to which it is the practice, in accordance with a union membership agreement, for the employee to belong to a specified trade union or one of a number of a specified trade unions.

1–668

(2) Every person who is, or is seeking to be, in employment to which this section applies shall have the right—
   (a) not to have an application for membership of a specified trade union unreasonably refused;
   (b) not to be unreasonably expelled from a specified trade union.

(3) The rights conferred by subsection (2) above are in addition to and not in substitution for any right which exists apart from that subsection; and, without prejudice to any remedy for infringement of any such other right, the remedies for infringement of a right conferred by that subsection shall be those provided by the following provisions of this section and section 5 below.

(4) A compalint may be presented to an industrial tribunal against a trade union by a person that an application by him for membership of the union has been unreasonably refused, or that he has been unreasonably expelled from the union, in contravention of subsection (2) above.

(5) On a complaint under this section, the question whether a trade union had acted reasonably or unreasonably shall be determined in accordance with equity and the substantial merits of the case, and in particular a union shall not be regarded as having acted reasonably only because it had acted in accordance with the requirements of its rules or unreasonably only because it has acted in contravention of them.

(6) A tribunal shall not entertain a complaint under this section unless it is presented to the tribunal before the end of the period of six months beginning with the date of the refusal or explusion, as the case may be, or within such further period as the tribunal considers reasonable in a case where it is satisfied that it was not reasonably practicable for the complaint to be presented before the end of the period of six months.

(7) Where a tribunal finds that a complaint under this section is well-founded, the tribunal shall make a declaration to that effect.

(8) An appeal shall lie to the Employment Appeal Tribunal on any question of law or fact arising from any decision of, or arising in any proceedings before, an industrial tribunal under this section.

(9) For the purposes of this section and section 5 below—
   (a) if an application for membership of a trade union has been neither granted nor rejected before the end of the period within which it might reasonably have been expected to be granted if it was to be granted, the application shall be treated as having been refused on the last day of that period, and
   (b) if under the rules of a trade union any person ceases to be a member of the union on the happening of an event specified in the rules, he shall be treated as having been expelled from the union.

(10) Any expression used in any provision of this section or section 5 below and in the 1974 Act has the same meaning in that provision as it has

in that Act, except that any reference in such a provision to a trade union includes a reference to a branch or section of a trade union.

(11) Any provision in an agreement shall be void in so far as it purports to exclude or limit the operation of, or to preclude any person from presenting a complaint or making an application under, this section or section 5 below; but this subsection shall not apply to an agreement to refrain from instituting or continuing proceedings where a conciliation officer has taken action in accordance with section 133(2) or (3) of the 1978 Act.

Compensation

1–669   **5.**—(1) A person who has made a complaint against a trade union under section 4 above which has been declared by an industrial tribunal or, on appeal by the Employment Appeal Tribunal to be well-founded may make an application in accordance with subsection (2) below for an award of compensation to be paid to him by the union.

(2) If at the time when the application under this section is made the applicant has been admitted or re-admitted to membership of the union against which he made the complaint, the application shall be to an industrial tribunal; and if at that time he has not been so admitted or re-admitted, the application shall be to the Employment Appeal Tribunal.

(3) An industrial tribunal or the Employment Appeal Tribunal shall not entertain an application for compensation under this section if it is made before the end of the period of four weeks beginning with the date of the declaration under section 4 above or after the end of the period of six months beginning with that date.

(4) Subject to the following provisions of this section, the amount of compensation awarded on an application under this section—
  (a) in the case of an application to an industrial tribunal, shall be such as the tribunal considers appropriate for the purpose of compensating the applicant for the loss sustained by him in consequence of the refusal or expulsion which was the subject of his complaint, and
  (b) in the case of an application to the Employment Appeal Tribunal, shall be such as the Appeal Tribunal considers just and equitable in all the circumstances.

(5) In determining the amount of compensation to be awarded under this section, the industrial tribunal or the Employment Appeal Tribunal shall apply the same rule concerning the duty of a person to mitigate his loss as applies to damages recoverable under the common law of England and Wales or of Scotland, as the case may be.

(6) Where the industrial tribunal or the Employment Appeal Tribunal finds that the refusal or expulsion which was the subject of the applicant's complaint was to any extent caused or contributed to by any action of the applicant, it shall reduce the amount of the compensation by such proportion as it considers just and equitable having regard to that finding.

(7) The amount of compensation awarded on an application to an industrial tribunal under this section shall not exceed the aggregate of—
  (a) an amount equal to thirty times the limit for the time being imposed by paragraph 8(1)(b) of Schedule 14 to the 1978 Act (maximum amount of a week's pay for purpose of calculating basic award in unfair dismissal cases), and
  (b) an amount equal to the limit for the time being imposed by section 75 of that Act (maximum compensatory award in such cases).

(8) The amount of compensation awarded on an application to the Employment Appeal Tribunal under this section shall not exceed the aggregate of—
  (a) the amount referred to in paragraph (a) of subsection (7) above, and
  (b) the amount referred to in paragraph (b) of that subsection, and
  (c) an amount equal to fifty-two times the limit for the time being imposed by paragraph 8(1)(a) of Schedule 14 to the 1978 Act (maximum amount of a week's pay for purpose of calculating additional award of compensation in unfair dismissal cases).

(9) An appeal shall lie to the Employment Appeal Tribunal on a question of law arising from any decision of, or arising in proceedings before, an industrial tribunal under this section.

. . . . . .

Other Rights of Employees

Guarantee payments
14.   1–670
(2) This section shall not have effect in relation to workless days (within the meaning of section 12 of that Act) falling before the commencement of this section except so far as they are relevant in determining entitlement to guarantee payments in respect of days falling after that time.

. . . . . .

Restrictions on Legal Liability

Picketing
16.—(1) [*Substitutes a new s.15 of the Trade Union and Labour Relations*   1–671
Act 1974. See ibid.]
(2) Nothing in section 13 of the 1974 Act shall prevent an act done in the course of picketing from being actionable in tort unless it is done in the course of attendance declared lawful by section 15 of that Act.
(3) In subsection (2) above "tort" has as respects Scotland the same meaning as in the 1974 Act.

Secondary action
17.—(1) Nothing in section 13 of the 1974 Act shall prevent an act from   1–672
being actionable in tort on a ground specified in subsection (1)(a) or (b) of that section in any case where—
  (a) the contract concerned is not a contract of employment, and
  (b) one of the facts relied upon for the purpose of establishing liability is that there has been secondary action which is not action satisfying the requirements of subsection (3), (4) or (5) below.
(2) For the purposes of this section there is secondary action in relation to a trade dispute when, and only when, a person—
  (a) induces another to break a contract of employment or interferes or induces another to interfere with its performance, or
  (b) threatens that a contract of employment under which he or another

is employed will be broken or its performance interfered with, or that he will induce another to break a contract of employment or to interfere with its performance.

if the employer under the contract of employment is not a party to the trade dispute.

(3) Secondary action satisfies the requirement of this subsection if—
   (a) the purpose or principal purpose of the secondary action was directly to prevent or disrupt the supply during the dispute of goods or services between an employer who is a party to the dispute and the employer under the contract of employment to which the secondary action relates; and
   (b) the secondary action (together with any corresponding action relating to other contracts of employment with the same employer) was likely to achieve that purpose.

(4) Secondary action satisfies the requirements of this subsection if—
   (a) the purpose or principal purpose of the secondary action was directly to prevent or disrupt the supply during the dispute of goods or services between any person and an associated employer of an employer who is a party to the dispute; and
   (b) the goods or services are in substitution for goods or services which but for the dispute would have fallen to be supplied to or by the employer who is a party to the dispute; and
   (c) the employer under the contract of employment to which the secondary action relates is either the said associated employer or the other party to the supply referred to in paragraph (a) above; and
   (d) the secondary action (together with any corresponding action relating to other contracts of employment with the same employer) was likely to achieve the purpose referred to in paragraph (a) above.

(5) Secondary action satisfies the requirements of this subsection if it is done in the course of attendance declared lawful by section 15 of the 1974 Act—
   (a) by a worker employed (or, in the case of a worker not in employment, last employed) by a party to the dispute, or
   (b) by a trade union official whose attendance is lawful by virtue of subsection (1)(b) of that section.

(6) In subsections (3)(a) and (4)(a) above—
   (a) references to the supply of goods or services between two persons are references to the supply of goods or services by one to the other in pursuance of a contract between them subsisting at the time of the secondary action; and
   (b) references to directly preventing or disrupting the supply are references to preventing or disrupting it otherwise than by means of preventing or disrupting the supply of goods or services by or to any other person.

(7) Expressions used in this section and in the 1974 Act have the same meanings in this section as in that Act; and for the purposes of this section an employer who is a member of an employers' association which is a party to a trade dispute shall by virtue of his membership be regarded as a party to the dispute if he is represented in the dispute by the association, but not otherwise.

(8) Subsection (3) of section 13 of the 1974 Act shall cease to have effect.

. . . . . .

Enactments ceasing to have effect

19. The following enactments shall cease to have effect, that is to say—
(*a*) section 1A of the 1974 Act (charter on freedom of the press);
(*b*) sections 11 to 16 of the 1975 Act (procedure for dealing with issues relating to recognition of trade unions); and
(*c*) section 98 of and Schedule 11 to the 1975 Act (extension of terms and conditions of employment) and the Road Haulage Wages Act 1938 (fixing of statutory remuneration).

Interpretation, minor and consequential amendments and repeals

20.—(1) In this Act—
"the 1974 Act" means the Trade Union and Labour Relations Act 1974;
"the 1975 Act" means the Employment Protection Act 1975;
"the 1978 Act" means the Employment Protection (Consolidation) Act 1978.

(2) Schedule 1 to this Act (which makes minor and consequential amendments) shall have effect.

(3) The enactments mentioned in Schedule 2 to this Act are hereby repealed to the extent specified in the third column of that Schedule.

Short title, commencement and extent

21.—(1) This Act may be cited as the Employment Act 1980.

(2) Sections 2, 4 to 19 and 20(2) and (3) of this Act, and Schedule 1 and 2, shall not come into operation until such day as the Secretary of State may appoint by order made by statutory instrument, and different days may be so appointed for different purposes.

(3) An order under this section may contain such transitional and supplementary provisions as appear to the Secretary of State to be necessary or expedient.

(4) Paragraph 7 of Schedule 1 to this Act shall extend to Northern Ireland, but otherwise this Act shall not extend there.

SCHEDULES

Section 17

SCHEDULE 1

Minor and Consequential Amendments

The Post Office Act 1969

1. In section 81(1) of the Post Office Act 1969 (exclusion of road haulage workers employed by Post Office from the workers in relation to whom wages councils may operate) the words from the beginning to "the Road Haulage Wages Act 1938; and" shall cease to have effect.

The Trade Union and Labour Relations Act 1974

2. In Schedule 1 to the 1974 Act, paragraph 32(2)(*a*) shall cease to have effect.

3. In Schedule 2 to the 1974 Act, in paragraph 32(1) (periodical re-examination of members' superannuation schemes) at the beginning there shall be inserted the words "Subject to paragraph 33A below" and after paragraph 33 there shall be inserted—

"33A. The Certification Officer, on the application of a trade union or employers' association, may exempt any members' superannuation scheme which it maintains from the requirements of paragraph 32 above if he is satisfied that, by reason of the small number of members to which the scheme is applicable or for any other special reasons, it is unnecessary for the scheme to be examined in accordance with those requirements.

33B. The Certification Officer may at any time revoke any exemption granted under paragraph 33A above if it appears to him that the circumstances by reason of which the exemption was granted have ceased to exist; and for the purposes of paragraph 32 above the relevant date next following the revocation shall be such date as the Certification Officer may direct."

The Employment Protection Act 1975

4. In section 6 of the 1975 Act after subsection (10) there shall be inserted—

"(10A) If the Service is of the opinion that the provisions of a Code of Practice to be issued under this section will supersede the whole or part of a Code previously issued by it under this section or by the Secretary of State under section 3 of the Employment Act 1980, it shall in the new Code state that on the day on which the new Code comes into effect in pursuance of an order under subsection (5) or (8) above the old Code or a specified part of it shall cease to have effect (subject to any transitional provisions or savings made by the order)."

5. In section 121(1) of the 1975 Act, for the words "98 to" there shall be substituted the words "99 to".

6. In section 126(1) of the 1975 Act, in the definition of "recognition", for the words from "has" to "above" there shall be substituted the words "in relation to a trade union, means the recognition of the union by an employer, or two or more associated employers, to any extent, for the purpose of collective bargaining".

7. In section 127(1) of the 1975 Act, after paragraph (*f*) there shall be inserted—
"(*ff*) the Employment Act 1980; and".

The Employment Protection (Consolidation) Act 1978

8. In section 15(5) of the 1978 Act, for the words "relevant periods" there shall be substituted the words "length of the period".

9. In section 32(1) of the 1978 Act, for "31" there shall be substituted "31A".

10. In section 55(5) of the 1978 Act after "64(1)(*a*)" there shall be inserted "64A".

11. In section 56 of the 1978 Act, after the word "then" there shall be inserted the words "subject to section 56A".

12. [*Repealed by the Employment Act 1982 (c.46), Sched. 4.*]

13. In section 66 of the 1978 Act (revocation of exclusion orders under section 65)—
   (*a*) subsection (1) shall cease to have effect; and
   (*b*) in subsection (2) for the words from "on" to "satisfied" there shall be substituted the words "at any time when an order under section 65 is in force in respect of a dismissal procedures agreement the Secretary of State is satisfied, whether on an application by any of the parties to the agreement or otherwise,".

14. [*Repealed by the Employment Act 1982 (c.46), Sched. 4.*]

15. In section 121(2)(*c*) of the 1978 Act, for the words "or 31(3)" there shall be substituted the words "31(3) or 31A(4)".

16. In section 128(4) of the 1978 Act, after the word "references" there shall be inserted the word "applications".

17. In section 133(1) of the 1978 Act, in paragraph (*a*) after "31" there shall be inserted "31A", and after paragraph (*c*) there shall be inserted—
"or
(*d*) arising out of a contravention, or alleged contravention, of section 4 of the Employment Act 1980".

18. In section 134 of the 1978 Act, for subsection (3) there shall be substituted—
"(3) Where—
   (*a*) a person claims that action has been taken in respect of which a complaint could be presented by him under section 67, and
   (*b*) before any complaint relating to that action has been so presented, a request is made to a conciliation officer (whether by that person or by the employer) to make his services available to them.
the conciliation officer shall act in accordance with subsections (1) and (2) above as if a complaint had been presented."

19. In section 136(5) of the 1978 Act after the words "subsection (1)" there shall be inserted the words "or under section 2, 4, or 5 or the Employment Act 1980".

20. In section 140 of the 1978 Act (restrictions on contracting out of 1978 Act) subsection (2)(*b*) shall cease to have effect.

21. In section 149 of the 1978 Act—
  (*a*) in subsection (1)(*c*), after "64(1)" there shall be inserted "64A (1)";
  (*b*) in subsection (2) after "58" there shall be inserted "58A".

22. In section 154 of the 1978 Act (orders, rules and regulations)—
  (*a*) in subsection (1) of the words "or an order under section 65 or 66" shall cease to have effect; and
  (*b*) in subsection (4) for the words from "section 96" to the end there shall be substituted the words "section 65, 66 or 96".

23. In the subsection set out in paragraph 2(1) of Schedule 2 to the 1978 Act, for the words from "the employer can" to the end there shall be substituted the words "in the circumstances (including the size and administrative resources of the employer's undertaking the employer would have been acting reasonably if she had not been absent from work; and that question shall be determined in accordance with equity and the substantial merits of the case."

24. In paragraphs 2(4) and 6(3) of Schedule 2 to the 1978 Act, for "58(3)" there shall be substituted "58(3) to (3E), 58A."

25. In paragraph 5 of Schedule 3 to the 1978 Act for the words "or 31" there shall be substituted the words "31 or 31A."

26. In paragraph 1(2)(*a*) of Schedule 9 to the 1978 Act, after the word "question" there shall be inserted the word "application."

27. In paragraph 7 of Schedule 9 to the 1978 Act for sub-paragraph (2) there shall be substituted—

  "(2) Any order for the payment of any sum made by an industrial tribunal in Scotland (or any copy of such an order certified by the Secretary of the Tribunals) may be enforced in like manner as an extract registered decree arbitral bearing a warrant for execution issued by the Sheriff Court of any Sheriffdom in Scotland."

28. In paragraph 18 of Schedule 11 to the 1978 Act after sub-paragraph (*a*) there shall be inserted—

  "(*aa*) with respect to the manner in which an application to the Appeal Tribunal under section 5 of the Employment Act 1980 may be made;

and after sub-paragraph (*c*) there shall be inserted—

  "(*d*) for the registration and proof of any award made on an application to the Appeal Tribunal under section 5 of the Employment Act 1980."

29. After paragraph 21 of Schedule 11 to the 1978 Act there shall be inserted—

  "21A.—(1) Any sum payable in England and Wales in pursuance of an award of the Appeal Tribunal under section 5 of the Employment Act 1980 which has been registered in accordance with the rules shall, if a county court so orders, be recoverable by execution issued from the county court or otherwise as if it were payable under an order of that court.

  (2) Any order by the Appeal Tribunal for the payment in Scotland of any sum in pursuance of such an award (or any copy of such an order certified by the Secretary of the Tribunals) may be enforced in like manner as an extract registered decree arbitral bearing a warrant for execution issued by the Sheriff Court of any Sheriffdom in Scotland."

30. In paragraph 23(1) of Schedule 11 to the 1978 Act, for the words from "section 14" to "those provisions" there shall be substituted the words "sections 31 and 32 of the Powers of Criminal Courts Act 1973 (powers of Crown Court in relation to fines and forfeited recognisance) shall have effect as if."

31. In paragraph 10 of Schedule 13 to the 1978 Act, for the words "section 47" there shall be substituted the words "section 45(1) or in pursuance of an offer made in the circumstances described in section 56A(2)."

32. In paragraph 11 of Schedule 13 to the 1978 Act after "64(1)(*a*)," there shall be inserted 64A(1)."

33. In paragraph 7(1) of Schedule 14 to the 1978 Act, after paragraph (*c*) there shall be inserted—

  "(*cc*) where the calculation is for the purposes of section 31A, he day of the appointment concerned;".

SCHEDULE 2

Repeals

Chapter	Short title	Extent of repeal
1 & 2 Geo. 6. c. 44.	The Road Haulage Wages Act 1938.	The whole Act.
12, 13 & 14 Geo. 6. c. 7.	The Wages Councils Act 1948.	In section (1) (c), the words from "Parts II and III" to the end, and Schedule 1.
1968 c. 73.	The Transport Act 1968.	Section 69 (4) (d). So much of Schedules 10 and 11 as amends the Road Haulage Wages Act 1938.
1969 c. 35.	The Transport (London) Act 1969.	In Schedule 3, paragraph 1 (2) (a).
1969 c. 48.	The Post Office Act 1969.	In section 81, in subsection (1), the words from the beginning to "the Road Haulage Wages Act 1938; and", and subsection (2).
1972 c. 68.	The European Communities Act 1972.	In paragraph 9 (4) of Schedule 4, the words from the beginning to "1938" and the words from "after" to "Part VI; and".
1974 c. 52.	The Trade Union and Labour Relations Act 1974.	Section 1A. Section 13 (3). In Schedule 1, in paragraph 32 (1) the words from "Except" to "below", and paragraph 32 (2). In Schedule 3, paragraph 4.
1975 c. 18.	The Social Security (Consequential Provisions) Act 1975.	In Schedule 2, paragraph 4.
1975 c. 60.	The Social Security Pensions Act 1975.	Section 31 (9).
1975 c. 71.	The Employment Protection Act 1975.	Sections 11 to 16. In section 17 (2), paragraph (b) and the word "or" immediately preceding it. In section 21 (5), paragraph (b) and the word "or" immediately preceding it. Section 98. Section 106 (1). In section 118 (2) (d), the words "16 (7) (b) or (c) or", the words from "or paragraph" to "this Act", the words "16 or" and the words from "or, as" to the end. In section 121 (1), the reference to section 16. In section 127 (1) (g), the words "in paragraphs (a) to (f)". Schedule 11. In Part IV of Schedule 16, paragraphs 4 and 17. In Schedule 17, paragraph 13.
1976 c. 3.	The Road Traffic (Drivers' Ages and Hours of Work) Act 1976.	In section 2 (3), the words from "the following" to "1938" and the word "and".
1976 c. 7.	The Trade Union and Labour Relations (Amendment) Act 1976.	Section 2.
1976 c. 79.	The Dock Work Regulation Act 1976.	In section 15 (1) in the definition of "recognised", the words from "and a union" to the end.

Chapter	Short title	Extent of repeal
1977 c. 3.	The Aircraft and Shipbuilding Industries Act 1977.	In section 56 (1), in the definition of "relevant trade union", the words from "or as" to the end.
1978 c. 36.	The House of Commons (Administration) Act 1978.	In Schedule 1, in paragraph 5 (6), the words "Part IV of".
1978 c. 44.	The Employment Protection (Consolidation) Act 1978.	In section 23, in subsection (1) (c), the words "which is not independent", and subsections (3) to (6). In section 25 (1), paragraph (b) and the word "and" immediately preceding it. In section 32 (1) (a), the words "not only" and the words from "but" to "1975". In section 33 (3), the word "and" at the end of paragraph (b). Section 58 (4). Section 66 (1). Section 73 (1) (c) and (8). Section 97. In section 135 (1), the words from "for the purpose" to the end. Section 140 (2) (b). In section 154 (1), the words "or an order under section 65 or 66". In Schedule 6, in paragraph 12 (2) (b), sub-paragraph (ii) and the word "or" immediately preceding it.
1979 c. 12.	The Wages Councils Act 1979.	In Schedule 6, paragraph 1.

COMPANIES ACT 1981

(1981 c.62)

An Act to amend the law relating to companies and business names.

[30th October 1981]

. . . . . .

The exemptions for individuals accounts

6.—(1) The directors of a company which is entitled to the benefit of the exemptions for individual accounts in respect of any accounting reference period may deliver copies of modified accounts to the registrar of companies in respect of that period instead of copies of the accounts of the company prepared in respect of that period under section 1 of the 1976 Act.

(2) The modifications permitted in the case of the accounts of a small company delivered to the registrar in respect of any accounting reference period are as follows—

    (a) subject to subsection (4) below, the directors may deliver to the registrar of companies a copy of a modified balance sheet prepared for the purposes of this section in respect of that period, instead of a copy of the company's balance sheet prepared in respect of that period under section 1 of the 1976 Act;

1–678

(b) the directors shall not be required under section 1(7)(a) of that Act to deliver to the registrar a copy of the company's profit and loss account prepared in respect of that period under that section;
(c) the information required by Schedule 8 to the 1948 Act to be given in notes to the accounts need not be so given, with the exception of any information required in relation to the accounts delivered to the registrar by any of the provisions of that Schedule mentioned in subsection (5) below; and
(d) the information required by section 196 of the 1948 Act (aggregate amounts of directors' salaries etc.) or section 6, 7 or 8 of the 1967 Act (detailed particulars of salaries etc., of directors and certain other employees) need not be given.

. . . . . .

Certain provisions of the Companies Acts to cease to have effect

1-679   **16.**—(1) Sections 17 and 18 of the 1967 Act (further information to be given in directors' reports) shall not apply to any directors' report attached in compliance with section 157 of the 1948 Act to accounts prepared under section 1 of the 1976 Act in compliance with section 149 of the 1948 Act unless the documents required to be comprised in those accounts for the purposes of section 1(6) to (8) of the 1976 Act include group accounts prepared in pursuance of paragraph 2 of Schedule 2 to this Act which state that they are prepared in compliance with section 152A of and Schedule 8A to the 1948 Act.

. . . . . .

Financial Assistance for Acquisition of Shares

Certain assistance for acquisition of shares prohibited

1-680   **42.**—(1) Subject to the following provisions of this section and sections 43 and 44 of this Act, where a person is acquiring or is proposing to acquire any shares in a company it shall not be lawful for the company or any of its subsidiaries to give financial assistance directly or indirectly for the purpose of that acquisition before or at the time as the acquisition takes place.

(2) Subject to the following provisions of this section and sections 43 and 44 of this Act, where a person has acquired any shares in a company and any liability has been incurred (by that or any other person) for the purpose of that acquisition it shall not be lawful for the company or any of its subsidiaries to give any financial assistance directly or indirectly for the purpose of reducing or dscharging the liability so incurred.

(3) Subsection (1) above shall not prohibit a company from giving any financial assistance for the purpose of any acquisition of shares in the company or its holding company if—
   (a) the company's principal purpose in giving the assistance is not to give it for the purpose of any such acquisition or the giving of the assistance for that purpose is but an incidental part of some larger purpose of the company; and
   (b) the assistance is given in good faith in the interests of the company.

(4) Subsection (2) above shall not prohibit a company from giving any financial assistance if—
   (a) the company's principal purpose in giving the assistance is not to

reduce or discharge any liability incurred by a person for the purpose of the acquisition of any shares in the company or its holding company or the reduction or discharge of any such liability is but an incidental part of some larger purpose of the company; and

(b) the assistance is given in good faith in the interests of the company.

(5) Subsections (1) and (2) above shall not prohibit—
- (a) any distribution of a company's assets by way of dividend lawfully made or any distribution made in the course of the winding up of the company;
- (b) the allotment of any bonus shares;
- (c) anything done in pursuance of an order of the court made under section 206 of the 1948 Act (compromises and arrangements with creditors and members);
- (d) anything done under an arrangement made between a company and its creditors which is binding on the creditors by virtue of section 306 of the 1948 Act;
- (e) anything done under an arrangement made in pursuance of section 287 of the 1948 Act (power of liquidator to accept shares, etc. as consideration for sale of property of company);
- (f) any reduction of capital confirmed by order of the court under section 68 of the 1948 Act;
- (g) a redemption or purchase of any shares made in accordance with sections 45 to 62 of this Act.

(6) Subsections (1) and (2) above shall not prohibit—
- (a) where the lending of money is part of the ordinary business of the company, the lending of money by the company in the ordinary course of its business;
- (b) the provision by a company in accordance with an employees' share scheme (within the meaning of section 87(1) of the 1980 Act) of money for the acquisition of fully paid shares in the company or its holding company;
- (c) the making by a company of loans to persons, other than directors, employed in good faith by the company with a view to enabling those persons to acquire fully paid shares in the company or its holding company to be held by themselves by way of beneficial ownership.

(7) Subsection (6) above shall authorise a public company to give financial assistance to any person only if the company has net assets which are not thereby reduced or, to the extent that those assets are thereby reduced, if the financial assistance is provided out of distributable profits.

(8) In this section "financial assistance" means—
- (a) financial assistance given by way of gift;
- (b) financial assistance given by way of guarantee, security or indemnity, other than an indemnity in respect of the indemnifier's own neglect or default, or by way of release or waiver;
- (c) financial assistance given by way of a loan or any other agreement under which any of the obligations of the person giving the assistance are to be fulfilled at a time when in accordance with the agreement any obligation of any other party to the agreement remains unfulfilled or by way of the novation of or the assignment of any rights arising under any loan or such other agreement; or

(d) any other financial assistance given by a company the net assets of which are thereby reduced to a material extent or which has not net assets.

In this subsection "net assets" has the same meaning as it has for the purposes of the 1980 Act.

(9) Any references in this section to a person incurring any liability shall be read as including a reference to his changing his financial position by making any agreement or arrangement (whether enforceable or unenforceable and whether made on his own account or with any other person) or by any other means.

(10) Any reference in this section to a company giving financial assistance for the purpose of reducing or discharging any liability incurred by any person for the purpose of the acquisition of any shares shall be read as including a reference to the company giving financial assistance for the purpose of wholly or partly restoring his financial position to what it was before the acquisition took place.

(11) For the purposes of subsection (7) above—
 (a) "net assets," in relation to the giving of financial assistance by any company, means the amount by which the aggregate amount of the company's assets exceeds the aggregate amount of its liabilities taking the amount of both assets and liabilities to be as stated in the company's accounting records immediately before the financial assistance is given; and
 (b) "liabilities" includes any amount retained as reasonably necessary for the purpose of providing for any liability or loss which is either likely to be incurred, or certain to be incurred but uncertain as to amount or as to the date on which it will arise.

(12) If a company acts in contravention of this section the company and any officer who is in default shall be liable—
 (a) on conviction on indictment, to a term of imprisonment not exceeding two years or a fine or both;
 (b) on summary conviction, to a term of imprisonment not exceeding six months or a fine not exceeding the statutory maximum, or both.

(13) Section 54 of the 1948 Act, which is superseded by the preceding provisions of this section, shall cease to have effect.

. . . . . .

SCHEDULE 1

. . . . . .

Information Supplementing the Profit and Loss Account

52. Paragraphs 53 to 57 below require information which either supplements the information given with respect to any particular items shown in the profit and loss account or otherwise provides particulars of income or expenditure of the company or of circumstances affecting the items shown in the profit and loss account.

. . . . . .

Particulars of staff

56.—(1) The following information shall be given with respect to the employees of the company—
 (a) the average number of persons employed by the company in the financial year; and

(b) the average number of persons employed within each category of persons employed by the company in the financial year; and

(2) The average number required by sub-paragraph (1)(a) or (b) above shall be determined by dividing the relevant annual number by the number of weeks in the financial year.

(3) The relevant annual number shall be determined by ascertaining for each week in the financial year—
  (a) for the purpose of sub-paragraph (1)(a) above, the number of persons employed under contracts of service by the company in that week (whether throughout the week or not);
  (b) for the purposes of sub-paragraph (1)(b) above, the number of persons in the category in question of persons so employed;
and, in either case, adding together all the weekly numbers.

(4) In respect of all persons employed by the company during the financial year who are taken into account in determining the relevant annual number for the purposes of sub-paragraph (1)(a) above there shall also be stated the aggregate amounts respectively of—
  (a) wages and salaries paid or payable in respect of that year to those persons;
  (b) for the purposes of sub-paragraph (1)(b) above, the number of persons
  (c) other pension costs so incurred;
save in so far as those amounts or any of them are stated in the profit and loss account.

(5) The categories of persons employed by the company by reference to which the number required to be disclosed by sub-pragraph (1)(b) above is to be determined shall be such as the directors may select, having regard to the manner in which the company's activities are organised.

Employment Act 1982

1–682

(1982 c.46)

An Act to provide for compensation out of public funds for certain past cases of dismissal for failure to conform to the requirements of a union membership agreement; to amend the law relating to workers, employers, trade unions and employers' associations; to make provision with respect to awards by industrial tribunals and awards by, and the procedure of, the Employment Appeal Tribunal; and for connected purposes.

[28th October 1982]

. . . . . .

Unfair Dismissal

Compensation for certain dismissals

2.—(1) The provisions of Schedule 1 shall have effect for the purpose of enabling the Secretary of State to make payments towards compensating individuals who in certain past cases have been dismissed for failure to conform to the requirements of a union membership agreement.

1–683

(2) The expenses incurred by the Secretary of State in consequence of that Schedule shall be defrayed out of money provided by Parliament.

. . . . . .

Union Membership or Recognition Requirements in Contracts

Prohibition on union membership requirements

12.—(1) Any term or condition of a contract for the supply of goods or

1–684

services is void in so far as it purports—
- (*a*) to require that the whole, or some part, of the work done for the purposes of the contract is to be done only by persons who are not members of trade unions or not members of a particular trade union; or
- (*b*) to require that the whole, or some part, of such work is to be done only by persons who are members of trade unions or members of a particular trade union.

(2) A person contravenes this subsection if, on the ground of union membership, he—
- (*a*) fails, in a case where he maintains (in whatever form) a list of approved suppliers of goods or services or a list of persons from whom tenders for the supply of goods or services may be invited to include the name of a particular person in that list;
- (*b*) terminates a contract for the supply of goods or services; or
- (*c*) does, in relation to a proposed contract for the supply of goods or services, any of the acts mentioned in subsection (3) below.

(3) The acts are—
- (*a*) excluding a particular person from the group of persons from whom tenders for the supply of the goods or services are invited;
- (*b*) failing to permit a particular person to submit such a tender;
- (*c*) otherwise determining not to enter into a contract with a particular person for the supply of the goods or services.

(4) For the purposes of subsection (2)(*a*) above a person (the "first person") fails to include the name of another person (the "supplier") in a list, on the ground of union membership, if the ground, or one of the grounds, for failing to include his name is either—
- (*a*) that if the supplier were to enter into a contract with the first person for the supply of goods or services work to be done for the purposes of the contract would, or would be likely to, be done by persons who were not members of trade unions or of a particular trade union; or
- (*b*) that if the supplier were to enter into such a contract work to be done for the purposes of the contract would, or would be likely to, be done by persons who were members of trade unions or of a particular trade union.

(5) For the purposes of subsection (2)(*b*) above, a person terminates a contract on the ground of union membership if the ground, or one of the grounds, for terminating it is either—
- (*a*) that work done, or to be done, for the purposes of the contract has been, or is likely to be, done by persons who are not members of trade unions or of a particular trade union; or
- (*b*) that work done, or to be done, for the purposes of the contract has been, or is likely to be, done by persons who are members of trade unions or of a particular trade union.

(6) for the purposes of subsection (2)(*c*) above, a person does an act on the ground of union membership if the ground, or one of the grounds, on which he does that act is either—
- (*a*) that, if the proposed contract were entered into with the person referred to in subsection (3) above, work to be done for the purposes of the contract would, or would be likely to, be done by

persons who are not members of trade unions or of a particular trade union; or

(b) that, if the proposed contract were entered into with that person, work to be done for the purposes of the contract would, or would be likely to, be done by persons who are members of trade unions or of a particular trade union.

(7) Subsection (2) above does not create an offence but the obligation to comply with it is a duty owed to each of the following—
 (a) in a case falling within subsection (2)(a) above, the person referred to in subsection (4) as the supplier;
 (b) in a case falling within subsection (2)(b) above, any other party to the contract;
 (c) in a case falling within subsection (2)(c) above, the person referred to in subsection (3) above; and
 (d) in any case, any other person who may be adversely affected by its contravention;

and any breach of that duty shall be actionable accordingly (subject to the defences and other incidents applying to actions for breach of statutory duty).

Prohibition on union recognition requirements

13.—(1) Any term or condition of a contract for the supply of goods or services is void in so far as it purports to require any party to the contract—
 (a) to recognise one or more trade unions (whether or not named in the contract) for the purpose of negotiating on behalf of workers, or any class of worker, employed by him; or
 (b) to negotiate or consult with, or with any official of, one or more trade unions (whether or not so named).

(2) A person contravenes this subsection if, on the ground of union exclusion, he acts in a manner falling within paragraph (a), (b) or (c) of section 12(2) of this Act.

(3) For the purposes of subsection (2) above, a person acts on the ground of union exclusion if the ground or one of the grounds for his action is that the person against whom it is taken does not, or is not likely to, recognise, negotiate or consult as mentioned in subsection (1) above.

(4) Subsection (2) above does not create an offence but the obligation to comply with it is a duty owed to each of the following–
 (a) the person against whom the action is taken; and
 (b) any other person who may be adversely affected by the contravention,

and any breach of that duty shall be actionable accordingly (subject to the defences and other incidents applying to actions for breach of statutory duty).

Pressure to impose union membership or recognition requirements

14.—(1) Nothing in section 13 of the 1974 Act shall prevent an act being actionable in tort in any case where a person induces, or attempts to induce, another—

(*a*) to incorporate in a contract to which that other person is a party, or proposed contract to which that other person intends to be a party, any term or condition which is, or would be, void by virtue of section 12(1) or 13(1) of this Act; or

(*b*) to contravene section 12(2) or 13(2);

and the act constitutes, or is one of a number of acts which together constitute, the inducement or attempted inducement.

(2) Nothing in section 13 of the 1974 Act shall prevent an act which interferes with the supply (whether or not under a contract) of goods or services, or can reasonably be expected to have such an effect, being actionable in tort in any case where subsection (3) below is satisfied and one of the facts relied upon for the purpose of establishing liability is that any person has—

(*a*) induced another to break a contract of employment or interfered or induced another to interfere with its performance; or

(*b*) threatened that a contract of employment under which he or another is employed will be broken or its performance interfered with, or that he will induce another to break a contract of employment or to interfere with its performance.

(3) This subsection is satisfied if—

(*a*) the reason, or one of the reasons, for doing the act is that work done or to be done in connection with the supply of the goods or services in question has been, or is likely to be, done by persons (other than persons employed by the relevant employer) who are not members of trade unions or of a particular trade union;

(*b*) the reason, or one of the reasons, for doing the act is that such work has been, or is likely to be, done by persons (other than persons employed by the relevant employer) who are members of trade unions or of a particular trade union); or

(*c*) the supplier of the goods or services in question is not the relevant employer and the reason, or one of the reasons, for doing the act is that the supplier does not, or is not likely to, recognise, negotiate or consult as mentioned in section 13.

(4) In subsection (3) above "the relevant employer" means the employer under the contract of employment mentioned in subsection (2) above.

Trade Disputes

Actions in tort against trade unions and employers' associations

15.—(1) Section 14 of the 1974 Act (immunity for trade unions and employers' associations from certain actions in tort) shall cease to have effect.

(2) Where proceedings in tort are brought against a trade union—

(*a*) on a ground specified in paragraph (*a*) or (*b*) of section 13(1) of the 1974 Act; or

(*b*) in respect of an agreement or combination by two or more persons to do or to procure the doing of an act which, if it were done without any such agreement or combination, would be actionable in tort on such a ground;

then, for the purpose of determining in those proceedings whether the union is liable in respect of the act in question, that act shall be taken to have been done by the union if, but only if, it was authorised or endorsed by a responsible person.

(3) For the purposes of this section, but subject to subsection (4) below, an act shall not be taken to have been authorised or endorsed by a responsible person unless it was authorised or, as the case may be, endorsed—
  (*a*) by the principal executive committee;
  (*b*) by any other person who is empowered by the rules to authorise or, as the case may be, endorse acts of the kind in question;
  (*c*) by the president or general secretary;
  (*d*) by any other official who is an employed official; or
  (*e*) by any committee of the union to whom an employed official regularly reports.

(4) An act shall not be taken, by virtue of subsection (3)(*d*) or (*e*) above, to have been authorised or endorsed by a responsible person if—
  (*a*) that person was, at the time in question, prevented by the rules from authorising or endorsing acts of the kind in question; or
  (*b*) the act has been repudiated by the principal executive committee or by the president or general secretary.

(5) For the purposes of subsection (4)(*b*) above, an act shall not be treated as repudiated unless—
  (*a*) it is repudiated as soon as is reasonably practicable after the purported authorisation or endorsement of the act has come to the knowledge of the principal executive committee or, as the case may be, of the president or general secretary; and
  (*b*) the person who purported to authorise or endorse the act has been notified in writing and without delay that it has been repudiated.

(6) An act shall not be treated as repudiated, notwithstanding subsection (5) above, if at any time after the union concerned purported to repudiate it the principal executive committee or president or general secretary has behaved in a manner which is inconsistent with the purported repudiation.

(7) In this section–
  "general secretary" means the official of the union concerned who holds the office of general secretary or, where there is no such office, who holds the office which is equivalent, or the nearest equivalent, to that of general secretary;
  "official" means an official of the union concerned; and "employed official" means, in relation to that union, an official who is employed by it;
  "president" means the official of the union concerned who holds the office of president or, where there is no such office, who holds the office which is equivalent, or the nearest equivalent, to that of president;
  "principal executive committee" means the principal committee of the union concerned exercising executive functions, by whatever name it is known;
  "rules" means the written rules of the union and any other written provisions forming part of the contract between a member and the other members (or, in the case of a special register body, between a member and the body).

(8) Where, for the purpose of any proceedings, an act is by virtue of this section taken to have been done by a trade union nothing in this section

shall affect the liability of any other person in those or any other proceedings in respect of that act.

Limit on damages awarded against trade unions in actions in tort

1–688   16.—(1) Subject to subsection (2) below, in any proceedings in tort brought against a trade union the amount which may be awarded against the union by way of damages in those proceedings shall not exceed the appropriate limit.

(2) Subsection (1) above does not apply to any proceedings—
- (*a*) for any of the following resulting in personal injury to any person, that is to say negligence, nuisance or breach of duty; or
- (*b*) without prejudice to paragraph (*a*) above, for breach of duty in connection with the ownership, occupation, possession, control or use of property (whether real or personal or, in Scotland, heritable or moveable).

(3) The appropriate limit is—
- (*a*) £10,000, if the union has less than 5,000 members;
- (*b*) £50,000, if it has 5,000 or more members but less than 25,000 members;
- (*c*) £125,000, if it has 25,000 or more members but less than 100,000 members; and
- (*d*) £250,000, if it has 100,000 or more members.

(4) The Secretary of State may by order vary any of the sums for the time being specified in subsection (3) above.

(5) An order under subsection (4) above—
- (*a*) shall be made by statutory instrument subject to annulment in pursuance of a resolution of either House of Parliament; and
- (*b*) may make such transitional provision as the Secretary of State considers appropriate.

(6) In this section—

"duty" means a duty imposed by any rule of law or by or under any enactment; and

"personal injury" includes any disease and any impairment of a person's physical or mental condition.

(7) For the purposes of this section, in any case where a trade union consists wholly or mainly of organisations or representatives of organisations, the members of such of those organisations as have their head or main office in Great Britain shall be treated as members of the union.

Recovery of sums awarded in proceedings involving trade unions and employers' associations

1–689   17.—(1) Where in any proceedings an amount is awarded by way of damages, costs or expenses—
- (*a*) against a trade union or employers' association;
- (*b*) against trustees in whom property is vested in trust for a trade union or employers' association, in their capacity as such and otherwise than in respect of a breach of trust on their part; or
- (*c*) against members or officials of a trade union or emloyers' association on behalf of themselves and all of the members of the union or association;

no part of that amount shall be recoverable by enforcement against any protected property.

(2) In this section "protected property" means any property—

(a) belonging to the trustees concerned otherwise than in their capacity as such;
(b) belonging to any member of the union or association concerned otherwise than jointly or in common with the other members;
(c) belonging to any official of the union or association concerned who is neither a member nor such a trustee;
(d) comprised in a political fund of the union concerned; or
(e) comprised in a provident benefits fund of the union concerned.

(3) In subsection (2) above—

"political fund" means a fund which is a political fund for the purposes of section 3 of the Trade Union Act 1913 and which is (and was at the time when the act in respect of which the proceedings are brought was done) subject to rules of the union which prevent property which is or has been comprised in the fund from being used for financing strikes or other industrial action;

"provident benefits" includes any payment, expressly authorised by the rules of the union, which is made to a member during sickness or incapacity from personal injury or while out of work, or to an aged member by way of superannuation, or to a member who has met with an accident or has lost his tools by fire or theft, and includes a payment in discharge or aid of funeral expenses on the death of a member or the wife of a member, or as provision for the children of a deceased member; and

"provident benefits fund" means a separate fund which is maintained in accordance with the rules of the union for the purpose only of providing provident benefits.

Meaning of "trade dispute"

18.—(1) Section 29 of the 1974 Act (meaning of "trade dispute") shall be amended as follows.

(2) In the opening words of subsection (1) (which define a "trade dispute" by reference to the parties to the dispute and its connection with certain matters)—
(a) for "between employers and workers" there shall be substituted "between workers and their employer";
(b) the words, "or between workers and workers," shall be omitted; and
(c) for "is connected with" there shall be substituted "relates wholly or mainly to".

(3) In subsection (2) (which extends the definition to certain disputes with a Minister of the Crown who does not employ the workers in question) for "employer and those workers" there shall be substituted "those workers and their employer".

(4) In subsection (3) (which extends the definition to disputes relating to matters occurring outside Great Britain) for "occurring outside Great Britain" there is substituted "occurring outside the United Kingdom, so long as the person or persons whose actions in the United Kingdom are said to be in contemplation or furtherance of a trade dispute relating to matters occurring outside the United Kingdom are likely to be affected in respect of one or more of the matters specified in subsection (1) of this section by the outcome of that dispute".

(5) Subsection (4) (which provides that a dispute with a trade union or employers' association is necessarily to be treated as a dispute to which workers or, as the case may be, employers are a party) shall be omitted.

(6) In subsection (6) for the definition of "worker" there is substituted—

" "worker", in relation to a dispute with an employer, means—
    (*a*) a worker employed by that employer; or
    (*b*) a person who has ceased to be employed by that employer where—
        (i) his employment was terminated in connection with the dispute; or
        (ii) the termination of his employment was one of the circumstances giving rise to the dispute.".

(7) The amendments made by this section do not affect the question whether an act done by a person is done by him in contemplation or furtherance of a dispute, whether he is a party to the dispute or not.

. . . . . .

Periods of Continuous Employment

Change of basis of computation of period of continuous employment

1–691   **20.**—(1) The amendments set out in Schedule 2 shall have effect for the following purposes—
    (*a*) amending enactments which confer rights by reference to the length of an employee's period of continuous employment so as to substitute for periods expressed in weeks or years of fifty-two weeks corresponding periods expressed in months or years of twelve months;
    (*b*) modifying the computation of an employee's period of continuous employment under Schedule 13 to the 1978 Act so as to provide for computing the length of the period in months and years of twelve months;
    (*c*) making minor and consequential amendments in connection with the purposes mentioned in paragraphs (*a*) and (*b*).

(2) The amendments set out in Schedule 2 shall not apply—
    (*a*) where the date by reference to which the length of an employee's period of continuous employment falls to be ascertained ("the qualification date") is before the commencement of this section, or
    (*b*) where the result would be to deprive a person of any right or entitlement which he would have had if the qualification date had fallen immediately before the commencement of this section.

(3) Subject to subsection (2), the amendments set out in Schedule 2 shall, so far as they relate to the computation of the length of a period of continuous employment, apply to periods before the commencement of this section as they apply to later periods.

(4) Nothing in this section shall affect—
    (*a*) any order made before the commencement of this section under section 18, 65 or 96 of the 1978 Act or any corresponding earlier enactment (exclusion of certain sections where equivalent protection afforded by collective agreement or wages order); or
    (*b*) the operation of any agreement or wages order to which such an order relates or the operation of any provision of the 1978 Act in relation to such an agreement or wages order.

Supplemental

Interpretation, minor and consequential amendments and repeals
21.—(1) In this Act—
"the 1974 Act" means the Trade Union and Labour Relations Act 1974;
"the 1975 Act" means the Employment Protection Act 1975;
"the 1976 Act" means the Trade Union and Labour Relations (Amendment) Act 1976;
"the 1978 Act" means the Employment Protection (Consolidation) Act 1978;
"the 1980 Act" means the Employment Act 1980;
"employers' association", "official" (in relation to a trade union), "special register body", "tort" (as respects Scotland), "trade union" and "worker" have the same meanings as in the 1974 Act.
(2) Schedule 3 to this Act (which makes minor and consequential amendments) shall have effect.
(3) The enactments mentioned in Schedule 4 to this Act are hereby repealed to the extent set out in the third column.

Short title, commencement and extent
22.—(1) This Act may be cited as the Employment Act 1982.
(2) This Act, except section 2 and Schedule 1, shall not come into operation until such day as the Secretary of State may appoint by order made by statutory instrument, and different days may be so appointed for different purposes.
(3) An order under this section may contain such transitional and supplemental provisions as appear to the Secretary of State to be necessary or expedient.
(4) Without prejudice to subsection (3) above—
(*a*) an order under this section bringing section 3 above into operation may provide that, for such period as may be specified in the order, section 58 of the 1978 Act (as substituted by section 3) shall have effect as if section 58(3)(*c*) applied only to a union membership agreement taking effect in relation to the employees in question after 14th August 1980; and
(*b*) an order under this section bringing section 10 above into operation may make corresponding provision in respect of section 23(2B) of the 1978 Act (as substituted by section 10(2) above).
(5) Paragraph 13(4) of Schedule 3 to this Act shall extend to Northern Ireland, but otherwise this Act shall not extend there.

SCHEDULES

Section 2   SCHEDULE 1

COMPENSATION FOR CERTAIN DISMISSALS

Power of Secretary of State to make payments
1. The Secretary of State may, if he thinks fit, pay to a person who satisfies the conditions specified in paragraph 2 an amount not exceeding that specified in paragraph 3.

Conditions of eligibility

2.—(1) A person may apply for compensation under this Schedule where—
   (*a*) he was dismissed from his employment on or after 16th September 1974 (when the 1974 closed shop provisions came into force) and before 15th August 1980 (when the 1980 amendments came into force);
   (*b*) he did not bring, or brought but did not succeed in, a complaint of unfair dismissal; and
   (*c*) if the 1980 amendments had been in force in relation to his dismissal (the law otherwise being as it was at the time), he would have been entitled by virtue of those amendments to succeed in a complaint of unfair dismissal.

(2) In this paragraph—
   "the 1974 closed shop provisions" means paragraph 6(5) of Schedule 1 to the 1974 Act, later amended by sections 1(*e*) and 3(5) of the 1976 Act and consolidated in subsection (3) of section 58 of the 1978 Act; and
   "the 1980 amendments" means the amendments of section 58 of the 1978 Act made by section 7 of, and paragraph 12 of Schedule 1 to, the 1980 Act, except so far as relating to the approval of union membership agreements by ballot, or, in relation to a dismissal occurring before 1st November 1978 (when section 58 came into force), corresponding amendments of paragraph 6 of Schedule 1 to the 1974 Act.

Maximum amount of compensation

3. The maximum amount which the Secretary of State may pay to a person in respect of his dismissal is the amount which that person would have been awarded if he had brought a successful complaint of unfair dismissal—
   (*a*) disregarding any question of an order for reinstatement or re-engagement;
   (*b*) assuming, in relation to a dismissal occurring before 1st June 1976, that the provisions of the 1975 Act were in force relating to the basic award of compensation; and
   (*c*) taking into account the actual loss sustained by him rather than such loss as might have been foreseen at the time,
together with interest from the date of the dismissal calculated at the rate from time to time in force under section 17 of the Judgments Act 1838.

Construction of references to date of dismissal

4.—(1) Subject to the following provisions of this paragraph, references in paragraphs 2 and 3 to the date of a dismissal are to the effective date of termination in relation to that dismissal as defined in section 55(4) of the 1978 Act.

(2) In ascertaining for the purposes of those paragraphs whether a dismissal occurred before the commencement of any provision of the 1975, 1978 or 1980 Acts, that is to say in ascertaining—
   (*a*) for the purpose of paragraph 2(1)(*a*) whether a person was dismissed before 15th August 1980,
   (*b*) for the purpose of paragraph 2(2) whether a dismissal occurred before 1st November 1978, or
   (*c*) for the purpose of paragraph 3(*b*) whether a dismissal occurred before 1st June 1976,
references to the date of the dismissal shall be construed in accordance with sub-paragraph (3) in the cases where that sub-paragraph applies.

(3) Where the notice required to be given by an employer by section 1(1) of the Contracts of Employment Act 1972 or section 49 of the 1978 Act (minimum period of notice) would, if duly given when notice of termination was given by the employer, or (where no notice was given) when the contract of employment was terminated by the employer, have expired on a date later than the effective date of termination as defined by section 55(4) of the 1978 Act, that later date shall be treated for the purposes mentioned in sub-paragraph (2) as the date of the dismissal.

Making an application

5. An application for compensation under this Schedule must be made in writing to the Secretary of State within twelve months from the passing of this Act or such further period as the Secretary of State may allow.

Reference of questions to appointed person

6.—(1) The Secretary of State may, if he thinks fit, before deciding an application for compensation under this Schedule, refer any question arising in connection with the application for inquiry and report by a person appointed by him under this paragraph.

(2) In any such case the applicant shall be informed of the identity of the appointed person and of the question or questions referred and shall be given an opportunity to make representations to the appointed person including oral representations if he so wishes.

(3) The Secretary of State may pay to any person attending at any place for the purpose of making such representations such travelling and other allowances as would be payable in connection with attendance at an industrial tribunal.

(4) A person may be appointed by the Secretary of State under this paragraph either for the purposes of a particular reference or for the purpose of such references as may from time to time be made to him; and the Secretary of State may pay to a person so appointed such remuneration and such travelling and other allowances as he may determine with the approval of the Treasury.

Consideration of application

7. In considering an application for compensation under this Schedule, the Secretary of State shall have regard to, but shall not be bound by—
   (a) the findings of any industrial tribunal in proceedings arising out of the dismissal in question; and
   (b) any report made in relation to the application by a person appointed under paragraph 6.

Notification of decision

8.—(1) The Secretary of State shall notify the applicant in writing of his decision.

(2) The notification shall be accompanied by a copy of any report made in relation to the application by a person appointed under paragraph 6.

Reconsideration of decision

9.—(1) The Secretary of State may, of his own motion or on the request of the applicant, reconsider his decision on any application for compensation under this Schedule on the ground that the decision was made in ignorance of, or was based on a mistake as to, some material fact.

(2) Where the Secretary of State decides of his own motion to reconsider a decision, he shall inform the applicant of that fact and of the grounds for reopening the case.

(3) A request by the applicant for reconsideration of the decision on his application must be made in writing to the Secretary of State within three months from the date on which the decision was notified to him, or such further period as the Secretary of State may allow.

(4) The provisions of paragraphs 6 to 8 shall, with the necessary modifications, apply in relation to the reconsideration of an application as they apply in relation to the original consideration of an application.

Liability to repay in certain cases

10.—(1) Where, for the purpose of obtaining compensation under this Schedule for himself or for another, any person misrepresents or fails to disclose any material fact, whether fraudulently or otherwise, the person to whom any such payment is in consequence made shall be liable to repay so much of it as the Secretary of State may direct, unless he can show that the misrepresentation or failure occurred without his connivance or consent.

(2) Except as provided by this paragraph, the reconsideration of a decision under paragraph 9 shall not give rise to a liability to repay.

(3) Any sum received by the Secretary of State by virtue of this paragraph shall be paid into the Consolidated Fund.

False statement an offence

11.—(1) It is an offence for a person to make, for the purpose of obtaining compensation under this Schedule for himself or for another, a statement which is false in a material particular and which he knows to be so false.

(2) An offence under this paragraph is punishable on summary conviction with a fine not exceeding £1,000.

Social Security and Housing Benefits Act 1982

(1982 c.24)

An Act to make provision for the payment of statutory sick pay by employers; to make new provision with respect to the grant of, and the payment of subsidies in respect of, rate rebates, rent rebates and rent allowances; to amend the law relating to social security and war pensions; to amend section 44 of the national Assistance Act 1948; and for connected purposes.

[28th June 1982]

Part I

Statutory Sick Pay

Employer's liability

1.—(1) Where an employee has a day of incapacity for work in relation to his contract of service with an employer, that employer shall, if the conditions set out in sections 2 to 4 of this Act are satisfied, be liable to make to him, in accordance with the following provisions of this Part, a payment (to be known as "statutory sick pay") in respect of that day.

(2) Any agreement shall be void to the extent that it purports—

(a) to exclude, limit or otherwise modify any provision of this Part; or

(b) to require an employee to contribute (whether directly or indirectly) towards any costs incurred by his employer under this Part.

(3) For the purposes of this Part a day shall not be treated as a day of incapacity for work in relation to any contract of service unless on that day the employee concerned is, or is deemed in accordance with regulations to be, incapable by reason of some specific disease or bodily or mental disablement of doing work which he can reasonably be expected to do under that contract.

(4) In any case where an employee has more than one contract of service with the same employer the provisions of this Part shall, except in such cases as may be prescribed and subject to the following provisions of this Part, have effect as if the employer were a different employer in relation to each contract of service.

The Qualifying Conditions

Period of incapacity for work

2.—(1) The first condition is that the day in question forms part of a period of incapacity for work.

(2) In this Part "period of incapacity for work" means any period of four or more consecutive days, each of which is a day of incapacity for work in relation to the contract of service in question.

(3) Any two periods of incapacity for work which are separated by a

period of not more than two weeks shall be treated as a single period of incapacity for work.

(4) No day of the week shall be disregarded in calculating any period of consecutive days for the purposes of this section.

(5) A day may be a day of incapacity for work in relation to a contract of service, and so form part of a period of incapacity for work, notwithstanding that—
  (*a*) it falls before the making of the contract or after the contract expires or is brought to an end; or
  (*b*) it is not a day on which the employee concerned would be required by that contract to be available for work.

Period of entitlement

3.—(1) The second condition is that the day in question falls within a period which is, as between the employee and his employer, a period of entitlement.

(2) For the purposes of this Part a period of entitlement, as between an employee and his employer, is a period beginning with the commencement of a period of incapacity for work and ending with whichever of the following first occurs—
  (*a*) the termination of that period of incapacity for work;
  (*b*) the day on which the employee reaches, as against the employer concerned, his maximum entitlement to statutory sick pay (determined in accordance with section 5 of this Act);
  (*c*) the day on which the employee's contract of service with the employer concerned expires or is brought to an end;
  (*d*) in the case of an employee who is, or has been, pregnant, the day immediately preceding the beginning of the disqualifying period.

(3) Schedule 1 to this Act has effect for the purpose of specifying circumstances in which a period of entitlement does not arise in relation to a particular period of incapacity for work.

(4) A period of entitlement as between an employee and an employer of his may also be, or form part of, a period of entitlement as between him and another employer of his.

(5) Regulations may provide, in relation to prescribed cases, for a period of entitlement to end otherwise than in accordance with subsection (2) above.

(6) In a case where the employee's contract of service first takes effect on a day which falls within a period of incapacity for work, the period of entitlement begins with that day.

(7) Regulations shall make provision as to an employer's liability under this Part to pay statutory sick pay to an employee in any case where the employer's contract of service with that employee has been brought to an end by the employer solely, or mainly, for the purpose of avoiding liability for statutory sick pay.

(8) Subsection (2)(*d*) above does not apply in relation to an employee who has been pregnant if her pregnancy terminated, before the beginning of the disqualifying period, otherwise than by confinement.

(9) In this section—
  "confinement" has the same meaning as in section 23 of the principal Act;

"disqualifying period" means the period of eighteen weeks beginning with the eleventh week before the expected week of confinement; and

"expected week of confinement" has the same meaning as in section 22 of the principal Act.

Qualifying days

1–699   **4.**—(1) The third condition is that the day in question is a qualifying day.

(2) The days which are, for the purposes of this part, to be qualifying days as between an employee and an employer of his (that is to say those days of the week on which he is required by his contract of service with that employer to be available for work or which are chosen to reflect the terms of that contract) shall be such day, or days, as may be agreed between the employee and his employer or, failing such agreement, determined in accordance with regulations.

(3) In any case where qualifying days are determined by agreement between an employee and his employer there shall, in each week (beginning with Sunday), be at least one qualifying day.

(4) A day which is a qualifying day as between an employee and an employer of his may also be a qualifying day as between him and another employer of his.

Limitations on Entitlement, etc.

Limitations on entitlement

1–700   **5.**—(1) Statutory sick pay shall not be payable for the first three qualifying days in any period of entitlement.

(2) An employee shall not be entitled, as against any one employer, to an aggregate amount of statutory sick pay in respect of any one period of entitlement, or tax year, which exceeds his maximum entitlement.

(3) The maximum entitlement as against any one employer is reached on the day on which the amount to which the employee has become entitled by way of statutory sick pay during the period of entitlement in question or, as the case may be, the aggregate amount to which he has become so entitled during the tax year in question first reaches or passes the entitlement limit.

(4) The entitlement limit is an amount equal to eight times the appropriate weekly rate set out in section 7 of this Act.

(5) Regulations may make provision for calculating the entitlement limit in any case where an employee's entitlement to statutory sick pay is calculated by reference to different weekly rates in the same tax year or period of entitlement.

Notification of incapacity for work

1–701   **6.**—(1) Regulations shall prescribe the manner in which, and the time within which, notice of any day of incapacity for work is to be given by or on behalf of an employee to his employer.

(2) An employer who would, apart from this section, be liable to pay an amount of statutory sick pay to an employee in respect of a qualifying day (the "day in question") shall be entitled to withhold payment of that amount if—

(a) the day in question is one in respect of which he has not been duly notified in accordance with regulations under subsection (1) above; or

(b) he has not been so notified in respect of any of the first three qualifying days in a period of entitlement (a "waiting day") and the day in question is the first qualifying day in that period of entitlement in respect of which the employer is not entitled to withhold payment—

(i) by virtue of paragraph (a) above; or

(ii) in respect of an earlier waiting day by virtue of this paragraph.

(3) Where an employer withholds any amount of statutory sick pay under this section—

(a) the period of entitlement in question shall not be affected; and

(b) for the purposes of calculating his maximum entitlement in accordance with section 5 of this Act, the employee shall not be taken to have become entitled to the amount so withheld.

Rate of Payment, etc.

Rate of payment

7.—(1) Statutory sick pay shall be payable by an employer at the weekly rate of—

(a) [£40·25], in a case where the employee's normal weekly earnings under his contract of service with that employer are not less than [£65];

(b) [£33·75], in a case where those earnings are less than [£65] but not less than [£48·50]; or

(c) [£27·20], in any other case.

(2) The amount of statutory sick pay payable by any one employer in respect of any day shall be the weekly rate applicable on that day divided by the number of days which are, in the week (beginning with Sunday) in which that day falls, qualifying days as between that employer and the employee concerned.

(3) The Secretary of State shall in the tax year 1982–1983, and in each subsequent tax year, review the sums specified in subsection (1)(a), (b) and (c) above for the purpose of determining whether they have retained their value in relation to the general level of prices obtaining in Great Britain.

(4) For the purposes of any such review the Secretary of State shall estimate the general level of prices in such manner as he thinks fit.

(5) Following any such review the Secretary of State may, in the tax year in which the review is carried out, prepare and lay before Parliament the draft of an order increasing one or more of the sums by such amount as he considers appropriate.

(6) If a draft order laid before Parliament in pursuance of this section is approved by resolution of each House, the Secretary of State shall make an order in the form of the draft.

(7) If on a review under this section the Secretary of State concludes that the general level of prices in Great Britain has risen during the period under review, but decides—

(a) not to prepare and lay before Parliament the draft or an order increasing one or more of the sums; or

(b) to prepare, and so lay, the draft of an order which provides for no increase in any one or more of the sums, or for an increase in any of them which differs from the appropriate amount;

he shall, unless in his opinion the amount by which that general level has risen, or, as the case may be, the amount by which an increase differs from the appropriate amount, is inconsiderable, lay before Parliament a report explaining his reasons for so deciding.

(8) If on a review under this section the Secretary of State concludes that the general level of prices in Great Britain has not risen during the period under review but decides to prepare and lay before Parliament the draft of an order increasing one or more of the sums, he shall lay before Parliament a report explaining his reasons for so deciding.

(9) In subsection (7) above "appropriate amount" means the amount which would, in the opinion of the Secretary of State, reflect the amount by which the general level of prices in Great Britain has risen during the period under review.

(10) A draft order prepared under subsection (5) above shall be framed so as to bring the increases in the sums to which it relates into force on the first day of the tax year beginning after the tax year in which the order is laid before Parliament in draft; and shall make such transitional provision as the Secretary of State considers expedient in respect of periods of entitlement running at that date.

AMENDMENT

The figures in square brackets in subs. (1) were substituted by the Statutory Sick Pay Uprating Order 1983 (S.I. 1983 No. 123).

Regulations as to method of payment, etc.

1–703   8.—(1) Regulations may prescribe the manner in which statutory sick pay may, and may not, be paid.

(2) Regulations may prescribe, in relation to any case where—
    (a) a decision has been made by an insurance officer, local tribunal or Commissioner in proceedings under this Part that an employee is entitled to an amount of statutory sick pay; and
    (b) the time for bringing an appeal against the decision has expired and either—
        (i) no such appeal has been brought; or
        (ii) such an appeal has been brought and has been finally disposed of;

the time within which that amount of statutory sick pay is to be paid.

(3) Regulations may make provision—
    (a) enabling a person to be appointed to exercise, on behalf of an employee who may be or become unable for the time being to act, any right or power which the employee may be entitled to exercise under this Part;
    (b) authorising a person so appointed to receive and deal with, on behalf of the employee, any sum payable by way of statutory sick pay;
    (c) in connection with an employee's death—
        (i) enabling proceedings on a question as to, or arising under this Part in connection with, entitlement to statutory sick pay to be begun or continued in his name;
        (ii) authorising payment or distribution of statutory sick

pay to or amongst persons claiming as his personal representatives, legatees, next of kin, or creditors (or, in any case where a deceased employed earner was illegitimate, to or amongst others); and

   (iii) dispensing with strict proof of the title of persons so claiming; and

 (*d*) adjusting amounts payable by way of statutory sick pay so as to avoid fractional amounts or facilitate computation.

(4) In subsection (3)(*c*)(ii) above "next of kin" means the persons who would take beneficially (or who, in Scotland, would be entitled to the moveable estate of the deceased) on an intestacy.

Recovery by employers of amounts paid by way of statutory sick pay

9.—(1) Regulations shall make provision—
 (*a*) entitling, except in prescribed circumstances, any employer who has made a payment of statutory sick pay to recover the amount so paid by making one or more deductions from his contributions payments; and
 (*b*) for the payment, in prescribed circumstances by or on behalf of the Secretary of State of sums to employers who are unable so to recover the whole, or any part, of any payments of statutory sick pay which they have made.

(2) In subsection (1)(*a*) above, "contributions payments", in relation to an employer, means any payments (other than payments arising under the National Insurance Surcharge Act 1976) which the employer is required, by or under any enactment, to make in discharge of any liability in respect of primary or secondary Class 1 contributions.

(3) Regulations under this section may, in particular,—
 (*a*) require employers who have made payments of statutory sick pay to furnish to the Secretary of State such documents and information, at such times, as may be prescribed; and
 (*b*) provide for any deduction made in accordance with the regulations to be disregarded for prescribed purposes.

(4) The power to make regulations conferred by paragraph 5 of Schedule 1 to the principal Act (power to combine collection of contributions with collection of income tax) shall include power to make such provision as the Secretary of State considers expedient in consequence of any provision made by or under this section.

(5) Provision made in regulations under paragraph 5 of Schedule 1, by virtue of subsection (4) above, may in particular require the inclusion—
 (*a*) in returns, certificates and other documents; or
 (*b*) in any other form of record;
which the regulations require to be kept or produced or to which those regulations otherwise apply, of such particulars relating to statutory sick pay as may be prescribed by those regulations.

(6) Where, in accordance with any provision of regulations made under this section, an amount has been deducted from an employer's contributions payments, the amount so deducted shall (except in such cases as may be prescribed) be treated for the purposes of any provision made by or under any enactment in relation to primary or secondary Class 1 contributions as having been—

(a) paid (on such date as may be determined in accordance with the regulations); and
(b) received by the Secretary of State;
towards discharging the liability mentioned in subsection (2) above.

(7) Any sums paid under regulations made by virtue of subsection (1)(b) above shall be paid out of the National Insurance Fund.

(8) Any employer who, in purporting to comply with any requirement imposed by regulations under this section—
(a) produces or furnishes, or causes or knowingly allows to be produced or furnished, any document or information which he knows to be false in a material particular; or
(b) recklessly produces or furnishes any document or information which is false in a material particular;
shall be guilty of an offence.

(9) A person guilty of an offence under subsection (8) above shall be liable, on summary conviction—
(a) in the case of an offence under paragraph (a), to a fine not exceeding £1,000 or to imprisonment for a term of not more than three months or to both; or
(b) in the case of an offence under paragraph (b), to a find not exceeding £500.

(10) Subsections (8) and (9) above shall apply, in place of the provision
(10) Subsections (8) and (9) above shall apply, in place of the provision made by section 98(2) of the Taxes Management Act 1970 (penalties for providing false information etc.) as applied by paragraph 5(2) of Schedule 1 to the principal Act, in relation to such requirements of the regulations made under paragraph 5 of Schedule 1 by virtue of subsection (4) above as may be specified in those regulations.

Relationship with Benefits and Other Payments, etc.

Relationship with benefits and other payments, etc.

1–705 10. Schedule 2 to this Act has effect with respect to the relationship between statutory sick pay and certain benefits and payments and for the purpose of modifying other enactments.

. . . . . .

Offences and penalties

1–706 20. Regulations may provide for contravention of, or failure to comply with, any provision contained in regulations made under section 8(2), 9(3)(a), 17(4) or 18 of this Act to be an offence under this Part and for the recovery, on summary conviction of any such offence, of penalties not exceeding—
(a) for any one offence, £200; or
(b) for an offence of continuing any such contravention or failure after conviction, £20 for each day on which it is so continued.

. . . . . .

Interpretation of Part I and supplementary provisions

1–707 26.—(1) In this Part—
"Commissioner" means a Social Security Commissioner and includes

a tribunal of Commissioners constituted under section 116 of the principal Act;

"contract of service" (except in paragraph (*a*) of the definition below of "employee") includes any arrangement providing for the terms of appointment of an employee;

"employed earner's employment" has the same meaning as in the principal Act;

"employee" means a person who is—
  (*a*) gainfully employed in Great Britain either under a contract of service or in an office (including elective office) with emoluments chargeable to income tax under Schedule E; and
  (*b*) over the age of 16;
but subject to regulations, which may provide for cases where any such person is not to be treated as an employee for the purposes of this Part and for cases where any person who would not otherwise be an employee for those purposes is to be treated as an employee for those purposes;

"employer", in relation to an employee and a contract of service of his, means the secondary contributor (within the meaning of section 4 of the principal Act) in relation to any earnings paid, or to be paid, to or for the benefit of that employee under that contract;

"insurance officer" means an officer appointed under section 97(1) of the principal Act;

"local office" means any office appointed by the Secretary of State as a local office for the purposes of this Part;

"local tribunal" means a tribunal established under section 97(2) of the principal Act;

"maternity allowance" means an allowance payable under section 22 of the principal Act;

"pensionable age" means, in the case of a man, 65 or, in the case of a woman, 60;

"period of entitlement" has the meaning given by section 3 of this Act;

"period of incapacity for work" has the meaning given by section 2 of this Act;

"period of interruption of employment" has the same meaning as it has in the principal Act by virtue of section 17(1)(*d*);

"prescribed" means prescribed by regulations;

"primary Class 1 contributions" and "secondary Class 1 contributions" have the same meaning as in the principal Act;

"qualifying day" has the meaning given by section 4 of this Act;

"week" means any period of seven days.

(2) For the purposes of this Part an employee's normal weekly earnings shall, subject to subsection (4) below, be taken to be his average weekly earnings in the relevant period under his contract of service with the employer in question.

(3) For the purposes of subsection (2) above, the expressions "earnings" and "relevant period" shall have the meaning given to them by regulations.

(4) In such cases as may be prescribed an employee's normal weekly earnings shall be calculated in accordance with regulations.

(5) Without prejudice to any other power to make regulations under this Part, regulations may specify cases in which , for the purposes of this Part or of such provisions of this Part as may be prescribed—

(a) two or more employers are to be treated as one;
(b) two or more contracts of service in respect of which the same person is an employee are to be treated as one.

(6) Regulations may provide for periods of work which begin on one day and finish on the following day to be treated, for purposes of this Part, as falling solely within one or other of those days.

(7) In this Part any reference to Great Britain includes a reference to the territorial waters of the United Kingdom adjacent to Great Britain.

. . . . . .

SCHEDULES

Section 3(3)

SCHEDULE 1

CIRCUMSTANCES IN WHICH PERIODS OF ENTITLEMENT DO NOT ARISE

1. A period of entitlement does not arise in relation to a particular period of incapacity for work in any of the circumstances set out in paragraph 2 below or in such other circumstances as may be prescribed.

2. The circumstances are that—
    (a) at the relevant date the employee is over pensionable age;
    (b) the employee's contract of service was entered into for a specified period of not more than three months;
    (c) at the relevant date the employee's normal weekly earnings are less than the lower earnings limit then in force under section 4(1)(a) of the principal Act;
    (d) the employee had—
        (i) in the period of 57 days ending immediately before the relevant date, at least one day which formed part of a period of interruption of employment; and
        (ii) at any time during that period of interruption of employment, an invalidity pension day (whether or not the day referred to in sub-paragraph (i) above);
    (e) in the period of 57 days ending immediately before the relevant date the employee had at least one day on which—
        (i) he was entitled to sickness benefit (or on which he would have been so entitled if he had satisfied the contribution conditions for sickness benefit mentioned in section 14(2)(a) of the principal Act); or
        (ii) she was entitled to a maternity allowance;
    (f) the employee has done no work for his employer under his contract of service;
    (g) on the relevant date there is, within the meaning of section 19 of the principal Act, a stoppage of work due to a trade dispute at the employee's place of employment;
    (h) before the relevant date the employee has reached his maximum entitlement to statutory sick pay as against the employer concerned, in the tax year in question; and
    (i) the employee is, or has been, pregnant and the relevant date falls within the disqualifying period (within the meaning of section 3(9) of this Act).

3. In this Schedule "relevant date" means the date on which a period of entitlement would begin in accordance with section 3 of this Act if this Schedule did not prevent it arising.

4.—(1) Paragraph 2(b) above does not apply in any case where—
    (a) at the relevant date the contract of service has become a contract for a period exceeding three months; or
    (b) the contract of service (the "current contract") was preceded by a contract of service entered into by the employee with the same employer (the "previous contract") and—
        (i) the interval between the date on which the previous contract ceased to have effect and that on which the current contract came into force was not more than eight weeks; and
        (ii) the aggregate of the period for which the previous contract had effect and

the period specified in the current contract (or, where that period has been extended, the specified period as so extended) exceeds thirteen weeks.

(2) For the purposes of sub-paragraph (1)(*b*)(ii) above, in any case where the employee entered into more than one contract of service with the same employer before the current contract, any of those contracts which came into effect not more than eight weeks after that date on which an earlier one of them ceased to have effect shall be treated as one with the earlier contract.

5.—(1) In paragraph 2(*d*) above "invalidity pension day" means a day—
   (*a*) for which the employee in question was entitled to an invalidity pension or a non-contributory invalidity pension; or
   (*b*) for which he was not so entitled but which was the last day of the invalidity pension qualifying period.

(2) In sub-paragraph (1)(*b*) above the "invalidity pension qualifying period" means the period mentioned in section 15(1) of the principal Act or, as the case may be, section 15(2) or 16(2) of the Social Security Pensions Act 1975 as falling within the period of interruption of employment referred to in that section.

6. For the purposes of paragraph 2(*f*) above, if an employee enters into a contract of service which is to take effect not more than eight weeks after the date on which a previous contract of service entered into by him with the same employer ceased to have effect, the two contracts shall be treated as one.

7. Paragraph 2(*g*) above does not apply in the case of an employee who proves that at no time on or before the relevant date did he participate in, or have a direct interest in, the trade dispute in question.

8. Paragraph 2(*i*) above does not apply in relation to an employee who has been pregnant if her pregnancy terminated, before the beginning of the disqualifying period, otherwise than by confinement (within the meaning of section 3(9) of this Act).

"employee": s.26.
"employer": s.26.
"invalidity pension day": para. 5.
"maximum entitlement": s.5.
"normal weekly earnings": s.26(2).
"pensionable age": s.26.
"period of entitlement": s.3.
"period of incapacity for work": s.2.
"period of interruption of employment": 1975 Act, s.17(1)(*d*).
"the principal Act": s.47.
"relevant date": para. 3.
"statutory sick pay": s.1.
"tax year": s.47.
"week": s.26.

Section 10   SCHEDULE 2   1–709

RELATIONSHIP WITH BENEFITS AND OTHER PAYMENTS, ETC.

. . . . . .

Contractual remuneration

. . . . . .

(2) Subject to sub-paragraph (3) below—
   (*a*) any contractual remuneration paid to an employee by an employer of his in respect of a day of incapacity for work shall go towards discharging any liability of that employer to pay statutory sick pay to that employee in respect of that day; and
   (*b*) any statutory sick pay paid by an employer to an employee of his in respect of a day of incapacity for work shall go towards discharging any liability of that employer to pay contractual remuneration to that employee in respect of that day.

PART II
STATUTORY INSTRUMENTS

Industrial Tribunals (England and Wales) Regulations 1965

(S.I. 1965 No. 1101)

Dated May 11, 1965, *and made by the Minister of Labour, after consultation with the Council on Tribunals, under the Industrial Training Act* 1964 (*c.* 16), *s.*12.

Title and commencement

1. These Regulations may be cited as the Industrial Tribunals (England and Wales) Regulations 1965 and shall come into operation on 31st May, 1965.

Interpretation

2. (1) In these Regulations, unless the context otherwise requires:—
"the Act" means the Industrial Training Act 1964;
"appellant" means a person who has appeal to a tribunal under the provisions of a levy order made under section 4 of the Act;
"the Board" means in relation to an appeal the respondent industrial training board;
"the clerk to the tribunal" means the person appointed by [the Secretary, or an Assistant Secretary, of the Tribunals][1] to act in that capacity at one or more hearings;
"hearing" means a sitting of a tribunal duly constituted for the purpose of receiving evidence, hearing addresses and witnesses or doing anything lawfully requisite to enable the tribunal to reach a decision on an appeal;
"levy" means a levy imposed under the Act;
"the Minister" means the Minister of Labour;
"the Office of the Tribunals" means the Central Office of the Industrial Tribunals (England and Wales);
["the panel of chairmen" means the panel of persons, being barristers or solicitors of not less than seven years' standing, appointed by the Lord Chancellor in pursuance of Regulation 5(2) of these Regulations;][2]
"the President" means the President of the Industrial Tribunals (England and Wales) or the person nominated by the Lord Chancellor to discharge for the time being the functions of the President;
"the Register of Appeals" means the Register of Industrial Levy Appeals and Decisions kept in pursuance of these Regulations;

---

[1] Substituted by the Industrial Tribunals (England and Wales) (Amendment) Regulations 1967 (S.I. 1967 No. 301).
[2] Added by the Industrial Tribunals (England and Wales) (Amendment) Regulations 1967 (S.I. 1967 No. 301).

"Rule" means a Rule of Procedure contained in [either Schedule][1] to these Regulations;

["the Secretary of the Tribunals" and "an Assistant Secretary of the Tribunals" mean respectively the persons for the time being acting as the Secretary or as an Assistant Secretary, of the Central Office of the Industrial Tribunals (England and Wales);][1]

"tribunal" means an industrial tribunal (England and Wales) established under these Regulations, and in relation to an appeal means the tribunal to which the appeal has been referred by the President [or by a member of the panel of chairmen for the time being nominated by the President].[2]

(2) [A form referred to by number in either Schedule to these Regulations means the form so numbered in the Appendix to that Schedule].[1]

(3) The Interpretation Act 1889 applies to the interpretation of these Regulations as it applies to the interpretation of an Act of Parliament.

President of Industrial Tribunals

2–004 3.—(1) There shall be a President of the Industrial Tribunals (England and Wales) who shall be appointed by the Lord Chancellor and shall be a barrister or solicitor of not less than seven years' standing.

[(2) The President shall vacate his office at the end of the completed year of service in the course of which he attains the age of seventy-two years.][3]

(3) The President may resign his office by notice in writing to the Lord Chancellor.

(4) If the Lord Chancellor is satisfied that the President is incapacitated by infirmity of mind or body from discharging the duties of his office, or if the President is adjudged bankrupt or makes a composition or arrangement with his creditors, the Lord Chancellor may revoke his appointment.

(5) The functions of the President under these Regulations may, if he is for any reason unable to act or during a vacancy in his office, be discharged by a person nominated for that purpose by the Lord Chancellor.

[*Establishment of Tribunals*

2–005 4.—(1) Such number of tribunals shall be established in England and Wales for the determination of appeals by persons assessed to a levy as the President may from time to time determine.

(2) The tribunals shall sit at such times and in such places as may from time to time be determined by the President or, in relation to any area specified by him in England and Wales, by a member of the panel of chairmen nominated by him to act in that area.][1]

Membership of Tribunals

2–006 5.—[(1) Subject to the provisions of paragraph (1A) of this Regulation, a tribunal shall consist of a chairman and two other members, but in the absence of any one member of a tribunal other than the chairman, an appeal may with the consent of the parties be heard in the absence of such member, and in that event the tribunal shall be deemed to be properly constituted.

(1A) A tribunal may consist of the President, the chairman of the tribunal or a member of the panel of chairmen for the time being nominated

---

[3] Substituted by the Industrial Tribunals (England and Wales) (Amendment) Regulations 1970 (S.I. 1970 No. 941).

for the purpose by the President, for any of the following purposes, that is to say—
(a) making an order dismissing the proceedings where the appellant or applicant has given written notice of the abandonment of his appeal or application;
(b) making an order allowing the appeal where the Board has given written notice that the appeal is not contested;
(c) deciding an appeal or application in accordance with the written agreement of the parties;
(d) dealing with any interlocutory matter or application;
(e) making an order for costs in connection with an order or decision mentioned in the foregoing sub-paragraphs of this paragraph.

(2) For each hearing the chairman shall be the President or a person selected from a panel of persons (being barristers or solicitors of not less than seven years' standing) appointed by the Lord Chancellor; such selection shall be made by the President or by a member of the said panel for the time being nominated by the President for the purpose, and that member may select himself.][1]

[(3) For each hearing the two members of a tribunal other than the chairman shall be selected by the President (or by a member of the panel of chairmen for the time being nominated by the President for the purpose), as to one member from a panel of persons appointed by the Secretary fo State after consultation with any organisation or association of organisations representative of employers, and as to the other member from a panel of persons appointed by the Secretary of State after consultation with any organisation or association of organisations representative of employed persons.][4]

(4) The President [(or a member of the panel of chairmen for the time being nominated by the President for the purpose)][2] may at any time select from the appropriate panel under another person in substitution for the chairman or other member of a tribunal previously selected [. . .][5] to hear an appeal.

(5) Members of panels constituted under these Regulations shall hold and vacate office under the terms of the instruments under which they are appointed, but may resign office by notice in writing in the case of a member of the panel of chairmen to the Lord Chancellor and in any other case to the Minister; and any such member who ceases to hold office shall be eligible for reappointment.

[*Procedure as to levy appeals*

6. The Rules of Procedure contained in Schedule 1 to these Regulations shall continue to have effect in relation to appeals by persons assessed to a levy under a levy order that came into operation before 13th March 1967, and the Rules of Procedure contained in Schedule 2 to these Regulations shall have effect in relation to appeals by persons assessed to a levy under a levy order coming into operation on or after that date.][1]

2–007

[*Proof of Decisions of Tribunals*

7. The production in any proceedings in any court of a document pur-

2–008

---

[4] Substituted by the Industrial Tribunals (Amendment) Regulations 1977 (S.I. 1977 No. 1473).

[5] Omitted by the Industrial Tribunals (England and Wales) (Amendment) Regulations 1967 (S.I. 1967 No. 301).

porting to be certified by the Secretary of the Tribunals to be a true copy of an entry of a decision in the Register of Appeals shall, unless the contrary is proved, be sufficient evidence of the document and of the facts stated therein.][2]

2–009

SCHEDULE 1

RULES OF PROCEDURE

Notice of Appeal

1. An appeal against an assessment to a levy shall be instituted by the appellant sending to the Secretary of the Tribunals in duplicate a written notice of appeal which shall be substantially in accordance with Form 1, and shall set out the grounds of the appeal.

Entering of appeal

2.—(1) Upon receiving a notice of appeal the Secretary of the Tribunals shall enter particulars of the appeal in the Register of Appeals, and shall forthwith send the duplicate notice to the Board, and shall inform the appellant and the Board in writing of the number of the appeal entered in the Register, which shall thereafter constitute the title of the appeal.

(2) Upon receiving the duplicate notice of appeal, the Board shall forthwith send to the Secretary of the Tribunals a copy of the assessment referred to therein.

Power to require further particulars

3.—(1) If the Board requires further particulars of the grounds on which the appellant intends to rely and of any facts and contentions relevant thereto, the Board may within 14 days of receiving the duplicate notice of appeal send to the appellant a notice specifying the particulars required by the Board and within the same time shall send a duplicate copy thereof to the Secretary of the Tribunals.

(2) The appellant shall within 14 days of the receipt of the notice send the further particulars to the Board and within the same time send a duplicate copy thereof to the Secretary of the Tribunals.

Power to require particulars of the assessment

4. The tribunal may at any time request the Board to furnish any particulars of the assessment which appear to be requisite for the decision of the appeal, and thereupon the Board shall send the particulars to the Secretary of the Tribunals and to the appellant.

Time and place of hearing

5. The President shall fix the date, time and place of the hearing of an appeal and the Secretary of the Tribunals shall not less than 14 days before the date so fixed send to the appellant and to the Board a notice substantially in accordance with Form 2.

The hearing

6.—(1) The hearing of an appeal shall take place in private, unless the tribunal determines at the request of the appellant to hear the appeal in public, but a member of the Council on Tribunals shall be entitled to attend the hearing of any appeal in his capacity as such member.

(2) If the appellant or the Board shall desire to submit representations in writing relating to an appeal for consideration by the tribunal at the hearing of such appeal the appellant or the Board, as the case may be, shall send such representations to the Secretary of the Tribunals not less than 7 days before the hearing and shall at the same time send a copy thereof to the other party.

Representation

7.—(1) The appellant may appear at the hearing of his appeal, and may be heard in person or be represented by counsel or solicitor or by any other person.

(2) The Board may appear at the hearing of an appeal, and may be represented by any member or officer thereof or by counsel or solicitor.

Procedure at hearing

8.—(1) The appellant and the Board shall be entitled to make opening statements, to call witnesses, to cross-examine any witnesses called by the other party and to address the tribunal.

(2) The appellant may if he so desires give evidence on his own behalf.

(3) If the appellant or the Board or both of them shall fail to appear or to be represented at the time and place fixed for the hearing of an appeal, the tribunal may dispose of the appeal in the absence of such party or parties or may adjourn the hearing to a later date: Provided that before disposing of an appeal in the absence of either or both parties the tribunal shall consider any representations submitted by such party or parties under Rule 6(2).

(4) The tribunal may require any witnesses to give evidence on oath or affirmation, and for that purpose the chairman may administer an oath or affirmation in due form.

Decision of tribunal

9.—(1) The decision of the tribunal may be taken by a majority thereof and, if in accordance with Regulation 5(1) the tribunal shall be constituted of two members only, the chairman shall have a second or casting vote.

(2) The decision of the tribunal shall be recorded in a document signed by the chairman which shall contain the reasons for the decision.

(3) The clerk to the tribunal shall transmit the document signed by the chairman to the Secretary of the Tribunals who shall as soon as may be enter it in the Register of Appeals, and shall send a copy of the entry to the appellant and the Board.

(4) The Register of Appeals shall be kept at the Office of the Tribunals and shall be open to the inspection of any person without charge at all reasonable hours.

(5) The chairman of the tribunal shall have power by certificate under his hand to correct any clerical mistake or error in a decision of the tribunal arising from any accidental slip or omission.

(6) A copy of any decision so corrected shall be sent by the clerk to the tribunal with the certificate of the chairman to the Secretary of the Tribunals who shall thereupon enter the correction in the Register of Appeals and shall send a copy of the corrected entry to the appellant and the Board.

Miscellaneous powers of tribunal

10.—(1) The tribunal may if it thinks fit:
  (*a*) extend the time appointed by these Rules for doing any act notwithstanding that the time appointed may have expired;
  (*b*) postpone the day or time fixed for, or adjourn the hearing of, any appeal;
  (*c*) at the request of the appellant or the Board by notice summon any person to appear before the tribunal to be examined;
  (*d*) if the appellant shall at any time give notice of the abandonment of his appeal, dismiss the appeal;
  (*e*) if the appellant and the Board agree in writing upon the terms of a decision to be made by the tribunal, decide accordingly.

(2) Subject to the provisions of these Rules the tribunal may regulate its own procedure.

(3) Any act other than the consideration of an appeal, required or authorised by these Rules to be done by the tribunal, may be done by, or on the direction of, the President or the chairman of the tribunal.

Applications

11.—(1) An application to the tribunal for an extension of the time appointed by these Rules for doing any act may be made by the appellant or the Board either before or after the expiration of the time so appointed.

(2) The appellant or the Board may at any time apply to the tribunal for directions on any matter arising in connection with an appeal.

(3) An application under the foregoing provisions of this Rule or for an extension of the time for appealing against an assessment to a levy shall be made by sending to the Secretary of the Tribunals in duplicate a notice of application which shall state the title of the appeal, or the number of the assessment if an appeal has not been instituted, and shall set out the grounds of the application.

Notices, etc.

12.—(1) Any notice required by these Rules shall be in writing, and all notices and docu-

ments required or authorised by these Rules to be sent or given to any person may be sent by the recorded delivery service or delivered—
   (a) in the case of a document directed to the Secretary of the Tribunals, to the Office of the Tribunals;
   (b) in the case of a document directed to a Board, to the office of the Board;
   (c) in the case of a document directed to the appellant, to his address for service specified in any notice given under these Rules, or to his last known address or place of business in the United Kingdom or, if the appellant is a company, to the company's registered office;
and if sent or given to the authorised representative of the appellant or the Board shall be deemed to have been sent or given to him or the Board as the case may be.
   (2) The appellant may at any time by notice to the Secretary of the Tribunals and to the Board change his address for service under these Rules.

2–010 # Industrial Tribunals (Improvement and Prohibition Notices Appeals) Regulations 1974

(S.I. 1974 No. 1925)

Dated November 18, 1974, *and made by the Secretary of State for Employment under the Trade Union and Labour Relations Act* 1974 (c. 52), *Sched.* 1, *para.* 21, *and the Health and Safety at Work etc. Act* 1974 (c. 37), *s.*24(2).

Citation and commencement

1. These Regulations may be cited as the Industrial Tribunals (Improvement and Prohibition Notices Appeals) Regulations 1974 and shall come into operation on 1st January 1975.

Interpretation

2–011   **2.**—(1) The Interpretation Act 1889 shall apply to the interpretation of these Regulations as it applies to the interpretation of an Act of Parliament.
   (2) In these Regulations, unless the context otherwise requires, the following expressions have the meanings hereby assigned to them respectively, that is to say—
   "appellant" means a person who has appealed to a tribunal under section 24 of the principal Act;
   "the clerk to the tribunal" means the person appointed by the Secretary of the Tribunals or an Assistant Secretary to act in that capacity at one or more hearings;
   "decision" in relation to a tribunal includes a direction under Rule 4 and any other order which is not an interlocutory order;
   "hearing" means a sitting of a tribunal duly constituted for the purpose of receiving evidence, hearing addresses and witnesses or doing anything lawfully requisite to enable the tribunal to reach a decision on any question;
   "improvement notice" means a notice under section 21 of the principal Act;

"inspector" means a person appointed under section 19(1) of the principal Act;

"nominated chairman" means a member of the panel of chairmen for the time being nominated by the President;

"the Office of the Tribunals" means the Central Office of the Industrial Tribunals (England and Wales);

"the panel of chairmen" means the panel of persons, being barristers or solicitors of not less than seven years' standing, appointed by the Lord Chancellor in pursuance of Regulation 5(2) of the Industrial Tribunal (England and Wales) Regulations 1965, as amended;

"party" means the appellant and the respondent;

"the President" means the President of the Industrial Tribunals (England and Wales) or the person nominated by the Lord Chancellor to discharge for the time being the functions of the President);

"the principal Act" means the Health and Safety at Work etc. Act 1974;

"prohibition notice" means a notice under section 22 of the principal Act;

"Regional Office of the Industrial Tribunals" means a regional office which has been established under the Office of the Tribunals for an area specified by the President;

"Register" means the Register kept in pursuance of the Industrial Tribunals (Labour Relations) Regulations 1974;

"respondent" means the inspector who issued the improvement notice or prohibition notice which is the subject of the appeal;

"Rule" means a Rule of Procedure contained in the Schedule to these Regulations;

"the Secretary of the Tribunals" and "an Assistant Secretary of the Tribunals" mean respectively the persons for the time being acting as the Secretary of the Office of the Tribunals and as the Assistant Secretary of a Regional Office of the Industrial Tribunals;

"tribunal" means an industrial tribunal (England and Wales) established in pursuance of the Industrial Tribunals (England and Wales) Regulations 1965, as amended, and in relation to any proceedings means the tribunal to which the proceedings have been referred by the President or by a nominated chairman.

Proceedings of tribunals

3. The Rules of Procedure contained in the Schedule to these Regulations shall have effect in relation to appeals to a tribunal under section 24 of the principal Act against improvement notices or prohibition notices relating to matters arising in England or Wales.

Proof of decisions of tribunals

4. The production in any proceedings in any court of a document purporting to be certified by the Secretary of the Tribunals to be a true copy of an entry of a decision in the Register shall, unless the contrary is proved, be sufficient evidence of the document and of the facts stated therein.

Regulation 3

SCHEDULE
Rules of Procedure

Notice of Appeal

1. An Appeal shall be commenced by the appellant sending to the Secretary of the Tribunals a notice of appeal which shall be in writing and shall set out:—
   (a) the name of the appellant and his address for the service of documents;
   (b) the date of the improvement notice or prohibition notices appealed against and the address of the premises or place concerned;
   (c) the name and address of the respondent;
   (d) particulars of the requirements or directions appealed against; and
   (e) the grounds of the appeal.

Time limit for bringing appeal

2.—(1) Subject to paragraph (2) of this Rule, the notice of appeal shall be sent to the Secretary of the Tribunals within 21 days from the date of the service on the appellant of the notice appealed against.

(2) A tribunal may extend the time mentioned above where it is satisfied on an application made in writing to the Secretary of the Tribunals either before or after the expiration of that time that it is not or was not reasonably practicable for an appeal to be brought within that time.

Action upon receipt of notice of appeal

3. Upon receiving a notice of appeal the Secretary of the Tribunals shall enter particulars of it in the Register and shall forthwith send a copy of it to the respondent and inform the parties in writing of the case number of the appeal entered in the Register (which shall thereafter constitute the title of the proceedings) and of the address to which notices and other communications to the Secretary of the Tribunals shall be sent.

Application for direction suspending the operation of a prohibition notice

4.—(1) Where an appeal has been brought against a prohibition notice and an application is made to the tribunal by the appellant in pursuance of section 24(3)(b) of the principal Act for a direction suspending the operation of the notice until the appeal is finally disposed of or withdrawn, the application shall be sent in writing to the Secretary of the Tribunals and shall set out:—
   (a) the case number of the appeal if known to the appellant or particulars sufficient to identify the appeal; and
   (b) the grounds on which the application is made.

(2) Upon receiving the application, the Secretary of the Tribunals shall enter particulars of it against the entry in the Register relating to the appeal and shall forthwith send a copy of it to the respondent.

Power to require attendance of witnesses and production of documents, etc.

5.—(1) A tribunal may on the application of a party made either by notice to the Secretary of the Tribunals or at the hearing—
   (a) require a party to furnish in writing to another party further particulars of the grounds on which he relies and of any facts and contentions relevant thereto;
   (b) grant to a party such discovery or inspection of documents as might be granted by a county court; and
   (c) require the attendance of any person as a witness or require the production of any document relating to the matter to be determined.

and may appoint the time at or within which or the place at which any act required in pursuance of this Rule is to be done.

(2) The tribunal shall not under paragraph (1) of this Rule require the production of any document certified by the Secretary of State as being a document of which the production would be against the interests of national security.

(3) A person on whom a requirement has been made under paragraph (1) of this Rule may apply to the tribunal either by notice to the Secretary of the Tribunals or at the hearing to vary or set aside the requirement.

(4) No such application to vary or set aside shall be entertained in a case where a time has been appointed under paragraph (1) of this Rule in relation to the requirement unless it is made before the time or, as the case may be, expiration of the time so appointed.

(5) Every document containing a requirement under paragraph (1)(b) or (c) of this Rule shall contain a reference to the fact that under paragraph 21(6) of Schedule 1 to the Trade

Union and Labour Relations Act 1974 any person who without reasonable excuse fails to comply with any such requirement shall be liable on summary conviction to a fine not exceeding £100.

Time and place of hearing and appointment of assessor

6.—(1) The President or a nominated chairman shall fix the date, time and place of the hearing of the appeal and of any application under Rule 4, and the Secretary of the Tribunals shall not less than 14 days (or such shorter time as may be agreed by him with the parties) before the date so fixed send to each party a notice of hearing which shall include information and guidance as to attendance at the hearing, witnesses, and the bringing of documents (if any), representation by another person and written representations.

(2) Where the President or a nominated chairman so directs, the Secretary of the Tribunals shall also send notice of the hearing to such persons as may be directed, but the requirement as to the period of notice contained in the foregoing paragraph of this Rule shall not apply to any such notices.

(3) The President or a nominated chairman may, if he thinks fit, appoint in pursuance of section 24(4) of the principal Act a person or persons having special knowledge or experience in relation to the subject matter of the appeal to sit with the tribunal as assessor or assessors.

The hearing

7.—(1) Any hearing of or in connection with an appeal shall take place in public unless the tribunal on the application of a party decides that a private hearing is appropriate for the purpose of hearing evidence which relates to matters of such a nature that it would be against the interests of national security to allow the evidence to be given in public or hearing evidence from any person which in the opinion of the tribunal is likely to consist of information the disclosure of which would be seriously prejudicial to the interests of the undertaking of the appellant or of any undertaking in which he works for reasons other than its effect on negotiations with respect to any of the matters mentioned in section 29(1) of the Trade Union and Labour Relations Act 1974.

(2) In cases to which the foregoing provisions of this Rule apply, a member of the Council on Tribunals in his capacity as such shall be entitled to attend the hearing.

Written representations

8. If a party shall desire to submit representations in writing for consideration by a tribunal at the hearing of the appeal, that party shall send such representations to the Secretary of the Tribunals not less than 7 days before the hearing and shall at the same time send a copy of it to the other party.

Right of appearance

9. At any hearing of or in connection with an appeal a party may appear before the tribunal in person or may be represented by counsel or by a solicitor or by any other person whom he desires to represent him, including in the case of the appellant a representative of a trade union or an employers' association.

Procedure at hearing

10.—(1) At any hearing of or in connection with an appeal a party shall be entitled to make an opening statement, to give evidence on his own behalf, to call witnesses, to cross-examine any witnesses called by the other party and to address the tribunal.

(2) If a party shall fail to appear or to be represented at the time and place fixed for the hearing of an appeal, the tribunal may dispose of the appeal in the absence of that party or may adjourn the hearing to a later date: Provided that before disposing of an appeal in the absence of a party the tribunal shall consider any written representations submitted by that party in pursuance of Rule 8.

(3) A tribunal may require any witness to give evidence on oath or affirmation and for that purpose there may be administered an oath or affirmation in due form.

Decision of tribunal

11.—(1) A decision of a tribunal may be taken by a majority thereof and, if the tribunal shall be constituted of two members only, the chairman shall have a second or casting vote.

(2) The decision of a tribunal shall be recorded in a document signed by the chairman which shall contain the reasons for the decision.

(3) The clerk to the tribunal shall transmit the document signed by the chairman to the Secretary of the Tribunals who shall as soon as may be enter it in the Register and shall send a copy of the entry to each of the parties.

(4) The specification of the reasons for the decision shall be omitted from the Register in any case in which evidence has been heard in private and the tribunal so directs and in that event a specification of the reasons shall be sent to the parties and to any superior court in any proceedings relating to such decision together with the copy of the entry.

(5) The Register shall be kept at the Office of the Tribunals and shall be open to the inspection of any person without charge at all reasonable hours.

(6) The chairman of a tribunal shall have power by certificate under his hand to correct in documents recording the tribunal's decisions clerical mistakes or errors arising therein from any accidental slip or omission.

(7) The clerk to the tribunal shall send a copy of any document so corrected and the certificate of the chairman to the Secretary of the Tribunals who shall as soon as may be make such correction as may be necessary in the Register and shall send a copy of the corrected entry or of the corrected specification of the reasons, as the case may be, to each of the parties.

(8) If any decision is—
  (a) corrected under paragraph (6) of this Rule; or
  (b) reviewed, revoked or varied under Rule 12; or
  (c) altered in any way by order of a superior court;
the Secretary of the Tribunals shall alter the entry in the Register to conform with any such certificate or order and shall send a copy of the new entry to each of the parties.

Review of tribunal's decision
12.—(1) A tribunal shall have power on the application of a party to review and to revoke or vary by certificate under the chairman's hand any of its decisions in a case in which a county court has power to order a new trial on the grounds that—
  (a) the decision was wrongly made as a result of an error on the part of the tribunal staff; or
  (b) a party did not receive notice of the proceedings leading to the decision; or
  (c) the decision was made in the absence of a party; or
  (d) new evidence has become available since the making of the decision provided that its existence could not have been reasonably known of or foreseen; or
  (e) the interests of justice require such a review.

(2) An application for the purposes of paragraph (1) of this Rule may be made at the hearing. If the application is not made at the hearing, such application shall be made to the Secretary of the Tribunals within 14 days from the date of the entry of a decision in the Register and must be in writing stating the grounds in full.

(3) An application for the purposes of paragraph (1) of this Rule may be refused by the chairman of the tribunal which decided the case, by the President or by a nominated chairman if in his opinion it has no reasonable prospect of success and he shall state the reasons for his opinion.

(4) If such an application is not refused under paragraph (3) of this Rule, it shall be heard by the tribunal and if it is granted the tribunal shall either vary its decision or revoke its decision and order a re-hearing.

(5) The clerk to the tribunal shall send to the Secretary of the Tribunals the certificate of the chairman as to any revocation or variation of the tribunal's decision under this Rule. The Secretary of the Tribunals shall as soon as may be make such correction as may be necessary in the Register and shall send a copy of the entry to each of the parties.

Costs
13.—(1) A tribunal may make an order that a party shall pay to another party either a specified sum in respect of the costs of or in connection with an appeal incurred by that other party or, in default of agreement, the taxed amount of those costs.

(2) Any costs required by an order under this Rule to be taxed may be taxed in the county court according to such of the scales prescribed by the county court rules for proceedings in the county court as shall be directed by the order.

Miscellaneous powers of tribunal
14.—(1) Subject to the provisions of these Rules, a tribunal may regulate its own procedure.

(2) A tribunal may, if it thinks fit—
  (a) postpone the day or time fixed for, or adjourn, any hearing;

(b) before granting an application under Rule 5 or 12 require the party making the application to give notice thereof to the other party;

(c) either on the application of any person or of its own motion, direct any other person to be joined as a party to the appeal (giving such consequential directions as it considers necessary), but may do so only after having given to the person proposed to be joined a reasonable opportunity of making written or oral objection;

(d) make any necessary amendments to the description of a party in the Register and in other documents relating to the appeal;

(e) if the appellant shall at any time give notice of the abandonment of his appeal, dismiss for the appeal;

(f) if the parties agree in writing upon the terms of a decision to be made by the tribunal, decide accordingly.

(3) Any act, other than the hearing of an appeal or of an application for the purposes of Rule 4 or 12(1) or the granting of an extension of time under Rule 2(2), required or authorised by these Rules to be done by a tribunal may be done by, or on the direction of, the President, the chairman of the tribunal or a nominated chairman.

(4) Rule 13 shall apply to an order dismissing proceedings under paragraph (2) of this Rule.

(5) Where the President so directs, any function of the Secretary of the Tribunals may be performed by an Assistant Secretary of the Tribunals and a notice of appeal under Rule 1, an application under Rule 4, and any other notice or other document required by these Rules to be sent to the Secretary of the Tribunals may be sent either to the Secretary of the Tribunals or to an Assistant Secretary of the Tribunals in accordance with such direction.

Notices, etc.

15.—(1) Any notice given under these Rules shall be in writing and all notices and documents required or authorised by these Rules to be sent or given to any person hereinafter mentioned may be sent by post (subject to paragraphs (3) and (4) of this Rule) or delivered to or at—

(a) in the case of a document directed to the Secretary of the Tribunals, the Office of the Tribunals or such other office as may be notified by the Secretary of the Tribunals to the parties;

(b) in the case of a document directed to a party, his address for service specified in the notice of appeal or in a notice under paragraph (2) of this Rule or (if no address for service is so specified), his last known address or place of business in the United Kingdom or, if the party is a corporation, the corporation's registered or principal office;

(c) in the case of a document directed to any person (other than a person specified in the foregoing provisions of this paragraph), his address or place of business in the United Kingdom, or if such a person is a corporation, the corporation's registered or principal office;

and if sent or given to the authorised representative of a party shall be deemed to have been sent or given to that party.

(2) A party may at any time by notice to the Secretary of the Tribunals and to the other party change his address for service under these Rules.

(3) Where a notice of appeal is not delivered, it shall be sent by the recorded delivery service.

(4) Where for any sufficient reason service of any document or notice cannot be effected in the manner prescribed under this Rule, the President or a nominated chairman may make an order for substituted service in such manner as he may deem fit and such service shall have the same effect as service in the manner prescribed under this Rule.

(5) In the case of an appeal to which the respondent is an inspector appointed otherwise than by the Health and Safety Executive, the Secretary of the Tribunals shall send to that Executive copies of the notice of appeal and the document recording the decision of the tribunal on the appeal.

Rehabilitation of Offenders Act 1974 (Exceptions) Order 1975   2–015

(S.I. 1975 No. 1023)

Dated June 24, 1975, and made by the Secretary of State for Home Affairs under the Rehabilitation of Offenders Act 1974 (c. 53), ss.4(4) and 7(4).

1. This Order may be cited as the Rehabilitation of Offenders Act 1974 (Exceptions) Order 1975 and shall come into operation on 1st July 1975.

2.—(1) In this Order "the Act" means the Rehabilitation of Offenders Act 1974.

(2) Where, by virtue of this Order, the operation of any of the provisions of the Act is excluded in relation to spent convictions the exclusion shall be taken to extend to spent convictions for offences of every description.

(3) Part IV of Schedule 1 to this Order shall have effect for the interpretation of expressions used in that Schedule.

(4) In this Order a reference to any enactment shall be construed as a reference to that enactment as amended, extended or applied by or under any other enactment.

(5) The Interpretation Act 1889 shall apply to the interpretation of this Order as it applies to the interpretation of an Act of Parliament.

3. None of the provisions of section 4(2) of the Act shall apply in relation to—
   (a) any question asked by or on behalf of any person, in the course of the duties of his office or employment, in order to assess the suitability—
      (i) of the person to whom the question relates for admission to any of the professions specified in Part I of Schedule 1 to this Order; or
      (ii) of the person to whom the question relates for any office or employment specified in Part II of the said Schedule 1; or
      (iii) of the person to whom the question relates or of any other person to pursue any occupation specified in Part III of the said Schedule 1 or to pursue it subject to a particular condition or restriction; or
      (iv) of the person to whom the question relates or of any other person to hold a licence, certificate or permit of a kind specified in Schedule 2 to this Order or to hold it subject to a particular condition or restriction,
   where the person questioned is informed at the time the question is asked that, by virtue of this Order, spent convictions are to be disclosed;
   (b) any question asked by or on behalf of any person, in the course of his duties as a person employed in the service of the Crown, the United Kingdom Atomic Energy Authority, the Civil Aviation Authority or the Post Office Corporation, in order to assess for the purpose of safeguarding national security, the suitability of the person to whom the question relates or of any other person for any office or employment where the person questioned is informed at the time the question is asked that, by virtue of this Order, spent convictions are to be disclosed for the purpose of safeguarding national security.

4. Paragraph (b) of section 4(3) of the Act shall not apply in relation to—
   (a) the dismissal or exclusion of any person from any profession specified in Part I of Schedule 1 to this Order;
   (b) any office, employment or occupation specified in Part II or Part III of the said Schedule 1;

(*c*) any action taken for the purpose of safeguarding national security.

5. Section 4(1) of the Act shall not apply in relation to any proceedings specified in Schedule 3 to this Order.

Articles 2(3), 3 and 4   SCHEDULE 1   2–016

EXCEPTED PROFESSIONS, OFFICES, EMPLOYMENTS AND OCCUPATIONS

PART I

Professions
1. Medical practitioner.
2. Barrister (in England and Wales), advocate (in Scotland), solicitor.
3. Chartered accountant, certified accountant.
4. Dentist, dental hygienist, dental auxiliary.
5. Veterinary surgeon.
6. Nurse, midwife.
7. Ophthalmic optician, dispensing optician.
8. Pharmaceutical chemist.
9. Registered teacher (in Scotland).
10. Any profession to which the Professions Supplementary to Medicine Act 1960 applies and which is undertaken following registration under that Act.

PART II

Offices and employments
1. Judicial appointments.
2. The Director of Public Prosecutions and any employment in his office.
3. Procurators Fiscal and District Court Prosecutors, and any employment in the office of a Procurator Fiscal or District Court Prosecutor or in the Crown Office.
4. Justices' clerks and their assistants.
5. Clerks (including depute and assistant clerks) and officers of the High Court of Justiciary, the Court of Session and the district court, sheriff clerks (including sheriff clerks depute) and their clerks and assistants.
6. Constables, persons appointed as police cadets to undergo training with a view to becoming constables and persons employed for the purposes of, or to assist the constables of, a police force established under any enactment; naval, military and air force police.
7. Any employment which is concerned with the administration of, or is otherwise normally carried out wholly or partly within the precincts of, a prison, remand centre, detention centre, Borstal institution or young offenders institution, and members of boards of visitors appointed under section 6 of the Prison Act 1952 or of visiting committees appointed under section 7 of the Prisons (Scotland) Act 1952.
8. Traffic wardens appointed under section 81 of the Road Traffic Regulations Act 1967 or section 9 of the Police (Scotland) Act 1967.
9. Probation officers appointed under Schedule 3 to the Powers of Criminal Courts Act 1973.
10. Any employment as a teacher in a school or establishment for further education and any other employment which is carried out wholly or partly within the precincts of a school or establishment for further education, being employment which is of such a kind to enable the holder to have access to persons under the age of 18 in attendance at the school or establishment for further education in the course of his normal duties.
11. Proprietors of independent schools.
12. Any employment by a local authority in connection with the provision of social services or by any other body in connection with the provision by it of similar services, being employment which is of such a kind as to enable the holder to have access to any of the following classes of person in the course of his normal duties, namely—
    (*a*) persons under the age of 18 or over the age of 65;
    (*b*) persons suffering from serious illness or mental disorder of any description;
    (*c*) persons addicted to alcohol or drugs;

(d) persons who are blind, deaf or dumb;
(e) other persons who are substantially and permanently handicapped by illness, injury or congenital deformity.

13. Any employment which is concerned with the provision of health services and which is of such a kind as to enable the holder to have access to persons in receipt of such services in the course of his normal duties.

14. Any employment by a youth club, local authority or other body which is concerned with the promotion of leisure or recreational activities for persons under the age of 18, being employment which is of such a kind as to enable the holder to have access to such persons in the course of his normal duties.

15. Any employment within a cadet force concerned with naval, military or air force training for persons under the age of 18, being employment which is of such a kind as to enable the holder to have access to such persons in the course, of his normal duties.

PART III

Regulated occupations

2–017

1. Firearms dealer.
2. Any occupation in respect of which an application to the Gaming Board for Great Britain for a licence, certificate or registration is required by or under any enactment.
3. Director, controller or manager of an insurance company—
    (a) in respect of which the Secretary of State's authorisation is required under section 3(1)(b) of the Insurance Companies Act 1974 for it to carry on insurance business; or
    (b) to which Part II of that Act applies.
4. Dealer in securities.
5. Manager or trustee under a unit trust scheme.
6. Any occupation which is concerned with—
    (a) the management of a place in respect of which the approval of the Secretary of State is required by section 1 of the Abortion Act 1967; or
    (b) in England and Wales, carrying on a nursing home in respect of which registration is required by section 187 of the Public Health Act 1936 or section 14 of the Mental Health Act 1959; or
    (c) in Scotland, carrying on a nursing home in respect of which registration is required under section 1 of the Nursing Homes Registration (Scotland) Act 1938 or a private hospital in respect of which registration is required under section 15 of the Mental Health (Scotland) Act 1960.
7. Any occupation which is concerned with carrying on an establishment in respect of which registration is required by section 37 of the National Assistance Act 1948 or section 61 of the Social Work (Scotland) Act 1968.
8. Any occupation in respect of which the holder, as occupier of premises on which explosives are kept, is required by any Order in Council made under section 43 of the Explosives Act 1875 to obtain from the police or a court of summary jurisdiction a certificate as to his fitness to keep the explosives.

2–018

PART IV

Interpretation

In this Schedule—

"certified accountant" means a member of the Association of Certified Accountants;

"chartered accountant" means a member of the Institute of Chartered Accountants in England and Wales or of the Institute of Chartered Accountants of Scotland;

"dealer in securities" means a person dealing in securities within the meaning of section 26(1) of the Prevention of Fraud (Investments) Act 1958;

"firearms dealer" has the meaning assigned to that expression by section 57(4) of the Firearms Act 1968;

"further education" has the meaning assigned to that expression by section 41 of the Education Act 1944 or, in Scotland, section 4 of the Education (Scotland) Act 1962;

"health services" means services provided under the National Health Service Acts 1946 to 1973 or the National Health Service (Scotland) Acts 1947 to 1973 and similar services provided otherwise than under the National Health Service;

"insurance company" has the meaning assigned to that expression by section 85 of the Insurance Companies Act 1974 and, in relation to an insurance company, "director" shall be construed in accordance with that section and "controller" and "manager" shall be construed in accordance with section 7 of that Act;

"judicial appointment" means an appointment to any office by virtue of which the holder has power (whether alone or with others) under any enactment or rule of law to determine any question affecting the rights, privileges, obligations or liabilities of any person;

"proprietor" and "independent school" have the meanings assigned to those expressions by section 114(1) of the Education Act 1944 or, in Scotland, section 145 of the Education (Scotland) Act 1962;

"registered teacher" means a teacher registered under the Teaching Council (Scotland) Act 1965 and includes a provisionally registered teacher;

"school" has the meaning assigned to that expression by section 114(1) of the Education Act 1944 or, in Scotland, section 145 of the Education (Scotland) Act 1962;

"social services", in relation to a local authority, means—
  (a) in England and Wales, services provided by the authority in discharging its social services functions within the meaning of the Local Authority Social Services Act 1970;
  (b) in Scotland, services provided by the authority in discharging functions referred to in section 2(2) of the Social Work (Scotland) Act 1968;

"teacher" includes a warden of a community centre, leader of a youth club or similar institution, youth worker and, in Scotland, youth and community worker;

"unit trust scheme" has the meaning assigned to that expression by section 26(1) of the Prevention of Fraud (Investments) Act 1958 and, in relation thereto, "manager" and "trustee" shall be construed in accordance with section 26(3) of that Act.

Article 3   SCHEDULE 2

EXCEPTED LICENCES, CERTIFICATES AND PERMITS

1. Firearm certificates and shot gun certificates issued under the Firearms Act 1968, and permits issued under section 7(1), 9(2) or 13(1)(c) of that Act.

2. Licences issued under section 25 of the Children and Young Persons Act 1933 (which relates to persons under the age of 18 going abroad for the purpose of performing or being exhibited for profit).

3. Certificates issued by the police or a court of summary jurisdiction under any Order in Council made under section 43 of the Explosives Act 1875 as to the fitness of a person to keep explosives for private use.

Article 5   SCHEDULE 3

EXCEPTED PROCEEDINGS

1. Proceedings in respect of a person's admission to, or disciplinary proceedings against a member of, any profession specified in Part I of Schedule 1 to this Order.

2. Proceedings before the Court of Appeal or the High Court in the exercise of their disciplinary jurisdiction in respect of solicitors.

3. Disciplinary proceedings against a constable.

4. Proceedings before the Gaming Board for Great Britain.

5. Proceedings under the Mental Health Act 1959 before any Mental Health Review Tribunal, or under the Mental Health (Scotland) Act 1960 before the Sheriff or the Mental Welfare Commission for Scotland.

6. Proceedings under the Firearms Act 1968 in respect of—
  (a) the registration of a person as a firearms dealer, the removal of a person's name from a register of firearms dealers or the imposition, variation or revocation of conditions of any such registration; or
  (b) the grant, renewal, variation or revocation of a firearm certificate; or
  (c) the grant, renewal or revocation of a shot gun certificate; or
  (d) the grant of a permit under section 7(1), 9(2) or 13(1)(c) of that Act.

7. Proceedings in respect of the grant, renewal or variation of a licence under section 25 of the Children and Young Persons Act 1933 (which relates to persons under the age of 18 going abroad for the purpose of performing or being exhibited for profit).

500   Rehabilitation of Offenders Act 1974 (Exceptions) Order 1975

8. Proceedings—
   (a) in respect of an application under section 3(1)(b) of the Insurance Companies Act 1974 for the Secretary of State's authorisation to carry on insurance business; or
   (b) in respect of a notice under section 38 or 39 of that Act (which relate to notification of the proposed exercise of certain powers conferred by the Act on the Secretary of State); or
   (c) under section 52 or 53 of that Act (which relate to the Secretary of State's approval of appointments in insurance companies).

9. Proceedings in respect of a determination by the Secretary of State as to the suitability of a person—
   (a) for employment as a teacher in a school or establishment for further education (within the meaning of paragraph 10 of Part II of Schedule 1 to this Order), or in determining the extent to which a person may be employed as such a teacher; or
   (b) to be the proprietor of an independent school (within the meaning of paragraph 11 of the said Part II),
(including proceedings before an Independent Schools Tribunal in respect of the above matters under section 72 of the Education Act 1944 or section 113 of the Education (Scotland) Act 1962).

10. Proceedings under the Prevention of Fraud (Investments) Act 1958 in respect of an application for, or revocation of,—
   (a) a licence to deal in securities; or
   (b) an order by the Secretary of State declaring a person to be an exempted dealer for the purposes of that Act; or
   (c) an order by the Secretary of State declaring a unit trust scheme to be an authorised unit trust scheme for the purposes of that Act,
(including proceedings under section 6 of that Act before the tribunal of inquiry constituted under that section in respect of a licence to deal in securities).

11. Proceedings in respect of an application for, or cancellation of,—
   (a) the Secretary of State's approval of a place under section 1 of the Abortion Act 1967; or
   (b) in England and Wales, registration in respect of a nursing home under section 187 of the Public Health Act 1936 or section 14 of the Mental Health Act 1959; or
   (c) in Scotland, registration in respect of a nursing home under section 1 of the Nursing Homes Registration (Scotland) Act 1938 or of a private hospital under section 15 of the Mental Health (Scotland) Act 1960.

12. Proceedings in respect of an application for, or cancellation of, registration under section 37 of the National Assistance Act 1948 or section 61 of the Social Work (Scotland) Act 1968 in respect of any such establishment as is mentioned in those sections.

13. Proceedings on an application to the police or a court of summary jurisdiction for a certificate under any Order in Council made under section 43 of the Explosives Act 1875 as to the fitness of the applicant to keep explosives.

14. Proceedings by way of appeal against, or review of, any decision taken by virtue of any of the provisions of this Order, on consideration of a spent conviction.

15. Proceedings held for the receipt of evidence affecting the determination of any question arising in any proceedings specified in this Schedule.

2–021   **Sex Discrimination (Formal Investigations) Regulations 1975**

(S.I. 1975 No. 1993)

Dated December 3, 1975, and made by the Home Secretary under the Sex Discrimination Act 1975 (c. 65), ss.58(3), 59(1), 67(2) and 82(1).

Citation and operation
   1. These Regulations may be cited as the Sex Discrimination (Formal

Investigations) Regulations 1975 and shall come into operation on 29th December 1975.

Interpretation
2.—(1) In these Regulations any reference to the Act is a reference to the Sex Discrimination Act 1975.

(2) Any reference to the Commission, in Regulations 4, 5 and 6 below, is a reference to the Equal Opportunities Commission except that, as respects any of the functions of the Commission in relation to a formal investigation which the Commission have delegated under section 57(3) of the Act, any such reference in Regulation 4 or 5 is a reference to the persons, being either Commissioners or Additional Commissioners, to whom those functions have been so delegated.

(3) The Interpretation Act 1889 shall apply for the interpretation of these Regulations as it applies for the interpretation of an Act of Parliament.

Service of notices
3. Any reference to a person being served with a notice, in Regulations 4, 5 and 6 below, is a reference to service of the notice on him being effected—
   (a) by delivering it to him; or
   (b) by sending it by post to him at his usual or last-known residence or place of business; or
   (c) where the person is a body corporate or is a trade union or employers' association within the meaning of the Trade Union and Labour Relations Act 1974, by delivering it to the secretary or clerk of the body, union or association at its registered or principal office or by sending it by post to that secretary or clerk at that office; or
   (d) where the person is acting by a solicitor by delivering it at, or by sending it by post to, the solicitor's address for service.

Notice of holding of formal investigation
4.—(1) Where, in pursuance of section 58 of the Act, notice of the holding of a formal investigation falls to be given by the Commission to a person named in the terms of reference for the investigation, that person shall be served with a notice setting out the terms of reference.

(2) Where the terms of reference for a formal investigation are revised, paragraph (1) shall apply in relation to the revised investigation and terms of reference as it applied to the original.

Requirement to furnish or give information or produce documents
5. Where, in pursuance of section 59(1) of the Act, the Commission require a person to furnish written information, give oral information or produce documents, that person shall be served with a notice in the form set out in Schedule 1 to these Regulations or a form to the like effect, with such variations as the circumstances may require.

Non-discrimination notice
6. Where, in pursuance of section 67(2) of the Act, the Commission issue a non-discrimination notice, the person to whom it is directed shall be served with a notice in the form set out in Schedule 2 to these Regulations

or a form to the like effect, with such variations as the circumstances may require.

2–022

SCHEDULE 1

REQUIREMENT TO FURNISH WRITTEN INFORMATION
OR GIVE ORAL EVIDENCE AND PRODUCE DOCUMENTS
(SEX DISCRIMINATION ACT 1975, s.59(1))

To A. B. of

For the purposes of the formal investigation being conducted by the Equal Opportunities Commission ("the Commission") the terms of reference of which [were given to you in a notice dated   ] [are set out in the Schedule hereto], you are hereby required, in pursuance of section 59(1) of the Sex Discrimination Act 1975 ("the Act") and subject to section 59(3) thereof, [to furnish such written information as is hereinafter described, namely, (*description of information*). The said information is to be furnished (*specify the time or times at which, and the manner and form in which, the information is to be furnished*).] [to attend at (*insert time*) on (*insert date*) at (*insert place*) and give oral information about (*or* give oral evidence about, and produce all documents in your possession or control relating to,) such matters as are hereinafter specified, namely (*specify matters*).]

Dated the . . . . day of 19   .

This notice was issued by the [Commission] [Commissioners/Commissioners and Additional Commissioners to whom the Commission have, in pursuance of section 57(3) of the Act and in relation to the investigation, delegated their functions under section 59(1)(*a*) thereof].

[Service of this notice was authorised by an order made in pursuance of section 59(2)(*a*) of the Act and dated (*insert date*), a copy of which is attached.]

[Having regard to the terms of reference of the investigation and the provisions of section 59(2)(*b*)/section 69 of the Act, service of this notice does not require the consent of the Secretary of State.]

C. D.
[Commissioner.]
[Chief Officer (*or other appropriate officer*)
of the Commission.]

[SCHEDULE

TERMS OF REFERENCE OF INVESTIGATION]

2–023

[SCHEDULE 2

NON-DISCRIMINATION NOTICE (SEX DISCRIMINATION ACT 1975, s.67)

To A. B. of

Whereas, in the course of a formal investigation, the Equal Opportunities Commission ("the Commission") have become satisfied that you were committing/had committed an act/acts to which section 67(2) of the Sex Discrimination Act 1975 ("the Act") applies, namely, (*insert particulars of act or acts*) [and are of the opinion that further such acts are likely to be committed unless changes are made in your practices or other arrangements as respects (*insert particulars*)].

Now, therefore, without prejudice to your other duties under the Act or the Equal Pay Act 1970, you are hereby required, in pursuance of section 67(2) of the Act, not to commit any such act as aforesaid or any other act which is [an unlawful discriminatory act by virtue of (*insert reference to relevant Part or provision of the Act*)] [a contravention of section 37 of the

Act] [an act which is a contravention of section 38/39/40 of the Act by reference to Part II/Part III thereof) [an act in breach of a term of a contract under which a person is employed, being a term modified or included by virtue of an equality clause within the meaning of the Equal Pay Act 1970].

In so far as compliance with the aforesaid requirement involves changes in any of your practices or other arrangements, you are further required, in pursuance of the said section 67(2), to inform the Commission [as hereinafter provided] that you have effected those changes and what those changes are [and to take the following steps for the purpose of affording that information to other persons concerned, namely *(specify steps to be taken)*].

[You are further required, in pursuance of section 67(3) of the Act, to furnish the Commission as hereinafter provided with the following information, to enable them to verify your compliance with this notice, namely, *(insert description of information required)*.]

[The information to be furnished by you to the Commission in pursuance of this notice shall be furnished as follows, namely, *(specify the time or times at which, and the manner and form in which, the information, or information of a particular description, is to be furnished)*.]

Dated the . . . . day of . . . . 19 .

This notice was issued by the Commission, the provisions of section 67(5) of the Act having been complied with.

C. D.
[Commissioner.]
[Chief Officer (*or other appropriate officer*)
of the Commission.]]

AMENDMENT
Sched. 2 was substituted by the Sex Discrimination (Formal Investigations) (Amendment) Regulations 1977 (S.I. 1977 No. 843).

Sex Discrimination (Question and Replies) Order 1975   2–024

(S.I. 1975 No. 2048)

Dated December 3, 1975, and made by the Home Secretary under the Sex Discrimination Act 1975 (c. 65), ss.74 and 81(4).

Citation and operation
1. This Order may be cited as the Sex Discrimination (Questions and Replies) Order 1975 and shall come into operation on 29th December 1975.

Interpretation
2.—(1) In this Order "the Act" means the Sex Discrimination Act 1975.
(2) In this Order any reference to a court is a reference to a county court in England or Wales or a sheriff court in Scotland and any reference to a tribunal is a reference to an industrial tribunal.
(3) The Interpretation Act 1889 shall apply to the interpretation of this Order as it applies to the interpretation of an Act of Parliament.

Forms for asking and answering questions
3. The forms respectively set out in Schedules 1 and 2 to this Order or forms to the like effect with such variation as the circumstances may require are, respectively, hereby prescribed as forms—

(a) by which a person aggrieved may question a respondent as mentioned in subsection (1)(a) of section 74 of the Act;
(b) by which a respondent may if he so wishes reply to such questions as mentioned in subsection (1)(b) of that section.

Period for service of questions—court cases
4. In proceedings before a court, a question shall only be admissible as evidence in pursuance of section 74(2)(a) of the Act—
   [(a) where it was served before those proceedings had been instituted, if it was so served during—
       (i) the period of six months beginning when the act complained of was done, or
       (ii) in a case to which section 66(5) of the Act applies, the period of eight months so beginning;]
   (b) where it was served when those proceedings had been instituted, if it was served with the leave of, and within a period specified by, the court.

Period for service of questions—tribunal cases
5. In proceedings before a tribunal, a question shall only be admissible as evidence in pursuance of section 74(2)(a) of the Act—
   (a) where it was served before a complaint had been presented to a tribunal, if it was so served within the period of three months beginning when the act complained of was done;
   (b) where it was served when a complaint had been presented to a tribunal, either if it was so served within the period of twenty-one days beginning with the day on which the complaint was presented or if it was so served later with leave given, and within a period specified, by a direction of a tribunal.

Manner of service of questions and replies
6. A question and any reply thereto may be served on the respondent or, as the case may be, on the person aggrieved—
   (a) by delivering it to him; or
   (b) by sending it by post to him at his usual or last-known residence or place of business; or
   (c) where the person to be served is a body corporate or is a trade union or employers' association within the meaning of the Trade Union and Labour Relations Act 1974, by delivering it to the secretary or clerk of the body, union or association at its registered or principal office or by sending it by post to the secretary or clerk at that office; or
   (d) where the person to be served is acting by a solicitor, by delivering it at, or by sending it by post to, the solicitor's address for service; or
   (e) where the person to be served is the person aggrieved, by delivering the reply, or sending it by post, to him at his address for reply as stated by him in the document containing the questions.

SCHEDULE 1

2–025

THE SEX DISCRIMINATION ACT 1975 s.74(1)(*a*)

QUESTIONNAIRE OF PERSONS AGGRIEVED

To .... (*name of person to be questioned*)

of ....(*address*)

1.—(1) I...................(*name of questioner*) of..(*address*) consider that you may have discriminated against me contrary to the Sex Discrimination Act 1975.

(2) (*Give date, approximate time and a factual description of the treatment received and of the circumstances leading up to the treatment.*)

(3) I consider that this treatment may have been unlawful [because ....
.... (*complete if you wish to give reasons, otherwise delete*)].

2. Do you agree that the statement in paragraph 1(2) above is an accurate description of what happened? If not, in what respect do you disagree or what is your version of what happened?

3. Do you accept that your treatment of me was unlawful discrimination by you against me? If not—
(*a*) why not,
(*b*) for what reason did I receive the treatment accorded to me, and
(*c*) how far did my sex or marital status affect your treatment of me?

4. (*Any other questions you wish to ask.*)

5. My address for any reply you may wish to give to the questions raised above is [that set out in paragraph 1(1) above] [the following address..].

.... (*signature of questioner*)

.... (*date*)

N.B. By virtue of section 74 of the Act this questionnaire and any reply are (subject to the provisions of the section) admissible in proceedings under the Act and a court or tribunal may draw any such inference as is just and equitable from a failure without reasonable excuse to reply within a reasonable period, or from an evasive or equivocal reply, including an inference that the person questioned has discriminated unlawfully.

SCHEDULE 2

2–026

THE SEX DISCRIMINATION ACT 1975 s.74(1)(*b*)

REPLY BY RESPONDENT

To .... (*name of questioner*)

of ....(*address*)

1. I...................(*name of person questioned*) of..(*address*) hereby acknowledge receipt of the questionnaire signed by you and dated ....
was served on me on..................... (*date*).

2. [I agree that the statement in paragraph 1(2) of the questionnaire is an accurate description of what happened.]
[I disagree with the statement in paragraph 1(2) of the questionnaire in that ....]

3. I accept/dispute that my treatment of you was unlawful discrimination by me against you.
[My reasons for so disputing are...The reason why you received the treatment accorded to you and the answers to the other questions in paragraph 3 of the questionnaire are ....]

4. (*Replies to questions in paragraph 4 of the questionnaire*)

[5. I have deleted (in whole or in part) the paragraph(s) numbered..................................

above, since I am unable/unwilling to reply to the relevant questions in the correspondingly numbered paragraph(s) of the questionnaire for the following reasons............................
....]

.... (*signature of person questioned*)
(*date*)

AMENDMENT
The words in square brackets in art. 4(*a*) were substituted by the Sex Discrimination (Questions and Replies) (Amendment) Order 1977 (S.I. 1977 No. 844).

2–027 **Labour Relations (Continuity of Employment) Regulations 1976**

(S.I. 1976 No. 660)

Dated April 27, 1976, and made by the Secretary of State for Employment under the Trade Union and Labour Relations Act 1974 (c. 42), Sched. 1, para. 30(3).

Citation, commencement and revocation
1.—(1) These Regulations may be cited as the Labour Relations (Continuity of Employment) Regulations 1976 and shall come into operation on 1st June 1976.
(2) As from that date the Industrial Relations (Continuity of Employment) Regulations 1972 shall cease to have effect.

Interpretation
2.—(1) The Interpretation Act 1899 shall apply to these Regulations as it applies to the interpretation of an Act of Parliament and as if these Regulations and the Regulations hereby revoked were Acts of Parliament.
(2) In these Regulations, unless the context otherwise requires—
"the 1965 Act" means the Redundancy Payments Act 1965;
"the 1974 Act" means the Trade Union and Labour Relations Act 1974;
"the 1975 Act" means the Employment Protection Act 1975; and
"the effective date of termination" has the same meaning as in paragraph 5(5) of Schedule 1 to the 1974 Act.

Application
3. These Regulations apply to any action taken in relation to the dismissal of an employee which consists—
(*a*) of the presentation by him of a complaint under paragraph 17 of Schedule 1 to the 1974 Act, or
(*b*) of his making a claim in accordance with a dismissals procedure agreement designated by an order under paragraph 13 of that Schedule, or
(*c*) of any action taken by a conciliation officer under paragraph 26(4) of that Schedule.

Continuity of employment where employee re-engaged
4.—(1) The provisions of this Regulation shall have effect to preserve

the continuity of a person's period of employment for the purposes of Schedule 1 to the Contracts of Employment Act 1972 and for the purposes of that Schedule as applied by the 1965 Act, the 1974 Act and the 1975 Act.

(2) If in consequence of any action to which these Regulations apply a dismissed employee is reinstated or re-engaged by his employer or by a successor or associated employer of the employer the continuity of that employee's period of employment shall be preserved and, accordingly, any week falling within the interval beginning with the effective date of termination and ending with the date of reinstatement or re-engagement, as the case may be, shall count in the computation of the employee's period of continuous employment.

Exclusion of operation of sections 24 and 24A of the 1965 Act where redundancy or equivalent payment repaid

5.—(1) Where in consequence of any action to which these Regulations apply a dismissed employee is reinstated or re-engaged by his employer or by a successor or associated employer of the employer and the terms upon which he is so reinstated or re-engaged include provision for him to repay the amount of a redundancy payment or an equivalent payment paid in respect of the relevant dismissal, sections 24 or 24A of the 1965 Act (which require the continuity of the period of employment to be treated as broken where a redundancy payment or an equivalent payment is paid and he is subsequently re-engaged) shall not apply if those provisions are complied with.

(2) For the purposes of this Regulation the cases in which a redundancy payment shall be treated as having been paid are cases mentioned in paragraphs (*a*) and (*b*) of section 24(3) of the 1965 Act.

Industrial Tribunals Awards (Enforcement in case of Death) Regulations 1976

2–028

(S.I. 1976 No. 663)

Dated April 29, 1976, and made by the Secretary of State for Employment under the Employment Protection Act 1975 (c. 71), Sched. 12, para. 3(2) and the Redundancy Payments Act 1965 (c. 62), Sched. 4, para. 21A(2).

Citation and commencement

1. These Regulations may be cited as the Industrial Tribunals Awards (Enforcement in case of Death) Regulations 1976 and shall come into operation on 1st June 1976.

Interpretation

2.—(1) The Interpretation Act 1889 shall apply to the interpretation of these Regulations as it applies to the interpretation of an Act of Parliament.

(2) In these Regulations, unless the context otherwise requires, the following expressions have the meanings hereby assigned to them respectively, that is to say—

"the 1965 Act" means the Redundancy Payments Act 1965, as amended by the Employment Protection Act 1975;
"the 1975 Act" means the Employment Protection Act 1975;
"employer" includes a successor of an employer or a personal representative of a deceased employer;
"the estate" means the estate of the deceased employee;
"the relevant provisions" means the provisions of the 1965 Act and the 1975 Act (including Schedule 12 thereto) conferring rights on employees, or connected therewith, and so much of the Trade Union and Labour Relations Act 1974, as amended by the 1975 Act and the Trade Union and Labour Relations (Amendment) Act 1976, as relates to unfair dismissal.

Application of Regulations
3. Where there is no personal representative of a deceased employee in proceedings arising under any of the relevant provisions in which an industrial tribunal makes any award, the terms of the award and the manner of its enforcement shall be governed by these Regulations.

Terms of the award
4. Where, in proceedings before an industrial tribunal arising under any of the relevant provisions, either—
(*a*) a person has been appointed under paragraph 3(1) of Schedule 12 to the 1975 Act or paragraph 21A(1) of Schedule 4 to the 1965 Act to institute or continue those proceedings on behalf of the estate; or
(*b*) an employee who is a party to those proceedings dies before the tribunal's award is made,
any award of the tribunal shall be made in favour of the estate.

Enforcement by person appointed
5. Where any person is appointed under paragraph 3(1) of Schedule 12 to the 1975 Act or paragraph 21A(1) of Schedule 4 to the 1965 Act to enforce an award made by an industrial tribunal in favour of the estate, or, as the case may be, in favour of an employee who has since died, that person may enforce such award on behalf of the estate without the grant of letters of administration or probate of any will or, in Scotland, confirmation and the receipt of that person shall be a sufficient discharge to the employer for any sum payable to the estate under the award.

Enforcement in other cases
6. Where Regulation 5 above does not apply, any award made in favour of the estate or in favour of an employee who has since died shall be enforceable on behalf of the estate by the person to whom a grant of letters of administration or probate or, in Scotland, confirmation is made in respect of that estate.

Safety Representatives and Safety Committees Regulations 1977
(S.I. 1977 No. 500)

Dated March 16, 1977, and made by the Secretary of State for Employment under the Health and Safety at Work etc. Act 1974 (c. 37), ss.2(4) and (7), 15(1), (3)(b) and (5)(b), 80(1) and (4) and 82(3)(a).

Citation and commencement
  1. These Regulations may be cited as the Safety Representatives and Safety Committees Regulations 1977 and shall come into operation on 1st October 1978.

Interpretation
  2.—(1) In these Regulations, unless the context otherwise requires—
   "the 1974 Act" means the Health and Safety at Work etc. Act 1974 as amended by the 1975 Act;
   "the 1975 Act" means the Employment Protection Act 1975;
   "employee" has the meaning assigned by section 53(1) of the 1974 Act and "employer" shall be construed accordingly;
   "recognised trade union" means an independent trade union as defined in section 30(1) of the Trade Union and Labour Relations Act 1974 which the employer concerned recognises for the purpose of negotiations relating to or connected with one or more of the matters specified in section 29(1) of that Act in relation to persons employed by him or as to which the Advisory, Conciliation and Arbitration Service has made a recommendation for recognition under the 1975 Act which is operative within the meaning of section 15 of that Act;
   "safety representative" means a person appointed under Regulation 3(1) of these Regulations to be a safety representative;
   "welfare at work" means those aspects of welfare at work which are the subject of health and safety regulations or of any of the existing statutory provisions within the meaning of section 53(1) of the 1974 Act;
   "workplace" in relation to a safety representative means any place or places where the group of groups of employees he is appointed to represent are likely to work or which they are likely to frequent in the course of their employment or incidentally to it.
  (2) The Interpretation Act 1889 shall apply to the interpretation of these Regulations as it applies to the interpretation of an Act of Parliament.
  (3) These Regulations shall not be construed as giving any person a right to inspect any place, article, substance or document which is the subject of restrictions on the grounds of national security unless he satisfies any test or requirement imposed on those grounds by or on behalf of the Crown.

Appointment of safety representatives
  3.—(1) For the purposes of section 2(4) of the 1974 Act, a recognised trade union may appoint safety representatives from amongst the employees in all cases where one or more employees are employed by an employer by whom it is recognised, except in the case of employees employed in a mine within the meaning of section 180 of the Mines and Quarries Act 1954 which is a coal mine.
  (2) Where the employer has been notified in writing by or on behalf of a trade union of the names of the persons appointed as safety representatives under this Regulation and the group or groups of employees they

represent, each such safety representative shall have the functions set out in Regulation 4 below.

(3) A person shall cease to be a safety representative for the purposes of these Regulations when—
 (a) the trade union which appointed him notifies the employer in writing that his appointment has been terminated; or
 (b) he ceases to be employed at the workplace but if he was appointed to represent employees at more than one workplace he shall not cease by virtue of this sub-paragraph to be a safety representative so long as he continues to be employed at any one of them; or
 (c) he resigns.

(4) A person appointed under paragraph (1) above as a safety representative shall so far as is reasonably practicable either have been employed by his employer throughout the preceding two years or have had at least two years' experience in similar employment.

Functions of safety representatives

4.—(1) In addition to his function under section 2(4) of the 1974 Act to represent the employees in consultations with the employer under section 2(6) of the 1974 Act (which requires every employer to consult safety representatives with a view to the making and maintenance of arrangements which will enable him and his employees to cooperate effectively in promoting and developing measures to ensure the health and safety at work of the employees and in checking the effectiveness of such measures), each safety representative shall have the following functions:—
 (a) to investigate potential hazards and dangerous occurrences at the workplace (whether or not they are drawn to his attention by the employees he represents) and to examine the causes of accidents at the workplace;
 (b) to investigate complaints by any employee he represents relating to that employee's health, safety or welfare at work;
 (c) to make representations to the employer on matters arising out of sub-paragraphs (a) and (b) above;
 (d) to make representations to the employer on general matters affecting the health, safety or welfare at work of the employees at the workplace;
 (e) to carry out inspections in accordance with Regulation 5, 6 and 7 below;
 (f) to represent the employees he was appointed to represent in consultations at the workplace with inspectors of the Health and Safety Executive and of any other enforcing authority;
 (g) to receive information from inspectors in accordance with section 28(8) of the 1974 Act; and
 (h) to attend meetings of safety committees where he attends in his capacity as a safety representative in connection with any of the above functions;
but, without prejudice to sections 7 and 8 of the 1974 Act, no function given to a safety representative by this paragraph shall be construed as imposing any duty on him.

(2) An employer shall permit a safety representative to take such time off with pay during the employee's working hours as shall be necessary for the purposes of—

(a) performing his functions under section 2(1) of the 1974 Act and paragraph 1(a) to (h) above;

(b) undergoing such training in aspects of those functions as may be reasonable in all the circumstances having regard to any relevant provisions of a code of practice relating to time off for training approved for the time being by the Health and Safety Commission under section 16 of the 1974 Act.

In this paragraph "with pay" means with pay in accordance with the Schedule to these Regulations.

Inspections of the workplace
5.—(1) Safety representatives shall be entitled to inspect the workplace or part of it if they have given the employer or his representative reasonable notice in writing of their intention to do so and have not inspected it, or that part of it, as the case may be, in the previous three months; and may carry out more frequent inspections by agreement with the employer.

(2) Where there has been a substantial change in the conditions of work (whether because of the introduction of new machinery or otherwise) or new information has been published by the Health and Safety Commission or the Health and Safety Executive relevant to the hazards of the workplace since the last inspection under this Regulation, the safety representatives after consultation with the employer shall be entitled to carry out a further inspection of the part of the workplace concerned notwithstanding that three months have not elapsed since the last inspection.

(3) The employer shall provide such facilities and assistance as the safety representatives may reasonably require (including facilities for independent investigation by them and private discussion with the employees) for the purpose of carrying out an inspection under this Regulation, but nothing in this paragraph shall preclude the employer or his representative from being present in the workplace during the inspection.

(4) An inspection carried out under section 123 of the Mines and Quarries Act 1954 shall count as an inspection under this Regulation.

Inspections following notifiable accidents, occurrences and diseases
6.—(1) Where there has been a notifiable accident or dangerous occurrence in a workplace or a notifiable disease has been contracted there and—

(a) it is safe for an inspection to be carried out; and

(b) the interests of employees in the group or groups which safety representatives are appointed to represent might be involved.

those safety representatives may carry out an inspection of the part of the workplace concerned and so far as is necessary for the purpose of determining the cause they may inspect any other part of the workplace; where it is reasonably practicable to do so they shall notify the employer or his representative of their intention to carry out the inspection.

(2) The employer shall provide such facilities and assistance as the safety representatives may reasonably require (including facilities for independent investigation by them and private discussion with the employees) for the purpose of carrying out an inspection under this Regulation; but nothing in this paragraph shall preclude the employer or his representative from being present in the workplace during the inspection.

(3) In this Regulation "notifiable accident or dangerous occurrence" and "notifiable disease" mean any accident, dangerous occurrence or disease,

Inspection of documents and provision of information

7.—(1) Safety representatives shall for the performance of their functions under section 2(4) of the 1974 Act and under these Regulations, if they have given the employer reasonable notice, be entitled to inspect and take copies of any document relevant to the workplace or to the employees the safety representatives represent with the employer is required by virtue of any relevant statutory provision within the meaning of section 53(1) of the 1974 Act except a document consisting of or relating to any health record of an identifiable individual.

(2) An employer shall make available to safety representatives the information, within the employer's knowledge, necessary to enable them to fulfil their functions except—
  (a) any information the disclosure of which would be against the interests of national security; or
  (b) any information which he could not disclose without contravening a prohibition imposed by or under an enactment; or
  (c) any information relating specifically to an individual, unless he has consented to its being disclosed; or
  (d) any information the disclosure of which would, for reasons other than its effect on health, safety or welfare at work, cause substantial injury to the employer's undertaking or, where the information was supplied to him by some other person, to the undertaking of that other person; or
  (e) any information obtained by the employer for the purpose of bringing, prosecuting or defending any legal proceedings.

(3) Paragraph (2) above does not require an employer to produce or allow inspection of any document or part of a document which is not related to health, safety or welfare.

Cases where safety representatives need not be employees

8.—(1) In the cases mentioned in paragraph (2) below safety representatives appointed under Regulation 3(1) of these Regulations need not be employees of the employer concerned; and section 2(4) of the 1974 Act shall be modified accordingly.

(2) The said cases are those in which the employees in the group or groups the safety representatives are appointed to represent are members of the British Actors' Equity Association or of the Musicians' Union.

(3) Regulations 3(3)(*b*) and (4) and 4(2) of these Regulations shall not apply to safety representatives appointed by virtue of this Regulation and in the case of safety representatives to be so appointed Regulation 3(1) shall have effect as if the words "from amongst the employees" were omitted.

Safety committees

9.—(1) For the purposes of section 2(7) of the 1974 Act (which requires an employer in prescribed cases to establish a safety committee if requested to do so by safety representatives) the prescribed cases shall be any cases in which at least two safety representatives request the employer in writing to establish a safety committee.

(2) Where an employer is requested to establish a safety committee in a

case prescribed in paragraph (1) above, he shall establish it in accordance with the following provisions—
 (a) he shall consult with the safety representatives who made the request and with the representatives of recognised trade unions whose members work in any workplace in respect of which he proposes that the committee should function;
 (b) the employer shall post a notice stating the composition of the committee and the workplace or workplaces to be covered by it in a place where it may be easily read by the employees;
 (c) the committee shall be established not later than three months after the request for it.

Power of Health and Safety Commission to grant exemptions
 10. The Health and Safety Commission may grant exemptions from any requirement imposed by these Regulations and any such exemption may be unconditional or subject to such conditions as the Commission may impose and may be with or without a limit of time.

Provisions as to Industrial Tribunals
 11.—(1) A safety representative may, in accordance with the jurisdiction conferred on industrial tribunals by paragraph 16(2) of Schedule 1 to the Trade Union and Labour Relations Act 1974, present a complaint to an industrial tribunal that—
 (a) the employer has failed to permit him to take time off in accordance with Regulation 4(2) of these Regulations; or
 (b) the employer has failed to pay him in accordance with Regulation 4(2) of and the Schedule to these Regulations.
 (2) An industrial tribunal shall not consider a complaint under paragraph (1) above unless it is presented within three months of the date when the failure occurred or within such further period as the tribunal considers reasonable in a case where it is satisfied that it was not reasonably practicable for the complaint to be presented within the period of three months.
 (3) Where an industrial tribunal finds a complaint under paragraph (1)(a) above well-founded the tribunal shall make a declaration of that effect and may make an award of compensation to be paid by the employer to the employee which shall be of such amount as the tribunal considers just and equitable in all the circumstances having regard to the employer's default in failing to permit time off to be taken by the employee and to any loss sustained by the employee which is attributable to the matters complained of.
 (4) Where on a complaint under paragraph (1)(b) above an industrial tribunal finds that the employer has failed to pay the employee the whole or part of the amount required to be paid under paragraph (1)(b), the tribunal shall order the employer to pay the employee the amount which it finds due to him.
 (5) Paragraph 16 of Schedule 1 to the Trade Union and Labour Relations Act 1974 (jurisdiction of industrial tribunals) shall be modified by adding the following sub-paragraphs:—
  "(2) An industrial tribunal shall have jurisdiction to determine complaints relating to time off with pay for safety representatives appointed under regulations made under the Health and Safety at Work etc. Act 1974".

2–032 Regulation 4(2) SCHEDULE

PAY FOR TIME OFF ALLOWED TO SAFETY REPRESENTATIVES

1. Subject to paragraph 3 below, where a safety representative is permitted to take time off in accordance with Regulation 4(2) of these Regulations, his employer shall pay him—
   (a) where the safety representative's remuneration for the work he would ordinarily have been doing during that time does not vary with the amount of work done, as if he had worked at that work for the whole of that time;
   (b) where the safety representative's remuneration for that work varies with the amount of work done, an amount calculated by reference to the average hourly earnings for that work (ascertained in accordance with paragraph 2 below).

2. The average hourly earnings referred to in paragraph 1(b) above are the average hourly earnings of the safety representative concerned or, if no fair estimate can be made of those earnings, the average hourly earnings for work of that description of persons in comparable employment with the same employer or, if there are no such persons, a figure of average hourly earnings which is reasonable in the circumstances.

3. Any payment to a safety representative by an employer in respect of a period of time off—
   (a) if it is a payment which discharges any liability which the employer may have under section 57 of the 1975 Act in respect of that period, shall also discharge his liability in respect of the same period under Regulation 4(2) of these Regulations;
   (b) if it is a payment under any contractual obligation, shall go towards discharging the employer's liability in respect of the same period under Regulation 4(2) of these Regulations;
   (c) if it is a payment under Regulation 4(2) of these Regulations shall go towards discharging any liability of the employer to pay contractual remuneration in respect of the same period.

2–033 # Race Relations (Formal Investigations) Regulations 1977

(S.I. 1977 No. 841)

Dated May 13, 1977, *and made by the Home Secretary under the Race Relations Act* 1976, (*c.* 74), *ss.*49(3), 50(1) *and* 58(2).

Citation and operation
1. These Regulations may be cited as the Race Relations (Formal Investigations) Regulations 1977 and shall come into operation on 13th June 1977.

Interpretation
2.—(1) In these Regulations any reference to the Act is a reference to the Race Relations Act 1976.

(2) Any reference to the Commission, in Regulations 4, 5 and 6 below, is a reference to the Commission for Racial Equality except that, as respects any of the functions of the Commission in relation to a formal investigation which the Commission have delegated under section 48(3) of the Act, any such reference in Regulation 4 or 5 is a reference to the persons, being either Commissioners or additional Commissioners, to whom those functions have been so delegated.

(3) The Interpretation Act 1889 shall apply for the interpretation of these Regulations as it applies for the interpretation of an Act of Parliament.

Service of notices
3. Any reference to a person being served with a notice, in Regulations 4, 5 and 6 below, is a reference to service of the notice on him being effected—
  (*a*) by delivering it to him; or
  (*b*) by sending it by post to him at his usual or last-known residence or place of business; or
  (*c*) where the person is a body corporate or is a trade union or employers' association within the meaning of the Trade Union and Labour Relations Act 1974 by delivering it to the secretary or clerk of the body, union or association at its registered or principal office or by sending it by post to that secretary or clerk at that office; or
  (*d*) where the person is acting by a solicitor by delivering it at, or by sending it by post to, the solicitor's address for service.

Notice of holding of formal investigation
4.—(1) Where, in pursuance of section 49 of the Act, notice of the holding of a formal investigation falls to be given by the Commission to a person named in the terms of reference for the investigation, that person shall be served with a notice setting out the terms of reference.
(2) Where the terms of reference for a formal investigation are revised, paragraph (1) shall apply in relation to the revised investigation and terms of reference as it applied to the original.

Requirement to furnish or give information or produce documents
5. Where, in pursuance of section 50(1) of the Act, the Commission require a person to furnish written information, give oral information or produce documents, that person shall be served with a notice in the form set out in Schedule 1 to these Regulations or a form to the like effect, with such variations as the circumstances may require.

Non-discrimination notice
6. Where, in pursuance of section 58(2) of the Act, the Commission issue a non-discrimination notice, the person to whom it is directed shall be served with a notice in the form set out in Schedule 2 to these Regulations or a form to the like effect, with such variations as the circumstances may require.

Regulation 5   SCHEDULE 1   **2–034**

Requirement to Furnish Written Information or Give Oral Evidence and Produce Documents (Race Relations Act 1976, s.50(1))

To A. B. of

For the purpose of the formal investigation being conducted by the Commission for Racial Equality ("the Commission") the terms of reference of which [were given to you in a notice dated   ] [are set out in the Schedule hereto], you are hereby required in pursuance of section 50(1) of the Race Relations Act 1976 ("the Act") and subject to section 50(3) thereof, [to furnish such written information as is hereinafter described, namely, [*description of information*). The said information is to be furnished (*specify the time or times at which, and the manner and form in which, the information is to be furnished*).] [to attend at (*insert time*) on (*insert date*) at (*insert place*) and give oral information about (*or* give oral evidence about, and produce all documents in your possession or control relating to,*)* such matters as are hereinafter specified, namely (*specify matters*).]

Dated the........................ day of....................... 19   .

This notice was issued by the [Commission] [Commissioners/Commissioners and additional

Commissioners to whom the Commission have, in pursuance of section 48(3) of the Act and in relation to the investigation, delegated their functions under section 50(1)(a) thereof].

[Service of this notice was authorised by an order made in pursuance of section 50(2)(a) of the Act and dated (*insert date*), a copy of which is attached.]

[Having regard to the terms of reference of the investigation and the provisions of section 50(2)(b)/section 60 of the Act, service of this notice does not require the consent of the Secretary of State.]

C. D.
[Commissioner.]
[Chief Officer (<i>or other appropriate officer</i>) of the Commission.]</p>

[SCHEDULE
TERMS OF REFERENCE OF INVESTIGATION]

2–035 Regulation 6   SCHEDULE 2

NON-DISCRIMINATION NOTICE (RACE RELATIONS ACT 1976, s.58)

To A. B. of

Whereas, in the course of a formal investigation, the Commission for Racial Equality ("the Commission") have become satisfied that you were committing/had committed an act/acts to which section 58(2) of the Race Relations Act 1976 ("the Act") applies, namely, (*insert particulars of act or acts*) [and are of the opinion that further such acts are likely to be committed unless changes are made in your practices or other arrangement as respects (*insert particulars*)].

Now, therefore, without prejudice to your other duties under the Act, you are hereby required, in pursuance of section 58(2) of the Act not to commit any such act as aforesaid or any act which is [an unlawful discriminatory act by virtue of (*insert reference to relevant Part or provision of the Act*)] [a contravention of section 28 of the Act] [an act which is a contravention of section 29/30/31 of the Act by reference to Part II/Part III thereof].

In so far as compliance with the aforesaid requirement involves changes in any of your practices or other arrangements, you are further required, in pursuance of the said section 58(2), to inform the Commission [as hereinafter provided] that you have effected those changes and what those changes are [and to take the following steps for the purpose of affording that information to other persons concerned, namely, (*specify steps to be taken*)].

[You are further required, in pursuance of section 58(3) of the Act, to furnish the Commission as hereinafter provided with the following information, to enable them to verify your compliance with this notice, namely, (*insert description of information required*).]

[The information to be furnished by you to the Commission in pursuance of this notice shall be furnished as follows, namely, (*specify the time or times at which, and the manner and form in which, the information, or information of a particular description is to be furnished*).]

Dated the.......................... day of 19   .

This notice was issued by the Commission, the provisions of section 58(5) of the Act having been complied with.

C. D.
[Commissioner.]
[Chief Officer (<i>or other appropriate officer</i>) of the Commission.]</p>

Race Relations (Questions and Replies) Order 1977

(S.I. 1977 No. 842)

Dated May 13, 1977, *and made by the Home Secretary under the Race Relations Act* 1976, (*c.* 74), *ss*.65 *and* 74(3).

Citation and operation

1. This Order may be cited as the Race Relations (Questions and Replies) Order 1977 and shall come into operation on 13th June 1977.

Interpretation

2.—(1) In this Order "the Act" means the Race Relations Act 1976.

(2) In this Order any reference to a court is a reference to a county court in England or Wales designated for the time being for the purposes of the Act by an order made by the Lord Chancellor under section 67(1) of the Act or a sheriff court in Scotland and any reference to a tribunal is a reference to an industrial tribunal.

(3) The Interpretation Act 1889 shall apply to the interpretation of this Order as it applies to the interpretation of an Act of Parliament.

Forms for asking and answering questions

3. The forms respectively set out in Schedules 1 and 2 to this Order or forms to the like effect with such variation as the circumstances may require are, respectively, hereby prescribed as forms—
 (*a*) by which a person aggrieved may question a respondent as mentioned in subsection (1)(*a*) of section 65 of the Act;
 (*b*) by which a respondent may if he so wishes reply to such questions as mentioned in subsection (1)(*b*) of that section.

Period for service of questions—court cases

4. In proceedings before a court, a question shall only be admissible as evidence in pursuance of section 65(2)(*a*) of the Act—
 (*a*) where it was served before those proceedings had been instituted, if it was so served during—
  (i) the period of six months beginning when the act complained of was done, or
  (ii) in a case to which section 57(5) of the Act applies, the period of eight months so beginning;
 (*b*) where it was served when those proceedings had been instituted, if it was served with the leave of, and within a period specified by, the court.

Period for service of questions—tribunal cases

5. In proceedings before a tribunal, a question shall only be admissible as evidence in pursuance of section 65(2)(*a*) of the Act—
 (*a*) where it was served before a complaint had been presented to a tribunal, if it was so served within the period of three months beginning when the act complained of was done;
 (*b*) where it was served when a complaint had been presented to a tribunal, either if it was so served within the period of twenty-one days beginning with the day of which the complaint was presented or if

it was so served later with leave given, and within a period specified, by a direction of a tribunal.

Manner of service of questions and replies

6. A question and any reply thereto may be served on the respondent or, as the case may be, on the person aggrieved—
   (*a*) by delivering it to him; or
   (*b*) by sending it by post to him at his usual or last-known residence or place of business; or
   (*c*) where the person to be served is a body corporate or is a trade union or employers' association within the meaning of the Trade Union and Labour Relations Act 1974, by delivering it to the secretary or clerk of the body, union or association at its registered or principal office or by sending it by post to the secretary or clerk at that office; or
   (*d*) where the person to be served is acting by a solicitor, by delivering it at, or by sending it by post to, the solicitor's address for service; or
   (*e*) where the person to be served is the person aggrieved, by delivering the reply, or sending it by post, to him at his address for reply as stated by him in the document containing the questions.

Article 3

SCHEDULE 1

THE RACE RELATIONS ACT 1976, s.65(1)(*a*)

QUESTIONNAIRE OF PERSON AGGRIEVED

To .... (*name of person to be questioned*)

of ....(*address*)

1. (1) I............................. (*name of questioner*) of...................................(*address*) consider that you may have discriminated against me contrary to the Race Relations Act 1976.

(2) (*Give date, approximate time and a factual description of the treatment received and of the circumstances leading up to the treatment.*)

(3) I consider that this treatment may have been unlawful [because ....

.... (*complete if you wish to give reasons, otherwise delete*)].

2. Do you agree that the statement in paragraph 1(2) above is an accurate description of what happened? If not, in what respect do you disagree or what is your version of what happened?

3. Do you accept that your treatment of me was unlawful discrimination by you against me? If not—
   (*a*) why not,
   (*b*) for what reason did I receive the treatment accorded to me, and
   (*c*) how far did considerations of colour, race, nationality (including citizenship) or ethnic or national origins affect your treatment of me?

4. (*Any other questions you wish to ask.*)

5. My address for any reply you may wish to give to the questions raised above is [that set out in paragraph 1(1) above] [the following address ....].

.... (*signature of questioner*)

.... (*date*).

N.B.—By virtue of section 65 of the Act this questionnaire and any reply can (subject to the provisions of the section) admissible in proceedings under the Act and a court or tribunal may draw any such inference as is just and equitable from a failure without reasonable excuse to reply within a reasonable period, or from an evasive or equivocal reply, including an inference that the person questioned has discriminated unlawfully.

Article 3   SCHEDULE 2   2–038

THE RACE RELATIONS ACT 1976, s.65(1)(*b*)

REPLY BY RESPONDENT

To.............................. (*name of questioner*) of..

....(*address*).

1. I............................(*name of person questioned*) of............................(*address*) hereby acknowledge receipt of the questionnaire signed by you and dated ....

which was served on me on................................ (*date*).

2. [I agree that the statement in paragraph 1(2) of the questionnaire is an accurate description of what happened.]

I disagree with the statement in paragraph 1(2) of the questionnaire in that ....]

3. I accept/dispute that any treatment of you was unlawful discrimination by me against you.
[My reasons for so disputing are... The reason why you received the treatment accorded to you and the answers to the other questions in paragraph 3 of the questionnaire are ....]

4. [*Replies to questions in paragraph* 4 *of the questionnaire.*]

[5. I have deleted (in whole or in part) the paragraph(s) numbered................................ above, since I am unable/unwilling to reply to the relevant questions in the correspondingly numbered paragraph(s) of the questionnaire for the following reasons ....]

.... (*signature of person questioned*)

.... (*date*)

Industrial Tribunals (Non-Discrimination Notices Appeals) Regulations 1977

2–039

(S.I. 1977 No. 1094)

Dated June 29, 1977, and made by the Secretary of State for Employment under the Trade Union and Labour Relations Act 1974 (c. 52), Sched. 1, Pt. III, para. 21.

Citation and commencement
1.—(1) These Regulations may be cited as the Industrial Tribunals (Non-Discrimination Notices Appeals) Regulations 1977 and shall come into operation on 5th August 1977.

(2) The Industrial Tribunals (Non-Discrimination Notices Appeals) Regulations 1975 shall cease to have effect except in relation to proceedings instituted before that date.

Interpretation
2.—(1) The Interpretation Act 1889 shall apply to these Regulations as it applies to an Act of Parliament as if these Regulations and the Regulations hereby revoked were Acts of Parliament.

(2) In these Regulations, unless the context otherwise requires, the following expressions have the meanings hereby assigned to them respectively, that is to say—

"the 1974 Act" means the Trade Union and Labour Relations Act 1974 as amended by the Employment Protection Act 1975 and the Trade Union and Labour Relations (Amendment) Act 1976;

"the 1975 Act" means the Sex Discrimination Act 1975;

"the 1976 Act" means the Race Relations Act 1976;

"appellant" means a person who has appealed to a tribunal under section 68 of the 1975 Act or, as the case may be, under section 59 of the 1976 Act;

"the clerk to the tribunal" means the person appointed by the Secretary of the Tribunals or an Assistant Secretary to act in that capacity at one or more hearings;

"decision" in relation to a tribunal includes a direction under section 68(3) of the 1975 Act or, as the case may be, under section 59(3) of the 1976 Act and any other order which is not an interlocutory order;

"hearing" means a sitting of a tribunal duly constituted for the purpose of receiving evidence, hearing addresses and witnesses or doing anything lawfully requisite to enable the tribunal to reach a decision on any question;

"non-discrimination notice" means a notice under section 67 of the 1975 Act or, as the case may be, under section 58 of the 1976 Act;

"nominated chairman" means a member of the panel of chairmen for the time being nominated by the President;

"the Office of the Tribunals" means the Central Office of the Industrial Tribunals (England and Wales);

"the panel of chairmen" means the panel of persons, being barristers or solicitors of not less than seven years' standing, appointed by the Lord Chancellor in pursuance of Regulation 5(2) of the Industrial Tribunals (England and Wales) Regulations 1965, as amended;

"party" means the appellant and the respondent;

"the President" means the President of the Industrial Tribunals (England and Wales) or the person nominated by the Lord Chancellor to discharge for the time being the functions of the President;

"Regional Office of the Industrial Tribunals" means a regional office which has been established under the Offices of the Tribunals for an area specified by the President;

"Register" means the Register kept in pursuance of the Industrial Tribunals (Labour Relations) Regulations 1974;

"respondent" means the Equal Opportunities Commission established under section 53 of the 1975 Act or, as the case may be, the Commission for Racial Equality established under section 43 of the 1976 Act;

"Rule" means a Rule of Procedure contained in the Schedule to these Regulations;

"the Secretary of the Tribunals" and "an Assistant Secretary of the Tribunals" mean respectively the persons for the time being acting as the Secretary of the Office of the Tribunals and as the Assistant Secretary of a Regional Office of the Industrial Tribunals;

"tribunal" means an industrial tribunal (England and Wales) established in pursuance of the Industrial Tribunals (England and Wales) Regulation 1965, as amended, and in relation to any proceedings means the tribunal to which the proceedings have been referred by the President or by a nominated chairman.

Proceedings of tribunals

3. The Rules of Procedure contained in the Schedule to these Regulations shall have effect in relation to appeals to a tribunal under section 68 of the 1975 Act and under section 59 of the 1976 Act against non-discrimination notices relating to matters arising in England and Wales.

Proof of decision of tribunals

4. The production in any proceedings in any court of a document purporting to be certified by the Secretary of the Tribunals to be a true copy of an entry of a decision in the Register shall, unless the contrary is proved, be sufficient evidence of the document and of the facts stated therein.

Regulation 3　　　　　　　　　SCHEDULE　　　　　　　　　2–040

RULES OF PROCEDURE

Notice of appeal

1. An appeal shall be commenced not later than six weeks after service of the non-discrimination notice, as specified in section 68(1) of the 1975 Act and in section 59(1) of the 1976 Act, by the appellant sending to the Secretary of the Tribunals a notice of appeal which shall be in writing and shall set out:—
    (a) the name of the appellant and his address for the service of documents;
    (b) the date of the non-discrimination notice appealed against;
    (c) the name and address of the respondent;
    (d) particulars of the requirements appealed against; and
    (e) the grounds of the appeal.

Action upon receipt of notice of appeal

2. Upon receiving a notice of appeal the Secretary of the Tribunals shall enter particulars of it in the Register and shall forthwith send a copy of it to the respondent and inform the parties in writing of the case number of the appeal entered in the Register (which shall thereafter constitute the title of the proceedings) and of the address to which notices and other communications to the Secretary of the Tribunals shall be sent.

Power to require attendance of witnesses and production of documents, etc.

3.—(1) A tribunal may on the application of a party made either by notice to the Secretary of the Tribunals or at the hearing—
    (a) require a party to furnish in writing to another party further particulars of the grounds on which he relies and of any facts and contentions relevant thereto;
    (b) grant to a party such discovery or inspection of documents as might be granted by a county court; and

(c) require the attendance of any person as a witness or require the production of any document relating to the matter to be determined.

and may appoint the time at or within which or the place at which any act required in pursuance of this Rule is to be done.

(2) The tribunal shall not under paragraph (1) of this Rule require the production of any document certified by the Secretary of State as being a document of which the production would be against the interests of national security.

(3) A person on whom a requirement has been made under paragraph (1) of this Rule may apply to the tribunal either by notice to the Secretary of the Tribunals or at the hearing to vary or set aside the requirement.

(4) No such application to vary or set aside shall be entertained in a case where a time has been appointed under paragraph (1) of this Rule in relation to the requirement unless it is made before the time or, as the case may be, expiration of the time so appointed.

(5) Every document containing a requirement under paragraph (1)(b) or (c) of this Rule shall contain a reference to the fact that under paragraph 21(6) of Part III of Schedule 1 to the 1974 Act any person who without reasonable excuse fails to comply with any such requirement shall be liable on summary conviction to a fine not exceeding £100.

Time and place of hearing

4.—(1) The President or a nominated chairman shall fix the date, time and place of the hearing of the appeal and the Secretary of the Tribunals shall not less than 14 days (or such shorter time as may be agreed by him with the parties) before the date so fixed send to each party a notice of hearing which shall include information and guidance as to attendance at the hearing, witnesses and the bringing of documents (if any), representation by another person and written representations.

(2) Where the President or nominated chairman so directs, the Secretary of the Tribunals shall also send notice of the hearing to such persons as may be directed, but the requirements as to the period of notice contained in the foregoing paragraph of this rule shall not apply to any such notices.

The hearing

5.—(1) Any hearing of or in connection with an appeal shall take place in public unless the tribunal on the application of a party decides that a private hearing is appropriate for the purpose of hearing evidence which relates to matters of such a nature that it would be against the interests of national security to allow the evidence to be given in public or hearing evidence from any person which in the opinion of the tribunal is likely to consist of information the disclosure of which would cause substantial injury to the undertaking of the appellant or of any undertaking in which he works for reasons other than its effect on negotiations with respect to any of the matters mentioned in section 29(1) of the 1974 Act.

(2) In cases to which the foregoing provisions of this Rule apply, a member of the Council on Tribunals in his capacity as such shall be entitled to attend the hearing.

Written representations

6. If a party shall desire to submit representations in writing for consideration by a tribunal at the hearing of the appeal, that party shall send such representations to the Secretary of the Tribunals not less than 7 days before the hearing and shall at the same time send a copy thereof to the other party.

Right of appearance

7. At any hearing of or in connection with an appeal a party may appear before the tribunal in person or may be represented by counsel or by a solicitor or by any other person whom he desires to represent him, including in the case of the appellant a representative of a trade union or an employers' association.

Procedure at hearing

8.—(1) At any hearing of or in connection with an appeal a party shall be entitled to make an opening statement, to give evidence, to call witnesses, to cross-examine any witnesses called by the other party and to address the tribunal.

(2) If a party shall fail to appear or to be represented at the time and place fixed for the

hearing of an appeal, the tribunal may dispose of the appeal in the absence of that party or may adjourn the hearing to a later date: Provided that before disposing of an appeal in the absence of a party the tribunal shall consider any written representation submitted by that party in pursuance of Rule 6.

(3) A tribunal may require any witness to give evidence on oath or affirmation and for that purpose there may be administered an oath or affirmation in due form.

Decision of tribunal

9.—(1) A decision of a tribunal may be taken by a majority thereof and, if the tribunal shall be constituted of two members only, the chairman shall have a second or casting vote.

(2) The decision of a tribunal shall be recorded in a document signed by the chairman which shall contain the reasons for the decision.

(3) The clerk to the tribunal shall transmit the document signed by the chairman to the Secretary of the Tribunals who shall as soon as may be enter it in the Register and shall send a copy of the entry to each of the parties.

(4) The specification of the reasons for the decision shall be omitted from the Register in any case in which evidence has been heard in private and the tribunal so directs and in that event a specification of the reasons shall be sent to the parties and to any superior court in any proceedings relating to such decision together with the copy of the entry.

(5) The Register shall be kept at the Office of the Tribunals and shall be open to the inspection of any person without charge at all reasonable hours.

(6) The chairman of a tribunal shall have power by certificate under his hand to correct in documents recording the tribunal's decisions clerical mistakes or errors arising therein from any accidental slip or omission.

(7) The clerk to the tribunal shall send a copy of any document so corrected and the certificate of the chairman to the Secretary of the Tribunals who shall as soon as may be make such corrections as may be necessary in the Register and shall send a copy of the corrected entry or of the corrected specification of the reasons, as the case may be, to each of the parties.

(8) If any decision is—
    (*a*) corrected under paragraph (6) of this Rule; or
    (*b*) reviewed, revoked or varied under Rule 10; or
    (*c*) altered in any way by order of a superior court.
the Secretary of the Tribunals shall alter the entry in the Register to conform with any such certificate or order and shall send a copy of the new entry to each of the parties.

Review of tribunal's decision

10.—(1) A tribunal shall have power on the application of a party to review and to revoke or vary by certificate under the chairman's hand any of its decisions in a case in which a county court has power to order a new trial on the ground that—
    (*a*) the decision was wrongly made as a result of an error on the part of the tribunal staff; or
    (*b*) a party did not receive notice of the proceedings leading to the decision; or
    (*c*) the decision was made in the absence of a party; or
    (*d*) new evidence has become available since the making of the decision provided that its existence could not have been reasonably known of or foreseen; or
    (*e*) the interests of justice require such a review.

(2) An application for the purposes of paragraph (1) of this Rule may be made at the hearing. If the application is not made at the hearing, such application shall be made to the Secretary of the Tribunals at any time from the date of the hearing until 14 days after the date on which the decision was sent to the parties and must be in writing stating the grounds in full.

(3) An application for the purposes of paragraph (1) of this Rule may be refused by the chairman of the tribunal which decided the case, by the President or by a nominated chairman if in his opinion it has no reasonable prospect of success and he shall state the reasons for his opinion.

(4) If such an application is not refused under paragraph (3) of this Rule, it shall be heard by the tribunal and if it is granted the tribunal shall either vary its decision or revoke its decision and order a re-hearing.

(5) The clerk to the tribunal shall send to the Secretary of the Tribunals the certificate of the chairman as to any revocation or variation of the tribunal's decision under this Rule. The Secretary of the Tribunals shall as soon as may be make such correction as may be necessary in the Register and shall send a copy of the entry to each of the parties.

Costs

11.—(1) A tribunal may make an order that a party shall pay to another party either a specified sum in respect of the costs of or in connection with an appeal incurred by that other party or, in default of agreement, the taxed amount of those costs.

(2) Any costs required by an order under this Rule to be taxed may be taxed in the county court according to such of the scales prescribed by the county court rules for proceedings in the county court as shall be directed by the order.

Miscellaneous powers of tribunal

12.—(1) Subject to the provision of these Rules, a tribunal may regulate its own procedure.

(2) A tribunal may, if it thinks fit—
   (*a*) postpone the day or time fixed for, or adjourn, any hearing;
   (*b*) before granting an application under Rule 3 or 10 require the party making the application to give notice thereof to the other party;
   (*c*) either on the application of any person or of its own motion, direct any other person to be joined as a party to the appeal (giving such consequential directions as it considers necessary), but may do so only after having given to the person proposed to be joined a reasonable opportunity of making written or oral objection;
   (*d*) make any necessary amendments to the description of a party in the Register and in other documents relating to the appeal;
   (*e*) if the appellant shall at any time give notice of the abandonment of his appeal, dismiss the appeal;
   (*f*) if the parties agree in writing upon the terms of a decision to be made by the tribunal decide accordingly.

(3) Any act, other than the hearing of an appeal or of an application for the purposes of Rule 10(1), required or authorised by these Rules to be done by a tribunal may be done by, or on the direction of, the President, the chairman of the tribunal or a nominated chairman.

(4) Rule 11 shall apply to an order dismissing proceedings under paragraph (2) of this rule.

(5) Any functions of the Secretary of the Tribunals may be performed by an Assistant Secretary of the Tribunals.

Notices, etc.

13.—(1) Any notice given under these Rules shall be in writing and all notices and documents required or authorised by these Rules to be sent or given to any person hereinafter mentioned may be sent by post (subject to paragraphs (3) and (4) of this Rule) or delivered to or at—
   (*a*) in a case of a document directed to the Secretary of the Tribunals, the Office of the Tribunals or such other office as may be notified by the Secretary of the Tribunals to the parties;
   (*b*) in the case of a document directed to a party, his address for service specified in the notice of appeal or in a notice under paragraph (2) of this Rule or (if no address for service is so specified), his last known address or place of business in the United Kingdom or, if the party is a corporation, the corporation's registered or principal office;
   (*c*) in the case of a document directed to any person (other than a person specified in the foregoing provisions of this paragraph), his address or place of business in the United Kingdom, or if such a person is a corporation, the corporation's registered or principal office;
and if sent or given to the authorised representative of a party shall be deemed to have been sent or given to that party.

(2) A party may at any time by notice to the Secretary of the Tribunals and to the other party change his address for service under these Rules.

(3) Where a notice of appeal is not delivered, it shall be sent by the recorded delivery service.

(4) Where for any sufficient reason service of any document or notice cannot be effected in the manner prescribed under this Rule, the President or a nominated chairman may make an order for substituted service in such manner as he may deem fit and such service shall have the same effect as service in the manner prescribed under this Rule.

Patents Rules 1978

2–041

(S.I. 1978 No. 216)

Dated February 17, 1978, and made by the Secretary of State for Trade under the Patents Act 1977 (c. 37), ss.14(4), (6) and (8), 25(5), 32(2), 72(3), 78(4), 92(3) and (4), 97(1)(d), 115(1) and (3) and 127, and Sched. 4, para. 14.

. . . . . .

Employees' inventions (Sections 40 to 43)

60.—(1) An application to the comptroller under section 40 for an award of compensation shall be made on Patents Form No. 26/77 and shall be accompanied by a copy thereof and a statement in duplicate setting out fully the facts relied upon.

(2) The prescribed period for the purposes of section 40(1) and (2) shall, in relation to proceedings before the comptroller, be that period which begins when the relevant patent is granted and which expires one year after it has ceased to have effect;

Provided that, where a patent has ceased to have effect by reason of a failure to pay any renewal fee within the period prescribed for the payment thereof and an application for restoration is made to the comptroller under section 28, the said period shall—
  (a) if restoration is ordered, continue as if the patent had remained continuously in effect; or
  (b) if restoration is refused, be treated as expiring one year after the patent ceased to have effect or six months after the refusal, whichever is the later.

(3) The comptroller shall send a copy of the application and statement to the employer who, if he wishes to contest the application, shall within three months of receiving them, file a counter-statement in duplicate setting out fully the grounds on which he disputes the employees' right to the relief sought, and the comptroller shall send a copy of the counter-statement to the employee.

(4) The employee may, within three months of the receipt of the copy of the counter-statement, file evidence in support of his case and shall send a copy of the evidence to the employer.

(5) Within three months of the receipt of the copy of the employee's evidence or, if the employee does not file any evidence, within three months of the expiration of the time within which the employee's evidence might have been filed, the employer may file evidence in support of his case and shall send a copy of the evidence to the employee; and within three months of the receipt of the copy of the employer's evidence, the employee may file evidence confined to matters strictly in reply and shall send a copy of that evidence to the employer.

(6) No further evidence shall be filed by either party except by leave or direction of the comptroller.

(7) The comptroller may give such directions as he may think fit with regard to subsequent procedure.

61.—(1) Where an award of compensation has been made to an employee under section 40(1) or (2), an application under section 41(8) to vary, discharge, suspend or revive any provision of the order shall be made on Patents Form No. 27/77 and shall be accompanied by a copy thereof and a statement setting out fully the facts relied upon and the relief which is sought.

(2) Thereafter the provision of rule 60(3) to (7) shall apply to an application made under section 41(8) by an employee as they apply to an application referred to in that rule and to an application made under section 41(8) by an employer as if references in those sub-rules to the employee were references to the employer and references to the employer were references to the employee.

2–042 **Industrial Tribunals (Rules of Procedure) Regulations 1980**

(S.I. 1980 No. 884)

Dated June 26, 1980, made by the Secretary of State in exercise of the powers conferred on him by paragraph 1 of Schedule 9 to the Employment Protection (Consolidation) Act 1978 and after consultation with the Council on Tribunals.

Citation, commencement and revocation

2–043 **1.**—(1) These Regulations may be cited as the Industrial Tribunals (Rules of Procedure) Regulations 1980 (and the Rules of Procedure contained in Schedule 1 to these Regulations may be referred to as the Industrial Tribunals Rules of Procedure 1980), and they shall come into operation on 1st October 1980.

(2) The Industrial Tribunals (Labour Relations) Regulations 1974 and the other Regulations mentioned in Schedule 2 to these Regulations shall cease to have effect on 1st October 1980 except in relation to proceedings instituted before that date.

Interpretation

2. In these Regulations, unless the context otherwise requires, the following expressions have the meaning hereby assigned to them respectively, that is to say—

"the 1966 Act" means the Docks and Harbours Act 1966;

"the 1978 Act" means the Employment Protection (Consolidation) Act 1978;

"applicant" means a person who in pursuance of Rule 1 has presented an originating application to the Secretary of the Tribunals for a decision of a tribunal and includes:—

(*a*) the Secretary of State, the Board or a licensing authority,

(*b*) a claimant or complainant,

(*c*) in the case of proceedings under section 51 of the 1966 Act, a person on whose behalf an originating application has been sent by a trade union, and

(*d*) in relation to interlocutory applications under these Rules, a person who seeks any relief;

"the Board" means the National Dock Labour Board as reconstituted under the Dock Work Regulation Act 1976;

"the clerk to the tribunal" means the person appointed by the Secretary of the Tribunals or an Assistant Secretary to act in that capacity at one or more hearings;

"court" means a magistrates' court or the Crown Court;

"decision" in relation to a tribunal includes a declaration, an order (other than an interlocutory order), a recommendation or an award of the tribunal but does not include an opinion given pursuant to a pre-hearing assessment held under Rule 6;

"hearing" means a sitting of a tribunal duly constituted for the purpose of receiving evidence, hearing addresses and witnesses or doing anything lawfully requisite to enable the tribunal to reach a decision on any question;

"licensing authority" means a body having the function of issuing licences under the 1966 Act;

"the Office of the Tribunals" means the Central Office of the Industrial Tribunals (England and Wales);

"the panel of chairmen" means the panel of persons, being barristers or solicitors of not less than seven years' standing, appointed by the Lord Chancellor in pursuance of Regulation 5(2) of the Industrial Tribunals (England and Wales) Regulations 1965;

"party" in relation to proceedings under section 51 of the 1966 Act means the applicant and the Board or the licensing authority with which or (as the case may be) any person with whom it appears to the applicant that he is in dispute about a question to which that section applies and, in a case where such a question is referred to a tribunal by a court, any party to the proceedings before the court in which the question arose;

"person entitled to appear" in relation to proceedings under section 51 of the 1966 Act means a party and any person who, under subsection (5) of that section, is entitled to appear and be heard before a tribunal in such proceedings;

"the President" means the President of the Industrial Tribunals (England and Wales) or the person nominated by the Lord Chancellor to discharge for the time being the functions of the President;

"Regional Chairman" means the chairman appointed by the President to take charge of the due administration of justice by tribunals in an area specified by the President, or a person nominated either by the President or the Regional Chairman to discharge for the time being the functions of the Regional Chairman;

"Regional Office of the Industrial Tribunals" means a regional office which has been established under the Office of the Tribunals for an area specified by the President;

"Register" means the Register of Applications and Decisions kept in pursuance of these Regulations;

"respondent" means a party to the proceedings before a tribunal other than the applicant, and other than the Secretary of State in proceedings under Parts III and VI of the 1978 Act in which he is not cited as the person against whom relief is sought;

"Rule" means a Rule of Procedure contained in Schedule 1 to these Regulations;

"the Secretary of the Tribunals" and "an Assistant Secretary of the Tribunals" means respectively the persons for the time being acting as the Secretary of the Office of the Tribunals and as the Assistant Secretary of a Regional Office of the Industrial Tribunals;

"tribunal" means an industrial tribunal (England and Wales) established in pursuance of the Industrial Tribunals (England and Wales) Regulations 1965 and in relation to any proceedings means the tribunal to which the proceedings have been referred by the President or a Regional Chairman.

Proceedings of tribunals
3. Except where separate Rules of Procedure, made under the provisions of any enactment, are applicable the Rules of Procedure contained in Schedule 1 to these Regulations shall have effect in relation to all proceedings before a tribunal where:—
  (*a*) the respondent or one of the respondents resides or carries on business in England or Wales; or
  (*b*) had the remedy been by way of action in the county court, the cause of action would have arisen wholly or in part in England or Wales; or
  (*c*) the proceedings are to determine a question which has been referred to the tribunal by a court in England or Wales; or
  (*d*) in proceedings under the 1966 Act they are in relation to a port in England and Wales.

Proof of decisions of tribunals
4. The production in any proceedings in any court of a document purporting to be certified by the Secretary of the Tribunals to be a true copy of an entry of a decision in the Register shall, unless the contrary is proved, be sufficient evidence of the document and of the facts stated therein.

Regulation 3

SCHEDULE 1

RULES OF PROCEDURE

Originating application
1.—(1) Proceedings for the determination of any matter by a tribunal shall be instituted by the applicant (or, where applicable, by a court) presenting to the Secretary of the Tribunals an originating application which shall be in writing and shall set out:—
  (*a*) the name and address of the applicant; and
  (*b*) the names and addresses of the person or persons against whom relief is sought or (where applicable) of the parties to the proceedings before the court; and
  (*c*) the grounds, with particulars thereof, on which relief is sought, or in proceedings under section 51 of the 1966 Act the question for determination and (except where the question is referred by a court) the grounds on which relief is sought.
(2) Where the Secretary of the Tribunals is of the opinion that the originating application does not seek or on the facts stated therein cannot entitle the applicant to a relief which a tribunal has power to give, he may give notice to that effect to the applicant stating the reasons for his opinion and informing him that the application will not be registered unless he states in writing that he wishes to proceed with it.
(3) An application as respects which a notice has been given in pursuance of the preceding paragraph shall not be treated as having been received for the purposes of Rule 2 unless the applicant intimates in writing to the Secretary of the Tribunals that he wishes to proceed with it; and upon receipt of such an intimation the Secretary of the Tribunals shall proceed in accordance with that Rule.

Action upon receipt of originating application
2. Upon receiving an originating application the Secretary of the Tribunals shall enter parti-

culars of it in the Register and shall forthwith send a copy of it to the respondent and inform the parties in writing of the case number of the originating application entered in the Register (which shall thereafter constitute the title of the proceedings) and of the address to which notices and other communications to the Secretary of the Tribunals shall be sent. Every copy of the originating application sent by the Secretary of the Tribunals under this paragraph shall be accompanied by a written notice which shall include information, as appropriate to the case, about the means and time for entering an appearance, the consequences of failure to do so, and the right to receive a copy of the decision. The Secretary of the Tribunals shall also notify the parties that in all cases under the provisions of any enactment providing for conciliation the services of a conciliation officer are available to them.

Appearance by respondent
3.—(1) A respondent shall within 14 days of receiving the copy originating application enter an appearance to the proceedings by presenting to the Secretary of the Tribunals a written notice of appearance setting out his full name and address and stating whether or not he intends to resist the application and,if so, setting out sufficient particulars to show on what grounds. Upon receipt of a notice of appearance the Secretary of the Tribunals shall forthwith send a copy of it to any other party.

(2) A respondent who has not entered an appearance shall not be entitled to take any part in the proceedings except—
  (i) to apply under Rule 13(1) for an extension of the time appointed by this Rule for entering an appearance;
  (ii) to make an application under Rule 4(1)(i);
  (iii) to make an application under Rule 10(2) in respect of Rule 10(1)(*b*);
  (iv) to be called as a witness by another person;
  (v) to be sent a copy of a decision or specification of reasons or corrected decision or specification in pursuance of Rule 9(3), 9(7) or 10(5).

(3) A notice of appearance which is presented to the Secretary of the Tribunals after the time appointed by this Rule for entering appearances shall be deemed to include an application under Rule 13(1) (by the respondent who has presented the notice of appearance) for an extension of the time so appointed. Without prejudice to Rule 13(4), if the tribunal grants the application (which it may do notwithstanding that the grounds of the application are not stated) the Secretary of the Tribunals shall forthwith send a copy of the notice of appearance to any other party. The tribunal shall not refuse an extension of time under this Rule unless it has sent notice to the person wishing to enter an appearance giving him an opportunity to show cause why the extension should be granted.

Power to require further particulars and attendance of witnesses and to grant discovery
4.—(1) A tribunal may—
  (*a*) subject to Rule 3(2), on the application of a party to the proceedings made either by notice to the Secretary of the Tribunals or at the hearing of the originating application, or
  (*b*) in relation to sub-paragraph (i) of this paragraph, if it thinks fit of its own motion—
    (i) require a party to furnish in writing to the person specified by the tribunal further particulars of the grounds on which he or it relies and of any facts and contentions relevant thereto;
    (ii) grant to the person making the application such discovery or inspection (including the taking of copies) of documents as might be granted by a county court; and
    (iii) require the attendance of any person (including a party to the proceedings) as a witness or require the production of any document relating to the matter to be determined, wherever such witness may be within Great Britain;
and may appoint the time at or within which or the place at which any act required in pursuance of this Rule is to be done.

(2) A party on whom a requirement has been made under paragraph (1)(i) or (1)(ii) of this Rule on an *ex parte* application, or (in relation to a requirement under paragraph 1(i)) on the tribunal's own motion, and a person on whom a requirement has been made under paragraph (1)(iii) may apply to the tribunal by notice to the Secretary of the Tribunal's before the appointed time at or within which the requirement is to be complied with to vary or set aside the requirement. Notice of an application under this paragraph to vary or set aside a requirement shall be given to the parties (other than the party making the application) and, where appropriate, in proceedings which may involve payments out of the Redundancy Fund or Maternity Pay Fund, the Secretary of State if not a party.

(3) Every document containing a requirement under paragraph (1)(ii) or (1)(iii) of this Rule shall contain a reference to the fact that under paragraph 1(7) of Schedule 9 to the 1978

Act, any person who without reasonable excuse fails to comply with any such requirement shall be liable on summary conviction to a fine not exceeding £100.

(4) If the requirement under paragraph (1)(i) or (1)(ii) of this Rule is not complied with, a tribunal, before or at the hearing, may dismiss the originating application, or, as the case may be, strike out the whole or part of the notice of appearance, and, where appropriate, direct that a respondent shall be debarred from defending altogether: Provided that a tribunal shall not so dismiss or strike out or give such a direction unless it has sent notice to the party who has not complied with the requirement giving him an opportunity to show cause why such should not be done.

Time and place of hearing and appointment of assessor

5.—(1) The President or a Regional Chairman shall fix the date, time and place of the hearing of the originating application and the Secretary of the Tribunals shall (subject to Rule 3(2)) not less than 14 days (or such shorter time as may be agreed by him with the parties) before the date so fixed send to each party a notice of hearing which shall include information and guidance as to attendance at the hearing, witnesses and the bringing of documents (if any), representation by another person and written representations.

(2) In any proceedings under the 1966 Act in which the President or a Regional Chairman so directs, the Secretary of the Tribunals shall also take such of the following steps as may be so directed, namely—

(a) publish in one or more newspapers circulating in the locality in which the port in question is situated notice of the hearing;

(b) send notice of the hearing to such persons as may be directed;

(c) post notices of the hearing in a conspicuous place or conspicuous places in or near the port in question;

but the requirement as to the period of notice contained in paragraph (1) of this Rule shall not apply to any such notices.

(3) Where in the case of any proceedings it is provided for one or more assessors to be appointed, the President or a Regional Chairman may, if he thinks fit, appoint a person or persons having special knowledge or experience in relation to the subject matter of the originating application to sit with the tribunal as assessor or assessors.

Pre-hearing assessment

6.—(1) A tribunal may at any time before the hearing (either, subject to Rule 3(2), on the application of a party to the proceedings made by notice to the Secretary of the Tribunals or of its own motion) consider, by way of a pre-hearing assessment, the contents of the originating application and entry of appearance, any representations in writing which have been submitted and any oral argument advanced by or on behalf of a party.

(2) If upon a pre-hearing assessment, the tribunal considers that the originating application is unlikely to succeed or that the contentions or any particular contention of a party appear to have no reasonable prospect of success, it may indicate that in its opinion, if the originating application shall not be withdrawn or the contentions or contention of the party shall be persisted in up to or at the hearing, the party in question may have an order for costs made against him at the hearing under the provisions of Rule 11. A pre-hearing assessment shall not take place unless the tribunal has sent notice to the parties to the proceedings giving them (and, where appropriate, in proceedings which may involve payments out of the Redundancy Fund or Maternity Pay Fund, the Secretary of State, if not a party) an opportunity to submit representations in writing and to advance oral argument at the pre-hearing assessment if they so wish.

(3) Any indication of opinion made in accordance with paragraph (2) of this Rule shall be recorded in a document signed by the chairman a copy of which shall be sent to the parties to the proceedings and a copy of which shall be available to the tribunal at the hearing.

(4) Where a tribunal has indicated its opinion in accordance with paragraph (2) of this Rule no member thereof shall be a member of the tribunal at the hearing.

The hearing

7.—(1) Any hearing of or in connection with an originating application shall take place in public unless in the opinion of the tribunal a private hearing is appropriate for the purpose of hearing evidence which relates to matters of such a nature that it would be against the interests of national security to allow the evidence to be given in public or hearing evidence from any person which in the opinion of the tribunal is likely to consist of—

(a) information which he could not disclose without contravening a prohibition imposed by or under any enactment; or (*b*) any information which has been communicated to him in confidence, or which he has otherwise obtained in consequence of the confidence reposed in him by another person; or

(*c*) information the disclosure of which would cause substantial injury to any undertaking of his or any undertaking in which he works for reasons other than its effect on negotiations with respect to any of the matters mentioned in section 29(1) of the Trade Union and Labour Relations Act 1974.

(2) A member of the Council on Tribunals shall be entitled to attend any hearing taking place in his capacity as such member.

(3) Subject to Rule 3(2), if a party shall desire to submit representations in writing for consideration by a tribunal at the hearing of the originating application that party shall present such representations to the Secretary of the Tribunals not less than 7 days before the hearing and shall at the same time send a copy to the other party or parties.

(4) Where a party has failed to attend or be represented at the hearing (whether or not he has sent any representations in writing) the contents of his originating application or, as the case may be, of his entry of appearance may be treated by a tribunal as representations in writing.

(5) The Secretary of State if he so elects shall be entitled to apply under Rules 4(1), 13(1) and (2), 15 and 16(1) and to appear as if he were a party and be heard at any hearing of or in connection with an originating application in proceedings in which he is not a party which may involve payments out of the Redundancy Fund or Maternity Pay Fund.

(6) Subject to Rule 3(2), at any hearing of or in connection with an originating application a party and any person entitled to appear may appear before the tribunal and may be heard in person or be represented by counsel or by a solicitor or by a representative of a trade union or an employers' association or by any other person whom he desires to represent him.

Procedure at hearing

8.—(1) The tribunal shall conduct the hearing in such manner as it considers most suitable to the clarification of the issues before it and generally to the just handling of the proceedings; it shall so far as appears to it appropriate seek to avoid formality in its proceedings and it shall not be bound by any enactment or rule of law relating to the admissibility of evidence in proceedings before the courts of law.

(2) Subject to paragraph (1) of this Rule, at the hearing of the originating application a party (unless disentitled by virtue of Rule 3(2), the Secretary of State, (if, not being a party, he elects to appear as provided in Rule 7(5)) and any other person entitled to appear shall be entitled to give evidence, to call witnesses, to question any witnesses and to address the tribunal.

(3) If a party shall fail to appear or to be represented at the time and place fixed for the hearing, the tribunal may, if that party is an applicant dismiss, or, in any case, dispose of the application in the absence of that party or may adjourn the hearing to a later date: Provided that before deciding to dismiss or disposing of any application in the absence of a party the tribunal shall consider any representations submitted by that party in pursuance of Rule 7(3).

(4) A tribunal may require any witness to give evidence on oath or affirmation and for that purpose there may be administered an oath or affirmation in due form.

Decision of tribunal

9.—(1) A decision of a tribunal may be taken by a majority thereof and, if the tribunal shall be constituted of two members only, the chairman shall have a second or casting vote.

(2) The decision of a tribunal shall be recorded in a document signed by the chairman which shall contain the reasons for the decision.

(3) The clerk to the tribunal shall transmit the document signed by the chairman to the Secretary of the Tribunals who shall as soon as may be enter it in the Register and shall send a copy of the entry to each of the parties and to the persons entitled to appear who did so appear and, where the originating application was sent to a tribunal by a court, to that court.

(4) The specification of the reasons for the decision shall be omitted from the Register in any case in which evidence has been heard in private and the tribunal so directs and in that event a specification of the reasons shall be sent to the parties and to any superior court in any proceedings relating to such decision together with a copy of the entry.

(5) The Register shall be kept at the Office of the Tribunals and shall be open to the inspection of any person without charge at all reasonable hours.

(6) Clerical mistakes in documents recording the tribunal's decisions, or errors arising in them from an accidental slip or omission, may at any time be corrected by the chairman by certificate under his hand.

(7) The clerk to the tribunal shall send a copy of any document so corrected and the certificate of the chairman to the Secretary of the Tribunals who shall as soon as may be make such correction as may be necessary in the Register and shall send a copy of the corrected entry

or of the corrected specification of the reasons, as the case may be, to each of the parties and to the persons entitled to appear who did so appear and, where the originating application was sent to the tribunal by a court, to that court.

(8) If any decision is—
   (a) corrected under paragraph (6) of this Rule,
   (b) reviewed, revoked or varied under Rule 10, or
   (c) altered in any way by order of a superior court,
the Secretary of the Tribunals shall alter the entry in the Register to conform with any such certificate or order and shall send a copy of the new entry to each of the parties and to the persons entitled to appear who did so appear and where the originating application was sent to the tribunal by a court, to that court.

Review of tribunal's decisions

10.—(1) A tribunal shall have power to review and to revoke or vary by certificate under the chairman's hand any decision on the grounds that—
   (a) the decision was wrongly made as a result of an error on the part of the tribunal staff; or
   (b) a party did not receive notice of the proceedings leading to the decision; or
   (c) the decision was made in the absence of a party or person entitled to be heard; or
   (d) new evidence has become available since the making of the decision provided that its existence could not have been reasonably known of or foreseen; or
   (e) the interests of justice require such a review.

(2) An application for the purposes of paragraph (1) of this Rule may be made at the hearing. If the application is not made at the hearing, such application shall be made by the Secretary of the Tribunals at any time from the date of the hearing until 14 days after the date on which the decision was sent to the parties and must be in writing stating th grounds in full.

(3) An application for the purposes of paragraph (1) of this Rule may be refused by the President or by the chairman of the tribunal which decided the case or by a Regional Chairman if in his opinion it has no reasonable prospect of success.

(4) If such an application is not refused under paragraph (3) of this Rule it shall be heard by the tribunal which decided the case or—
   (a) where it is not practicable for it to be heard by that tribunal, or
   (b) where the decision was made by a chairman acting alone under Rule 12(4);
by a tribunal appointed either by the President or a Regional Chairman, and if it is granted the tribunal shall either vary the decision or revoke the decision and order a rehearing.

(5) The clerk to the tribunal shall send to the Secretary of the Tribunals the certificate of the chairman as to any revocation or variation of the tribunal's decision under this Rule. The Secretary of the Tribunals shall as soon as may be make such correction as may be necessary in the Register and shall send a copy of the entry to each of the parties and to the persons entitled to appear who did so appear and where the originating application was sent to a tribunal by a court, to that court.

Costs

11.—(1) Subject to paragraphs (2), (3) and (4) of this Rule, a tribunal shall not normally make an award in respect of the costs or expenses incurred by a party to the proceedings but where in its opinion a party (and if he is a respondent whether or not he has entered an appearance) has in bringing or conducting the proceedings acted frivolously, vexatiously or otherwise unreasonably the tribunal may make—
   (a) an order that that party shall pay to another party (or to the Secretary of State, if, not being a party, he has acted as provided in Rule 7(5)) either a specified sum in respect of the costs or expenses incurred by that other party (or, as the case may be, by the Secretary of State), or the whole or part of those costs or expenses as taxed (if not otherwise agreed);
   (b) an order that that party shall pay to the Secretary of State the whole, or any part, of any allowances (other than allowances paid to members of tribunals or assessors) paid by the Secretary of State under paragraph 10 of Schedule 9 to the 1978 Act to any person for the purposes of, or in connection with, his attendance at the tribunal.

(2) Where the tribunal has on the application of a party to the proceedings postponed the day or time fixed for or adjourned the hearing, the tribunal may make orders against or, as the case may require, in favour of that party as at paragraph (1)(a) and (b) of this Rule as respects any costs or expenses incurred or any allowances paid by that party as a result of the postponement or adjournment.

(3) Where, on a complaint of unfair dismissal in respect of which—
   (i) the applicant has expressed a wish to be reinstated or re-engaged which has been communicated to the respondent at least 7 days before the hearing of the complaint, or

(ii) the proceedings arise out of the respondent's failure to permit the applicant to return to work after an absence due to pregnancy or confinement,
any postponement or adjournment of the hearing has been caused by the respondent's failure, without a special reason, to adduce reasonable evidence as to the availability of the job from which the applicant was dismissed, or, as the case may be, which she held before her absence, or of comparable or suitable employment, the tribunal shall make orders against that respondent as at paragraph (1)(*a*) and (*b*) of this Rule as respects any costs or expenses incurred or any allowances paid as a result of the posponement or adjournment.

(4) In any proceedings under the 1966 Act a tribunal may make—
  (*a*) an order that a party, or any other person entitled to appear who did so appear, shall pay to another party or such person either a specified sum in respect of the costs or expenses incurred by that other party or person or the whole or part of those costs or expenses as taxed (if not otherwise agreed);
  (*b*) an order that a party, or any other person entitled to appear who did so appear, shall pay to the Secretary of State a specified sum in respect of the whole, or any part, of any allowances (other than allowances paid to members of tribunals) paid by the Secretary of State under paragraph 10 of Schedule 9 to the 1978 Act to any person for the purpose of, or in connection with, his attendance at the tribunal.

(5) Any costs required by an order under this Rule to be taxed may be taxed in the county court according to such of the scales prescribed by the county court rules for proceedings in the county court as shall be directed by the order.

Miscellaneous powers of tribunal

12.—(1) Subject to the provisions of these Rules, a tribunal may regulate its own procedure.

(2) A tribunal may, if it thinks fit,—
  (*a*) extend the time appointed by or under these Rules for doing any act notwithstanding that the time appointed may have expired;
  (*b*) postpone the day or time fixed for, or adjourn, any hearing (particularly as respects cases under the provisions of any enactment providing for conciliation for the purpose of giving an opportunity for the complaint to be settled by way of conciliation and withdrawn);
  (*c*) if the applicant shall at any time give notice of the withdrawal of his originating application, dismiss the proceedings;
  (*d*) except in proceedings under the 1966 Act, if both or all the parties (and the Secretary of State, if, not being a party, he has acted as provided in Rule 7(5)) agree in writing upon the terms of a decision to be made by the tribunal, decide accordingly;
  (*e*) at any stage of the proceedings order to be struck out or amended any originating application or notice of appearance or anything in such application or notice of appearance on the grounds that it is scandalous, frivolous or vexatious;
  (*f*) on the application of the respondent, or of its own motion, order to be struck out any originating application for want of prosecution; Provided that before making any order under (*e*) or (*f*) above the tribunal shall send notice to the party against whom it is proposed that any such order should be made giving him an opportunity to show cause why such an order should not be made.

(3) Subject to Rule 4(2), a tribunal may, if it thinks fit, before granting an application under Rule 4 or Rule 13 require the party (or, as the case may be, the Secretary of State) making the application to give notice of it to the other party or parties. The notice shall give particulars of the application and indicate the address to which and the time within which any objection to the application shall be made being an address and time specified for the purposes of the application by the tribunal.

(4) Any act other than the holding of a pre-hearing assessment under Rule 6, the hearing of an originating application, or the making of an order under Rule 10(1), required or authorised by these Rules to be done by a tribunal may be done by, or on the direction of, the President or the chairman of the tribunal, or any chairman being a member of the panel of chairmen.

(5) Rule 11 shall apply to an order dismissing proceedings under paragraph (2)(*c*) of this Rule.

(6) Any functions of the Secretary of the Tribunals other than that mentioned in Rule 1(2) may be performed by an Assistant Secretary of the Tribunals.

Extension of time and directions

13.—(1) An application to a tribunal for an extension of the time appointed by these Rules for doing any act may be made by a party either before or after the expiration of any time so appointed.

(2) Subject to Rule 3(2), a party may at any time apply to a tribunal for directions on any matter arising in connection with the proceedings.

(3) An application under the foregoing provisions of this Rule shall be made by presenting to the Secretary of the Tribunals a notice of application, which shall state the title of the proceedings and shall set the grounds of the application.

(4) The Secretary of the Tribunals shall give notice to both or all the parties (subject to Rule 3(2) of any extension of time granted under Rule 12(2)(*a*) or any directions given in pursuance of this Rule.

Joinder and representative respondents

14.—(1) A tribunal may at any time either upon the application of any person or, where appropriate of its own motion, direct any person against whom any relief is sought to be joined as a party to the proceedings, and give such consequential directions as it considers necessary.

(2) A tribunal may likewise, either upon such application or of its own motion, order that any respondent named in the originating application or subsequently added, who shall appear to the tribunal not to have been, or to have ceased to be, directly interested in the subject of the originating application, be dismissed from the proceedings.

(3) Where there are numerous persons having the same interest in an originating application, one or more of them may be cited as the person or persons against whom relief is sought, or may be authorised by the tribunal, before or at the hearing, to defend on behalf of all the persons so interested.

Consolidation of proceedings

15. Where there are pending before the industrial tribunals two or more originating applications, then, if at any time upon the application of a party or of its own motion it appears to a tribunal that—
   (*a*) some common question of law or fact arises in both or all the originating applications, or
   (*b*) the relief claimed therein is in respect of or arises out of the same set of facts, or
   (*c*) for some other reason it is desirable to make an order under this Rule,
the tribunal may order that some (as specified in the order) or all of the originating applications shall be considered together, and may give such consequential directions as may be necessary: Provided that the tribunal shall not make an order under this Rule without sending notice to all parties concerned giving them an opportunity to show cause why such an order should not be made.

Transfer of proceedings

16.—(1) Where there is pending before the industrial tribunals an originating application in respect of which it appears to the President or a Regional Chairman that the proceedings could be determined by an industrial tribunal (Scotland) established in pursuance of the Industrial Tribunals (Scotland) Regulations 1965 and that the originating application would more conveniently be determined by such a tribunal, the President or a Regional Chairman may, at any time upon the application of a party or of his own motion, with the consent of the President of the Industrial Tribunals (Scotland), direct that the said proceedings be transferred to the Office of the Industrial Tribunals (Scotland): Provided that no such direction shall be made unless notice has been sent to all parties concerned giving them an opportunity to show cause why such a direction should not be made.

(2) Where proceedings have been transferred to the Office of the Industrial Tribunals (England and Wales) under Rule 16(1) of the Industrial Tribunals (Rules of Procedure) (Scotland) Regulations 1980 they shall be treated as if in all respects they had been commenced by an originating application pursuant to Rule 1.

Notices, etc.

17.—(1) Any notice given under these Rules shall be in writing.

(2) All notices and documents required by these Rules to be presented to the Secretary of the Tribunals may be presented at the Office of the Tribunals or such other office as may be notified by the Secretary of the Tribunals to the parties.

(3) All notices and documents required or authorised by these Rules to be sent or given to any person hereinafter mentioned may be sent by post (subject to paragraph (5) of this Rule) or delivered to or at—
   (*a*) in the case of a notice or document directed to the Secretary of the State in proceedings to which he is not a party, the offices of the Department of Employment at Caxton

House, Tothill Street, London SW1H 9NA or such other office as may be notified by the Secretary of State;
(b) in the case of a notice or document directed to the Board, the principal office of the Board;
(c) in the case of a notice or document directed to a court, the office of the clerk of the court;
(d) in the case of a notice or document directed to a party:—
  (i) his address for service specified in the originating application or in a notice of appearance or in a notice under paragraph (4) of this Rule; or
  (ii) if no address for service has been so specified, his last known address or place of business in the United Kingdom or, if the party is a corporation, the corporation's registered or principal office in the United Kingdom or, in any case, at such address or place outside the United Kingdom as the President or a Regional Chairman may allow;
(e) in the case of a notice or document directed to any person (other than a person specified in the foregoing provisions of this paragraph), his address or place of business in the United Kingdom, or if such person is a corporation, the corporation's registered or principal office in the United Kingdom;
and if sent or given to the authorised representative of a party shall be deemed to have been sent or given to that party.

(4) A party may at any time by notice to the Secretary of the Tribunals and to the other party or parties (and, where appropriate, to the appropriate conciliation officer) change his address for service under these Rules.

(5) The recorded delivery service shall be used instead of the ordinary post:—
(a) when a second set of documents or notices is to be sent to a respondent who has not entered an appearance under Rule 3(1);
(b) for service of an order made under Rule 4(1)(iii) requiring the attendance of a witness or the production of a document.

(6) Where for any sufficient reason service of any document or notice cannot be effected in the manner prescribed under this Rule, the President or a Regional Chairman may make an order for substituted service in such manner as he may deem fit and such service shall have the same effect as service in the manner prescribed under this Rule.

(7) In proceedings brought under the provisions of any enactment providing for conciliation the Secretary of the Tribunals shall send copies of all documents and notices to a conciliation officer who in the opinion of the Secretary is an appropriate officer to receive them.

(8) In proceedings which may involve payments out of the Redundancy Fund or Maternity Pay Fund, the Secretary of the Tribunals shall, where appropriate, send copies of all documents and notices to the Secretary of State notwithstanding the fact that he may not be a party to such proceedings.

(9) In proceedings under the Equal Pay Act 1970, the Sex Discrimination Act 1975 or the Race Relations Act 1976 the Secretary of the Tribunals shall send to the Equal Opportunities Commission or, as the case may be, the Commission for Racial Equality copies of all documents sent to the parties under Rule 9(3), (7) and (8) and Rule 10(5).

Regulation 1 SCHEDULE 2

REGULATIONS REVOKED

Statutory Instrument	Title	Extent of revocation
1974/1386	The Industrial Tribunals (Labour Relations) Regulations 1974	
1976/661	The Industrial Tribunals (Labour Relations) (Amendment) Regulations 1976	The whole Regulations except as respects proceedings instituted before 1st October, 1980.
1977/911	The Industrial Tribunals (Labour Relations) (Amendment) Regulations 1977	

1978/991 The Industrial Tribunals
(Labour Relations)
(Amendment) Regulations 1978

Funds for Trade Union Ballots Regulations 1980

(S.I. 1980 No. 1252)

Dated August 18, 1980, and made by the Secretary of State in exercise of the powers conferred on him by section 1 of the Employment Act 1980 and of all other powers enabling him in that behalf.

AMENDMENT
The words in square brackets in these regulations were added or substituted by the Funds for Trade Union Ballots (Amendment) Regulation 1982 (S.I. 1982 No. 1108).

Citation and commencement
1. These Regulations may be cited as the Funds for Trade Union Ballots Regulations 1980 and shall come into operation on 1st October 1980.

Interpretation
2. In these Regulations—
["the post" means a postal service provided by the Post Office or a postal service which by reason of a licence granted under section 68(1) of the British Telecommunications Act 1981 or of an order made under section 69(1) of that Act does not constitute an infringement of the privilege conferred on the Post Office by section 66(1) of that Act, and cognate expressions shall be construed accordingly;]
"the Scheme" means the scheme made by these Regulations;
"the 1964 Act" means the Trade Union (Amalgamations, etc.) Act 1964.

Scope of the Scheme
3. Subject to Regulations 5 to 7 below, the Scheme applies to a ballot if—
   (*a*) the purpose of the question, or of each of the questions, to be voted upon falls within the purposes mentioned in Regulation 4 below; or
   (*b*) the purpose of one or more of the questions to be voted upon falls within the said purposes and each other question to be voted upon relates to the same issue as a question the purpose of which falls within the said purposes.
4. The purposes referred to in Regulation 3 above are—

(a) obtaining a decision or ascertaining the views of members of a trade union as to the calling or ending of a strike or other industrial action;
(b) carrying out an election provided for by the rules of a trade union to the principal committee having the executive responsibility for managing the affairs of the trade union, whether known as the executive committee or by any other name;
(c) carrying out an election provided for by the rules of a trade union to the positions of president, chairman, secretary or treasurer of the trade union or to any position which the person elected will hold as an employee of the trade union;
(d) amending the rules of a trade union;
(e) obtaining a decision in accordance with the 1964 Act on a resolution to approve an instrument of amalgamation or transfer.
[(f) obtaining a decision or ascertaining the views of members of a trade union as to the acceptance or rejection of a proposal made by an employer which relates in whole or in part to remuneration (whether in money or money's worth), hours of work, level of performance, holidays or pensions.]

5. The Scheme applies only to ballots which are so conducted as to secure, so far as reasonably practicable, that those voting may do so in secret.

6. The Scheme does not apply to a ballot if the arrangements for the conduct of the ballot do not—
(a) require those voting to do so by marking a voting paper; and
(b) provide that those voting shall individually return the voting paper by post to the trade union conducting the ballot or to another person responsible for counting the votes.

7. The Scheme applies to a ballot if the end of the period for voting falls on or after 1st October 1980 but nothing in this Regulation shall enable the Certification Officer to make payments in respect of expenditure incurred before 1st August 1980.

Application for payments

8.—(1) An independent trade union claiming to have incurred expenditure on a ballot to which the Scheme applies may apply to the Certification Officer.

(2) An application under paragraph (1) above shall be made in such form and shall be accompanied by such other documents as the Certification Officer may require.

9. If the Certification Officer is satisfied that an application under paragraph (1) of Regulation 8 above is in respect of a ballot to which the Scheme applies he shall proceed in accordance with the following Regulations.

Conditions to be satisfied if payment is to be made

10. Except as provided in Regulation 12 below the Certification Officer shall not make any payments under Regulations 13 to 16 below if—
(a) on consideration of any matter which has come to his notice, he is of the opinion that any of the conditions mentioned in Regulation 11 below have not been satisfied; or
(b) any assurance he requests from the trade union relating to the said conditions is not given.

11. The conditions referred to in Regulation 10 above are—

(a) that the holding of the ballot was not in contravention of the rules of the trade union;
(b) that any requirements in the rules of the trade union as to conduct of the ballot were complied with;
(c) in the case of a ballot containing a question for the purpose of ascertaining the views of members of a trade union as to the calling or ending of a strike or other industrial action, that, so far as reasonably practicable, the ballot was conducted so as to secure that all members likely to be called upon to participate in the action, or participating in the action, as the case may be, were entitled to vote;
(d) that those entitled to vote were allowed to vote without interference or constraint;
(e) that, so far as reasonably practicable, those entitled to vote had a fair opportunity of voting;
(f) that where the votes on any question have not been counted, the decision not to count them was taken because of a change in circumstances occurring after the first day on which voting papers were despatched or given to persons entitled to vote which materially affected the issue to which the question related;
(g) that where the votes cast have been counted, they have been fairly counted.
[(h) in the case of a ballot containing a question within paragraph (f) of Regulation 4 above, that only persons who were union members and were affected by the proposal were entitled to vote.]

12.—(1) If the Certification Officer is of the opinion that the conditions mentioned in Regulation 11 were not satisfied only because the condition mentioned in paragraph (b) of that Regulation was not satisfied he may make payments towards the expenditure incurred in respect of the ballot if he is of the opinion that the failure to comply with the requirements referred to therein had no significant effect upon the proper conduct of the ballot.

(2) If the ballot has been conducted for the purpose of obtaining a decision in accordance with the 1964 Act on a resolution to approve an instrument of amalgamation or transfer—
(a) the condition mentioned in paragraph (a) of Regulation 11 above does not apply to the ballot;
(b) the condition mentioned in paragraph (b) of Regulation 11 above does not apply to any failure to comply with the rules of the trade union which is sanctioned by section 2 of the 1964 Act;
(c) if arrangements have been made under section 2(2) of the 1964 Act the Certification Officer shall not make any payments under Regulations 13 to 16 below if—
  (i) on consideration of any matter which has come to his notice, he is of the opinion that the manner in which the vote was taken was not in accordance with the arrangements and that in consequence there was a significant effect upon the proper conduct of the ballot, or,
  (ii) any assurance he requests from the trade union relating to the manner in which the vote was taken is not given.

Payments towards stationery and printing expenditure
13.—(1) The Certification Officer shall make a payment towards the

expenditure incurred by the trade union on stationery and printing in respect of—
  (a) voting papers, envelopes for sending out and returning voting papers and any additional envelopes used for the purpose of helping to secure the secrecy of the voting;
  (b) that part of any material enclosed with the voting papers which explains the matter to which the question to be voted upon relates or the procedure for voting.

(2) The amount of the payment referred to in paragraph (1) above shall, if the Certification Officer considers the expenditure incurred to have been reasonable, be the amount spent, or, if he considers the expenditure incurred to have been unreasonable, the amount which he considers would have been reasonable.

Payment towards postal costs

14.—(1) If the post has been used to send voting papers to persons entitled to vote, the Certification Officer shall make a payment towards the postal expenditure incurred by the trade union in sending to the persons entitled to vote the voting papers, envelopes and material referred to in Regulation 13 above in respect of which a payment is payable.

(2) [*Repealed by S.I. 1982 No. 1108.*]

15.—(1) The Certification Officer shall make a payment towards the postal expenditure (if any) incurred by the trade union in paying for the persons entitled to vote to return their voting papers by post.

(2) [*Repealed by S.I. 1982 No. 1108.*]

[**15A.** Subject to Regulation 16 below, the amount of the payments referred to in Regulations 14 and 15 above shall be—
  (a) to the extent that second class post or a cheaper postal means was used, the amount spent on such use;
  (b) to the extent that a means more expensive than second class post was used, the amount which would have been spent if second class post had been used, or, if the Certification Officer considers the use of the more expensive means to have been reasonable in the circumstances, the amount spent on such use.]

16. If the Certification Officer considers that additional postal expenditure has been incurred by the use of paper of a greater quantity or heavier quality than is reasonable, a payment made under Regulation 14 or 15 above shall not include the amount of the additional postal expenditure so incurred.

Provisions as to payments

17. The Certification Officer shall not make any payments until the expiration of a period of six weeks beginning with whichever is the last of the following dates—
  (a) the date on which the results relating to the questions asked in the ballot in respect of which the votes were counted have been made available to the persons entitled to vote;
  (b) the date on which an application is made under Regulation 8 above;
  (c) in the case of a ballot conducted for the purposes of the 1964 Act where the amalgamating or transferor trade union has passed a resolution approving the instrument of amalgamation or transfer and an application has been made to register the instrument or the

Certification Officer has reason to believe that such an application will be made, the date of registration of the instrument or, if a complaint is made under section 4 of the 1964 Act and the Certification Officer makes an order under subsection (3) of that section specifying steps which must be taken before he will entertain any application to register the instrument, the date on which the order is made.

18. All payments shall be made to the applicant trade union.

Arrangements to hold ballots

19. The Scheme applies to arrangements to hold a ballot which is not proceeded with if voting papers have been despatched or given to persons entitled to vote before the decision not to proceed with the ballot is taken and, accordingly, in relating to arrangements to which the Scheme applies by virtue of this Regulation, these Regulations shall have effect with such modifications as may be appropriate.

Special provisions as to amalgamations and tranfers of engagements

20. If an amalgamating or transferor trade union has passed a resolution approving an instrument of amalgamation or transfer under section 1 of the 1964 Act which is registered and, having incurred expenditure in respect of a ballot, has either made application under Regulation 8 above before the date of registration of the instrument, or, being eligible to make such an application, has not done so before that date, and the amalgamated or transferee trade union is an independent trade union, then—

(*a*) with effect from the date of registration of the instrument the amalgamated or transferee trade union shall be treated for the purposes of the Scheme other than Regulations 10 to 12 above as if, in a case where an application under Regulation 8 has been made before that date, it were the applicant trade union and in that case and the case where no such application has been made it had incurred the expenditure in respect of the ballot;

(*b*) an assurance following a request by the Certification Officer pursuant to Regulations 10(*b*) or 12(2)(*c*)(ii) above shall be treated as being given by the amalgamation or transferor trade union if given by a person who was an officer of that union immediately before the date of registration of the instrument.

Special provisions as to section 2 of the Employment Act 1980

21. If on complaint presented under section 2 of the Employment Act 1980 in respect of a ballot an industrial tribunal has made an award of compensation to be paid to a trade union and the Scheme applies to that ballot, the Certification Officer shall on an application under Regulation 8 above reduce the total of the payments made under Regulation 13 to 16 above by so much of the award as he considers relates to the expenditure in respect of which payments are to be made under the said Regulations.

Employment Appeal Tribunal Rules 1980

(S.I. 1980 No. 2035)

Dated December 18, 1980, and made by the Lord Chancellor, in execise of the powers conferred on him by paragraph 17 of Schedule 11 of the Employment Protection (Consolidation) Act 1978 and after consultation with the Lord President of the Court of Session.

Citation and commencement

1.—(1) These Rules may be cited as the Employment Appeal Tribunal Rules 1980 and shall come into operation on 1st February 1981.

(2) The Employment Appeal Tribunal Rules 1976 shall cease to have effect except in relation to appeals instituted before that date.

Interpretation

2. In these Rules, unless the context otherwise requires—
"the Act" means the Employment Protection (Consolidation) Act 1978 and a section or Schedule referred to by number means the section or Schedule so numbered in the Act;
"the Appeal Tribunal" means the Employment Appeal Tribunal established under section 87 of the Employment Protection Act 1975 and continued in existence under section 135 of the Act and includes the President, a judge, a member or the Registrar acting on behalf of the Tribunal;
"judge" means a judge of the Appeal Tribunal nominated under section 135(2)(*a*) or (*b*) and includes a judge nominated under paragraph 5 or 6 and a judge appointed under paragraph 8 of Schedule 11 to act temporarily in the place of a judge of the Tribunal;
"member" means a member of the Appeal Tribunal appointed under section 135(2)(*c*) and includes a member appointed under paragraph 7 of Schedule 11 to act temporarily in the place of a member appointed under that section;
"the President" means the judge appointed under section 135(4) to be President of the Appeal Tribunal and includes a judge nominated under paragraph 4 of Schedule 11 to act temporarily in his place;
"the Registrar" means the person appointed to be Registrar of the Appeal Tribunal and includes any officer of the Tribunal authorised by the President to act on behalf of the Registrar;
"the Secretary of Industrial Tribunals" means the person acting for the time being as the Secretary of the Central Office of the Industrial Tribunals (England and Wales), or, as may be appropriate, of the Central Office of the Industrial Tribunals (Scotland);
"the Certification Officer" means the person appointed to be the Certification Officer under section 7(1) of the Employment Protection Act 1975;
"taxing officer" means any officer of the Appeal Tribunal authorised by the President to assess costs or expenses.

Institution of appeal

3.—(1) Every appeal to the Appeal Tribunal shall be instituted by serving on the Tribunal, within 42 days of the date on which the document recording the decision or order appealed from was sent to the appellant, a notice of appeal in, or substantially in accordance with Form 1, 2 or 3 in the Schedule to these Rules, together with a copy of the said decision or order.

(2) Where it appears to the Registrar that the grounds of appeal stated in the notice of appeal do not give the Appeal Tribunal jurisdiction to entertain the appeal, he shall notify the appellant accordingly informing him of the reasons for the opinion and, subject to paragraphs (3) and (5) of this rule, no further action shall be taken on the appeal.

(3) Where notification has been given under paragraph (2) of this rule, the appellant may serve a fresh notice of appeal within the time remaining under paragraph (1) or within 28 days from the date on which the Registrar's notification was sent to him, whichever is the longer period.

(4) Where the appellant serves a fresh notice of appeal under paragraph (3) of this rule the Registrar shall consider such fresh notice of appeal with regard to jurisdiction as though it were an original notice of appeal lodged pursuant to paragraph (1) of this rule.

(5) Where an appellant expresses dissatisfaction in writing with the reasons given by the Registrar, under paragraph (2) of this rule, for his opinion that the grounds of appeal stated in a notice of appeal do not give the Appeal Tribunal jurisdiction to entertain the appeal, the Registrar shall place the papers before the President or a judge for his direction as to whether any further action should be taken on the appeal.

Service of notice of appeal

2–055
4. On receipt of notice under rule 3, the Registrar shall seal the notice with the Appeal Tribunal's seal and shall serve a sealed copy on the appellant and on—
- (*a*) every person who, in accordance with rule 5, is a respondent to the appeal; and
- (*b*) the Secretary of Industrial Tribunals in the case of an appeal from an industrial tribunal; or
- (*c*) the Certification Officer in the case of an appeal from any of his decisions; or
- (*d*) the Secretary of State in the case of an appeal under section 36 or Part VI of the Act or Part IV of the Employment Protection Act 1975 to which he is not a respondent.

Respondents to appeals

5. The respondents to an appeal shall be—
- (*a*) in the case of an appeal from an industrial tribunal or from a decision of the Certification Officer under section 3 of the Trade Union Act 1913 or section 4 of the Trade Union (Amalgamations, etc.) Act 1964, the parties (other than the appellant) to the proceedings before the industrial tribunal or the Certification Officer;
- (*b*) in the case of an appeal against a decision of the Certification Officer under section 4 or 5 of the Trade Union Act 1913, section 8 of the Trade Union and Labour Relations Act 1974 or section 8 of the Act, that Officer.

Respondent's answer and notice of cross-appeal

2–056
6.—(1) The Registrar shall, as soon as practicable, notify every respondent of the date appointed by the Appeal Tribunal by which any answer under this rule must be delivered.

(2) A respondent who wishes to resist an appeal shall, within the time

appointed under paragraph (1) of this rule, deliver to the Appeal Tribunal an answer in writing in, or substantially in accordance with, Form 4 in the Schedule to these Rules, setting out the grounds on which he relies, so, however, that it shall be sufficient for a respondent to an appeal referred to in rule 5(*a*) who wishes to rely on any ground which is the same as a ground relied on by the industrial tribunal or the Certification Officer for making the decision or order appealed from to state that fact in his answer.

(3) A respondent who wishes to cross-appeal may do so by including in his answer a statement of the grounds of his cross-appeal, and in that event an appellant who wishes to resist the cross-appeal shall, within a time to be appointed by the Appeal Tribunal, deliver to the Tribunal a reply in writing setting out the grounds on which he relies.

(4) The Registrar shall serve a copy of every answer and reply to a cross-appeal on every party other than the party by whom it was delivered.

(5) Where the respondent does not wish to resist an appeal, the parties may deliver to the Appeal Tribunal an agreed draft of an order allowing the appeal and the Tribunal may, if it thinks it right to do so, make an order allowing the appeal in the terms agreed.

Disposal of appeal
7.—(1) The Registrar shall, as soon as practicable, give notice of the arrangements made by the Appeal Tribunal for hearing the appeal to—
   (*a*) every party to the proceedings; and
   (*b*) the Secretary of Industrial Tribunals in the case of an appeal from an industrial tribunal; or
   (*c*) the Certification Officer in the case of an appeal under section 36 or Part VI of the Act or Part IV of the Employment Protection Act 1975 to which he is not a respondent.

(2) Any such notice shall state the date appointed by the Appeal Tribunal by which any interlocutory application must be made.

Application under section 5(2) of the Employment Act 1980
8. Every application to the Appeal Tribunal for an award of compensation for unreasonable exclusion or expulsion from a trade union shall be made in writing in or substantially in accordance with Form 5 in the Schedule to these Rules and shall be served on the Tribunal together with a copy of the decision or order declaring that the applicant's complaint against the trade union was well-founded.

9. If on receipt of an application under rule 8 it becomes clear that at the time the application was made the applicant had been admitted or re-admitted to membership of the union against which the complaint was made, the Registrar shall forward the application to the Central Office of Industrial Tribunals.

Service of application
10. On receipt of an application under rule 8, the Registrar shall seal it with the Appeal Tribunal's seal and shall serve a sealed copy on the applicant and on the respondent trade union and the Secretary of Industrial Tribunals.

Appearance by respondent trade union
11. A respondent trade union wishing to resist an application shall within 14 days of receiving the sealed copy of the application enter an appearance

by serving on the Appeal Tribunal a notice of appearance in, or substantially in accordance with, Form 6 in the Schedule to these Rules and setting out the grounds on which the union relies.

12. On receipt of the notice of appearance the Registrar shall serve a copy of it on the applicant.

Disposal of application

13.—(1) The Registrar shall, as soon as practicable, give notice to the parties to the application of the arrangements made by the Appeal Tribunal for hearing the application.

(2) Any such notice shall state the date appointed by the Appeal Tribunal by which any interlocutory application must be made.

Joinder of parties

14. The Appeal Tribunal may, on the application of any person or of its own motion, direct that any person not already a party to the proceedings be added as a party, or that any party to proceedings shall cease to be a party, and in either case may give such consequential directions as it considers necessary.

Interlocutory applications

15.—(1) An interlocutory application may be made to the Appeal Tribunal by giving notice in writing specifying the directions or order sought.

(2) On receipt of a notice under paragraph (1) of this rule, the Registrar shall serve a copy on every other party to the proceedings who appears to him to be concerned in the matter to which the notice relates and shall notify the applicant and every such party of the arrangements made by the Appeal Tribunal for disposing of the application.

Disposal of interlocutory applications

16.—(1) Every interlocutory application made to the Appeal Tribunal shall be considered in the first place by the Registrar who will have regard to the just and economical disposal of the application and to the expense which may be incurred by the parties in attending an oral hearing.

(2) Every interlocutory application shall be disposed of by the Registrar except that any matter which he thinks should properly be decided by the President or a judge should be referred by him to the President or a judge, who may dispose of it himself or refer it in whole or in part to the Appeal Tribunal as required to be constituted by paragraph 16 of Schedule 11 or refer it back to the Registrar with such directions as he thinks fit.

Appeals from Registrar

17.—(1) Where an application is disposed of by the Registrar in pursuance of rule 16(2) any party aggrieved by his decision may appeal to a judge and in that case the judge may determine the appeal himself or refer it in whole or in part to the Appeal Tribunal as constituted by paragraph 16 of Schedule 11.

(2) Notice of appeal under paragraph (1) of this rule may be given to the Appeal Tribunal, either orally or in writing, within three days of the decision appealed from the Registrar shall notify every other party who

appears to him to be concerned in the appeal and shall inform every such party and the appellant of the arrangements made by the Tribunal for disposing of the appeal.

Hearing of interlocutory applications
18. The Appeal Tribunal may sit either in private or in public for the hearing of any interlocutory application.

Appointment for direction
19.—(1) Where it appears to the Appeal Tribunal that the future conduct of any proceedings would thereby be facilitated, the Tribunal may (either of its own motion or on application) at any stage in the proceedings appoint a date for a meeting for directions as to their future conduct and thereupon the following provisions of this rule shall apply.
(2) The Registrar shall give to every party in the proceedings notice of the date appointed under paragraph (1) of this rule and any party applying for directions shall, if practicable, before that date give to the Appeal Tribunal particulars of any direction for which he asks.
(3) The Registrar shall take such steps as may be practicable to inform every party of any directions applied for by any other party.
(4) On the date appointed under paragraph (1) of this rule, the Appeal Tribunal shall consider every application for directions made by any party and any written representations relating to the application submitted to the Tribunal and shall give such directions as it thinks fit for the purpose of securing the just, expeditious and economical disposal of the proceedings, including, where appropriate, directions in pursuance of rule 30, for the purpose of ensuring that the parties are enabled to avail themselves of opportunities for conciliation.
(5) Without prejudice to the generality of paragraph (4) of this rule, the Appeal Tribunal may give such directions as it thinks fit as to—
(*a*) the amendment of any notice, answer or other document;
(*b*) the admission of any facts or documents;
(*c*) the admission in evidence of any documents;
(*d*) the mode in which evidence is to be given at the hearing;
(*e*) the consolidation of the proceedings with any other proceedings pending before the Tribunal;
(*f*) the place and date of the hearing.
(6) An application for further directions or for the variation of any directions already given may be made in accordance with rule 15.

Appeal Tribunal's power to give directions
20. The Appeal Tribunal may either of its own motion or on application, at any stage of the proceedings, give any party directions as to any steps to be taken by him in relation to the proceedings.

Default by parties
21. If a respondent to any proceedings fails to deliver an answer or, in the case of an application made under section 5(2) of the Employment Act 1980, a notice of appearance within the time appointed under these Rules, or if any party fails to comply with an order or direction of the Appeal Tribunal, the Tribunal may order that he be debarred from taking any further part in the proceedings, or may make such other order as it thinks just.

Attendance of witnesses and production of documents

22.—(1) The Appeal Tribunal may, on the application of any party, order any person to attend before the Tribunal as a witness or to produce any document.

(2) No person to whom an order is directed under paragraph (1) of this rule shall be treated as having failed to obey that order unless at the time at which the order was served on him there was tendered to him a sufficient sum of money to cover his costs of attending before the Appeal Tribunal.

Oaths

23. The Appeal Tribunal may, either of its own motion or on application, require any evidence to be given on oath.

Oral hearings

24.—(1) Subject to paragraph (2) of this rule, an oral hearing at which any proceedings before the Appeal Tribunal are finally disposed of shall take place in public before such members of the Tribunal as (subject to paragraph 16 of Schedule 11) the President may nominate for the purpose.

(2) The Appeal Tribunal may sit in private to conduct proceedings which in the opinion of the Tribunal—
- (*a*) relate to matters of such a nature that it would be against the interests of national security to allow the proceedings to be conducted in public; or
- (*b*) in the course of which, evidence is likely to be given (wholly or in part) of information which—
   - (i) the person giving the evidence could not disclose without contravening a prohibition imposed by or under an enactment; or
   - (ii) has been communicated to that person in confidence or which he has otherwise obtained in consequence of the confidence reposed in him by another person; or
   - (iii) of information the disclosure of which would cause substantial injury to an undertaking of the person giving the evidence or any undertaking in which he works for reasons other than its effect on any negotiations with respect to any of the matters mentioned in section 29(1) of the Trade Union and Labour Relations Act 1974.

Drawing up, reasons for, and enforcement of orders

25.—(1) Every order of the Appeal Tribunal shall be drawn up by the Registrar and a copy, sealed with the seal of the Tribunal, shall be served by the Registrar on every party to the proceedings to which it relates and—
- (*a*) in the case of an order disposing of an appeal from an industrial tribunal, on the Secretary of the Industrial Tribunals; or
- (*b*) in the case of an order disposing of an appeal from the Certification Officer, on that Officer.

(2) The Appeal Tribunal shall, on the application of any party made within 14 days after the making of an order finally disposing of any proceedings, give its reason in writing for the order unless it was made after the delivery of a reasoned judgment.

(3) Subject to any order made by the Court of Appeal or Court of Session and to any directions given by the Appeal Tribunal, an appeal from the Tribunal shall not suspend the enforcement of any order made by it.

Review of decisions and correction of errors

26.—(1) The Appeal Tribunal may, either of its own motion or on application, review any order made by it and may, on such review, revoke or vary that order on the grounds that—
- (*a*) the order was wrongly made as the result of an error on the part of the Tribunal or its staff;
- (*b*) a party did not receive proper notice of the proceedings leading to the order; or
- (*c*) the interests of justice require such review.

(2) An application under paragraph (1) above shall be made within 14 days of the date of the order.

(3) A clerical mistake in any order arising from an accidental slip or omission may at any time be corrected by, or on the authority of, a judge or member.

Costs or expenses

27.—(1) Where it appears to the Appeal Tribunal that any proceedings were unnecessary, improper or vexatious or that there has been unreasonable delay or other unreasonable conduct in bringing or conducting the proceedings the Tribunal may order the party at fault to pay any other party the whole or such part as it thinks fit of the costs or expenses incurred by that other party in connection with the proceedings.

(2) Where an order is made under paragraph (1) of this rule, the Appeal Tribunal may assess the sum to be paid, or may direct that it be assessed by the taxing officer, from whose decision an appeal shall lie to a judge.

(3) Rules 17 and 18 shall apply to an appeal under paragraph (2) of this rule as they apply to an appeal from the Registrar.

(4) The costs of an assisted person shall be taxed in accordance with Schedule 2 to the Legal Aid Act 1974 by a Taxing Master of the Supreme Court.

Service of documents

28.—(1) Any notice or other document required or authorised by these Rules to be served on, or delivered to, any person may, be sent to him by post to his address for service or, where no address for service has been given, to his registered office, principal place of business, head or main office or last known address, as the case may be, and any notice or other document required or authorised to be served on, or delivered to, the Appeal Tribunal may be sent by post or delivered to the Registrar—
- (*a*) in the case of a notice instituting proceedings, at the central office of any other offices of the Tribunal; or
- (*b*) in any other case, at the office of the Tribunal in which the proceedings in question are being dealt with in accordance with rule 32(2).

2–060

(2) Any notice or other document required or authorised to be served on, or delivered to, an unincorporated body may be sent to its secretary, manager or other similar officer.

(3) Every document served by post shall be assumed, in the absence of evidence to the contrary, to have been delivered in the normal course of post.

(4) The Appeal Tribunal may inform itself in such manner as it thinks fit of the posting of any document by an officer of the Tribunal.

Conciliation

29. Where at any stage of any proceedings it appears to the Appeal Tribunal that there is a reasonable prospect of agreement being reached between the parties, the Tribunal may take such steps as it thinks fit to enable the parties to avail themselves of any opportunities for conciliation, whether by adjourning any proceedings or otherwise.

Time

30.—(1) The time prescribed by these Rules or by order of the Appeal Tribunal for doing any act may be extended (whether it has already expired or not) or abridged, and the date appointed for any purpose may be altered, by order of the Tribunal.

(2) Where the last day for the doing of any act falls on a day on which the appropriate office of the Tribunal is closed and by reason thereof the act cannot be done on that day, it may be done on the next day on which that office is open.

(3) An application for an extension of the time prescribed for the doing of an act, including the institution of an appeal under rule 8, shall be heard and determined as an interlocutory application under rule 16.

Tribunal offices and allocation of business

31.—(1) The central office and any other office of the Appeal Tribunal shall be open at such times as the President may direct.

(2) Any proceedings before the Tribunal may be dealt with at the central office or at such other office as the President may direct.

Non-compliance with, and waiver of, rules

32.—(1) Failure to comply with any requirements of these Rules shall not invalidate any proceedings unless the Appeal Tribunal otherwise directs.

(2) The Tribunal may, if it considers that to do so would lead to the more expeditious or economical disposal of any proceedings or would otherwise be desirable in the interests of justice, dispense with the takings of any step required or authorised by these Rules, or may direct that any such steps be taken in some manner othan than that prescribed by these Rules.

SCHEDULE

Rule 3

FORM 1

Notice of Appeal from Decision of Industrial Tribunal
1. The appellant is (*name and address of appellant*).
2. Any communication relating to this appeal may be sent to the appellant at (*appellant's address for service, including telephone number if any*).
3. The appellant appeals from:
(*here give particulars of the decision of the industrial tribunal from which the appeal is brought*)

on the following question of law:
(*here set out the question of law on which the appeal is brought*).
4. The parties to the proceedings before the industrial tribunal, other than the appellant, were (*name and addresses of other parties to the proceedings resulting in decision appealed from*).
5. The appellant's grounds of appeal are
(*here state the grounds of appeal*).
6. A copy of the industrial tribunal's decision is attached to this notice.

Date   Signed

Rule 3

FORM 2

Notice of Appeal from Decision of Certification Officer

1. The appellant is (*name and address of appellant*).
2. Any communication relating to this appeal may be sent to the appellant at (*appellant's address for service, including telephone number if any*).
3. The appellant appeals from:
(*here give particulars of the decision of the industrial tribunal from which the appeal is brought*).
4. The appellant's grounds of appeal are:
(*here state the grounds of appeal*).
5. A copy of the Certification Officer's decision is attached to this notice.

Date   Signed

Rule 3

FORM 3

Notice of Appeal from Decision of Industrial Tribunal under Section 4(8) *of the Employment Act* 1980

1. The appellant is (*name and address of appellant*).
2. Any communication relating to this appeal may be sent to the appellant at (*appellant's address for service, including telephone number if any*).
3. The appellant appeals from:
(*here give particulars of the decision of the industrial tribunal from which the appeal is brought*).
4. The appellant's grounds of appeal are:
(*here state the grounds of appeal*).
5. In so far as the appeal relates to the findings of fact by the industrial tribunal, the appellant states
(*a*) that the following findings of fact by the industrial tribunal were wrong:
(*b*) and that the industrial tribunal should have found the facts to be as follows.
6. A copy of the industrial tribunal decision is attached to this notice.

Date   Signed

Rule 6

FORM 4

Respondent's Answer

1. The respondent is (*name and address of respondent*).
2. Any communication relating to this appeal may be sent to the respondent at (*respondent's address for service, including telephone number if any*).
3. The respondent intends to resist the appeal of (here give the name of appellant). The

grounds on which the respondent will rely are [the grounds relied upon by the industrial tribunal/Certification Officer for making the decision or order appealed from] [and] [the following grounds];
(*here set out any grounds which differ from those relied upon by the industrial tribunal or Certification Officer, as the case may be*).

4. The respondent cross-appeals from:
(*here give particulars of the decision appealed from*).

5. The respondent's grounds of appeal are:
(*here state the grounds of appeal*).

Date   Signed

Rule 8

FORM 5

Application to the Employment Appeal Tribunal for Compensation for Unreasonable Exclusion or Repulsion from a Trade Union

1. My name is
My address is

2. Any communication relating to this application may be sent to me at
(*here state address for service, including telephone number if any*).

3. My complaint against the (*state the name and address of the trade union*) was declared to be well-founded by:
(*state tribunal or court*)
on
(*give date of the decision or order*).

4. I have not been admitted/re-admitted to membership of the above named trade union and hereby apply for compensation on the following grounds.

Date   Signed

N.B.—A copy of the decision or order declaring the complaint against the trade union to be well-founded must be enclosed with this application.

Rule 11

FORM 6

Notice of Appearance to Application to Employment Appeal Tribunal for Compensation for Unreasonable Exclusion or Expulsion from a Trade Union

1. The respondent trade union is (*name and address of union*).

2. Any communication relating to this application may be sent to the respondent at (*respondent's address for service, including telephone number if any*).

3. The respondent intends to resist the application of:
(*here give name of the applicant*)
the grounds on which the respondent will rely are as follows.

4. State whether or not the applicant had been admitted or re-admitted to membership on or before the date of application.

Date   Signed
                  Position in union

Transfer of Undertakings (Protection of Employment) Regulations 1981
(S.I. 1981 No. 1794)

Citation, commencement and extent

1.—(1) These Regulations may be cited as the Transfer of Undertakings (Protection of Employment) Regulations 1981.

(2) These Regulations, except Regulations 4 to 9 and 14, shall come into operation on 1st February 1982 and Regulations 4 to 9 and 14 shall come into operation on 1st May 1982.

(3) These Regulations, except Regulations 11(10) and 13(3) and (4), extend to Northern Ireland.

Interpretation

2.—(1) In these Regulations—
"collective agreement", "employers' association", and "trade union" have the same meanings respectively as in the 1974 Act or, in Northern Ireland, the 1976 Order;
"collective bargaining" has the same meaning as it has in the 1975 Act or, in Northern Ireland, the 1976 Order;
"contract of employment" means any agreement between an employee and his employer determining the terms and conditions of his employment;
"employee" means any individual who works for another person whether under a contract of service or apprenticeship or otherwise but does not include anyone who provides services under a contract for services and references to a person's employer shall be construed accordingly;
"the 1974 Act", "the 1975 Act", "the 1978 Act" and "the 1976 Order" mean, respectively, the Trade Union and Labour Relations Act 1974, the Employment Protection Act 1975, the Employment Protection (Consolidation) Act 1978 and the Industrial Relations (Northern Ieland) Order 1976;
"recognised", in relation to a trade union, means recognised to any extent by an employer, or two or more associated employers (within the meaning of the 1978 Act, or, in Northern Ireland, the 1976 Order), for the purpose of collective bargaining;
"relevant transfer" means a transfer to which these Regulations apply and "transferor" and "transferee" shall be construed accordingly; and
"undertaking" includes any trade or business but does not include any undertaking or part of an undertaking which is not in the nature of a commercial venture.

(2) References in these Regulations to the transfer of part of an undertaking are references to a transfer of a part which is being transferred as a business and, accordingly, do not include references to a transfer of a ship without more.

(3) For the purposes of these Regulations the representative of a trade union recognised by an employer is an official or other person authorised to carry on collective bargaining with that employer by that union.

A relevant transfer

3.—(1) Subject to the provisions of these Regulations, these Regulations apply to a transfer from one person to another of an undertaking situated immediately before the transfer in the United Kingdom or a part of one which is so situated.

(2) Subject as aforesaid, these Regulations so apply whether the transfer is effected by sale or by some other disposition or by operation of law.

(3) Subject as aforesaid, these Regulations so apply notwithstanding—
  (a) that the transfer is governed or effected by the law of a country or territory outside the United Kingdom;
  (b) that persons employed in the undertaking or part transferred ordinarily work outside the United Kingdom;
  (c) that the employment of any of those persons is governed by any such law.

(4) It is hereby declared that a transfer of an undertaking or part of one may be effected by a series of two or more transactions between the same parties, but in determining whether or not such a series constitutes a single transfer regard shall be had to the extent to which the undertaking or part was controlled by the transferor and transferee respectively before the last transaction, to the lapse of time between each of the transactions, to the intention of the parties and to all the other circumstances.

(5) Where, in consequence (whether directly or indirectly) of the transfer of an undertaking or part of one which was situated immediately before the transfer in the United Kingdom, a ship within the meaning of the Merchant Shipping Act 1894 registered in the United Kingdom ceases to be so registered, these Regulations shall not affect the right conferred by section 5 of the Merchant Shipping Act 1970 (right of seamen to be discharged when ship ceases to be registered in the United Kingdom) on a seaman employed in the ship.

Transfer by receivers and liquidators

4.—(1) Where the receiver of the property or part of the property of a company or, in the case of a creditors' voluntary winding up, the liquidator of a company transfers the company's undertaking, or part of the company's undertaking (the "relevant undertaking") to a wholly owned subsidiary of the company, the transfer shall for the purposes of these Regulations be deemed not to have been effected until immediately before—
  (a) the transferee company ceases (otherwise than by reason of its being wound up) to be a wholly owned subsidiary of the transferor company; or
  (b) the relevant undertaking is transferred by the transferee company to another person;

whichever first occurs, and, for the purposes of these Regulations, the transfer of the relevant undertaking shall be taken to have been effected immediately before that date by one transaction only.

(2) In this Regulation—
  "creditors' voluntary winding up" has the same meaning as in the Companies Act 1948 or, in Northern Ireland, the Companies Act (Northern Ireland) 1960; and
  "wholly owned subsidiary" has the same meaning as it has for the purposes of section 150 of the Companies Act 1948 and section 144 of the Companies Act (Northern Ireland) 1960.

Effect of relevant transfer on contracts of employment, etc.

5.—(1) A relevant transfer shall not operate so as to terminate the contract of employment of any person employed by the transferor in the undertaking or part transferred but any such contract which would otherwise have been terminated by the transfer shall have effect after the transfer as if originally made between the person so employed and the transferee.

(2) Without prejudice to paragraph (1) above, on the completion of a relevant transfer—
  (*a*) all the transferor's rights, powers, duties and liabilities under or in connection with any such contract, shall be transferred by virtue of this Regulation to the transferee; and
  (*b*) anything done before the transfer is completed by or in relation to the transferor in respect of that contract or a person employed in that undertaking or part shall be deemed to have been done by or in relation to the transferee.

(3) Any reference in paragraph (1) or (2) above to a person employed in an undertaking or part of one transferred by a relevant transfer is a reference to a person so employed immediately before the transfer, including, where the transfer is effected by a series of two or more transactions, a person so employed immediately before any of those transactions.

(4) Paragraph (2) above shall not transfer or otherwise affect the liability of any person to be prosecuted for, convicted of and sentenced for any offence.

(5) Paragraph (1) above is without prejudice to any right of an employee arising apart from these Regulations to terminate his contract of employment without notice if a substantial change is made in his working conditions to his detriment; but no such right shall arise by reason only that, under that paragraph, the identity of his employer changes unless the employee shows that, in all the circumstances, the change is a significant change and is to his detriment.

Effect of relevant transfer on collective agreements

6. Where at the time of a relevant transfer there exists a collective agreement made by or on behalf of the transferor with a trade union recognised by the transferor in respect of any employee whose contract of employment is preserved by Regulation 5(1) above, then,—
  (*a*) without prejudice to section 18 of the 1974 Act or Article 63 of the 1976 Order (collective agreements presumed to be unenforceable in specified circumstances) that agreement, in its application in relation to the employee, shall, after the transfer, have effect as if made by or on behalf of the transferee with that trade union, and accordingly anything done under or in connection with it, in its application as aforesaid, by or in relation to the transferor before the transfer, shall, after the transfer, be deemed to have been done by or in relation to the transferee; and
  (*b*) any order made in respect of that agreement, in its application in relation to the employee, shall, after the transfer, have effect as if the transferee were a party to the agreement.

Exclusion of occupational pensions schemes

7. Regulations 5 and 6 above shall not apply—
  (*a*) to so much of a contract of employment or collective agreement as relates to an occupational pension scheme within the meaning of the Social Security Pensions Act 1975 or the Social Security Pensions (Northern Ireland) Order 1975; or

(b) to any rights, powers, duties or liabilities under or in connection with any such contract or subsisting by virtue of any such agreement and relating to such a scheme or otherwise arising in connection with that person's employment and relating to such a scheme.

Dismissal of employee because of relevant transfer

2–069   **8.**—(1) Where either before or after a relevant transfer, any employee of the transferor or transferee is dismissed, that employee shall be treated for the purposes of Part V of the 1978 Act and Articles 20 to 41 of the 1976 Order (unfair dismissal) as unfairly dismissed if the transfer or a reason connected with it is the reason or principal reason for his dismissal.

(2) Where an economic, technical or organisational reason entailing changes in the workforce of either the transferor or the transferee before or after a relevant transfer is the reason or principal reason for dismissing an employee—
   (a) paragraph (1) above shall not apply to his dismissal; but
   (b) without prejudice to the application of section 57(3) of the 1978 Act or Article 22(10) of the 1976 Order (test of fair dismissal), the dismissal shall for the purposes of section 57(1)(b) of that Act and Article 22(1)(b) of that Order (substantial reason for dismissal) be regarded as having been for a substantial reason of a kind such as to justify the dismissal of an employee holding the position which that employee held.

(3) The provisions of this Regulation apply whether or not the employee in question is employed in the undertaking or part of the undertaking transferred or to be transferred.

(4) Paragraph (1) above shall not apply in relation to the dismissal of any employee which was required by reason of the application of section 5 of the Aliens Restriction (Amendment) Act 1919 to his employment.

Effect of relevant transfer on trade union recognition

2–070   **9.**—(1) This Regulation applies where after a relevant transfer the undertaking or part of the undertaking transferred maintains an identity distinct from the remainder of the transferee's undertaking.

(2) Where before such a transfer an independent trade union is recognised to any extent by the transferor in respect of employees of any description who in consequence of the transfer become employees of the transferee, then, after the transfer—
   (a) the union shall be deemed to have been recognised by the transferee to the same extent in respect of employees of that description so employed; and
   (b) any agreement for recognition may be varied or rescinded accordingly.

Duty to inform and consult trade union representatives

2–071   **10.**—(1) In this Regulation and Regulation 11 below "an affected employee" means, in relation to a relevant transfer, any employee of the transferor or the transferee (whether or not employed in the undertaking or the part of the undertaking to be transferred) who may be affected by the transfer or may be affected by measures taken in connection with it; and references to the employer shall be construed accordingly.

(2) Long enough before a relevant transfer to enable consultations to take place between the employer of any affected employees of a description in respect of which an independent trade union is recognised by him and that union's representatives, the employer shall inform those representatives or—
 (a) the fact that the relevant transfer is to take place, when, approximately, it is to take place and the reasons for it; and
 (b) the legal, economic and social implications of the transfer for the affected employees; and
 (c) the measures which he envisages he will, in connection with the transfer, take in relation to those employees or, if he envisages that no measures will be so taken, that fact; and
 (d) if the employer is the transferor, the measures which the transferee envisages he will, in connection with the transfer, take in relation to such of those employees as, by virtue of Regulation 5 above, become employees of the transferee after the transfer or, if he envisages that no measures will be so taken, that fact.

(3) The transferee shall give the transferor such information at such a time as will enable the transferor to perform the duty imposed on him by virtue of paragraph (2)(*d*) above.

(4) The information which is to be given to the representatives of a trade union under this Regulation shall be delivered to them, or sent by post to an address notiied by them to the employer, or sent by post to the union at the address of its head or main office.

(5) Where an employer of any affected employees envisages that he will, in connection with the transfer, be taking measures in relation to any such employees of a description in respect of which an independent trade union is recognised by him, he shall enter into consultations with the representatives of that union.

(6) In the course of those consultations the employer shall—
 (a) consider any representations made by the trade union representatives; and
 (b) reply to those representations and, if he rejects any of those representations, state his reasons.

(7) If in any case there are special circumstances which render it not reasonably practicable for an employer to perform a duty imposed on him by any of the foregoing paragraphs, he shall take all such steps towards performing that duty as are reasonably practicable in the circumstances.

Failure to inform or consult

11.—(1) A complaint that an employer has failed to inform or consult a representative of a trade union in accordance with Regulation 10 above may be presented to an industrial tribunal by that union.

(2) If on a complaint under paragraph (1) above a question arises whether or not it was reasonably practicable for an employer to perform a particular duty or what steps he took towards performing it, it shall be for him to show—
 (a) that there were special circumstances which rendered it not reasonably practicable for him to perform the duty; and
 (b) that he took all such steps towards its performance as were reasonably practicable in those circumstances.

(3) On any such complaint against a transferor that he had failed to perform the duty imposed upon him by virtue of paragraph 2(*d*) or, so far as relating thereto, paragraph (7) of Regulation 10 above, he may not show

2–072

that it was not reasonably practicable for him to perform the duty in question for the reason that the transferee had failed to give him the requisite information at the requisite time in accordance with Regulation 10(3) above unless he gives the transferee notice of his intention to show that fact; and the giving of the notice shall make the transferee a party to the proceedings.

(4) Where the tribunal finds a complaint under paragraph (1) above well-founded it shall make a declaration to that effect and may—
   (a) order the employer to pay appropriate compensation to such descriptions of affected employees as may be specified in the award; or
   (b) if the complaint is that the transferor did not perform the duty mentioned in paragraph (3) above and the transferor (after giving due notice) shows the facts so mentioned, order the transferee to pay appropriate compensation to such descriptions of affected employees as may be specified in the award.

(5) An employee may present a complaint to an industrial tribunal on the ground that he is an employee of a description to which an order under paragraph (4) above relates and that the transferor or the transferee has failed, wholly or in part, to pay him compensation in pursuance of the order.

(6) Where the tribunal finds a complaint under paragraph (5) above well-founded it shall order the employer to pay the complainant the amount of compensation which it finds is due to him.

(7) Where an employer, in failing to perform a duty under Regulation 10 above, also fails to comply with the requirements of section 99 of the 1975 Act or Article 49 of the 1976 Order (duty of employer to consult trade union representatives on redundancy)—
   (a) any compensation awarded to an employee under this Regulation shall go to reduce the amount of remuneration payable to him under a protective award subsequently made under Part IV of that Act or Part IV of that Order and shall also go towards discharging any liability of the employer under, or in respect of a breach of, the contract of employment in respect of a period falling wihin the protected period under that award; and
   (b) conversely any remuneration so payable and any payment made to the employee by the employer under, or by way of damages for breach of, that contract in respect of a period falling within the protected period shall go to reduce the amount of any compensation which may be subsequently awarded under this Regulation;
but this paragraph shall be without prejudice to section 102(3) of that Act and Article 52(3) of that Order (avoidance of duplication of contractual payments and remuneration under protective awards).

(8) An industrial tribunal shall not consider a complaint under paragraph (1) or (5) above unless it is presented to the tribunal before the end of the period of three months beginning with—
   (a) the date on which the relevant transfer is completed, in the case of a complaint under paragraph (1);
   (b) the date of the tribunal's order under paragraph (4) above, in the case of a complaint under paragraph (5);
or within such further period as the tribunal considers reasonable in a case where it is satisfied that it was not reasonably practicable for the complaint to be presented before the end of the period of three months.

(9) Section 129 of the 1978 Act (complaint to be sole remedy for breach

of relevant rights) and section 133 of that Act (functions of conciliation officer) and Articles 58(2) and 62 of the 1976 Order (which make corresponding provision for Northern Ireland) shall apply to the rights conferred by this Regulation and to proceedings under this Regulation as they apply to the rights conferred by that Act or that Order and the industrial tribunal proceedings mentioned therein.

(10) An appeal shall lie and shall lie only to the Employment Appeal Tribunal on a question of law arising from any decision of, or arising in any proceedings before, an industrial tribunal under or by virtue of these Regulations; and section 13(1) of the Tribunals and Inquiries Act 1971 (appeal from certain tribunals to the High Court) shall not apply in relation to any such proceedings.

(11) In this Regulation "appropriate compensation" means such sum not exceeding two weeks' pay for the employee in question as the tribunal considers just and equitable having regard to the seriousness of the failure of the employer to comply with his duty.

(12) Schedule 14 to the 1978 Act or, in Northern Ireland, Schedule 2 to the 1976 Order shall apply for calculating the amount of a week's pay for any employee for the purposes of paragraph (11) above; and, for the purposes of that calculation, the calculation date shall be—

(a) in the case of an employee who is dismissed by reason of redundancy (within the meaning of section 81 of the 1978 Act or, in Northern Ireland, section 11 of the Contracts of Employment and Redundancy Payments Act (Northern Ireland) 1965) the date which is the calculation date for the purposes of any entitlement of his to a redundancy payment (within the meaning of that section) or which would be that calculation date if he were so entitled;

(b) in the case of an employee who is dismissed for any other reason, the effective date of termination (within the meaning of section 55 of the 1978 Act or, in Northern Ireland, Article 21 of the 1976 Order) of his contract of employment;

(c) in any other case, the date of the transfer in question.

Restriction on contracting out

12. Any provision of any agreement (whether a contract of employment or not) shall be void in so far as it purports to exclude or limit the operation of Regulation 5, 8 or 10 above or to preclude any person from presenting a complaint to an industrial tribunal under Regulation 11 above.

Exclusion of employment abroad or as a dock worker

13.—(1) Regulation 8, 10 and 11 of these Regulations do not apply to employment where under his contract of employment the employee ordinarily works outside the United Kingdom.

(2) For the purpose of this Regulation a person employed to work on board a ship registered in the United Kingdom shall, unless—

(a) the employment is wholly outside the United Kingdom, or

(b) he is not ordinarily resident in the United Kingdom,

be regarded as a person who under his contract ordinarily works in the United Kingdom.

(3) Nothing in these Regulations applies in relation to any person employed as a registered dock worker unless he is wholly or mainly engaged in work which is not dock work.

(4) Paragraph (3) above shall be construed as if it were contained in section 145 of the 1978 Act.

Consequential amendments
14.—(1) In section 4(4) of the 1978 Act (written statement to be given to employee on change of his employer), in paragraph (*b*), the reference to paragraph 17 of Schedule 13 to that Act (continuity of employment where change of employer) shall include a reference to these Regulations.

(2) In section 4(6A) of the Contracts of Employment and Redundancy Payments Act (Northern Ireland) 1965, in paragraph (*b*), the reference to paragraph 10 of Schedule 1 to that Act shall include a reference to these Regulations.

Statutory Sick Pay (General) Regulations 1982

(S.I. 1982 No. 894)

Dated June 30, 1982 *and made by the Secretary of State under ss.1(3) and* (4), 3(5) *and* (7), 4(2), 5(5), 6(1), 8(1) *to* (3), 17(4), 18(1), 20 *and* 26(1) *and in Schedule* 2 *paras.* 2(3) *and* 3(2) *of the Social Security and Housing Benefits Act* 1982. *They come into force on April* 6, 1983.

Citation, commencement and interpretation
1.—(1) These regulations may be cited as the Statutory Sick pay (General) Regulations 1982, and shall come into operation on 6th April 1983.

(2) In these regulations—
"the Act" means the Social Security and Housing Benefits Act 1982;
"Part I" means Part I of the Act;
and other expressions, unless the context otherwise requires, have the same meaning as in Part I.

(3) Unless the context otherwise requires, any reference—
  (*a*) in these regulations to a numbered section or Schedule is a reference to the section or Schedule, as the case may be, of or to the Act bearing that number;
  (*b*) in these regulations to a numbered regulation is a reference to the regulation bearing that number in these regulations; and
  (*c*) in any of these regulations to a numbered paragraph is a reference to the paragraph bearing that number in that regulation.

Persons deemed incapable of work
2.—(1) A person who is not incapable of work of which he can reasonably be expected to do under a particular contract of service may be deemed to be incapable of work of such a kind by reason of some specific disease or bodily or mental disablement for any day on which either—
  (*a*) (i) he is under medical care in respect of a disease or disablement as aforesaid,
     (ii) it is stated by a registered medical practitioner that for precautionary or convalescent reasons consequential on such

disease or disablement he should abstain from work, or from work of such a kind, and

(iii) he does not work under that contract of service, or

(b) he is excluded from work, or from work of such a kind, on the certificate of a Medical Officer for Environmental Health and is under medical observation by reason of his being a carrier, or having been in contact with a case, of infectious disease.

(2) A person who at the commencement of any day is, or thereafter on that day becomes, incapable of work of such a kind by reason of some specific disease or bodily or mental disablement, and

(a) on that day, under that contract of service, does no work, or no work except during a shift which ends on that day having begun on the previous day; and

(b) does no work under that contract of service during a shift which begins on that day and ends on the next,

shall be deemed to be incapable of work of such kind by reason of that disease or bodily or mental disablement throughout that day.

Period of entitlement ending or not arising

3.—(1) In a case where an employee is detained in legal custody or sentenced to a term of imprisonment (except where the sentence is suspended) on a day which in relation to him falls within a period of entitlement, that period shall end with that day.

(2) A period of entitlement shall not arise in relation to a period of incapacity for work where at any time on the first day of that period of incapacity for work an employee in question is in legal custody or sentenced to or undergoing a term of imprisonment (except where the sentence is suspended).

Contract of service ended for the purpose of avoiding liability for statutory sick pay

4.—(1) The provisions of this regulation apply in any case where an employer's contract of service with an employee is brought to an end by the employer solely or mainly for the purpose of avoiding liability for statutory sick pay.

(2) Where a period of entitlement is current on the day on which the contract is brought to an end, the employer shall be liable to pay statutory sick pay to the employee until the occurrence of an event which, if the contract had still been current, would have caused the period of entitlement to come to an end under section 3(2)(a), (b) or (d) or regulation 3(1), [of these regulations or regulation 10(2) of the Statutory Sick Pay (Mariners, Airmen and Persons Abroad) Regulations 1982] or (if earlier) until the date on which the contract would have expired.

AMENDMENT

The words in square brackets were inserted by S.I. 1982 No. 1349, reg. 10(3).

Qualifying days

5.—(1) In this regulation "week" means a period of 7 consecutive days beginning with Sunday.

(2) Where an employee and an employer of his have not agreed which

day or days in any week are or were qualifying days, the qualifying day or days in that week shall be—
   (a) the day or days on which it is agreed between the employer and the employee that the employee is or was required to work (if not incapable) for that employer or, if it is so agreed that there is or was no such day,
   (b) the Wednesday, or, if there is no such agreement between the employer and employee as mentioned in sub-paragraph (a),
   (c) every day, except that or those (if any) on which it is agreed between the employer and the employee that none of that employer's employees are or were required to work (any agreement that all days are or were such days being ignored).

Calculation of entitlement limit

6.—(1) Where an employee's entitlement to statutory sick pay is calculated by reference to different weekly rates in the same period of entitlement or tax year, the entitlement limit shall be calculated in the manner described in paragraphs (2) and (3), or, as the case may be, (4) and (5); and where a number referred to in paragraph (2)(b) or (d) or (4)(a)(ii) or (d)(ii) is not a whole number, it shall be calculated to the nearest hundredth, 5 thousandths being reckoned as one hundredth.

(2) For the purpose of determining whether an employee has reached his maximum entitlement to statutory sick pay in respect of a period of entitlement, there shall be calculated—
   (a) the amount of statutory sick pay to which the employee became entitled during the part of the period of entitlement before the change in the weekly rate;
   (b) the number by which the weekly rate (before the change) must be multiplied in order to produce the amount mentioned in sub-paragraph (a);
   (c) the amount of statutory sick pay to which the employee has so far become entitled during the part of the period of entitlement after the change in the weekly rate; and
   (d) the number by which the weekly rate (after the change) must be multiplied in order to produce the amount mentioned in sub-paragraph (c);
   (e) the sum of the amounts mentioned in sub-paragraphs (a) and (c); and
   (f) the sum of the numbers mentioned in sub-paragraphs (b) and (d).

(3) When the sum mentioned in paragraph (2)(f) reaches 8, the sum mentioned in paragraph (2)(e) reaches the entitlement limit.

(4) For the purpose of determining whether an employee has reached his maximum entitlement to statutory sick pay in respect of a tax year, there shall be calculated—
   (a) in respect of each period of entitlement (or part of such a period) in that tax year except the one which is current when the calculation is being made—
       (i) the amount of statutory sick pay to which the employee became entitled, and
       (ii) the number by which the weekly rate applicable to that period must be multiplied in order to produce the amount mentioned in head (i);
   (b) the sum of the amounts mentioned in sub-paragraph (a)(i) calculated in respect of all the periods of entitlement in question;

(c) the sum of the numbers mentioned in sub-paragraph (a)(ii) calculated in respect of all the periods of entitlement in question;
(d) in respect of the period of entitlement which is current when the calculation is being made—
  (i) the amount of statutory sick pay to which the employee has so far become entitled, and
  (ii) the number by which the weekly rate applicable to that period must be multiplied in order to produce the amount mentioned in head (i);
(e) the sum of the sum mentioned in sub-paragraph (b) and the amount mentioned in sub-paragraph (d)(i);
(f) the sum of the sum mentioned in sub-paragraph (c) and the number mentioned in sub-paragraph (d)(ii).

(5) When the sum first mentioned in paragraph (4)(f) reaches 8, the sum first mentioned in paragraph (4)(e) reaches the entitlement limit.

Time and manner of notification of incapacity for work

7.—(1) Subject to paragraph (2), notice of any day of incapacity for work shall be given by or on behalf of an employee to his employer—
(a) in a case where the employer has decided on a time limit (not being one which requires the notice to be given earlier than the end of the first qualifying day in the period of incapacity for work which includes that day of incapacity for work) and taken reasonable steps to make it known to the employee, within that time limit; and
(b) in any other case, on or before the seventh day after that day of incapacity for work.

(2) Notice of any day of incapacity for work may be given later than as provided by paragraph (1) where there is good cause for giving it later, so however that it shall in any event be given on or before the 91st day after that day.

(3) A notice contained in a letter which is properly addressed and sent by prepaid post shall be deemed to have been given on the day on which it was posted.

(4) Notice of any day of incapacity for work shall be given by or on behalf of an employee to his employer—
(a) in a case where the employer has decided on a manner in which it is to be given (not being a manner which imposes a requirement such as is specified in paragraph (5)) and taken reasonable steps to make it known to the employee, in that manner; and
(b) in any other case, in any manner, so however that unless otherwise agreed between the employer and employee it shall be given in writing.

(5) The requirements mentioned in paragraph (4)(a) are that notice shall be given—
(a) personally;
(b) in the form of medical evidence;
(c) more than once in every 7 days during a period of entitlement;
(d) on a document supplied by the employer; or
(e) on a printed form.

Manner in which statutory sick pay may not be paid

8. Statutory sick pay may not be paid in kind or by way of the provision of board or lodging or of services or other facilities.

Time limits for paying statutory sick pay

2–084 9.—(1) In this regulation, "pay day" means a day on which it has been agreed, or it is the normal practice, between an employer and an employee of his, that payments by way of remuneration are to be made, or, where there is no such agreement or normal practice, the last day of a calendar month.

(2) In any case where—
- (*a*) a decision has been made by an insurance officer, local tribunal or Commissioner in proceedings under Part I that an employee is entitled to an amount of statutory sick pay; and
- (*b*) the time for bringing an appeal against the decision has expired and either—
    - (i) no such appeal has been brought; or
    - (ii) such an appeal has been brought and has been finally disposed of,

that amount of statutory sick pay is to be paid within the time specified in paragraph (3).

(3) Subject to paragraphs (4) and (5), the employer is required to pay the amount not later than the first pay day after—
- (*a*) where an appeal has been brought, the day on which the employer receives notification that it has been finally disposed of;
- (*b*) where leave to appeal has been refused and there remains no further opportunity to apply for leave, the day on which the employer receives notification of the refusal; and
- (*c*) in any other case, the day on which the time for bringing an appeal expires.

(4) Subject to paragraph (5), where it is impracticable, in view of the employer's methods of accounting for and paying remuneration, for the requirement of payment referred to in paragraph (3) to be met by the pay day referred to in that paragraph, it shall be met not later than the next following pay day.

(5) Where the employer would not have remunerated the employee for his work on the day of incapacity for work in question (if it had not been a day of incapacity for work) as early as the pay day specified in paragraph (3) or (if it applies) paragraph (4), the requirement shall be met on the first day on which the employee would have been remunerated for his work on that day.

Persons unable to act

2–085 10.—(1) Where in the case of any employee—
- (*a*) statutory sick pay is payable to him or he is alleged to be entitled to it;
- (*b*) he is unable for the time being to act; and
- (*c*) either—
    - (i) no receiver has been appointed by the Court of Protection with power to receive statutory sick pay on his behalf, or
    - (ii) in Scotland, his estate is not being administered by any tutor, curator or other guardian acting or appointed in terms of law,

the Secretary of State may, upon written application to him by a person who, if a natural person, is over the age of 18, appoint that person to exercise, on behalf of the employee, any right to which he may be entitled under Part I and to deal on his behalf with any sums payable to him.

(2) Where the Secretary of State has made an appointment under paragraph (1)—
   (a) he may at any time in his absolute discretion revoke it;
   (b) the person appointed may resign his office after having given one month's notice in writing to the Secretary of State of his intention to do so; and
   (c) the appointment shall terminate when the Secretary of State is notified that a receiver or other person to whom paragraph (1)(c) applies has been appointed.

(3) Anything required by Part I to be done by or to any employee who is unable to act may be done by or to the person appointed under this regulation to act on his behalf, and the receipt of the person so appointed shall be a good discharge to the employee's employer for any sum paid.

Rounding to avoid fractional amounts
11. Where any payment of statutory sick pay is made and the statutory sick pay due for the period for which the payment purports to be made includes a fraction of a penny, the payment shall be rounded up to the next whole number of pence.   2–086

Days not to be treated as, or as parts of, periods of interruption of employment
12. In a case to which paragraph 3 of Schedule 2 applies, the day of incapacity for work mentioned in sub-paragraph (1)(b) of that paragraph shall not be, or form part of, a period of interruption of employment where it is a day which, by virtue of section 17(1) or (2) of the Social Security Act 1975 or any regulations made thereunder, is not to be treated as a day of incapacity for work.   2–087

Records to be maintained by employers
13. Every employer shall maintain for 3 years after the end of each tax year a record, in relation to each employee of his, of—   2–088
   (a) any day in that tax year which was one of 4 or more consecutive days on which, according to information supplied by or on behalf of the employee, the employee was incapable by reason of some specific disease or bodily or mental disablement of doing work which he could reasonably be expected to do under any contract of service between him and the employer, whether or not he would normally have been expected to work on that day;
   (b) any day recorded under paragraph (a) for which the employer did not pay statutory sick pay to the employee;
   (c) the reason why he did not; and
   (d) the days which were qualifying days as between that employer and that employee in each period of entitlement which fell wholly or partly in that tax year.

Provision of information in connection with determination of questions
14. Any person claiming to be entitled to statutory sick pay, or any other person who is a party to proceedings arising under Part I, shall, if he receives notification from the Secretary of State that any information is required from him for the determination of any question arising in connection therewith, furnish that information to the Secretary of State within 10 days of receiving that notification.   2–089

Provision of information by employers to employees

2–090 **15.**—(1) In a case which falls within paragraph (*a*), (*b*) or (*c*) of section 18(3) (provision of information by employers in connection with the making of claims for sickness and other benefits), the employer shall furnish to his employee, in writing on a form approved by the Secretary of State for the purpose, the information specified in paragraph (2), (3) or (4) below respectively within the time specified in the appropriate one of those paragraphs.

(2) In a case which falls within paragraph (*a*) (no period of entitlement arising in relation to a period of incapacity for work) of section 18(3)—
  (*a*) the information mentioned in paragraph (1) is a statement of all the reasons why, under the provisions of paragraph 1 of Schedule 1 and regulations made thereunder, a period of entitlement does not arise; and
  (*b*) it shall be furnished not more than 7 days after the day on which the employer is notified by or on behalf of the employee of the employee's incapacity for work on the fourth day of the period of incapacity for work.

(3) In a case which falls within paragraph (*b*) (period of entitlement ending but period of incapacity for work continuing) of section 18(3)—
  (*a*) the information mentioned in paragraph (1) above is a statement of the reason why the period of entitlement ended; and
  (*b*) it shall be furnished not more than 7 days after the day on which the period of entitlement ended or, if earlier, on the day on which it is already required to be furnished under paragraph (4).

(4) In a case which falls within paragraph (*c*) (period of entitlement expected to end before period of incapacity for work ends, on certain assumptions) of section 18(3)—
  (*a*) the information mentioned in paragraph (1) above is a statement of the reason why the period of entitlement is expected to end; and
  (*b*) it shall be furnished on or before the seventh day before the period of entitlement is expected to end, or, if later, the seventh day after the first day on which the employer could have known that the circumstances mentioned in paragraph (*c*) of section 18(3) existed.

(5) For the purposes of section 18(3)(*c*)(i) (period for which the period of incapacity for work is to be assumed to continue to run) the prescribed period shall be 14 days.

Meaning of "employee"

2–091 **16.**—(1) In a case where, and in so far as, a person over the age of 16 is treated as an employed earner by virtue of the Social Security (Categorisation of Earners) Regulations 1978, he shall be treated as an employee for the purposes of Part I and in a case where, and in so far as, such a person is treated otherwise than as an employed earner by virtue of those regulations, he shall not be treated as an employee for the purposes of Part I.

(2) A person who is in employed earner's employment within the meaning of the Social Security Act 1975 but whose employer—
  (*a*) does not fulfil the conditions prescribed in regulation 119(1)(*b*) of the Social Security (Contributions) Regulations 1979 as to residence or presence in Great Britain, or
  (*b*) is a person who, by reason of any international treaty to which the United Kingdom is a party or of any international convention binding the United Kingdom—

(i) is exempt from the provisions of the Social Security Act 1975, or

(ii) is a person against whom the provisions of that Act are not enforceable,

shall not be treated as an employee for the purposes of Part I.

Meaning of "earnings"

17.—(1) In this regulation "secondary contributor" means a person who is, or but for the provisions of the Social Security Act 1975 relating to the lower earnings limit would be, liable to pay a secondary contribution under section 4 of that Act.

(2) For the purposes of section 26(2), the expression "earnings" refers to gross earnings and includes any remuneration or profit derived from a person's employment, except any payment in so far as it is—

(*a*) a payment on account of the person's earnings in respect of that employment, which comprises or represents, and does not exceed in amount, sums which have previously been included in his earnings for the purposes of section 26(2);

(*b*) a payment in respect of a period of holiday, where the sum paid is derived directly or indirectly from a fund to which more than one secondary contributor contributes and the management and control of which are not vested in those secondary contributors, or where the person making the payment is entitled to be reimbursed from such a fund;

(*c*) a payment of or in respect of a gratuity or offering—

(i) where the payment is not made directly or indirectly by the secondary contributor and the sum paid does not comprise or represent sums previously paid to the secondary contributor; or

(ii) where the payment is not directly allocated by the secondary contributor to the employee;

(*d*) any payment in kind or by way of the provision of board or lodging or of services or other facilities;

(*e*) a payment made to or by trustees, where

(i) in the case of a payment to trustees, the share thereof which that person is entitled to have paid to him, or

(ii) in the case of a payment by trustees, the amount to be so paid, is or may be dependent upon the exercise by the trustees of a discretion or the performance by them of a duty arising under the trust;

(*f*) any payment of earnings in respect of employed earner's employment which a secondary contributor is required to make under regulation 3(2)(*e*) of the Occupational Pension Schemes (Recognition of Schemes) (No. 2) Regulations 1973;

(*g*) any payment by way of a pension;

(*h*) a payment of a fee in respect of employment as a minister of religion which does not form part of the stipend or salary paid in respect of that employment;

(*i*) a payment to defray or a contribution towards expenses incurred by persons for whom facilities are provided under section 15 of the Disabled Persons (Employment) Act 1944 in travelling to and from the place where they are employed or where training is provided;

(*j*) a payment by way of or derived from shares appropriated under a profit sharing scheme to which the provisions of Chapter III of Part III of the Finance Act 1978 (profit sharing schemes) apply.

2–092

For the purposes of section 26(2) the expression "earnings" includes also—
  (a) any sum payable by way of maternity pay or payable by the Secretary of State in pursuance of section 40 of the Employment Protection (Consolidation) Act 1978 in respect of maternity pay;
  (b) any sum which is payable by the Secretary of State by virtue of section 122(3)(a) of that Act in respect of arrears of pay and which by virtue of section 42(1) of that Act is to go towards discharging a liability to pay maternity pay;
  (c) any sum payable by way of pay in pursuance of an order for reinstatement or re-engagement under that Act;
  (d) any sum payable by way of pay in pursuance of an order under that Act for the continuation of a contract of employment;
  (e) any sum payable by way of remuneration in pursuance of a protective award under the Employment Protection Act 1975;
  (f) any sum payable to any employee under the Temporary Short-time Working Compensation Scheme administered under powers conferred by the Employment Subsidies Act 1978;
  (g) any sum paid in satisfaction of any entitlement to statutory sick pay.
(4) Where goods or services are supplied by an employee and earnings paid to or for the benefit of that employee in respect of that employment include the remuneration for the supply of those goods or services, and on that supply value added tax is chargeable, there shall, for the purposes of section 26(2), be excluded from the calculation of those earnings an amount equal to the value added tax so chargeable.
(5) For the avoidance of doubt, in the calculation for the purposes of section 26(2) of earnings paid to or for the benefit of an employee, there shall be disregarded—
  (a) any payment by way of a redundancy payment;
  (b) any specific and distinct payment of, or contribution towards, expenses actually incurred by an employee in carrying out his employment.

Payments to be treated or not to be treated as contractual remuneration
18. For the purposes of paragraph 2(1) and (2) of Schedule 2 to the Act those things which are included within the expression "earnings" by regulation 17 (except paragraph (3)(g) thereof) shall be, and those things which are excluded from that expression by that regulation shall not be, treated as contractual remuneration.

Normal weekly earnings
19.—(1) For the purposes of section 26(2) and (4), an employee's normal weekly earnings shall be determined in accordance with the provisions of this regulation.
(2) In this Regulation—
  "the critical date" means the first day of the period of entitlement in relation to which a person's normal weekly earnings fall to be determined, or, in a case to which paragraph 2(c) of Schedule 1 applies, the relevant date within the meaning of Schedule 1;
  "Normal pay day" means a day on which the terms of an employee's contract of service require him to be paid, or the practice in his employment is for him to be paid, if any payment is due to him; and

"day of payment" means a day on which the employee was paid.

(3) Subject to paragraph (4), the relevant period (referred to in section 26(2)) is the period between—

(a) the last normal pay day to fall before the critical date; and

(b) the last normal pay day to fall at least 8 weeks earlier than the normal pay day mentioned in sub-paragraph (a),

including the normal pay day mentioned in sub-paragraph (a) but excluding that first mentioned in sub-paragraph (b).

(4) In a case where an employee has no identifiable normal pay day, paragraph (3) shall have effect as if the words "day of payment" were substituted for the words "normal pay day" in each place where they occur.

(5) In a case where an employee has normal pay days at intervals of or approximating to one or more calendar months (including intervals of or approximating to a year) his normal weekly earnings shall be calculated by dividing his earnings in the relevant period by the number of calendar months in that period (or, if it is not a whole number, the nearest whole number), multiplying the result by 12 and dividing by 52.

(6) In a case to which paragraph (5) does not apply and the relevant period is not an exact number of weeks, the employee's normal weekly earnings shall be calculated by dividing his earnings in the relevant period by the number of days in the relevant period and multiplying the result by 7.

(7) In a case where the normal pay day mentioned in sub-paragraph (a) or paragraph (3) exist but that first mentioned in sub-paragraph (b) of that paragraph does not yet exist, the employee's normal weekly earnings shall be calculated as if the period for which all the earnings under his contract of service received by him before the critical date represented payment were the relevant period.

(8) In a case where neither of the normal pay days mentioned in paragraph (3) yet exists, the employee's normal weekly earnings shall be the remuneration to which he is entitled, in accordance with the terms of his contract of service, for, as the case may be—

(a) a week's work; or

(b) a number of calendar months' work, divided by that number of months, multiplied by 12 and divided by 52.

Treatment of one or more employers as one

20.—(1) In a case where the earnings paid to an employee in respect of 2 or more employments are aggregated and treated as a single payment of earnings under regulation 12(1) of the Social Security (Contributions) Regulations 1979, the employers of the employee in respect of those employments shall be treated as one for all purposes of Part I.

(2) Where 2 or more employers are treated as one under the provisions of paragraph (1), liability for the statutory sick pay payable by them to the employee shall be apportioned between them in such proportions as they may agree or, in default of agreement, in the proportions which the employee's earnings from each employment bear to the amount of the aggregated earnings.

(3) Where a contract of service ("the current contract") was preceded by a contract of service entered into between the same employer and employee ("the previous contract"), and the interval between the date on which the previous contract ceased to have effect and that on which the current contract came into force was not more than 8 weeks, then for the

purposes of establishing the employee's maximum entitlement within the meaning of section 5 (limitation on entitlement to statutory sick pay in any one period of entitlement or tax year), the provisions of Part I shall not have effect as if the employer were a different employer in relation to each of those contracts of service.

Treatment of more than one contract of service as one
21. Where 2 or more contracts of service exist concurrently between one employer and one employee, they shall be treated as one for all purposes of Part I except where, by virtue of regulation 11 of the Social Security (Contributions) Regulations 1979, the earnings from those contracts of service are not aggregated for the purposes of earnings-related contributions.

Penalties
22. Any person who without reasonable excuse contravenes or fails to comply with any provision of regulation 9, 13, 14 or 15 shall be guilty of an offence under Part I, and liable on summary conviction to a penalty not exceeding—
  (*a*) for any one offence, £200; or
  (*b*) for an offence of continuing any such failure after conviction, £20 for each day on which it is so continued.

Funds for Trade Union Ballots Order 1982

(S.I. 1982 No. 953)

Dated July 9, 1982 and made by the Secretary of State, in exercise of the powers conferred on him by section 1(3) of the Employment Act 1980 and of all other powers enabling him in that behalf.

Citation and commencement
1. This Order may be cited as the Funds for Trade Union Ballots Order 1982 and shall come into operation on 16th July 1982.

2. The following purpose is hereby specified as a purpose within subsection (3) of section 1 of the 1980 Act:—
  "Obtaining a decision or ascertaining the views of members of a trade union as to the acceptance or rejection of a proposal made by an employer in relation to the contractual terms and conditions upon which or the other incidents of the relationship whereby a person works or provides services for the employer."

PART III

EUROPEAN MATERIALS

European Economic Community

Treaty of Rome

. . . . .

ARTICLE 117

Member States agree upon the need to promote improved working conditions and an improved standard of living for workers, so as to make possible their harmonisation while the improvement is being maintained.

They believe that such a development will ensure not only from the functioning of the common market, which will favour the harmonisation of social systems, but also from the procedures provided for in this Treaty and from the approximation of provisions laid down by law, regulation or administrative action.

ARTICLE 118

Without prejudice to the other provisions of this Treaty and in conformity with its general objectives, the Commission shall have the task of promoting close cooperation between Member States in the social field, particularly in matters relating to:
—employment;
—labour law and working conditions;
—basic and advanced vocational training;
—social security;
—prevention of occupational accidents and diseases;
—occupational hygiene;
—the right of association, and collective bargaining between employers and workers.

To this end, the Commission shall act in close contact with Member States by making studies, delivering opinions and arranging consultations both on problems arising at national level and on those of concern to international organisation.

Before delivering the opinions provided for in this Article, the Commission shall consult the Economic and Social Committee.

ARTICLE 119

Each Member State shall during the first stage ensure and subsequently maintain the application of the principle that men and women should receive equal pay for equal work.

For the purpose of this Article, "pay" means the ordinary basic of minimum wage or salary and any other consideration, whether in cash or in kind, which the worker receives, directly or indirectly, in respect of his employment from his employer.

Equal pay without discrimination based on sex means:
(a) that pay for the same work at piece rates shall be calculated on the basis of the same unit of measurement;
(b) that pay for work at time rates shall be the same for the same job.

ARTICLE 120

3–004 Member States shall endeavour to maintain the existing equivalence between paid holiday schemes.

ARTICLE 121

3–005 The Council may, acting unanimously and after consulting the Economic and Social Committee, assign to the Commission tasks in connection with the implementation of common measures, particularly as regards social security for the migrant workers referred to in Articles 48 to 51.

ARTICLE 122

3–006 The Commission shall include a separate chapter on social development within the Community in its annual report to the Assembly.

The Assembly may invite the Commission to draw up reports on any particular problems concerning social conditions.

3–007 **Council Directive 75/117 of February 10, 1975**

On the Approximation of the Laws of the Member States Relating to the Application of the Principle of Equal Pay for Men and Women

(O.J. 1975, L45/19)

THE COUNCIL OF THE EUROPEAN COMMUNITIES,
Having regard to the Treaty establishing the European Economic Community, and in particular Article 100 thereof;
Having regard to the proposal from the Commission;
Having regard to the Opinion of the European Parliament;
Having regard to the Opinion of the Economic and Social Committee;
Whereas implementation of the principle that men and women should receive equal pay contained in Article 119 of the Treaty is an integral part of the establishment and functioning of the common market;
Whereas it is primarily the responsibility of the Member States to ensure the application of this principle by means of appropriate laws, regulations and administrative provisions;

Whereas the Council resolution of January 21, 1974 (C13/1) concerning a social action programme, aimed at making it possible to harmonise living and working conditions while the improvement is being maintained and at achieving a balanced social and economic development of the Community, recognised that priority should be given to action taken on behalf of women as regards access to employment and vocational training and advancement, and as regards working conditions, including pay;

Whereas it is desirable to reinforce the basic laws by standards aimed at facilitating the practical application of the principle of equality in such a way that all employees in the Community can be protected in these matters;

Whereas differences continue to exist in the various Member States despite the efforts made to apply the resolution of the conference of the Member States of December 30, 1961 on equal pay for men and women and whereas, therefore, the national provisions should be approximated as regards application of the principle of equal pay.

HAS ADOPTED THIS DIRECTIVE:

Article 1

3–008

The principle of equal pay for men and women outlined in Article 119 of the Treaty, hereinafter called "principle of equal pay," means, for the same work or for work to which equal value is attributed, the elimination of all discrimination on grounds of sex with regard to all aspects and conditions of remuneration.

In particular, where a job classification system is used for determining pay, it must be based on the same criteria for both men and women and so drawn up as to exclude any discrimination on grounds of sex.

Article 2

3–009

Member States shall introduce into their national legal systems such measures as are necessary to enable all employees who consider themselves wronged by failure to apply the principle of equal pay to pursue their claims by judicial process after possible recourse to other competent authorities.

Article 3

3–010

Member States shall abolish all discrimination between men and women arising from laws, regulations or administrative provisions which is contrary to the principle of equal pay.

Article 4

3–011

Member States shall take the necessary measures to ensure that provisions appearing in collective agreements, wage scales, wage agreements or individual contracts of employment which are contrary to the principle of equal pay shall be, or may be declared, null and void or may be amended.

Article 5

3–012

Member States shall take the necessary measures to protect employees against dismissal by the employer as a reaction to a complaint within the undertaking or to any legal proceedings aimed at enforcing compliance with the principle of equal pay.

Article 6

3–013

Member States shall, in accordance with their national circumstances and legal systems, take the measures necessary to ensure that the principle of equal pay is applied. They shall see that effective means are available to take care that this principle is observed.

Article 7

3–014 Member States shall take care that the provisions adopted pursuant to this Directive, together with the relevant provisions already in force, are brought to the attention of employees by all appropriate means, for example at their place of employment.

Article 8

3–015 1. Member States shall put into force the laws, regulations and administrative provisions necessary in order to comply with this Directive within one year of its notification and shall immediately inform the Commission thereof.

2. Member States shall communicate to the Commission the texts of the laws, regulations and administrative provisions which they adopt in the field covered by this Directive.

Article 9

3–016 Within two years of the expiry of the one-year period referred to in Article 8, Member States shall forward all necessary information to the Commission to enable it to draw up a report on the application of this Directive for submission to the Council.

Article 10

3–017 This Directive is addressed to the Member States.
Done at Brussels, February 10, 1975.

3–018
Council Directive 75/129 of February 17, 1975

On the Approximation of the Laws of the Member States Relating to Collective Redundancies

(O.J. 1975, L48/29)

THE COUNCIL OF THE EUROPEAN COMMUNITIES,
Having regard to the Treaty establishing the European Economic Community, and in particular Article 100 thereof;
Having regard to the proposal from the Commission;
Having regard to the Opinion of the European Parliament;
Having regard to the Opinion of the Economic and Social Committee;
Whereas it is important that greater protection should be afforded to workers in the event of collective redundancies while taking into account the need for balanced economic and social development within the Community;
Whereas, despite increasing convergence, differences still remain between the provisions in force in the Member States of the Community concerning the practical arrangements and procedures for such redundancies and the measures designed to alleviate the consequences of redundancy for workers;
Whereas these differences can have a direct effect on the functioning of the common market;

Whereas the Council resolution of January 21, 1974 (O.J. 1974, C13/1) concerning a social action programme makes provision for a Directive on the approximation of Member States' legislation on collective redundancies;

Whereas this approximation must therefore be promoted while the improvement is being maintained within the meaning of Article 117 of the Treaty,

HAS ADOPTED THIS DIRECTIVE:

Section I—Definitions and scope

Article 1

1. For the purposes of this Directive:
    (*a*) "collective redundancies" means dismissals effected by an employer for one or more reasons not related to the individual workers concerned where, according to the choice of the Member States, the number of redundancies is:
    —either, over a period of 30 days:
        (i) at least 10 in establishments normally employing more than 20 and less than 100 workers;
        (2) at least 10 per cent. of the number of workers in establishments normally employing at least 100 but less than 300 workers;
        (3) at least 30 in establishments normally employing 300 workers or more;
    —or, over a period of 90 days, at least 20, whatever the number of workers normally employed in the establishments in question;
    (*b*) "workers' representatives" means the workers' representatives provided for by the laws or practices of the Member States.
2. This Directive shall not apply to:
    (*a*) collective redundancies effected under contracts of employment concluded for limited periods of time or for specific tasks except where such redundancies take place prior to the date of expiry or the completion of such contracts;
    (*b*) workers employed by public administrative bodies or by establishments governed by public law (or, in Member States where this concept is unknown, by equivalent bodies);
    (*c*) the crews of sea-going vessels;
    (*d*) workers affected by the termination of an establishment's activities where that is the result of a judicial decision.

Section II—Consultation procedure

Article 2

1. Where an employer is contemplating collective redundancies, he shall begin consultations with the workers' representatives with a view to reaching an agreement.
2. These consultations shall, at least, cover ways and means of avoiding collective redundancies or reducing the number of workers affected, and mitigating the consequences.
3. To enable the workers' representatives to make constructive pro-

posals the employer shall supply them with all relevant information and shall in any event give in writing the reasons for the redundancies, the number of workers to be made redundant, the number of workers normally employed and the period over which the redundancies are to be effected.

The employer shall forward to the competent public authority a copy of all the written communications referred to in the preceding sub-paragraph.

Section III—Procedure for collective redundancies

ARTICLE 3

3–021   1. Employers shall notify the competent public authority in writing of any projected redundancies.

This notification shall contain all relevant information concerning the projected collective redundancies and the consultations with workers' representatives provided for in Article 2, and particularly the reasons for the redundancies, the number of workers to be made redundant, the number of workers normally employed and the period over which the redundancies are to be effected.

2. Employers shall forward to the workers' representatives a copy of the notification provided for in paragraph 1.

The workers' representatives may send any comments they may have to the competent public authority.

ARTICLE 4

3–022   1. Projected collective redundancies notified to the competent public authority shall take effect not earlier than 30 days after the notification referred to in Article 3(1) without prejudice to any provisions governing individual rights with regard to notice of dismissal.

Member States may grant the competent public authority the power to reduce the period provided for in the preceding subparagraph.

2. The period provided for in paragraph 1 shall be used by the competent public authority to seek solutions in the problems raised by the projected collective redundancies.

3. Where the initial period provided for in paragraph 1 is shorter than 60 days, Member States may grant the competent public authority the power to extend the initial period to 60 days following notification where the problems raised by the projected collective redundancies are not likely to be solved within the initial period.

Member States may grant the competent public authority wider powers of extension.

The employer must be informed of the extension and the grounds for it before expiry of the initial period provided for in paragraph 1.

Section IV—Final provisions

ARTICLE 5

3–023   This Directive shall not affect the right of Member States to apply or to introduce laws, regulations or administrative provisions which are more favourable to workers.

ARTICLE 6

1. Member States shall bring into force the laws, regulations and administrative provisions needed in order to comply with this Directive within two years following its notification and shall forthwith inform the Commission thereof.

2. Member States shall communicate to the Commission the texts of the laws, regulations and administrative provisions which they adopt in the field covered by this Directive.

ARTICLE 7

Within two years following expiry of the two year period laid down in Article 6, Member States shall forward all relevant information to the Commission to enable it to draw up a report for submission to the Council on the application of this Directive.

ARTICLE 8

This Directive is addressed to the Member States.
Done at Brussels, February 17, 1975.

Council Directive 76/207 of February 9, 1976

On the Implementation of the Principle of Equal Treatment for Men and Women as Regards Access to Employment, Vocational Training and Promotion, and Working Conditions

(O.J. 1976, L39/40)

THE COUNCIL OF THE EUROPEAN COMMUNITIES

Having regard to the Treaty establishing the European Economic Community, and in particular Article 235 thereof,

Having regard to the proposal from the Commission,

Having regard to the opinion of the European Parliament,

Having regard to the opinion of the Economic and Social Committee,

Whereas the Council, in its resolution of January 21, 1974 concerning a social action programme, included among the priorities action for the purpose of achieving equality between men and women as regards access to employment and vocational training and promotion and as regards working conditions, including pay;

Whereas, with regard to pay, the Council adopted on February 10, 1975 Directive 75/117 on the approximation of the laws of the Member States relating to the application of the principle of equal pay for men and women;

Whereas Community action to achieve the principle of equal treatment for men and women in respect of access to employment and vocational training and promotion and in respect of other working conditions also appears to be necessary; whereas, equal treatment for male and female workers constitutes one of the objectives of the Community, in so far as the harmonisation of living and working conditions while maintaining their improvement are *inter alia* to be furthered; whereas the Treaty does not confer the necessary specific powers for this purpose;

Whereas the definition and progressive implementation of the principle of equal treatment in matters of social security should be ensured by means of subsequent instruments.

HAS ADOPTED THIS DIRECTIVE.

Article 1

3–025   1. The purpose of this Directive is put into effect in the Member States the principle of equal treatment for men and women as regards access to employment, including promotion, and to vocational training and as regards working conditions and, on the conditions referred to in paragraph (2), social security. This principle is hereinafter referred to as "the principle of equal treatment."

2. With a view to ensuring the progressive implementation of the principle of equal treatment in matters of social security, the Council, acting on a proposal from the Commission, will adopt provisions defining its substance, its scope and the arrangements for its application.

Article 2

3–026   1. For the purposes of the following provisions, the principle of equal treatment shall mean that there shall be no discrimination whatsoever on grounds of sex either directly or indirectly by reference in particular to marital or family status.

2. This Directive shall be without prejudice to the right of Member States to exclude from its field of application those occupational activities and, where appropriate, the training leading thereto, for which, by reason of their nature or the context in which they are carried out, the sex of the worker constitutes a determining factor.

3. This Directive shall be without prejudice to measures to promote equal opportunity for men and women, in particular by removing existing inequalities which affect women's opportunities in the areas referred to in Article 1(1).

Article 3

3–027   1. Application of the principle of equal treatment means that there shall be no discrimination whatsoever on grounds of sex in the conditions, including selection criteria, for access to all jobs or posts, whatever the sector or branch of activity, and to all levels of the occupational hierarchy.

2. To this end, Member States shall take the measures necessary to ensure that:

- (*a*) any laws, regulations and administrative provisions contrary to the principle of equal treatment shall be abolished;
- (*b*) any provisions contrary to the principle of equal treatment which are included in collective agreements, individual contracts of employment, internal rules of undertakings or in rules governing the independent occupations and professions shall be, or may be declared, null and void or may be amended;
- (*c*) those laws, regulations and administrative provisions contrary to the principle of equal treatment when the concern for protection which originally inspired them is no longer well founded shall be revised; and that where similar provisions are included in collective agreements labour and management shall be requested to undertake the desired revision.

Article 4

Application of the principle of equal treatment with regard to access to all types and to all levels, of vocational guidance, vocational training, advanced vocational training and retraining, means that Member States shall take all necessary measures to ensure that:

    (*a*) any laws, regulations and administrative provisions contrary to the principle of equal treatment shall be abolished;

    (*b*) any provisions contrary to the principle of equal treatment which are included in collective agreements, individual contracts of employment, internal rules of undertakings or in rules governing the independent occupations and professions shall be, or may be declared, null and void or may be amended;

    (*c*) without prejudice to the freedom granted in certain Member States to certain private training establishments, vocational guidance, vocational training, advanced vocational training and retraining shall be accessible on the basis of the same criteria and at the same levels without any discrimination on grounds of sex.

3–028

Article 5

1. Application of the principle of equal treatment with regard to working conditions, including the conditions governing dismissal, means that men and women shall be guaranteed the same conditions without discrimination on grounds of sex.

2. To this end, Member States shall take the measures necessary to ensure that:

    (*a*) any laws, regulations and administrative provisions contrary to the principle of equal treatment shall be abolished;

    (*b*) any provisions contrary to the principle of equal treatment which are included in collective agreements, individual contracts of employment, internal rules of undertakings or in rules governing the independent occupations and professions shall be, or may be declared, null and void or may be amended;

    (*c*) those laws, regulations and administrative provisions contrary to the principle of equal treatment when the concern for protection which originally inspired them is no longer well founded shall be revised; and that where similar provisions are included in collective agreements labour and management shall be requested to undertake the desired revision.

3–029

Article 6

Member States shall introduce into their national legal systems such measures as are necessary to enable all persons who consider themselves wronged by failure to apply to them the principle of equal treatment within the meaning of Articles 3, 4 and 5 to pursue their claims by judicial process after possible recourse to other competent authorities.

3–030

Article 7

Member States shall take the necessary measures to protect employees against dismissal by the employer as a reaction to a complaint within the

3–031

undertaking or to any legal proceedings aimed at enforcing compliance with the principle of equal treatment.

ARTICLE 8

3–032   Member States shall take care that the provisions adopted pursuant to this Directive, together with the relevant provisions already in force, are brought to the attention of employees by all appropriate means, for example at their place of employment.

ARTICLE 9

3–033   1. Member States shall put into force the laws, regulations and administrative provisions necessary in order to comply with this Directive within 30 months of its notification and shall immediately inform the Commission thereof.

However, as regards the first part of Article 3(2)(c) and the first part of Article 5(2)(c), Member States shall carry out a first examination and if necessary a first revision of the laws, regulations and administrative provisions referred to therein within four years of notification of this Directive.

2. Member States shall periodically assess the occupational activities referred to in Article 2(2) in order to decide, in the light of social developments, whether there is justification for maintaining the exclusions concerned. They shall notify the Commission of the results of this assessment.

3. Member States shall also communicate to the Commission the texts of laws, regulations and administrative provisions which they adopt in the field covered by this Directive.

ARTICLE 10

3–034   Within two years following expiry of the 30-month period laid down in the first sub-paragraph of Article 9(1), Member States shall forward all necessary information to the Commission to enable it to draw up a report on the application of this Directive for submission to the Council.

ARTICLE 11

3–035   This Directive is addressed to the Member States.
Done at Brussels, February 9, 1976.

3–036   ## Council Directive 77/187 of February 14, 1977

On the Approximation of the Laws of the Member States Relating to the Safeguarding of Employees' Rights in the Event of Transfers of Undertakings, Businesses or Parts of Businesses

(O.J. 1977, L61/26)

THE COUNCIL OF THE EUROPEAN COMMUNITIES
Having regard to the Treaty establishing the European Economic Community, and in particular Article 100 thereof.
Having regard to the proposal from the Commission,
Having regard to the opinion of the European Parliament,
Having regard to the opinion of the Economic and Social Committee,

Whereas economic trends are bringing in their wake, at both national and Community level, changes in the structure of undertakings, through transfers of undertakings, businesses or parts of businesses to other employers as a result of legal transfers or mergers;

Whereas it is necessary to provide for the protection of employees in the event of a change of employer, in particular, to ensure that their rights are safeguarded;

Whereas differences still remain in the Member States as regards the extent of the protection of employees in this respect and these differences should be reduced;

Whereas these differences can have a direct effect on the functioning of the common market;

Whereas it is therefore necessary to promote the approximation of laws in this field while maintaining the improvement described in Article 117 of the Treaty,

HAS ADOPTED THIS DIRECTIVE:

Section I—Scope and definitions

Article 1

1. This Directive shall apply to the transfer of an undertaking, business or part of a business to another employer as a result of a legal transfer or merger.

2. This Directive shall apply where and in so far as the undertaking, business or part of the business to be transferred is situated within the territorial scope of the Treaty.

3. This Directive shall not apply to sea-going vessels.

Article 2

For the purposes of this Directive:
- (a) "transferor" means any natural or legal person who, by reason of a transfer within the meeting of Article 1(1), ceases to be the employer in respect of the undertaking, business or part of the business;
- (b) "transferee" means any natural or legal person who, by reason of a transfer within the meaning of Article 1(1), becomes the employer in respect of the undertaking, business or part of the business;
- (c) "representatives of the employees" means the representatives of the employees provided for by the laws or practice of the Member States, with the exception of members of administrative, governing or supervisory bodies of companies who represent employees on such bodies in certain Member States.

Section II—Safeguarding of employee's rights

Article 3

1. The transferor's rights and obligations arising from a contract of employment or from an employment relationship existing on the date of a transfer within the meaning of Article 1(1) shall, by reason of such transfer, be transferred to the transferee.

Member States may provide that, after the date of transfer within the meaning of Article 1(1) and in addition to the transferee, the transferor shall continue to be liable in respect of obligations which arose from a contract of employment or an employment relationship.

2. Following the transfer within the meaning of Article 1(1), the transferee shall continue to observe the terms and conditions agreed in any collective agreement on the same terms applicable to the transferor under that agreement, until the date of termination or expiry of the collective agreement or the entry into force or application of another collective agreement.

Member States may limit the period for observing such terms and conditions, with the proviso that it shall not be less than one year.

3. Paragraphs (1) and (2) shall not cover employees' rights to old-age, invalidity or survivors' benefits under supplementary company or intercompany pension schemes outside the statutory social security schemes in Member States.

Member States shall adopt the measures necessary to protect the interests of employees and of persons no longer employed in the transferor's business at the time of the transfer within the meaning of Article 1(1) in respect of rights conferring on them immediate or prospective entitlement to old-age benefits, including survivors' benefits, under supplementary schemes referred to in the first sub-paragraph.

ARTICLE 4

1. The transfer of an undertaking, business or part of a business shall not in itself constitute grounds for dismissal by the transferor or the transferee. This provision shall not stand in the way of dismissals that may take place for economic, technical or organisational reasons entailing changes in the workforce.

Member States may provide that the first sub-paragraph shall not apply to certain specific categories of employees who are not covered by the laws or practice of the Member States in respect of protection against dismissal.

2. If the contract of employment or the employment relationship is terminated because the transfer within the meaning of Article 1(1) involves a substantial change in working conditions to the detriment of the employee, the employer shall be regarded as having been responsible for termination of the contract of employment or of the employment relationship.

ARTICLE 5

1. If the business preserves its autonomy, the status and function, as laid down by the laws, regulations or administrative provisions of the Member States, of the representatives or of the representation of the employees affected by the transfer within the meaning of Article 1(1) shall be preserved.

The first sub-paragraph shall not apply if, under the laws, regulations, administrative provisions or practice of the Member States, the conditions necessary for the re-appointment of the representatives of the employees or for the reconstitution of the representation of the employees are fulfilled.

2. If the term of office of the representatives of the employees affected by a transfer within the meaning of Article 1(1) expires as a result of the

transfer, the representatives shall continue to enjoy the protection provided by the laws, regulations, administrative provisions or practice of the Member States.

Section III—Information and consultation

ARTICLE 6

1. The transferor and the transferee shall be required to inform the representatives of their respective employees affected by a transfer within the meaning of Article 1(1) of the following:
    — the reasons for the transfer,
    — the legal, economic and social implications of the transfer for the employees,
    — measures envisaged in relation to the employees.

The transferor must give such information to the representatives of his employees in good time before the transfer is carried out.

The transferee must give such information to the representatives of his employees in good time, and in any event before his employees are directly affected by the transfer as regards their conditions of work and employment.

2. If the transferor or the transferee envisages measures in relation to his employees, he shall consult his representatives of the employees in good time on such measures with a view to seeking agreement.

3. Member States whose laws, regulations or administrative provisions provide that representatives of the employees may have recourse to an arbitration board to obtain a decision on the measures to be taken in relation to employees may limit the obligations laid down in paragraphs (1) and (2) to cases where the transfer carried out gives rise to a change in the business likely to entail serious disadvantages for a considerable number of the employees.

The information and consultations shall cover at least the measures envisaged in relation to the employees.

The information must be provided and consultations take place in good time before the change in the business as referred to in the first sub-paragraph is effected.

4. Member States may limit the obligations laid down in paragraphs (1), (2) and (3) to undertakings or businesses which, in respect of the number of employees, fulfil the conditions for the election or designation of a collegiate body representing the employees.

5. Member States may provide that where there are no representatives of the employees in an undertaking or business, the employees concerned must be informed in advance when a transfer within the meaning of Article 1(1) is about to take place.

Section IV—Final provisions

ARTICLE 7

This Directive shall not affect the right of Member States to apply or introduce laws, regulations or administrative provisions which are more favourable to employees.

ARTICLE 8

1. Member States shall bring into force the laws, regulations and admin-

istrative provisions needed to comply with this Directive within two years of its notification and shall forthwith inform the Commission thereof.

2. Member States shall communicate to the Commission the texts of the laws, regulations and administrative provisions which they adopt in the field covered by this Directive.

Article 9

Within two years following expiry of the two-year period laid down in Article 8, Member States shall forward all relevant information to the Commission in order to enable it to draw up a report on the application of this Directive for submission to the Council.

Article 10

This Directive is addressed to the Member States.
Done at Brussels, February 14, 1977.

COUNCIL OF EUROPE

European Convention on Human Rights and Fundamental Freedoms 1953

. . . . . .

Article 9

1. Everyone has the right to freedom of thought, conscience and religion; this right includes freedom to change his religion or belief, and freedom, either alone or in community with others and in public or private, to manifest his religion or belief, in worship, teaching, practice and observance.

2. Freedom to manifest one's religion or beliefs shall be subject only to such limitations as are prescribed by law and are necessary in a democratic society in the interests of public safety, for the protection of public order, health or morals, or for the protection of the rights and freedoms of others.

Article 10

1. Everyone has the right to freedom of expression. This right shall include freedom to hold opinions and to receive and impart information and ideas without interference by public authority and regardless of frontiers. This Article shall not prevent States from requiring the licensing of broadcasting, television or cinema enterprises.

2. The exercise of these freedoms, since it carries with it duties and responsibilities, may be subject to such formalities, conditions, restrictions or penalties as are prescribed by law and are necessary in a democratic society, in the interests of national security, territorial integrity or public safety, for the prevention of disorder or crime, for the protection of health or morals, for the protection of the reputation or rights of others, for preventing the disclosure of information received in confidence, or for maintaining the authority and impartiality of the judiciary.

Article 11

1. Everyone has the right to freedom of peaceful assembly and to free-

dom of association with others, including the right to form and to join trade unions for the protection of his interests.

2. No restrictions shall be placed on the exercise of these rights other than such as are prescribed by law and are necessary in a democratic society in the interests of national security or public safety, for the prevention of disorder or crime, for the protection of health or morals or for the protection of the rights and freedoms of others. This Article shall not prevent the imposition of lawful restrictions on the exercise of these rights by members of the armed forces, of the police or of the administration of the State.

Article 14

The enjoyment of the rights and freedoms set forth in this Convention shall be secured without discrimination on any ground such as sex, race, colour, language, religion, political or other opinion, national or social origin, association with a national minority, property, birth or other status.

European Social Charter 1965

. . . . . .

The Right to Bargain Collectively

Article 6

With a view to ensuring the effective exercise of the right to bargain collectively, the Contracting Parties undertake:
(1) to promote joint consultation between workers and employers;
(2) to promote where necessary and appropriate, machinery for voluntary negotiations between employers or employers' organisations and workers' organisations, with a view to the regulation of terms and conditions of employment by means of collective agreements;
(3) to promote the establishment and use of appropriate machinery for conciliation and voluntary arbitration for the settlement of labour disputes; and recognise:
(4) the right of workers and employers to collective action in cases of conflicts of interest, including the right to strike, subject to obligations that might arise out of collective agreements previously entered into.

. . . . . .

The Right of Employed Women to Protection

Article 8

With a view to ensuring the effective exercise of the right of employed women to protection, the Contracting Parties undertake:
(1) to provide either by paid leave, by adequate social security benefits or by benefits from public funds for women to take leave before and after childbirth up to a total of at least 12 weeks;

[(2) to consider it as unlawful for an employer to give a woman notice of dismissal during her absence on maternity leave or to give her notice of dismissal at such a time that the notice would expire during such absence;

(3) to provide that mothers who are nursing their infants shall be entitled to sufficient time off for this purpose;]
- (4) (*a*) to regulate the employment of women workers on night work in industrial employment
  - (*b*) to prohibit the employment of women workers in underground mining, and, as appropriate, on all other work which is unsuitable for them by reason of its dangerous, unhealthy, or arduous nature.

Note: The paragraphs in square brackets have not been accepted by the United Kingdom.

PART IV

REPEALED LEGISLATION

Trade Union Act 1871

(34 & 35 Vict. c.31)

An Act to amend the Law relating to Trade Unions.

[29th June 1871.]

. . . . . .

Criminal Provisions

Trade union not criminal

2. The purposes of any trade union shall not, by reason merely that they are in restraint of trade be deemed to be unlawful so as to render any member of such trade union liable to criminal prosecution for conspiracy or otherwise.

Trade union not unlawful for civil purposes

3. The purposes of any trade union shall not, by reason merely that they are in restraint of trade, be unlawful so as to render void or voidable any agreement or trust.

Trade union contracts, when not enforceable

4. Nothing in this Act shall enable any court to entertain any legal proceedings instituted with the object of directly enforcing or recovering damages for the breach of any of the following agreements, namely,

(1) Any agreement between members of a trade union as such, concerning the conditions on which any members for the time being of such trade union shall or shall not sell their goods, transact business, employ, or be employed:

(2) Any agreement for the payment by any person of any subscription or penalty to a trade union:

(3) Any agreement for the application of the funds of a trade union—
 (*a*) To provide benefits to members; or
 (*b*) To furnish contributions to any employer or workman not a member of such trade union, in consideration of such employer or workman acting in conformity with the rules or resolutions of such trade union; or
 (*c*) To discharge any fine imposed upon any person by sentence of a court of justice; or

(4) Any agreement made between one trade union and another; or

(5) Any bond to secure the performance of any of the above-mentioned agreements.

But nothing in this section shall be deemed to constitute any of the above-mentioned agreements unlawful.

Conspiracy and Protection of Property Act 1875

[38 & 39 VICT. c.86]

An Act for amending the Law relating to Conspiracy, and to the Protection of Property, and for other purposes.

[13th August 1875.]

. . . . . .

Conspiracy, and Protection of Property

Amendment of law as to conspiracy in trade disputes

3. An agreement or combination by two or more persons to do or procure to be done any act in contemplation or furtherance of a trade dispute . . . shall not be indictable as a conspiracy if such act committed by one person would not be punishable as a crime.

[¹ An act done in pursuance of an agreement or combination by two or more persons shall, if done in contemplation or furtherance of a trade dispute, not be actionable unless the act, if done without any such agreement or combination, would be actionable.]

Nothing in this section shall exempt from punishment any persons guilty of a conspiracy for which a punishment is awarded by any Act of Parliament.

Nothing in this section shall affect the law relating to riot, unlawful assembly, breach of the peace, or sedition, or any offence against the State or the Sovereign.

A crime for the purposes of this section means an offence punishable on indictment, or an offence which is punishable on summary conviction, and for the commission of which the offender is liable under the statute making the offence punishable to be imprisoned either absolutely or at the discretion of the court as an alternative for some other punishment.

Where a person is convicted of any such agreement or combination as aforesaid to do or procure to be done any act which is punishable only on summary conviction, and is sentenced to imprisonment, the imprisonment shall not exceed three months, or such longer time, if any, as may have been prescribed by the statute for the punishment of the said act when committed by one person.

AMENDMENT
The words in square brackets were inserted by the Trade Disputes Act 1906 (6 Edw. 7 c. 47), s.1.

Breach of contract by persons employed in supply of gas or water

4. Where a person employed by a municipal authority or by any company or contractor upon whom is imposed by Act of Parliament the duty, or who have otherwise assumed the duty of supplying any city borough town or place, or any part thereof, with gas or water, wilfully and maliciously breaks a contract of service with that authority or company or contractor, knowing or having reasonable cause to believe that the probable consequences of his so doing, either alone or in combination with others, will be to deprive the inhabitants of that city, borough, town, place, or part, wholly or to a great extent of their supply of gas or water, he shall on conviction thereof by a court of summary jurisdiction, or on indictment as hereinafter mentioned be liable either to pay a penalty not exceeding twenty pounds or to be imprisoned for a term not exceeding three months, with or without hard labour.

Every such municipal authority, company, or contractor as is mentioned in this section shall cause to be posted up, at the gasworks or waterworks, as the case may be, belonging to such authority or company or contractor, a printed copy of this section in some conspicuous place where the same may be conveniently read by the persons employed, and as often as such copy becomes defaced obliterated or destroyed, shall cause it to be renewed with all reasonable despatch.

If any municipal authority or company or contractor make default in complying with the provisions of this section in relation to such notice as aforesaid, they or he shall incur on summary conviction a penalty not exceeding five pounds for every day during which such default continues, and every person who unlawfully injures, defaces, or covers up any notice so posted up as aforesaid in pursuance of this Act, shall be liable on summary conviction to a penalty not exceeding forty shillings.

Trade Disputes Act 1906

4–008

(6 EDW. 7 c.47)

An Act to provide for the regulation of Trades Unions and Trade Disputes.

[21st December 1906.]

. . . . . .

Peaceful picketing

2.—(1) It shall be lawful for one or more persons, acting on their own behalf or on behalf of a trade union or of an individual employer or firm in contemplation or furtherance of a trade dispute, to attend at or near a house or place where a person resides or works or carries on business or happens to be, if they so attend merely for the purpose of peacefully obtaining or communicating information, or of peacefully persuading any person to work or abstain from working.

4–009

[*Subs.* (2) *rep.* 17 & 18 *Geo.* 5. *c.* 42 (*S.L.R.*)]

Removal of liability of interfering with another person's business, &c.

3. An act done by a person in contemplation or furtherance of a trade dispute shall not be actionable on the ground only that it induces some other person to break a contract of employment or that it is an interference with the trade, business, or employment of some other person, or with the right of some other person to dispose of his capital or his labour as he wills.

4–010

Prohibition of actions of tort against trade unions

4. (1) An action against a trade union, whether of workmen or masters, or against any members or officials thereof on behalf of themselves and all other members of the trade union in respect of any tortious act alleged to have been committed by or on behalf of the trade union, shall not be entertained by any court.

4–011

(2) Nothing in this section shall affect the liability of the trustees of a trade union to be sued in the events provided for by the Trade Union Act,

1871, section nine, except in respect of any tortious act committed by or on behalf of the union in contemplation or in furtherance of a trade dispute.

Short title and construction

4–012   5.—(1) This Act may be cited as the Trade Disputes Act, 1906, and the Trade Union Acts, 1871 and 1876, and this Act may be cited together as the Trade Union Acts, 1871 to 1906.

(2) In this Act the expression "trade union" has the same meaning as in the Trade Union Acts, 1871 and 1876, and shall include any combination as therein defined, notwithstanding that such combination may be the branch of a trade union.

(3) In this Act and in the Conspiracy and Protection of Property Act, 1875, the expression "trade dispute" means any dispute between employers and workmen, or between workmen and workmen, which is connected with the employment or non-employment, or the terms of the employment, or with the conditions of labour, of any person, and the expression "workmen" means all persons employed in trade or industry, whether or not in the employment of the employer with whom a trade dispute arises. . . .

4–013   # Trade Union and Labour Relations Act 1974

(1974 c.52)

. . . . . .

Restrictions on Legal Liability and Legal Proceedings

Acts in contemplation or furtherance of trade disputes
13.—. . . .
(2) For the avoidance of doubt it is hereby declared that an act done by a person in contemplation or furtherance of a trade dispute is not actionable in tort on the ground only that it is an interference with the trade, business or employment of another person, or with the right of another person to dispose of his capital or his labour as he wills.

(3) For the avoidance of doubt it is hereby declared that—
  (*a*) an act which by reason of subsection (1) or (2) above is itself not actionable;
  (*b*) a breach of contract in contemplation or furtherance of a trade dispute;
shall not be regarded as the doing of an unlawful act or as the use of unlawful means for the purpose of establishing liability in tort.

. . . . . .

Immunity of trade unions and employers' associations to actions in tort

4–014   14.—(1) Subject to subsection (2) below, no action in tort shall lie in respect of any act—

(a) alleged to have been done by or on behalf of a trade union which is not a special register body or by or on behalf of an unincorporated employers' association; or
(b) alleged to have been done, in connection with the regulation of relations between employers or employers' associations and workers or trade unions, by or on behalf of a trade union which is a special register body or by or on behalf of an employers' association which is a body corporate; or
(c) alleged to be threatened or to be intended to be done as mentioned in paragraph (a) or (b) above;

against the union or association in its own name, or against the trustees of the union or association, or against any members or officials of the union or association on behalf of themselves, and all other members of the union or association.

(2) Subsection (1) above shall not affect the liability of a trade union or employers' association to be sued in respect of the following, if not arising from an act done in contemplation or furtherance of a trade dispute, that is to say—
(a) any negligence, nuisance or breach of duty (whether imposed on them by any rule of law or by or under any enactment) resulting in personal injury to any person; or
(b) without prejudice to paragraph (a) above, breach of any duty so imposed in connection with the ownership, occupation, possession, control or use of property (whether real or personal or, in Scotland, heritable or moveable).

(3) In this section "personal injury" includes any disease and any impairment of a person's physical or mental condition.

Peaceful picketing

15. It shall be lawful for one or more persons in contemplation or furtherance of a trade dispute to attend at or near— 4–015
(a) a place where another person works or carries on business; or
(b) any other place where another person happens to be, not being a place where he resides,

for the purpose only of peacefully obtaining or communicating information, or peacefully persuading any person to work to abstain from working.

. . . . . .

Meaning of trade dispute

29.—(1) In this Act "trade dispute" means a dispute between employers and workers, or between workers and workers, which is connected with one or more of the following, that is to say— 4–016
(a) terms and conditions of employment, or the physical conditions in which any workers are required to work;
(b) engagement or non-engagement, or termination or suspension of employment or the duties of employment, of one or more workers;
(c) allocation of work or the duties of employment as between workers or groups of workers;
(d) matters of discipline;
(e) the membership or non-membership of a trade union on the part of a worker;
(f) facilities for officials of trade unions; and

(g) machinery for negotiations or consultation, and other procedures, relating to any of the foregoing matters, including the recognition by employers or employers' associations of the rights of a trade union to represent workers in any such negotiation or consultation or in the carrying out of such procedures.

PART V
APPENDICES

APPENDIX 1

E.A.T Practice Direction
Appeal Procedure 5–001

Dated February 17, 1981, and made by the President of the Employment Appeal Tribunal

1. The Employment Appeal Tribunal Rules 1980 (S.I. 1980 No. 2035) (hereinafter called "The Rules") came into operation on February 1, 1981.

2. By virtue of paragraph 7(2) of Schedule 11 to the Employment Protection (Consolidation) Act 1978, the Appeal Tribunal has power, subject to the Rules, to regulate its own procedure.

3. Where the Rules do not otherwise provide, the following procedure will be followed in all appeals to the Appeal Tribunal.

4. *Appeals out of time*

(a) By virtue of rule 3(1) of the Rules every appeal under section 136 of the Employment Protection (Consolidation) Act 1978 or section 4 of the Employment Act 1980 to the Employment Appeal Tribunal shall be instituted by serving on the tribunal, within 42 days of the date on which the document recording the decision or order appealed from was sent to the appellant, a notice of appeal as prescribed in the Rules.

(b) Every notice of appeal not delivered within 42 days of the date on which the document recording the decision or order appealed from was sent to the appellant must be accompanied by an application for an extension of time, setting out the reasons for the delay.

(c) Applications for an extension of time for appealing cannot be considered until a notice of appeal has been presented.

(d) Unless otherwise ordered, the application for extension of time will be considered and determined as though it were an interlocutory application.

(e) In determining whether to extend the time for appealing, particular attention will be paid to the guidance contained in *Marshall* v. *Harland & Wolff Ltd.* [1972] I.C.R. 97, and to whether any excuse for the delay has been shown.

(f) It is not necessarily a good excuse for delay in appealing that legal aid has been applied for, or that support is being sought, (*e.g.* from the Equal Opportunities Commission, or from a trade union. In such cases the intending appellant should at the earliest possible moment, and at the latest within the time limit for appealing, inform the registrar, and the other party, of his

intentions, and seek the latter's agreement to an extension of time for appealing.
- (g) Time for appealing runs from the date on which the document recording the decision or order of the industrial tribunal was sent to the appellant, notwithstanding that the assessment of compensation has been adjourned, or an application has been made for a review.
- (h) In any case of doubt or difficulty, notice of appeal should be presented in time, and an application made to the registrar for directions.

5. *Institution of Appeal*
   - (a) Subject to Rule 3(2) of the Rules, if it appears to the registrar that a Notice of Appeal or application gives insufficient particulars or lacks clarity either as to the question of law or the grounds of an appeal, the registrar may postpone his decision under that Rule pending amplification or clarification of the Notice of Appeal, as regards the question of law or grounds of appeal, by the intended appellant.
   - (b) An appellant will not ordinarily be allowed to contend that "the decision was contrary to the evidence," or that "there was no evidence to support the decision," or to advance similar contentions, unless full and sufficient particulars identifying the particular matters relied upon have been supplied to the Appeal Tribunal.
   - (c) It will not be open to the parties to reserve a right to amend, alter or add to any pleading. Any such right is not inherent and may only be exercised if permitted by order for which an interlocutory application should be made as soon as the need for alteration is known.

6. *Special Procedure*
   - (a) Where an appeal has not been rejected pursuant to Rule 3(2) but nevertheless the Appeal Tribunal considers that it is doubtful whether the grounds of appeal disclose an arguable point of law, the president or a judge may direct that the matter be set down before a Division of the Appeal Tribunal for hearing of a preliminary point to enable the appellant to show cause why the appeal should not be dismissed on the ground that it does not disclose a fairly arguable point of law.
   - (b) The respondent will be given notice of the hearing but since it will be limited to the preliminary point he will not be required to attend the hearing or permitted to take part in it.
   - (c) If the appellant succeeds in showing cause, the hearing will be adjourned and the appeal will be set down for hearing before a different Division of the Appeal Tribunal in the usual way.
   - (d) If the appellant does not show cause, the appeal will be dismissed.
   - (e) The decision as to whether this procedure will be adopted in any particular case will be in the discretion of the president or a judge.

7. *Interlocutory Applications*
   - (a) On receipt of an interlocutory application the registrar will sub-

mit a copy of the application to the other side, and will indicate that if it is not intended to oppose the application it may be unnecessary for the parties to be heard and that the appropriate order may be made in their absence. Where the application is opposed the registrar will also in appropriate cases give the parties an opportunity of agreeing to the application being decided on the basis of written submissions.

(b) Save where the president or a judge directs otherwise, every interlocutory application to strike out pleadings or to debar a party from taking any further part in the proceedings pursuant to Rules 16 or 21 will be heard on the day appointed for the hearing of the appeal, but immediately preceding the hearing thereof.

8. *Meeting for directions*

On every appeal from the decision of the certification officer, and, if necessary, on any other appeal, so soon as the answer is delivered, or if a cross-appeal, the reply, the registrar will appoint a day when the parties shall meet on an appointment for directions and the appeal tribunal will give such directions, including a date for hearing, as it deems necessary.

9. *Right to inspect the register and certain documents and to take copies*

Where, pursuant to the direction dated March 31, 1976, a document filed at the Employment Appeal Tribunal has been inspected and a photographic copy of the document is bespoken, a copying fee of 25p for each page will be charged.

10. *Listing of appeals*

A. *England and Wales*

(a) When the respondent's answer has been received and a copy served on the appellant, the case will be put in the list of cases for hearing. At the beginning of each calendar month a list will be prepared of cases to be heard on specified dates in the next following calendar month. That list will also include a number of cases which are liable to be taken in each specified week of the relevant month. The parties or their representatives will be notified as soon as the list is prepared. When cases in the list with specified dates are settled or withdrawn, cases warned for the relevant week will be substituted and the parties notified as soon as possible.

(b) A party finding that the date which has been given causes serious difficulties may apply to the listing officer before the 15th of the month in which the case first appears in the list. No change will be made unless the listing officer agrees, but every reasonable effort will be made to accommodate parties in difficulties. Changes after the 15th of the month in which the list first appears will not be made other than on application to the President of the Employment Appeal Tribunal; arrangements for the making of such an application should be made through the listing officer.

(c) Other cases may be put in the list by the listing officer with the consent of the parties at shorter notice, *e.g.* where other cases have been settled or withdrawn or where it appears that they will take less time than originally estimated. Parties who wish their cases to be taken as soon as possible and at short notice should notify the listing officer.

(d) Each week an up-to-date list for the following week will be prepared including any changes which have been made (in particular specifying cases which by then have been given fixed dates).

(e) The monthly list and the weekly list will appear in the Daily Cause List and will also be displayed in Room 6 at the Royal Courts of Justice and at No. 4, St. James's Square, London, S.W.1. It is important that parties or their advisers should inspect the weekly list as well as the monthly list.

(f) If cases are settled or to be withdrawn notice should be given at once to the listing officer so that other cases may be given fixed dates.

B. *Scotland*

When the respondent's answer has been received and a copy served on the appellant both parties will be notified in writing that the appeal will be ready for hearing in approximately six weeks. The proposed date of hearing will be notified to the parties three or four weeks ahead. Any party who wishes to apply for a different date must do so within seven days of receipt of such notification. Thereafter a formal notice of the date fixed for the hearing will be issued not less than 14 days in advance. This will be a peremptory diet. It will not be discharged except by the judge on cause shown.

11. *Admissiblity of documents*
    (a) Where, pursuant to rules 9 or 13 an application is made by a party to an appeal to put in at the hearing of the appeal any document which was not before the industrial tribunal, including a note of evidence given before the industrial tribunal (other than the chairman's note), the application shall be submitted in writing with copies of the document(s) sought to be made admissible at the hearing.
    (b) The registrar will forthwith communicate the nature of the application and of the document(s) sought to be made admissible to the other party and where appropriate, to the chairman of the industrial tribunal, for comment.
    (c) A copy of the comment will be forwarded to the party making the application, by the registrar who will either dispose of it in accordance with the Rules or refer it to the appeal tribunal for a ruling at the hearing. In the case of comments received from the chairman of the industrial tribunal a copy will be sent to both parties.

12. *Complaints of bias, etc.*
    (a) The appeal tribunal will not normally consider complaints of bias or of the conduct of an industrial tribunal unless full and sufficient particulars are set out in the grounds of appeal.
    (b) In any such case the registrar may inquire of the party making the complaint whether it is the intention to proceed with the complaint in which case the registrar will give appropriate directions for the hearing.
    (c) Such directions may include the filing of affidavits dealing with the matters upon the basis of which the complaint is made or for the giving of further particulars of the complaint on which the party will seek to rely.
    (d) On compliance with any such direction the registrar will communicate the complaint together with the matters relied on in

support of the complaint to the chairman of the industrial tribunal so that he may have an opportunity of commenting upon it.
(e) No such complaint will be permitted to be developed upon the hearing of the appeal, unless the appropriate procedure has been followed.
(f) A copy of any affidavit or direction for particulars to be delivered thereunder will be communicated to the other side.

13. *Exhibits and documents for use at the hearing*
   (a) The appeal tribunal will prepare copies of all documents for use of the judges and members at the hearing in addition to those which the registrar is required to serve on the parties under the Rules. It is the responsibility of parties or their advisers to ensure that all documents submitted for consideration at the hearing are capable of being reproduced legibly by photographic process.
   (b) In Scotland a copy of the Chairman's Notes will not be supplied to the parties except on application to the Appeal Tribunal on cause shown. In England and Wales copies will only be sent to the parties if in the view of the Appeal Tribunal all or part of such notes are necessary for the purpose of the appeal or on application to the tribunal on cause shown. Chairman's Notes are supplied for the use of the Appeal Tribunal and not for the parties to embark on a "fishing" expedition to establish further grounds of appeal.
   (c) It is the duty of parties and their solicitors to ensure that only those documents which are relevant to the point of law raised in the appeal, and which are likely to be referred to, are included in the documents before the tribunal.
   (d) It will be the responsibility of the parties or their advisers to ensure that all exhibits and documents used before the industrial tribunal, and which are considered to be relevant to the appeal, are sent to the appeal tribunal immediately on request. This will enable the appeal tribunal to number and prepare sufficient copies, together with an index, for the judges and members at least a week before the day appointed for the hearing.
   (e) A copy of the index will be sent to the parties or their representatives prior to the hearing so that they may prepare their bundles in the same order.

TRANSCRIPTS

The Employment Appeal Tribunal issued the following Practice Direction on September 1, 1981:
Where the tribunal at the hearing does not direct that a judgment be transcribed, a transcription will only be provided free of charge to a party

to the appeal if application is made at the hearing or within 14 days of the hearing [1981] I.C.R. 690, E.A.T.

Appendix 2

5–006

Codes of Practice

Industrial Relations Act 1971 Code of Practice

This Code of Practice was laid before Parliament on January 19, 1972, under the Industrial Relations Act 1971, s.3(1), and came into operation on February 28, 1972.

Note: Selected paragraphs are set out below, viz. 40–46 and 120–129.

Status and security of employees

5–007 40. As far as is consistent with operational efficiency and the success of the undertaking management should:
  (i) provide stable employment, including reasonable job security for employees absent through sickness or other causes beyond their control;
  (ii) avoid unnecessary fluctuations in the level of earnings of employees.
  41. Where practicable, management should provide occupational pension and sick pay schemes.
  42. Differences in the conditions of employment and status of different categories of employee and in the facilities available to them should be based on the requirements of the job. The aim should be progressively to reduce and ultimately to remove differences which are not so based. Management, employees and their representatives and trade unions should co-operate in working towards this objective.
  43. In deciding how and when the changes mentioned in paragraphs 41 and 42 are to be introduced, their cost should be taken into account as part of total labour costs.
  44. Responsibility for deciding the size of the work force rests with management. But before taking the final decision to make any substantial reduction, management should consult employees or their representatives, unless exceptional circumstances make this impossible.
  45. A policy for dealing with reductions in the work force, if they become necessary, should be worked out in advance so far as practicable and should form part of the undertaking's employment policies. As far as is consistent with operational efficiency and the success of the undertaking, management should, in consultation with employee representatives, seek to avoid redundancies by such means as:
  (i) restrictions on recruitment;
  (ii) retirement of employees who are beyond the normal retiring age;
  (iii) reductions in overtime;
  (iv) short-time working to cover temporary fluctuations in manpower needs;

(v) retraining or transfer to other work.

46. If redundancy becomes necessary, management in consultation, as appropriate, with employees or their representatives, should:
   (i) give as much warning as practicable to the employees concerned and to the Department of Employment;
   (ii) consider introducing schemes for voluntary redundancy, retirement, transfer to other establishments within the undertaking, and a phased rundown of employment;
   (iii) establish which employees are to be made redundant and the order of discharge;
   (iv) offer help to employees in finding other work in co-operation, where appropriate, with the Department of Employment, and allow them reasonable time off for the purpose;
   (v) decide how and when to make the facts public, ensuring that no announcement is made before the employees and their representatives and trade unions have been informed.

. . . . . .

GRIEVANCE AND DISPUTES PROCEDURES

120. All employees have a right to seek redress for grievances relating to their employment. Each employee must be told how he can do so (see para. 60).

121. Management should establish, with employee representatives or trade unions concerned, arrangements under which individual employees can raise grievances and have them settled fairly and promptly. There should be a formal procedure, except in very small establishments where there is close personal contact between the employer and his employees.

122. Where trade unions are recognised, management should establish with them a procedure for settling collective disputes.

123. Individual grievances and collective disputes are often dealt with through the same procedure. Where there are separate procedures they should be linked so that an issue can, if necessary, pass from one to the other, since a grievance may develop into a dispute.

Individual grievance procedures

124. The aim of the procedure should be to settle the grievance fairly and as near as possible to the point of origin. It should be simple and rapid in operation.

125. The procedure should be in writing and provide that:
   (i) the grievance should normally be discussed first between the employee and his immediate superior;
   (ii) the employee should be accompanied at the next stage of the discussion with management by his employee representative if he so wishes;
   (iii) there should be a right of appeal.

Collective disputes procedures

126. Disputes are broadly of two kinds:
   (i) disputes of right, which relate to the application or interpretation of existing agreements or contracts of employment;
   (ii) disputes of interest, which relate to claims by employees or pro-

5–008

posals by management about terms and conditions of employment.

127. A procedure for settling collective disputes should be in writing and should:
  (i) state the level at which an issue should first be raised;
  (ii) lay down time limits for each stage of the procedure, with provision for extension by agreement;
  (iii) preclude a strike, lock-out, or other form of industrial action until all stages of the procedure have been completed and a failure-to-agree formally recorded.

128. The procedure should have the following stages:
  (i) employee representatives should raise the issue in dispute with management at the level directly concerned;
  (ii) failing settlement, it should be referred to a higher level within the establishment;
  (iii) if still unsettled, it should be referred to further agreed stages, for example, to a stage of an industry-wide procedure, or to a higher level within the undertaking.

129. Independent conciliation and arbitration can be used to settle all types of dispute if the parties concerned agree that they should. Arbitration by the Industrial Arbitration Board or other independent arbitrators is particularly suitable for settling disputes of right, and its wider use for that purpose is desirable. Where it is used the parties should undertake to be bound by the award.

Code of Practice on
Disciplinary Practice and Procedures in Employment

This Code, issued pursuant to s.6(1) and (8) of the Employment Protection Act 1975, came into effect, by order of the Secretary of State, on June 20, 1977.

Introduction

5–009 This Code supersedes paragraph 130 to 133 (inclusive) of the Code of Practice in effect under Part I of Schedule 1 to the Trade Union and Labour Relations Act 1974, which paragraphs shall cease to have effect on the date on which this Code comes into effect.

1. This document gives practical guidance on how to draw up disciplinary rules and procedures and how to operate them effectively. Its aim is to help employers and trade unions as well as individual employees—both men and women—wherever they are employed regardless of the size of the organisation in which they work. In the smaller establishments it may not be practicable to adopt all the detailed provisions, but most of the features listed in paragraph 10 could be adopted and incorporated into a simple procedure.

Why have disciplinary rules and procedures?

5–010 2. Disciplinary rules and procedures are necessary for promoting fairness and order in the treatment of individuals and in the conduct of industrial relations. They also assist an organisation to operate effectively. Rules set standards of conduct at work; procedure helps to ensure that the standards are adhered to and also provides a fair method of dealing with alleged failures to observe them.

3. It is important that employees know what standards of conduct are expected of them and the Contracts of Employment Act 1972 (as amended by the Employment Protection Act 1975) requires employees to provide written information for their employees about certain aspects of their disciplinary rules and procedures.[1]

4. The importance of disciplinary rules and procedures has also been recognised by the law relating to dismissals, since the grounds for dismissal and the way in which the dismissal has been handled can be challenged before an industrial tribunal.[2] Where either of these is found by a tribunal to have been unfair the employer may be ordered to re-instate or re-engage the employees concerned and may be liable to pay compensation to them.

Formulating policy

5. Management is responsible for maintaining discipline within the organisation and for ensuring that there are adequate disciplinary rules and procedures. The initiative for establishing these will normally lie with management. However, if they are to be fully effective the rules and procedures need to be accepted as reasonable both by those who are to be covered by them and by those who operate them. Management should therefore aim to secure the involvement of employees and all levels of management when formulating new or revising existing rules and procedures. In the light of particular circumstances in different companies and industries trade union officials[3] may or may not wish to participate in the formulation of the rules but they should participate fully with management in agreeing the procedural arrangements which will apply to their members and in seeing that these arrangements are used consistently and fairly.

5–011

Rules

6. It is unlikely that any set of disciplinary rules can cover all circumstances that may arise: moreover the rules required will vary according to particular circumstances such as the type of work, working conditions and size of establishment. When drawing up rules the aim should be to specify clearly and concisely those necessary for the efficient and safe performance of work and for the maintenance of satisfactory relations within the workforce and between the employees and management. Rules should not be so general as to be meaningless.

5–012

---

[1] Contracts of Employment Act 1972, s.4(2), as amended by Employment Protection Act 1975, Sched. 16, Part II, requires employers to provide employees with a written statement of the main terms and conditions of their employment. Such statements must also specify any disciplinary rules applicable to them and indicate the person to whom they should apply if they are dissatisfied with any disciplinary decision. The statement should explain any further steps which exist in any procedure for dealing with disciplinary decisions or grievances. The employer may satisfy these requirements by referring the employees to a reasonably accessible document which provides the necessary information.

[2] The Trade Union and Labour Relations Act 1974, Sched. 1, para. 21(4), as amended by the Employment Protection Act 1975, Sched 16, Part III, specifies that a complaint of unfair dismissal has to be presented to an Industrial Tribunal before the end of the three-month period beginning with the effective date of termination.

[3] Throughout this Code, trade union official has the meaning assigned to it by s.30(1) of the Trade Union and Labour Relations Act 1974 and means, broadly, officers of the union, its branches and sections, and anyone else, including fellow employees, appointed or elected under the union's rules to represent members.

7. Rules should be readily available and management should make every effort to ensure that employees know and understand them. This may be best achieved by giving every employee a copy of the rules and by explaining them orally. In the case of new employees this should form part of an induction programme.

8. Employees should be made aware of the likely consequences of breaking rules and in particular they should be given a clear indication of the type of conduct which may warrant summary dismissal.

Essential features of disciplinary procedures

5–013
9. Disciplinary procedures should not be viewed primarily as a means of imposing sanctions. They should also be designed to emphasise and encourage improvements in individual conduct.

10. Disciplinary procedures should:
   (a) Be in writing.
   (b) Specify to whom they apply.
   (c) Provide for matters to be dealt with quickly.
   (d) Indicate the disciplinary actions which may be taken.
   (e) Specify the levels of management which have the authority to take the various forms of disciplinary action, ensuring that immediate superiors do not normally have the power to dismiss without reference to senior management.
   (f) Provide for individuals to be informed of the complaints against them and be given an opportunity to state their case before decisions are reached.
   (g) Give individuals the right to be accompanied by a trade union representative or by a fellow employee of their choice.
   (h) Ensure that, except for gross misconduct, no employees are dismissed for a first breach of discipline.
   (i) Ensure that disciplinary action is not taken until the case has been carefully investigated.
   (j) Ensure that individuals are given an explanation for any penalty imposed.
   (k) Provide a right of appeal and specify the procedure to be followed.

The procedure in operation

5–014
11. When a disciplinary matter arises, the supervisor or manager should first establish the facts promptly before recollections fade, taking into account the statements of any available witnesses. In serious cases consideration should be given to a brief period of suspension while the case is investigated and this suspension should be with pay. Before a decision is made or penalty imposed the individual should be interviewed and given the opportunity to state his or her case and should be advised of any rights under the procedure, including the right to be accompanied.

12. Often supervisors will give informal oral warnings for the purpose of improving conduct when employees commit minor infringements of the established standards of conduct. However, where the facts of a case appear to call for disciplinary action, other than summary dismissal, the following procedure should normally be observed:
   (a) In the case of minor offences the individual should be given a formal oral warning or if the issue is more serious, there should be a written warning setting out the nature of the offence and the likely consequences of further offences. In either case the individual should be

Codes of Practice

advised that the warning constitutes the first formal stage of the procedure.
(b) Further misconduct might warrant a final written warning which should contain a statement that any recurrence would lead to suspension or dismissal or some other penalty, as the case may be.
(c) The final step might be disciplinary transfer, or disciplinary suspension without pay (but only if these are allowed for by an express or implied condition of the contract of employment), or dismissal, according to the nature of the misconduct. Special consideration should be given before imposing disciplinary suspension without pay and it should not normally be for a prolonged period.

13. Except in the event of an oral warning, details of any disciplinary action should be given in writing to the employee and if desired, to his or her representative. At the same time the employee should be told of any right of appeal, how to make it and to whom.

14. When determining the disciplinary action to be taken the supervisor or manager should bear in mind the need to satisfy the test of reasonableness in all the circumstances. So far as possible, account should be taken of the employee's record and any other relevant factors.

15. Special consideration should be given to the way in which disciplinary procedures are to operate in exceptional cases. For example:
 (a) *Employees to whom the full procedure is not immediately available.* Special provisions may have to be made for the handling of disciplinary matters among the nightshift workers, workers in isolated locations or depots or others who may pose particular problems for example because no one is present with the necessary authority to take disciplinary action or no trade union representative is immediately available.
 (b) *Trade union offences.* Disciplinary action against a trade union official can lead to a serious dispute if it is seen as an attack on the union's functions. Although normal disciplinary standards should apply to their conduct as employees, no disciplinary action beyond an oral warning should be taken until the circumstances of the case have been dscussed with a senior trade union representative or full-time official.
 (c) *Criminal offences outside employment.* These should not be treated as automatic reasons for dismissal regardless of whether the offence has any relevant to the duties of the individual as an employee. The main considerations should be whether the offence is one that makes the individual unsuitable for his or her type of work or unacceptable to other employees. Employees should not be dismissed solely because a charge against them is pending or because they are absent through having been remanded in custody.

Appeals

16. Grievance procedures are sometimes used for dealing with disciplinary appeals though it is normally more appropriate to keep the two kinds of procedure separate since the disciplinary issues are in general best resolved within the organisation and need to be dealt with more speedily than others. The external stages of a grievance procedure may however, be the appropriate machinery for dealing with appeals against disciplinary action where a final decision within the organisation is contested or where the matter becomes a collective issue between management and a trade union.

17. Independent arbitration is sometimes an appropriate means of resolving disciplinary issues. Where the parties concerned agree, it may constitute the final stage of procedure.

Records

5–016
18. Records should be kept, detailing the nature of any breach of disciplinary rules, the action taken and reasons for it, whether an appeal was lodged, its outcome and any subsequent developments. These records should be carefully safeguarded and kept confidential.

19. Except in agreed special circumstances breaches of disciplinary rules should be disregarded after a special period of satisfactory conduct.

Further action

5–017
20. Rules and procedures should be reviewed periodically in the light of any developments in employment legislation or industrial relations practice and, if necessary, revised in order to ensure their continuing relevance and effectiveness. Any amendments and additional rules imposing new obligations should be introduced only after reasonable notice has been given to all employees and, where appropriate, their representatives have been informed.

5–018
Code of Practice on
Disclosure of Information to Trade Unions for Collective Bargaining Purposes

This Code, issued with the authority of Parliament, came into effect, by order of the Secretary of State, on August 22, 1977.

Introduction

1. Under the Employment Protection Act 1975 the Advisory, Conciliation and Arbitration Service (ACAS) may issue Codes of Practice containing such practical guidance as the Service thinks fit for the purpose of promoting the improvement of industrial relations. In particular, the Service has a duty to provide practical guidance on the application of sections 17 and 18 of the Act in relation to the disclosure of information by employers to trade unions for the purpose of collective bargaining.

2. The Act and the Code apply to employers operating in both the public and private sectors of industry. They do not apply to collective bargaining between employers' associations and trade unions, although the parties concerned may wish to follow the guidelines contained in the Code.

3. The information which employers may have a duty to disclose under section 17 is information which it would be in accordance with good industrial relations practice to disclose. In determining what would be in accordance with good industrial relations practice regard is to be had to any relevant provisions of the Code. However, the Code imposes no legal obligations on an employer to disclose any specific item of information. Failure to observe the Code does not by itself render anyone liable to proceedings,

but the Act requires any relevant provisions to be taken into account in proceedings before the Central Arbitration Committee.[4]

This Code supersedes paragraph 96–98 (inclusive) of the Code of Practice in effect under Part 1 of Schedule 1 to the Trade Union and Labour Relations Act 1974, which paragraphs shall cease to have effect on the date on which this Code comes into effect.

Provisions of the Act

4. The Act places a general duty on an employer to disclose at all stages of collective bargaining information requested by representatives of independent trade unions. The unions must be either recognised by the employer for collective bargaining purposes, or fall within the scope of an ACAS recommendation for recognition. The representative of the union is an official or other person authorised by the union to carry on such collective bargaining.

5. The information requested has to be in the employer's possession, or in the possession of any associated employer, and must relate to the employer's undertaking. The information to be disclosed is that without which a trade union representative would be impeded to a material extent in bargaining and which it would be in accordance with good industrial relations practice to disclose for the purpose of collective bargaining. In determining what is in accordance with good industrial relations practice, any relevant provisions of this Code are to be taken into account.

6. No employer is required to disclose any information which: would be against the interests of national security; would contravene a prohibition imposed by or under an enactment; was given to an employer in confidence, or was obtained by the employer in consequence of the confidence reposed in him by another person; relates to an individual unless he has consented to its disclosure; would cause substantial injury to the undertaking (or national interest in respect of Crown employment) for reasons other than its effect on collective bargaining; or was obtained for the purpose of any legal proceedings.

7. In providing information the employer is not required to produce original documents for inspection or copying. Nor is he required to compile or assemble information which would entail work or expenditure out of reasonable proportion to the value of the information in the conduct of collective bargaining. The union representative can request that the information be given in writing by the employer or be confirmed in writing. Similarly, an employer can ask the trade union representative to make the request for information in writing or confirm it in writing.

8. If the trade union considers that an employer has failed to disclose to its representatives information which he was required to disclose by section 17 of the Act, it may make a complaint to the Central Arbitration Committee.[5] The Committee may ask the Advisory, Conciliation and Arbitration Service to conciliate. If conciliation does not lead to a settlement of the complaint the Service shall inform the Committee accordingly who shall proceed to hear and determine the complaint. If the complaint is upheld by the Committee it is required to specify the information that should have been disclosed and a period of time within which the employer ought to disclose the information. If the employer does not disclose the

5–019

---

[4] Employment Protection Act 1975, ss.17(1)(*b*), 17(4) and 6(11).
[5] Further information can be obtained from the Secretary of the Committee at 1 The Abbey Garden, London SW1P 3SE.

information within the specified time the union may present a further complaint to the Committee and may also present a claim for improved terms and conditions. If the further complaint is upheld by the Committee an award, which would have effect as part of the contract of employment, may be made against the employer on the terms and conditions specified in the claim, or other terms and conditions which the Committee considers appropriate.

Providing information

9. The absence of relevant information about an employer's undertaking may to a material extent impede trade unions in collective bargaining; particularly if the information would influence the formulation, presentation or pursuance of a claim, or the conclusion of an agreement. The provision of relevant information in such circumstances would be in accordance with good industrial relations practice.

10. To determine what information will be relevant negotiators should take account of the subject-matter of the negotiations and the issues raised during them; the level at which negotiations take place (department, plant, division, or company level); the size of the company; and the type of business the company is engaged in.

11. Collective bargaining within an undertaking can range from negotiations on specific matters arising daily at the work place affecting particular sections of the workforce, to extensive periodic negotiations on terms and conditions of employment affecting the whole workforce in multiplant companies. The relevant information and the depth, detail and form in which it could be presented to negotiators will vary accordingly. Consequently, it is not possible to compile a list of items that should be disclosed in all circumstances. Some examples of information relating to the undertaking which could be relevant in certain collective bargaining situations are given below:
  (i) *Pay and benefits*: principles and structure of payment systems; job evaluation systems and grading criteria; earnings and hours analysed according to work-group, grade, plant, sex, out-workers and homeworkers, department or division, giving, where appropriate, distributions and make-up of pay showing any additions to basic rate or salary; total pay bill; details of fringe benefits and non-wage labour costs.
  (ii) *Conditions of service*: policies on recruitment, redeployment, redundancy, training, equal opportunity, and promotion; appraisal systems; health, welfare and safety matters.
  (iii) *Manpower*: numbers employed analysed according to grade, department, location, age and sex; labour turnover; absenteeism; overtime and short-time; manning standards; planned changes in work methods, materials, equipment or organisation; available manpower plans; investment plans.
  (iv) *Performance*: productivity and efficiency data; savings from increased productivity and output; return on capital invested; sales and state of order book.
  (v) *Financial*: cost structures; gross and net profits; sources of earnings; assets; liabilities; allocation of profits; details of government financial assistance; transfer prices; loans to parent or subsidiary companies and interest charged.

12. These examples are not intended to represent a check list of infor-

mation that should be provided for all negotiations. Nor are they meant to be an exhaustive list of types of information as other items may be relevant in particular negotiations.

Restrictions on the duty to disclose

13. Trade unions and employers should be aware of the restrictions on the general duty to disclose information for collective bargaining.[6]

14. Some examples of information which if disclosed in particular circumstances might cause substantial injury are: cost information, on individual products; detailed analysis of proposed investment, marketing or pricing policies; and price quotas or the make-up of tender prices. Information which has to be made available publicly, for example under the Companies Acts, would not fall into this category.

15. Substantial injury may occur if, for example, certain customers would be lost to competitors, or suppliers would refuse to supply necessary materials, or the ability to raise funds to finance the company would be seriously impaired as a result of disclosing certain information. The burden of establishing a claim that disclosure of certain information would cause substantial injury lies with the employer.

5–021

Trade union responsibilities

16. Trade unions should identify and request the information they require for collective bargaining in advance of negotiations whenever practicable. Misunderstandings can be avoided, costs reduced, and time saved, if requests state as precisely as possible all the information required, and the reasons why the information is considered relevant. Requests should conform to an agreed procedure. A reasonable period of time should be allowed for employers to consider a request and to reply.

17. Trade unions should keep employers informed of the names of the representatives authorised to carry on collective bargaining on their behalf.

18. Where two or more trade unions are recognised by an employer for collective bargaining purposes they should co-ordinate their requests for information whenever possible.

19. Trade Unions should review existing training programmes or establish new ones to ensure negotiators are equipped to understand and use information effectively.

5–022

Employers' responsibilities[7]

20. Employers should aim to be as open and helpful as possible in meeting trade union requests for information. Where a request is refused, the reasons for the refusal should be explained as far as possible to the trade union representatives concerned and be capable of being substantiated should the matter be taken to the Central Arbitration Committee.

21. Information agreed as relevant to collective bargaining should be made available as soon as possible once a request for the information has been made by an authorised trade union representative. Employers should present information in a form and style which recipients can reasonably be expected to understand.

5–023

---

[6] Employment Protection Act 1975, s.18. See paras. 6 and 7 of this Code.
[7] The Stock Exchange has drawn attention to the need for employers to consider any obligations which they may have under their Listing Agreement.

Joint arrangements for disclosure of information

5–024   22. Employers and trade unions should endeavour to arrive at a joint understanding on how the provisions on the disclosure of information can be implemented most effectively. They should consider what information is likely to be required, what is available, and what could reasonably be made available. Consideration should also be given to the form in which the information will be presented, when it should be presented and to whom. In particular, the parties should endeavour to reach an understanding on what information could most appropriately be provided on a regular basis.

23. Procedures for resolving possible disputes concerning any issues associated with the disclosure of information should be agreed. Where possible such procedures should normally be related to any existing arrangements within the undertaking or industry and the complaint, conciliation and arbitration procedure described in the Act.[8]

5–025

Code of Practice on
Time off for Trade Union Duties and Activities

This Code, issued with the authority of Parliament, came into effect, by order of the Secretary of State, on April 1, 1978.

Introduction

1. Under section 6 of the Employment Protection Act 1975 (referred to hereafter as the Act) the Advisory, Conciliation and Arbitration Service (ACAS) has a duty to provide practical guidance on the time off to be permitted by an employer.
    (a) to a trade union official in accordance with section 57 of the Act; and
    (b) to a trade union member in accordance with section 58 of the Act.
This code is intended to provide such guidance.

2. Section 57 of the Act requires an employer to permit an employee of his or hers, who is an official of an dependent trade union which is recognised by the employer,[9] to take reasonable paid time off during the employee's working hours for the purpose of enabling the employee.
    (a) to carry out those duties which are concerned with industrial relations between his or her employer and any associated employer[10] and their employees; or
    (b) to undergo training in aspects of industrial relations which is
        (i) relevant to the carrying out of those duties; and

---

[8] Employment Protection Act 1975, ss.19 to 21. See para. 8 of this Code.

[9] s.62 of the Act provides that a trade union shall be treated as recognised not only if it is recognised for the purposes of collective bargaining but also if ACAS has made a recommendation for recognition which is operative within the meaning of s.15 of the Act.

[10] Any two employers are to be treated as associated if one is a company of which the other (directly or indirectly) has control, or if both are companies of which a third person (directly or indirectly) has control: Trade Union and Labour Relations Act 1974, s.30(5). This definition is appropriate to the private sector of employment.

(ii) approved by the Trades Union Congress or by the independent trade union of which he or she is an official.

3. An employer who permits an employee time off under this section is required to pay him or her for the time off taken. Where the employee's pay does not vary with the amount of work done, the employer is required by the Act to pay the employee as if he or she had worked during the period when the time off was taken. Where the employee's pay does vary according to the amount of work done then payment for the time off permitted is to be calculated by reference to the average hourly earnings for the work the employee is employed to do.

4. For the purposes of section 57 of the Act the word "official" means an employee who has been elected or appointed in accordance with the rules of the union to be a representative of all or some of the union's members in a particular company or workplace.

5. Section 58 of the Act requires an employer to permit an employee of his or hers who is a member of an appropriate trade union[11] to take reasonable time off during the employee's working hours for the purpose of taking part in any trade union activity to which the section applies. Trade union activities to which the section applies are any activities of an appropriate trade union of which the employee is a member; and any activities in relation to which the employee is acting as a representative of such a union; but excluding activities which themselves consist of industrial action whether or not in contemplation or furtherance of a trade dispute. There is no requirement under section 58 that union members or representatives be paid for time off taken on union activities.

6. The amount of time off under sections 57 and 58 of the Act, the purposes for which, the occasions on which and any conditions subject to which time off may so be taken are those that are reasonable in all the circumstances having regard to any relevant provisions of this Code of Practice.

7. Sections 57 and 58 of the Act provide that a trade union official or member may present a complaint to an industrial tribunal that his or her employer has failed to permit the taking of time off as required by these sections or, in the case of an official, to pay him or her the whole or part of any amount required by the Act to be paid. Such complaints may be resolved by conciliaton by ACAS, and is such a resolution is achieved no tribunal hearing will be necessary. This Code will be taken into account in determining any question arising during tribunal proceedings on sections 57 and 58, although failure to observe any provision of the Code will not of itself render a person liable to any proceedings.

General considerations for time off arrangements

8. The general purpose of the statutory provisions on time off for trade union duties and activities is to aid and improve the conduct of industrial relations. These provisions apply to all employers without exception as to size or type of business or service. But trade unions should be aware of the wide variety of circumstances and the different operational requirements

---

[11] "Appropriate trade union" for the purposes of the section means, in relation to an employee of any description, an independent trade union which, in respect of that description of employee, either is recognised by his or her employer or is the subject of an operative ACAS recommendation for recognition.

which will have to be taken into account in any arrangements for dealing with time off. For example, some employers face particular exigencies of production, services and safety in process industries. Others operate in the special circumstances of the small firm. In enterprises large and small the workforce may be fragmented. Proper regard will therefore have to be paid to particular operational requirements and obligations of different industries and services.

9. Union officials and members may face particular problems of effective representation and communication, and employers in their turn should be aware of these. They may arise, for example, from the differing hours or shifts worked by members in a single negotiating area; from employment part-time; from the scattered or isolated locations of workplaces and, particularly in the case of some married women, from domestic commitments which limit the possibilities of active participation in their union outside the workplace and outside the hours of normal day working.

10. To take account of this wide variety of circumstances and problems, employers and unions should reach agreement on arrangements for handling time off in ways appropriate to their own situations. Subsequent advice in the Code should be read in the light of this primary point of guidance which ACAS considers fundamental to the proper operation of time off facilities. The absence of a formal agreement dealing specifically with time off for trade union duties and activities should not of itself preclude the granting of release.

11. Employers and unions, at the appropriate level, will need to review jointly their current time off provision bearing in mind the statutory requirements, this Code of Practice and the particular workplace circumstances. Where existing arrangements meet these requirements and are working to the satisfaction of both parties they need not be changed. In some situations time off arrangements will have to be revised and it may be helpful to set out any such revised arrangements in formal agreements.

12. Arrangements for the handling of time off for union duties, industrial relations training and union activities should accord with agreed procedures for negotiation, consultation, grievance handling and dispute settlement. Agreements on time off and on other facilities for union representation should be consistent with wider agreements which should deal with such matters of workplace representation as constituencies, number of representatives and the form of any joint credentials.

Trade union officials duties concerned with industrial relations

13. In addition to his or her work as an employee a trade union official may have important duties concerned with industrial relations. An official's duties are those duties pertaining to his or her role in the jointly agreed procedures or customary arrangements for consultation, collective bargaining and grievance handling, where such matters concern the employer and any associated employer and their employees. To perform these duties properly an official should be permitted to take reasonable paid time off during working hours for such purposes as

   (a) collective bargaining with the appropriate level of management;
   (b) informing constituents about negotiations or consultations with management;
   (c) meetings with other lay officials or with full-time union officers on matters which are concerned with industrial relations between his or her employer and any associated employer and their employees;

(d) interviews with and on behalf of constituents on grievance and discipline matters concerning them and their employer;
(e) appearing on behalf of constituents before an outside official body, such as an industrial tribunal, which is dealing with an industrial relations matter concerning the employer; and
(f) explanations to new employees whom he or she will represent of the role of the union in the workplace industrial relations structure.

Training of officials in aspects of industrial relations

14. To carry out their duties effectively officials need to possess skills and knowledge. In addition to the practical experience obtained from holding office officials should undertake training in relevant subjects when necessary.

15. Training should be relevant to the industrial relations duties of an official. It should be approved by the TUC or the official's union. An official's industrial relations duties will vary according to the collective bargaining arrangements at the place of work, the structure of the union and the role of the official. Accordingly there is no universally applicable syllabus for training.

16. An official who has duties concerned with industrial relations should be permitted to take reasonable paid time off work for initial basic training and such training should be arranged as soon as possible after the official is elected or appointed.

17. An official should be permitted to take reasonable paid time off work for further training relevant to the carrying out of his or her duties concerned with industrial relations where he or she has special responsibilities or where such training is necessary to meet circumstances such as changes in the structure or topics of negotiation at the place of employment or legislative changes affecting industrial relations.

18. When the trade union has identified a need for basic or further training and wishes an official to receive training it should inform management what training it has approved for the purpose and, if the employer asks for it, supply a copy of the syllabus or prospectus indicating the contents of the training course or programme.

19. The number of officials receiving training from any one place of employment at any one time should be that which is reasonable in the circumstances, bearing in mind such factors as the operational requirements of the employer and the availability of relevant courses. Trade unions should normally give at least a few weeks' notice of their nominations for training.

20. Unions and management should endeavour to reach agreement on the appropriate numbers and arrangements and should refer any problem which may arise to the relevant procedure.

Trade union activities

21. To operate effectively and democratically trade unions need the active participation of members in certain union activities. A member should therefore be permitted to take reasonable time off during working hours for union activities such as taking part, as a representative, in meetings of official policy-making bodies of the union such as the executive committee or annual conference, or representing the union on external bodies such as the committees of industrial training boards.

5–028

5–029

22. Members should be permitted to take reasonable time off during working hours for such purposes as voting at the workplace in union elections. Also there may be occasions when it is reasonable for unions to hold meetings of members during working hours because of the urgency of the matter to be discussed or where to do so would not adversely affect production or services. Employers may also have an interest in ensuring that meetings are representative.

Conditions relating to time off

23. For time off arrangements to work satisfactorily the trade union should ensure that its officials are fully aware of their role, responsibilities and functions. The union should inform management, in writing, as soon as possible after officials are appointed or have resigned and should ensure that officials receive any appropriate written credentials promptly. Management at all levels should be familiar with agreements and arrangements relating to time off.

24. Management should make available to officials the facilities necessary for them to perform their duties efficiently and to communicate effectively with members, fellow lay officials and full-time officers. Such facilities may include accommodation for meetings, access to a telephone, notice boards and, where the volume of the official's work justifies it, the use of office facilities.

25. Management is responsible for maintaining production and service to customers, and for making the operational arrangements for time off. Union officials should bear in mind management's problems in discharging these responsibilities. The union official who seeks time off should ensure that the appropriate management representative is informed as far in advance as is reasonable in the circumstances. The official should indicate the nature of the business for which time off is required, the intended location and the expected period of absence. Management and the union should seek to agree arrangements, where necessary, for other employees to cover the work of officials or members taking time off.

26. Where it is necessary for the union to hold meetings of members during working hours it should seek to agree the arrangements with management as far in advance as is practicable. Where such meetings necessarily involve a large proportion of employees at the workplace at any one time, management and unions should agree on a convenient time which minimises the effects on production or service—for example, towards the end of the shift or the working week or just before or after a meal break.

27. When a number of members needs time off at any one time there should be agreement to leave at work such members as are essential for safety or operational reasons—for example, to keep premises open to the public or to provide necessary manning in a continuous process firm.

28. Management may want time off work for union duties or activities to be deferred because, for example, problems of safety or of maintenance of production or service would ensue if time off were taken at a particular time. The grounds for postponement should be made clear and parties should endeavour to agree on an alternative time for the union duty or activity. In considering postponement parties should weigh the urgency of the matter for which time off is required against the seriousness of any problems arising.

29. The union official and union member should not unduly or unnecessarily prolong the time they are absent from work on union duties or activities.

30. A dispute or grievance in relation to time off work for union duties or activities should be referred to the relevant procedure.

Industrial action

31. Management and unions have a responsibility to use agreed procedures to resolve problems constructively and avoid industrial action. Time off should be provided for this purpose. Satisfactory time off arrangements are particularly needed where communication and co-operation between management and unions are in danger of breaking down. Where industrial action has not occurred employers and unions should avoid hastily altering these arrangements since to do so may change relationships.

5–031

32. A distinction should be made between situations where an official is engaged in industrial action along with his or her constituents and those where the official is not—for example, where only some of the constituents are taking unofficial action. Where an official is not taking part in industrial action but represents members involved, normal arrangements for time off with pay for the official should apply.

33. There is no obligation on employers to permit time off for union activities which themselves consist of industrial action but where a group of members not taking part in such action is directly affected by other people's industrial action these members and their officials may need to seek the agreement of management to time off for an emergency meeting.

Health and Safety Commission's Code of Practice on Safety Representatives

5–032

This Code has been approved by the Health and Safety Commission under the provisions of s.16 of the Health and Safety at Work etc. Act 1974 and came into effect on October 1, 1978. The Code is followed by Guidance Notes.

1. The Safety Representatives and Safety Committees Regulations 1978 concern safety representatives appointed in accordance with section 2(4) of the Act and cover;
    (a) prescribed cases in which recognised trade unions may appoint safety representatives from amongst the employees;
    (b) prescribed functions of safety representatives.

Section 2(6) of the Act requires employers to consult with safety representatives with a view to the making and maintenance of arrangements which will enable him and his employees to co-operate effectively in promoting and developing measures to ensure the health and safety at work of the employees, and in checking the effectiveness of such measures. Under section 2(4) safety representatives are required to represent the employees in those consultations.

2. This Code of Practice has been approved by the Health and Safety Commission with the consent of the Secretary of State for Employment. It relates to the requirements placed on safety representatives by section 2(4) of the Act and on employers by the regulations and takes effect on the date the regulations come into operation.

3. The employer, the recognised trade unions concerned and safety representatives should make full and proper use of the existing agreed industrial relations machinery to reach the degree of agreement necessary to

achieve the purpose of the regulations and in order to resolve any differences.

Interpretation

5–033 4. (a) In this Code, "the 1974 Act" means the Health and Safety at Work etc. Act 1974 and "the Regulations" means the Safety Representatives and Safety Committees Regulations 1978;
  (b) words and expressions which are defined in the Act or in the Regulations have the same meaning in this Code unless the context requires otherwise.

Functions of safety representatives

5–034 5. In order to fulfill their functions under section 2(4) of the Act safety representatives should:
  (a) take all reasonably practicable steps to keep themselves informed of:
    (i) the legal requirements relating to the health and safety of persons at work, particularly the group or groups of persons they directly represent,
    (ii) the particular hazards of the workplace and the measures deemed necessary to eliminate or minimise the risk deriving from these hazards, and
    (iii) the health and safety policy of their employer and the organisation and arrangements for fulfilling that policy;
  (b) encourage co-operation between their employer and his employees in promoting and developing essential measures to ensure the health and safety of employees and in checking the effectiveness of these measures.
  (c) bring to the employer's notice normally in writing any unsafe or unhealthy conditions or working practices or unsatisfactory arrangements for welfare at work which come to their attention whether on an inspection or day to day observation. The report does not imply that all other conditions and working practices are safe and healthy or that the welfare arrangements are satisfactory in all other respects.
  Making a written report does not preclude the bringing of such matters to the attention of the employer or his repesentative by a direct oral approach in the first instance, particularly in situations where speedy remedial action is necessary. It will also be appropriate for minor matters to be the subject of direct oral discussion without the need for a formal written approach.

Information to be provided by employers

5–035 6. The regulations require employers to make information within their knowledge available to safety representatives necessary to enable them to fulfil their functions. Such information should include:
  (a) information about the plans and performance of their undertaking and any changes proposed in so far as they affect the health and safety at work of their employees;
  (b) information of a technical nature about hazards to health and safety precautions deemed necessary to eliminate or minimise them, in

respect of machinery, plant, equipment, processes, systems of work and substances in use at work, including any relevant information provided by consultants or designers or by the manufacturer, importer or supplier of any article or substance used, or poposed to be used, at work by their employees;
(c) information which the employer keeps relating to the occurrence of any accident, dangerous occurrence or notifiable industrial disease and any statistical records relating to such accidents, dangerous occurrences or cases of notifiable industrial disease;
(d) any other information specifically related to matters affecting the health and safety at work of his employees, including the results or any measurements taken by the employer or persons acting on his behalf in the course of checking the effectiveness of his health and safety arrangements.
(e) information on articles or substances which an employer issues to homeworkers.

GUIDANCE NOTES

Appointment and functioning of safety representatives
1. The Safety Representatives and Safety Committees Regulations 1978, made under section 2(4) of the Health and Safety at Work etc. Act 1974, prescribe the cases in which recognised trade unions may appoint safety representatives, specify the functions of such safety representatives, and set out the obligations of employers towards them.

2. The Code of Practice, approved by the Commission under section 16 of the Act and issued in amplification of those regulations, gives guidance on how safety representatives should fulfil their statutory functions, and guidance to employers regarding the information which they should make available to safety representatives to enable them to fulfil their functions.

3. The Commission have decided that it would be wrong to try and make regulations which cater in detail for the wide variety of circumstances in which they will have to be applied. Accordingly, the purpose of the regulations and the Code of Practice is to provide a framework within which each undertaking can develop effective working arrangements. To supplement this statutory framework these guidance notes are being issued which the Commission hope will be of help to employers, to trade unions, to safety representatives and to members of safety committees.

4. This part of the guidance notes offers advice to all who are concerned with the appointment and functioning of safety representatives. Advice regarding safety committees is given at paragraph 2A–162.

5–036

Appointment of safety representatives
5. The regulations provide that recognised trade unions may appoint safety representatives to represent the employees. The Commission have decided that recognition for this purpose must be on the same basis as in the Trade Union and Labour Relations Act 1974 and the Employment Protection Act 1975. Any disputes between employers and trade unions about this matter should be dealt with under the provisions of the Employment Protection Act.

6. The Commission expect that such unions would normally appoint representatives to represent a group or groups of workers of a class for which the union has negotiating rights. The limitation of representation to a particular group or groups should not, however, be regarded as a hindrance to

5–037

the raising by that representative of general matters affecting the health and safety of employees as a whole.

7. Equally, these general principles do not preclude the possibility of a safety representative representing, by mutual agreement between the appopriate unions, more than one group or groups of employees (*e.g.* in a small workplace or within the organisation of a small employer when the number of recognised trade unions is high relative to the total numbers employed).

8. When consideration is being given to the numbers of safety representatives to be appointed in a particular case the guidance given by the Commission in paragraph 3 of the Code of Practice should be borne in mind. Appropriate criteria would include:
   (a) the total numbers employed;
   (b) the variety of different occupations;
   (c) the size of the workplace and the variety of workplace locations;
   (d) the operation of shift systems;
   (e) the type of work activity and the degree and character of the inherent dangers.

9. At certain undertakings there will be a particular need for flexibility of approach both to the question of the group or groups of the employees the safety representative represents and to the numbers of safety representatives which might be appropriate in particular circumstances. Examples of such circumstances might include:
   (a) workplaces with rapidly changing situations and conditions as the work develops and where there might be rapid changes in the level of manpower, *e.g.* building and construction sites, shipbuilding and ship repairing, docks.
   (b) workplaces from which the majority of employees go out to their actual place of work and subsequently report back, *e.g.* goods and freight depots, builders' yards, service depots of all kinds.
   (c) workplaces where there is a wide variety of different work activities going on within a particular location.
   (d) workplaces with a specially high process risk, *e.g.* construction sites at particular stages—demolition, excavations, steel erection, etc., and some chemical works and research establishments.
   (e) workplaces where the majority of employees are employed in low risk activities, but where one or two processes or activities or items of plant have special risks connected with them.

10. The regulations require that appointed safety representatives normally have either worked for their present employer throughout the preceding two years or have had at least two years experience in similar employment. This is to ensure that those who are appointed have the kind of experience and knowledge of their particular type of employment necessary to enable them to make a responsible and practical contribution to health and safety in their employment. Circumstances may, however, arise where it will not be reasonably practicable that the appointed safety representative shall possess such experience (*e.g.* where the employer or workplace location is newly established, or where work is of short duration, or where there is a high labour turnover).

Functions of safety representatives

5–038   11. It is provided in the regulations that no function given to a safety representative shall be construed as imposing any duty on him other than duties he may have as an employee under sections 7 and 8 of the Act. For example, a safety representative, by accepting, agreeing with or not objecting to a course of action taken by the employer to deal with a health or safety hazard, does not take upon himself any legal responsibility for that course of action. In addition, the commission have directed that the Health and Safety Executive shall not institute criminal proceedings against any safety representative for any act or omission by him in respect of the performance of functions assigned to him by the regulations or indicated by the Code of Practice. Similar arrangements have been made with the other enforcing authorities.

12. Recognised trade unions will have well established methods of communication within a workplace, or within a particular employer's undertaking. These will be the appropriate channels by which the appointed safety representatives can keep the members of the group or groups which they represent informed on all matters of consequence affecting their health, safety and welfare at work. Appointed safety representatives will also need to establish close relationships with the other appointed safety representatives, including those appointed by trade unions other than their own, for example, in order to look at hazardous situations, develop a common approach, and responsibility complementary to their responsibility for the group or groups they represent directly.

13. It is important that safety representatives should be able to take matters up with management without delay. They must therefore have ready access to the employer or his representatives; who those should be will be determined in the light of local circumstances. It may not be desirable to specify one individual for all contacts, bearing in mind that hazards could involve differing degrees of urgency and importance. The need is to ensure that safety representatives have a clear idea as to who is authorised to act as the employers' representative for the purpose of these regulations.

14. Safety representatives should record when they have made an inspection. Specimens of the kinds of *pro forma* which might be adopted by safety representatives both to record that an inspection has been made and to draw the employer's attention to an unsafe or unhealthy condition, etc., are given on page 19. A copy of each completed form should be given to the employer. These forms may be purchased from offices of the Health and Safety Executive.

15. Section 28(8) of the H.S.W. Act requires inspectors to give certain types of infomation to employees and employers. Where safety representatives have been appointed under the regulations, they are the appropriate persons to receive this information on behalf of the employees.

EXAMPLES OF PRO-FORMA

A. Sample of suggested form to be used for recording that an inspection by a safety representative(s) has taken place.

Date of inspection	Area or workplace inspected	Name(s) of safety representative(s) taking part in inspection

[*This record does not imply that the conditions are safe and healthy or that the arrangements for welfare at work are satisfactory.*]
Signature(s) of safety representative(s) ....

Date ....

B. Sample of suggested form to be used for notifying to the employer, or his representative, unsafe and unhealthy conditions and working practices and unsatisfactory arrangements for welfare at work.

Date of inspection or matter observed	Particulars of matter(s) notified to employer or his representative (include location where appropriate)	Name(s) of safety representative notifying matter(s) to employer (or his representative)	Remedial action taken (with date) or explanation if not taken

[*This report does not imply that the conditions are safe and healthy or that the arrangements for welfare at work are satisfactory in all other respects.*]

Signature(s) of safety representative(s) ....

Date ....

Signature of employer ....
(or his representative)

Date ....

Inspections by safety representatives

5–040 16. The regulations deal with the frequency of formal inspections by the appointed safety representatives. In some circumstances where a high risk activity or rapidly changing circumstances are confined to a particular area of a workplace or sector of an employee's activities it may be appropriate for more frequent inspections of that area or sector to be agreed.

17. In providing for formal inspection of the workplace by the appointed safety representatives the regulations require that they shall give reasonable notice to the employer of their intention to do so. In the Commission's view it is desirable that the employer and the safety representatives should plan a programme of formal inspections in advance, which will itself fulfil the conditions as to notice. Variations in this planned programme should of course be subject to agreement.

18. The Commission see advantages in formal inspections being jointly carried out by the employer or his representatives and safety representatives, but this should not prevent safety representatives from carrying out independent investigations or private discussion with employees. The safety representatives should co-ordinate their work to avoid unnecessary duplication. It will often be appropriate for the safety officer or specialist advisers to be available to give technical advice on health and safety matters which may arise during the course of the inspection.

19. There are various forms which the formal inspection may take and it will be for the appointed safety representatives to agree with their employer about this, but the Commission consider that the following types of inspection, or a combination of any or all of them over a period of time, may be appropriate in the fulfilment of this function.
   (a) *safety tours*—general inspections of the workplace;
   (b) *safety sampling*—systematic sampling of particular dangerous activities, processes or areas;
   (c) *safety surveys*—general inspections of the particular dangerous activities, processes or area.

The numbers of safety representatives taking part in any one formal inspection should be a matter for agreement between the appointed safety representatives and their employer in the light of their own particular circumstances and the nature of the inspection.

20. At large workplaces it may be impracticable to conduct a formal inspection of the entire workplace at a single session or for the complete inspection to be carried out by the same group of safety representatives. In these circumstances arrangements may be agreed between the employer (or his representative) and the appointed safety representatives for the inspection to be carried out by breaking it up into manageable units (*e.g.* on a departmental basis). It may also be appropriate, as part of the planned programme, for different groups of safety representatives to carry out inspections in different parts of the workplace either simultaneously or at different times but in such a manner as to ensure complete coverage before the next round of formal inspections becomes due. There may be special circumstances in which appointed safety representatives and their employer will wish to agree a different frequency of inspections for different parts of the same workplace (*e.g.* where there are areas or activities of especially high risk).

21. Where safety representatives have made a written report to the employer in accordance with paragraph 5(*c*) of the Code of Practice, appropriate remedial action will normally be taken by the employer. Where remedial action is not considered appropriate or cannot be taken within a reasonable period of time, or the form of remedial action is not acceptable to the safety representatives, then the employer or his representative should explain the reasons and give them in writing to the safety representatives. A suggested method for this is to record it in Form B (para. 2A–158). Where remedial action has been taken, the safety representatives who notified the matter(s) should be given the opportunity to make any necessary reinspection in order to satisfy themselves that the matter(s) notified have received appropriate attention and they should also be afforded the opportunity to record their views on this aspect.

22. Such action should be publicised throughout the workplace and to other appropriate parts of the employer's organisations—if necessary the whole—by the normal channels of communication. It may also be appropriate that they should be brought to the specific attention of the safety committee, if one exists.

23. For the purpose of ascertaining the circumstances of a notifiable accident, dangerous occurrence, or notifiable disease, it will be necessary for the representatives to examine any relevant machinery, plant, equipment or substances in the workplace. It is the Commission's view that the main purpose of the examination should be to determine the causes so that the possibility of action to prevent a recurrence can be considered. For this reason it is important that the approach to the problem should be a joint one by the employer and the safety representatives.

It may be necessary, following an accident or dangerous occurrence for the employer to take urgent steps to safeguard against further hazards. If he does this he should notify the safety representative of the action he has taken and confirm this in writing.

24. Such examinations may include visual inspection, and discussions with persons who are likely to be in the possession of relevant information and knowledge regarding the circumstances of the accident or occurrence. The examination must not, however, include interference with any evidence or the testing of any machinery, plant, equipment or substance which could disturb or destroy the factual evidence before any inspector from the appropriate enforcing authority has had the opportunity to investigate as thoroughly as is necessary the circumstances of the accident or occurrence.

25. In the course of the performance of their functions, in particular concerning formal inspections of the workplace and examinations following notifiable accidents, dangerous occurrences, or notifiable diseases, safety representatives have rights under the regulations to inspect and take copies of relevant documents which the employer is required to keep in accordance with the Act and other relevant statutory provisions.

Safety representatives should in exercising this right have regard to the reasonableness of time off as well as any other circumstances with which the employer may be faced in producing such documents.

26. Where technical matters are involved the appointed safety representatives may find that the necessary expertise is available within the undertaking. The employer and the safety representatives may wish to seek advice from outside the undertaking, for example from appropriate universities or polytechnics. The Commission considers that arrangements should be agreed as to the persons from such institutions who may be called upon. If the representatives wish to have advice from their own technical advisers, such advisers may be called in where this has been agreed in advance with the employer. A copy of any report specifically relating to health or safety matters made to the safety representatives should also be available to the employer.

Obligations of employers

5–041   27. Employers have a duty under section 2(2)(c) of the 1974 Act to provide such information, instruction and training as is reasonably practicable, to ensure the health and safety at work of all their employees. Appointed safety representatives will need to be given information and knowledge over and above that necessary for employees generally to enable them to play an informed part in promoting health and safety at work. The recognised trade unions responsible for appointing safety representatives will make their own arrangements for the information and guidance of their appointed safety representatives as to how they will carry out their functions.

. . . . . .

SAFETY COMMITTEES

5–042   1. The Safety Representatives and Safety Committees Regulations 1978 prescribe the cases in which an employer shall establish a safety committee. These guidance notes are concerned with such committees.

2. The Commission believe that the detailed arrangements necessary to fulfil this particular requirement of the Act should evolve from discussion and negotiation between employers and the appointed safety representatives who are best able to interpret the needs of the particular workplace or places with which the committee is to concern itself. These guidance notes are, however, issued by the Commission to provide background advice to those involved in the setting up and functioning of such committees. Although the title "Safety Committees" might suggest functions limited to purely safety matters, the opening words of the Act refer to "health, safety and welfare of persons at work": and safety committees should therefore be concerned with all relevant aspects of these matters in the working environment.

3. Circumstances will vary greatly between one workplace and another. Now that the Act covers virtually all persons at work, safety committees

will be set up to deal with work situations as varied as that between a foundry and a forest or a construction site and a general hospital. Each situation must be looked at carefully by those involved in it and systems for safety, including safety committees, will need to be developed to take full account of all the relevant circumstances.

4. Although the relationship of the safety committee to other works committees is a matter for local organisation, it is necessary to ensure that the work of the safety committee has a separate identity, and that safety matters do not become interposed in the agenda for other meetings.

5. Safety committees are most likely to prove effective where their work is related to a single establishment rather than to a collection of geographically distinct places. There may be a place for safety committees at group or company level for larger organisations; this will apply where relevant decisions are taken at a higher level than the establishment. In general, it should be unnecessary for an employer to appoint duplicate committees for the same workplace, *e.g.* representing different levels of staff. In large workplaces, however, a single committee may either be too large, or if kept small, may become too remote. In these circumstances, it may be necessary to set up several committees with adequate arrangements for co-ordination between them.

Objectives and functions of safety committees

6. Under section 2(7) of the H.S.W. Act, safety committees have the function of keeping under review the measures taken to ensure the health and safety at work of the employees. In carrying out this function safety committees ought to consider the drawing up of agreed objectives or terms of reference.

An objective should be the promotion of co-operation between employers and employees in instigating, developing and carrying out measures to ensure the health and safety at work of the employees.

7. Within the agreed basic objectives certain specific functions are likely to become defined. These might include:
   (a) The study of accident and notifiable diseases, statistics and trends, so that reports can be made to management on unsafe and unhealthy conditions and practices, together with recommendations for corrective action.
   (b) Examination of safety audit reports on a similar basis.
   (c) Consideration of reports and factual information provided by inspectors of the enforcing authority appointed under the Health and Safety at Work Act.
   (d) Consideration of reports which safety representatives may wish to submit.
   (e) Assistance in the development of works safety rules and safe systems of work.
   (f) A watch on the effectiveness of the safety content of employee training.
   (g) A watch on the adequacy of safety and health communication and publicity in the workplace.
   (h) The provisions of a link with the appropriate inspectorates of the enforcing authority.

8. In certain instances safety committees may consider it useful to carry out an inspection by the committee itself. But it is management's responsibility to take executive action and to have adequate arrangements for

regular and effective checking for health and safety precautions and for ensuring that the declared health and safety policy is being fulfilled. The work of the safety committees should supplement these arrangements; it cannot be a substitute for them.

Membership of safety committees

9. The membership and structure of safety committees should be settled in consultation between management and the trade union representatives concerned through the use of the normal machinery. The aim should be to keep the total size as reasonably compact as possible and compatible with the adequate representation of the interests of management and all the employees, including safety representatives. The number of management representatives should not exceed the number of employees' representatives.

10. Management representatives should not only include those from line management but such others as works engineers and personnel managers. The supervisory level should also be represented. Management representation should be aimed at ensuring:
   (a) adequate authority to give proper consideration to views and recommendations;
   (b) the necessary knowledge and expertise to provide accurate information to the committee on company policy, production needs and on technical matters in relation to premises, processes, plant, machinery and equipment.

11. In undertakings where a company doctor, industrial hygienist or safety officer/adviser is employed, they should be ex-officio members of the safety committee. Other company specialists, such as project engineers, chemists, organisation and methods staff and training officers might be co-opted for particular meetings when subjects on which they have expertise are to be discussed.

12. It should be fully understood that a safety representative is not appointed by the safety committee or vice versa, but the relationship between safety representatives and the safety committee should be a flexible but intimate one. Neither is responsible to, or for, the other. The aim should be to form the most effective organisation appropriate in the particular undertakings, and in particular effective co-ordination between the work of the committee and the safety representatives.

13. It should be the practice for membership of safety committees to be regarded as part of an individual's normal work. As a consequence he or she should suffer no loss of pay through attendance at meetings of safety committees or at other agreed activities such as inspections undertaken by, or on behalf of, such committees.

14. The purpose of studying accidents is to stop them happening again; it is not the committees' business to allocate blame, its job should be:
   (a) to look at the facts in an impartial way;
   (b) to consider what sort of precautions might be taken;
   (c) to make appropriate recommendations.

15. There are advantages in looking at not only legally notifiable cases but also at selected groups of minor injuries. The records for such injuries can yield valuable information if it is extracted and analysed.

16. The committee may well be able to:
   (a) advise on the appropriateness and adequacy of the rules for safety and health proposed by management; and/or

(b) draw attention to the need to establish rules for a particular hazardous work activity or class of operations.

Adherence to these rules will also be secured more easily if employees appreciate the reasons for having them and know that their representatives have been consulted in the making of them.

17. Where written reports have been made by safety representatives following inspections, they may be brought to the attention of the safety committee. In such cases the committee may suggest suitable publicity.

18. An essential condition to the effective working of a safety committee is good communications between management and the committee and between the committee and the employees. In addition, there must be a genuine desire on the part of management to tap the knowledge and experience of its employees and an equally genuine desire on the part of the employees to improve the standards of health and safety at the workplace.

19. The effectiveness of a joint safety committee will depend on the pressure and influence it is able to maintain on all concerned. The following activities could assist in maintaining the impetus of a committee's work:
   (a) regular meetings with effective publicity of the committee's discussions and recommendations;
   (b) speedy decisions by management on the committee's recommendations, where necessary promptly translated into action and effective publicity;
   (c) participation by members of the safety committee in periodical joint inspection;
   (d) development of ways of involving more employees.

The conduct of safety committees

20. Safety committees should meet as often as necessary. The frequency of meetings will depend on the volume of business, which in turn is likely to depend on local conditions, the size of the workplace, numbers employed, the kind of work carried out and the degree of risk inherent. Sufficient time should be allowed during each meeting to ensure full discussion of all business.

21. Meetings should not be cancelled or postponed except in very exceptional circumstances. Where postponement is absolutely necessary an agreed date for the next meeting should be made and announced as soon as possible.

22. The dates of the meetings should as far as possible be arranged well in advance, even to the extent of planning a programme six months or a year ahead. In these circumstances all members of the committee should be sent a personal copy of the programme giving the dates of the meetings. Notices of the dates of meetings should also be published where all employees can see them. A copy of the agenda and any accompanying papers should be sent to all committee members at least one week before each meeting.

23. Committees may wish to draw up additional rules for the conduct of meetings. These might include procedures by which committees might reach decisions.

24. In certain undertakings it might be useful for the safety committee to appoint sub-committees to study particular health and safety problems.

25. Agreed minutes of each meeting should be kept and a personal copy supplied to each member of the committee as soon as possible after the meeting to which they relate and a copy sent to each safety representative appointed for workplaces covered by the committee. A copy of the

minutes should be sent to the most senior executive responsible for health and safety; and arrangements should be made to ensure that the Board of Directors is kept informed generally of the work of the committee. An adequate number of copies of the minutes should be displayed, or made available by other means, along with any other information which the employer provides whether required by statute or not.

5–045

Code of Practice on Picketing

This Code was issued with the authority of Parliament (resolutions passed on November 13, 1980, *by the House of Commons and by the House of Lords). It came into effect, by order of the Secretary of State, on December* 17, 1980. *See Employment Code of Practice (Picketing) Order 1980* (S.I. 1980 No. 1757).

Section A

INTRODUCTION

1. The Code is intended to provide practical guidance on picketing in trade disputes for those who may be contemplating, organising or taking part in a picket and for those who as employers or workers or members of the general public may be affected by it.

2. There is no legal "right to picket" as such but peaceful picketing has long been recognised as being lawful. However, the law imposes certain limits on how and where lawful picketing can be undertaken so as to ensure that there is proper protection for those who may be affected by picketing, including those who want to go to work normally.

3. It is a *civil* wrong, actionable in the civil courts, to persuade someone to break his contract of employment or to secure the breaking of a commercial contract. But the law exempts from this liability those acting in contemplation or furtherance of a trade dispute, including pickets, provided that they are picketing only at their own place of work.[12] The *criminal* law, however, applies to pickets just as it applies to everyone else: they have no exemption from the provisions of the criminal law (*e.g.* as to obstruction and public order).

4. The Code outlines the law on picketing (although it is of course for the courts and industrial tribunals to interpret and apply the law in particular cases). Sections B and C outline the provisions of the civil and criminal law respectively and Section D describes the role of the police in enforcing the law. The Code—in Sections E, F and G—also gives guidance on good practice in the conduct of picketing.

5. The Code itself imposes no legal obligations and failure to observe it

---

[12] Subject additionally in cases of secondary action to the limitations described in paragraph 9 below.

does not by itself render anyone liable to proceedings. But section 3(8) of the Employment Act 1980 provides that any provisions of the Code are to be admissible in evidence and taken into account in proceedings before any court or industrial tribunal or the Central Arbitration Committee where they consider them relevant.

Section B

PICKETING AND THE CIVIL LAW

6. Section 15 of the Trade Union and Labour Relations Act 1974 (as amended by the Employment Act 1980) provides the basic rules for lawful industrial picketing: 5–046
  (i) it may only be undertaken in contemplation or furtherance of a trade dispute;
  (ii) it may only be carried out by a person *attending at or near his own place of work*; a trade union official in addition to attending at or near his own place of work may also attend at or near the place of work of a member of his trade union whom he is accompanying on the picket line and whom he represents;
  (iii) its only purpose must be peacefully obtaining or communicating information or peacefully persuading a person to work or not to work.

7. Picketing commonly involve persuading employees to break their contracts of employment by not going into work and, by disrupting the business of the employer who is being picketed, interfering with his commercial contracts with other employers. If pickets follow the rules outlined in paragraph 6 they are protected by section 13 of the Trade Union and Labour Relations Act 1974 (as amended)[13] from being sued in the civil courts for these civil wrongs. These rules are explained more fully in paragraphs 10 to 19 below.

8. These rules apply in the normal cases where employees picket at their own place of work in support of a dispute with their own employer. Cases may arise, however, where employees picket at their own place of work in support of a dispute between another employer and his employees, for example, where employees at one place are involved in a strike in support of a dispute elsewhere and have mounted a picket line at their own place of work in the course of that strike.

9. In such cases the picketing, in order to be protected, must further satisfy the requirements of lawful secondary action contained in section 17 of the Employment Act 1980. (These are described in detail in the Annex). In practice this means that these pickets will have to target their picketing precisely on the supply of goods or services between their employer and the employer in dispute. If they impose or threaten an indiscriminate blockade on their employer's premises, they will be liable to be sued in the civil courts.

In contemplation or furtherance of a trade dispute
10. Picketing is lawful only if it is carried out in contemplation or further- 5–047

---

[13] Unless otherwise stated by the Trade Union and Labour Relations (Amendment) Act 1976.

ance of a trade dispute. A trade dispute is defined in section 29 of the Trade Union and Labour Relations Act 1974 (as amended). It covers all the matters which normally occasion disputes between employers and workers such as terms and conditions of employment, the allocation of work, matters of discipline, trade union recognition and membership or non-membership of a trade union.

Attendance at or near his own place of work

11. It is lawful for a person to induce a breach of contract in the course of picketing only if he pickets at or near his own place of work.

12. "At or near his own place of work" is not defined in statute. In general, however, except for those covered by paragraphs 13 and 14 below, lawful picketing normally involves attendance at an entrance to or exit from the factory, site or office at which the picket works. It does not enable a picket to attend lawfully at an entrance to or exit from any place of work which is not his own, even if those who work there are employed by the same employer or covered by the same collective bargaining arrangements. The law does not protect anyone who pickets without permission on or inside any part of premises which are private property. Pickets who trespass may be sued in the civil courts.

13. Section 15 of the 1974 Act (as amended by the Employment Act 1980) distinguishes two specific groups of employees:

those (*e.g.* mobile workers) who work at more than one place; and

those for whom it is impracticable to picket at their own place of work because of its location.

It declares that it is lawful for such workers to picket those premises of their employer from which they work or from which their work is administered. In the case of lorry drivers, for example, this will usually mean in practice those premises of their employer from which their vehicles operate.

14. Special provisions also govern people who are not in employment and who have lost their jobs for reasons connected with the dispute which has occasioned the picketing. This might arise, for example, where the dismissal of a group of employees has led directly to a strike, or where in the course of a dispute an employer has terminated his employees' contracts of employment because those employees refuse to work normally. In such cases section 15 declares that it is lawful for a worker to picket *at his former place of work*. This does not apply, however, to any workers who have subsequently found a job at another place of work. Such workers may only picket lawfully at their new place of work in the course of a dispute with their new employer or in the course of lawful secondary action.

Trade union officials

15. For the reasons described in Section F it is often helpful to the orderly organisation and conduct of picketing for a trade union official to be present on a picket line where his members are picketing. Section 15 of the 1974 Act (as amended by the Employment Act 1980) therefore makes it lawful for a trade union official to picket at any place of work provided that:

(i) he is accompanying members of his trade union who are picketing lawfully at or near their own place of work; and

(ii) he personally represents those members within their trade union.

If these conditions are satisfied then a trade union official has the same legal protection as other pickets who picket lawfully at or near their own place of work.

16. Under section 15 of the 1974 Act (as amended by the Employment Act 1980) an official[14]—whether a lay official or an employee of the union—is regarded for this purpose as representing only those members of his union whom he has been specifically appointed or elected to represent. An official cannot, therefore, claim that he represents a group of members simply because they belong to his trade union. He must represent and be responsible for them in the normal course of his trade union duties. For example, it is lawful for an official (such as a shop steward) who represents members at a particular place of work to be present on a picket line where those members are picketing lawfully; for a branch official to be present only where members of his branch are lawfully picketing; for a regional official to be present only where members of his region are lawfully picketing; for a national official who represents a particular trade group or section within the union, to be present wherever members of that trade group or section are lawfully picketing; and for a national official such as a General Secretary or President who represents the whole union to be present wherever any members of his union are picketing lawfully.

17. Trade union officials may, of course, picket lawfully at their own place of work, whether or not their members are also picketing. However, to be entitled to picket at a place of work other than their own, they must satisfy the conditions laid down in section 15 of the Trade Union and Labour Relations Act 1974 (as amended by the Employment Act 1980) and described in paragraphs 15 and 16 above.

Lawful purposes of picketing

18. The only purposes of picketing declared lawful by section 15 are: 5–050
   peacefully obtaining and communicating information; and
   peacefully persuading a person to work or not to work.

Pickets may, therefore, seek to explain their case to those entering or leaving the picketed premises and to ask them not to enter or leave the premises where the dispute is taking place. This may be done verbally or it may involve the distribution of leaflets or the carrying of banners or placards putting the pickets' case. Pickets have, however, no powers to require other people to stop or to compel them to listen or to do what they have asked them to do. A person who decides to cross a picket line must be allowed to do so.

19. Picketing which is accompanied by, for example, violent, threatening or obstructive behaviour goes beyond peaceful persuasion and is therefore unlawful. As explained in Section C, a picket who threatens or intimidates someone, or obstructs an entrance to a workplace, or causes a breach of the peace commits a criminal offence. But in addition pickets who commit such criminal offences, may forfeit their immunity under the civil law and may be liable to be sued for inducing or threatening to induce a breach of contract.

Seeking redress

20. An employer or an employee whose contracts are interfered with by 5–051
picketing which does not comply with the rules described in paragraphs

---

[14] As defined in section 30 of the Trade Union and Labour Relations Act 1974 (as amended by the Employment Protection Act 1975).

10–19 above has a civil law remedy. He may start an action for damages against those responsible and also ask the court to make an order[15] stopping the unlawful picketing.

21. An order will normally be sought against the person on whose instructions or advice the picketing is taking place, but it will usually apply not only to him but to any others acting on his behalf or on his instructions. Thus an organiser of picketing cannot avoid liability by, for example, changing the members of the picket line each day. Moreover, if a person knows that such an order has been made against someone and yet aids and abets him in breaking it, he may be in contempt of court himself and liable to be punished by the court.

Section C

PICKETING AND THE CRIMINAL LAW

5–052

22. If a picket commits a criminal offence he is just as liable to be prosecuted as any other member of the public who breaks the law. The immunity provided under the civil law does not protect him in any way.

23. The criminal law protects the right of every person to go about his lawful daily business free from interference by others. No one is under any obligation to stop when a picket asks him to do so or, if he does stop, to comply with the picket's request, for example, not to go into work. Everyone has the right, if he wishes to do so, to cross a picket line in order to go into his place of work or to deliver or collect goods. A picket may exercise peaceful persuasion but if he goes beyond that and tries by means other than peaceful persuasion to deter another person from exercising those rights he may commit a criminal offence.

24. Among other matters it is a criminal offence for pickets (as for others)

> to use threatening or abusive language or behaviour directed against any person, whether a worker seeking to cross a picket line, an employer, an ordinary member of the public or the police;
>
> to use or threaten violence to a person or his family;
>
> to intimidate a person by threatening words or behaviour which cause him to fear harm or damage if he fails to comply with the picket's demands;
>
> to obstruct the highway or the entrance to premises or to seek physically to bar the passage of vehicles or persons by lying down in the road, linking arms across or circling in the road, or jostling or physically restraining those entering or leaving the premises;
>
> to be in possession of an offensive weapon;
>
> intentionally or recklessly to damage property;
>
> to engage in violent, disorderly or unruly behaviour or to take any action which is likely to lead to a breach of the peace;
>
> to obstruct a police officer in the execution of his duty.

25. A picket has no right under the law to require a vehicle to stop or to be stopped. The law allows him only to ask a driver to stop by words or

---

[15] An injunction in England and Wales and an interdict in Scotland.

signals. A picket may not physically obstruct a vehicle if the driver decides to drive on or, indeed, in any other circumstances. A driver must—as on all other occasions—exercise due care and attention when approaching or driving past a picket line, and may not drive in such a manner as to give rise to a reasonably foreseeable risk or injury.

Section D

ROLE OF THE POLICE

26. It is not the function of the police to take a view of the merits of a particular trade dispute. They have a general duty to uphold the law and keep the peace, whether on the picket line or elsewhere. The law gives the police discretion to take whatever measures may reasonably be considered necessary to ensure that picketing remains peaceful and orderly.

27. The police have *no* responsibility for enforcing the *civil* law. An employer cannot require the police to help in identifying the pickets against whom he wishes to seek an order from the civil court. Nor is it the job of the police to enforce the terms of an order. Enforcement of an order on the application of a plaintiff is a matter for the court and its officers. The police may, however, decide to assist the officers of the court if they think there may be a breach of the peace.

28. As regards the *criminal* law the police have considerable discretionary powers to limit the number of pickets at any one place where they have reasonable cause to fear disorder.[16] The law does not impose a specific limit on the number of people who may picket at any one place; nor does this Code affect in any way the discretion of the police to limit the number of people on a particular picket line. It is for the police to decide, taking into account all the circumstances, whether the number of pickets at any particular place is likely to lead to a breach of the peace. If a picket does not leave the picket line when asked to do so by the police, he is liable to be arrested for obstruction either of the highway or of a police officer in the execution of his duty if the obstruction is such as to cause, or be likely to cause, a breach of the peace.

Section E

LIMITING NUMBERS OF PICKETS

29. The main cause of violence and disorder on the picket line is excessive numbers. Wherever large numbers of people with strong feelings are involved there is a danger that the situation will get out of control and that those concerned will run the risk of arrest and prosecution.

30. This is particularly so whenever people seek by sheer weight of numbers to stop others going into work or delivering or collecting goods.

---

[16] In *Piddington* v. *Bates* (1960) the High Court upheld the decision of a police constable in stances of that case to limit the number of pickets to two.

In such cases, what is intended is not peaceful persuasion, but obstruction, if not intimidation. Such a situation is often described as "mass picketing." In fact, it is not picketing in its lawful sense of an attempt at peaceful persuasion and may well result in a breach of the peace or other criminal offences. Moreoever, anyone seeking to demonstrate support for those in dispute should keep well away from any picket line so as not to create the risk of a breach of the peace or other criminal offence being committed on that picket line.

31. Large numbers on a picket line are also likely to give rise to fear and resentment amongst those seeking to cross that picket line even where no criminal offence is committed. They exacerbate disputes and sour relations not only between management and employees but between the pickets and their fellow employees. Accordingly pickets and their organisers should ensure that in general the number of pickets does not exceed six at any entrance to a workplace; frequently a smaller number will be appropriate.

Section F

ORGANISATION OF PICKETING

Functions of the picket organiser

5–055

32. An experienced person, preferably a trade union official who represents those picketing, should always be in charge of the picket line. He should have a letter of authority from his union which he can show to police officers or to people who want to cross the picket line. Even when he is not on the picket line himself he should be available to give the pickets advice if a problem arises.

33. An organiser of pickets should maintain close contact with the police. Advance consultation with the police is always in the best interests of all concerned. In particular the organiser and the pickets should seek directions from the police on the number of people who should be present on the picket line at any one time and on where they should stand in order to avoid obstructing the highway.

34. The other main functions of the picket organiser should be:
- to ensure that pickets understand the law and the provisions of this Code and that the picketing is conducted peacefully and lawfully;
- to be responsible for distributing badges or armbands, which authorised pickets should wear so that they are clearly identified;
- to ensure that employees from other places of work do not join the picket line and that any offers of support on the picket line from outsiders are refused;
- to remain in close contact with his own union office, and with the offices of other unions if they are involved in the picketing;
- to ensure that such special arrangements as may be necessary for essential supplies or maintenance (see paragraph 38) are understood and observed by the pickets.

Consultation with other trade unions

35. Where several unions are involved in a dispute, they should consult each other about the organisation of any picketing. It is important that they

should agree how the picketing is to be carried out, how many pickets there should be from each union and who should have overall responsibility for organising them.

Right to cross picket lines

36. Everyone has the right to decide for himself whether he will cross a picket line. Disciplinary action should not be taken or threatened by a union against a member on the ground that he has crossed a picket line which is not authorised or which was not at the member's place of work. Under section 4 of the Employment Act 1980 exclusion or expulsion from a union in a closed shop on such grounds may be held to be unreasonable.

Section G

ESSENTIAL SUPPLIES AND SERVICES

37. Pickets should take very great care to ensure that their activities do not cause distress, hardship or inconvenience to members of the public who are not involved in the dispute. Pickets should take particular care to ensure that the movement of essential goods and supplies, the carrying out of essential maintenance of plant and equipment and the provision of services essential to the life of the community are not impeded, still less prevented. Arrangements to ensure this should be agreed in advance between the unions and employers concerned.

38. The following list of essential supplies and services is provided as an illustration but it is not intended to be comprehensive:

supplies for the production, packaging, marketing and/or distribution of medical and pharmaceutical products;

supplies essential to health and welfare institutions, *e.g.* hospitals, ole people's homes;

heating fuel for schools, residential institutions and private residential accommodation;

other supplies for which there is a crucial need during a crisis in the interests of public health and safety (*e.g.* chlorine, lime and other agents for water purification; industrial and medical gases; sand and salt for road gritting purposes);

supplies of goods and services necessary to the maintenance of plant and machinery;

supplies for the production, packaging, marketing and/or distribution of food and animal feeding stuffs;

the operation of essential services, such as police, fire, ambulance, medical and nursing services, air safety, coastguard and air sea rescue services and services provided by voluntary bodies (*e.g.* Red Cross and St. John's ambulances, meals on wheels, hospital car service) and mortuaries, burial and cremation services.

5–056

Annex
SECONDARY ACTION AND PICKETING

5–057   1. This Annex amplifies the description of lawful secondary action in paragraph 9 of Section B (Picketing and the Civil Law).

2. It is lawful for employees who are in dispute with their own employer to picket peacefully at their own place of work. As the Code explains such pickets have immunity from civil actions if in the course of picketing they interfere with contracts.

3. Anyone who contemplates picketing at his own place of work in furtherance of a dispute between another employer and his workers is subject to separate and more restrictive provisions. In such cases picketing must satisfy the requirement of section 17 of the Employment Act 1980 (as set out in paragraphs 4 and 5 below).

4. If such pickets interfere only with contracts of employment then they are protected by the statutory immunity. If, however, they also interfere with commercial contracts (by means, for example, of inducing breaches of contracts of employment), their activities will be immune from civil proceedings only if:
   (a) their employer is a supplier to, or customer of, the employer in dispute under a contract to provide goods or services; and
   (b) the principal purpose of the picketing is directly to prevent or disrupt the supply of goods or services during the dispute between their employer and the employer in dispute; and
   (c) the picketing is likely to achieve that purpose.

5. Employees of an associated employer[17] of the employer in dispute and of suppliers and customers of that associated employer may also picket lawfully at their own place of work if:
   (a) their principal purpose is to disrupt the supply of goods and services between the associated employer and his supplier or customer; and
   (b) those goods or services are in substitution for goods or services which but for the dispute would have been supplied to or by the employer in dispute; and
   (c) the secondary action is likely to achieve the purpose in (a) above.

6. In practice this means that any picketing by employees who are not in dispute with their own employer must be very specifically targeted
   in the case of customers and suppliers of the employer in dispute, on the business being carried out during the dispute between the customer or supplier and the employer in dispute; or
   in the case of the associated employer, on work which has been transferred from the employer in dispute because of the dispute.
There is no immunity for interfering with commercial contracts by indiscriminate picketing at customers and suppliers or at associated employers of the employer in dispute.

5–058
Code of Practice on
Closed Shop Agreements and Arrangements

This Code was issued with the authority of Parliament (resolutions passed

---

[17] Two employers are associated if one is a company of which the other has control or both are companies of which a third has control (s.30(5) of the Trade Union and Labour Relations Act 1974).

on April 13, 1983, by the House of Commons and on April 14, 1983 by the House of Lords). It came into effect, by order of the Secretary of State, on May 18, 1983.

CONTENTS

PARA.

SECTION A
Introduction.. 00

SECTION B
The closed shop and the law:
(a) *Legal rights of individuals* 00
(b) *Other protection for non-union employees: union labour only requirements* 00

SECTION C
Practical guidance on closed shop agreements and arrangements:
(a) *Before a closed shop is considered* 00
(b) *Scope and content of agreements*..................................... 00
(c) *Review of closed shop agreements and secret ballots*...... 00
(d) *Operations of new or existing agreements*....................... 00

SECTION D
Union treatment of members and applicants........................... 00

SECTION E
The closed shop and the freedom of the press......................... 00

ANNEX A
Definition of a union membership agreement......................... 00

ANNEX B
Those entitled to vote in a ballot on a closed shop agreement 00

Section A

INTRODUCTION

1. The purpose of the Code is to provide practical guidance on questions which arise out of the formulation and operation of closed shop agreements[18]—that is collective agreements that have the effect of requiring employees to be, or remain, members of one or more unions.

2. The Code applies to all employment and to all closed shops whether these are written agreements or informal arrangements which have grown up between employer and union. It applies to closed shops already in existence as well as those which might be proposed for the future.

3. Changes in existing practices and written agreements required to meet

---

[18] Closed shop agreements in the Code are union membership agreements as defined by s.30 of the Trade Union and Labour Relations Act 1974 as amended in 1976. That definition covers both agreement and arrangements requiring employees to become or remain union members. (See Annex for the full definition and how it is to be applied for the purpose of s.7 of the Employment Act 1980).

the standards set by the Code should be adopted in the light of the Code's general approach—and that of the 1980 and 1982 Employment Acts, which it complements. This is that any agreement or practice on union membership should protect basic individual rights; should enjoy the overwhelming support of those affected; and should be flexibly and tolerantly applied.

4. Section B of the Code outlines the provisions of the law on the closed shop as it now stands (although it is of course for the courts and industrial tribunals to interpret and apply the law in particular cases); Sections C, D and E provide practical guidance concerning the operation of closed shops and related matters.

5. The Code itself imposes no legal obligations and failure to observe it does not by itself render anyone liable to proceedings. But section 3(8) of the Employment Act provides that any provisions of the Code are to be admissible in evidence and taken into account in proceedings before any court or industrial tribunal or the Central Arbitration Committee where they consider them relevant.

Section B

THE CLOSED SHOP AND THE LAW

5–059   6. The law in relation to the closed shop is to be found principally in the Employment Protection (Consolidation) Act 1978 and in the Employment Acts 1980 and 1982.

(*a*) *Legal Rights of Individuals*

Unfair dismissal or action short of dismissal

5–060   7. As from 1 November 1984[19] employees who work under a closed shop agreement which has not been "approved" in a ballot will have the following rights:

   a right not to be dismissed for the reason that they are not members of a trade union;

   a right not to have other action (known legally as "action short of dismissal") taken by their employer to compel them to remain or become union members.

From 1 November 1984 a closed shop agreement will count as "approved" at any given date only if in the five years preceding that date it has been supported in a secret ballot. The required levels of support in the ballot depend upon the date the agreement took, or takes effect. They are as follows:

   (*a*) Agreements which took or take effect after 14 August 1980
      —if the agreement has *never* been "approved" in a ballot, 80 per cent. or more of those entitled to vote;
      —if the agreement has previously been "approved" in a ballot, 80 per cent. or more of those entitled to vote *or* 85 per cent. or more of those voting.
   (*b*) Agreements which took effect on or before 14 August 1980

---

[19] The relevant provision will come into effect on tless the Secretary of State brings the date forward by order. The provision will not, however, take effect before 1 November 1983.

—80 per cent. or more of those entitled to vote *or* 85 per cent. or more of those voting.

8. Already, employees who work under a closed shop agreement which came into effect after 14 August 1980 have the rights set out in paragraph 7 if the agreement has not been "approved" in a secret ballot by 80 per cent. or more of those entitled to vote.

9. Furthermore, even if a closed shop agreement has been "approved" in a ballot in accordance with the requirements in paragraphs 7 or 8 is not yet subject to a balloting requirement[20] the rights set out in paragraph 7 apply where:

- the employee genuinely objects on grounds of conscience or other deeply-held personal conviction to being a member of any trade union whatsoever or of a particular union; or
- the employee belonged to the class of employees covered by the closed shop agreement before it took effect and has at no time subsequently been a member of a trade union in accordance with the agreement; or
- the employee works under an "approved" closed shop agreement which took effect after 14 August 1980, was entitled to vote in the first or only ballot through which the closed shop agreement was approved and has not been a member of a trade union in accordance with the agreement since the day that ballot was held; or
- the employee at the time of dismissal[21] *either* has been found by an industrial tribunal to have been unreasonably excluded or expelled from the trade union to which he was required to belong under the closed shop agreement (see paragraph 18 below) *or* has a complaint of unreasonable exclusion or explusion by that union pending before a tribunal[22]; or
- the employee has qualifications relating to his job which make him subject to a written code of conduct and
    —*either* has been expelled from his trade union because he refused to strike or take other industrial action on the grounds that this would have breached his code of conduct;
    —*or* has refused to belong to the union concerned on the grounds that membership, would have required him to take industrial action in breach of the code.

10. Employees who have the rights set out in paragraph 7 also have the right not to be dismissed for refusing to make a payment in lieu of union membership and the right not to have action short of dismissal taken by their employer to compel them to make such a payment. Deduction by the employer of a sum of money in lieu of union membership from their wages or salary will count as action short of dismissal taken to compel them to make such a payment.

11. Employees who work outside a closed shop automatically have the rights set out in paragraph 7. The law gives similar rights to employees who are dismissed or who suffer action short of dismissal because of their actual

---

[20] Because it came into effect on or before 14 August 1980.
[21] Where the dismissal was with notice, the time of dismissal means the time when notice was given.
[22] This does not apply, however, if by the "effective date of termination"
the industrial tribunal's decision had been overturned on appeal; or
the employee had become a member of the union concerned at some point after making his complaint to the tribunal; or
the employee had turned down a chance of rejoining the union since making his complaint.

or proposed membership of a trade union or because of their participation in trade union activities at an appropriate time.

12. Whether or not they work under a closed shop agreement employees have a right not to be chosen for redundancy on the grounds that they are not union members. The law also gives employees the right not to be chosen for redundancy on the grounds that they are union members or have participated in trade union activities at an appropriate time.

Remedies

5–061   13. An employee who considers that any of the rights set out in paragraphs 7–12 above have been infringed may complain to an industrial tribunal within a period of three months[23] after the action complained of. If the dismissed employee's complaint is upheld the tribunal may award compensation.[24] Alternatively the tribunal may make an order requiring the employer to reinstate or re-engage the individual, and to compensate him for any loss during the interruption of his employment. In a case of action short of dismissal the tribunal will make a declaration that the complaint is well-founded and may award compensation. A complaint that any of the rights set out in paragraphs 7–11 above has been infringed can be made to a tribunal irrespective of the age or length of service of, or the number of hours worked by, the employee concerned.

14. In addition an employee who considers that he has been unfairly dismissed for non-membership of a trade union can apply to a tribunal for "interim relief"; *i.e.* an order requiring the continuation of his contract of employment pending a full hearing of his unfair dismissal complaint. An application for interim relief must be made within seven days of dismissal.

Statutory requirements concerning secret ballots

5–062   15. A ballot on the continuation or introduction of a closed shop agreement will be valid only if it is conducted in such a way as to ensure that, so far as reasonably practicable, all those entitled to vote have an opportunity of voting and of doing so in secret. Annex B sets out who is entitled to vote in such a ballot.

16. Unless a closed shop agreement has been "approved" within the previous five years by the required percentage (see paragraphs 7–8 above) in a secret ballot which satisfies these conditions, employers will have no defence against unfair dismissal claims or complaints of action short of dismissal if they dismiss non-union employees for the reason that they are not members of a trade union or if they take action short of dismissal against such employees to compel them to remain or become union members.

Joinder

17. An employer who faces a complaint of unfair dismissal or action short of dismissal may have dismissed the employee concerned or taken the

---

[23] A tribunal may consent to examine a complaint presented after three months if it considers that it was not reasonably practicable for it to be presented within three months.

[24] Compensation for unfair dismissal for non-membership of a union, or for trade union membership or activities, is normally payable at a higher rate than compensation for general unfair dismissal.

action complained of as a result of pressure, in the form of actual or threatened industrial action, exercised by a trade union or person because the employee was not a member of a trade union. If the employer or the employee making the complaint claims there was such pressure either of them may ask for the union or other person concerned to be "joined"[25] (*i.e.* brought in as a party) to the proceedings. If the tribunal upholds the complaint and finds the claim of pressure well-founded, it may order all or part of any award of compensation to be paid by the union or other person "joined," instead of by the employer. A request by either an employer or by a person who brings a complaint to "join" a trade union or other person in this way will be granted by the tribunal if it is made before the hearing begins, but may be refused if it is not made until after the hearing has started.

Unreasonable exclusion or expulsion from a union

18. The Employment Act 1980 provides individuals with statutory rights in relation to their unions. Any person who is employed or is seeking employment in a job where it is the practice, in accordance with a closed shop agreement, to require membership of a specified trade union or one of a number of unions, has the right not to have an application for membership of the union unreasonably refused and the right not to be unreasonably expelled from that trade union.

19. An individual may present a complaint to an industrial tribunal against a trade union that he has been unreasonably excluded or expelled from that union, within a period of six months[26] of that refusal or expulsion. The tribunal will decide whether the expulsion or exclusion concerned was reasonable or not in accordance with equity and the substantial merits of the case and will not base its decision solely on whether the union has acted in accordance with its own rules. The tribunal must have regard in reaching its decision to the guidance in Section D of this Code on trade union treatment of members and applicants where it considers this guidance relevant. If the tribunal finds the complaint well-founded it will make a declaration that the exclusion or expulsion was unreasonable.

20. Where such a declaration has been made by the tribunal, or by the Employment Appeal Tribunal on appeal, the person who made the complaint may make an application for compensation from the union concerned for any loss he has suffered. Such an application may not be made before the end of the period of four weeks following the date of declaration or after the end of the period of six months following the date of the declaration.

21. If, following the tribunal's declaration, the complainant has been admitted or re-admitted to the union by the time he applies for compensation, the application shall be to the industrial tribunal which may award compensation to be paid by the union up to a statutory maximum.

22. If, following the declaration, the complainant has not been admitted or re-admitted to the union, the application shall be to the Employment Appeal Tribunal which may award compensation to be paid by the union up to a higher maximum which is also fixed by the legislation.

---

[25] Sisted in Scotland.
[26] A tribunal may consent to examine a complaint presented after six months if it considers that it was not reasonably practicable for it to be presented within six months.

Common law rights

5–064   23. The provisions of the 1980 Act do not in any way detract from existing rights under the common law. At common law a person may complain to the courts either that action taken against him by a trade union is contrary to its own rules or that in expelling or otherwise disciplining him the union did not act in accordance with the requirements of natural justice.

(b) Other Protection for Non-Union Employees: Union Labour Only Requirements

24. In addition to the protection which the law provides specifically for employees who work in a closed shop the 1982 Employment Act also:
—declares void requirements in contracts which oblige a contractor to employ only union labour in the performance of the contract;
—makes it a breach of statutory duty to impose such requirments in the drawing up of tender lists and the awarding of contracts;
—removes immunity from the organisers of industrial action which is designed to put pressure on an employer to impose or enforce such requirements[27] or which is designed to prevent work in connection with the supply of goods or services being carried out by people who are not union members.

25. It is, therefore, unlawful to attempt to impose union membership on the employees of another employer by insisting that contractors use union labour only or excluding non-union firms from tender lists. In addition, it is unlawful to organise any form of industrial action by the employees of one employer in order to force another employer to employ only union labour.

Section C

PRACTICAL GUIDANCE ON CLOSED SHOP AGREEMENTS AND ARRANGEMENTS

(a) Before a Closed Shop is Considered

5–065   26. Before there is any question of negotiating on proposals for a closed shop, employers and trade unions should take account of the following factors.

Employers

5–066   27. Closed shop agreements, like other collective agreements, require the participation of both parties. Employers are under no obligation to agree to the introduction or continuation of a closed shop, notwithstanding that it has been endorsed in a ballot of employees.

28. Employer's associations may be able to advise on the implications of a closed shop agreement for industrial relations in the industry or locality generally. They should be consulted by their members at an early stage.

---

[27] The Act makes similar provision for requirements which oblige a contractor to recognise, negotiate or consult with trade unions.

29. Employers should expect a union to show a very high level of membership before agreeing to consider the introduction of a closed shop.

30. Employers should acquaint themselves with the legislation (see Section B above). In particular they should be aware of the provisions of the legislation on closed shop ballots (see paragraphs 7–8 and 15–16 above). They should also consider the liabilities which they are likely to incur if their employees' statutory rights are infringed as a result of the operation of closed shop agreements.

31. The employer should have special regard to the interests of particular groups of staff who as members of professional associations are subject to their own code of ethics or conduct. Where the obligations imposed by such a code are incompatible with the full range of union activities including, for example, participation in industrial action endangering health or safety, the employees concerned should be exempted from any requirement to join a union whose rules do not respect such obligations. Such employees may in any case have statutory rights under the 1982 Employment Act (see paragraph 9 above).

32. The employer should also carefully consider the effects of a closed shop on his future employment policy and on industrial relations. In particular, he should consider whether a closed shop is likely to lead to his employees being obliged to take industrial action against their will.

Unions

33. Before seeking a closed shop a union should be recognised and should already have recruited voluntarily a very high proportion of the employees concerned.

5–067

34. A union should be sure that its members who would be affected themselves favour a closed shop. High union membership among those to be covered by the proposed closed shop agreement is not in itself a sufficient indication of their views on this question and indeed some employees might decide to leave their union if a closed shop was in prospect.[28] A union should always consider carefully whether an agreement allowing them sole recognition or bargaining rights might not be a more satisfactory arrangement.

35. A trade union should also consider the liabilities it may incur (see paragraph 17 above) if employees' statutory rights are infringed as a result of the operation of a closed shop agreement.

36. A union should not start negotiations for a closed shop agreement which excludes other unions with a membership interest in the area concerned before the matter has been resolved with the other unions. If affiliated to the TUC, the union should have regard to the relevant TUC guidance on this matter.

37. Disagreements over the arrangements for a secret ballot to test the support for a close shop agreement (see paragraphs 46–48 below), or disagreements over the precise terms of an agreement which arise after the attainment of the required level of support in such a ballot, should be dealt with where appropriate in accordance with the disputes procedure to which the firm and union are parties. The conciliation services of the Advisory, Conciliation and Arbitration Service will be available.

---

[28] See paragraph 9 above.

(b) Scope and Content of Agreements

5–068 38. Written closed shop agreements are always to be preferred to unwritten closed shop arrangements and any new agreements should be in writing. All written agreements should be clearly drafted.

39. In addition the agreement should:
   (i) indicate clearly the class of employees to be covered. This can be done by reference, for example, to the grade or location or bargaining unit concerned. The agreement should not necessarily cover all employees at a location or in a grade. Some examples of groups which may well be excluded are professional, managerial, personnel or part-time employees. All exclusions or exemptions should be clearly stated in the agreement;
   (ii) not require employees in any of the categories described in paragraph 9 to be members of a trade union;
   (iii) specify a reasonable period within which employees should join the union;
   (iv) make clear that, where an individual has been excluded or expelled by his union, no other action, whether by the union or the employer, will be taken against him before any appeal or complaint regarding the exclusion or explusion has been determined; and that where he is found by an industrial tribunal to have been unreasonably excluded or expelled by his union (see paragraph 18 above) he will have no action taken against him by the employer;
   (v) provide that an employee will not be dismissed if expelled from his union for refusal to take part in industrial action;
   (vi) set out clearly how complaints or disputes arising from the agreement are to be resolved. It should provide appropriate procedures which give the individual concerned an adequate right to be heard and enable any question about non-membership of a union to be fairly tested. Such procedures can usefully provide for independent conciliation or arbitration so long as the terms of refernce of any arbitration make clear that the statutory requirements in Section B above cannot be over-ridden;
   (vii) provide for periodic reviews and secret ballots to comply with the statutory provisions on ballots for new and existing closed shops (see paragraphs 7–8 and 15–16 above);
   (viii) provide that either party can terminate the agreement by giving a specified period of notice, which should not exceed 3 months;
   (ix) provide that, notwithstanding any period of notice specified in the agreement, the closed shop will cease to have effect immediately if it is not approved in a secret ballot in accordance with the requirements set out in paragraphs 7–8 and 15–16 above).

40. It is open to the parties to agree that an alternative to union membership would be the payment to a charity by individual non-unionists of a sum equivalent to the union membership subscription. However, such an agreement cannot limit the statutory rights of individuals described in paragraphs 7–12 above.

41. Where other unions have a known interest in the area to be covered by the agreement, it may specify as appropriate membership of unions other than those actually party to it. Where unions affiliated to the TUC find themselves in a dispute which has not been settled locally or within the industry they should refer the issue to the TUC.

(c) Review of Closed Shop Agreements and Secret Ballots

Periodic review

42. All closed shop agreements, whether new or existing, or whether covering a firm or industry should be subject to periodic review and secret ballot.

43. Reviews should take place at least every five years, and more frequently if changes of the following types occur:
> where there is evidence that the support of the employees for the closed shop has declined;
> where there has been a change in the parties to the agreement;
> where there is evidence that the agreement or parts of it are not working satisfactorily;
> when there is a change in the law affecting the closed shop, such as the 1980 and 1982 Employment Acts.

44. If as a result of a review the employer and union favour continuing the agreement, they should ensure that it is revised to conform to the requirements set out in paragraphs 38–39 above and that it has the support of the employees to whom it currently applies. The degree of support should be tested by means of a secret ballot. If the agreement is thought no longer to serve the purpose for which it was intended or there is evidence of insufficient support or there is evidence of insufficient support among those covered by the agreement, the parties should agree to allow it to lapse. And either party, having given any period of notice specified in an agreement (subject to paragraph 39(viii and ix) above), can terminate it.

45. Closed shop agreements which require people to belong to a trade union before they can be employed (the pre-entry closed shop) may particularly infringe the freedom of individuals to work. No new agreements of this type should be contemplated and where they currently exist the need for their continuation should be carefully reviewed as soon as possible and regularly thereafter.

Secret ballots

46. The statutory requirements concerning secret ballots on closed shop agreements are set out in paragraphs 7–8 and 15–16 above. A secret ballot, conducted in conformity with these requirements, should be held at least every five years on the question of whether an existing closed shop agreement should continue and a ballot should be held where any new closed shop agreement is proposed.

47. The following guidelines should be observed in relation to such a ballot:
  (i) A proposed closed shop agreement
      The terms of a proposed agreement should be worked out before it is put to the test of a ballot of those to be affected by it.
  (ii) The definition of the electorate
      The electorate should be all the members of the class of employee to be covered by the proposed or existing closed shop including those who are not union members.
  (iii) Informing the electorate
      Steps should be taken to ensure that each employee affected is

aware of the intention to hold a ballot and of the terms of the agreement and any other relevant information a reasonable time before the date of the ballot. Suitable arrangements should be made to inform those members of the electorate who might otherwise not have access such information due to sickness or absence from work or for other reasons.

(iv) The framing of the question

The ballot form should be clear and simple. The question asked should be limited to the single issue of whether or not, in the case of an existing agreement, the closed shop agreement should continue to apply to the employees covered by it or, in the case of a new agreement, whether or not membership of the union(s) party to the proposed agreement or otherwise specified in it (see paragraph 41 above) should be a requirement for employees in the class of employment it would cover. If several questions are asked or other issues raised in the ballot this may confuse the outcome.

(v) Method of balloting

Under the 1982 Act the ballot should be conducted so as to ensure that, so far as reasonably practicable, all those entitled to vote have an opportunity of voting and of doing so in secret (see paragraph 15 above). Either a workplace or a postal ballot may meet these requirements. In the case of a workplace ballot arrangements should be made for those absent from work for any reason at the date(s) of the ballot to register their vote.

(vi) Holding the ballot

Before the ballot can be held, decisions will be needed on such matters as the method of distributing the ballot forms and arranging for their return and counting, the time to be allowed for voting, and the persons charged with conducting the ballot. Greater confidence will result if the ballot is independently conducted and this will help to ensure that the statutory requirements regarding secrecy are not infringed.

(vii) Other matters

Agreement should also be reached in advance on such matters as the procedure for handling disputes about eligibility, spoilt votes and any other issues, and the safe keeping of ballot papers until an agreed destruction date.

48. The law specifies minimum levels of support for the approval of new and existing closed shop agreements by secret ballot (see paragaphs 7–8 above). However, this does not prevent an employer from deciding that the required majority should be higher than the statutory minimum—or that there must be a minimum percentage turn-out—before he agrees to introduce such a radical change in his employee's terms and conditions of employment or to continue an existing agreement. Employers should agree with the union on the figure appropriate in their case before the ballot and make this known to those entitled to vote.

(d) Operation of New or Existing Agreements

Those in scope of or parties to agreements

49. Closed shop agreements should be applied flexibly and tolerantly and with full regard to the interests of individuals.

50. Before any potential new employee is recruited he should be informed of any requirement to become a union member under a closed

shop agreement and have his attention drawn to the existence of statutory rights in relation to the closed shop.

51. Employers and unions should not contemplate any disciplinary action before procedures for resolving disputes and grievances which arise under the agreement are exhausted.

52. Employers and unions should take no action against an employee who has been expelled or excluded from a union until any appeal under union appeal procedures has been determined and any industrial tribunal proceedings concerning the exclusion or expulsion have been completed. Where such proceedings result in a declaration by a tribunal that an employee has been unreasonably expelled or excluded from his union no action should be taken against him by the employer or unions concerned (see paragraph 9 above).

Those not in scope of or parties to agreements

53. Employers and unions who have negotiated a closed shop, and employees in scope of it, should not impose unreasonable requirements on those who are not parties or in scope of the agreement. There should be no attempt, by formal or informal means to impose a requirement of union membership on the employees of contractors, suppliers and customers of an employer. The imposition of such requirements is unlawful under the 1982 Employment Act (see paragraphs 24–25 above). 5–072

Section D

UNION TREATMENT OF MEMBERS AND APPLICANTS

54. Union decisions on exclusion or expulsion from membership in a closed shop should be taken only after all rules and procedures have been fully complied with. 5–073

Union rules and procedures

55. In handling admissions to membership, unions should adopt and apply clear and fair rules covering: 5–074
- who is qualified for membership;
- who has power to consider and decide upon applications;
- what reasons will justify rejecting an application;
- the appeals procedure open to a rejected applicant;
- the power to admit applicants where an appeal is upheld.

56. When determining whom they might accept into membership the factors to which unions may have regard include the following:
- whether the person applying for membership of a union or section of it has the appropriate qualifications for the type of work done by members of the union or section concerned;
- whether, because of the nature of the work concerned, for example acting, the number of applicants or potential applicants has long been and is likely to continue to be so great as to pose a serious threat of undermining negotiated terms and conditions of employment;
- whether the TUC's principles and procedures governing relations

between unions or any findings of a TUC Dispute Committee are relevant.

57. In handling membership discipline, unions should adopt and apply clear and fair rules covering:

    the offences for which the union is entitled to take disciplinary action and the penalties applicable for each of these offences;

    the procedure for hearing and determining complaints in which offences against the rules are alleged;

    a right to appeal against the imposition of any penalty;

    the procedure for the hearing of appeals against any penalty by a higher authority comprised of persons other than those who imposed the penalty;

    the principle that a recommendation for expulsion should not be made effective so long as a member is genuinely pursuing his appeal.

58. Union procedures on exclusion or expulsion should comply with the rules of natural justice. These include giving the individual member fair notice of the complaint against him, a reasonable opportunity of being heard, a fair hearing and an impartial decision.

59. Unions affiliated to the Trades Union Congress should bear in mind its guidance on these matters, and inform individuals of the appeals procedure the TUC provide for those expelled or excluded from membership of a union.

60. In general voluntary procedures are to be preferred to legal action and all parties should be prepared to use them. However, since an individual may face consderable economic loss or adverse social consequences as a result of exclusion or expulsion from a union it would be unreasonable to expect him to defer his application to a tribunal.[29] Unions should therefore not consider taking action likely to lead to an individual losing his job until their own procedures have been fully used and any decision of an external body has been received. Any decision of the Independent Review Committee of the TUC should be fully taken into account.

Industrial action

61. Disciplinary action should not be taken or threatened by a union against a member on the grounds of his refusal to take part in industrial action called for by the union:

    (*a*) where there were reasonable grounds for believing that the industrial action was unlawful[30] or that it involved a breach of statutory duty or the criminal law; or that it constituted a serious risk to public safety, health or property; or

    (*b*) where the member believed that the industrial action contravened his professional or other code of ethics;

    (*c*) where the industrial action was in breach of a procedure agreement; or

    (*d*) where the industrial action had not been affirmed in a secret ballot.

62. Furthermore, disciplinary action should not be taken or threatened

---

[29] Complaints of unreasonable exclusion or expulsion to a tribunal are subject to a time limit of six months (see paragraph 19 above).

[30] *i.e.* industrial action which does not have immunity under the Trade Union and Labour Relations Act 1974 as amended by the 1976, 1980 and 1982 Acts.

by a union against a member on the ground that he has crossed a picket line which it had not authorised or which was not at the member's place or work.

Section E

THE CLOSED SHOP AND THE FREEDOM OF THE PRESS

5–076

The freedom of the press[31] to collect and publish information and to publish comment and criticism is an essential part of our democratic society. All concerned have a duty to ensure that industrial relations are conducted so as not to infringe or jeopardise this principle.

57. Journalists, wherever employed, should enjoy the same rights as other employees to join trade unions and participate in their activities. However, the actions of unions must not be such as to conflict with the principle of press freedom. In particular any requirement on journalists to join a union creates the possibility of such a conflict.

58. Individual journalists may genuinely feel that membership of a trade union is incompatible with their need to be free from any serious risk of interference with their freedom to report or comment. This should be respected by employers and unions.

59. A journalist should not be disciplined by a trade union for anything he has researched or written for publication in accordance with generally accepted professional standards.

60. Editors should be free to decide whether to become or remain a member of any trade union.

61. Within the agreed basic policy of the publication:
    (i) Editors have final responsibility for the content of the publications. An editor should not be subjected to improper pressure—that is, any action or threat calculated to induce him to distort news, comment or criticism, or contrary to his judgment, to publish or to suppress or to modify news, comment or criticisms.
    (ii) The editor should be free to decide whether or not to publish any material submitted to him from any source. He should exercise this right responsibly with due regard for the interests of the readers of the publication and the employment or opportunities of employment of profeesional journalists.

Annex A

THE DEFINITION OF A UNION MEMBERSHIP AGREEMENT

5–077

Section 30 of the Trade Union and Labour Relations Act 1974 (as amended in 1976) says
    "union membership agreement" means an agreement or arrangement which—

---

[31] For the purpose of this Code, the press includes newspapers, periodicals and news agencies.

(a) is made by or on behalf of, or otherwise exists between, one or more independent trade unions and one or more employers or employers' associations; and

(b) relates to employees of an identifiable class; and

(c) has the effect in practice of requiring the employees for the time being of the class to which it relates (whether or not there is a condition to that effect in their contract of employment) to be or become a member of the union or one of the unions which is or are parties to the agreement or arrangement or of another specified independent trade union;

and references in this definition to a trade union include references to a branch or section of a trade union; and a trade union is specified for the purposes of, or in relation to, a union membership agreement if it is specified in the agreement or is accepted by the parties to the agreement as being the equivalent of a union so specified."

Section 58A(6) of the Employment Protection (Consolidation) Act 1978 (contained in section 3 of the Employment Act 1982) has the effect that for the purpose of determining whether or not an employee belongs to the relevant class of employees entitled to vote in a ballot on a closed shop,[32] any attempt by the parties to the agreement to define the class by reference to employees' membership of non-membership of a union, by objection to membership, shall be disregarded by tribunals.

Annex B

THOSE ENTITLED TO VOTE IN A BALLOT ON A CLOSED SHOP AGREEMENT

5–078 Those entitled to vote in a closed shop ballot are all the members of the class of employees covered by the closed shop agreement, including those who are not union members, who are in the employment of the employer on the day of the ballot or, in a case where voting takes place over more than one day, on a "qualifying day" which must be specified by the person conducting the ballot. This qualifying day must not fall after the last voting day or an unreasonably long time before it. If a ballot takes place over more than one day, all those entitled to vote must, so far as reasonably practicable, know which day has been specified as the qualifying day before they cast their votes.

---

[32] See Annex B.

Code of Practice on Race Relations

This Code was issued by the Commission for Racial Equality under section 47 of the Race Relations Act 1976. It comes into effect, by order of the Secretary of State, on April 1, 1983 by virtue of the Race Relations Code of Practice Order 1983 (S.I. 1983 No. 1081).

INTRODUCTION

1. The Purpose and Status of the Code s. 47(1)

1.1 This Code aims to give practical guidance which will help employers, trade unions, employment agencies and employees to understand not only the provisions of the Race Relations Act and their implications, but also how best they can implement policies to eliminate racial discrimination and to enhance equality of opportunity.

1.2 The Code does not impose any legal obligations itself, nor is it an authoritative statement of the law—that can only be provided by the courts and tribunals. If, however, its recommendations are not observed this may result in breaches of the law where the act or omission falls within any of the specific prohibitions of the Act. Moreover its provisions are admissible in evidence in any proceedings under the Race Relations Act before an Industrial Tribunal and if any provision appears to the Tribunal to be relevant to a question arising in the proceedings it must be taken into account in determining that question. If employers take the steps that are set out in the Code to prevent their employees from doing acts of unlawful discrimination they may avoid liability for such acts in any legal proceedings brought against them. *References to the appropriate Sections of the Race Relations Act 1976 are therefore given in the margin to the Code.*

[margin: s. 47(10), s. 47(11), s. 32]

1.3 Employees of all racial groups have a right to equal opportunity. Employers ought to provide it. To do so is likely to involve some expenditure, at least in staff time and effort. But if a coherent and effective programme of equal opportunity is developed it will help industry to make full use of the abilities of its entire workforce. It is therefore particularly important for all those concerned—employers, trade unions and employees alike—to co-operate with goodwill in adopting and giving effect to measures for securing such equality. We welcome the commitment already made by the CBI and TUC to the principle of equal opportunity. The TUC has recommended a model equal opportunity clause for inclusion in collective agreements and the CBI has published a statement favouring the application by companies of constructive equal opportunity policies.

1.4 A concerted policy to eliminate both race and sex discrimination often provides the best approach. Guidance on equal opportunity between men and women is the responsibility of the Equal Opportunities Commission.

2. The Application of the Code

2.1 The Race Relations Act applies to all employers. The Code itself is not restricted to what is required by law, but contains recommendations as well. Some of its detailed provisions may need to be adapted to suit particular circumstances. Any adaptations that are made, however, should be fully consistent with the Code's general intentions.

2.2 Small Firms

In many small firms employers have close contact with their staff and there will therefore be less need for formality in assessing whether equal opportunity is being achieved, for example, in such matters as arrangements for monitoring. Moreover it may not be reasonable to expect small firms to have the resources and administrative systems to carry out the Code's detailed recommendations. In complying with the Race Relations Act, small firms should, however, ensure that their practices are consistent with the Code's general intentions.

3. Unlawful Discrimination s.4

5–078/3   3.1 The Race Relations Act 1976 makes it unlawful to discriminate against a person, directly or indirectly, in the field of employment.

s. 1(1)(a)   Direct discrimination consists of treating a person, on racial grounds,[33] less favourably than others are or would be treated in the same or similar circumstances.

s. 1(2)   Segregating a person from others on racial grounds constitutes less favourable treatment.

s. 1(1)(b)   3.2 Indirect discrimination consists of applying in any circumstances covered by the Act a requirement or condition which, although applied equally to persons of all racial groups, is such that a considerably smaller proportion of a particular racial group can comply with it and it cannot be shown to be justifiable on other than racial grounds. Possible examples are:
— a rule about clothing or uniforms which disproportionately disadvantages a racial group and cannot be justified;
— an employer who requires higher language standards than are needed for safe and effective performance of the job.

3.3 The definition of indirect discrimination is complex, and it will not be spelt out in full in every relevant Section of the Code. Reference will be only to the terms 'indirect discrimination' or 'discriminate indirectly'.

s. 2   3.4 Discrimination by victimisation is also unlawful under the Act. For example, a person is victimised if he or she is given less favourable treatment than others in the same circumstances because it is suspected or known that he or she has brought proceedings under the Act, or given evidence or information relating to such proceedings, or alleged that discrimination has occurred.

4. The Code and Good Employment Practice

5–078/4   Many of the Code's provisions show the close link between equal opportunity and good employment practice. For example, selection criteria which are relevant to job requirements and carefully observed selection procedures not only help to ensure that individuals are appointed according to their suitability for the job and without regard to racial group; they are also part of good employment practice. In the absence of consistent selection procedures and criteria, decisions are often too subjective and racial discrimination can easily occur.

5. Positive Action

5–078/5   Opportunities for employees to develop their potential through encouragement, training and careful assessment are also part of good employment practice. Many employees from the racial minorities have potential which,

---

[33] Racial grounds are the grounds of race, colour, nationality—including citizenship—or ethnic or national origins, and groups defined by reference to these grounds are referred to as racial groups.

perhaps because of previous discrimination and other causes of disadvantage, they have not been able to realise, and which is not reflected in their qualifications and experience. Where members of particular racial groups have been under-represented over the previous twelve months in particular work, employers and specified training bodies are allowed under the Act to encourage them to take advantage of opportunities for doing that work and to provide training to enable them to attain the skills needed for it. In the case of employers, such training can be provided for persons currently in their employment (as defined by the Act) and in certain circumstances for others too, for example if they have been designated as training bodies. This Code encourages employers to make use of these provisions, which are covered in detail in paragraphs 1.44 and 1.45.

ss. 37, 38

6. Guidance Papers

The guidance papers referred to in the footnotes contain additional guidance on specific issues but do not form part of the statutory Code.

5–078/6

PART 1

The Responsibilities of Employers

1.1 Responsibility for providing equal opportunity for all job applicants and employees rests primarily with employers. To this end it is recommended that they should adopt, implement and monitor an equal opportunity policy to ensure that there is no unlawful discrimination and that equal opportunity is genuinely available.[34]

5–078/7

1.2 This policy should be clearly communicated to all employees—e.g. through notice boards, circulars, contracts of employment or written notifications to individual employees.

Equal Opportunity Policies

1.3 An equal opportunity policy aims to ensure:
  (a) that no job applicant or employee receives less favourable treatment than another on racial grounds;
  (b) that no applicant or employee is placed at a disadvantage by requirements or conditions which have a disproportionately adverse effect on his or her racial group and which cannot be shown to be justifiable on other than racial grounds;
  (c) that, where appropriate and where permissible under the Race Relations Act, employees of under-represented racial groups are given training and encouragement to achieve equal opportunity within the organisation.

5–078/8

---

[34] The CRE has issued guidance papers on equal opportunity policies: "Equal Opportunity in Employment" and "Monitoring an Equal Opportunity Policy".

1.4 In order to ensure that an equal opportunity policy is fully effective, the following action by employers is recommended:
  (a) allocating overall responsibility for the policy to a member of senior management;
  (b) discussing and, where appropriate, agreeing with trade union or employee representatives the policy's contents and implementation;
  (c) ensuring that the policy is known to all emloyees and if possible, to all job applicants;
  (d) providing training and guidance for supervisory staff and other relevant decision makers, (such as personnel and line managers, foremen, gatekeepers and receptionists) to ensure that they understand their position in law and under company policy;
  (e) examining and regularly reviewing existing procedures and criteria and changing them where they find that they are actually or potentially unlawfully discriminatory;
  (f) making an initial analysis of the workforce and regularly monitoring the application of the policy with the aid of analyses of the ethnic origins of the workforce and of job applicants in accordance with the guidance in paragraphs 1.34–1.35.

Recruitment, Promotion, Transfer, Training & Dismissal

Sources of Recruitment
Advertisements

5–078/9

s. 29

1.5 When advertising job vacancies it is unlawful for employers:
to publish an advertisement which indicates, or could reasonably be understood as indicating, an intention to discriminate against applicants from a particular racial group. (For exceptions see the Race Relations Act).

1.6 It is therefore recommended that:
  (a) employers should not confine advertisements unjustifiably to those areas or publications which would exclude or disproportionately reduce the numbers of applicants of a particular racial group;
  (b) employers should avoid prescribing requirements such as length of residence or experience in the UK and where a particular qualification is required it should be made clear that a fuly comparable qualification obtained overseas is as acceptable as a UK qualification.

1.7 In order to demonstrate their commitment to equality of opportunity it is recommended that where employers send literature to applicants, this should include a statement that they are equal opportunity employers.

Employment Agencies

1.8 When recruiting through employment agencies, job centres, careers offices and schools, it is unlawful for employers:

s. 30

s. 31

  (a) to give instructions to discriminate, for example by indicating that certain groups will or will not be preferred. (For exceptions see the Race Relations Act);
  (b) to bring pressure on them to discriminate against members of a particular racial group. (For exceptions, as above).

1.9 In order to avoid indirect discrimination it is recommended that

Codes of Practice

employers should not confine recruitment unjustifiably to those agencies, job centres, careers offices and schools which, because of their particular source of applicants, provide only or mainly applicants of a particular racial group.

Other Sources

1.10 It is unlawful to use recruitment methods which exclude or disproportionately reduce the numbers of applicants of a particular racial group and which cannot be shown to be justifiable. It is therefore recommended that employers should not recruit through the following methods:
  (*a*) recruitment, solely or in the first instance, through the recommendations of existing employees where the workforce concerned is wholly or predominantly white or black and the labour market is multi-racial;
  (*b*) procedures by which applicants are mainly or wholly supplied through trade unions where this means that only members of a particular racial group, or a disproportionately high number of them, come forward.

Sources for Promotion and Training

1.11 It is unlawful for employers to restrict access to opportunities for promotion or training in a way which is discriminatory. It is therefore recommended that:
  —job and training vacancies and the application procedure should be made known to all eligible employees, and not in such a way as to exclude or disproportionately reduce the numbers of applicants from a particular racial group.

ss. 4, 28

Selection for Recruitment, Promotion, Transfer, Training and Dismissal

1.12 It is unlawful to discriminate,[35] not only in recruitment, promotion, transfer and training, but also in the arrangements made for recruitment and in the ways of affording access to opportunities for promotion, transfer or training.

5–078/10

Selection Criteria and Tests

1.13 In order to avoid direct or indirect discrimination it is recommended that selection criteria and tests are examined to ensure that they are related to job requirements and are not unlawfully discriminatory (See Introduction para. 3.2). For example:
  (*a*) a standard of English higher than that needed for the safe and effective performance of the job or clearly demonstrable career pattern should not be required, or a higher level of educational qualification than is needed;
  (*b*) in particular, employers should not disqualify applicants

ss. 4, 28

---

[35] It should be noted that discrimination in selection to achieve "racial balance" is not allowed. The clause in the 1968 Race Relations Act which allowed such discrimination for the purpose of securing or preserving a reasonable balance of persons of different racial groups in the establishment is not included in the 1976 Race Relations Act.

because they are unable to complete an application form unassisted unless personal completion of the form is a valid test of the standard of English required for safe and effective performance of the job;

(c) overseas degrees, diplomas and other qualifications which are comparable with UK qualifications should be accepted as equivalents, and not simply be assumed to be of an inferior quality;

(d) selection tests which contain irrelevant questions or exercises on matters which may be unfamiliar to racial minority applicants should not be used (for example, general knowledge questions on matters more likely to be familiar to indigenous applicants);

(e) selection tests should be checked to ensure that they are related to the job's requirements, i.e. an individual's test markings should measure ability to do or train for the job in question.

Treatment of Applicants, Shortlisting, Interviewing and Selection

1.14 In order to avoid direct or indirect discrimination it is recommended that:

(a) gate, reception and personnel staff should be instructed not to treat casual or formal applicants from particular racial groups less favourably than others. These instructions should be confirmed in writing;

(b) in addition, staff responsible for shortlisting, interviewing and selecting candidates should be:
—clearly informed of selection criteria and of the need for their consistent application;
—given guidance or training on the effects which generalised assumptions and prejudices about race can have on selection decisions;
—made aware of the possible misunderstandings that can occur in interviews between persons of different cultural background;

(c) wherever possible, shortlisting and interviewing should not be done by one person alone but should at least be checked at a more senior level.

Genuine Occupational Qualification

ss. 5, 5(2)(d)

1.15 Selection on racial grounds is allowed in certain jobs where being of a particular racial group is a genuine occupational qualification for that job. An example is where the holder of a particular job provides persons of a racial group with personal services promoting their welfare, and those services can most effectively be provided by a person of that group.

Transfers and Training

5–078/11

s. 4(2)(b)

1.16 In order to avoid direct or indirect discrimination it is recommended that:

(a) staff responsible for selecting employees for transfer to other jobs should be instructed to apply selection criteria without unlawful discrimination;

(b) industry or company agreements and arrangements of custom and practice on job transfers should be examined and amended if they are found to contain requirements or conditions which appear to be indirectly discriminatory. For example, if

employees of a particular racial group are concentrated in particular sections, the transfer arrangements should be examined to see if they are unjustifiably and unlawfully restrictive and amended if necessary;
(c) staff responsible for selecting employees for training, whether induction, promotion or skill training should be instructed not to discriminate on racial grounds;
(d) selection criteria for training opportunities should be examined to ensure that they are not indirectly discriminatory.

Dismissal (including redundancy) and Other Detriment

1.17 It is unlawful to discriminate on racial grounds in dismissal, or other detriment to an employee.
It is therefore recommended that: s. 4(2)(c)
(a) staff responsible for selecting employees for dismissal, including redundancy, should be instructed not to discriminate on racial grounds;
(b) selection criteria for redundancies should be examined to ensure that they are not indirectly discriminatory.

Performance Appraisals

1.18 It is unlawful to discriminate on racial grounds in appraisals of s. 4(2)
employee performance.
1.19 It is recommended that:
(a) staff responsible for performance appraisals should be instructed not to discriminate on racial grounds;
(b) assessment criteria should be examined to ensure that they are not unlawfully discriminatory.

Terms of Employment, Benefits, Facilities and Services s.4(2)

1.20 It is unlawful to discriminate on racial grounds in affording terms of 5–078/12
employment and providing benefits, facilities and services for employees.
It is therefore recommended that:
(a) all staff concerned with these aspects of employment should be instructed accordingly;
(b) the criteria governing eligibility should be examined to ensure that they are not unlawfully discriminatory.
1.21 In addition, employees may request extended leave from time to time in order to visit relations in their countries of origin or who have emigrated to other countries. Many employers have policies which allow annual leave entitlement to be accumulated, or extra unpaid leave to be taken to meet these circumstances. Employers should take care to apply such policies consistently and without unlawful discrimination.

Grievance, Disputes and Disciplinary Procedures s.4(2) & s.2

1.22 It is unlawful to discriminate in the operation of grievance, disputes 5–078/13
and disciplinary procedures, for example by victimising an individual through disciplinary measures because he or she has complained about racial discrimination, or given evidence about such a complaint. Employers should not ignore or treat lightly grievances from members of particular racial groups on the assumption that they are over-sensitive about discrimination.

1.23 It is recommended that:
in applying disciplinary procedures consideration should be given to the possible effect on an employee's behaviour of the following:
—racial abuse or other racial provocation;
—communication and comprehension difficulties;
—differences in cultural background or behaviour.

Cultural and Religious Needs

5–078/14 1.24 Where employees have particular cultural and religious needs which conflict with existing work requirements, it is recommended that employers should consider whether it is reasonably practicable to vary or adapt these requirements to enable such needs to be met. For example, it is recommended that they should not refuse employment to a turbanned Sikh because he could not comply with unjustifiable uniform requirements.
Other examples of such needs are:
(*a*) observance of prayer times and religious holidays[36];
(*b*) wearing of dress such as sarees and the trousers worn by Asian women.

ss. 4(2), 28 1.25 Although the Act does not specifically cover religious discrimination, work requirements would generally be unlawful if they have a disproportionately adverse effect on particular racial groups and cannot be shown to be justifiable.[37]

Communications and Language Training for Employees

5–078/15 1.26 Although there is no legal requirement to provide language training, difficulties in communication can endanger equal opportunity in the workforce. In addition, good communications can improve efficiency, promotion prospects and safety and health and create a better understanding between employers, employees and unions. Where the workforce includes current employees whose English is limited it is recommended that steps are taken to ensure that communications are as effective as possible.
1.27 These should include, where reasonably practicable:
(*a*) provision of interpretation and translation facilities, for example, in the communication of grievance and other procedures, and of terms of employment;
(*b*) training in English language and in communication skills[38];
(*c*) training for managers and supervisors in the background and culture of racial minority groups;
(*d*) the use of alternative or additional methods of communication, where employees find it difficult to understand health and safety requirements, for example:
—safety signs; translation of safety notices;
—instructions through interpreters;
—instruction combined with industrial language training.

---

[36] The CRE has issued a guidance paper entitled—"Religious Observance by Muslim Employees".

[37] Genuinely necessary safety requirements may not constitute unlawful discrimination.

[38] Industrial language training is provided by a network of Local Education Authority units throughout the country. Full details of the courses and the comprehensive services offered by these units are available from the National Centre for Industrial Language Training, The Havelock Centre, Havelock Road, Southall, Middx.

Instructions and Pressure to Discriminate

1.28 It is unlawful to instruct or put pressure on others to discriminate on racial grounds.
  (a) An example of an unlawful instruction is:
    —an instruction from a personnel or line manager to junior staff to restrict the numbers of employees from a particular racial group in any particular work;
  (b) An example of pressure to discriminate is:
    —an attempt by a shop steward or group of workers to induce an employer not to recruit members of particular racial groups, for example by threatening industrial action.

1.29 It is also unlawful to discriminate in response to such instructions or pressure.

1.30 The following recommendations are made to avoid unlawful instructions and pressure to discriminate:
  (a) guidance should be given to all employees, and particularly those in positions of authority or influence on the relevant provisions of the law;
  (b) decision-makers should be instructed not to give way to pressure to discriminate;
  (c) giving instructions or bringing pressure to discriminate should be treated as a disciplinary offence.

Victimisation

1.31 It is unlawful to victimise individuals who have made allegations or complaints of racial discrimination or provided information about such discrimination, for example, by disciplining them or dismissing them. (See Introduction, para 3.4.)

1.32 It is recommended that:
  —guidance on this aspect of the law should be given to all employees and particularly to those in positions of influence or authority.

Monitoring Equal Opportunity[39]

1.33 It is recommended that employers should regularly monitor the effects of selection decisions and personnel practices and procedures in order to assess whether equal opportunity is being achieved.

1.34 The information needed for effective monitoring may be obtained in a number of ways. It will best be provided by records showing the ethnic origins of existing employees and job applicants. It is recognised that the need for detailed information and the methods of collecting it will vary according to the circumstances of individual establishments. For example, in small firms or in firms in areas with little or no racial minority settlement it will often be adequate to assess the distribution of employees from personal knowledge and visual identification.

1.35 It is open to employers to adopt the method of monitoring which is best suited to their needs and circumstances, but whichever method is adopted, they should be able to show that it is effective. In order to achieve

---

[39] See the CRE's guidance paper on "Monitoring an Equal Opportunity Policy".

the full commitment of all concerned the chosen method should be discussed and agreed, where appropriate, with trade union or employee representatives.

1.36 Employers should ensure that information on individuals' ethnic origins is collected for the purpose of monitoring equal opportunity alone and is protected from misuse.

1.37 The following is the comprehensive method recommended by the CRE[40]

Analyses should be carried out of:
>   (a) the ethnic composition of the workforce of each plant, department, section, shift and job category, and changes in distribution over periods of time;
>   (b) selection decisions for recruitment, promotion, transfer and training, according to the racial group of candidates, and reasons for these decisions.

1.38 Except in cases where there are large numbers of applicants and the burden on resources would be excessive, reasons for selection and rejection should be recorded at each stage of the selection process, e.g. initial shortlisting and final decisions. Simple categories of reasons for rejection should be adequate for the early sifting stages.

1.39 Selection criteria and personnel procedures should be reviewed to ensure that they do not include requirements or conditions which constitute or may lead to unlawful indirect discrimination.

1.40 This information should be carefully and regularly analysed and, in order to identify areas which may need particular attention, a number of key questions should be asked.

1.41 Is there evidence that individuals from any particular racial group:
>   (a) do not apply for employment or promotion, or that fewer apply than might be expected?
>   (b) are not recruited or promoted at all, or are appointed in a significantly lower proportion than their rate of application?
>   (c) are under-represented in training or in jobs carrying higher pay, status or authority?
>   (d) are concentrated in certain shifts, sections or departments?

1.42 If the answer to any of these questions is yes, the reasons for this should be investigated. If direct or indirect discrimination is found action must be taken to end it immediately.

1.43 It is recommended that deliberate acts of unlawful discrimination by employees are treated as disciplinary offences.

Positive Action[41] *s.38*

1.44 Although they are not legally required, positive measures are allowed by the law to encourage employees and potential employees and provide training for employees who are members of particular racial groups which have been under-represented[42] in particular work. (See

---

[40] This is outlined in detail in "Monitoring an Equal Opportunity Policy".

[41] The CRE has issued a guidance paper on Positive Action, entitled—"Equal Opportunity in Employment—Why Positive Action?"

[42] A racial group is under-represented if, at any time during the previous twelve months, either there was no one of that group doing the work in question, or there were disproportionately few in comparison with the group's proportion in the workforce at that establishment, or in the population from which the employer normally recruits for work at that establishment.

Introduction, para. 5.) Discrimination at the point of selection for work, however, is not permissible in these circumstances.

1.45 Such measures are important for the development of equal opportunity. It is therefore recommended that, where there is under-representation of particular racial groups in particular work, the following measures should be taken wherever appropriate and reasonably practicable:
- (*a*) job advertisements designed to reach members of these groups and to encourage their applications: for example, through the use of the ethnic minority press, as well as other newspapers;
- (*b*) use of the employment agencies and careers offices in areas where these groups are concentrated;
- (*c*) recruitment and training schemes for school leavers designed to reach members of these groups;
- (*d*) encouragement to employees from these groups to apply for promotion or transfer opportunities;
- (*e*) training for promotion or skill training for employees of these groups who lack particular expertise but show potential: supervisory training may include language training.

PART 2

THE RESPONSIBILITIES OF INDIVIDUAL EMPLOYEES

2.1 While the primary responsibility for providing equal opportunity rests with the employer, individual employees at all levels and of all racial groups have responsibilities too. Good race relations depend on them as much as on management, and so their attitudes and activities are very important.

2.2 The following actions by individual employees would be unlawful:
- (*a*) discrimination in the course of their employment against fellow employees or job applicants on racial grounds, for example, in selection decisions for recruitment, promotion, transfer and training;   s. 4   s. 33
- (*b*) inducing, or attempting to induce other employees, unions or management to practise unlawful discrimination. For example, they should not refuse to accept other employees from particular racial groups or refuse to work with a supervisor of a particular racial group;   s. 31
- (*c*) victimising individuals who have made allegations or complaints of racial discrimination or provided information about such discrimination. (See Introduction, para. 3.4.)   s. 2

2.3 To assist in preventing racial discrimination and promoting equal opportunity it is recommended that individual employees should:
- (*a*) co-operate in measures introduced by management designed to ensure equal opportunity and non-discrimination;
- (*b*) where such measures have not been introduced, press for their introduction (through their trade union where appropriate);
- (*c*) draw the attention of management and, where appropriate, their trade unions to suspected discriminatory acts or practices;

(d) refrain from harassment or intimidation of other employees on racial grounds, for example, by attempting to discourage them from continuing employment. Such action may be unlawful if it is taken by employees against those subject to their authority.

2.4 In addition to the responsibilities set out above individual employees from the racial minorities should recognise that in many occupations advancement is dependent on an appropriate standard of English. Similarly an understanding of the industrial relations procedures which apply is often essential for good working relationships.

2.5 They should therefore:
- (a) where appropriate, seek means to improve their standards of English;
- (b) co-operate in industrial language training schemes introduced by employers and/or unions;
- (c) co-operate in training or other schemes designed to inform them of industrial relations procedures, company agreements, work rules, etc;
- (d) where appropriate, participate in discussions with employers and unions, to find solutions to conflicts between cultural or religious needs and production needs.

PART 3

The Responsibilities of Trade Unions

5–078/21

3.1 Trade unions, in common with a number of other organisations, have a dual role as employers and providers of services specifically covered by the Race Relations Act.

s. 11

3.2 In their role as employer, unions have the responsibilities set out in Part 1 of the Code. They also have a responsibility to ensure that their representatives and members do not discriminate against any particular racial group in the admission or treatment of members, or as colleagues, supervisors, or subordinates.

3.3 In addition, trade union officials at national and local level and shop-floor representatives at plant level have an important part to play on behalf of their members in preventing unlawful discrimination and in promoting equal opportunity and good race relations. Trade unions should encourage and press for equal opportunity policies so that measures to prevent discrimination at the workplace can be introduced with the clear commitment of both management and unions.

Admission of Members

5–078/22

3.4 It is unlawful for trade unions to discriminate on racial grounds:
- (a) by refusing membership;

s. 11(2)
- (b) by offering less favourable terms of membership.

Treatment of Members s.11(3)

3.5 It is unlawful for trade unions to discriminate on racial grounds against existing members:

(a) by varying their terms of membership, depriving them of membership or subjecting them to any other detriment; s. 11(3)
(b) by treating them less favourably in the benefits, facilities or services provided. These may include:
    training facilities;
    welfare and insurance schemes;
    entertainment and social events;
    processing of grievances;
    negotiations;
    assistance in disciplinary or dismissal procedures.

3.6 In addition, it is recommended that unions ensure that in cases where members of particular racial groups believe that they are suffering racial discrimination, whether by the employer or the union itself, serious attention is paid to the reasons for this belief and that any discrimination which may be occurring is stopped.

Disciplining Union Members who Discriminate

3.7 It is recommended that deliberate acts of unlawful discrimination by union members are treated as disciplinary offences. 5–078/23

Positive Action s.38(3), (4) & (5)

3.8 Although they are not legally required, positive measures are allowed by the law to encourage and provide training for members of particular racial groups which have been under-represented[43] in trade union membership or in trade union posts. (Discrimination at the point of selection, however, is not permissible in these circumstances.)

3.9 It is recommended that, wherever appropriate and reasonably practicable, trade unions should:
(a) encourage individuals from these groups to join the union. Where appropriate, recruitment material should be translated into other languages;
(b) encourage individuals from these groups to apply for union posts and provide training to help fit them for such posts.

Training and Information

3.10 Training and information play a major part in the avoidance of discrimination and the promotion of equal opportunity. It is recommended that trade unions should: 5–078/24
(a) provide training and information for officers, shop stewards and representatives on their responsibilities for equal opportunity. This training and information should cover:
    the Race Relations Acts and the nature and causes of discrimination;

---

[43] A racial group is under-represented in trade union membership, if at any time during the previous twelve months no persons of that group were in membership, or disproportionately few in comparison with the proportion of persons of that group among those eligible for membership. Under-representation in trade union posts applies under the same twelve month criteria, where there were no persons of a particular racial group in those posts or disproportionately few in comparison with the proportion of that group in the organisation. s. 38(3)

s. 38(4)

the backgrounds of racial minority groups and communication needs;
the effects of prejudice;
equal opportunity policies;
avoiding discrimination when representing members.
(*b*) ensure that members and representatives, whatever their racial group, are informed of their role in the union, and of industrial relations and union procedures and structures. This may be done, for example:
through translation of material;
through encouragement to participate in industrial relations courses and industrial language training.

Pressure to Discriminate s.31
3.11 It is unlawful for trade union members or representatives to induce or to attempt to induce those responsible for employment decisions to discriminate:
(*a*) in the recruitment, promotion, transfer, training or dismissal of employees;
(*b*) in terms of employment, benefits, facilities or services.
3.12 For example, they should not:
(*a*) restrict the numbers of a particular racial group in a section, grade or department;
(*b*) resist changes designed to remove indirect discrimination, such as those in craft apprentice schemes, or in agreements concerning seniority rights or mobility between departments.

Victimisation
3.13 It is unlawful to victimise individuals who have made allegations or complaints of racial discrimination or provided information about such discrimination. (See Introduction, para. 3.4.)

Avoidance of Discrimination
3.14 Where unions are involved in selection decisions for recruitment, promotion, training or transfer, for example through recommendation or veto, it is unlawful for them to discriminate on racial grounds.
3.15 It is recommended that they should instruct their members accordingly and examine their procedures and joint agreements to ensure that they do not contain indirectly discriminatory requirements or conditions, such as:
unjustifiable restrictions on transfers between departments or irrelevant and unjustifiable selection criteria which have a disproportionately adverse effect on particular racial groups.

Union Involvement in Equal Opportunity Policies
3.16 It is recommended that:
(*a*) unions should co-operate in the introduction and implementation of full equal opportunity policies, as defined in paras. 1.3 & 1.4;
(*b*) unions should negotiate the adoption of such policies where they have not been introduced or the extension of existing policies where these are too narrow;
(*c*) unions should co-operate with measures to monitor the progress of equal opportunity policies, or encourage management

to introduce them where they do not already exist. Where appropriate (See paras. 1.33–1.35) this may be done through analysis of the distribution of employees and job applicants according to ethnic origin;

(d) where monitoring shows that discrimination has occurred or is occurring, unions should co-operate in measures to eliminate it;

(e) although positive action[44] is not legally required, unions should encourage management to take such action where there is under-representation of particular racial groups in particular jobs, and where management itself introduces positive action representatives should support it;

(f) similarly, where there are communication difficulties, management should be asked to take whatever action is appropriate to overcome them.

PART 4

THE RESPONSIBILITIES OF EMPLOYMENT AGENCIES

4.1 Employment agencies, in their role as employers, have the responsibilities outlined in Part 1 of the Code. In addition, they have responsibilities as suppliers of job applicants to other employers.

4.2 It is unlawful for employment agencies: (For exceptions see Race Relations Act)

(a) to discriminate on racial grounds in providing services to clients; — s. 14(1)

(b) to publish job advertisements indicating, or which might be understood to indicate that applications from any particular group will not be considered or will be treated more favourably or less favourably than others; — s. 29

(c) to act on directly discriminatory instructions from employers to the effect that applicants from a particular racial group will be rejected or preferred or that their numbers should be restricted; — s. 14(1)

(d) to act on indirectly discriminatory instructions from employers i.e. that requirements or conditions should be applied that would have a disproportionately adverse effect on applicants of a particular racial group and which cannot be shown to be justifiable. — s. 14(1) & s. 1(1)(b)

4.3 It is recommended that agencies should also avoid indicating such conditions or requirements in job advertisements unless they can be shown to be justifiable. Examples in each case may be those relating to educational qualifications or residence.

4.4 It is recommended that staff should be given guidance on their duty not to discriminate and on the effect which generalised assumptions and

---

[44] See 1.44—Positive Action recommendations.

prejudices can have on their treatment of members of particular racial groups.

4.5 In particular staff should be instructed:
  (a) not to ask employers for racial preferences;
  (b) not to draw attention to racial origin when recommending applicants unless the employer is trying to attract applicants of a particular racial group under the exceptions in the Race Relations Act;
  (c) to report a client's refusal to interview an applicant for reasons that are directly or indirectly discriminatory to a supervisor, who should inform the client that discrimination is unlawful. If the client maintains this refusal the agency should inform the applicant of his or her right to complain to an industrial tribunal and to apply to the CRE for assistance. An internal procedure for recording such cases should be operated;
  (d) to inform their supervisor if they believe that an applicant, though interviewed, has been rejected on racial grounds. If the supervisor is satisfied that there are grounds for this belief, he or she should arrange for the applicant to be informed of the right to complain to an industrial tribunal and to apply to the CRE for assistance. An internal procedure for recording such cases should be operated;
  (e) to treat job applicants without discrimination. For example, they should not send applicants from particular racial groups to only those employers who are believed to be willing to accept them, or restrict the range of job opportunities for such applicants because of assumptions about their abilities based on race or colour.

4.6 It is recommended that employment agencies should discontinue their services to employers who give unlawful discriminatory instructions and who refuse to withdraw them.

4.7 It is recommended that employment agencies should monitor the effectiveness of the measures they take for ensuring that no unlawful discrimination occurs. For example, where reasonably practicable they should make periodic checks to ensure that applicants from particular racial groups are being referred for suitable jobs for which they are qualified at a similar rate to that for other comparable applicants.

APPENDIX 3

5–079

TUC Disputes Principles and Procedures

Incorporating changes made by the 1979 Trades Union Congress

SECTION I

RELATIONS BETWEEN UNIONS

TUC Principles Governing Relations Betwen Unions

Preface

5–079 The following Principles constitute a code of conduct accepted as morally binding by affiliated organisations. They are not intended by such organisations or by the Trades Union Congress to be a legally enforceable contracts. The Principles include the main text and the Notes and both are to be read together as having equal status and validity.

Principle 1

Each union shall consider developing joint working agreements with unions with whom they are in frequent contact, and in particular developing (a) procedures for resolving particular issues and (b) specific arrangements concerning spheres of influence, transfers of members and benefit rights, recognition of cards, and demaracation of work. Unions should also ensure that members and officials are made fully aware of the terms of existing agreements, and of the importance of following the agreed procedures for the avoidance and settlement of disputes.

5–080

NOTES ON PRINCIPLE 1

(a) *Procedures for resolving particular issues* are usually between two unions, cover all the members, and are capable of dealing with any issue that arises between the two unions. They normally provide for an issue that arises between the two unions. They normally provide for an unresolved issue to be processed through the district, regional and national levels of the procedure. They may also provide for arbitration by a third party (for example, by the TUC) if the final stage of the procedure has been exhausted without agreement being reached. Such agreements may also incorporate joint standing committees to review relations between the unions and to promote closer working arrangements.

(b) *Specific arrangements* concerning:
    (i) spheres of influence (trade union organisation and representation);
    (ii) transfers of members and benefit rights;
    (iii) recognition of cards;
    (iv) demaracation of work

are usually between two unions but may be on a wider basis (for example, between a number of unions on the trade union side of a joint negotiating body), particularly when they relate to spheres of influence concerning trade union organisation. They generally apply to members in a particular establishment or industry though in the case of agreements they will normally apply to all the members of the signatory unions.

(c) *Advice and assistance*: The General Council will assist unions in drawing up such arrangements and procedures and, if requested, will be pleased to arrange meetings between unions.

(d) *Mergers*: Mergers between affiliated unions in frequent contact with one another are in general a desirable means of strengthening trade union organisation and the General Council will therefore be glad to provide advice and assistance to unions considering mergers.

Affiliated unions should consult other affiliates with an interest when they are considering a merger with a non-affiliated organisation. In the event of disagreement it is open to any affiliated union involved to refer the matter to the TUC for advice and conciliation but not adjudication by a Dispute Committee unless by agreement between all the affiliated unions concerned.

Affiliated unions will of course appreciate that it is a matter of good trade union practice not to intervene in any way in a ballot being conducted by other unions about a merger.

(e) *Sole negotiating rights and union membership agreements*: When making sole negotiating rights or union membership agreements or arrangements affiliated unions should have regard to the interest of other unions which may be affected and should consider their position in the drafting of such agreements. Where unions cannot resolve these matters between themselves they may be referred to the TUC for advice and conciliation and if necessary to a Dispute Committee for adjudication.

Principle 2

5–081   No one who is or has recently been a member of any affiliated union should be accepted into membership in another without inquiry of his present or former union. The present or former union shall be under an obligation to reply within 21 days of the inquiry, stating:
 (a) Whether the applicant has tendered his resignation;
 (b) Whether he is clear on the books;
 (c) Whether he is under discipline or penalty;
 (d) Whether there are any other reasons why the applicant should not be accepted.

If the present or former union objects to the transfer, and the inquiring union considers the objection to be unreasonable, the inquiring union shall not accept the application into membership but shall maintain the status quo with regard to membership. If the problem cannot be mutually resolved it should be referred to the TUC for adjudication.

A union should not accept an applicant into membership if no reply has been received 21 days after the inquiry, but in such circumstances a union may write again to the present or former union, sending a copy of the letter to the head office of the union if the correspondence is with a branch, stating that if no reply is received within a further 14 days they intend to accept the applicant into membership. Where the union to which application is being made is dealing directly with the head office of the present or former union, a copy of this communication may be sent to the TUC.

NOTES ON PRINCIPLE 2
 (a) Where unions are in frequent contact, they should advise one another of the appropriate level at which membership inquiries should be made.
 (b) No member should be allowed to escape his financial obligations by leaving one union while in arrears and by joining another.
 (c) The reference to "recently" in the first sentence of Principle 2 shall normally be understood to apply to applicants who have contributed to an affiliated union during the preceding 52 weeks. Unions should however appreciate that this is intended merely as a guide and much difficulty will be avoided if inquiries are made in all cases where previous trade union membership is known.

Principle 3

5–082   Each union shall use an inquiry form as proposed by the General Council in the case of all inquiries under Principle 2 above, and forward reasoned replies on any such form as they may receive from an inquiring union.

NOTES ON PRINCIPLE 3

A model of the inquiry form is [below]. It will help to avoid difficulties if inquiries are always made by use of the model inquiry form and a separate form is used in respect of each individual.

Principle 4

A union shall not accept a member of another union where that union objects to the transfer (see Principle 2 above), or where inquiry shows that the member is:
   (a) under discipline;
   (b) engaged in a trade dispute;
   (c) in arrears with contributions.

5–083

NOTES ON PRINCIPLE 4

(a) It should be a general understanding that both national and local officials of trade unions should refrain from speaking or acting adversely to the interests of any other union during any period in which the members of the latter union are participating in a trade dispute. Much trouble could be avoided if unions about to participate in a trade dispute would take care to inform other unions whose members would be likely to be affected thereby. (See Congress Rule II on pp. 25–26).

(b) With regard to the question of arrears in (c) above, a number of affiliated unions have a rule or rules excluding members who have been in arrears for a specified period of time. However, although a union with such a rule regards an individual in such arrears as being no longer a member entitled to participate in the work of the union, it does not necessarily mean that the union regards the individual as being automatically free to join another organisation. Any union which considers that another union has unreasonably objected to a transfer on the grounds of arrears (or for any other reason) should not therefore accept an individual into membership, but should refer the matter to the TUC for adjudication.

Principle 5

No union shall commence organising activities at any establishment or undertaking in respect of any grade or grades of workers in which another union has the majority of workers employed and negotiates wages and conditions, unless by arrangement with that union.

5–084

NOTES ON PRINCIPLE 5

Where a union has membership but does not have a majority in respect of any grade or grades of workers and/or does not negotiate terms and conditions of employment for such grade or grades, another union wishing to organise should engage in consultation as soon as it is aware (or has drawn to its attention by the existing union) that another union has membership in the grade or grades concerned before it commences organising activities. If there is no agreement, and the matter is referred by either union to the TUC and a Disputes Committee adjudicates, the Disputes Committee will have regard to the following factors:
   (i) the efforts which the union opposing the entry of another union or unions has itself made in trying to secure or retain a majority membership, the period over which any such efforts have been made, the extent and causes of any difficulties encountered by that union, and the likely prospect of that union securing or regaining a majority membership and/or negotiating rights;

(ii) any existing collective bargaining or other representation arrangements in the establishment, company or industry.

Principle 6

5–085　Each union shall include in its membership form questions on the lines of the TUC model form in regard to past or present membership of another union.

The essential questions on the model form are as follows:

Are you, or have you been a member of any other trade union or unions? (*See Note below.*) Give the name of the union or unions, together with the name of the branch or branches of that union or those unions of which you are or were formerly a member. (*See Note below.*)

If you are a member of any other trade union and are not in benefit, please state the amount of your arrears.

Each union should also include in its membership form a note pointing out that dual *membership* is valid only if the two unions concerned have jointly agreed to it.

NOTE ON PRINCIPLE 6

Failure by a union to include the necessary questions and note on its application form will make it impossible for a union to pursue the course of inquiry laid down, and will be regarded by a Disputes Committee as an important factor in determining any complaint brought against such a union.

Principle 7

5–086　In cases of inter-union disputes (whether relating to trade union membership, trade union recognition, demarcation of work, or any other difficulty) no official strike should take place before the TUC has been able to examine the issue.

If a dispute (short of a strike) emerges between two or more unions there is an obligation on the unions concerned to notify the TUC forthwith of the circumstances so that it can be dealt with by a TUC Disputes Committee.

Principle 8

5–087　If an inter-union dispute has led to an authorised stoppage of work there is an obligation on the union or unions concerned to take immediate and energetic steps to get their members to resume normal working; the union or unions concerned are also required to notify the TUC as soon as possible of the dispute and of the steps they have taken, or are taking, to secure a resumption of work.

Employment Protection Act 1975

5–088　The Employment Protection Act enables an independent trade union to refer a recognition issue to the Advisory, Conciliation and Arbitration Service (ACAS) which may, after investigation, make a recommendation about recognition. In some circumstances, however, more than one union may have an interest and unions should continue to follow the Principles and Procedures set out in this booklet.

An affiliated union should not therefore invoke the Act's procedure on recognition without consultation and agreement with any other affiliated union with an interest in the matter and should in any event notify the TUC of its intention to proceed with a section 11 reference in sufficient time for inquiries to be made as to whether any other unions have an interest in the matter. Where there is a disagreement between affiliated unions about a claim for recognition the matter should be resolved through the TUC Disputes Procedures.

Guidance on the various provisions of the Employment Protection Act, including recognition, is set out in a series of booklets which are available from the TUC.

Regulations Governing Procedure in Regard to Disputes Between Affiliated Organisations

A. In the event of a dispute arising between affiliated unions, there should be a normal maximum period of eight weeks in which the unions concerned should have made efforts to resolve the issues between them including a meeting at national level (see note on time limits).

B. On receiving a complaint the General Secretary or any person to whom he delegates authority shall ascertain whether the complainant union has taken the matter up with the head office of the respondent union, and no dispute between unions shall be heard by a Disputes Committee (see Regulation E below) until the General Secretary or any person to whom he delegates authority is assured that the unions have made an effort to settle the dispute between themselves including holding a meeting between national officials, although in exceptional circumstances this requirement may be waived.

In a case of alleged poaching, the effort at settlement should include an examination of the specific cases.

C. If there is machinery within the industry for the settlement of disputes, no dispute between unions shall be heard by a Disputes Committee unless the General Secretary or any person to whom he delegates authority is assured that such machinery has been tried and has failed to settle the dispute, although in exceptional circumstances this requirement may be waived.

D. Where it appears to the General Secretary or any person to whom he delegates authority that agreement might be reached by conciliation at an informal conference under the chairmanship of a member of the General Council or the General Secretary or any person appointed by the General Secretary, efforts shall be made to persuade the disputants to follow this method. If the unions concerned agree to attend an informal conference, they will be expected to agree within 14 *days* on a date for the conference which is convenient to the TUC and the unions.

E. Where he considers it appropriate, the General Secretary may refer a dispute between affiliated organisations to a Disputes Committee. A Disputes Committee shall consist of not less than three persons appointed by or under the authority of the General Secretary, being members of a panel comprising all members of the General Council and experienced union officials nominated by affiliated organisations. A member of the General Council shall act as Chairman of a Disputes Committee. Where the General Secretary or the General Council decides that an investigation on the spot will be useful, the Disputes Committee shall, so far as is practicable, include members of the panel who live in a region adjacent to the locality of the dispute. No person shall be appointed as a member of a

5–089

Disputes Committee who is himself, or who is a member of a union which is, immediately involved in the dispute.

F. There shall be a Secretary to the Disputes Committees of the Congress ("the Secretary'), appointed by the General Secretary. The Secretary may delegate any of his duties or functions under these Regulations to such persons as he sees fit, provided always that the Secretary shall remain responsible therefore to the General Secretary.

G. The Secretary shall require the complainant union to furnish (if they have not already done so) explicit particulars of the complaint.

(1) In a case of alleged poaching of members the following particulars shall be provided, so far as applicable to the case:
  (a) the names of the persons concerned, their places of work, and their grade or occupation;
  (b) the date of joining the complainant union;
  (c) the date up to which contributions have been paid;
  (d) arrears, if any; and
  (e) letters of resignation or application for transfer, if any.

In ordinary circumstances there shall be no hearing by a Disputes Committee until these particulars or at least (a), (b), (c) and (d) are in the hands of the Secretary.

(2) In cases concerning recognition, demarcation or wages and conditions of employment the complainant union shall provide the following particulars, so far as they are relevant to the case:
  (f) its agreement(s) with the employer or federation of employers concerned;
  (g) the extent of membership among the grade of workers concerned;
  (h) its agreement(s) with the union(s) with whom it is in dispute; and
  (i) a description of the work in dispute.

H. Subject to Regulations A, B, C, D, and G, above, the complaint with full particulars shall be conveyed by the TUC to the respondent union with a request for their comments. The respondent union shall send a considered reply to the TUC within 21 *days*.

(1) In a complaint of poaching, the respondent union shall be asked definitely whether the workers concerned are members of their union and if so, shall be required to provide the following particulars:
  (a) original application forms;
  (b) the date of acceptance into the union (if not included above);
  (c) applications for transfers, if any.

(2) In cases concerning recognition, demarcation of work, or wages and conditions of employment the respondent union shall provide the following particulars, so far as they are relevant to the case:
  (d) its agreement(s) with the employer or federation or employers concerned;
  (e) the extent of its membership among the grade of workers concerned;
  (f) its agreement(s) with the union(s) with whom it is in dispute; and
  (g) a description of the work in dispute.

I. The reply of the respondent union shall be sent by the TUC to the complainant union which shall within 21 *days* inform the TUC whether it wishes to pursue the complaint.

J. Where a union wishes to pursue the complaint the TUC will inform the respondent union, and both unions will be expected to agree within 14 *days* on a date for a Disputes Committee hearing which is convenient to the TUC and the unions.

K. The General Secretary shall be empowered in the case of unnecessary or wilful delay on the part of either union at any stage in the procedure to fix a date for a Disputes Committee hearing.

L. In addition to the information provided under the preceding Regulations, unions shall endeavour (wherever possible) to submit a written statement of their case to the Secretary at least seven days before the date of the hearing.

M. At the hearing of the complaint before the Disputes Committee no new complaint may be raised without the consent of the Disputes Committee. In the event of such a consent being granted the disputants shall be given a fair opportunity to prepare and present their cases on the new matter.

N. At the hearing, corroborative evidence may be produced. Originals or copies of all documents read or quoted by the disputants shall be handed to the Secretary and copies of such documents supplied to the other disputants and to the Disputes Committee.

O. A Disputes Committee shall investigate the causes and circumstances of the dispute and shall give to the disputants a full opportunity to submit factual information and to present their views to the Disputes Committee. With the agreement of the disputants the Disputes Committee may discuss the dispute with such local union representatives and management representatives as it considers appropriate. The Disputes Committee shall otherwise conduct its proceedings in such manner as it sees fit.

P. The basic approach of the Disputes Committee shall be to seek to obtain an agreed settlement, whether of a permanent or an interim character, which is acceptable to all the disputants; and the Disputes Committee may at any time make such recommendations as it sees fit. But whenever the Disputes Committee considers it to be necessary, it shall make an award. In deciding the dispute the Disputes Committee shall have general regard to the interests of the trade union Movement and to the declared principles or declared policy of Congress but shall in particular be guided by the *Principles Governing Relations Between Unions* (currently set out in the booklet, *TUC Disputes Principles and Procedures*), as amended by the General Council and adopted by the Congress from time to time.

Q. The General Secretary shall send copies of the award of the Disputes Committee to all the disputants and to the General Council.

Time Limits

This note summarises the time limits to which reference is made in the above Regulations.

The 1979 Congress decided that time limits should be introduced at each stage of the Disputes Procedures. Unions will be expected to have regard to these time limits. However, they are not to be regarded as fixed times for carrying out the various stages of the procedure; rather unions should aim to complete the various stages in less than the maximum time which is laid down.

The time limits are as follows:

—a maximum period of *eight weeks* in which the unions concerned should have made efforts to resolve the issues between them including a meeting at national level. (Even where unions deal with disputes at, say, three levels—district, region and national—it does not seem unreasonable that a local meeting should be held within two weeks and any subsequent meeting within three weeks at each stage) (Regulation A).

—if the matter is reported to the TUC, and the TUC is satisfied that it has obtained the information from the complainant union as required under Regulation G, it will send it to the respondent union which shall send a considered reply to the TUC within 21 *days* (Regulation H).

—the TUC will send the reply of the respondent union to the complainant union which shall within 21 *days* inform the TUC whether it wishes to pursue the complaint (Regulation I).

—where a union wishes to pursue the complaint the TUC will inform the respondent union and both unions will be expected to agree within 14 *days* on a date for a conciliation meeting or a Dispute Committee hearing which is convenient to the TUC and the unions (Regulations D and J).

The Role of TUC Disputes Committees in Disputes Between Affiliated Organisations

5–091 A Disputes Committee's basic approach will be to seek to obtain a settlement, whether of a permanent or an interim character, which is acceptable to all the parties involved. Depending on the circumstances, terms of a permanent or interim settlement may be accompanied by or embodied in a formal award or recommendation.

Where the Committee find, having regard to Principles 7 and 8, that there should have been no stoppage of work, they will require the union or unions concerned to take energetic steps to obtain a resumption of work.

Disputes between unions fall wholly or mainly into one of four categories:

(a) a difference about the union to which a particular individual or group of workers should belong (*membership*);
(b) a difference about which unions should be recognised (*recognition*);
(c) a difference about which union members should carry out particular work (*demarcation*);
(d) a difference about the policy which should be purused in respect of terms and conditions of employment (*wages and conditions*).

In respect of cases (c) *demarcation* and (d) *wages and conditions* the solution will usually depend upon subsequent agreement with the employer, and as a consequence the Disputes Committee's decision will probably take the form of a *recommendation*. The Committee will seek to establish that the parties to the dispute are prepared to act on the recommendation without delay, and if the employer indicates that he is prepared to accept the TUC's findings an award will be made.

In respect of cases (a) *membership* and (b) *recognition* the Committee will make an *award* if discussions do not lead to a solution which is acceptable to the unions concerned.

SECTION II

DISPUTES BETWEEN EMPLOYERS AND UNIONS

NOTIFICATION OF DISPUTES

5–092 Apart from the requirements of Principles 7 and 8 on unions to avoid stoppages of work arising from inter-union disputes, the union or unions concerned have the obligation to notify the TUC of any dispute, constitutional or unconstitutional, authorised or unauthorised, between a union and an employer, which involves directly or indirectly large bodies of workers, or which, if protracted, may have serious consequences.

Most industrial disputes are of short duration and involve few workers either directly or indirectly, and the General Council recognise the difficulties that may arise in deciding whether a particular dispute is of such a nature that it falls into the category described in the previous paragraph. Moreover, the union or unions concerned will be making every effort to secure a speedy settlement. Therefore, the only general advice that can be given to unions on the question of disputes involving only small numbers of workers is to notify the TUC of any dispute where they themselves cannot be certain that it will be settled speedily and will not have wider repercussions.

Action by the TUC

Even before notification by the union or unions directly concerned, the TUC may take an initiative. In all cases, whatever the source of information, the TUC General Secretary will discuss with the union or unions concerned the causes and circumstances of the dispute, and whether the stage has been reached where it would be appropriate for the TUC to give assistance towards the settlement of the dispute. 5–093

The TUC will expect the union or unions concerned to ensure that every effort is made to settle the dispute through the normal procedures at local, district and national level in the industry.

The possibility of assistance being given by the Advisory Conciliation and Arbitration Service will also be considered in cases where this appears to be suitable.

Where it has been decided that the TUC should take action to assist in the settlement of a dispute the General Secretary of the TUC will decide on the most appropriate method of resolving the issue. Because of the importance of maintaining a flexible approach this may take various forms, ranging from informal discussions to consideration by a Disputes Committee.

Where a dispute with an employer is considered by a Disputes Committee, the Committee will normally make a recommendation and will seek to establish that the parties to the dispute are prepared to act on it without delay. The recommendation may also include suggestions for changes in the negotiating arrangements and/or the disputes procedure to help to avoid a similar difficulty occurring in future.

If it is found in a particular case that there is a strong element of inter-union difficulty, and if the employer indicates that he will be prepared to accept the TUC's findings, the Committee may make an award.

Section III

Compliance with Decisions and TUC Rules 11, 12 and 13

Implementation of Awards of Disputes Committee
The 1956 Congress decided "that in view of the imperative need to maintain effective machinery for the settlement of inter-union disputes it was 5–094

necessary for all affiliated unions to amend their rules to enable Executives to exclude a member if required to do so in order to conform to an award of a Disputes Committee."

Model Rule

The "Model Rule" is given below in the form endorsed by the 1976 Congress.

"Notwithstanding anything in these rules (the Executive*) may by giving six weeks' notice in writing terminate the membership of any member if necessary in order to comply with a decision of a Disputes Committee of the Trades Union Congress."

* The name to be inserted here must be the exact name of the authority to be vested with the power to act in accordance with the rule, *e.g.* Executive Committee, Executive Council, etc.

NOTE: The 1976 Congress agreed on a slight amendment to the Model Rule by changing "the Disputes Committee" to "a Disputes Committee." Affiliated unions were recommended to amend their rules at an appropriate occasion.

Compliance with Decisions

Affiliated unions are required to act in accordance with the procedure set out in rule 11 and rule 12 and to abide by decisions of the General Council and Disputes Committees.

The General Council will require the union or unions concerned to satisfy them that they have done all that they can reasonably be expected to do to secure compliance with such a decision, including taking action within their own rules if necessary.

Any refusal on the part of an affiliated union to give effect to a decision will be dealt with under rule 11, 12 or 13 as may be appropriate.

Advice

If, in a particular case, a union is in doubt about its obligations under rule 11 and rule 12, about its capacity to give effect to those obligations, or about the course of action it should follow in accordance with this procedure, the TUC's advice should be sought.

TUC Rules 11, 12 and 13

TUC rules 11, 12 and 13 are set out below in the form agreed at the annual Trades Union Congress in September 1976.

RULE 11

INDUSTRIAL DISPUTES

5–095 (a) It shall be an obligation upon the affiliated organisations to keep the General Secretary informed with regard to matters arising between them and their employers and/or between one organisation and another, including unauthorised and unconstitutional stoppages of work, in particular where such matters may involve directly or indirectly large bodies of workers. The General Council or the General Secretary shall (if either should consider it necessary) disseminate the information as soon as possible to all organisations which are affiliated to the Congress and which may be either directly or indirectly affected.

(b) The general policy of the General Council shall be that unless requested to do so by the affiliated organisation or organisations concerned, neither the General Council nor the General Secretary shall intervene so long as there is a prospect of whatever difference may exist on the matters in question being amicably settled by means of the machinery of negotiation existing in the trades affected.

(c) If, however, a situation has arisen, or is likely to arise, in which other bodies of workpeople affiliated to Congress might be involved in a stoppage of work or their wages, hours and conditions of employment imperilled, the General Council or the General Secretary may investigate the matter by calling representatives of the organisation or organisations concerned into consultation, and may use their influence or his influence (as the case may be) to effect a just settlement of the difference. In this connection the General Council or the General Secretary, having given an opportunity to each organisation concerned to present its views on the matter and having ascertained the facts relating to the difference, may tender their or his considered opinion and advice thereon to the organisation or organisations concerned. Should the organisation or organisations refuse such assistance or advice, the General Secretary shall duly report thereon to the General Council and/or the General Council shall duly report thereon to Congress or deal with the organisation under Clauses (b), (c), (d) and (h) of rule 13.

(d) Whenever the General Council intervenes in relation to a matter within the provision of clause (a) of this rule, and the organisation or organisations concerned accept the assistance and advice of the General Council, and where despite the efforts of the General Council the policy of the employers enforces a stoppage of work by strike or lock-out, the General Council shall forthwith take steps to organise on behalf of the organisation or organisations concerned all such moral and material support as the circumstances of the dispute may appear to justify.

Rule 12

Disputes Between Affiliated Organisations

(a) Where disputes arise or threaten to arise between affiliated organisations, the General Council or the General Secretary shall use their or his influence (as the case may be) to promote a settlement.

(b) It shall be an obligation on the affiliated organisation or organisations concerned to notify the General Secretary when an official stoppage of work is contemplated in any dispute between affiliated organisations, whether relating to trade union recognition, trade union membership, demarcation of work, or any other difficulty. No affiliated organisation shall authorise such a stoppage of work until the dispute has been dealt with under the provisions of clauses (e) to (h) of this rule.

(c) Where a dispute between unions has led to an unauthorised stoppage of work, it shall be an obligation of the affiliated organisation or organisations concerned to take immediate and energetic steps to obtain a resumption of work.

(d) The affiliated organisation or organisations concerned shall notify the General Secretary as soon as possible of any stoppage of work which

5–096

involves directly or indirectly large bodies of workers or which, if protracted, may have serious consequences. In addition to such notiication, the affiliated organisation or organisations concerned shall inform the General Secretary of the causes and circumstances of the dispute and of the steps taken or proposed by it or by them to secure a resumption of work.

(e) Either upon notification from an affiliated organisation as required by clause (b) or clause (d) of this rule, or upon the application of an affiliated organisation, or whenever he considers it to be necessary, the General Secretary may investigate cases of dispute or disagreement between affiliated organisations and may decide on the most appropriate method of resolving the issue. Where he considers it appropriate, the General Secretary may refer any such case to a Disputes Committee of the Congress for resolution in accordance with the regulations governing procedure in regard to disputes between affiliated organisations (as amended by the General Council and adopted by the Congress from time to time). In the event of such a reference, the General Secretary may summon affiliated organisations to appear as parties before a Disputes Committee and shall require such organisations to submit to that Committee any information which he or the Committee considers to be essential to enable the Committee to adjudicate upon the case.

(f) If an affiliated organisation refuses or fails to respond to a summons by the General Secretary to appear before a Disputes Committee, the General Secretary shall investigate the circumstances of such a refusal or failure by calling representatives of the organisation into consultation and inviting the organisation to give reasons for its conduct. If, after such investigation, the General Secretary does not withdraw his summons and the organisation persists in its refusal or failure to appear before the Disputes Committee the General Secretary shall report the matter to the General Council who may deal with the organisation under clause (h) of this rule as if it were a case of failure by that organisation to comply with an award of a Disputes Committee.

(g) If an organisation which is a party to a dispute fails or refuses to submit its case to a Disputes Committee as provided by this rule, the Disputes Committee may proceed to make an award in the absence of that organisation and in any event it shall not be permissible for that organisation to raise the dispute at any Annual Congress.

(h) Affiliated organisations summoned by the General Secretary to appear as parties before a Disputes Committee shall be bound by any award of the Disputes Committee and shall comply forthwith with such award. Should any such organisation refuse or fail forthwith to carry into effect such an award (in whole or in part) th General Council having received the award may report on the matter as they think fit to all affiliated organisations, and/or may either:

  (i) deal with the organisation under clauses (b), (c), (d) and (h) of the rule 13; or
  (ii) report the matter to the next Annual Congress to be dealt with as that Congress may decide.

Rule 13

Conduct of Affiliated Organisations

(a) If at any time there appears to the General Council to be justification for an investigation into the conduct of any affiliated organisation on the grounds that the activities of such organisation may be detrimental to the interests of the trade union Movement or contrary to the declared principles or declared policy of the Congress, the General Council shall summon such organisation to appear by duly appointed representatives before them or before such Committee as the General Council considers appropriate in order that such activities may be investigated. In the event of the organisation failing to attend, the investigation shall proceed in its absence.

(b) If after an investigation under
    (i) clause (a) of this rule; or
    (ii) an investigation under clause (c) of rule 11; or
    (iii) an investigation and report to the General Council by the General Secretrary under clause (f) of rule 12; or
    (iv) an investigation by a Disputes Committee under clauses (e) and (g) of rule 12 and a refusal or failure to comply with its award under clause (h) of rule 12;

it appears to the General Council that the activities of the organisation may be detrimental to the interests of the trade union Movement or contrary to the declared principles or declared policy of Congress, the General Council shall notify the organisation of that fact, specifying the grounds on which that charge is made and inviting the organisation to present its views to the General Council. If, after considering those views, the General Council decide that the said activities are detrimental to the interests of the trade union Movement or contrary to the declared principles or declared policy of Congress, the General Council shall direct the organisation to discontinue such activities forthwith and undertake not to engage therein in the future.

(c) Should the organisation disobey such direction, or fail to give such undertaking, the General Council are hereby empowered in their discretion to order that the organisation be forthwith suspended from membership of the Congress until the next Annual Congress.

(d) The General Council shall submit a report upon the matter to the next Annual Congress.

(e) No affiliated organisation shall circularise, either in writing or by general oral communication, other affiliated organisations upon any matter concerning the business of the Congress, without first securing the General Council's authorisation for such circularisation.

(f) Should any such unauthorised circularisation take place concerning a motion for the Agenda of the Annual Congress or any Special Congress or Conferences, and the General Council after investigation decide that those responsible for such motion connived at, or were party to, or concerned with such circularisation, the motion shall not be included in the Agenda.

(g) The General Council may investigate any violation of the provision of clauses (e) and (f), and if after such investigation they decide that any organisation has acted deliberately in such violation they may deal with the organisation by investigation, suspension and report under the terms of clauses (b), (c) and (d) of this rule.

(h) Any affiliated organisation dealt with under this rule shall have the right to appeal to the next Annual Congress and may appoint delegates in accordance with rules 17 and 18 to represent the organisation upon the appeal and at the Annual Congress if the appeal is allowed. Congress shall upon such appeal have final authority to deal with the matter by way of readmission, further suspension or exclusion from membership of the Congress.

INDEX

ACCOUNT,
  meaning of, 1–117
ADVERTISEMENTS, 1–226
  meaning of, 1–266, 1–409
  racial discrimination, and, 1–365
ADVISORY, CONCILIATION AND ARBITRATION SERVICE, 1–276 *et seq.*
  advice, 1–289
  allowances, 1–333
  arbitration, 1–288
  Central Arbitration Committee, 1–295
  certification as independent trade union, 1–293
  Certification Officer, 1–292
  Codes of Practice, 1–291
  conciliation, 1–277
  constitution of, 1–331
  custody of documents, 1–294
  expenses, 1–333
  inquiry, 1–290
  remuneration, 1–333
  sums payable on retirement, 1–333
AGRICULTURAL WAGES ACTS,
  amendments of, 1–302
AGRICULTURAL WAGES BOARD,
  powers of, 1–334
AGRICULTURAL WAGES ORDERS, 1–140
AMALGAMATED UNION,
  meaning of, 1–128
ANTE-NATAL CARE,
  time off work for, 1–459
APPEALS,
  disciplinary procedures, and, 5–015
  improvement notice, and, 1–160
  prohibition notice, and, 1–160
APPORTIONMENT, 1–018 *et seq.*
  rents, of, 1–019, 1–024
APPRENTICESHIP,
  bankruptcy, and, 1–083
ARTIFICERS,
  contracts for hiring,
    current coin of realm, in, 1–002
AUDITORS, 1–195
  appointment of, 1–195
  qualifications of, 1–195
  removal of, 1–195

BALLOTS, 1–665 *et seq.*
  arrangements to hold, 2–051

BALLOTS—*cont.*
  funds for, 2–098
    conditions to be satisfied, 2–049
    regulations, 2–047, 2–051
    payments towards stationery and printing expenditure, 2–050
    postal costs, 2–050
  secret, 1–665
    employer's premises, on, 1–666
    union membership agreement, as to, 1–488
BANK,
  meaning of, 1–117
BANKNOTES,
  payment of wages in, 1–008
BANKRUPTCY, 1–069
  amendment of Acts of 1913 and 1914, 1–104
  explanation of Act of 1914, s.33, 1–098
  preferential claim in case of apprenticeship, 1–083
  priority of debts, 1–082
BARTER, 1–051
BREACH OF CONTRACT, 1–027
  injury, involving, 1–027
BUSINESS,
  change of ownership, 1–528

CASH,
  payment in, 1–051
CENTRAL ARBITRATION COMMITTEE, 1–295 *et seq.*, 1–144
  constitution of, 1–332
  determination of award, 1–300
  determination of claim, 1–300
CENTRAL CO-ORDINATING COMMITTEES, 1–641
CERTIFICATION OFFICER,
  meaning of, 1–079
  notice of appeal from decision of, form, 2–062
CHARITIES,
  racial discrimination, and, 1–369/1
  sex discrimination, and, 1–231
CIVIL SERVANT,
  redundancy rebate of, 1–544, 1–545
CLOSED SHOP, 5–058 *et seq.*
  ballot on,
    entitlement to vote, 5–078
  Code of Practice, 5–058 *et seq.*

CLOSED SHOP—*cont.*
common law rights, and, 5–064
content of agreements, 5–068
employers, and, 5–066
freedom of the press, and, 5–076
industrial action, and, 5–075
joinder of actions, and, 5–062
operation of new or existing
  agreements, 5–071, 5–072
periodic review of, 5–069
practical guidance on, 5–065, 5–072
remedies, and, 5–061
scope of arrangements, 5–068
secret ballots, and, 5–062, 5–070
trade unions, and, 5–067
unfair dismissal, and, 5–060
union procedures, and, 5–074
union rules, and, 5–074
COIN,
payment of wages in, 1–004, 1–005
COLLECTIVE AGREEMENTS, 1–180
meaning of, 1–192
redundancy on, 1–311
COLLECTIVE BARGAINING, 3–042
COLLECTIVE DISPUTES PROCEDURES,
5–008
COLLECTIVE REDUNDANCIES, 3–018
  et seq.
consultation procedure, 3–020
final provisions, 3–023
meaning of, 3–019
procedure for, 3–021, 3–022
COMMISSION FOR RACIAL EQUALITY,
  1–376 *et seq.*, 1–412
annual reports, 1–380
assistance by, 1–397
assistance to organisations, 1–378
Codes of Practice, 1–381, 5–078/1 *et
  seq. See also* RACE RELATIONS.
duties of, 1–376
education, 1–379
establishment of, 1–376
investigations, 1–382, 1–386
research, 1–379
staff, 1–413
COMPANIES, 1–102 *et seq.*, 1–133 *et seq.*,
  1–656 *et seq.*, 1–678 *et seq.*
accounts,
  employees receiving more than
    £20,000 a year, particulars of,
    1–133
employees,
  power to provide for, 1–662
exemptions for individual accounts,
  1–678
preferential payments,
  amendments as to, 1–103
winding up, 1–103

COMPENSATION,
unfair dismissal, and, 1–503, 1–510
CONCILIATION OFFICES, 1–566, 1–567
general provisions, 1–312
CONDITIONS OF EMPLOYMENT,
criminal liability, 1–636
false entries in records, 1–639
notices, 1–636
offices, 1–638
power to fix, 1–630, 1–631
power to obtain information, 1–640
records, 1–636
reports on, 1–642
CONFINEMENT, 1–461
dismissal, and, 1–484
redundancy payment, and, 1–520
CONSPIRACY, 1–026 *et seq.*, 1–421 *et seq.*
amendment of law, 4–006
exemptions from liability, 1–422
meaning of, 1–421
penalties, and, 1–030, 1–423
regulations as to evidence, 1–032
restrictions on institution of
  proceedings for, 1–424
summary proceedings, and, 1–031
CONTINUOUS EMPLOYMENT,
computation of, 1–582
periods of,
  computation of, 1–691
CONTRACT,
fixed term, for, 1–575
illegality of, 1–100
meaning of, 1–015
CONTRACT OF EMPLOYMENT,
continuation of,
  orders for, 1–512
meaning of, 1–192, 1–584
CONTRACTING OUT, 1–573
restrictions on, 1–319
CORPORATION,
offences by, 1–318
COURTS OF INQUIRY, 1–085, 1–086
counsel, appearance by, 1–089
expenses of, 1–087
reports of, 1–086
solicitor, appearance by, 1–089
CROWN,
application of sex discrimination
  provisions to, 1–269
employment protection, and, 1–321
employment under, 1–194
racial discrimination, and, 1–406
CROWN EMPLOYMENT, 1–571
meaning of, 1–090
transfer to, 1–529

DAMAGED GOODS,
deductions from wages, and, 1–060

Index

DAMAGES,
  trade unions, awarded against,
    limit on damages, 1–688
DEATH,
  employee, of, 1–581
  employer, of, 1–581
DIRECTORS, 1–656 *et seq.*
  contracts of employment, 1–658
  duties of, 1–656 *et seq.*
  interests of employees, having regard
    to, 1–657
  service contracts of, inspection of,
    1–134
  shadow, 1–661
  substantial contracts with, disclosure
    of, 1–659
DIRECTORS' REPORTS,
  health and safety at work, and, 1–164
DISCIPLINARY PRACTICE, 5–009 *et seq.*
DISCIPLINARY PROCEDURES, 5–009
    et seq.
  appeals, 5–015
  essential features of, 5–013
  formulating policy, 5–011
  further action, 5–017
  operation of, 5–014
  reasons for, 5–010
  records of, 5–016
  rules of, 5–012
DISCLOSURE OF INFORMATION, 5–018 *et
    seq.*
  employers' responsibilities, 5–023
  joint arrangements for, 5–024
  restrictions on duty, 5–021
  trade union responsibilities, 5–022
  trade unions, to, 5–018 *et seq.*
DISCRIMINATION, 1–208. *See also*
    RACIAL DISCRIMINATION; SEX
    DISCRIMINATION.
DISMISSAL,
  compensation for, 1–694
  confinement, and, 1–484
  fairness of, 1–486
  industrial dispute, and, 1–492
  lock-out, and, 1–492
  meaning of, 1–483
  period of absence, during, 1–594
  pregnancy, on ground of, 1–490
  procedures agreement, 1–496, 1–497
  redundancy, on ground of, 1–489
  replacement employee, of, 1–491
  strike, and, 1–492
  teacher in aided school, 1–514
  termination of employment by
    statute, and, 1–549
  trade union membership, and, 1–487
  written statement of reasons for,
    1–481

DISMISSAL PROCEDURES AGREEMENT,
  meaning of, 1–584
DISPUTES PROCEDURES, 5–008
DOCK WORKERS, 1–577
DOMESTIC SERVANTS, 1–012
  redundancy payments, and, 1–533

EARNINGS,
  meaning of, 2–092
EDUCATION,
  deduction from wages, and, 1–048
ELECTIVE BODIES,
  sex discrimination, and, 1–234
EMERGENCY,
  issue of proclamations of, 1–095
EMERGENCY POWERS, 1–094, 1–097
EMERGENCY REGULATIONS, 1–096
EMPLOYED PERSON,
  meaning of, 1–117
EMPLOYEE,
  death of, 1–313, 1–338, 1–581, 1–606
    redundancy payments, and, 1–609
  meaning of, 1–192, 1–707, 2–091
  paid by person other than employer,
    1–550
  rights in period of notice, 1–595
  security of, 5–007
  status of, 5–007
EMPLOYEES' INVENTIONS, 1–415
  compensation for, 1–416, 1–417
  contracts relating to, 1–418
EMPLOYEES' SHARE SCHEME,
  meaning of, 1–663
EMPLOYER,
  advance of money by, 1–014
  death of, 1–313, 1–338, 1–581, 1–606
    redundancy payments, and, 1–608
  duty to consult trade union
    representatives on redundancy,
    1–303
  failure to disclose information,
    complaint of, 1–298, 1–299
  general duty to disclose information,
    1–296
  goods supplied by,
    wages, and, 1–006
  insolvency of. *See* INSOLVENCY.
  meaning of, 1–015, 1–192, 1–707
  neglect by, 1–028
  penalty for entering into illegal
    contract, 1–009
  production of contract by, 1–064
EMPLOYERS' ASSOCIATION,
  administrative provisions, 1–195
  annual returns, 1–174
  auditors, of, 1–174
  duty to keep accounting records,
    1–173

EMPLOYERS' ASSOCIATION—*cont.*
  incorporation, cessation of, 1–181
  list of, 1–171
  meaning of, 1–072, 1–190
  members' superannuation schemes, 1–174
  offences, 1–175
  registered, 1–172
  superannuation schemes, 1–196
  unincorporated, 1–169
EMPLOYMENT,
  meaning of, 1–191, 1–266
EMPLOYMENT AGENCIES ACT 1973,
  amendments of, 1–339
EMPLOYMENT AGENCY,
  racial discrimination, and, 1–361
  sex discrimination, and, 1–218
EMPLOYMENT AND TRAINING ACT 1973,
  amendments of, 1–340
EMPLOYMENT APPEAL TRIBUNAL, 1–568, 1–569, 1–604, 2–052 *et seq.*
  appeal procedure, 5–001
    institution of, 2–054
  application for compensation, forms, 2–062
  costs, 2–059
  expenses, 2–059
  interlocutory applications, 2–057, 2–058
  listing of appeals, 5–001
  membership of, 1–604
  notice of appeal, service of, 2–055
  notice of cross-appeal, 2–056
  offices, 2–061
  oral hearings, 2–059
  pensions, 1–605
  remuneration, 1–605
  respondent's answer, 2–056
    form of, 2–062
  respondents to appeals, 2–055
  rules, 2–052 *et seq.*
  service of application, 2–057
  service of documents, 2–060
  time, 2–061
  waiver of rules, 2–061
EMPLOYMENT LEGISLATION,
  power to extend, 1–328
EMPLOYMENT PROTECTION, 1–276 *et seq.*
  consolidation, 1–427 *et seq.*
  financial provisions, 1–324
  Northern Ireland, and, 1–329
EMPLOYMENT PROTECTION ACT 1975,
  effect of, 5–088
EMPLOYMENT PROTECTION LEGISLATION,
  extension of, 1–570
EQUAL OPPORTUNITIES COMMISSION, 1–238 *et seq.*, 1–273
  annual reports, 1–241

EQUAL OPPORTUNITIES COMMISSION—*cont.*
  Codes of Practice, 1–242
  disclosure of information, restriction on, 1–247
  duties of, 1–238
  education, 1–239
  establishment of, 1–238
  formal investigations,
    power to conduct, 1–243
    recommendations and reports, 1–246
  health and safety legislation, review of, 1–240
  power to obtain information, 1–245
  research, 1–239
  terms of reference, 1–244
EQUAL PAY, 1–135 *et seq.*
  abolition of discrimination, and, 3–010
  application of principle, 3–013
  collective agreements, 1–138, 3–011
  complaint, and,
    dismissal, and, 3–012
  equal treatment,
    disputes as to, 1–137
    enforcement of, 1–137
    men and women in same employment, 1–136
  Europeran Economic Community, and, 3–007 *et seq.*
  meaning of, 3–008
  pay structures, 1–138
  pensions, 1–141
  remedies for failure of, 3–009
  service pay, 1–142
  wages regulation orders, 1–139
ESTATE AGENT,
  meaning of, 1–266
EUROPEAN CONVENTION ON HUMAN RIGHTS AND FUNDAMENTAL FREEDOMS, 3–041
EUROPEAN ECONOMIC COMMUNITY, 3–001 *et seq.*
  collective redundancy, and, 3–018 *et seq.*
  equal pay, 3–007 *et seq.*
  sex discrimination, 3–024 *et seq.*
  transfer of undertakings, and, 3–036 *et seq.*
EUROPEAN MATERIALS, 3–001 *et seq.*
EUROPEAN SOCIAL CHARTER 1965, 3–042
EXPECTED WEEK OF CONFINEMENT. *See* CONFINEMENT.
  meaning of, 1–584

FINE,
  deduction from wages, and, 1–059

Index 685

FIXED TERM,
  contract for, 1–575
FREEDOM OF THE PRESS,
  closed shop, and, 5–076

GAS,
  supply of,
    breach of contract, and, 4–007
GENERAL NOTICE,
  meaning of, 1–266, 1–409
GOVERNMENT OF OVERSEAS TERRITORY,
  employment under, 1–546
  meaning of, 1–547
GREAT BRITAIN,
  employment outside, 1–574
  meaning of, 1–266
GRIEVANCE PROCEDURES, 5–008
GUARANTEE PAYMENT, 1–438, 1–444, 1–670
  amount of, 1–441
  calculation of, 1–440
  complaint to industrial tribunal, 1–443
  right to, 1–438

HEALTH AND SAFETY AT WORK, 1–146 et seq.
  application to Crown, 1–163
  appointment of inspectors, 1–155
  directors' reports, 1–164
  duty not to charge employees, 1–153
  employees, 1–151
  employers, 1–147, 1–148
  enforcement, 1–154
  general duties, 1–147, 1–153
  imminent danger,
    power to deal with, 1–161
  improvement notices, 1–157, 1–159
    appeal against, 1–160
  interference with things provided, 1–152
  manufactures,
    articles and substances, 1–150
  notices,
    service of, 1–162
  powers of inspectors, 1–156
  premises, 1–149
  prohibition notices, 1–158, 1–159
    appeal against, 1–160
  self-employed, 1–147
HEALTH AND SAFETY AT WORK ACT 1974,
  amendments of, 1–341
HOLDING COMPANY,
  meaning of, 1–106
HOMEWORKERS,
  meaning of, 1–644
HOUSE OF COMMONS STAFF, 1–572
  employment protection, and, 1–322

HOUSING BENEFITS, 1–695 et seq.
HUSBANDRY,
  servant in, 1–045

INCAPACITATED PERSON,
  permits to, 1–632
INDEPENDENT TRADE UNION,
  meaning of, 1–192, 1–584
INDUSTRIAL ACTION,
  avoidance of, 5–031
  closed shop, and, 5–075
INDUSTRIAL COURTS, 1–084, 1–093
INDUSTRIAL DISPUTE,
  dismissal, and, 1–492
  information to TUC General Secretary, 5–095
  redundancy payment, and, 1–526
INDUSTRIAL RELATIONS,
  Codes of Practice,
    issue by Secretary of State, 1–667
INDUSTRIAL RELATIONS ACT 1971,
  Code of Practice, 5–006
  repeal of, 1–166
INDUSTRIAL TRIBUNALS, 1–561 et seq.
  awards,
    enforcement, 2–028
  effect of repeals, and, 1–184
  establishment of, 2–005
  general provisions, 1–312
  membership of, 2–006
  non-discrimination notices,
    appeals, 2–039
    procedure, 2–040
  notice of appeal from,
    form, 2–062
  power to confer jurisdiction on, 1–564
  President of, 2–004
  procedure, 1–602
  procedure as to levy appeals, 2–007
  proceedings of, 2–012
  proof of decisions of, 2–008, 2–012
  racial discrimination, and, 1–388, 1–390
  recoupment of benefits, and, 1–565
  reference to,
    pay statement, and, 1–437
  rules of procedure, 2–009, 2–014, 2–042, 2–046
  regulations, 2–001 et seq
  sex discrimination, and, 1–249
  time off work, and, 1–457
  unfair dismissal, and, 1–498
INFIRM PERSON,
  permit to, 1–632

INJUNCTION,
   ex parte, 1–179
INJURY,
   breach of contract involving,
      1–027
INSOLVANCY,
   employer, of, 1–554 *et seq*.
INTERDICT, 1–179
INTIMIDATION, 1–029
INVENTION,
   employee's, 1–415
      compensation for, 1–416, 1–417

JOB,
   meaning of, 1–584

LABOUR RELATIONS,
   continuity of employment,
      regulations, 2–027
LAY-OFF,
   redundancy payment, and, 1–521,
      1–522, 1–523, 1–608
LOCK-OUT,
   dismissal, and, 1–492

MAGISTRATE,
   disqualification of, 1–056
MALICIOUSLY,
   meaning of, 1–034
MANPOWER SERVICES COMMISSION,
   racial discrimination, and, 1–362
   sex discrimination, and, 1–219
MARINERS, 1–576
MATERIAL DATE,
   meaning of, 1–483
MATERNITY, 1–461 *et seq*.
   right to return to work, 1–473,
      1–475
MATERNITY PAY, 1–462, 1–472
   rebate, 1–467
MATERNITY PAY FUND,
   financing of, 1–301
MEN,
   sex discrimination against, 1–205. *See
      also* SEX DISCRIMINATION.
MERCHANT SEAMEN, 1–320
MIDWIVES, 1–223
MINE CLUB FUNDS,
   preferential payments, and,
      1–109
MINEWORKERS, 1–224
MINISTERS OF RELIGION,
   sex discrimination, and, 1–222
MISCONDUCT,
   redundancy payment, and, 1–526

NATIONAL HEALTH SERVICE EMPLOYERS,
   1–597

NATIONAL INDUSTRIAL RELATIONS
      COURT,
   abolition of,
      effect of, 1–183
      power to compensate for loss of
         office, 1–186
NATIONAL SECURITY,
   racial discrimination, and, 1–376
   sex discrimination, and, 1–237
NEGLECT,
   employer, by, 1–028
NON-DISCRIMINATION NOTICE, 1–253,
      1–256
   appeal against, 1–254
   form of, 2–035
   issue of, 1–253
   register of, 1–256
NORMAL WEEKLY EARNINGS,
   calculation of, 2–094
NORMAL WORKING HOURS,
   calculation of, 1–583, 1–611
NORTHERN IRELAND,
   employment protection, and, 1–329
NOTICE,
   minimum period of, 1–477, 1–478

OCCUPATIONAL PENSION SCHEME,
   payment of unpaid contributions to,
      1–556
   transfer of undertakings, and,
      2–068
OFFICER,
   meaning of, 1–192
OFFICIAL,
   meaning of, 1–192
ORIGINAL CONTRACT OF EMPLOYMENT,
   meaning of, 1–584

PARTNERSHIP,
   racial discrimination, and, 1–357
   sex discrimination by, 1–214
   Truck Acts, and, 1–010
PATENTS, 1–414
PATENTS RULES, 2–041
PAY,
   week's, calculation of, 1–611, 1–612
PAY STATEMENT,
   fixed deductions, standing statement
      of, 1–435
   itemised, 1–434
PEACEFUL PICKETING, 4–009, 4–015
PENSION RIGHTS,
   redundancy payments, and, 1–531
PENSIONS, 1–202
   contracting-out certificates, 1–202
   equal pay, and, 1–141

PERIOD OF EMPLOYMENT,
  computation of, 1–610
PICKETING, 1–671, 5–045 *et seq.*
  attendance at or near own place of
    work, 5–048
  civil law, and, 5–046 *et seq.*
  Code of Practice, 5–045
  contemplation or furtherance of trade
    dispute, 5–047
  criminal law, and, 5–052
  essential supplies and services,
    5–056
  lawful purposes of, 5–050
  limiting numbers, 5–054
  organisation of, 5–055
  peaceful, 1–177
  role of police, 5–053
  secondary action, and, 5–057
  seeking redress, and, 5–051
  trade union officials, 5–049
POLICE,
  picketing, and, 5–053
  racial discrimination, and, 1–363
  sex discrimination, and, 1–220
POLICE SERVICE,
  meaning of, 1–192, 1–578
PREFERENTIAL PAYMENTS,
  Stannaries cases, in, 1–108
  winding up, in, 1–107
PREGNANCY, 1–461
  dismissal on ground of, 1–490
PREMIUMS,
  employers not to receive, 1–635
PENSION OFFICERS,
  sex discrimination, and, 1–220
PROFIT AND LOSS ACCOUNT,
  information supplementing, 1–681

QUALIFYING BODY,
  racial discrimination, and, 1–359
  sex discrimination by, 1–216

RACE RELATIONS, 1–347 *et seq.*
  Code of Practice, 5–078/1 *et seq.*
    advertisements, and, 5–078/9
    application of, 5–078/2
    disciplinary procedures, and,
      5–078/13
    dismissal, 5–078/9, 5–078/11
      selection for, 5–078/10
    disputes procedures, and, 5–078/13
    employees,
      cultural needs of, 5–078/14
      language training, 5–078/15
      religious needs of, 5–078/14
      responsibilities of, 5–078/20
    employment agencies, 5–078/9
    responsibilities of, 5–078/28

RACE RELATIONS—*cont.*
  Code of Practice—*cont.*
    equal opportunity, monitoring of,
      5–078/18
    equal opportunity policies, 5–078/8
    genuine occupational qualification,
      and, 5–078/10
    good employment practice, 5–078/4
    grievance procedures, and,
      5–078/13
    guidance papers, 5–078/6, 5–078/7,
      5–078/19
    indirect discrimination, 5–078/3,
      5–078/18
    instructions to discriminate,
      5–078/16
    pressure to discriminate, 5–078/16
    promotion, and, 5–078/9
      selection for, 5–078/10
    purpose and status of, 5–078/1
    racial minorities, and, 5–078/5
    recruitment, and, 5–078/9
      selection for, 5–078/10
    small firms, 5–078/2
    terms of employment, 5–078/12
    trade unions,
      discrimination, pressure to,
        5–078/25
      members of, training and
        information, 5–078/24
      members of, discipline of,
        5–078/23
      members of, treatment of,
        5–078/22
      membership of, 5–078/22
      responsibilities of, 5–078/21
      training, and, 5–078/9, 5–078/11
        selection for, 5–078/9, 5–078/10
      transfer, and, 5–078/9
        selection for, 5–078/10
      under-represented racial groups,
        5–078/5, 5–078/8
      unlawful discrimination, 5–078/3
      victimisation, discrimination by,
        5–078/3, 5–078/17
    formal investigations, 2–033, 2–035
    questions and replies,
      order, 2–036, 2–038
RACIAL DISCRIMINATION, 1–347 *et seq.*
  acts done under statutory authority,
    1–375
  advertisements, 1–365
  aggrieved persons, help for, 1–398
  aiding unlawful acts, 1–369
  charities, 1–369/1
  Commission for Racial Equality. *See*
    COMMISSION FOR RACIAL
    EQUALITY.

RACIAL DISCRIMINATION—*cont.*
  conciliation in employment cases, 1–389
  contract workers, 1–354
  contracts,
    revision of, 1–403
    validity of, 1–403
  Crown, application to, 1–406
  education, and, 1–370
  employers, by, 1–351, 1–356
  employers and principals, liability of, 1–368
  employment agencies, and, 1–361
  evidence of, 1–401
  indirect access to benefits, and, 1–374
  industrial tribunals, jurisdiction of, 1–388
  instructions to, 1–366
  local authority,
    general statutory duty, 1–402
  Manpower Services Commission, and, 1–362
  national security, and, 1–376
  non-discrimination notice, 1–391
    appeal against, 1–392
    investigation as to, 1–393
    register of, 1–394
  partnership, and, 1–357
  persistent, 1–395
  police, 1–363
  practices, 1–364
  preliminary action in employment cases, 1–397
  pressure to, 1–367
  proceedings, period within which to bring, 1–400
  qualifying bodies, and, 1–359
  questionnaire of person aggrieved, 2–037
  reply by respondent, 2–038
  restriction of proceedings for breach of Act, 1–387
  seamen recruited abroad, 1–356
  trade union, and, 1–358
  training, and, 1–370, 1–371, 1–372, 1–373
  victimisation, 1–349
  vocational training bodies, and, 1–360
  welfare, and, 1–370
RACIAL GROUNDS,
  meaning of, 1–350
RACIAL GROUP,
  meaning of, 1–350
REDUNDANCY,
  collective. *See also* COLLECTIVE REDUNDANCIES.

REDUNDANCY—*cont.*
  collective—*cont.*
    European Economic Community, and, 3–018 *et seq.*
    collective agreement on, 1–311
    complaint by trade union, 1–305
    dismissal on ground of, 1–489
    duty of employer to consult trade unions, 1–303
    duty of employer to notify Secretary of State, 1–304
    meaning of, 1–326
    notices,
      provisions as to, 1–552
      offences in relation to, 1–553
    protective award, 1–305
      entitlement under, 1–306
      complaint by employer, and, 1–307
      reduction of rebate on failure to notify, 1–308
REDUNDANCY FUND, 1–536, 1–542
  calculation of payments to employees out of, 1–600
REDUNDANCY PAYMENT,
  adaptation of provisions, 1–593
  calculation of, 1–596
  claims for, 1–534
  confinement, and, 1–520
  death of employee, and, 1–609
  death of employer, and, 1–608
  dismissal by employer, 1–517
  domestic servants, 1–533
  employer's notice, expiry of,
    anticipation by employee of, 1–519
  exemption orders, 1–530
  industrial dispute, and, 1–526
  lay-off, and, 1–521, 1–522, 1–523, 1–608
  misconduct, and, 1–526
  pension rights, and, 1–531
  public offices, 1–532
  rebates in respect of, 1–598
  re-engagement, and, 1–518
  reference of questions to industrial tribunal, 1–525
  relevant date, the, 1–524
  renewal of contract, and, 1–518
  right to, 1–515, 1–516
  short-time, and, 1–521, 1–522, 1–523, 1–608
  written particulars of, 1–535
REDUNDANCY REBATE, 1–537
  civil servant, of, 1–544, 1–545
RE-ENGAGEMENT,
  order for, 1–500
    compensation, and, 1–502
REFEREES,
  statutory provisions relating to, 1–603

Index

REHABILITATION OF OFFENDERS, 1–200, 2–015
  effect of rehabilitation, 1–201
  excepted licences, 2–019
  excepted professions, 2–016
  regulated occupations, 2–017
REINSTATEMENT,
  order for, 1–500
  compensation, and, 1–502
RELEVANT DATE, THE,
  meaning of, 1–524
REMUNERATION,
  apportionment of, 1–634
  computation of, 1–633
RENT,
  apportionment of, 1–018 *et seq*.
REPEALED LEGISLATION, 4–001 *et seq*.

SAFETY COMMITTEES, 2–031, 5–042, 5–044
  conduct of, 5–044
  functions of, 5–042
  membership of, 5–043
  objectives of, 5–042
SAFETY REPRESENTATIVES, 2–029, 5–032 *et seq*.
  appointment of, 2–029, 5–036, 5–037
  functioning of, 5–036, 5–038
  functions of, 2–029, 5–034
  information to be provided by employers, 5–035
  inspection of documents, 2–030
  inspections by, 5–040
  inspections of workplace, 2–029
  obligations of employers, 5–041
  pay for time off allowed for, 2–032
  provision of information, 2–030
SCOTTISH AGRICULTURAL WAGES BOARD,
  powers of, 1–336
SEAMEN, 1–035
  racial discrimination, and, recruited abroad, 1–356
SECONDARY ACTION, 1–672
SECRET BALLOT,
  closed shop, and, 5–070
SEX DISCRIMINATION, 1–203 *et seq*.
  advertisements, 1–226
  aiding unlawful acts, 1–230
  assistance by Equal Opportunities Commission, 1–261
  charities, 1–231
  claims under Part III of Act, 1–252
  complaint under section 63 of Act, 1–251
  conciliation, 1–250
  contract workers, 1–212
  Crown, application to, and, 1–269

SEX DISCRIMINATION—*cont*.
  discriminatory practices, 1–225
  dismissal, protection against, and, 3–031
  educational admissions, transitional exemption orders, 1–272
  elective bodies, 1–234
  employers, by, 1–209, 1–213
  employers and principals, 1–229
  employment,
    meaning of, 1–213
  employment agencies, 1–218
  enforcement, 1–248 *et seq*.
  Equal Pay Act 1970, and, 1–211
  European Economic Community Directive, 3–024, 3–035
  formal investigations, 2–021, 2–023
    non-discrimination notice, 2–023
    oral evidence, 2–022
    written information, 2–022
  genuine occupational qualification, and, 1–210
  help for aggrieved persons, 1–260
  indirect access to benefits, 1–235
  industrial tribunals, 1–249
  instructions to discriminate, 1–227
  Manpower Services Commission, 1–219
  married persons, 1–206
    meaning of, 1–208
  men, against, 1–205
  midwives, and, 1–223
  mineworkers, 1–224
  ministers of religion, 1–222
  national security, 1–237
  orders, 1–265
  partnership, by, 1–214
  persistent, 1–257
  police, 1–220
  preliminary action in employment cases, 1–259
  pressure to discriminate, 1–228
  prison officers, 1–221
  proceedings, period within which to bring, 1–262
  qualifying bodies, and, 1–216
  question and replies, 2–024
  questionnaire of persons aggrieved, 2–025
  reply by respondent, 2–026
  removal, 1–093
  revision of contracts, 1–263
  statutory authority, acts done under, and, 1–236
  trade unions, 1–215, 1–234
  training, 1–232, 1–233
  validity of contracts, 1–263

SEX DISCRIMINATION—cont.
  victimisation, and, 1–207
  vocational training bodies, and,
    1–217
  women, against, 1–204
  working conditions and, 3–029
SHARES,
  acquisition of,
    financial assistance for, 1–680
SHORT-TIME,
  redundancy payment, and, 1–521,
    1–522, 1–523, 1–608
SOCIAL SECURITY, 1–695 et seq.
  pensions, 1–202
STANNARIES CASES,
  preferential payments in, 1–108
STATE IMMUNITY, 1–4216
  contracts of employment, 1–4216
STATUTORY COMPENSATION SCHEME,
  1–551
STATUTORY JOINT INDUSTRIAL COUNCILS,
  1–626 et seq.
  abolition of, 1–628
  constitution, 1–652
  conversion of wages councils to,
    1–626
  disputes between employers' and
    workers' representatives, 1–627
  orders relating to, 1–649
STATUTORY SICK PAY, 1–696 et seq.
  avoiding liability for, 2–079
  calculation of entitlement limit, 2–081
  contract of service, treatment as more
    than one, 2–096
  employer,
    liability of, 1–696
    records to be maintained by, 2–088
  employers,
    treatment as more than one, 2–095
  entitlement, periods of, 1–698
    arising of, 1–708
    limitations on, 1–700
  manner in which not paid, 2–083
  normal weekly earnings, 2–094
  notification of incapacity for work,
    1–701, 2–082
  offences, 1–706
  payments treated as contractual
    remuneration, 2–093
  penalties, 1–706, 2–097
  period of entitlement ending or not
    arising, 2–078
  period of incapacity for work, 1–697
  periods of interruption of
    employment, 2–087
  persons deemed incapable of work,
    2–077
  persons unable to act, 2–085

STATUTORY SICK PAY—cont.
  provision of information, 2–089,
    2–090
  qualifying days, 1–699, 2–080
  rate of payment, 1–702
  regulations, 2–076 et seq.
  regulations as to method of payment,
    1–703
  relationship with benefits, 1–705,
    1–709
  recovery by employers, 1–704
  rounding to avoid fractional amounts
    2–086
  time limits for paying, 2–084
STRIKE,
  dismissal, and, 1–492
  employer's notice to terminate
    contract, during, 1–543
SUBSIDIARY,
  meaning of, 1–106
SUPERANNUATION SCHEME,
  meaning of, 1–644
SUPPLEMENTARY BENEFIT,
  trade dispute, and, 1–314
SUSPENSION FROM WORK,
  medical grounds, on, 1–445
    calculation of remuneration, 1–447
    complaint to industrial tribunal,
      1–448

TERMINATION OF CONTRACT,
  constructive, 1–527
  implied, 1–527
TERMINATION OF EMPLOYMENT, 1–477 et
  seq.
  minimum period of notice, 1–477
TERMS OF EMPLOYMENT, 1–428 et seq.
  changes in, 1–430
  contracts in writing, exclusions to,
    1–431
  particulars of, 1–428
    written, 1–428
  power to fix, 1–630, 1–631
  reports on, 1–642
THRIFT SCHEME,
  meaning of, 1–644
TIME OFF,
  trade union duties, for, 5–025
    conditions relating to, 5–030
    general considerations, 5–026
    training of officials, 5–028
TIME OFF WORK, 1–454 et seq.
  ante-natal care, 1–459
  arrangements for training, 1–458
  industrial tribunal, and, 1–457
  looking for work, 1–458
  public duties, 1–456
  trade union duties, 1–454, 1–455

Tools,
  deduction from wages for sharpening, 1–049
Trade Disputes,
  acts in contemplation or furtherance of, 1–176, 4–013
  inquiry into, 1–085
  meaning of, 1–191, 1–327, 1–690, 4–016
Trade Union and Labour Relations Act 1974,
  amendments of, 1–343
Trade Unions, 1–070 et seq., 4–001 et seq.
  actions in tort against,
    limit on damages, 1–688
  activities, 1–449, 5–029
    compensation, and, 1–452
  administrative provisions, 1–195
  amalgamations, 1–120 et seq.
    complaints to Certification Officer, 1–123
    disposal of property on, 1–124
    Northern Ireland, 1–132
    regulations, 1–126
    resolution for, 1–121
  annual returns, 1–174
  approval of rules, 1–074
  auditors, 1–174
  ballots,
    funds for, order, 2–098
    regulations, 2–047, 2–051
    secret, 1–665. See also Ballots.
  carrying out duties of,
    time off work, and, 1–454, 1–455
  ceasing to be incorporated, 1–181
  change of name, 1–125
  civil purposes, unlawful for, 4–003
  closed shop, and, 5–067. See also Closed Shop.
  conduct of, 5–097
  contracts,
    not enforceable, when, 4–004
  disclosure of information to,
    collective bargaining purposes, for, 5–018 et seq. See also Disclosure of Information.
  disputes between,
    regulations governing procedure in regard to, 5–089
    role of TUC Disputes Committee, 5–091
    TUC, and, 5–096
  Disputes Committee,
    decisions of, 5–094
  disputes procedures,
    time limits, 5–090

Trade Unions—cont.
  duty to keep accounting records, 1–173
  employers, and,
    disputes will, 5–092
      action by TUC, 5–093
  exemption from contributions to political fund, 1–077
  expulsion from, 1–668
    compensation, and, 1–669
  funds, application of,
    political purposes, for, 1–073
  immunity of, 4–014
  independent,
    certification as, 1–293
  inter-union disputes, 5–086, 5–087
  list of, 1–171
  meaning of, 1–072, 1–190
  members' superannuation schemes, 1–174
  membership, 1–449
    compensation, and, 1–452
    dismissal, and, 1–487
  membership agreement,
    ballot as to, 1–488
    definition of, 5–077
  membership form, 5–085
  nominations by members of, 1–194
  notice of objection to contribute towards political object, 1–075
  objects of, 1–071
  offences, 1–175
  political fund,
    exemption notice,
      form of, 1–081
  power to alter rules of, 1–182
  powers of, 1–071
  pressure to impose membership requirements, 1–686
  proceedings,
    sums awarded, 1–689
    recovery of sums awarded, 1–689
  prohibition on membership requirements, 1–684
  property of, 1–169
  racial discrimination, and, 1–358
  recognition requirements, 1–685
  registered, 1–172
  relations between, 5–079 et seq.
  restrictions on contracting out, 1–194
  right to terminate membership of, 1–170
  sex discrimination by, 1–215, 1–234
  status of, 1–167
  superannuation schemes, 1–196
  time off for duties, 5–025
  tort, and,
    prohibition of actions, 4–011

TRADE UNIONS—*cont.*
transfer of membership, 5–083
transfers of engagement, 1–120 *et seq.*
  disposal of property on, 1–124
  Northern Ireland, 1–132
  power to alter rules of transferee organisation, and, 1–122
  regulations, 1–126
unreasonable exclusion or expulsion from, 5–063
TUC DISPUTES PRINCIPLES AND PROCEDURES, 5–079 *et seq.*
TRAINING,
  meaning of, 1–266
TRANSFER OF UNDERTAKINGS, 2–063 *et seq.*
  collective agreements, effect on, 2–667
  consultation, 3–039
  dismissal of employee, and, 2–069
  dock workers, and, 2–074
  duty to consult trade union representatives, 2–071
    failure to, 2–072
  effect of, 2–066
  employee's rights, safeguarding of, 3–038
  employment abroad, and, 2–074
  European Economic Community Directive, 3–036 *et seq.*
  information, 3–039
  liquidator, by, 2–065
  occupational pension schemes, and, 2–068
  receiver, by, 2–065
  relevant, 2–064
  restriction on contracting out, and, 2–073
  trade union recognition, effect on, 2–070
TREATY OF ROME, 3–001 *et seq.*
  co-operation between Member States, 3–002
  equal pay, 3–003
  paid holidays, 3–004
  social development, 3–006
  social security for migrant workers, 3–005
  working conditions, 3–001
TRUCK ACT 1831, 1–001 *et seq.*
  application of, 1–043
  exceptions to, 1–013
  liability under, 1–053
  inspectors appointed under, duties of, 1–067
  service of summons under, 1–011

UNEMPLOYMENT BENEFIT,
  trade dispute, and, 1–314
UNFAIR DISMISSAL, 1–482 *et seq.*
  adaptation of provisions, 1–592
  closed shop, and, 5–060
  compensation for, 1–503, 1–510, 1–683
  death during notice period, 1–607
  industrial tribunal, complaint to, 1–498
  interim relief, and, 1–511, 1–513
  pressure on employer, 1–493
  qualifying period, 1–494, 1–495
  remedies for, 1–499, 1–607
  upper age limit, 1–494
UNION MEMBERSHIP AGREEMENT,
  meaning of, 1–192. *See also* TRADE UNIONS.

VOCATIONAL TRAINING BODY,
  racial discrimination, and, 1–360
  sex discrimination by, 1–217

WAGES,
  advance of, 1–044
  banknotes, payment in, 1–008
  damaged goods, and, 1–060
  deduction of fines from, 1–059
  deductions from,
    audit of, 1–050
    recovery of, 1–063
  enforcement of order for, 1–036
  goods supplied by employer, and, 1–006
  materials, deductions in respect of, 1–061
  meaning of, 1–015, 1–117
  order for goods as deduction from, 1–046
  payment in coin, 1–004, 1–005
  payment of, 1–110 *et seq.*
  payment otherwise than in cash, request for, 1–111
    cancellation of, 1–113
    absence, in case of, 1–114
  spending at particular shop, contract for, 1–047
  stipulations as to expenditure, 1–003
WAGES COUNCILS, 1–616 *et seq.*
  abolition of, 1–620
  advisory committees, 1–624
    provisions as to, 1–651
  applications for abolition of, 1–621
  applications for orders, 1–618
  constitution of, 1–650
  duty to consider references by government departments, 1–625
  establishment of, 1–617

Index

WAGES COUNCILS—*cont.*
  orders relating to, 1–649
  power to extend legislation, 1–643
  proceedings, references as to
    establishment of, 1–619
  revocation of orders, 1–622
  variation of field of operation of,
    1–620
  variation of orders, 1–622
WAGES REGULATION ORDERS, 1–139
WATER,
  supply of,
    breach of contract, and, 4–007
WEEK,
  meaning of, 1–584

WEEK'S PAY, A,
  calculation of, 1–583, 1–611, 1–612
WINDING UP,
  company, of, 1–103
  preferential payments, 1–107
WOMEN,
  employed,
    right to protection, of, 3–042
  sex discrimination against, 1–204
WORK,
  no compulsion to, 1–178
WORKER,
  meaning of, 1–191, 1–644
WORKMAN,
  meaning of, 1–043